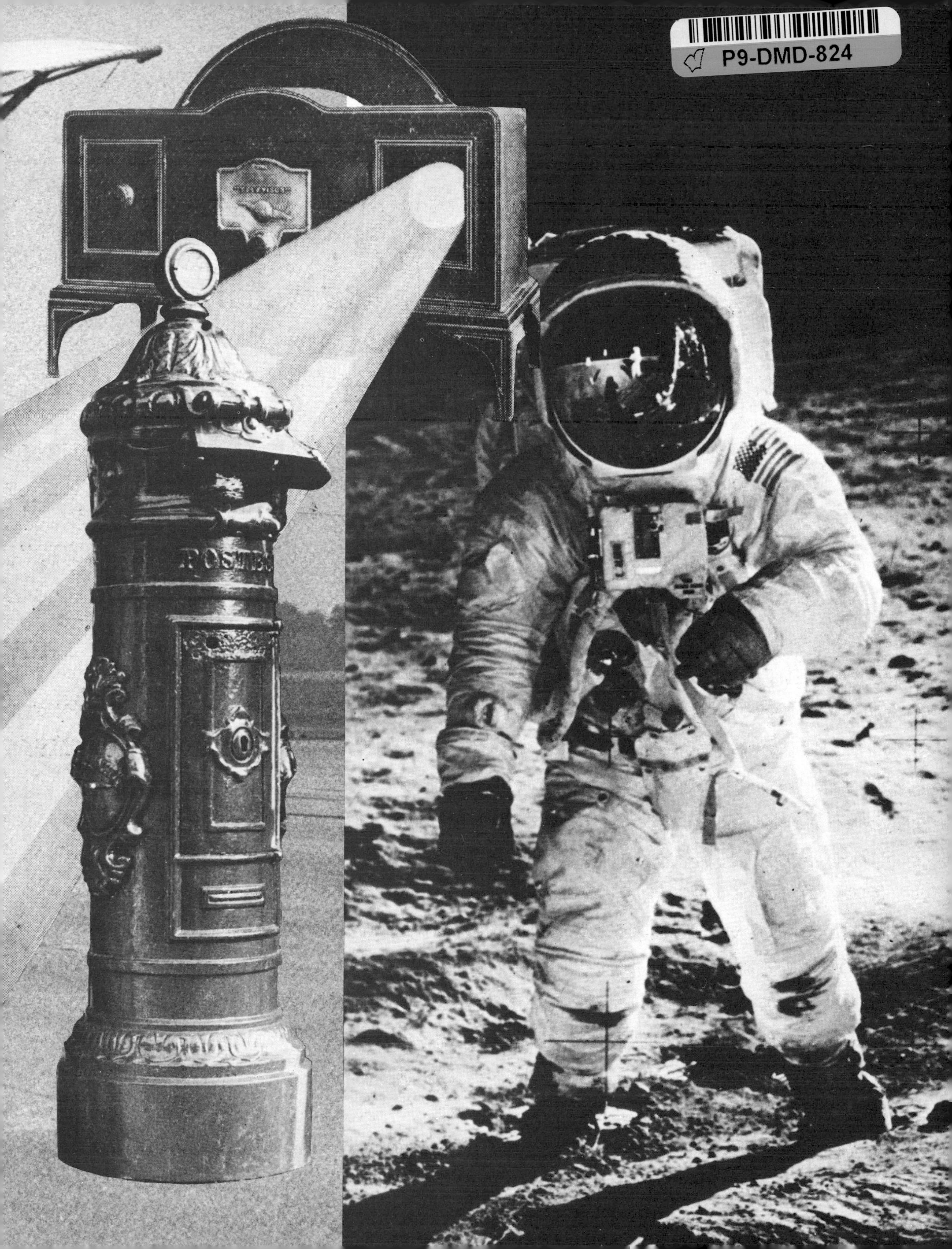
P9-DMD-824

THE BOOK OF FIRSTS

THE BOOK OF FIRSTS

Patrick Robertson

CONTENTS

Clarkson N. Potter, Inc./Publisher NEW YORK
Distributed by Crown Publishers, Inc

Designed and produced by
Rainbird Reference Books Limited
Marble Arch House, 44 Edgware Road,
London W.2

House Editor: Sue Unstead
Designer: Frank Phillips
Picture Researcher: Elly Beintema

Text filmset in Century Schoolbook by
Jarrold & Sons Ltd, Norwich, England,
and the book printed and bound by
Cox and Wyman Ltd, Fakenham, Norfolk,
England

First published 1974

First American edition published 1974
by Clarkson N. Potter Inc., New York

Library of Congress Catalog Card Number
74-77149

PRINTED IN GREAT BRITAIN

INTRODUCTION

The Book of Firsts is not an encyclopedia of inventions. Had it been intended as such, then I would have listed many more scientific discoveries and technological innovations. Rather, the purpose of the book is to provide a chronology of a wide range of 'firsts' that have contributed to life as it is lived today, particularly those that have served to alter society in some greater or lesser degree.

'First', as used here, means the first in the modern world; the listing of an item does not preclude the possibility that it may have been known to ancient civilizations in some earlier form.

Originally it was hoped to be able to include an expanded entry on every item listed in the Chronology, but limitations of space have made this impracticable. The entries in the text have not been chosen on the basis of the importance of their subject-matter, because this would have meant repeating much information that is readily accessible in other reference books. Instead, I have selected the subjects that I believe have the greatest appeal to a majority of readers and also those which have received little attention in the past. This is the justification for including such items as beauty contest, motels and film reviews, while omitting the electric telegraph, the steam-engine and the introduction of State education.

Many historians have warned against the danger of ever describing anything as 'the first'. Their caution is not wholly misplaced, because a great many innovations have been wrongly attributed or mistakenly heralded as first in their field simply because they have attracted more attention than any predecessor. Although I have attempted to look beyond popular mythology and to question doubtful claims, I would not be so rash as to claim this work as definitive. Seldom is it possible to be unhesitatingly certain that any particular endeavour is entirely original, and the findings in this book represent the earliest that I have been able to identify positively. As far as attribution is concerned, the question I have attempted to answer is 'Who did it first in practical terms?', not 'Who expounded the principle that enabled it to be done?' – since, generally, the man to accomplish something for the first time in practical form, particularly in the field of invention, has drawn on the ideas of earlier workers in the same field. Or to put it another way, not 'Who had the idea?' but 'Who made the idea work?'

Corrections and supplementary information for possible inclusion in a later edition will always be welcome, though I would ask readers to bear in mind that the book does not cover the ancient world and that generally a 'first' only has social significance if it has been widely imitated.

Wellington, NZ 1963
Richmond, Surrey 1974

Patrick Robertson

ACKNOWLEDGMENTS

The author gratefully acknowledges the help he has received from the following individuals and organizations:

John Abraham; Altonaer Museum, Hamburg; Amateur Athletic Assoc.; American Institute of Public Opinion; American Museum, Bath; R.L. Andrews; Angelsea Education Committee; Archives des Assemblée Nationale, Paris; Atlantic Steam Navigation Co; Australian Broadcasting Commission; Automatic Vending Assoc. of Britain; Aveling-Barford Ltd; Avery Historical Museum; D.G. Banwell; Barton Transport; IG Farbenfabrik Bayer; BBC; Bernhard Historisches Bildarchiv; BFW-Fokker; Albert R. Bochroch; Haldeen Braddy; British Caledonian Airways; British Canoe Union; British Dental Assoc.; British Esperanto Assoc.; British Film Institute; British Medical Assoc.; British Overseas Airways; British Rail; British Transport Archives; Peter Bull; Bundespost Archiv, Berlin; Henry Button; Dr Laurence R. Campbell; Canterbury Royal Museum; CBS; Citroën; City of London Sanitation Dept; Norman Clare; Brian Coe; COI; Capt. E. de W.S. Colver; R.J. Constable; Thos Cook Ltd; Countryside Commission; Courtaulds Ltd; Miss M.E. Crooke; Cross and Cockade Soc.; Christopher Crouch; *Daily Mail*; *Daily Mirror*; *Daily Telegraph*; Daimler-Benz AG; Timothy d'Arch Smith; Miss Louisiana Dart; Alec Davis; R.V. Decarau; Department of Education and Science; Department of the Environment; Detroit Police; Deutsches Institut für Filmkunde; Dublin Stock Exchange; Dr Henry Durrant; Ecole Nationale Vétérinaire de Lyon; EMI Ltd; Fédération Aéronautique Internationale; Fédération Française d'Athletisme; Ferranti Co; B.R. Fincken; Ford Foundation; Foreign and Commonwealth Office; Foreningen Til Ski-Idrettens Fremme, Oslo; John Fraser; G.L. Frow; J.S. Fry & Sons; Martha A. Gable; Garter King of Arms; G.N. Georgano; B.F. George; Charles Gibbs-Smith; Girard-Perregaux SA; Douglas Graham; Mrs Allison H. Greenlees; Girl Guides Assoc.; Guernsey, States of; Guide Dogs for the Blind Assoc.; Hamburger Feuerkasse; Hans Bredow Institut, Hamburg; Col J.R. Henderson; Henkel et Cie GMBH; Percival F. Hinton; Mrs Ingrid Holford; Rathbone Holme; Holmenkollen Ski Museum; Home Office; Maj. K.E. Hunt; Stanley K. Hunter; Inner London Education Authority; Institute of the American Musical; Institution of Royal Engineers; Instytut Kultury Polskiej; Internationales Zeitungsmuseum der Stadt Aachen; ITA; Rev. Victor James; Jockey Club; T.E. Kermeen; Prof. Glen Kleine; Kodak Museum; Miles Monroe Kreuger; Dr E.B. Kurtz; Langenscheidt; Liverpool Housing Dept; London Stock Exchange; Los Angeles Police; Tom Mahoney; Manchester College, Oxford; Mander and Mitchenson Theatre Archive; Manx Museum; Mariners' Museum, Newport News; Marconi Co; Martin-Baker Aircraft Co; Sir Peter Masefield; Didier Masson; Maj. W.G. McMinnies; Norris McWhirter; Hon. S. Merrifield; Methodist Research Centre; Michelin et Cie; Military Historical Society; Ministère d'Etat chargé de la Défence Nationale, Paris; Ministère de la Santé Publique, Paris; Ministry of Defence; Ministry of Transport; R.P. Moore; Morgan Guaranty Co; Musée de l'Air; Musée National de la Voiture et du Tourisme; Musée du Tabac, Ville de Bergerac; Museo Leonardo da Vinci, Milan; Museum of Childhood, Edinburgh; Museum of English Rural Life, Reading; Lewis Napleton; National Army Museum; National Maritime Museum; National Motor Museum; NBC; Nestlé Alimentana SA; New Zealand Post Office; Louis Nierynck; Northern Stock Exchange; Ohio Agricultural Research Center; Old Etonian Assoc.; Omnibus Soc.; Ordnance Survey; Passport Office; Patent Office; Philadelphia Board of Education; Gale Pedrick; Philco Corp; Roy Plomley; Potato Chip Institute International; P & O; Prefecture de Paris; Psywar Society; W.R. Puglise; Henry Racinais; Lord Reith; Col Paul A. Rockwell; Duncan Ross; Royal Aero Club; Royal Aeronautical Soc; Royal Cane Club; Royal Horticultural Soc.; Royal Institution of British Architects; Royal Institution of Chartered Surveyors; Royal National Institute for the Blind; Royal National Lifeboat Institution; Royal Society of Arts; Royal Television Soc.; Ruston Paxman Diesels Ltd; Paul Rutledge; SAAB-Scania; Mme Schiaparelli; Albert Schwinges; Science Museum; Scout Assoc.; Michael Sedgwick; Shrewsbury School; Siegen Archives; Siemens Ltd; Mrs Julia Singer; Peter Singer; Keith Skone; Tony Slide; Smiths Food Group; W.H. Smith & Son; Smithsonian Institution; Social Surveys (Gallup Poll) Ltd; Society of Chiropodists; Spalding Gentlemen's Soc.; Frank Staff; Ernest Stanley; R.L. Steiner; H. von Stephanitz; Jack D. Stewart; Stiftung Technorama der Schweiz; G.C. Stonelake; Sunderland Museum; Supramar AG; Sussex Constabulary; Svenska Filminstitutet; C.J. Swallow; Tauchnitz; Temple Grove School; H.R. Tennant; Tom Todd; Touring Club de France; Twyford School; Unitarian General Assembly; Victoria and Albert Museum; Victoria State Electoral Office; Verein für Deutsche Schäferhunde; Lawrence Verney; Veteran Car Club; Hans Vogt; Mrs Audrey Wadowska; Dale L. Walker; Walthamstow Museum; Washington State University; Wellcome Institute; Western Electric Co; E.A. Westwood; W.M. Whiteman; Paul Whitfield; William Penn Charter School; Geoffrey Wilson; Bryan Wolf; John Youell; Zeiss.

I would also like to thank the Librarians and staff of the following libraries:

Aberdeen; Alexander Turnbull Library, Wellington, NZ; Amherst College; Atlantic City; Australian National Library, Canberra; Baltimore; Bibliothèque Nationale; Birmingham; Bolton; Bradford; Brighton; Canterbury; Cardiff; Chetham's Library, Manchester; Chicago; Dallas; Derby; Douglas I.o.M.; Dundee; Dun Laoghaire; East Molesey; Edinburgh; Folkestone; Godalming; Greenock; Guildhall Library; House of Commons; Huntingdon; Indianapolis; Iowa State Univ.; Islington; Keighley; Kimberley, SA; Kungliga Biblioteket, Stockholm; Leamington Spa; Liechtensteinische Landesbibliothek; Library of Congress; Liverpool; London Library; Maitland, NSW; Manchester; McGill Univ.; Mitchell Library, Sydney; Mitchell Library, Glasgow; Newcastle-upon-Tyne; New York Public Library; Nottingham; Nürnberg Stadbibliotek; Oxford; Philadelphia Free Library; Pontypool; Portsmouth; Pretoria, SA; San Luis Obispo; Scarborough; South Australian Parliament; Springfield, Ill.; Southampton; Stroud; Tokyo; Troy, NY; Uppsala Stadsbibliotek; Wellington, NZ; Victorian Parliament; Victoria State Library, Melbourne; Wandsworth; Westminster Central Reference Library; Wolverhampton; Yale University.

Special thanks are due to my researchers, Miss Iona Rhys Jones and Miss Elly Beintema; and to my wife Karla for her unfailing support and encouragement.

The use of 'GB' in the text and chronology refers to the British Isles prior to 6 December 1922 and to Great Britain and Northern Ireland after that date.

Unless otherwise indicated, the prefix 'Motor' refers throughout to vehicles driven by an internal-combustion engine or by an electric motor. Similarly the terms 'Aeroplane' and 'Aircraft' signify a powered heavier-than-air machine capable of sustained and controlled flight.

The first recorded
ABORTION CLINIC
in Britain was advertised on the back page of the *Morning Post* for 28 April 1780 in the following terms:

PREGNANCY.
To the Ladies:
Any Lady whose situation may induce her to seek or require a temporary retirement may be accommodated agreeable to her wishes in the house of a gentleman of eminence in the profession, whose honour and secrecy may be depended on, and where every vestige of pregnancy is obliterated . . .
Letters (post paid) addressed to A.B., No 23, Fleet Street, will be attended to.

The first
ABORTION, COUNTRY TO LEGALIZE
was the USSR under a decree of 1920. Although in effect the decree allowed abortion on demand, physicians were ordered to discourage patients from having the operation, particularly in the case of first pregnancies. They were not, however, allowed to refuse an abortion unless the pregnancy had lasted more than two and a half months. Despite the official policy of limiting abortion as much as possible, the practice grew to such an extent that in 1934 there were a reported 700,000 legal abortions in the RSFSR alone. In order to remedy this situation the original decree was revoked in 1936 and a new law introduced restricting the carrying out of abortions to cases where pregnancy endangered life, was calculated to be a serious threat to the health of the patient, or where the child was likely to inherit a specified disease. These conditions remained in force until 1955, when abortion on demand was reintroduced subject to certain safeguards. The current rate of surgical abortions in the USSR is approximately 6 million p.a.

The first country to introduce legalized abortion on medico-social grounds was Iceland under Law No. 38 of 28 January 1935. This law decreed that abortion might be carried out within the first 28 weeks of pregnancy if its continuance was clearly demonstrated to constitute a threat to the physical or mental well-being of the patient. Most of the western European nations who have legalized abortion have followed Iceland's example and prescribed medico-social conditions. The only parts of the world in which abortions are allowed on demand are the USSR, Hungary and three States of the USA – Hawaii, Alaska and New York.
GB: The Abortion Act received the Royal Assent on 27 October 1967 and came into effect on 27 April 1968. The Bill, the eighth presented to Parliament, had been introduced by Mr David Steel, Liberal MP for Roxburgh, Selkirk and Peebles.

The first
ADVERTISEMENT, PHOTOGRAPHICALLY ILLUSTRATED
was placed by the Harrison Patent Knitting Machine Co of Portland Street, Manchester, in the 11 November 1887 issue of *The Parrot*, a locally published humorous periodical, and depicted the Company's display stand and attendant staff at the Manchester Jubilee Exhibition. The photograph, a whole-page halftone, was reproduced by the Meisenbach process, and the advertisement handled by Messrs Pratt & Co, advertising agents, Manchester.

The world's first photographically illustrated advertisement, Manchester, 1887

16 THE PARROT. November 11, 1887.

VIEWS IN OLD MANCHESTER at the RECENT JUBILEE EXHIBITION.

OPENING OF NEW AND LARGER PREMISES, 133, PORTLAND STREET, Corner of Oxford Street
Opposite the old shop.
The Harrison Patent Knitting Machine Co., 128, Portland Street, Manchester.

The first
AERIAL CROP-DUSTING
was carried out on behalf of the Ohio Agricultural Experimental Station by Lt John B. Macready, then holder of the world altitude record, who used a Curtiss JN6 light aircraft to dust a 6-acre catalpa grove infested with leaf caterpillars, at Troy, Ohio on 3 August 1921. Powdered arsenate of lead was released from a specially designed hopper secured to the side of the fuselage of the aircraft, which flew at a height of 20–35ft above the ground; 175lb of powder were distributed over the 4,815 trees in the orchard in six 9sec discharges. Thus the actual time spent on the work of dusting was less than 1min.

Two days after the experiment C.R. Neillie, the Cleveland entomologist who had first suggested the idea, was able to report that 'evidences of the wholesale destruction of the insects were everywhere apparent' and that not more than 1% remained alive on the trees.

The first commercially operated crop-dusting service was offered by Huff-Daland Dusters Inc, founded in 1925 at Macon, Ga. by C.E. Woolman, who used a Petrel aircraft to discharge calcium arsenate over Georgia cotton plantations infested with boll-weevil.

The first
AERIAL PROPAGANDA
raid took place in May 1806. Admiral Thomas Cochrane, 10th Earl of Dundonald, had been asked, in common with a number of other naval commanders, to distribute a quantity of 'printed proclamations addressed to the French people'. The Admiralty suggested that the leaflets should be handed to French fishermen encountered near the coast, with instructions to pass them on to their countrymen. Cochrane did not share Their Lordships' cynical – or perhaps naïve – assessment of the French fishing fleet's willingness to aid and abet the enemy, and sought a surer means of landing his cargo in France. The previous year he had conducted a series of experiments aboard HMS *Pallas* with enormous kites designed to supplement sail-power and give the ship greater impetus. Borrowing from this idea, the Admiral had a number of smaller kites constructed. The leaflets were attached in bundles at spaced intervals along a

slow-burning fuse, so that they would be released every mile or so as the ship progressed along the coast. The system worked, and Cochrane reported that the proclamations 'became widely distributed over the country'.
AERIAL PROPAGANDA RAID BY AIRCRAFT: the first was made by the Italian Servizi Aeronautici over Libya during the Italo-Turkish War of 1911–12. The leaflet, signed 'Cavena' and dated Tripoli, 15 January 1912, was addressed to the Arabs of Tripolitania, and promised a gold napoleon and a sack of wheat or barley to every man who surrendered.
GB: The first British propaganda leaflet to be distributed by aircraft was prepared by Lt-Col Swinton, and printed in Paris at the offices of the *Continental Daily Mail* in October 1914. It contained a budget of war news, designed to convince German soldiers that they were facing imminent defeat, and seeking to persuade them that they were being forced to fight only 'to satisfy the grasping war-lusts of the militarists'.

The first
AERIAL WARFARE
operations were carried out by the Italian Army Aviation Corps over Libya during the Italo-Turkish War of 1911–12. The original strength of the unit that arrived at Tripoli on 19 October 1911, was 10 officers, 29 troopers and 9 aircraft (2 Blériots, 2 Etrichs, 2 Henri Farmans and 3 Nieuports), later supplemented by some Deperdussins and several airships. The organization under which the aerial campaign in Libya was conducted, consisted of an Aeroplane Battalion, an Airship Battalion (in operation 4 March 1912), a factory for construction and repairs, and a laboratory for experimental work. The functions performed by the Corps were fivefold: aerial reconnaissance, photogrammetry, artillery ranging, leaflet raids (*see* Aerial Propaganda) and bombing from the air. Thus the only two major uses of the aeroplane in modern warfare that were not foreshadowed during the Libyan campaign were the transport of troops and supplies, obviously beyond the capacity of the ultra-light aircraft of 1911, and aerial combat. It is more than likely that fighting in the air would have taken place had the enemy succeeded in its attempt to acquire aircraft.
AERIAL OPERATION CARRIED OUT BY AN AEROPLANE IN WARFARE: the first was a reconnaissance flight made by Capt. Piazza, commander of the air base at Tripoli, who flew over the Turkish encampment at Azizia on 23 October 1911 in a Blériot XI *bis* (*see also* Aeroplane Reconnaissance).
AIR RAID: the first took place on 1 November 1911, when Lt Giulio Gavotti took off from Tripoli in an Etrich monoplane and dropped a $4\frac{1}{2}$lb Citelli-type bomb on the Turkish position at Ain Zara. After encircling the camp to estimate the effect of the detonation, he flew to the oasis at Tagiura and released his three remaining bombs.

A second raid on Ain Zara three days later brought a strong protest from the Turks that the Italians were contravening the Geneva Convention, and a considerable discussion ensued on the ethics of air bombardment, not only in the Turkish and Italian Press, but also in the newspapers of many non-aligned countries.
CASUALTY IN AERIAL WARFARE: the first occurred on 31 March 1912, when Capt. Montu was wounded by gunfire from the Arab encampment at Tobruk while dropping bombs from the observer's seat. The aircraft was being piloted by Lt Rossi and was flying at a height of 1,800ft when four bullets struck the fuselage, one of them hitting his passenger.

No Italian air crew were killed during the Libyan campaign, though one of their number, Lt Moizo, earned the unenviable distinction of becoming the first pilot to be captured in warfare when his Nieuport made a forced landing near Azizia on 11 September 1912. Moizo had been the first pilot to arrive in Tripoli and during his 11 months on active service had made 82 sorties, more than any other member of the Aviation Corps. It was reported about this time that the longest an airman could last under war conditions was six months, and that he would then require a 'considerable period of recuperation before he can take up military flying again'.
PILOT TO BE KILLED IN WARFARE: the first was a Bulgarian, M. Popoff, who was reported by Reuter's Correspondent in Sofia, in a dispatch dated 3 November 1912, to have been shot down 'recently' while making a reconnaissance flight over Adrianople.
AERIAL ATTACK ON SHIPPING first took place in 1913, but could have been in either of two different wars. Towards the end of the 1st Balkan War, a Farman biplane, belonging to the Royal Hellenic Navy and used for reconnaissance, is known to have dropped four hand-grenades on vessels of the Turkish fleet lying in the Dardanelles. This would have been before May. The other bombing attack at sea during that year took place during General Carranza's campaign against General Huerta in Mexico. Carranza secured the services of a French-born American citizen called Didier Masson, who became a one-man air force in the loyalist cause. Flying a Curtiss biplane, brought over in parts by mule train across the Rio Grande, Masson launched an attack on a Huerta gunboat as it lay in the Bay of Guaymas, releasing a number of canisters of explosive which he claimed caused a certain amount of damage to the vessel.

Apart from the three campaigns already noted, aircraft were employed in several other wars prior to 1914 – by the French and Spanish in their respective Moroccan campaigns, and during the 2nd Balkan War (1913), which was also the first conflict to see aircraft being used by both sides. In April 1914, a few weeks before the outbreak of World War I, the Americans gained a baptism of fire in the air when a short campaign was mounted against Mexico. One Curtiss seaplane and two Curtiss flying-boats were sent to Vera Cruz aboard the *Birmingham* and the *Mississippi* (*see* Aircraft Carrier) and flew ship-to-shore reconnaissance missions.

The only Englishman known to have served as a combatant pilot before World War I was Snowdon Hedley, who had qualified at Brooklands in 1911. During the 1st Balkan War of 1912–13, he joined the Bulgarian Army Aviation Corps and is reputed to have bombed Adrianople from a Farman box-kite biplane during the siege.
AIR BATTLE: the earliest recorded, albeit one-sided, is shrouded in the anonymity of a scrupulously censored Reuter's dispatch dated 15 August 1914:

In another place a French aeroplane yesterday encountered a German aeroplane. The French pilot chased the German, firing with a Browning. The German aviator did not reply, but fled.

The first decisive aerial engagement, resulting in the death of the enemy, took place on 5 October 1914, when Joseph Frantz, of the French Air Corps' V24 fighter squadron, encountered a German Aviatik while returning from a reconnaissance over enemy lines in his Voisin biplane. Frantz's mechanic, Quenault, had charge of a Hotchkiss machine-gun mounted in the nacelle of the machine; the Aviatik's observer was armed only with a rifle, which he had difficulty in aiming as the aircraft's tail was in the line of fire. Quenault riddled the German aeroplane with bullets until the Hotchkiss jammed, at which moment the Aviatik burst into flames and crashed behind the French lines. The battle was watched by ground troops of both sides, who climbed on to the parapets of their trenches to obtain a better view. The German aviators, first to be killed in air-to-air combat, were Wilhelm Sclienting of Alterdorf and Fritz von Zangen of Darmstadt. A letter found in the dead pilot's pocket, addressed to his mother, was delivered to a near-by German airfield by a French aircraft, a mark of compassion that became customary during the early period of the air war, when duels in the sky were still fought with a certain *élan* and without malice to the enemy.

For the first offensive operation by British forces in the air (19 August 1914) *see* Aeroplane Reconnaissance.

The first British aircraft shot down in warfare was an Avro of No. 5 Squadron RFC, which had left Maubeuge on a reconnaissance at 10.16am on 22 August 1914, and crashed near Mons some time later, after being hit by ground fire. The crew, Lts V. Waterfall and C. G. G. Bayley, were the first British fliers to be killed in action.

The first attack on an enemy aircraft was made by Lts L. A. Strange and Penn-Gaskell of No. 5 Squadron RFC in a Henri Farman, equipped with a Lewis gun and 300 rounds of ammunition, the first 'fighter' aircraft to go into action. With Strange at the controls, they took off from Maubeuge in pursuit of a German Albatross shortly before 2.30pm on 22 August 1914. Owing to the weight of the machine-gun, the Henri Farman was unable to climb above 3,500ft, but Penn-Gaskell was able to loose off several bursts of ammunition before the enemy aeroplane climbed into the sky and made good its escape.

The first occasion on which a British aircraft is definitely known to have shot down its opponent occurred on 22 November 1914, when Lts L. A. Strange and F. G. Small of No. 5 Squadron RFC engaged an Albatross at a height of 6,500ft. The British aviators were flying an Avro, equipped, against orders, with a Lewis gun, Strange having been ordered to desist from his machine-gun experiments after the episode described above. Two drums of ammunition were emptied into the enemy machine before it side-slipped away and made a forced landing behind Allied lines, close to Neuve-Église. The German pilot and his observer were uninjured, despite the fact that their aircraft had been hit in 20 different places. They were taken prisoner by their adversaries, who had landed near by. A number of other German aircraft had been forced to land on earlier occasions, but this was generally effected by a number of British aeroplanes 'buzzing' their opponent, and not, as far as is known, by armed combat.

BOMB ATTACK BY A BRITISH AIRCRAFT: the first was made over Lessines at 11.30am on 24 August 1914, when Capt. H. C. Jackson and Lt E. L. Conran of No. 3 Squadron RFC sighted three German aircraft on the ground and aimed a single bomb at them. It detonated wide of the mark.

The first effective attack from the air was made on 28 August 1914 by Lt. L. A. Strange of No. 5 Squadron RFC, who dropped a home-made petrol bomb on to a German truck as it proceeded along a road near Mons. The vehicle swerved off the road and caught fire; flaming petrol was splashed over a following truck, which also began to burn.

The first effective air raid by British aircraft on specified targets was carried out by two Sopwith Tabloids of the RNAS on 8 October 1914, Squadron Commander Spenser Grey launching an attack on Cologne, and Flt-Lt R. L. Marix aiming for Düsseldorf. In both instances their objective was the Zeppelin sheds. Marix located his target without difficulty and dived at the sheds, releasing his bombs from a height of 600ft. An inflated Zeppelin inside immediately exploded into flame and within 30sec the roof of the building had collapsed, sending enormous flames licking 500ft into the air. Grey was less fortunate, heavy mist preventing him from finding the Cologne sheds, but he was able to drop his bombs on the main railway station instead.

AIR RAID ON BRITISH SOIL: the first was made on Dover by Lt von Prondynski in a Taube monoplane on 24 December 1914. He dropped a single bomb, from a height of 5,000ft, which landed in the grounds of St James's Rectory, blowing a hole in the lawn and breaking the windows. Fragments of the bomb were mounted on a shield and presented to HM King George V.

The first casualties sustained in an air raid over Britain were caused by the attack on Great Yarmouth by the *L3* Zeppelin, which dropped six 110lb bombs and a number of incendiaries at 8.30pm on 19 January 1915. The first two people killed were Samuel Smith, a 50-year-old shoemaker, struck down outside his house at St Peter's Plain, and 72-year-old Miss Martha Taylor, who died 'as she was going for her supper'. Three other persons were injured.

See also Aerial Propaganda; Aeroplane, Jet; Aeroplane Reconnaissance; Aircraft Carrier.

The first
AEROGRAMME

was devised by the Iraq Director of Posts, Douglas Gumbley, and registered at Stationers' Hall in London under his own copyright in February 1933. They were first issued for postal use by the Iraq Post Office on 15 July 1933.

GB: The first pre-stamped aerogramme for civilian use was introduced by the GPO on 18 June 1943. This had been preceded by an unstamped air-letter form, first issued on 25 November 1942, and intended primarily for Forces Mail, though civilians could also use them for writing to other civilians overseas, provided that a 6d stamp was affixed. Pale blue replaced a murky grey as the standard British aerogramme colour in 1950, the postal rate remaining unchanged at 6d until 1966.

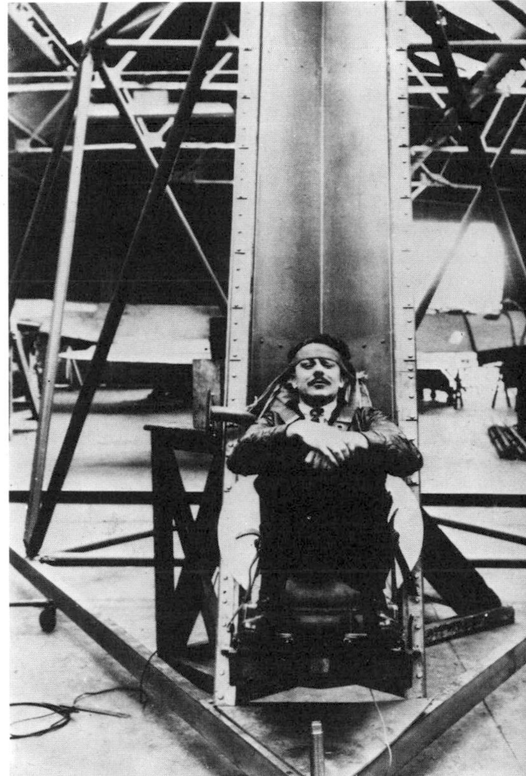

Bernard Lynch prepared for the first British live test shot, January 1945

The first
AEROPLANE EJECTION SEAT

was a compressed-air operated device fitted to the experimental German Heinkel He 280 jet fighter, which made its maiden flight at Rostock-Marienehe on 2 April 1941. The first emergency ejection was made over Rechlin, Germany on 13 January 1942, when the prototype crashed, due to heavy icing. The pilot, Maj. Schenk, ejected at 7,875ft, and made a safe landing. The He 280 did not go into production, as Government contracts were cancelled in favour of the Messerschmitt Me 262 jet fighter.

The first aircraft fitted with an ejection seat fired by an explosive charge was the Swedish-built Saab 21, which flew for the first time on 30 July 1943. This ballistic system of ejection completely superseded the use of compressed-air cylinders, and SAAB can claim credit for developing in practical form the principle upon which nearly all modern ejection seats are operated.

The first production aircraft to become operational with an ejection seat as standard equipment was the Heinkel He 162, which made its maiden flight on 6 December 1944, and went into service with the German Luftwaffe Squadron L/JG1 at Leck-Holstein on 14 April 1945. Powder-charged ballistic-catapult-type seats were fitted to a total of 116 pre-production and production aircraft. The Saab 21, which had been developed earlier than the He 162, did not become operational with the Royal Swedish Air Force until December 1945.

GB: The first ejection seat was developed independently of the German and Swedish systems by James Martin of the Martin-Baker Aircraft Co, Denham, Buckinghamshire between 1944 and 1946. The first man to be ejected was Aircraft-Fitter Benny Lynch. According to his own account, 'everyone in the factory elected me as the person it was hardest to kill'. On 24 July 1946, Lynch bailed out from a Meteor jet fighter flying at 8,000ft above Chalgrove Aerodrome, Oxfordshire, and landed in the back-yard of a public house. He was recovered intact from the bar.

The first British pilot to use his ejection seat in an emergency was Armstrong Whitworth test pilot J.O. Lancaster, who made a successful escape from the experimental AWA 52 delta-wing jet when it went out of control 4,000ft above Coventry on 30 May 1949.

The first
AEROPLANE FLIGHT

sustained and controlled in a powered aircraft, was made by Orville Wright in the 12hp Flyer I at Kill Devil Hills, Kittyhawk, N. Car. at 10.35am on 17 December 1903. The flight lasted for 12sec at a height of 8–12ft and an air speed of 30–35mph. It was witnessed by Orville Wright's brother and co-inventor Wilbur and by five coastguards. Three other flights were made the same day, the longest by Wilbur, who covered 852ft in 59sec, or more than half-a-mile air distance. The following day's Press reports treated the announcement of the conquest of the air with levity, and in Britain the news was carried by only one newspaper, the *Daily Mail*.

GB: The first flight in Britain was made on 16 October 1908, by the American showman and inventor 'Colonel' Samuel Franklin Cody, in his Army Aeroplane No. 1 at the Balloon Corps Factory, Farnborough. He flew 1,390ft and was airborne for 27sec. A week earlier Wilbur Wright had flown nearly 50 miles in France.

The first
AEROPLANE FLIGHT WITH A PASSENGER

took place at Kill Devil Hills, Kittyhawk, N. Car. on 14 May 1908, when Wilbur Wright carried his mechanic, Charles W. Furnas at Dayton, Ohio, on a 1,968ft flight of 29sec duration in the Wright Flyer III.

GB: The first Englishman to fly as a passenger was Griffith Brewer, a patent agent and keen amateur balloonist, who accompanied Wilbur Wright on two circuits of the airfield at Le Mans on 8 October 1908. He wrote of his experience: 'During the first flight I remember wondering whether we should really rise from the rail, and then a feeling of elation when the grass slipped away backwards and downwards and the machine seemed to be sitting on nothing. But the predominant sense was one of wonder that the same man could calmly invent such a mechanism and yet fly it with such consummate skill!'

The first woman to fly as an aeroplane passenger was the French sculptress, Mme Thérèse Peltier, who was taken for a short flight by Léon Delagrange in a Voisin at Turin on 8 July 1908.

The first aeroplane passenger to fly in Britain was Col J.E. Capper, RE, Officer Commanding Balloon Sections, who was piloted by S.F. Cody for a 2-mile flight over Laffan's Plain in his British Army Aeroplane No. 1 on 14 August 1909. Mrs Cody became the first woman passenger in Britain on the same day, and Mrs Capper the first British woman passenger in Britain on 27 September 1909.

PAYING PASSENGERS in Britain were first able to book joy-rides at Hendon and Brooklands during the summer of 1911 through Messrs Keith Prowse & Co, who enjoyed the sole agency. Short flights cost 2gns, while longer ones – three circuits of the aerodrome culminating in a gliding descent – could be had for an extra guinea.

The first fare-paying passenger flight to a specific destination took place on 17 May 1911 when J.V. Martin flew a passenger from Brooklands to Hendon on a G.W. Farman.

The first
AEROPLANE TO BE HIJACKED

was the Cathay Pacific Airways Catalina flying-boat *Miss Macao*, which was seized by a gang of Chinese bandits led by a peasant called Wong-yu Man, shortly after taking off from Macao during a scheduled flight to Hong Kong on 16 June 1948. The motive for the hijacking was to ransom the passengers, but the pilot resisted, the hijackers fired their weapons and the flying-boat crashed. The only survivor was the bandit leader Wong-yu Man. Although at first foul play was not suspected, when salvage-teams recovered the bullet-riddled fuselage, the police placed an informer in the bed next to Wong-yu Man in his Hong Kong hospital. With the aid of a tape-recorder the full story of the world's first aerial hijacking was pieced together from remarks made by the perpetrator to his fellow 'patient'.

GB: The first hijack of a British plane took place near Beirut, Lebanon on 9 September 1970, when guerrillas of the Popular Front for the Liberation of Palestine forced the pilot of a London-bound BOAC Super VC-10, carrying 114 passengers, to land at an airstrip in the desert north-east of Amman, Jordan. Here a Swissair DC8 and a TWA Boeing 707 were already being held with 184 passengers as hostages for hijacker Leila Khaled, then in detention in London, and other Arab Nationalist prisoners in Germany and Switzerland. Civil war subsequently broke out in Jordan and the three hijacked airliners were blown up by the Palestine Nationalists. The hostages were returned safely to their own countries in exchange for Miss Khaled and other detainees.

The first
AEROPLANE, JET (TURBOJET)

was the Heinkel He 178, which was powered by a centrifugal-flow engine designed by Dr Hans von Ohain, and first flown by Flug Kapitan Erich Warsitz at Rostock-Marienehe, Germany early on the morning of 24 August 1939. A longer flight took place three days later, often described as the first. Dr Ohain had joined Heinkel in 1936 and his first test-bed turbojet engine, designated 'He S1', was run the following year. The experiments were carried out in secret without the knowledge of the German Air Ministry, and it was not until October 1939 that the He 178 was officially demonstrated before high-ranking officers of the Luftwaffe.

GB: The first turbojet aircraft was the Gloster-Whittle E.28/39, designed by FO (later Sir) Frank Whittle and test flown for the first time at Cranwell by Flt Lt P.E.G. Sayer on 15 May 1941. The Gloster-Whittle was the first turbojet to fly with a performance superior to any piston-engined aircraft and attained speeds of up to 466mph. Whittle had taken out his first patent for a gas-turbine system of jet propulsion in 1930 while still a cadet at Cranwell. He

Messerschmitt Me 262A

subsequently formed a company called 'British Power Jets Ltd' to exploit his patents, and the first test-bed run of the experimental Whittle Unit took place on 12 April 1937.
TURBOJET AIRCRAFT IN SERIES PRODUCTION and the first *JET FIGHTER USED IN WARFARE* was the Messerschmitt Me 262A, of which the prototype made its maiden jet-powered flight at Leipheim, 18 July 1942. It was powered by Junkers Jumo 004 engines giving a maximum speed of 540mph, and armed with four MK 108 30mm short-barrelled guns. Thirteen pre-production A-1 fighters were delivered to test centres at Lechfeld and Rechlin for service evaluation in March and April 1944, followed by the first production models in May. In June 1944 the world's first operational jet-fighter unit, Erprobungskommando EK 262, was formed at Lechfeld under Hauptmann Werner Thierfelder.

The first jet fighter to engage an enemy in combat was an Me 262, from the EK 262 experimental unit at Lechfeld, which intercepted a Mosquito of 544 Squadron RDF over Munich on 25 July 1944. The pilot of the British plane, Flt Lt Wall, evaded five firing passes from the Me 262 before escaping into a cloudbank.
GB: The first production model and the first jet fighter was the Gloster Meteor F Mk 1, of which the prototype, designated 'F9/40', was first flown at Cranwell by Michael Daunton on 5 March 1943. The first two production models of the Meteor, powered by twin Rolls-Royce W.2B/23 Welland 1 engines, were delivered to 616 Squadron RAF at Culmhead, Somerset on 12 July 1944. A fortnight later the Squadron moved to Manston, Kent and on 27 July, Meteors were flown in a combat operation for the first time. The RAF's first jet pilot to score a 'kill' was FO Dean, who deflected and grounded a V-1 flying-bomb on 4 August.
JET BOMBER: the first was the Messerschmidt Me 262A-2 *Sturmvogel* (Stormbird), delivered to the Kommando Schenk at Rheine for evaluation in June 1944. The first operational jet-bomber unit was 3. Staffel of I./KG 51, which arrived at Juvincourt, near Rheims with five *Sturmvögel* in August. It was at Hitler's personal insistence that this bomber version of the Me 262 was produced, though the basic design was plainly unsuitable for such a role.
GB: The first British-designed jet bomber was the English Electric Canberra B Mk 1, powered by Rolls-Royce Avon RA2 engines, of which the prototype was test flown at Warton by Wing Cdr R. P. Beaumont on 13 May 1949. The first production model was delivered to 101 Squadron RAF at Binbrook on 25 May 1951.
JET-TO-JET AERIAL COMBAT first took place over North Korea on 8 November 1950, when Lt Russell John Brown of the US Air Force, flying a Lockheed F-80 jet fighter, engaged and destroyed a Soviet MiG-15.

The first
AEROPLANE MANUFACTURING COMPANY
for the production of powered aircraft was the firm of Voisin Frères, established in la rue de la Ferme, Billancourt, France in November 1906 by 26-year-old Gabriel Voisin and his brother Charles, 24. Their cash assets at the time they decided to found a new industry, Gabriel remembered in his autobiography, amounted to 4 or 5 francs in the bank and some loose change. There were originally two employees, a former boat-builder called Métayer and a cabinet-maker named Brost. The company's first order was received in December 1906 from a M. Florencie, inventor of a flapping-wing ornithopter, but the machine was based on unsound principles and failed to leave the ground. The brothers' first successful, commercially built aircraft was a box-kite biplane of their own design powered by a 50hp eight-cylinder Antoinette engine, which was ordered the same month by Paris sculptor Léon Delagrange and test flown by Charles Voisin at Bagatelle on 30 March 1907. The aircraft was handed over to the customer the same day and this date can be regarded as marking the birth of the world-wide aviation industry.
GB: The first aircraft-manufacturer in Britain was Howard T. Wright, who together with his automobile-distributor brother Warwick, set up a workshop under a rented railway arch at Battersea in 1907 and began work on a helicopter ordered by Signor Capone of Naples. This pioneer product of the British aircraft industry was powered by a 30hp Antoinette engine driving twin two-bladed lifting rotors; although it succeeded in lifting a weight of 1,250lb during tethered trials at Norbury Golf Links in February 1908, it never succeeded in achieving free flight. The first conventional powered aircraft produced by the firm was a biplane with a 50hp Métallurgique water-cooled engine built to the order of Malcolm Seton-Karr in 1908 and exhibited at the Olympia Aero Show the following year. The price of the aircraft was £1,200 and it had a maximum speed of 35mph. Although recognized as a brilliant designer, Howard Wright lacked the business acumen to run a successful aviation company, and he gave up manufacture in 1910 to join the Coventry Ordnance Works.

The first
AEROPLANE EQUIPPED WITH RADIO
was flown over the racetrack at Sheepshead Bay, N.Y. on 27 August 1910, by the Canadian pilot J. A. D. McCurdy, who transmitted the following message to the ground station operated by H. M. Horton: 'Another chapter in aerial achievement is hereby written in the receiving of this first message ever recorded from an aeroplane in flight.'
GB: The first aeroplane to be equipped with radio was a Bristol Boxkite flown on reconnaissance by the distinguished actor Robert Loraine during the British Army's autumn manœuvres on Salisbury Plain on 27 September 1910. The 14lb radio was designed and installed in the aircraft by Thorne Baker. The aerial was wound round the wooden supports between the main-planes of the machine. (McCurdy had employed a long trailing aerial.) The pilot operated the transmitter from a key strapped to his left knee, using his right hand for the controls. A temporary receiving station was set up in the Bristol hangar at Larkhill, and Thorne Baker was able to take down simple messages of one or two words transmitted in Morse at distances of up to one mile. Ground-to-air communication was maintained with a hand-lamp.

The first complete and coherent

message transmitted from an aircraft beyond visual range of the receiving station was sent by Capt. Brenôt of the French Army from a position between Saint-Cyr and Rambouillet, some 35 miles from the Eiffel Tower radio station, early in July 1911.

The first British service aircraft to be equipped with radio was a Flanders monoplane, which carried out experiments at the Army Aircraft Factory, Farnborough, and at Brooklands Aviation Ground in 1912 using a Marconi 6V battery-operated tuned-spark transmitter. At the outbreak of war in 1914 the RFC and RNAS had a total of 16 aircraft and 2 airships with spark transmitters.

AIRBORNE RADIO IN WARFARE, the first use of, took place on 24 September 1914, when Lts D.S. Lewis and B.T. James of No. 4 Squadron RFC directed artillery-fire from the air during the 1st Battle of the Aisne. The radio log for that date begins at 4.02pm with the message 'A very little short. Fire! Fire!' and concludes at 4.42pm with the words 'I am coming home now.' Both officers were killed in action shortly after.

AIRBORNE RADIO TELEPHONE: the first was Wireless Telephone Mark I, designed by former Marconi engineer Maj. C.E. Prince and demonstrated from air to ground before Lord Kitchener in France, February 1916. Shortly after this, Maj. Prince succeeded in communicating from ground to air in an experiment carried out at Brooklands Aviation Ground. The pilot, Lt J.M. Furnival, was circling the aerodrome at 50mph when the message came over: 'Hullo, Furnie. If you hear me now it will be the first time speech has ever been communicated to an aeroplane in flight.' Furnival acknowledged by dipping his wing.

The first squadron to be equipped with two-way radio telephones was London Defence Squadron (No. 141) RFC in 1917. Training and installation was under the direction of Wireless Officer F.S. Mockford, who was to win greater renown after the war as the originator of the Mayday distress signal.

CIVIL AIRLINER TO BE EQUIPPED WITH RADIO: the first was the DH 42 G-EALU operated by Aircraft Transport & Travel Ltd between London and Paris in 1919. The AD I/S set was installed by Marconi's.

The first
AEROPLANE RECONNAISSANCE
was made in a single-seater Henri Farman biplane by Capt. Marconnet and Lt Fequant of the French Army on 9 June 1910. With Fequant at the controls, the reconnaissance mission took the two aviators on a record-breaking 2½hr, 145km flight from the Camp de Châlons at Mourmelon to Vincennes. Capt. Marconnet, squeezed into the narrow space between the pilot's seat and the engine, used a hand-held camera to take a series of reconnaissance photographs of the roads, railways, towns and countryside beneath.

GB: The first reconnaissance mission was flown on 24 September 1910 by Capt. Bertram Dickson during the British Army's autumn military manœuvres on Salisbury Plain. Having succeeded in locating the 'Blue Army', he was captured on landing his Bristol Boxkite aircraft in 'enemy territory' and subsequently interviewed by the Home Secretary, Winston Churchill, who displayed great interest in the possibilities of reconnaissance aircraft in warfare. After reading the *Daily Mail* Air Correspondent's account of Bertram Dickson's exploit, the actor Robert Loraine rushed down to Salisbury Plain from London and took to the air on behalf of the 'Blue Army', making the first reconnaissance report by wireless (*see* Aeroplane equipped with Radio).

AEROPLANE RECONNAISSANCE IN WARFARE was first flown during the Italo-Turkish War of 1911–12 by Capt. Piazza, commander of the air base at Tripoli. He took off from Tripoli in a Blériot XI *bis* on 23 October 1911 and flew over the Turkish encampment at Aziza, causing consternation and alarm in the enemy ranks. This was the first use of aircraft in the history of warfare. Three days later the Italians became the first to use aircraft in battle, when Capt. Piazza and Lt Gavotti flew a reconnaissance mission over enemy lines at the Battle of Sciara-Sciat and directed gunfire from the battleship *Carlo Alberto* and from the Italian mountain artillery.

GB: The first aeroplane reconnaissance in warfare was made on 19 August 1914 by Capt. (later Air Marshal Sir) Philip Joubert de la Ferté of No. 3 Squadron RFC, flying a Blériot XI monoplane, and Lt Gilbert Mapplebeck of No. 4 Squadron RFC, in a B.E.2; they were detailed to fly over Nivelle and Genappe to see if Belgian forces were in the area, and to search for German cavalry round Gembloux.

PHOTO RECONNAISSANCE FLIGHT IN WARFARE: the first was made during the Tripolitanian campaign (*see above*) by Capt. Piazza of the Italian Servizi Aeronautici in a Blériot XI *bis*, which he flew over enemy positions on 24 February 1912, and again the following day. Shortly afterwards Commandant Sulsi became the first to employ a ciné camera for photo reconnaissance, filming an enemy encampment from the airship P.3. During the course of the year, Italian Servizi Aeronautici fliers undertook an extensive aerial survey of both their own and enemy territory, and assembled the results into a photographic *carte démonstrative.*

The first
AIR CHARTER HOLIDAY
was arranged by the Polytechnic Touring Association of London in 1932 in response to the Government appeal not to spend money abroad following the financial crisis of the previous year. By chartering an aircraft to fly holiday-makers to Switzerland, and lodging them at the PTA's own chalets at Seeburg, Lucerne, 95% of the currency expended returned to Britain. The first party of 24 tourists left Croydon by Imperial Airways Heracles airliner on the 5hr flight to Basle in May. Inclusive cost of a seven-day holiday in Switzerland was approximately £12–£14, or £16–£18 for a fortnight. The plea made by the PTA in their brochure to a public yet to become air-minded – "But air travel IS safe . . .' – proved itself justified, and a more ambitious package tour of seven European capitals was arranged the same year, carrying the venturesome air tourist aloft to Amsterdam, Berlin, Vienna, Budapest, Rome, Paris, and back to London, a 14-day round trip of 2,829 miles by Heracles airliner. Over 900 PTA tourists were taken to the Continent by air in 1932.

The following year passenger air transport recovered from the effects of the slump, and Imperial Airways being unwilling to charter its aircraft, air holidays were discontinued until after World War II.

The first
AIRCRAFT CARRIER
The first naval vessel to be equipped with a (temporary) flight-deck was the US light cruiser *Birmingham*, from which exhibition pilot Eugène Ely took off in a 50hp Curtiss pusher biplane at 3.16pm on 14 November 1910, while the ship lay at anchor in Chesapeake Bay. He landed 2½ miles away at Willoughby Spit, near Norfolk, Va.

The first landing on the deck of a ship was performed by Ely at 11.01am on 18 January 1911, when he touched down on a 120ft-long platform erected on the stern of the armoured cruiser *Pennsylvania*, moored in San Francisco Bay. His Curtiss aircraft was fitted with three pairs of spring-loaded hooks on the undercarriage, designed to engage a series of 22 cables stretched between sandbags across the flight-deck at 3ft intervals. This arrester system brought the plane to a halt after a deck run of only 30 ft.

GB: The first ship of the Royal Navy fitted with a flight-deck was HMS *Africa* in December 1911. In a secret experiment made on 10 January 1912, Lt Charles Samson took off in a Short S.38 biplane while the *Africa* lay at anchor in Sheerness Harbour and alighted in the water.

TAKE-OFF FROM A SHIP UNDER WAY anywhere in the world was first made from HMS *Hibernia* by Lt Samson in a Short S.38, while the vessel was moving at a speed of 10½ knots during a Review of the Fleet by HM King George V at Weymouth on 8 May 1912.

SHIP OF THE ROYAL NAVY IN REGULAR USE AS AN AIRCRAFT CARRIER: the first was HMS *Hermes*, a light cruiser adapted for this purpose towards the end of 1912 by the addition of a short flight-deck over her bow. She carried two RNAS seaplanes, which were launched from the flight-deck on trolleys. It was from this carrier that Lt Samson made the first trials with a folding-wing aircraft the following year, an idea that had originated with the First Lord of the Admiralty, Winston Churchill.

AIRCRAFT CARRIERS IN WARFARE, the first use of, took place in April 1914, when the US battleship *Mississippi* and the cruiser *Birmingham* were ordered to Vera Cruz with five US Navy seaplanes. The aircraft were used to make reconnaissance flights over the Mexican lines, being lowered over the side of their carriers for take-off from the water.

The first Royal Navy aircraft carriers used in warfare were the former Channel steamers *Empress*, *Engadine* and *Riviera*, converted into seaplane carriers in 1914, primarily for coastal defence. The first carrier-launched air raid was made from these craft as they lay off Heligoland on 25 December 1914, seven seaplanes under the command of Cdr C. L'Estrange Malone (*see* Communist Party, MP) flying to Cuxhaven to bomb the Zeppelin sheds of the German naval base.

CATAPULT LAUNCHING from a ship at sea was first made on 5 November 1915, when an AB-2 flying-boat of the US Navy took off from the stern of the battleship *North Carolina* as she lay anchored in Pensacola Bay, Fla.

The first warship in the world built as an aircraft carrier, though not originally designed as such, was HMS *Ark Royal*, a 366ft-long vessel of 7,020 tons displacement, launched at Blyth in September 1914, and commissioned on 9 December following. Intended as a merchantman, she was acquired by the Admiralty while under construction and converted for use as a carrier with below-deck hangers accommodating 10 seaplanes. The *Ark Royal* was dispatched to the Dardanelles immediately on completing her trials and conducted her first offensive operation on arrival at Tenedos on 17 February 1915, when one of her aircraft took off on a reconnaissance mission.

The first warship built for the use of wheeled-aircraft was HMS *Furious*, a 19,100 tons displacement combination battle cruiser/carrier, which joined the Fleet on completion in June 1917. At this time she had only a take-off deck, her six wheeled-aircraft being expected to proceed to a land base on fulfilment of a mission, but in November 1917 she returned to dock for installation of a landing-deck. A notable feature of the *Furious* was her hydraulic lifts for raising aircraft from hangar to flight-deck.

AIRCRAFT CARRIER TO BE DESIGNED AND COMPLETED AS SUCH: the first was the Japanese Navy's 7,470 tons displacement *Hosho*, which was laid down on 19 December 1919, and made its first sea trials off Tateyama on 30 November 1922. She carried 21 aircraft and had a maximum speed of 25 knots.

GB: The first purpose-designed aircraft carrier was the 10,850 tons displacement HMS *Hermes*, which although laid down in January 1918, nearly two years before the *Hosho*, was not completed until July 1923. Twenty-five aircraft were carried; maximum speed was 25 knots.

JET AIRCRAFT TO TAKE OFF FROM AND LAND ABOARD AN AIRCRAFT CARRIER: the first was an XFD-1 Phantom which was flown from the USS *Franklin D. Roosevelt* by Lt-Cdr James J. Davidson as she lay off Cape Henry, Va. on 21 July 1946. The deck-run for take-off was 460ft.

The first carrier-based squadron of jet aircraft was US Navy Squadron 17-A, comprising 16 Phantoms, which qualified for cruiser operation aboard the USS *Saipan* on 5–7 May 1948.

NUCLEAR-POWERED AIRCRAFT CARRIER: the first was the 72,500 tons displacement USS *Enterprise*, launched at Newport News, Va., on 24 September 1960, and commissioned on 25 November 1961. Fitted with eight pressurized water-cooled nuclear reactors, she was the most powerful warship ever built (approx. 300,000hp), as well as the largest (1,101½ft long) and the costliest (($445 million). The total complement of the *Enterprise* was 440 officers and 4,160 enlisted men. She was designed to carry 100 aircraft, and her flight-deck was described as being the size of four American football pitches.

The first
AIR FORCE
unit was the Aeronautical Division of the Office of the Chief Signal Officer of the US Army, established under the command of Capt. Charles de Forest Chandler on 1 July 1907. The original strength of the force was one officer, one NCO and one enlisted man. A contract was placed with the Wright brothers for an aircraft that had to be capable of a speed of at least 36mph, and able to remain in the air continuously for at least one hour. The biplane was delivered to Fort Myer,

The world's first air force with the world's first military aircraft, 1909

Va. for flight tests in August 1908, but crashed the following month. A new Wright Flyer was constructed and, after successful flight trials, formally handed over to the Aeronautics Division on 2 August 1909. It was then taken to College Park, Md., where it made its maiden flight as the world's first regularly commissioned military aircraft. The first pilot officer to solo was 2nd Lt Frederic E. Humphreys, who made two circuits of the field at College Park in 3min on 26 October 1909. Although the first to show heavier-than-air aircraft a formal military recognition, the US Army was slow to develop its aviation resources and by the outbreak of war in Europe in 1914 it could boast no more than six aeroplanes.

The first nation to build up an effective force of military aircraft was France, which by the end of 1910 had 34 fully qualified Army pilots, another 20 under instruction, and 32 service aircraft. By the summer of 1911, French air power had increased to 100 aircraft and a comparable number of pilots. At the beginning of 1912 the number had doubled, with 234 aircraft and nearly 300 pilots.

GB: The first military aircraft acquired by the British Army was a Wright biplane presented to the War Office by the Hon. C.S. Rolls and delivered to the Balloon Corps Factory at Farnborough in June 1910. As there were no qualified military pilots available, the machine was folded up and stored in a corner of a large airship hangar. (Earlier experiments with military aircraft, designed by Lt Dunne and Samuel Cody, had been discontinued by the War office due to mounting costs, and the machines were returned to their inventors.) The first aircraft purchased by the War Office for service use were a Henri Farman *type-militaire* two-seater and a Paulhan biplane, both of which were ordered from the Aircraft Supply Co in November 1910, following the Larkhill trials noted below.

The first military pilot to fly officially for the Army was Capt. Bertram Dickson, who performed a reconnaissance mission during the autumn manœuvres at Larkhill on 24 September 1910. His aircraft was a Bristol Boxkite lent to the War Office by the British & Colonial Aeroplane Co. Both Capt. Dixon and Lt L.D.L. Gibbs, who began flying on reconnaissance the following day in his own clipped-wing racing Farman, had learned to fly privately in France; their initial reception at Larkhill by those of their brother officers schooled in a more traditional mode of warfare was far from encouraging. None of the senior officers in command took the trouble to give them any instructions and the role to be played by aircraft in the manœuvres was left entirely to their own initiative. Their striking successes in identifying the positions of the 'enemy' from the air, combined with the personal interest shown by the visiting Home Secretary, Winston Churchill, and by General French, helped to change the climate of opinion to such an extent that an immediate result of the exercises was a decision by the War Office to 'enlarge the scope of the work hitherto carried out at the Balloon School . . . by affording opportunities for aeroplaning'.

SERVING OFFICERS TO BE TRAINED AS PILOTS: three lieutenants of the Royal Navy and one member of the Royal Marine Artillery were selected from some 200 applicants and seconded to Eastchurch for flight training on 1 March 1911. Instruction was given on two Short biplanes. The first officers to qualify as pilots were Lt Charles Rumney Samson (*see* Aircraft Carrier) and Lt A.M. Longmore on 24 April, followed by Lt R. Gregory and Lt G.V. Wildman Lushington of the Royal Marines on 1 May.

AVIATION UNIT OF THE BRITISH ARMY, the first, and the lineal ancestor of the RAF was the Air Battalion, Royal Engineers, re-formed from the Balloon Section, RE on 1 April 1911. The original strength of the Battalion, commanded by Maj. Sir Alexander Bannerman RE, was 14 officers, 23 NCOs, 153 men of the Royal Engineers, 2 buglers, 4 riding-horses, 32 draught-horses, miscellaneous kites, balloons and airships and 5 aeroplanes. Four of the aircraft, a Wright, Farman, Paulhan and de Havilland, were biplanes, and one, a Blériot, was a monoplane. All were already part of the establishment of the Balloon Corps Factory at Farnborough, which now became the Army Aircraft Factory. Officers applying for transfer to the Air Battalion were recommended to be bachelors under 161lb in weight and over 30yr old. Desirable qualifications were stated to be good eyesight, medical fitness, the ability to map-read and make field sketches, immunity from sea-sickness (a practical consideration) and a knowledge of foreign languages. The role assigned to the Air Battalion was solely one of reconnaissance, as little regard was paid in military circles to the aircraft's potential as an active weapon of war. It was superseded by the Royal Flying Corps, formed on 13 May 1912. The RFC was conceived as an independent service and not as an adjunct to the Army or Navy, though in practice the War Office and the Admiralty regarded the Military and Naval Wing of the RFC respectively each as their special preserve.

INDEPENDENT AIR FORCE: the first to be effectively established, subordinate to neither naval or military command, was the Royal Air Force, formed by amalgamation of the Royal Flying Corps and the Royal Naval Air Service on 1 April 1918.

The first
AIR HOSTESS

was Miss Ellen Church, a Registered Nurse from Iowa, who on 15 May 1930 welcomed her first 11 passengers aboard a United Airlines tri-motor Boeing 80A at Oakland Airport, Calif., preparatory to the five-stage flight to Cheyenne, Wyo. Nurse Church, a private pilot herself, had written to the airline a month or two previously suggesting that suitably qualified young ladies like herself might be employed as cabin attendants. She was not only engaged, but given the task of selecting and training seven other girls for the same work. Aspiring applicants had to be Registered Nurses of 25 or under, weigh not more than 115lb and were not to exceed 5ft 4in in height. The chosen few won themselves the right to wear a chic woollen twill uniform with grey and silver buttons, a salary of $125 a month, and the sometimes doubtful pleasure of spending a basic

Ellen Church, the first air hostess

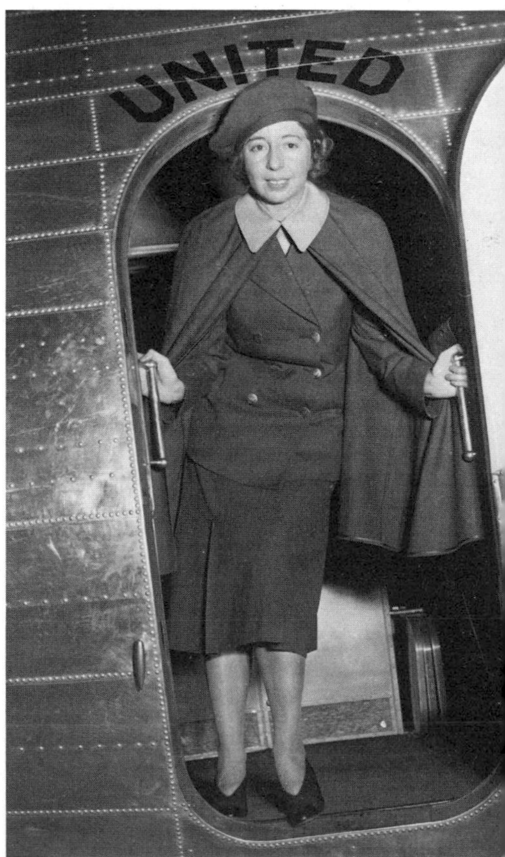

100hr flying a month in an unheated and unpressurized aircraft. Their duties, which were not confined to the air, included carrying the passengers' baggage, cleaning the interior of the aeroplane, helping the pilot and mechanics to push the machine in and out of hangars, and wielding a refuelling hose. At each embarkation point they collected tickets and once in the air dispensed unvarying meals of fruit cocktail, fried chicken and rolls, and tea or coffee. Scheduled time for the 950-mile flight was 18hr, but according to one of the pioneer hostesses it generally took something closer to 24. At the beginning Miss Church and the other seven ex-nurses suffered undisguised hostility from the pilots and the even fiercer resentment of their wives, who deluged the airline with letters demanding that the girls should go. Expressions of appreciation from passengers weighed more heavily with United, and the girls stayed, harbingers of a new profession for women.

Outside the USA the first air hostesses were recruited by Air France in 1931, and these were also the first to fly on international routes. Swissair followed suit in 1934, KLM a year later, and Lufthansa in 1938.

GB: The first air hostess was Miss Rosamond Gilmour of Croydon, Surrey, who commenced flying duties on 10 May 1943 on a BOAC shuttle-service flight made by Frobisher aircraft operating between Whitchurch, Somerset and Shannon Airport, Eire, and connecting with the flying-boat base at near-by Foynes. In July she and four other girls began working on the Foynes–Lisbon run. They were outfitted with a dark blue uniform with rose-coloured sleeve stripes and epaulettes, brass buttons and stout brogue shoes. Catering under conditions of wartime rationing was relatively simple, meals consisting of sandwiches, cold snacks and hot drinks from a Thermos flask. One duty seldom required of a later generation of air stewardesses, however, was the fastening and unfastening of passengers' seat-belts, a task they were not entrusted to do for themselves. Qualifications for the job included nursing experience, ability to cook (presumably with a view to expanded peacetime operation), an educated voice, poise and infinite patience, but, stated BOAC austerely, 'glamour girls are definitely not required'.

The first
AIRLINE
to establish scheduled passenger service by aeroplane was the St Petersburg–Tampa Airboat Line of St Petersburg, Fla., which commenced flight operations on 1 January 1914. Passengers were carried across the 20-mile-wide Tampa Bay one at a time in a Benoist flying-boat piloted by Tony Jannus. The fare was $5 and saved the affluent and intrepid a 36-mile journey round the bay by road. The service continued for four months, with two flights a day.

The first operational airline in Europe, and the first in the world to achieve a sustained service, was Germany's DLR (Deutsche Luft-Reederei), which began flying between Berlin and Weimar on a regular daily schedule on 6 February 1919. It would appear that only mail and newspapers were carried on the initial flights, but by 28 February a total of 19 passengers had made the journey. The aircraft used were open-cockpit LVG CIV biplanes, which meant that passengers had to be issued with flying-suits, helmets and goggles, and fur-lined flying-boots. Shortly, however, DLR began using AEG JII biplanes with a five-seater passenger compartment. Further internal routes opened up during the course of 1919 included Berlin–Hamburg (1 March), Berlin–Hanover–Rotthausen (15 April) and Berlin–Warnemünde (15 April). One standard airline feature that had been pioneered by DLR before the end of the year was the adoption of a corporate emblem for display on their aircraft, and this symbol – a crane rising in flight – is still used as the fleet emblem of Lufthansa.

GB: The first scheduled civil airline service in Britain was maintained between Alexander Park, Manchester and Blackpool/Southport by A. V. Roe & Co from 10 May to 30 September 1919. Average flying speed of the two-seater (later converted to four-seater) single-engine Avro biplanes was 70mph, and the 50-mile flight was generally completed in a little under the hour. A total of 8,730 route miles were flown that summer and 194 out of 222 scheduled flights completed at fares of 2gns single and 4gns return.

A more extensive internal airline service was inaugurated the same month by the North Sea Aerial Navigation Co, which opened up its first route, Hartlepool–Hull, on 26 May 1919, and followed this during the summer with services linking Hull–Leeds–Hounslow (for London), and Scarborough–Hull–Harrogate. The aircraft were Blackburn Kangaroos. While Avro's services out of Manchester catered principally for holidaymakers, North Sea's speedy link between London and the North attracted the custom of businessmen whose time meant money.

INTERNATIONAL AIRLINE SERVICE, the first, was instituted between Paris and Brussels on a weekly schedule by Lignes Aériennes Farman on 22 March 1919. The pilot of the Farman F.60 Goliath used was M. Bossoutrot, flying time 2hr 50min, and the fare 365 francs.

GB: The first international airline service out of Britain, and the first in the world on a daily schedule, began with Air Transport & Travel's 9.10am flight from London (Hounslow) to Paris (Le Bourget) on 25 August 1919. A converted DH4a biplane bomber piloted by Lt E. H. Lawford carried newspapers, a consignment of leather, several brace of grouse, some jars of Devonshire cream and George Stevenson-Reece, who paid a single fare of £21 for the 2½hr journey. The cost of travelling by rail and boat to Paris at this date was £3 8s 5d.

INTERCONTINENTAL AIRLINE SERVICE, the first, was operated by Lignes Aériennes Latécoère, which began flying Breguet 14s on the Toulouse–Barcelona–Tangier route on 1 September 1919, with an extension to Casablanca from April 1920.

On the American continent the first airline to start operations after World War I was the S. des T.A. Guyanais of French Guiana in November 1919; this marked a trend by which it was often the less-developed countries with inadequate rail services that were in the forefront of civil aviation development. In the USA, where ground communications were a model of efficiency, there were no sustained aerial passenger services before 1926. America, the birthplace of the aeroplane, was thus the last of the advanced nations of the world to enter the field of commercial aviation as a means of passenger transport, though having done so, she was quick to realize the 'flying bus' concept of the airliner. Whereas in Europe air travel before World War II was generally confined to those whose time was valuable enough to justify paying fares four or five times in excess of the cost by surface transport, and was commensurately luxurious, the American airlines aimed to provide a reliable and cheap, though somewhat less comfortable service that would offer an economic alternative to rail travel.

MEALS IN FLIGHT: the first attempt at providing such a service was made by Handley Page Transport and took the form of pre-packed lunch-boxes offered on their London–Paris flights from 11 October 1919. The price was 3s.

A number of different airlines have claimed the distinction of having been the first to serve hot meals in flight, but it would appear that this was, appropriately, a French innovation. Possibly first, and certainly among the earliest, was Air Union, which was

offering an elaborate five-course lunch with choice of wines *c.* 1925.
GB: The first cooked meals were served on Imperial Airways' luxury 'Silver Wing' flights from London to Paris, commencing on 1 May 1927. The three-engined Armstrong Whitworth Argosies used on this service were furnished with a galley at the rear of the aircraft from which lunch could be provided for up to 18 passengers.
AIRLINE STEWARD: the first was Jack Sanderson, who started duty on a de Havilland 34 operated by Daimler Airways between London and Paris on 2 April 1922. Steward Sanderson was killed in an air crash the following year.
1ST- OR 2ND-CLASS TRAVEL: the first airline to offer a choice at varying fares was Imperial Airways on the London–Paris route in October 1927. First-class passengers were carried in 'Silver Wing' Argosies with steward service for £9 return and made the trip in 2hr 30min; 2nd-class passengers paid £7 10s return for a 2hr 50min flight in a Handley Page biplane without food or drinks *en route.*
AIRLINE TRAVEL-BAGS, in use by 1935, were given away free to passengers flying on KLM's Amsterdam–Djakarta service, provided they were travelling the whole 9,000-mile distance.
TRANSATLANTIC AIRLINE SERVICE: the first across the North Atlantic began with the inaugural passenger flight of Pan American Airways' Boeing 314 flying-boat *Yankee Clipper* between Botwood, Newfoundland and Southampton in 18hr 42min on 27–28 June 1939. Her 19 passengers enjoyed a standard of accommodation that has not been surpassed since on scheduled air-routes. The aircraft had separate passenger cabins, a dining-saloon, ladies' dressing-room, recreation lounge, sleeping-berths and a bridal suite. The fare was £140 return.
GB: The first commercial North Atlantic passenger service by a British airline was flown by BOAC Lockheed Constellations from London to New York commencing 1 July 1946. Scheduled flying time was 19hr 45min.
JET (TURBO) AIRLINE SERVICE: the first was inaugurated by BOAC with the flight of de Havilland Comet, G-ALYP, from London to Johannesburg (6,724 miles) in 23hr 34min on 2–3 May 1952.

The first jet services across the North Atlantic were flown between London and New York by BOAC Comet 4, G-APDC (pilot Capt. R.E. Millichap), and from New York to London by BOAC Comet 4, G-APDB (pilot Capt. T.B. Stoney), both on 4 October 1958. The NY–London run established a new Atlantic record of 6hr 11min.

Jet service to Australia began with a BOAC Comet 4 flight from London to Sydney on 1 November 1959.

See also Aeroplane to be Hijacked; Airmail; Film: In-Flight Movie; Helicopter: Passenger Service.

The first
AIRLINE DISASTER
on a scheduled passenger flight occurred at Golders Green, a suburb of north London, shortly after noon on Tuesday, 14 December 1920. The airliner, belonging to Handley Page Continental Air Services, had just left Cricklewood Aerodrome for Paris, carrying a two-man crew and six passengers. It crashed into the back of a newly built house, 6 Basinghill, The Ridgeway, and fell in flames into the garden. Four of the passengers managed to jump clear just before the aircraft hit the ground, two of them surviving unhurt, and the other two being only slightly injured. The other occupants of the plane were all killed.
COLLISION BETWEEN AIRLINERS first took place on 7 April 1922, when a Farman Goliath operated by the French airline Grands Express flew into the path of a Daimler Airways DH 18 over Poix in northern France.

The first
AIRMAIL
flight (official) was made by Henri Pecquet in a Humber-Sommer biplane at the United Provinces Exhibition, Allahabad, India on 18 February 1911. A load of 6,000 letters and cards was flown 5 miles from Allahabad to Naini Junction, and then sent on by rail.
GB: By arrangement with the Post Office the Graham-White Aviation Co operated an experimental service between Hendon and Windsor (19 miles) from 9 to 26 September 1911. The first consignment of mail was carried in a Blériot monoplane piloted by Gustav Hamel, one of four pilots who airlifted a total of 25,000 letters and 90,000 postcards during the three weeks of the service.

The first regular commercially operated airmail service was inaugurated in the German Colony of South West Africa with a Roland biplane which made its initial mail-carrying flight between Swakopmund and Windhoek on 18 May 1914. The service came to a premature end when Union troops invaded the country on the outbreak of World War I.
INTERNATIONAL AIRMAIL SERVICE (experimental) was first operated by Italian military aircraft between Brindisi, Italy and Valona, Albania, May–June 1917. The first regular international airmail service was the Austrian civil airmail inaugurated under the direction of A.R. von Marwil, a former fighter pilot, on 11 March 1918. Mail was carried by Hansa-Brandenburg C I transports from Vienna to Lvov (then Lemberg) and Proskurov, via Cracow, with a branch service from Proskurov to Odessa. From 4 July 1918 the route was extended to Budapest. The service ended with the collapse of the Austro-Hungarian Empire in November 1918.
GB: The first regular civil airmail was inaugurated by Air Transport & Travel between Hounslow and Paris on 10 November 1919. The mail was surcharged at the rate of 2s 6d an ounce,

Taking aboard the airmail at Hendon, 1911

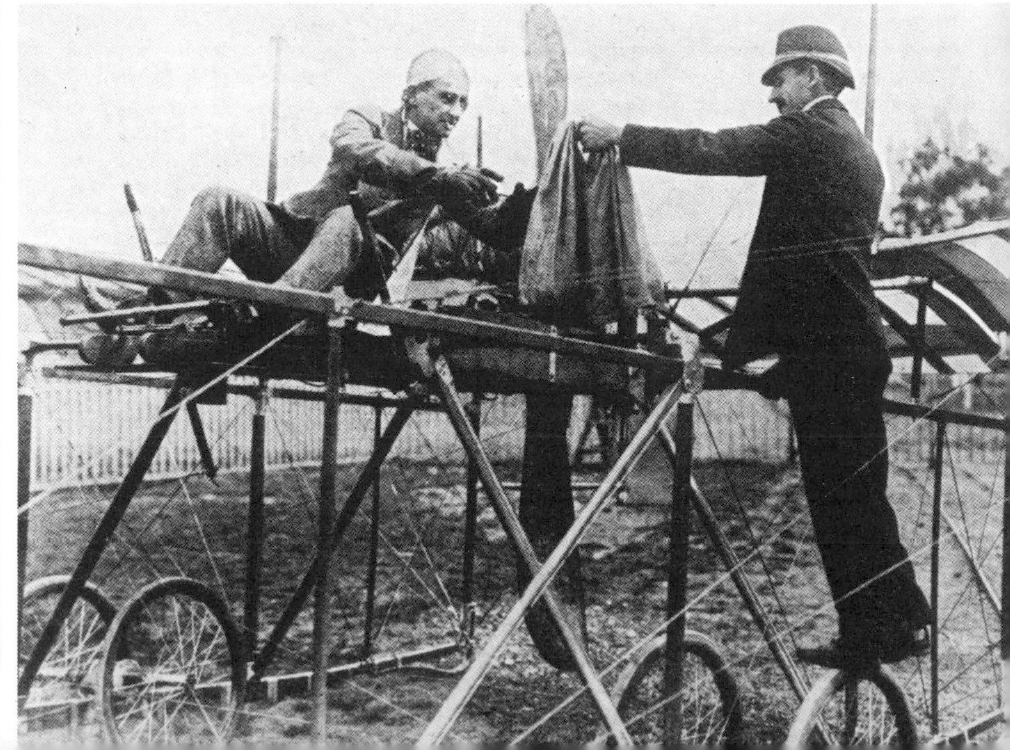

of which 2s went to the airline. These high rates tended to discourage potential users, and during the early months of the service an average of only 45 letters a day were carried.
TRANSATLANTIC AIRMAIL (successful) was first flown by Capt. John Alcock and Lt Whitten-Brown in a Vickers Vimy from St John's, Newfoundland to Clifden, Ireland on 14 June 1919. Earlier the same year an attempt by Harry Hawker and Cdr Mackenzie-Grieve had ended when they were forced to ditch in the sea, abandoning the mails when they were rescued. Several days later a passing ship succeeded in extracting the mail from the fuselage of the still-drifting aircraft, and the sea-stained letters marked 'First Transatlantic Air Post' were ultimately delivered to their destinations.

The first regular transatlantic airmail was inaugurated by Deutsche Lufthansa between Berlin and Buenos Aires, via Stuttgart, Seville, Bathurst and Natal, Brazil on 3 February 1934. Initially the service was run every 14 days; from May 1935 weekly. Delivery time was four days.

The first regular North Atlantic airmail service was inaugurated by Pan American Airways between New York and Lisbon/Marseilles on 20 May 1939. Flying time for the Boeing 314 flying-boats was 29hr.
GB: Inaugurated by BOAC between Southampton and Montreal/New York on 4 August 1939. Two Short S.30 flying-boats, *Cabot* and *Caribou*, maintained a weekly service until the end of September, when the war halted operations.
JET AIRMAIL: the first service was inaugurated by an Avro Canada Jetliner between Toronto and New York on 18 April 1950.
PAR AVION AIRMAIL STICKERS: the first were imperforate labels or *etiquettes* printed in black on magenta paper for use on letters carried by the French civil airmail service inaugurated between Paris and Saint-Nazaire in August 1918. *Etiquettes* continue to be inscribed *Par Avion* in all countries as French is the language recognized by the Universal Postal Union.
GB: Available at post offices 10 August 1920.

See also Aerogramme; Postage Stamps, Airmail

The first
AIR TROOP TRANSPORT
operation took place during the Kurdish uprising in April 1923, when a fully equipped fighting force of 280 Sikh troops was flown by the RAF from Kingarban to Kirkuk, Iraq in 12-seater Vickers Vernon transports. Each man carried a rifle and 15lb of equipment, and the aircraft bore an additional load of 30,000 rounds of small-arms ammunition. The time taken to transport the whole force over the 75-mile distance was a day and a half, or about 10 flying-hours – a journey normally occupying five days on the march.

The first use of long-range air troop transport took place in June 1932, when 21 Vickers Victoria transports, belonging to 70 and 216 Squadron RAF, flew the 1st Northamptonshire Regiment from Egypt to Iraq, once again in ferment, in two airlifts during the course of six days.
AERIAL INVASION: the first took place between August and October 1936, when 20 Junkers 52/3 Mg bomber-transports of the German Luftwaffe Transport Squadron under the command of Oberleutnant Rudolf Freiherr von Moreau were used to carry 8,899 Moorish troops, 44 field-guns, 90 machine-guns and 137 tons of ammunition from Spanish Morocco to Seville in Spain in support of General Franco.

The first
AMBULANCE
was designed in 1792 by Baron Dominique Jean Larrey, Napoleon's personal surgeon, as a means of removing wounded men from the field of battle without their sustaining further injury from jolting over rough ground in the unsprung carts previously employed. Together with the Chief Surgeon of the French Army, Pierre François Percy, Larrey established an ambulance corps consisting of field surgeons, stretcher-bearers and his 'one-horse flying ambulances'. Each division was equipped with 12 ambulances mounted on springs. They were used for the first time in Napoleon's Italian campaign of 1796–7.
GB: Sprung wagons for the transfer of wounded from the battlefield were attached to the Commissariat Train in the Peninsular War during 1812 at the instigation of Sir James McGrigor, Inspector of Hospitals during the campaign. There was little development of this rudimentary ambulance service during the Napoleonic Wars, since the Duke of Wellington refused to sanction the formation of a British equivalent to the French Ambulance Corps.

The first ambulance unit of the British Army was the Hospital Conveyance Corps, raised in 1854 for service in the Crimea. Members of the Corps, all of whom were military pensioners, were charged with maintaining the ambulance service, acting as stretcher-bearers and serving as orderlies in field hospitals. They were given no training in ambulance-work and were described by Ensign Robert Lindsay, later the first Chairman of the British Red Cross Society, as 'rascally old pensioners who got drunk on the brandy and wine provided for the sick'.

There was little organized attempt at providing a civilian ambulance service in Britain until the founding of the Ambulance Association of the British National Society for Aid to the Sick and Wounded in 1877. Originally, the Association confined its activities to First Aid, but about a year later an ambulance corps was established at Margate, Kent with a single-wheeled litter for transport. From this small beginning grew the Invalid Transport Corps of the Ambulance Association, which was equipped in 1883 with a special rubber-tyred one-horse ambulance designed by John Furley. The vehicle had accommodation for four stretcher cases and attendants.
MOTOR AMBULANCE: the first was a Daimler-engined vehicle exhibited by Panhard et Levassor at the Salon du Cycle held in the Palais de l'Industrie, Paris, in December 1895. There is no record that it carried patients.

The first motor ambulance in regular

Larrey's ambulance volante, *1792*

service was acquired by the French 9th Army Corps in July 1900. The first civilian motor ambulance was introduced at Alençon, France the same year. The *Autocar* reported: 'A motor quadricycle is coupled to an ambulance of the Lagogue pattern. The motor man and the doctor use the quadricycle, and the patient is the sole occupant of the ambulance.

GB: A Straker and Squire motor ambulance was acquired by the Royal Army Medical Corps in November 1905.

The first civilian motor ambulance was delivered to the South Western Ambulance Station of the Metropolitan Asylums Board on 16 December 1905. It had been built to order by Messrs James and Browne of 395 Oxford Street, for a price of £465. The ambulance was put into regular service for conveying scarlet-fever patients from their homes to the isolation hospitals on 11 February 1906.

MOTOR AMBULANCES USED IN WARFARE: the first were 10 Italian Army vehicles employed during the Italo-Turkish War in Tripoli, at the Battle of Zanzur on 8 June 1912. The ambulances carried 70 wounded to the field hospital at Gargaresh and another 40 dead to the cemetery.

The first
ANAESTHETIC

for a surgical operation was administered by Dr Crawford Long of Jefferson, Ga., who removed a cyst from the neck of a student, James Venable, while he was insensible under ether on 30 March 1842. The bill for the world's first practical application of anaesthesia was $2.25. Ether had been introduced to the isolated community of Jefferson by an itinerant science lecturer who would demonstrate the effects of the gas at his exhibitions. The young people of the town, unbeknown to their parents, persuaded Dr Long to let them try it out for themselves, and he readily gave them whiffs of ether and joined in the fun at their mild intoxication. Realizing that a stronger dose of the gas could have the effect of deadening a person's consciousness, Long persuaded Venable to undergo the experiment with entirely successful results. Altogether he performed nine operations with ether, including the amputation of a Negro boy's finger, but not without arousing a fierce opposition from the older citizens of Jefferson, who suspected him of sorcery. At length he was persuaded to desist when a deputation called on him and bluntly threatened him with lynching if he continued his activities. He played no further part in the development of anaesthesia and his pioneering role remained quite unknown until investigated by the Georgia State Medical Society in 1852.

DENTAL EXTRACTION UNDER AN ANAESTHETIC was first performed by Dr John M. Riggs of Hartford, Conn. at the request of Dr Horace Wells, who wished to establish the pain-killing effect of nitrous oxide (laughing gas). The anaesthetic was administered to Wells on 11 December 1844 by a travelling showman and demonstrator of laughing gas, Gardner Colton; Riggs was enabled to remove a healthy tooth quite painlessly. Wells was overjoyed and declared that the event marked 'a new era in tooth pulling'. What he did not know was that nitrous oxide had to be mixed with oxygen to be applied effectively and safely, and though he performed some 40 extractions with the gas, of which half were successful, he abandoned his experiments after a patient had nearly died from an overdose. Meanwhile, William Morton, Wells's one-time partner, had achieved painless dentistry with rectified sulphuric ether in September 1846 and the continuous development of anaesthesia can be dated from this time.

ANAESTHESIA IN MAJOR SURGERY: the first application was made at Massachusetts General Hospital, Boston on 16 October 1846, when Dr John Collins Warren excised a tumour from the jaw of a 20-year-old printer called Gilbert Abbott. It was with the greatest reluctance that Warren had been persuaded by William Morton, the Boston dentist, who administered the ether, to agree to the experiment. A plaque on the wall of the theatre records: 'The patient declared that he had felt no pain during the operation and was discharged well December 7. Knowledge of this discovery spread from this room throughout the civilized world and a new era for surgery began.' The word 'anaesthesia' was coined by Oliver Wendell Holmes in a letter to Morton dated 21 November 1846.

GB: News of Morton's successful use of ether as an anaesthetic reached England in a letter addressed to Dr Francis Boott from Dr Henry Bigelow of Boston dated 28 November 1846. Before sending the letter on to Robert Liston, the foremost surgeon in London at the time, Boott called on the services of a young dentist named James Robinson in order to satisfy himself of the efficacy of Morton's method. On 19 December 1846 Boott administered the vapour to a Miss Lonsdale, while Robinson performed the first dental extraction under anaesthesia in Britain. The whole operation occupied the space of 3min and the patient said afterwards that she had experienced no pain, only 'a heavenly dream'. Boott and Robinson then set about devising a practical ether-inhaler, which they began producing commercially on 10 January 1847.

The first surgical operation under anaesthesia was performed at University College Hospital, London, on 21 December 1846 by Robert Liston, who amputated the leg of a servant called James Churchill suffering from a putrescent wound. The ether was administered on this occasion by William Squire.

CHILD TO BE BORN ALIVE WITH THE AID OF ANAESTHESIA: the first was Wilhelmina Carstairs, daughter of Dr William Carstairs of the Indian Medical Service, delivered under chloroform administered to her mother by Dr James Young Simpson at 19 Albany Street, Edinburgh on 9 November 1847. Contrary to popular legend, the child was not christened 'Anaesthesia', a misconception derived from the fact that Dr Simpson, seeing a photograph of Wilhelmina at the age of 17 and admiring her air of sanctity, observed 'Ah! Saint Anaesthesia.'

LOCAL ANAESTHETIC: the pain-killing properties of cocaine were first discovered by Karl Koller of the Allgemeines Krankenhaus, Vienna, while he was working with Sigmund Freud on the use of the drug as a treatment for morphine addiction. It was first demonstrated as an anaesthetic on the eye of a patient from the Heidelberg Clinic by Josef Brettauer of Trieste, using a vial of cocaine forwarded by Koller, at the Heidelberg Congress of Ophthamology on 15 September 1884.

Local anaesthesia by injection or neuro-regional anaesthesia was introduced by William Halstead of Johns Hopkins University, Baltimore in 1885.

The first
APPENDIX OPERATION

for the removal of an infected appendix was performed in Philadelphia on 27 April 1887 by George Thomas Morton, son of William Morton, pioneer of anaesthesia (*q.v.*). The patient was a 26-year-old man in an advanced stage of acute appendicitis, whose life was undoubtedly saved by the operation. Nearly all early appendicectomies were carried out in cases where the appendix had already ruptured and were performed only as an ultimate resort. The idea of operating in the early stages of appendicitis was introduced by an Irish-American surgeon, John Benjamin Murphy of Chicago, who operated on a young workman called Monhan at Cook County Hospital on 2 March 1889, only 8hr after the patient had first complained of abdominal pains.

GB: The first appendicectomy was

performed at the London Hospital on 29 June 1888 by Prof. Frederick Treves, who was later to carry out the same operation on King Edward VII shortly before his Coronation in 1902.

The first
ART EXHIBITION
was held by the Académie de Peinture et de Sculpture at the Palais-Royale in Paris, from 9 to 23 April 1667. They were continued biennially, though after 1671 the exhibition was usually held in the Grande Galerie of the Louvre, then a royal palace.
GB: The Annual Exhibition of United Artists was held under the auspices of the Society of Arts at their room in the Strand, 21 April–8 May 1760. Although the artists had intended to charge an admission fee of 1s, the Society rejected this proposal, and instead 6,582 catalogues were sold at 6d each. There were 130 exhibits, and the 69 artists represented included Sir Joshua Reynolds, Richard Wilson and Paul Sandby. Some of the more distinguished exhibitors subsequently formed themselves into The Society of Artists of Great Britain and held a separate exhibition at Spring Gardens, Charing Cross in 1761. The following year the Society arranged the first exhibition in Britain at which a charge for admission (1s) was made, and the first at which all the paintings on display were for sale – the prices being set by the committee.
EXHIBITION OF CHILDREN'S ART: the first in Britain was held annually by the London School Board commencing in 1877.

The first
ART GALLERY
in Britain that was freely open to the public was the Dulwich College Picture Gallery, opened in 1814 with approximately 510 paintings housed in a building specially designed for the purpose by Sir John Soane. The nucleus of the collection had been formed by Edward Alleyn, a retired Elizabethan actor who founded Alleyn's College of God's Gift (now Dulwich College) in 1619. At his death in 1626 he bequeathed 39 pictures to the College. The collection was augmented by a further bequest of 80 pictures made by the actor William Cartwright in 1686. The decision to build a public art gallery was taken by the Governors following the major gift of 371 pictures received under the Bourgeois Bequest in 1811. Originally admission to the gallery was by tickets obtainable without charge from various art-dealers in London and Croydon, but this formality was done away with in 1858.
PAINTINGS PURCHASED BY THE NATION: the first for public display were 38 works from the Angerstein Collection, for which the Government paid £57,000 in 1824. These went on exhibition at the British Institution's rooms at 52 Pall Mall on 10 May of the same year. After a number of additions had been made to the national art collection, it was removed to the newly built National Gallery in Trafalgar Square, which was opened on 9 April 1838.

The first
ARTIFICIAL INSEMINATION
The earliest successful experiment on an animal was conducted by the Italian Abbé Lazare Spallanzani in 1779, when he injected the semen of a spaniel into the genital tract of a female hunting-dog. A litter of three cross-bred puppies was born 62 days later.
HUMAN ARTIFICIAL INSEMINATION was conducted first by M. Thouret, Doyen of the Medical Faculty at Paris University, who made an intra-vaginal injection of sperm on his sterile wife in 1785 with a tin syringe. This resulted in the birth of a healthy baby, the achievement being described by Thouret in an anonymous pamphlet.
GB: The first doctor in England to practise artificial insemination was Dr John Hunter, who used it on a wealthy and aristocratic female patient whose husband suffered from hypospadias. The case was initially reported by Everard Home in 1799, but the actual date it was carried out is not known. Dr Hunter died in 1793.

The first artificial insemination with semen other than that of the husband (AID, or Artificial Insemination with Donor) was conducted by Prof. Pancoast of Philadelphia on a chloroformed woman without her knowledge in 1884. This was done at the request of the husband, who was himself sterile.

The first
ARTISTE'S AGENT
was Ambrose Maynard, who established an office at 20 Waterloo Road, London in 1858 to specialize in bookings for music-hall performers. Maynard had originally been a comic singer and knew the difficulties faced by artistes working in the provinces who wanted to obtain London engagements. For the consideration of 1s he would enter a performer's name on his list of artistes 'at liberty', and circulate it round the London managers. Although there was no shortage of applicants willing to pay this small fee, at first the managers refused to have anything to do with Maynard or his register. Then one day an artiste booked to appear at a certain hall was unable to appear, and the proprietor found himself in need of a replacement at short notice. Maynard, happening to be in the right place at the right time, heard of the manager's dilemma and immediately sent along one of his clients, a serio-comic called Julia Weston, who filled the breach so admirably that other managers looking for talent began to use Maynard's services.

The first
ASPIRIN
was introduced commercially in powder form by the Bayer AG of Leverkusen, Germany in May 1899. Acetylsalicylic acid ('Aspirin' was a registered tradename) had been synthesized as early as 1853 by an Alsatian chemist, Karl Gerhardt; it was not until 1897 that Dr Felix Hoffman of Bayer succeeded in producing it in a form sufficiently pure to be employed therapeutically. Originally it was only available in Germany on prescription. Aspirin tablets were first retailed by Bayer in packets of 20 in 1915.
GB: Bayer Aspirin was first marketed in 1905. It continued to be imported from Germany until 1914, when manufacture in Britain was undertaken by W.J. Bush & Co.

The first
ATHLETICS MEETING
of modern times was organized at Shrewsbury, England by the Royal Shrewsbury School Hunt in 1840. The only positive information on this meeting is contained in a series of letters written nearly 60 years later by C.T. Robinson, who was a boy at the school from 1838 to 1841. The field where it was held was the site of the Shrewsbury cattle-market, and was used by the boys on non-market days for playing rounders, quoits and 'Prisoners' Bars'. Members of the Hunt competing in the races were given the names of horses and assigned to 'owners'. Robinson himself ran as Mr Kenyon's 'Capt'n Pops', which was the name of a real racehorse of the day. The only event mentioned is a 'Derby', won by a boy called 'Nigger' Kearsley, but it seems reasonable to suppose that this was a full-scale meeting on the evidence of an account of the RSS Hunt Races held in February 1843. The events on this later occasion – most probably the fourth in a series of annual meetings – comprised five foot-races of varying distances, and a hurdle-race over eight 3ft hurdles. Two of the races were open events, while the others were restricted to 'horses' under a certain height, e.g. 'The Severn Stakes of 4d each for horses under 5ft 6ins. Twice round and a distance. Second horse to save his stake.'

While such light-hearted sport cannot be said to have been more than an athletics meeting in embryo, it clearly had more in common with modern athletics than the rural games held at village fairs and wakes, or the races between running footmen or professional walkers that had been popular during the 18th century. No evidence has been found to support the contention that an organized athletics meeting was held at the Royal Military Academy, Sandhurst in either 1812 or 1825. The 1840 Shrewsbury meeting undoubtedly represents the earliest-recorded occasion on which trained athletes came together to compete in a number of prearranged races held on the same day. Shrewsbury was followed by Eton, which instituted annual sprints, hurdle-races and a steeplechase in 1845. The Royal Military Academy, Woolwich, had its first sports day in 1849, and annual athletics meetings were begun at Kensington Grammar School in 1852, at Harrow and Cheltenham in 1853, Rugby in 1856 and Winchester in 1857.

The first university meeting was held by Exeter College, Oxford in the autumn of 1850, and, like the school sports preceding it, was confined to track events. The following year's meeting, however, is believed to have been the first to have included a high-jump and a long-jump competition. Outside the schools and universities, athletics was pioneered by the Honourable Artillery Company at Finsbury in 1858.

ATHLETICS CLUB: the first was the Mincing Lane AC, founded by a group of City businessmen in June 1863. The first club meeting was held at the West London Rowing Club grounds, Brompton on 9 April 1864. Later the same year the first challenge-cup competitions were instituted, one for the 220yd sprint and another for the 10-mile walk. The club changed its name to the London AC in 1866.

INTER-VARSITY ATHLETICS MEETING: the first was held between Oxford and Cambridge at Christchurch cricket ground, Oxford on 3 March 1864. The result was a tie, each team winning four events. The winner of the high jump cleared 5ft 6in; the winner of the long jump leaped 18ft. The third Oxford and Cambridge meeting in 1866 is notable for the first introduction of 'Throwing the Hammer' – an ancient form of contest in Scotland – as a field event in a modern athletics meeting.

NATIONAL ATHLETICS CHAMPIONSHIP: the first was inaugurated by the Amateur Athletic Club and held at Beaufort House, Walham Green on 23 March 1866. The times and distances achieved there were the first officially recognized British athletic records.

INDOOR ATHLETICS MEETING: the first was held by the New York AC at the Empire Skating Rink, 63rd Street and 3rd Avenue on 11 November 1868. This was also the first athletics meeting held in the USA. William B. Curtis, who had helped found the New York AC two months earlier, introduced the first pair of spiked running-shoes at the meeting, and four competitors wore them in seven different events.

GB: The first indoor meeting was the Amateur Athletic Association Indoor Championships, held at the Empire Pool and Sports Arena, Wembley on Saturday, 6 April 1935.

ATHLETICS TRACK (purpose built): the first was laid down at Lillie Bridge, West Kensington by the Amateur Athletic Club in 1868. One lap equalled one-third of a mile.

RELAY RACE: the first was run experimentally at Berkeley, Calif. on 17 November 1883, when a demonstration team clocked a time of 9min 51sec over four half-mile laps. It was not until March 1893 that the first competitive relay-race was contested between two teams from the University of Pennsylvania.

GB: A 2-mile relay event, styled the 'Flying Squadron Race', was run at Stamford Bridge in September 1895, with Finchley Harriers winning against Ranelagh Harriers in a time of 8min 57·4sec.

ATHLETE TO USE THE CROUCH START: the first is generally said to have been Charles Sherrill of Yale University, the US 100yd Champion. He was induced to try out this new method of starting for sprint-races in May 1888 by his coach, Mike Murphy. It has been claimed, however, that a New Zealand Maori called Bobby MacDonald was using the crouch start at athletics meetings in Scotland as early as 1884. The first English runner to adopt the technique was T.L. Nicholas, who won the AAA 440yd championship from a crouch start in 1890. Starting-blocks were patented by American coach George Bresnahan in 1927. The first runner to use them in Britain was Guyanan-born J.E. London of Poly Harriers, *c.* 1929.

The first
ATOMIC POWER STATION
was established at Obninsk, 55 miles from Moscow, and began producing electrical current for industrial undertakings and for agricultural purposes on 27 June 1954. It had a useful capacity of 5,000kW.

GB: The first large-scale atomic power station in the world was Calder Hall, Cumberland, which began generating on 20 August 1956, the date on which the first turbine was brought into operation. It was formally opened by HM Queen Elizabeth II on 17 October 1956, when power was first fed into the grid of the Central Electricity Authority. The plant comprised 4 graphite-moderated, gas-cooled reactors with their associated heat-exchangers, 2 turbine-halls and 4 cooling-towers. Calder Hall was designed to generate some 90,000kW of electrical power and at the same time to manufacture plutonium, an artificial nuclear fuel, for military purposes.

The first
AUTOBIOGRAPHY
in the English language was 'A book of songs and sonnetts with longe discoorses sett with them, of the chylds lyfe, together with a young mans lyfe, and entering into the old mans lyfe', written by the Elizabethan composer Thomas Whythorne, probably in 1576. The prose passages chronicle the author's schooldays as a chorister at Magdalen College School, student-days under the musician John Heywood, his adult life as a music-master in many of the great houses of England, and his eventual appointment as Master of Music to Archbishop Parker. The unpublished manuscript was discovered by James Osborn and auctioned at Sotheby's in 1955. It is now in the Bodleian Library, Oxford.

The first
BABY-INCUBATOR
for the post-natal care of premature and weakly infants was devised by Dr Alexandre Lion of Nice in 1891. The air in the incubator was purified through a filter and kept constantly fresh by means of a fan ventilator, while the temperature was regulated automatically by a thermostatic control.

Shortly after perfecting his invention Dr Lion established his first 'Oeuvre Maternelle des Couveuses d'Enfants' at Nice, and this was followed by similar establishments at Bordeaux, Marseilles, Lyons and Paris. The Nice clinic was supported partly by charitable contributions and partly by a subsidy from the municipality. In Paris the public were admitted to inspect the incubated babies for 50 centimes a head, and this was sufficient to cover the nurses' wages of 60 francs a month and other expenses.

Dr Lion claimed a 72% success rate;

137 out of the 185 children reared in the incubators at Nice during the first three years surviving infancy. None of the 185, he considered, would have lived in the ordinary course of events. Babies too weak to swallow naturally were fed through the nose with a specially moulded spoon, or breast-fed through a tube attached to the nipple of the wet-nurse. 'Black women often take care of white babies', noted an English reporter, 'and white women take care of black babies, as occasion requires.'
GB: Dr Lion introduced his Couveuses to London in 1897.

The first
BABY SHOW
was held at Springfield, Ohio on 14 October 1854. There were 127 exhibits, including one of five months that weighed 27lb and another that was a 17th child. The winner was the 10-month-old offspring of William Romner of Vienna, Clark County, Ohio, who was awarded a service of silver plate. The prevailing spirit of mutual admiration was unfortunately marred when one of the judges had the temerity to define a baby as 'an alimentary canal with a loud noise at one end and no sense of responsibility at the other'.

The first
BAKED BEANS
reference to, is a recipe included in Mrs S.M. Child's *The Frugal Housewife*, Boston, 1829. 'A pound of pork is enough for a quart of beans', she wrote, 'and that is a large dinner for a common family.' At this time the marriage of baked beans to tomato sauce was still more than half a century away (*see below*), molasses being used as a binder. In rural New England during the mid-19th century their preparation was attended by a certain amount of ceremony, culminating in what was known as the 'baked-bean festival' on Saturday nights. The beans were put into earthenware pots to soak overnight, and seasoned early the next morning with mustard, salt-pork and blackstrap molasses. The pots, wrapped in coloured napkins, were then carried by the children through the streets at dawn to the local bakery, where they were labelled and put into an oven to cook all day. The children returned in the evening to collect the beans for the family feast.
CANNED BAKED BEANS were first produced by the Burnham & Morrill Co of Portland, Maine in 1875 for the benefit of their fishing fleet, the men having expressed a desire to enjoy at sea the same Saturday-night pleasure as on shore.

Baked beans in tomato sauce, the form in which they are eaten in England, were introduced in the USA in 1880. Canning by the Van Camp Packing Co began at Indianapolis in 1891.
GB: Baked beans were test marketed by the Pittsburgh firm of H.J. Heinz in the north of England in 1905. Advertising was aimed mainly at working-class housewives and sought to persuade them that baked beans would constitute a cheap and nourishing meal for their menfolk returning from work. The canned beans continued to be imported from America until 1928, when manufacture began at the H.J. Heinz plant at Harlesden. A recent survey showed that 84% of housewives buy baked beans regularly, and with sales exceeding a million cans a day, the British people consume twice as many baked beans *per capita* as the Americans.

The first
BALLET
to rely on mime and gestures to the exclusion of either speech or song was John Weaver's *The Loves of Mars and Venus*, presented at the Theatre Royal, Drury Lane on 2 March 1717 with Louis Dupré dancing the part of Mars, Mrs Santlow as Venus, and Weaver himself in the role of Vulcan. The music was written by two different composers, Richard Firbank, who was responsible for the 'Dancing Airs', and Henry Symonds, a member of the King's Band of Musicians, who was commissioned to compose the 'Symphonies'. The latter's contribution was intended to reflect 'the Passions and Affections of the Characters'. The production was mounted on a shoestring budget, because the Manager of Drury Lane, Colley Cibber, was reluctant to invest very much in a completely untried form of entertainment. As far as the public were concerned, Weaver's innovation was a considerable success. He himself, having more exacting standards than his audience, admitted that he was not wholly satisfied with the performance of the dancers, who, it seems, were somewhat bewildered by Weaver's *avant-garde* choreography. 'I must confess', he wrote afterwards, 'that I have in this entertainment too much inclin'd to the Modern Dancing.'

Weaver was the first to liberate ballet from opera and give it an independent existence as an art form. Although it may appear an anomaly that England, which won little distinction in the world of dance until the present century, should have been the birthplace of the classical *ballet d'action*, there are some sound historical reasons for this early development. England had established a tradition of popular dramatic entertainment earlier than most continental countries. Dance in England, too, had a wider currency in the Court entertainments of the 16th and 17th centuries than was general in Europe, though it must be said that ballet in its primitive form, as an interlude in operas and masques, saw its earliest flowering in France and Italy.

The first *ballet d'action* to be performed on the public stage in continental Europe was Marie Sallé's *Pygmalion*, which had been premièred at Covent Garden in January 1734 and was opened in Paris later the same year by François Riccobini at the Théâtre-Italien. From France the ballet was introduced to Russia, where the Imperial Theatre School was established under the direction of the ballet-master Landé in 1751. It was from this fertile soil that the classical ballet was destined to return to its birthplace, England, when in 1911 the Diaghilev troupe took London by storm, causing a revival of interest in dance that ended a century of stagnation. So barren had the 19th century been in the chronicle of English ballet that the term 'ballet-dancer' had been debased to mean, at best, a performer in pantomime, and at its worst a euphemism for the kind of harlot who pretended connections with the stage.
CHOREOGRAPHER TO INTRODUCE THE USE OF POINTES: the first was Charles Didelot for his ballet *Zéphyr et Flore*, originally presented at the Theatre Royal, Drury Lane in 1796. The dancers were enabled to rise on their *pointes* by special machinery, also used to carry them up into the air and away into the wings. Once it had been established as a graceful and desirable element of the dance, the use of *pointes* was found to be perfectly feasible without the aid of artificial supports of this kind. Didelot's *Zéphyr et Flore* is also notable as the first ballet in which the male lead lifts his partner, and for its introduction of the *pas de deux* as a 'conversation' between two dancers.
BALLET TUTU: the first was designed by A.E. Chalon (or according to some authorities, the painter Eugène Lami) for Filippo Taglioni's *La Sylphide*, which opened at the Paris Opéra on 12 March 1832, and was presented at Covent Garden on 26 July the same year. In both productions the *première danseuse*, Marie Taglioni, and the *corps de ballet* were similarly attired in these simple white muslin costumes, with a low *décolletage*, skirts half way down the calf, and the arms left bare. This marked a radical departure from the elaborate ballet dress formerly in vogue and remains, with some modification, the standard 'neutral' costume for romantic ballet to the present day. James Laver has pointed out that the

ballet tutu was in fact but a 'slight theatricalization' of the fashionable dress of the 1830s.

The first wheel-shaped tutu was worn by the Italian ballerina Virginia Zucchi when she danced the name-part in *La Fille du Pharaon* at the Imperial Theatre, St Petersburg in 1885.
See also Television Ballet.

The first
BALLOT, VOTE BY
in Parliamentary elections was introduced by the Legislative Council of the Colony of Victoria under the Electoral Act which became law on 19 March 1856. Proposals to adopt a secret ballot had been rejected five years earlier by E. Deas Thomson, then Colonial Secretary, who said the very notion was 'not only unconstitutional, but un-British'. The man who finally succeeded in securing its adoption was William Nicholson, a Cumberland grocer who had emigrated to Victoria in 1841, was Mayor of Melbourne in 1850, and was to be Premier of the Colony in 1859. His motion in favour of the secret ballot was carried by 33 votes to 25 on 18 December 1855 and in consequence the Government was obliged to resign. Although returned to office, they were forced to respond to the majority will and allow for the passage of the measure.

The first Parliamentary election to be held by secret ballot was the General Election for the Victorian Legislative Council held on 27 August 1856. In the meantime, South Australia had introduced its own ballot law, which received the Governor's Assent on 2 April 1856, and the other Australian colonies followed suit – New South Wales and Tasmania in 1858, Queensland in 1859, and Western Australia somewhat tardily in 1879. The first American State to adopt the Australian system was Massachusetts in 1888.
GB: Voting by ballot was introduced by Act on 13 July 1872. The first Parliamentary election held under the provisions of the Act took place at Pontefract on 15 August 1872, when H. E. Childers was re-elected 'very peacefully'. The first use of the secret ballot in a General Election was in 1874. Despite the fact that there was no longer compulsion to vote as directed by squire or landlord, the former Liberal majority of 112 was converted into a Conservative majority of 48.

The first
BALL-POINT PEN
for writing on paper was devised in 1938 by a Hungarian hypnotist, sculptor and journalist, Lasalo Biro, who at this time happened to be editing a Government-sponsored cultural magazine in Budapest. During the course of a visit to the printers of the magazine, Biro was struck by the advantage of a quick-drying ink for use in pens, and constructed the prototype ball-point to this end. Shortly afterwards he escaped from Hungary to Paris in the face of the encroaching Nazi menace, and from thence to Argentina in 1940. Here he continued to work on his idea for a pen that would not blot and patented it on 10 June 1943. About the same time he met a visiting Englishman, Henry Martin, who had arrived in Buenos Aires on a mission for the British Government. Martin was impressed with the invention, which he saw as an answer to the problem experienced by air crews having to make navigational calculations at high altitudes. Biro's ball-point, he found, was in no way affected by changes of air pressure or atmosphere. Accordingly he acquired the British rights, and in 1944 began producing ball-points for the RAF in a disused aircraft hangar near Reading. His staff of 17 girls turned out 30,000 finished pens the first year.

The first commercially produced ball-point on regular sale was produced under the Biro patents by the Eterpen Co of Buenos Aires early in 1945. Biro had been imprudent enough not to patent his pen in the USA, and an American businessman lost no time in doing so.

Advertised as the 'first pen that writes underwater', the American version won an immediate response when it went on sale, priced $12.50, at Gimbel's of New York on 29 October 1945. It was reported that nearly 10,000 had been sold before closing time.
GB: The production of ball-points for public consumption was started by Henry Martin, whose London-based Miles-Martin Pen Co launched its 55s Biro for Christmas 1945. By 1949 sales of ball-points had already outstripped fountain-pens.

The first successful 'throw-away'-ball-point was the Bic Crystal, introduced into Britain from France in June 1958. Priced at 1s, sales during 1959 totalled 53 million, or approximately one to every man, woman and child in the country.

The first
BARBED WIRE
was patented by Lucien B. Smith of Kent, Ohio on 25 June 1867. The barbs protruded from small blocks of wood strung along the wire strand. No example of Smith's wire has yet been located and it cannot therefore be certain that it was ever manufactured. The following year, however, a patent was taken out by M. Kelly for a twisted two-strand wire with diamond-shaped barbs; this was advertised as providing 'a strong thorney hedge'. Fences made of 'Kelly's Diamond' are still standing in some parts of America. The invention of barbed wire was a prerequisite to the opening up of the American West, since there was insufficient timber for fencing in its vast cattle-ranches.

Barbed-wire collecting is one of the more esoteric forms of antiquarian pursuit, yet to catch on in Europe, but already a growing activity in the South-western States of the USA. Over 1,500 different varieties of wire have been identified by collectors, and rare examples have been known to fetch as much as $65 per 18in piece at auction.
GB: Barbed wire would appear to have been introduced into Britain prior to 1878, when it was the subject of a law-suit for the first time.
BARBED WIRE FOR DEFENCE
was first used by US forces in Cuba during the Spanish-American War of 1898.

The first
BEAUTY CONTEST
was the 'Concours de Beauté' held at Spa in Belgium on 19 September 1888. The initial judging was done from photographs of the 350 contestants, of whom 21 were chosen to appear at the finals. The contest was conducted with the utmost propriety and discretion. 'The finalists were not allowed to be seen by the people', said a Scandinavian journal. 'They lived in a separate wing and were driven in closed carriages to the hall, where their charms were judged.' First prize of 5,000 francs went to an 18-year-old Creole from Guadeloupe called Bertha Soucaret. 'It is said', the same paper continued, 'that Miss Soucaret will now go on the stage; of course, beauty opens every door.'
GB: The earliest recorded contest in Britain was a 'Blonde and Brunette Beauty Show', the final of which took place on the stage of the Olympia Theatre, Newcastle upon Tyne, on Saturday, 23 December 1905. The competition was open to girls of 16 and over and at the end of the 'Grand Finale' the winner, whose name unfortunately is not recorded, was presented with a gold bangle and bracelet.

The first international beauty contest in Britain was held at the Pier Hippodrome in Folkestone on 14 August 1908 and attracted 6 English entries, 3 French, 1 Irish, 1 Austrian, 1 American and 'a number of fisher girls from Boulogne'. The latter appear not to have been included among the official French contingent, presumably because they had not been through any eliminating rounds. The admission price of 4s entitled each spectator to three voting coupons, the whole audience

The procession of competitors at the first beauty contest, Spa, 1888. The winner, a Negress, is not shown.

being empanelled as judges. The winner of the first prize, a Spencer piano, was 18-year-old Miss Nellie Jarman, a shop-keeper's daughter from East Molesey, Surrey. The reporter from the *Folkestone Herald* declared that it was only too apparent that the audience were determined to have a native-born winner.

BATHING BEAUTY CONTEST: the first in which competitors were judged in swimsuits was held at Atlantic City for the title of Miss America on 7 September 1921. The practice of naming beauty queens after their country originated with this, the first of the annual national beauty contests, and was the inspiration of *Atlantic City Press* reporter Herb Test. The first Miss America, Margaret Gorman, was only 15 years old when she was chosen to enter the contest as Miss Washington, D.C. and still a pupil at Western High School in Georgetown. A blue-eyed blonde with an amazingly slender 30–25–32 figure, Miss Gorman remains the youngest, slightest and shortest (5ft 1in) contestant ever to have won the Miss America title.

MISS WORLD CONTEST: the first was organized in 1951 by Eric Morley, Publicity Officer of Mecca Ltd, in response to a request by his management to devise an event of international interest to coincide with the Festival of Britain celebrations. For the initial contest, held at the Lyceum Ballroom off the Strand on 19 April, there were 30 contestants, but only 5 from overseas countries. An original feature of the competition was that all the girls paraded in bikinis (*q.v.*) – a type of swimwear new to Britain at that date. The winner of the title and the £1,000 prize that accompanied it was Miss Sweden, 21-year-old Kiki Haakonson, daughter of a Stockholm policeman.

The first
BICYCLE

was invented by Kirkpatrick Macmillan, blacksmith of Courthill, Dumfries, in 1839. The 57lb vehicle was constructed with a curved wooden frame, the front of which was carved with a horse's head, and had iron-tyred wheels of 32in diameter in the front and 42in in the rear. The pedals were connected by cranks to the rear wheel, and driven by a forward and backward motion of the feet. There is no evidence that Macmillan foresaw his machine as the precursor of a great industry, and it seems that he built it solely as an efficient means of getting himself about, often riding the 14 miles from Courthill to Dumfries. In 1842 he rode to Glasgow, unwittingly establishing another first by committing the earliest recorded cycling offence. The *Glasgow Herald* for 10 June reported that Macmillan 'on entering Glasgow at the finish of a 40 mile ride, knocked over a child owing to the crowd of people to see his novel iron horse. He was fined five shillings at Gorbals Police Court.'

About this time Macmillan's niece, Mary Marchbank, took to riding his machine and so became the first lady cyclist.

BICYCLE-MANUFACTURER: the first was Pierre Michaux, coachbuilder of the Cité Godot de Mauroy, Paris. The genesis of the industry was described by his son Henri in a letter to *Le Vélo* in 1893:

In the month of March, 1861 . . . a hat-maker, Monsieur Brunel of the rue de Verneuil, Paris, brought his Vélocifère [hobby-horse] to my father for the front wheel to be repaired. The same evening my brother Ernest, 19 years of age, took the machine out for a trial on the avenue Montaigne. 'I can balance myself alright, but it is quite as tiring to hold my legs up as to give the impulsion on the ground with my feet', he said to my father in my presence on returning home. 'Well then', observed my father, 'fix two small supports on each side of the front fork of the wheel and once started, as you can balance yourself on the machine, you can rest your legs; or, better still, to rest your feet, adopt a cranked axle in the hub of the front wheel, and then you can make the wheel revolve as if you were turning the handle and crank of a grindstone!' My brother put my father's idea into execution and afterwards fitted pedals which were also due to the ingenuity of Pierre Michaux; but it was his son Ernest who carried out the first work.

The company established to manufacture the pedal velocipede was called 'La Compagnie Parisienne Ancienne Maison Michaux et Cie'. Two models were produced in 1861, presumably as patterns, and regular series production commenced the following year, when 142 cycles were manufactured and sold.

GB: The first production models for sale in Britain were imported from France in January 1869 by C. Spencer, the proprietor of a gymnasium in Old Street, who advertised 'Parisian' velocipedes at £10 and £14, and thus became the first cycle-dealer. By May of the same year the bicycle was already sufficiently established for *The Times* to head its report of a comic singer being fined for furious driving on the pavement: 'A New Terror to the Streets'.

The first manufacturing concern in Britain was the Coventry Machinists Co, established by Josiah Turner on 10 May 1869 to produce bicycles for sale in France. Export orders ceased with the outbreak of the Franco–Prussian War the following year, and the company was obliged to cultivate a home market.

LIGHTWEIGHT ALL-METAL MACHINE: the first was patented in 1870 by James Starley and William Hillman of the Coventry Machinists Co; this, the Ariel cycle, was also the first with wire-spoked tension wheels. To demonstrate the machine, the two inventors undertook to ride 96 miles from London to Coventry in a day, a feat they accomplished with no time to spare, arriving at Starley's house just as the Cathedral clock struck midnight. It was marketed in September 1871 at a price of £8, or £12 with speed-gear.

LADIES' BICYCLE: the first was patented by Samuel Webb Thomas in

1870, and was designed to be ridden side-saddle.

Series production of ladies' bicycles began in 1874 when James Starley and Hillman brought out a specially adapted version of their Ariel cycle. Like the Thomas prototype, it was a side-saddle model, fitted with a complex pedal and crank mechanism and extremely difficult to balance, which probably accounts for its failure to attract much custom. The Ariel was an 'ordinary' or 'penny-farthing' bicycle, and a fall could cause serious injury.

The first ladies' bicycle with dropped frame, designed to be ridden in the modern manner, was a safety bicycle with chain-driven rear wheel patented by H. J. Lawson in 1884.

CHAIN-DRIVEN SAFETY BICYCLE: the first was designed by H. J. Lawson in 1873 and ridden in the streets of Brighton the following year. Lawson's machine had small wooden wheels of 23in diameter, earning it the nickname of the 'Sussex Dwarf'. In 1879 he produced an improved model called the 'Bicyclette', though again the wheels were of different size, the front measuring 40in diameter and the rear 24in. It was exhibited at the Stanley Show at Holborn Town Hall in February 1880 and this was probably the date that it was launched on the market by the Tangent & Coventry Tricycle Co of Coventry (later Rudge) as the world's first commercially manufactured safety bicycle. Rival manufacturers referred to the ungainly looking machine as 'the Crocodile' and the small numbers sold gave them little cause for anxiety.

The true forerunner of the modern safety was the Rover Safety, exhibited by John Kemp Starley at the Stanley Show in January 1885. This model had wheels of equal diameter, a diamond frame, and geared-up chain-drive; a conception so advanced that it could probably be ridden today without exciting undue comment or attention. Starley's Rover set an established pattern for bicycle design, which underwent no radical changes until Alex Moulton's revolutionary mini-wheeled machine made its appearance over 60 years later.

MOULTON BICYCLE: the first was designed by Alex Moulton of Bradford-on-Avon in 1958, and offered to Raleigh Industries for evaluation the following year. Raleigh turned it down, being of the opinion that the unusual looking machine with its miniature 16in wheels and low centre of gravity would never catch on with the public. Moulton then began production on his own account at Bradford-on-Avon, and to the surprise of the cycle industry the new machine immediately found favour with businessmen and others who might normally be expected to use a more sophisticated form of transport. Among those who found the Moulton ideal for beating London traffic was Quintin Hogg (Lord Hailsham), who used his to cycle to the House of Commons. In 1962 John Woodburn of Reading cycled from Cardiff to London on a Moulton in 6hr 44min, beating the existing record for the 162-mile journey by 18min. The final vindication of Moulton's revolutionary design came in 1967, when Raleigh Industries admitted that their original decision had been wrong, and took over the Bradford concern, retaining Alex Moulton as consultant.

See also Pneumatic Tyre.

The first
BIKINI

swimsuit was designed by French *couturier* Louis Reard and first modelled by a dancer called Micheline Bernardi at a Paris fashion show held on 5 July 1946, four days after the Americans had detonated an atomic bomb at Bikini Atoll in the Pacific. The word 'bikini' was used by M. Reard to express the idea of 'the ultimate'. The prototype bikini was made of cotton printed with a newspaper design. Pictures of Mlle Bernardi reclining in the new creation were widely circulated and it was reported that she subsequently received 50,000 fan letters.

GB: A combination of climate and clothing-coupons probably accounted for the bikini's late appearance in Britain. The first intimation of its arrival was a report in the *News of the World* for 25 June 1950, which described how a Mrs Yvonne Goodman had made an unsuccessful attempt to wear a home-made bikini on Hampstead Heath. She was approached by police, who informed her: 'Your costume does not conform to regulations. You must put clothes on at once. You cannot swim in that costume.'

The first
BIRTH CONTROL: CONTRACEPTIVE SHEATH OR CONDOM

is attributed to Gabriel Fallopius, Professor of Anatomy at Padua University from 1551 until his death in 1562, and first described in his posthumously published *De Morbo Gallico* of 1564. The linen sheath, which Fallopius claimed to have tried out on 1,100 different men, was designed to be worn over the glans of the penis and it was necessary to insert it beneath the foreskin to keep it in place. Fallopius intended his invention as a preventive against venereal disease and its contraceptive properties were incidental. There is no known reference in literature to the use of the sheath other than as a prophylactic until 1655, when an anonymous Parisian publication titled *L'Escole Des Filles* recommended a linen contraceptive to prevent the passage of the semen.

Although by the end of the 17th century the use of contraceptive techniques was fairly widespread among the upper classes in France, it was the intra-uterine sponge rather than the male sheath that won most favour. Writing to her daughter in 1671, Mme de Sévigné described the condom as 'an armour against enjoyment and a spider web against danger'.

GB: A veiled but not over-ambiguous reference to the manufacture and sale of contraceptive sheaths is contained in William Burnaby's play of 1701 titled *The Ladies' Visiting Day*. In the third act there is an arch exchange between Sir Testly Dolt and Lady Lovetoy over the latter's patronage of 'Mrs Phillips'. Although this is the earliest-known allusion to Mrs Phillips, later in the century, she, or more likely her heirs, successors and imitators, all of whom appear to have traded under the same name, became widely celebrated as purveyors of condoms.

The earliest explicit reference to the condom by name is made in a poem of 1706 titled 'A Scots Answer to a British Vision'. Another poem published two years later – 'Almonds for Parrots' – provides an insight into early marketing methods, with an allusion to the

A sport not yet revived in our permissive society. The object of this 18th-century game was to see who could blow up a contraceptive into the biggest balloon!

honest 'Condon' sellers who perambulated 'St James's Park, Spring-Garden, the Play-House and the Mall'.

In England, as on the Continent, it was originally used as a prophylactic. The contraceptive utility of the sheath had, however, been recognized as early as 1723, the year that White Kennett, son of the Bishop of Peterborough, spoke in his satirical poem 'Armour' of the condom emancipating young women from the fear of 'big belly, and the squalling brat'.

The oldest surviving contraceptive sheaths date from *c.* 1800 and were found in a locked box in the muniment-room of an English country-house in the 1950s. Made of the dried gut of a sheep, they would have required soaking in water before use. It was this kind of condom that Casanova described as an 'English overcoat' in his *Memoirs*, adding that they were generally tied at the base with pink ribbon, a necessary precaution, since a wet length of animal intestine would have had limited elasticity. It could also be porous, hence the sound commercial advice given by the 'Cundum Warehouse' of St Martin's Lane in 1744 that it was safer to wear two. No record of rubber sheaths exists before 1888, when a rubber-trade journal denounced them as a disgrace to a respectable industry. It seems probable, though, that they existed at least a decade earlier than this, even if the contemporary climate of public morality did not lend itself to references in print.

LOCAL AUTHORITY IN BRITAIN TO OFFER FREE CONTRACEPTIVES ON THE RATES: the first was Hounslow Borough Council, with effect from 1 April 1972. There was no restriction on the type of contraceptives provided, nor on the marital status of those eligible – applicants had only to be resident in Hounslow and 16 years of age.

The first
BIRTH CONTROL: ORAL CONTRACEPTIVE

was produced by Dr Gregory Pincus of the Worcester Foundation for Experimental Biology at Shrewsbury, Mass. In 1950 he was invited to undertake research on behalf of the Planned Parenthood Movement to devise an ideal contraceptive, defined as 'harmless, entirely reliable, simple, practical, universally applicable and aesthetically satisfactory to both husband and wife'. Pincus and co-worker Dr John Rock spent five years in developing an oral contraceptive to meet these requirements from the compounds progestin and oestrogen. The first clinical tests were made in 1954.

The first large-scale oral contraceptive tests with Dr Pincus's pill were initiated in 1956 at San Juan, Puerto Rico, where 1,308 women involved in a slum-clearance scheme volunteered to participate. Of this number 811 were put on Conovid and 497 on Uvulen. At the end of the three-year trial, out of the 830 women remaining in the test group, only 17 had become pregnant.

The first commercially produced oral contraceptive was Enovid 10, marketed by the G. D. Searle Drug Co of Skokie, Ill. on 18 August 1960.

GB: The first field test was carried out with the co-operation of 50 Birmingham women by Searle Laboratories in 1960. The first commercially available oral contraceptive in Britain was Conovid 5 mg, launched on 1 January 1961.

The first
BLOOD TRANSFUSION

to a human being was carried out on 12 June 1667 by Jean-Baptiste Denys, Professor of Philosophy and Mathematics at Montpellier University and personal physician to Louis XIV. The patient was a boy of 15 suffering from a severe fever who had already been bled 20 times 'to assuage the excessive heat'. In order to compensate for this loss of blood, Denys gave him a transfusion of 9oz of blood from the carotid artery of a lamb. According to the Professor his patient responded to this extremely dangerous experiment by displaying 'a clear and smiling countenance' and eventually recovered. Others were not so fortunate, and after one of Denys's victims had died as a result of receiving animal's blood, the practice was prohibited in France and fell into disrepute elsewhere.

GB: The first transfusion was made in a spirit of scientific inquiry by Dr Richard Lower and Dr Edmund King, both members of the Royal Society, at Arundel House on 23 November 1667. The subject of the experiment was 32-year-old Arthur Coga, a somewhat disreputable Bachelor of Divinity, who for the consideration of £1 consented to risk his life by receiving 12oz of blood from a sheep, and was apparently none the worse for the experience. The two learned doctors were delighted and persuaded him to undergo a second transfusion, which was carried out on 14 December of the same year. Perhaps fortunately for medical science, this seemingly easy way of making money went to Coga's head and brought an end to the venture. 'The effects of the transfusion are not to be seen,' wrote Sir Philip Skippon in a letter to a friend, 'the coffee-houses having endeavoured to debauch the fellow, and so consequently discredit the Royal Society and make the experiment ridiculous.'

The first transfusion of human blood was performed in September 1818 by the brilliant 28-year-old Dr Thomas Blundell, of Guy's Hospital, London. Blundell used a syringe of his own invention to inject some 12–14oz of fresh blood from several different donors, but his patient was in a moribund state and already beyond hope of recovery. Another 10 years were to pass before he succeeded in saving the life of a patient by this means and by that time others had preceded him.

The first recorded instance of a patient's life being saved by a blood transfusion occurred in London in 1825, when a Dr Doubleday gave 14oz of blood to a woman suffering from a severe internal haemorrhage. After receiving only 6oz she sat up in bed and announced 'I feel as strong as a bull.' Her pulse rate subsequently fell from 140 to 104.

Although this case demonstrated that blood transfusion could be effective if carefully regulated, there were still two major obstacles to be overcome before it had any chance of general acceptance. Foremost was ignorance of incompatibility, and not until Karl Landsteimer of Vienna discovered blood groups in 1900 was it possible for doctors to match the donor to the patient. Several years were to pass before this knowledge was applied in a practical manner, but in 1907 the Norwegian scientist Jansky made the first reliable classification of blood groups, and the following year Dr Reuben Ottenberg of New York instituted the practice of making blood tests before a transfusion.

The other major difficulty was blood clotting, a factor which had probably helped to save some of the unfortunate subjects of those gruesome experiments with animal blood, since it prevented more than a few ounces from entering the blood-stream. The answer to this lay with the chemical sodium citrate, which acts as an anti-coagulant and enables blood to be decanted into bottles ready for use, so that a transfusion can be given without the presence of the donor. The citrate method was discovered by the Belgian surgeon A. Hustin, who performed the first indirect transfusion with blood stored in this way at the l'Hôpital Sant-Jean in Brussels on 27 March 1914.

Although citrate would prevent clotting, the problem of preserving blood-supplies for more than a few hours remained. This was overcome in 1917 by Dr Oswald Robertson, an American physician serving with the Canadian forces on the Western Front, who conceived the idea of storing blood corpuscles in jars of glucose, in much the same way as jam is preserved. The blood was collected behind the lines from Group O donors and then brought under refrigeration to the RAMC Casualty Clearing Station near Doullens by ambulance. There, under Dr Robertson's supervision, it was stored in a cool dug-out until required, the blood corpuscles needing only the addition of a saline solution to be ready for use.

BLOOD DONORS: the first panel was set up in 1921 by Dr P.L. Oliver, who arranged for four volunteers from the Camberwell Division of the London Branch of the British Red Cross Society to donate their blood at King's College Hospital. This was the beginning of the London Blood Transfusion Service, which provided a register of donors who were prepared to respond to a call for blood from any of the London hospitals in an emergency. At first the demand was small, only 26 requests for blood being made in 1924, but five years later the number had increased to 5,333.

BLOOD BANK: the first was established in 1931 by Prof. Sergei Yudin at the Sklifosovsky Institute, Moscow's central emergency service hospital. The term 'blood bank' was coined by Bernard Fantus, who set up America's first centralized depot for the storage of blood at Cook County Hospital, Chicago in 1937.

PRE-NATAL BLOOD TRANSFUSION: the first was performed by Prof. George Green on a child born to Mrs E. McLeod at the National Women's Hospital, Auckland, NZ on 20 September 1963. A similar transfusion was carried out for the first time in Britain at Lewisham Hospital in August 1964.

The first
BOOK CLUB

offering books at specially reduced prices was the Left Book Club, which issued its first monthly selection, Maurice Thorez's *France Today and the People's Front*, to 5,000 subscribers in May 1936. The Club was launched by the London publisher Victor Gollancz with the purpose of producing a series of cheap, hitherto unpublished books on the questions of Fascism, poverty and the threat of war. The original selection committee comprised John Strachey, Harold Laski and Gollancz himself. Each book chosen was published in a special Club edition with orange limp cloth binding at 2s 6d, and simultaneously issued as a hardback for normal retail distribution at three or four times the Club price.

The first book club dealing in general literature for a non-specialist membership was the Readers Union, founded in 1937 and now the oldest surviving club of its kind.

The first
BOOK DUST-JACKET

was issued with *The Keepsake*, 1833, an annual published by Longman, London in November 1832. It was pale buff, with a decorative border enclosing the title printed in red, and advertisements for other Longman publications on the back. The spine was plain. This unique book-jacket was discovered by the English bibliophile John Carter in 1934, and predated by 28 years the earliest book-jacket reported hitherto. It was lost in 1952 while being taken to the Bodleian Library in Oxford and no other example has ever been found.

PICTORIAL DUST-WRAPPER: the first was issued with an edition of Bunyan's *Pilgrim's Progress* published by Longman in 1860. The illustration reproduced on the buff wrapper was a woodcut by Charles Bennett, also contained in the book itself.

The Keepsake jacket of 1832 and *The Pilgrim's Progress* jacket of 1860, as well as the half dozen or so examples known to have been issued between these dates, were all designed to completely enclose the book. The earliest-known example of a book-jacket of the modern kind (i.e. with flaps folding in between cover and end-papers, leaving the edges of the pages free, and with the title printed on the spine) was issued with Noel Paton's *Poems by a Painter*, published by Blackwood of Edinburgh in 1861.

PUBLISHERS KNOWN TO HAVE USED 'BLURBS' ON THEIR BOOK-JACKETS: the first were Harper and Dodd Mead, both of New York. Three examples survive from 1899 – Harper's *Admiral George Dewey*, by John Barrett, and their *The Enchanted Type-writer*, by J.K. Bangs, and Dodd Mead's *Janice Meredith* by P.L. Ford.

The word 'blurb' was coined by American author Gelett Burgess in 1907. At the American Booksellers' Association banquet that year he defined the verb 'to blurb' as 'to make a sound like a publisher' and added 'A blurb is a check drawn on Fame, and it is seldom honored.'

The first
BOOK TOKENS

were launched towards the end of 1932 by the National Book Council with the slogan 'The Gift is Mine, The Choice is Thine.' The idea had been conceived in 1926 by Harold Raymond of Chatto & Windus, but it was several years before he could secure the co-operation of the booksellers. Book tokens have since been introduced in most countries of the Western world with the notable exception of the USA, where it has been found impossible to devise a workable scheme.

The first
BOWLER HAT

was made in 1849 by Thomas and William Bowler, felt-hat makers of Southwark Bridge Road, London in fulfilment of an order placed with them by Lock & Co of St James's on behalf of their customer William Coke of Holkham, Norfolk. Coke intended the 'bowler' as protection from low overhanging branches when out shooting. On 17 December 1849, Coke travelled up to London to try the new hat on. Before taking delivery, however, he placed the hat on the floor and stamped on it. Although no customer had ever had the temerity to conduct such an experiment on Lock's premises before, he stamped on it again before placing the undamaged hat on his head and inquiring the price, which was 12s. Although the hat soon acquired the name of the original craftsmen, Lock's still to this day prefer to call it a Coke in honour of the customer who first wore one.

The first
BOYS' CLUB

was the Cyprus Boys' Club, Kennington, London, established under the direction of the Rev. Daniel Elsdale in October 1872. The earliest report of its activities appears in the *St John's Parish Magazine:*

This Club has now been open for three weeks, in Beulah Hall, for 1½ hours on Thursday and Friday, and 2 hours on Saturdays: and from the number that attend seems to be much appreciated. The boys have a few games and, by the kindness of some friends, a Bagatelle Table was bought last week. There are 25 or 30 boys who generally attend. Tea and coffee, bread and butter are supplied. The club is free to Sunday and Night School boys, also to the Band boys: others are charged 1d a night. Two gentlemen kindly superintend each night and have little or no trouble with the boys.

The Club continued in existence until World War I.

The first
BOY SCOUT MOVEMENT

originated with an experimental camp held on Brownsea Island, Poole, Dorset by Lt-Gen (Sir) Robert Baden-Powell from 29 July to 9 August 1907. Twenty boys were invited to try out the new 'Game of Scouting', of whom nine were members of the Bournemouth and Poole Boys' Brigade companies, and the remainder were sons of Baden-Powell's own friends. They were formed into four patrols – Curlews, Ravens, Wolves and Bulls – to carry out a range of activities that included woodcraft, observation, swimming, knot-tying,

The Boy Scouts

BE PREPARED

This is to certify that the 1st Glasgow Troop of Boy Scouts is duly registered at Headquarters

Signed on behalf of the Council by [illegible] Secretary.

Dated Jan 26 [illegible]

The proof of the 1st Glasgow's claim to be the first Boy Scout Troop – a registration certificate dated 26 January 1908

cooking, physical jerks, boat and fire drill, night patrols and a game called 'Harpooning the Whale', that consisted of harpooning a floating log from a boat. Although there were no uniforms, at B.-P.'s direction the boys wore shorts – unusual for the period – and a badge based on the north point of the compass. This last was borrowed from the 5th Dragoon Guards and remains the official insignia of the Scout Movement. The bullet-riddled Union Jack that had flown during the Siege of Mafeking was raised over the camp.

The continuous development of the movement began with the publication of the first fortnightly 4d part of Baden-Powell's *Scouting for Boys* on 16 January 1908. It was not the author's intention to found a national youth organization, but rather to provide guidance for boys who wanted to train themselves in the frontier skills that he himself had learned while soldiering in various parts of the Empire. The movement grew quite spontaneously, boys in all parts of the country – though principally those from middle- and lower middle-class suburbs – banding themselves into patrols to put into practice the advice imparted by B.-P. in his book.

The earliest Scout Troop of which there is definitive evidence was the 1st Glasgow, which has in its possession an official registration certificate retrospectively dated to 26 January 1908. This troop was originally founded in September 1907 by Mr Robert Young as an association of Glasgow schools OTC members who had met and formed friendships at their annual summer camp. Soon afterwards B.-P. visited Capt. Young and persuaded him to introduce the Scouting methods previously tried out at the Brownsea camp. The cadets having accepted this idea, the association was renamed the 1st Glasgow Scout Troop and formed into four patrols, each of which represented one of the four schools from which membership of the troop was drawn – Hillhead High, Glasgow High, Glasgow Academy and Kelvinside Academy.

Other claims to priority have been advanced on behalf of three troops organized at Nottingham by B.-P. himself on 4 February 1908, and the Sunderland troop founded by Col Vaux during the same month. The latter, known as the 'Lambton Street Troop (Vaux's Own)', was made up of members of the Sunderland Waifs' Rescue Agency and Street Vendors' Club, most of whom were newspaper-boys from poor homes. In May 1908 they held what may well have been the first-ever Scout troop camp, spending a month under canvas at Grindon, Co Durham, where they were joined by the Kangaroo Patrol of the 1st Hampstead Troop. The newsboys were compensated for loss of earnings while attending the camp by an *ex gratia* payment of 5s a week made to them by Col Vaux. It has been claimed that it was the success of this camp that decided B.-P. to proceed with the formal organization of the movement. This had been effected by the end of the year with the opening of a permanent headquarters at 116–118 Victoria Street, London, and the appointment of two Scout Inspectors.

Membership of the world-wide Scout Movement passed 10 million for the first time in 1964. It is now the largest international voluntary organization (other than religious bodies) in the world.

See also Girl Guides.

The first *BREAKFAST CEREAL*

ready to eat, was Shredded Wheat, produced by Henry D. Perky at Denver, Colo. in 1893. At first the product was sold locally in Denver and Colorado Springs, but in 1895 Perky founded the Natural Food Co and commenced manufacture on a factory scale at Worcester, Mass. A lawyer by profession, Perky was a martyr to dyspepsia and it was after encountering a fellow sufferer in a Nebraska hotel, a man who ate whole boiled wheat with milk for breakfast, that he was inspired with the Shredded Wheat idea.

FLAKED BREAKFAST CEREAL: the first was Granose Flakes, prepared from wheat by Dr John Kellogg of the Battle Creek Sanitarium, Mich. and announced in the February 1895 issue of *Food Health.*

CORN FLAKES were first introduced in 1898 by Dr Kellogg's brother William, and manufactured by the Sanitas Food Co of Battle Creek.

GB: The first breakfast cereal was Force wheat flakes, introduced from Canada by the Force Food Co in June 1902.

BRIDGE
probably originated in Turkey, where the first laws of the game were compiled by an English visitor to Constantinople, Mr John Collinson, *c*. 1885. On his return to London he published a pamphlet titled *Biritch, or Russian Whist* in February 1886. The Russian origin he ascribed to the game is unsupported by any evidence and the word 'Biritch' does not exist in any language.

Writing in 1906 a well-known exponent of the game, William Dalton, suggested that it may have been played in England even earlier than Collinson's return from Turkey.

We have received a letter from a well-known Greek gentleman, now resident in London, in which we are assured that the writer can remember the game of Bridge, very much in its present form, being regularly played among a colony of Greeks, settled in Manchester, of whom his own father was one, as far back as the seventies of the last century. The only important point of difference between the game as it was then played and as it is played now was, that the value of No Trumps was 10 points per trick instead of 12, and that the four aces in one hand counted 80 above the line instead of 100 as at present. Also, the lead of a heart, in answer to a double of No Trumps by the leader's partner, which is commonly supposed to have originated in America, was the general custom.

The Greek gentleman was identified as a Mr Scaramanga.

Bridge was little known in England until the autumn of 1894, when Lord Brougham introduced the game at the Portland Club, after learning it in Cairo. The first official laws were issued by a joint committee of the Turf and Portland Clubs in July of the following year, and within a few months it had totally ousted whist, the traditional game of London's clubland, and threatened to do the same to amateur theatricals at country-house parties. A similar metamorphosis was meanwhile taking place in New York, whence Mr Henry Barbey had introduced the game from Paris in April 1892.
AUCTION BRIDGE is traditionally believed to have been the invention of three Anglo-Indian civilians marooned in a remote hill station in 1902 with no fourth man to make up the usual table. The first printed reference to the game is contained in a letter to *The Times* of 16 January 1903 from a Mr Oswald Crawford, lately returned from India. The following year John Doe published his *Auction Bridge* in Allahabad and in 1906 the new version of the game was adopted by the Bath Club and regularized for four-handed play.
CONTRACT BRIDGE was first played under the name of 'Saac', the initials of the four men who devised it at Poona in 1912. The first rules were published by Sir Hugh Clayton in the *Times of India* on 15 July 1914, but the game was slow to catch on in England before the laws were codified by a committee of the Portland Club in December 1929.

Contract Bridge had an independent American origin in 1925, when the American millionaire Harold S. Vanderbilt learned to play the French game of Plafond aboard a steamship plying between Los Angeles and Havana in May of that year. Making his own adaptation of the rules, he introduced the game under its present name of Contract Bridge at the Whist Club in New York.
INTERNATIONAL BRIDGE MATCH: the first was held on 15 September 1930 at Almack's, London, between a British team captained by Lt-Col Walter Buller and an American team captained by Ely Culbertson. The USA won the match of 200 deals by 4,845 points.

The first
BUILDING SOCIETY
reference to, appeared in the following advertisement published in *Aris's Birmingham Gazette* on 13 July 1778:

To be sold by Auction, at the Golden Cross, Snow Hill, on Wednesday the 22nd of this Instant July, between the hours of Seven and Nine in the Evening, Three Shares or Parts in a Building Society. Enquire for Particulars at the said Golden Cross.

Two other advertisements for the same Society appear on 26 October 1778 and 29 March 1779. The latter refers to the building society held at Mr Richard Ketley's, the Golden Cross Inn, Snow Hill, and offers three shares on which £80 had already been advanced. Although nothing is known about the subscription rates of the Society, Mr Seymour J. Price, in his scholarly work on the origin of the movement (*Building Societies: their origin and history*, London, 1958), surmised from this figure that Ketley's Society may have been in existence for a period of three to five years. He suggests that 'in the absence of any information to the contrary, it would certainly be reasonable to consider 1775 as the year in which the modern building society movement originated'.

The early building society movement was centred in the north of England and the Midlands. It is estimated that by the end of the century some 50 building societies had come into existence, of which not a single example was in the London area.

The first houses positively identifiable as having been built through the agency of a building society are the 20 cottages of Club Row, Longridge, Lancashire, erected in blocks of four for the members of the Longridge Building Society between 1793 and 1804. The average cost of each house was £97 8s 6d, though with allowances for interest on the capital sums invested by the Society, each member paid out only £75 3s in fees and subscriptions.

Like all the early building societies, the Longridge venture was a terminating society, i.e. the Society was founded with the intention of providing a house for each of its members, whose numbers were limited by the articles of foundation. The order in which the houses were allocated on completion was decided by ballot and when every member was housed and all liabilities discharged, the Society was dissolved. The members of the Longridge Society were probably representative of the movement as a whole, consisting as they did of respectable artisans and yeomen bent on self-help and prepared to subscribe the not-inconsiderable sum of 2s 6d a week towards realizing the ideal of home ownership. The activity of the early terminating societies was limited to the actual building of new houses, and they did not buy existing property.

While the movement continued to rely on the terminating principle, it was not possible for a society to cater to the interests of more than a limited number of members or to extend its benefits beyond the immediate locality it was designed to serve. It was not until 1846 that a distinguished actuary, Arthur Strachey, then Secretary of the Western Life Assurance & Annuity Society, devised a viable plan for the establishment of permanent building societies, which he published the following year under the title *Treatise on Benefit Building Societies*. It is not possible to identify the first permanent building society, as a number of terminating societies already in existence adopted Strachey's plan in 1846 and succeeding years. The innovation led to an immediate expansion of the building society movement and some of the 2,000 societies founded in the next decade are among the largest operating today.

The earliest-known society in the USA, the Oxford Provident Building Association of Philadelphia County, was established by three English immigrants on 3 January 1831.

The first
BUSES
were eight-seater vehicles known as *carrosses à cinq solz*. They were intro-

duced in Paris by a company formed under Royal Patent in January 1662 by the French philosopher and scientist, Blaise Pascal and his friend and chief financial backer, the Duc de Roannez. A scheduled service began between the Porte de Saint-Antoine and the Porte du Luxembourg on 18 March 1662, four vehicles running in one direction and three in the other at 7–8min intervals. It was stressed by the Commissaire at the inauguration ceremony that the *carrosses* would leave punctually whether full or empty, an innovation in itself. The fare was a flat-rate 5 sous for the whole or any part of the journey, though later a circular route was added with intermediate fare stages.

At first the idea of an urban system of public transport was greeted with great enthusiasm, except by the soldiers and peasant classes who were excluded from using the service under the terms of the Patent. Aristocrats were known to leave their carriages at one of the termini and brave the discomforts of sharing a confined space with seven others of humbler birth, solely for the novelty of the experience. Even the King himself indulged the popular fancy, and became one of the few reigning monarchs who have ever travelled by bus.

By 5 July, a further four routes had been opened, but then the craze began to wane, and as the aristocracy reverted to a more conventional mode of travel, the bourgeoisie ceased to ape their superiors and made a virtue of walking to save the fare. When Pascal died in August, a bare five months after the start of the enterprise, the *carrosses* were already running half empty, though the undertaking contrived to stay alive until the aged Duc de Roannez surrendered his monopoly nearly 20 years later. Buses were not reintroduced to Paris, or any other part of the world, until 1819, when Jacques Lafitte began operating a fleet of buses each carrying 16–18 passengers.

The word 'omnibus' was coined by Stanislas Baudry, the proprietor of hot-water baths in a suburb of Nantes, who began running a special service for his patrons from la place du Commerce in the centre of the city in 1823. Finding that his vehicles were being used by people living in the suburb as well as bathers, he decided to extend his operations and cast about for a word that would suitably express the public nature of his service. The terminus in la place du Commerce was outside a shop kept by a M. Omnes, whose sign bore the slogan 'Omnes Omnibus', and Baudry, appreciating that 'omnibus' could equally well be translated as 'for everybody' as 'for everything', borrowed the word for his own purpose.

GB: The first regular scheduled bus service was introduced on 4 July 1829 by George Shillibeer, a London coach-builder who had at one time worked for Lafitte in Paris. Shillibeer operated two 22-seat rear-entrance buses drawn by three horses abreast 'after the French fashion' on a route from the 'Yorkshire Stingo' in Marylebone Road, London, to the Bank via New Road (now Euston Road and City Road). The original conductors, both sons of naval officers, were dressed in midshipman uniforms, and further tone was given to the undertaking by the provision of newspapers and magazines for the amusement and edification of passengers. The fare was 1s for the full distance, or 6d for any intermediate stage.

SELF-PROPELLED OMNIBUS: the first was the 10-seat steam-driven *Infant*, built by Walter Hancock and put into service experimentally 'as a means of dissipating . . . prejudices' (it was not licensed to carry paying passengers) between Stratford and the City in 1831. The first scheduled service for paying passengers was inaugurated by the London & Paddington Steam Carriage Co on 22 April 1833, when Hancock's 14-seat *Enterprise* began plying between Paddington and the City. During the next three and a half years the Company's steam-buses carried 12,761 passengers without mishap and travelled 4,200 route miles, but were finally driven off the road by unnecessarily harsh restrictions on their use.

DOUBLE-DECKER BUS: the first was built by Adams and Co of Bow, London, for the Economic Conveyance Co in April 1847, and had accommodation for 14 upper-deck passengers sitting back to back on the roof. Those riding on top were charged half-fare. The year 1851 saw the general introduction of double-decker buses as proprietors hastened to add the 'knife-board' (so named after the piece of wood wrapped in emery-paper used for cleaning knives) to accommodate the vast increase of passengers caused by the Great Exhibition. If all the seats were occupied, passengers were allowed to sit on the edge of the roof with their legs dangling over the side, provided they were prepared to pay for any windows they smashed with their boots.

The first motor bus in the world to enter regular passenger service, 1895

BUSES WITH AN ENCLOSED UPPER DECK: the first were four Commer vehicles introduced by Widnes Corporation on 9 April 1909. In London there were police restrictions against roofed-in upper decks, and it was not until 2 October 1925 that the enclosed NS type went into service.

The first totally enclosed double-decker – top deck, staircase and driver's cab – was ST1, introduced by the London General Omnibus Co (LGOC) on their 11A route in 1930.

PETROL-DRIVEN MOTOR BUS: the first was a 5hp Benz single-deck enclosed landau, which began running on a 15km route – Siegen–Netphen–Deuz – in the North Rhineland on 18 March 1895. Operated by a local co-operative, the Netphener Omnibus Co, the bus could seat six to eight passengers inside and another two outside on the driver's box. The driver was Hermann Golze from Netphen. A second, exactly similar bus came into service on 1 July 1895. They maintained an average speed (without stops) of 14kph and took 1hr 20min for the complete journey. The fare was 70Pf and intermediate stages cost 20Pf. The buses were heated inside for winter comfort, a luxury not afforded by the Post-Wagon which previously had constituted the sole means of public transport on the route. On the other hand passengers could be called upon to get out and help push the bus uphill whenever required. High operating costs and frequent breakdowns combined to render the service uneconomic and it closed down on 20 December 1895. The two vehicles had carried 10,600 fare-paying passengers during the time they had been on the road.

GB: The first motor-bus service was advertised in the *Bradford Observer* for 25 September 1897: 'The Yorkshire Motor Car Co Ltd., Albert Buildings, Bradford. Motor omnibuses daily from Town Hall to Four Lane Ends.'

The service was run by J.E. Tuke (*see also* Car Hire), using a covered Daimler wagonette. The fare for the 2-mile distance was 6d. It is not known how long the service was maintained and, apart from the paid advertisement quoted above, this epoch-making event in the annals of British transport passed completely unnoticed by Bradford's three newspapers.

FULL-SIZE PETROL OMNIBUS WITH CONVENTIONAL BUS BODY: the first known in regular service was a 16hp 6-ton single-deck Tenting Omnibus seating 18 passengers, which was running between Nantes and Velheuil, France by March 1898.

GB: The first full-size petrol buses, also the first London motor buses in scheduled service, were two steel-tyred 12hp German Daimlers with 26-seat Bayley double-decker bodies, introduced by the Motor Traction Co on a route from Kennington to Victoria Station via Westminster Bridge on 9 October 1899. The route was changed to Kennington–Oxford Circus the following year, but the service could not be maintained and the buses were withdrawn in December 1900. The fare on both routes was 2d for the distance and 1d for intermediate stages.

After the initial period of experimentation, the motor bus began to establish itself as a paying proposition on London routes from 1905 onwards, and gradually ousted the horse-drawn bus. By 31 October 1910, there were 1,142 horse-drawn buses and 1,142 motor buses licensed in London. A year later the London General Omnibus Co, then the largest single operator, withdrew its last horse bus. The last London horse bus of all ceased running over Waterloo Bridge in 1916. Known as the 'Flea Box', the fare was ½d and it has been tersely described as being 'small and having dirty looking red velvet curtains'. The last horse bus in Britain ceased running between Wickhambrook and Newmarket in 1932 when one of the horses died.

See also Motor Coach; Motor-coach Tour; Pneumatic Tyres, Bus.

The first
BUS CONDUCTRESS

was Miss Kate Barton, who began working for her father's bus company, Barton Transport of Beeston, Nottinghamshire, on the Long Eaton–Nottingham route in 1909. Her sisters Ruth and Edith joined the firm as conductresses in 1911, after trying factory-work and domestic service and finding neither to their liking. They wore long green coats on duty and Kate Barton sported a male conductor's peaked cap, the other girls preferring to go bareheaded as they were proud of their long hair. As long hours on cold buses were considered bad for them, an improvised heating system was installed in one of the Durham Churchill buses operated by Barton's, the exhaust-pipe being run through the interior of the bus to radiate the passenger compartment. Late-night runs were unpopular, Edith recalls, as they had to contend with drunks; at other times it was over-amorous passengers that provided a hazard. Kate Barton left the buses when she married in 1918, and her sisters shortly afterwards.

The first conductresses employed on London buses were recruited in February 1916 as a wartime measure to enable more men to be released for the Services.

The first
CAESARIAN SECTION

by which both mother and baby survived is alleged to have been performed on the wife of Jacob Nufer, a sow-gelder of Sigershauffen, Switzerland, in 1500. The operation was carried out by Jacob himself with his sow-gelding instruments. According to François Rosset's text on Caesarian section, published in Paris in 1581, Frau Nufer lived to the age of 77 and subsequent to the operation was delivered of a pair of twins and four other children, all by normal delivery. This remarkable post-operative history has caused some authorities to cast doubt on the authenticity of the episode.

GB: The first successful Caesarian section was performed at Charlemont, Ireland in January 1738 by an illiterate local midwife, Mary Donally, who used a razor to deliver her patient, Alice O'Neal, of a healthy child. The mother had been 12 days in labour at the time of the operation. Having cut through the abdominal wall and opened up the uterus, Mary Donally removed the child, placenta and membrane and then held the lips of the incision together with her hands while neighbours went a mile in search of silk and a tailor's needle. The wound was dressed with white of egg after stitching and Alice made such a rapid recovery that she was able to go about her normal business on the 27th day after the operation.

The first successful Caesarian section to be performed by a qualified medical practitioner in Britain took place at Blackburn, Lancashire in 1793, when Dr James Barlow delivered a child from a patient with a fractured pelvis.

The first
CANNED FOOD

The principle by which perishable foods could be preserved in sealed containers was discovered by Parisian confectioner Nicolas Appert. He developed a commercially practicable process in response to an offer made by the French Government in 1795 of a 12,000-franc prize for an improved method of food conservation. Appert himself did not use metal canisters, but employed glass bottles. It is generally accepted, however, that the present-day canning industry owes its inception to Appert's pioneer work in the art of preservation. The first independent test of his products was made in 1804, when the Minister of Marine directed that samples should be sent for appraisal to the naval station at Brest. The bottles were kept for three months before opening. The Marine Prefect then submitted the following report to the Board of Health in Paris:

The broth in bottles was good; the broth included with boiled beef, in a special vessel, good also but weak; the beef itself very edible.
The beans and green peas, prepared both with and without meat, have all the freshness and the agreeable flavour of freshly picked vegetables.

During the course of the same year Appert established a factory at Massy, just outside Paris, and laid out a market-garden on the adjoining land in order to grow his own fruit and vegetables for bottling.

The use of tinplate cans for preserving food on a commercial scale was pioneered by Messrs Donkin & Hall, who established the world's first cannery at Blue Anchor Road, Bermondsey in 1812. Appert's principal difficulty had been in sealing the bottles – he used up to five layers of cork cut so that the pores ran horizontally – and it was to solve this problem that Bryan Donkin and John Hall decided to experiment with tin cans. For the sum of £1,000 they acquired the rights of a patent, taken out in 1810 by Peter Durand, that covered the use of 'vessels of tin or other metals' for food preservation.

Messrs Donkin & Hall submitted their first canned foods to high-ranking officers of the Army and Navy for trial in 1813. One of these 'tasters' was Lord Wellesley, later Duke of Wellington, whose secretary wrote to say that he had found the preserved beef very good. Unfortunately the writer was tactless enough to add that His Lordship could not reply himself as he was indisposed. Favourable reports having been received the authorities ordered supplies for a number of overseas stations the following year, including St Helena and the West Indies. Donkin & Hall's 'Preserved Meat' and 'Vegetable Soup' also formed part of the provisions aboard HMS *Isabella* and HMS *Alexander*, which set out on an expedition to Baffin's Bay under the command of John Ross in 1814.

A list of the supplies delivered to the Admiralty Victualling Depot by Donkin, Hall & Gamble (as the firm had become) between March and December 1818 gives an indication of the range of canned foods then available. The Admiralty order, totalling 23,779 cans, included the following: Mess Beef, Corned Round of Beef, Roasted Beef, Seasoned Beef, Boiled Mutton, Seasoned Mutton, Boiled Veal, Roasted Veal, Veal and Vegetables, Soup and Bouilli, Vegetable Soup, Mess Beef and Vegetables, Concentrated Soup.

Vegetables on their own had made their appearance by 1824, when Capt. W. E. Parry ordered 12,000lb of canned carrots and 8,000lb of canned parsnips for his second voyage in search of a North-West Passage. Two cans from this expedition – one a 4lb tin of Roast Veal, the other a 2lb tin of Carrots and Gravy – were brought back to England and preserved intact until 1936, when they were opened by scientists of the International Tin Research and Development Council. The contents of the 112-year-old veal tin were fed to young rats and an adult cat without any adverse effects. The carrots had the appearance of freshly cooked vegetables on opening, but had a metallic smell and taste. They were sliced and packed in their own juice, no gravy being evident.

The cans used by Donkin, Hall & Gamble were filled through a small aperture in the top, which was then sealed with a soldered disc. Manufacture was by hand, and in the 1840s it was recorded that 60 canisters a day was the maximum output of an expert craftsman. The can-opener being unknown at this time, directions on the label of the can read: 'Cut round on the top near to the outer edge with a chisel and hammer . . .'.

Although canned foods became available in English shops in 1830, their exterior appearance remained as starkly utilitarian as the goods supplied on contract, and it was left to the more sales-conscious Americans to realize the need for attractive packaging. The earliest-known coloured pictorial label was designed for Messrs Reckhow & Larne of New York, probably in the 1860s, and depicts a dish of tomatoes in red and green against a sky-blue background. The sole surviving example of this label was found on an empty tin can in an old house at Salem, Ind.

The word 'can' was adopted for the first time as an abbreviation of 'canister' by the book-keepers of the Boston cannery of Underwood in 1839.

See also Baked Beans.

The first *CAPITAL PUNISHMENT, COUNTRIES TO EFFECTIVELY ABOLISH*

in time of peace were Russia and Finland in 1826. The Tsar Nicholas I, who had succeeded his brother Alexander I in December 1825, was afforded an early opportunity to demonstrate his attitude towards the death penalty. The Decembrist Revolution, which broke out immediately on his ascending the throne, was put down after a brief conflict, and 579 of those involved were brought to trial. Out of this number, nearly half were acquitted; of the remainder, 31 were exiled to Siberia, 85 imprisoned and most of the others subjected to some form of restraint. Only 5 of the ringleaders were hanged, an extraordinary display of clemency for the time. Order having been restored, the Tsar issued a proclamation declaring that he was against the death penalty in principle and stating his intention that in future all such sentences would be commuted to exile to Siberia, with the exception of those imposed for acts of treason.

These provisions applied equally to Finland, then under the domain of Russia. When Finland became autonomous in 1882 a penal code was drawn up that sanctioned the death penalty for certain offences, but in practice this was always commuted. Though capital punishment was not proscribed by law until 1949, the last occasion on which the death penalty was carried out in Finland was in 1824.

In Russia the principle of commuting death sentences automatically has been in abeyance since the Communists assumed power in 1917. Capital punishment was only recognized in Soviet law, however, in 1936, when it was sanctioned for offences against the State – a category that was given the broadest interpretation and included such crimes as petty theft of State property and expressions of dissatisfaction with the Government.

The first country in the British Commonwealth to abolish capital punishment was New Zealand in 1936.

GB: The movement for the abolition of capital punishment in Britain began in 1868, when Mr Gilpin MP introduced a Bill to that effect in the House of Commons. It was defeated by 127 votes to 23 on 21 April 1868.

The death penalty was held in abeyance between August 1955 and March 1957, convicted murderers being automatically reprieved. On 9 November 1965 an Act abolishing capital punishment came into force, largely due to the efforts of Sidney Silverman MP. The last offenders to suffer the death penalty in Britain were Peter Anthony Allen and John Robson Walby, who were executed at Strangeways Gaol, Manchester on 13 August 1964.

NB: A number of official Government and UN publications have stated that capital punishment was first abolished in Liechtenstein in 1798. There is no evidence that the death penalty has ever been legally in abeyance at any time in Liechtenstein's history and it is today one of the last remaining countries in western Europe to retain capital punishment.

The first *CARAVANS*

providing living accommodation were probably first used by continental showmen at the beginning of the 19th century. Few records of their use have come down to us, but it is known that an elaborate *voiture nomade* containing a kitchen, dining-room and bedroom was built in Paris for the circus-proprietor Antoine Franconi during the early 1830s. Prior to 1800 the term 'caravan' was used in English and French to signify a stage-wagon or a kind of rude carriage designed for carrying servants. The word is derived from the Persian *karwan*, meaning 'a company of travellers'.

GB: The earliest record of a living-wagon in Britain, albeit fictional, is

Sir Samuel and Lady Baker embarking on the first caravan holiday – Cyprus, 29 January 1879 ▶

Charles Dickens's description of Mrs Jarley's caravan in *The Old Curiosity Shop*, which was published in 1840. Mrs Jarley was proprietress of a travelling waxworks; her caravan 'a smart little house upon wheels, with white dimity curtains festooning the windows, and window-shutters of green picked out with panels of staring red'. Inside it was divided into kitchen and living-room, the latter 'partitioned off at the further end as to accommodate a sleeping-place, constructed after the fashion of a berth on board ship'.

It was not until some 20 to 30 years later that what is nowadays regarded as the traditional carved and decorated gypsy wagon began to make its appearance on the English highways. George Borrow, the repository of most of the known facts about mid-19th-century gypsy life, makes no allusions to them in his earlier novels, and it is only in *Romano Lavo-Lil* (1873) that he gives definite indication that they were then coming into use. The majority of gypsies lived in bender tents prior to this time and many continued to do so until the end of the century.

CARAVAN TOUR: the first man to take a tour for pleasure was Sir Samuel White Baker, the discoverer of Lake Albert, who purchased a gypsy wagon in London in 1878, to take with him to Cyprus on a holiday and fact-finding trip. Before leaving England he had it painted, varnished and fitted out by Messrs Glover of Dean Street, Soho, London. 'This van', Baker wrote, 'was furnished with a permanent bed; shelves or wardrobe beneath; a chest of drawers; table to fall against the wall when not in use, lockers for glass and crockery, stove and chimney, and in fact resembled a ship's cabin, nine feet six inches long, by five feet eight inches wide.' Accompanied by his wife, half a dozen servants and three spaniels, Sir Samuel left Larnaca for a six months' tour of the island on 29 January 1879. As the caravan had to be drawn by oxen, progress was naturally exceedingly slow, but the comfort he and Lady Baker were able to enjoy at night compensated for some of the frustrations of the day. At their first overnight halt he noted: 'The gypsy van presented such a picture of luxury that if the world were girded by a good road instead of a useless equator, I should like to be perpetually circum-vanning it.'

CARAVAN BUILT SPECIALLY FOR HOLIDAY TOURING: the first was the 12ft-long 2-ton *Wanderer*, designed for his own use by Dr Gordon Stables RN, the prolific author of boys' adventure stories, and delivered by the Bristol Wagon Co in the spring of 1885. This contained two compartments, a kitchen fitted with a Rippingille cooking-range, and a living-room furnished with a sofa upholstered in strong blue railway repp, bunk, lockers, table, chiffonier, piano-stool, gilt candle-brackets, Persian rug, music-rack and a small harmonium. Dr Stables occupied the bunk, while his valet Foley used to make up a bed on the floor. The coachman John slept in a tent outside. Foley's principal job during their 1,300-mile tour of Britain in 1885 was to travel in advance of the caravan on a tricycle and warn other road-users of its approach.

Dr Gordon Stables's 'land yacht' Wanderer, *built in 1885*

TRAILER CARAVAN: the first, designed for motor haulage, was built in 1897 by Jeantaud of Paris for Prince Oldenburg, uncle of the Tsar of Russia. The two-wheel trailer, in which he proposed touring the Caucasus, was drawn by a 30hp De Dion steam-tractor, and the whole massive combination, nearly 30ft long, was claimed to be capable of speeds up to 19mph. The double folding-doors let on to a side corridor, in imitation of railway-carriage practice. The most luxurious caravan ever built up to that time, it contained a number of striking and novel features, such as running water in the kitchen, an up-to-date water-closet, a cage for dogs slung underneath the wagon, and a promenade deck on the roof furnished with chairs for sitting out. The roof also accommodated a reservoir and a coke-bunker carrying fuel sufficient for a run of 500km. The outside was painted pale green and the inside was panelled with polished mahogany. Cost of tractor and trailer together was £1,200.

MOTOR CARAVAN: the first was a 25hp petrol-driven vehicle built in 1901–2 by Panhard et Levassor of Paris at a cost of £3,000, for Dr E.E. Lehwess, a German who hoped to become the first man to drive round the world. The canary-yellow *Passe-Partout* set out on this expedition from London in April 1902, and travelled across Europe via Paris, Berlin, Warsaw and St Petersburg. Disaster struck in the form of cracked cylinders at a place near Nizhni-Novgorod (Gorki), and the caravan was abandoned in a snowdrift, having completed one-fifth of its projected journey.

GB: Messrs Marshall & Co of Clayton, Manchester, manufacturers of the Belsize car, built a 30hp motor caravan with five bunks for an unnamed customer in 1903. Such vehicles were looked at askance by some of the high priests of the then burgeoning motor-car cult. They were designed, sniffed the *Motor Year Book 1905*, 'for those misguided folk who imagine that motoring has something to do with carrying your home about with you'.

REGULAR DEALER IN TRAILER CARAVANS: the first was G. J. Hay-Moulder, who founded Grosvenor Caravans in Chelsea in 1919 to sell ex-Red Cross and ex-WD Mobile Headquarters caravans that he converted for recreational use.

REGULAR MANUFACTURER OF TRAILER CARAVANS for touring: the first was Eccles Motor Transport Ltd of Gosta Green, Birmingham, which exhibited their prototype model outside the Motor Show at Olympia in December 1919. (For some long-forgotten reason Eccles were not allowed to display it inside.) Built of steel, with mahogany panelling inside and felt insulation, this first-ever production-model trailer had sleeping accommodation for two, a Primus cooker, basin, meat-safe, fireproof compartment and damp-proof locker for bedding. Only a single order was received during the course of the Motor Show, from Sybil, Dowager Viscountess Rhondda. On the basis of this sale the initial production series of 50 trailers was laid down and the price advertised as £300. Early models were distinctly 'cottagy' in appearance, with bulbous sides, lantern roofs and bow-windows with lattice panes. Streamlining was introduced by the caravan industry *c.* 1930.

CARAVAN HIRE SERVICE: the first was operated by the Auto-Salon-Luxe of Ostend, Belgium, which began letting out a four-berth 'luxury Pullman caravan' in 1920 to persons wishing to tour the battlefields of Flanders. The vehicle, built something like a yacht and equipped with an electric kitchen, had been constructed to the order of a Belgian nobleman the previous year, but the transaction had fallen through.

GB: Initiated by the Holiday Caravan Co of Woodstock Road, Oxford, which acquired 36 Eccles caravans in the summer of 1924 and, despite a disastrously wet holiday season, succeeded in letting them all. A 'canvas lean-to dining room' and a 'Ford folding boat' could be hired as extras.

The first
CARBON PAPER

was invented by Ralph Wedgwood of London, who secured a patent on 7 October 1806 for 'apparatus for producing duplicates of writings'. This described the process of saturating thin paper with ink, and drying it out between sheets of blotting-paper. The date at which Wedgwood started manufacture is not known, but during the 1820s he had a successful business at 4 Rathbone Place, Oxford Street.

The first
CARDIAC SURGERY

The first operation involving a suture of the heart itself was performed by Louis Rehn at Frankfurt City Hospital on 9 September 1896. The patient, a 22-year-old gardener's assistant called William Justus, had been stabbed to the heart by an unknown assailant after a tavern brawl. A wound 1·5cm long was found in the right ventricle, from which there was active bleeding. It was closed with three silk sutures and the blood removed from the pleural and pericardial cavities, the patient making a complete recovery. Out of the 124 cases of cardiac surgery coming to Rehn's notice during the ensuing 10 years, about 40% of the patients survived; formerly mortality among victims of heart wounds had been almost 100%.

HEART TRANSPLANT: the first was performed by Prof. Christian Barnard at Groote Schuur Hospital, Cape Town, SA on 2 December 1967, when Louis Waskansky, a wholesale grocer suffering from chronic heart disease, received the heart of a 25-year-old traffic victim, Denise Darvali. The operation took 6hr and Prof. Barnard worked with a team of 30 doctors and nurses. Waskansky died of pneumonia 18 days later.

The first
CARPET-SWEEPER

of practical design was patented by Melville R. Bissell of Grand Rapids, Mich. on 19 September 1876. Proprietor of a china-shop, Bissell suffered from headaches caused by his allergy to the dusty straw used for packing his wares. His solution to the dust menace lay in a sweeper with a sprung brush roller that responded to pressure on the handle. Most of the parts were made by women working on piece-rates at home and assembled by Mr and Mrs Bissell, who formed the Bissell Carpet Sweeper Co to market their product.

The first
CASH-REGISTER

was patented by James J. Ritty of Dayton, Ohio on 4 November 1879. Ritty owned a saloon on Main Street in Dayton, and constant pilfering by his bartenders so undermined his health that he took a sea voyage to Europe to recover. While on board the liner his attention was attracted by a machine used to record the number of revolutions made by the propellers; it was this that gave him the idea from which the basic principle of the cash-register is derived. After taking out the patent he continued to work on improvements and in 1884 the National Cash Register Co was formed to exploit his invention.

The first
CATAMARAN

was the *Experiment*, built at Dublin for Sir William Petty, a founder-member of the Royal Society, and launched on 22 December 1662. The vessel was 30 tons burthen, carried 5 guns, and was crewed by 30 men. In January 1663 it won the first open yacht race, and the following July beat the Dublin Packet in the first sea-going race, Dublin–Holyhead. It is recorded that Charles II, himself a keen yachtsman, considered the *Experiment* a great joke, but declined to accept a challenge from Sir William.

The first
CHARITY WALK

was organized in aid of the World Refugee Fund by Kenneth Johnson of Letchworth, Hertfordshire and held on 26 December 1959. The intended route was along the Icknield Way from Letchworth to Yatesbury, Wiltshire. Twenty men and one girl each paid 1s to enter, and sponsors guaranteed so much a mile. Ten of the participants gave up after 13 miles, 3 after 22 miles, 1 after 25 miles, 4 on reaching Princes Risborough, and the remaining 3, including Johnson himself, covered 50 miles, giving up at Ewelme, Oxfordshire. About £20 was raised.

The first
CHARTER FLIGHT

took place on 28 June 1911, the day that the liner *Olympic* left New York on the return half of her maiden voyage across the Atlantic. Among the passengers was a Philadelphia merchant, W. A. Burpee, who had broken his spectacles shortly before the ship sailed and sent them to Wanamaker's for repair. Just before the *Olympic* left harbour he sent a wireless message to the store asking them to forward the spectacles to his address in London. An executive of Wanamaker's had heard that the celebrated English aviator Tom Sopwith was in New York with his Howard Wright biplane, and suggested that the firm charter the aircraft to deliver Burpee's spectacles, which had already been repaired. Sopwith agreed to the terms offered and set off in pursuit of the *Olympic*, then a few miles out to sea. He overhauled the vessel and, flying low, dropped the carefully wrapped package on to the deck.

GB: The first charter flight in Britain, the first international charter flight and the first passenger charter flight was made on 21 May 1914 by Princess Ludwig von Löwestein-Wertheim, who chartered a Handley Page H.P.7 biplane from the Northern Aircraft Co to fly her to Paris for an urgent social engagement. The charter plane left Hendon at 7.30am despite poor visibility. At Eastbourne, fog over the Channel forced them to land and wait, and they only reached Calais at 4.30pm. Despite the fact that the Princess missed her engagement, she was so delighted with the experience that she determined to fly the Atlantic and commissioned Frederick Handley Page to build a suitable transatlantic aircraft. But for the outbreak of war it is possible that the Princess would have succeeded in her ambition to be the first person to cross the Atlantic by aeroplane.

The first
CHAUFFEUR
in Britain was Edward J. Thompson of Worthing, Sussex, who was employed by the Hon. Evelyn Ellis to drive the Panhard Levassor which he imported from Paris in June 1895. Mr Thompson had the distinction of driving one of the first half dozen petrol cars to run on English roads, but it is not recorded whether he was required to drive the Daimler fire-engine also owned by his employer.

The first
CHEQUE
known to have been drawn on a British bank was for the sum of £400 made payable to a Mr Delboe by Nicholas Vanacker and dated London, 16 February 1659. It was paid through Messrs Clayton & Morris, bankers, law scriveners and estate agents of Cornhill. The original cheque is preserved in the archives of the National Westminster Bank. It is made out in almost exactly the style of a modern cheque, the amount being written out first in words and then in figures.
PRINTED CHEQUE: the earliest surviving is one issued by Hoare's Bank and filled in for the amount of £5,000 made payable to David Roberts by John Calcroft, Army Agent, 4 March 1763.
CHEQUES WITH PERFORATED COUNTERFOILS: the first were issued by Hoare's Bank on 5 July 1864.
CHEQUE MADE OUT IN BRITISH DECIMAL CURRENCY: the first was for the sum of £50.30 payable to London Linen Supply Ltd by Mr N. Hickmet on behalf of Gatwick Manor Ltd and dated 4 March 1968. It was cleared by the Westminster Bank, Crawley, Sussex on 7 March.

The first
CHEWING-GUM
commercially produced, was the 'State of Maine Pure Spruce Gum', manufactured by John Curtis on a Franklin stove in the kitchen of his home at Bangor, Maine in 1848. He moved to Portland in 1850 and began production of paraffin gums under names like 'Sugar Cream', 'White Mountain', 'Four-in-Hand', 'Biggest and Best' and 'Licorice Lulu'. At the same time his range of spruce gums was extended to include 'American Flag', 'Trunk Spruce', 'Yankee Spruce' and '200 Lump Spruce'.

The first chewing-gum manufactured from chicle was produced by a Staten Island photographer called Thomas Adams. He started experimenting with chicle as a substitute for rubber in moulded goods in 1870, but was forced to abandon the idea. Chewing on a lump of his surplus stock one day, he conceived the notion of adding flavouring and selling it as gum. Although warned by a prominent manufacturer of spruce gums that the product was bound to fail, Adams commenced a small factory in 1872. Within 20 years he was operating from a six-storey plant employing 250 hands.
CHEWING-GUM SOLD FROM VENDING-MACHINES: the first was Tutti-Frutti Gum in 1888. The machines were installed on station platforms of the New York Elevated Railroad by Thomas Adams of the Adams Gum Co.
GB: Beeman's Pepsin Chewing Gum, first manufactured at Merton, Surrey in 1894. It failed to catch on with the upper strata of society, to which Beeman's addressed their advertising, and gum-chewing cannot be said to have become part of the Victorian way of life. Chewing-gum was reintroduced to Britain by Wrigley's in 1911, though as sweetshops refused to handle the product it could only be sold in vending machines.

The first
CHILDREN'S BOOK
published in English (other than school-books) was *A Booke in Englyssh Metre, of the great Marchante Man called Dives Pragmaticus, very preaty for Children to reade*, printed by Alexander Lacy, London, 1563. A small quarto of eight pages, it contains a series of rhymes, chiefly about the traders or shopkeepers who were invited to purchase stocks from Dives's extensive range of wares:

Dripping pans, pot hooks, old cats and kits;
And preaty fine dogs, without fleas or nits.
Axes for butchers, and fine glass for wives:
Medicines for rats to shorten their lives.

The first publisher to specialize in children's books was John Newbery (*see also* Children's Fiction; Children's Magazine), who commenced a thriving business in London in 1744 with the publication of *A Little Pretty Pocket Book intended for the Instruction and Amusement of Little Master Tommy and Pretty Miss Polly*. Newbery introduced a kind of premium offer with this book that may have helped to ensure its success – the little volume on its own cost 6d, but for an extra 2d 'Master Tommy' was entitled to a red and black ball to go with it, and 'Miss Polly' a red and black pincushion. A letter addressed to the children from Jack the Giant Killer – contained in the book – explained that they should stick a pin in the red half of their respective toys for every good deed performed, and a pin in the black side for every act of mischief.
CHILDREN'S BOOK WITH A PRINTED COLOUR ILLUSTRATION: the first was Mary M. Sherwood's *Caroline Mordaunt*, published by William Darton, London, 1835, which had a coloured frontispiece by George Baxter.

The first
CHILDREN'S FICTION
original work of, to be printed in the English language, was *The History of Little Goody Two-Shoes; Otherwise called, Mrs Margery Two-Shoes*, of which the earliest surviving copy, published by John Newbery at the Bible and Sun in St Paul's Churchyard (*see also* Children's Magazine), belongs to the 3rd edition and is dated 1766. The authorship of the novel is as questionable as the date of its first publication, though most authorities suggest the name of Oliver Goldsmith, who was closely associated with Newbery in a number of his enterprises.
A rags to riches story, it follows the progress of Miss Margery Meanwell, otherwise Goody Two-Shoes, from the time her father is evicted from his farm by the rascally Sir Timothy Gripe and she is left with but one shoe. A recurring theme through the book is the reliance placed by many of the characters on Dr James's Fever Powder – indeed Goody's father dies from the lack of it. This was a patent medicine manufactured by John Newbery himself, who never lost an opportunity of combining literature and advertisement in the same profitable blend.

The first
CHILDREN'S LIBRARY
was the Bingham Library for Youth, begun in January 1803 with a stock of 150 volumes at Salisbury, Conn. by a bookseller called Caleb Bingham and intended for the exclusive use of children from 9 to 16 years of age. Deprived of books in his own youth, he hoped to give other children the opportunities for reading that he had lacked. The Bingham Library was also notable as being one of the first libraries to receive municipal support.
GB: The first library for children in

Britain was started at the Campfield Reference Library, Manchester early in 1862 by the Principal Librarian, R.W. Smiles, who decided to set apart two tables reserved exclusively for children and provided a special stock of 115 volumes for their use. These included such works as Chambers's *Library for the Young* and a selection of bound magazines, principally of an improving nature.

CHILDREN'S LENDING LIBRARY: the first in Britain and the first children's library to be housed in its own separate premises was opened in Shakespeare Street, Nottingham by the City of Nottingham Public Libraries on 10 January 1883 and continued in use until 1932. The earliest catalogue extant is dated 1889 and names Miss Emma Hill as the Children's Librarian. In that year the library contained 3,500 volumes and there were some 2,000 members.

The first
CHILDREN'S MAGAZINE

was *The Lilliputian Magazine; or the Young Gentleman and Lady's Golden Library*, edited by the children's-book publisher John Newbery at the Bible and Sun in St Paul's Churchyard and probably first issued in June 1751. The opening number contains an announcement that it will be continued monthly, price 3d.

In accordance with its title, the magazine was truly Lilliputian, measuring only 4×2½in. It contained short stories, riddles, jokes, songs and pictures, and unlike its early 19th-century successors, was designed solely to entertain, not for moral uplift. The final issue, dated 3 July 1752, contains a list of members of the 'Lilliputian Society' (i.e. the juvenile subscribers), from which it is apparent that the magazine circulated on both sides of the Atlantic, as many of the children resided in Maryland.

MAGAZINE EXCLUSIVELY FOR BOYS: the first was the *Boy's Own Magazine*, founded and edited by S.O. Beeton, husband of Isabella Beeton of *Household Management* fame, and published monthly, price 2d, commencing January 1855. Containing stories by popular authors like Mayne Reid, biographies of great heroes, articles on sport, and adventures with savages, villains and fierce animals, all copiously illustrated, it proved an instant success and achieved a circulation of 40,000 by 1862. Beeton ran the first prize competitions for children in this paper, the winners receiving silver pencil-cases valued at 21s.

The first
CHIROPODISTS

originated as corn-cutters, who are first mentioned in English by Thomas Nashe in his *Strange Newes, of the intercepting certaine letters . . .*, London, 1593. This work contains the phrase 'Broome boyes, and cornecutters (or whatsouer trade is more contemptible)'. Contempt was indeed the general lot of these early specialists in foot care, who generally led a wandering life, plying their trade at fairs or in the streets.

The first chiropodist to style himself as such was David Low, who had established the first hotel (*q.v.*) in London in 1774, but abandoned the catering trade in 1780 to take up corn-cutting (which at a guinea a visit may have been more lucrative). In 1785 he published a text on the foot called *Chiropodologia*, in which the word 'chiropodist' makes its first dated appearance in print, though it also featured on his trade-cards, which may have been issued earlier. The *European Magazine*, which reviewed the book in its issue for June 1785, considered Low's adoption of the term 'an absurdity and needless affectation of learning'.

The first specialized training in chiropody was offered by the New York School of Chiropody, established by the Pedic Society of the State of New York in 1910. The first 14 qualified chiropodists, including one woman, graduated from the School in 1913.

The first positive recognition of chiropody as a profession in the USA came with the granting of the medical degree M.Cp. to four students of the Garreston Teaching Hospital at Temple University, Philadelphia in June 1916.

The first
CHOCOLATE, DRINKING

reference to in Britain, is an advertisement in the *Publick Adviser* of 16–22 June 1657 informing the public that

> *in Bishopsgate Street, in Queen's Head Alley, at a Frenchman's house, is an excellent West India drink called Chocolate to be sold, where you may have it ready at any time, and also unmade at reasonable rates.*

Chocolate, as opposed to cocoa (*q.v.*), was prepared from a number of ingredients additional to the crushed cacao bean; generally arrowroot, sago and refined sugar were added, though the less reputable manufacturers of the first half of the 19th century were not above using umber or red earth to adulterate their product. Cadbury's chocolate of the early 1860s comprised only one-fifth cocoa powder, the rest being made up of potato starch, sago, flour and treacle. The flour was intended to counteract the grease of the cocoa butter. This unpromising beverage was described by one Cadbury Director as 'a comforting gruel'.

The first
CHOCOLATE, EATING

produced on a factory scale was manufactured by 23-year-old François-Louis Cailler at Vevey, Switzerland in 1819. This was also the first eating-chocolate to be prepared and sold in blocks. The origins of eating-chocolate are obscure, but it is apparent that French and Italian confectioners were producing it on a very limited scale before Cailler introduced machine methods of manufacture. The Italian chocolate was generally made in thick rolls and then sliced.

GB: The earliest-known reference to eating-chocolate is contained in an advertisement for Fry's Chocolate Lozenges that appeared in *Butler's Medicine Chest Directory* for 1826. They were described as 'a pleasant and nutritious substitute for food in travelling, or when unusual fasting is caused by irregular periods of meal times'. It was only in 1853, with the introduction of their Chocolate Cream Stick, that Fry's began producing chocolate purely as a confectionary line; in the meantime John Cadbury's first price-list of 1842 had advertised 'French Eating Chocolate' at 2s a slab. It is not known whether this was Cadbury's own product, made according to the French style, or imported French chocolate.

MILK CHOCOLATE was first manufactured by Daniel Peter, F.-L. Cailler's son-in-law, at Vevey, Switzerland in 1875.

GB: By Cadbury's of Bournville in 1905.

BOXES OF ASSORTED CHOCOLATES were introduced in Britain by Cadbury's in 1866. Chocolat des Délices aux Fruits contained a selection of

The genesis of chocolate-box art – Cadbury's dragees, 1868

orange, lemon, raspberry and almond soft centres, while Cadbury's Flavoured Bonbons included cinnamon-, almond-, lemon- and spice-flavoured chocolates. The earliest-known pictorial chocolate box, an unlabelled Fry's assortment, dates from 1868 and depicts a group of children in a goat-carriage. The real father of 'chocolate-box art', though, was Richard Cadbury, who executed the first specially produced commercial design in the autumn of 1868. This was a portrait of his six-year-old daughter, reproduced in the form of an oleograph and stuck on the lids of 4oz oval boxes of Cadbury's dragees.

The first
CHRISTMAS CARD
was designed in 1843, at the suggestion of (Sir) Henry Cole, by John Calcott Horsley RA, later to become famous for his campaign against the use of nude models by artists, which earned him the nickname 'Clothes-Horsley'. The design depicted three generations of a Victorian family party sitting round the festive board, their glasses raised to the absent guest, otherwise the recipient. This charming and seemingly innocuous little scene gave rise to heated denunciations on the grounds that the card encouraged alcoholism and drunkenness. According to tradition Henry Cole commissioned the card because pressure of business had prevented him from writing to all his friends at Christmas, as was his usual custom. One thousand were printed by Messrs Jobbins of Warwick Court, Holborn from a lithographic stone, each on a single piece of pasteboard measuring 5×3¼in, and coloured by hand. All those surplus to the requirements of Cole and Horsley were sold by the printer, Joseph Cundall, at Summerly's Home Treasury Office, 12 Old Bond Street, London for 1s each.

Although a few other examples of similar cards are known to have been published in succeeding years, regular commercial production did not start until the London printing firm of Charles Goodall & Sons entered the field. The Christmas-card industry, wrote the Victorian artist 'Luke Limmer' (John Leighton),

began in 1862, the first attempts being the size of the ordinary gentleman's address card, on which was simply put 'A Merry Christmas' and 'A Happy New Year'; after that there came to be added robins and holly branches, embossed figures and landscapes. Having made the original designs for these, I have the originals before me now; they were produced by Goodall & Son. Seeing a growing want, and the great sale obtained abroad, this house produced [1868] a 'Little Red Riding Hood', a 'Hermit and his Cell', and many other subjects in which snow and the robin played a part.

The traffic in pasteboard greetings during December had grown to a sufficient volume by 1871 for a leading daily newspaper to complain of people trying to outdo each other in the number they received (dependent of course on the number they sent) and the 'subsequent delay in legitimate correspondence'. Not surprisingly such immoderate enthusiasm by the middle classes soon caused a reaction among their social betters, and in 1873 the first advertisement apologizing for 'not sending Christmas cards this year' appeared in the personal column of *The Times*.

The GPO adopted the slogan 'Post Early For Christmas' for the first time in 1880.

CHARITY CHRISTMAS CARDS, which now account for approximately 20% of the total sold, originated with

124 THE ILLUSTRATED LONDON NEWS. [Dec. 25, 1847

NO. 1. CONUNDRUM AND ANSWER.

Y is a like a
cause E has a his

As a skater was sporting his elegant make in the Regent's-park, he was asked this con:—
"Why is this sheet of ice like a Canada lake?" D'ye give it up?"—
Because it's the lake you're on (Lake Huron).

2. One person tells another that he can put something into his right hand, which it is impossible the other can put in his left.—How is this to be done?

3. Which are the only two words in the English language wherein the five vowels follow each other in their proper order?

ANSWER: ABSTEMIOUS AND FACETIOUS.

4. How must a circle be drawn round a person placed in the centre of a room, so that he will not be able to jump out of it, though his legs should be free?

5. CONUNDRUM AND ANSWER.

W is a like a
W it's hard

Easily Tired.—Produce a small stick, and tell some person present that he will be completely tired before he has carried it out of the room. If he deny your assertion take a penknife, and having cut with it a small piece the size of a grain of corn, desire him to take that out first; upon his return, give him a similar piece, and so on, until he confesses himself tired. This will soon be the case, as it is evident at he rate you can cut up the stick it will take him some months to carry it out of tthe room.

PICTURE PROVERBS.

"GREAT CRY AND LITTLE WOOL." "A FRIEND IN-KNEED IS A FRIEND INDEED."

"AS A MAN MAKES HIS BED, SO MUST HE LIE ON IT." "PAY AS YOU GO."

PRAISE THE SEA, BUT KEEP ON LAND." "IT'S NOT THE GAY COAT MAKES THE GENTLEMAN."

ALL IS FISH THAT COMES TO THE NET."

6. What is that which never was seen, felt, nor heard, never was, and never will be, and yet has a name?

7. CONUNDRUM AND ANSWER.

Y is like the V
cause ITS

The Dancing Pea.—Take a piece of tobacco-pipe, break it off even at the end, and with a knife or file work the hole rather larger, so that there may be a little hollow for the pea (which should be perfectly round) to rest in. Place the other end of the pipe in your mouth, hold your head back, and, keeping the pipe quite perpendicular, commence blowing gently, and the pea will dance about, leaping up sometimes to the height of two or three inches.

CONS UPON CATS.

8. WHAT IS MOST LIKE A CAT LOOKING OUT OF WINDOW?

9. WHY IS A CAT STANDING ON ITS HIND LEGS, LIKE THE FALLS OF NIAGARA?

10. My First's a little busy thing
My Second ladies do,
Impelled by love their flight to wing
My Whole—say, what are you?
An animal of swiftest pace,
Endowed with beauty, strength, and grace.

10. What is that which is above all human imperfections, and yet shelters the weakest and wickedest, as well as the wisest of mankind

11. CONUNDRUMS AND ANSWERS.

Y is a like the
Both make a Na

Wine and Water.—In a wine-glass, half full of water, drop a piece of bread, about as big as the top of your finger. Gently pour some wine upon it, and the two liquids will continue separate, the water remaining at the bottom of the glass and the wine floating on its surface.

12. Why is a child with a cold in its head like a stormy day in winter

13. When is a man thinner than a lath?

14. CONUNDRUM AND ANSWER.

W is a Debt
W E has a is paid 4

PICTURE PROVERBS.

"ALL ARE NOT HUNTERS THAT BLOW THE HORN." "A CONTENTED MIND IS A CONTINUAL FEAST."

"BETTER LATE THAN NEVER."

"ANYTHING FOR A QUIET LIFE." "HE IS WISE WHO SPEAKS LITTLE."

15. Four things there are, all of a height
One of them crossed, the rest upright:
Take three away, and you will find
Exactly ten remain behind;
But, if you cut the four in twain,
You'll find one half doth eight contain.

16. I went to a wood and got it—I sat down to look for it, and brought it home because I could not find it. What was this wonderful thing?

17. Pray, youngsters who in witty things delight,
Say what's invisible, yet never out of sight?

18. How should a candle be placed so that every person shall see it except although he shall not be blindfolded or prevented from examining every pa the room, neither shall the candle be hidden?

SNAP DRAGON.

19. CONUNDRUM AND ANSWER.

Y is a busy-body like a

R
Both a

20. Who swallowed a street, and where?

21. When does a pieman shed scalding tears?

22. Why is learning like

" A BOWL OF PUNCH."

23. What word is that which is made shorter by adding another syllable to

24. I'll throw an egg against a wall,
And it shall neither break nor fall
How is this?

25. What snuff-taker is that whose box gets fuller the more snuff he takes

25. CONUNDRUM AND ANSWER.

WHY R entitled to be ranked as great navigators

Answer.—Because they are always

CROSSING THE LINE.

26. Why is a melancholy young lady the pleasantest of all companions?

27. Why are fish in a thriving state like fish made to imitate them?

28. Who was the first whistler, and what tune did he whistle?

29. CONUNDRUM AND ANSWER.

Y is a like a
cause he thing

30. When was the King of Prussia the longest man living?

31. Why is the fire like the Aphis Vastator?

32. What is the difference between fish alive and live fish?

A FAREWELL.

A +
A hap

(Answers in our next.)

London: Printed and published at the Office, 198, Strand, in the Parish of St. Clement Danes, in the County of Middlesex, by William Little, 198, Strand, aforesaid.—Saturday, December 25, 1847.

the UNICEF card for Christmas 1949, designed by 7-year-old Jitka Samkova of Rudolfo, Czechoslovakia. Like many other villages in Czechoslovakia, Rudolfo had been devastated in the war and there was at the time a severe shortage of food, medicines and other basic necessities. UNICEF helped to feed the hungry population of the village and organized a campaign to fight tuberculosis. In gratitude to the organization, Jitka painted a picture of gaily dressed children dancing round a maypole. She used a sheet of glass to work on as there was no paper available. The scene, she explained, 'means joy, going round and round'. Her teacher entered the painting for a UNICEF competition; winning first prize, it attracted the attention of the Director of the organization and was subsequently made into UNICEF's first Christmas card.

The first
CHRISTMAS CRACKER
reference to, is contained in Albert Smith's story 'Delightful People', which appeared in the *Mirror* for 26 June 1841. The earliest-known illustration of a cracker featured in the Christmas 1847 issue of the *Illustrated London News* and effectively disposes of the claim of one prominent modern manufacturer to have invented crackers in 1860. Prior to World War I, crackers often followed a topical theme – there were Darwinian crackers, Arctic exploration, motor, Press, aeroplane, cinema, telephone, suffragette, Charlie Chaplin and even Leap Year crackers, which included miniature marriage certificates and wedding-rings.

The first
CHRISTMAS-DAY DIP IN THE SERPENTINE
in London's Hyde Park, a tradition that has been delighting stay-at-home newspaper readers since the birth of news photography, was inaugurated by intrepid members of the Serpentine Swimming Club in 1864.

The first
CHRISTMAS NUMBER OF A MAGAZINE
was a special 16-page supplement to the *Illustrated London News* published on 23 December 1848. It contained a Christmas lyric by Charles McKay entitled 'Under the Holly Bow', pictures of 'Grandpapa's Christmas Hamper' and 'Making the Christmas Pudding', a drawing by Leech titled 'Fetching Home the Christmas Dinner', and a scene showing a young audience enjoying a magic-lantern show. There was also a page of satirical predictions for the coming year, and a spirited attack on the commercialization of Christmas by one signing himself 'Oldest Inhabitant', who vituperated: 'Thirty or forty years ago . . . people knew it was Christmas without being told so by advertisement.'

◀ *The earliest picture of a Christmas cracker, 1847 – 13 years before the date claimed for its invention*

The first
CHRISTMAS TREE
recorded, was seen by an unidentified visitor to Strasbourg, who wrote in 1605: 'For Christmas they have fir-trees in their rooms, all decorated with paper roses, apples, sugar, gold and wafers.'

It has been suggested that the Christmas tree may have been known in Alsace as early as 1521. Here it was customary on May Day to set up decorated fir trees known as *Maien*. The municipal account books of the small Alsatian town of Schlettstadt indicate that not only was there an upsurge of activity among the local foresters just before May Day during the 15th and 16th centuries, but also that in three specific years – 1521, 1546 and 1556 – a similar number of Christmas *Maien* were also cut.

The earliest reference to a lighted Christmas tree is contained in a letter written by Lieselotte von der Pfalz, Comtesse d'Orléans in 1660, in which she stated that it was the custom in Hanover to decorate box trees with candles at Christmastide.

GB: The first known Christmas tree was erected at Queen's Lodge, Windsor by Queen Charlotte, the German-born wife of George III, for a party she held on Christmas Day 1800 for the children of the leading families in Windsor. Her biographer, Dr John Watkins, described the scene:

in the middle of the room stood an immense tub with a yewtree placed in it, from the branches of which hung bunches of sweetmeats, almonds, and raisins, in papers, fruits and toys, most tastefully arranged, and the whole illuminated by small wax candles. After the company had walked round and admired the tree, each child obtained a portion of the sweets which it bore, together with a toy, and then all returned home quite delighted.

Christmas trees were a firmly established Royal institution in Britain long before the custom spread to the general populace. Queen Adelaide always had one for her Christmas Eve parties in the Dragon Room at Brighton Pavilion, and the young Princess Victoria recorded her delight at the Christmas tree at Kensington Palace in 1832. In less exalted circles it is known that German merchants had introduced the Christmas tree to Manchester by 1822, though it is doubtful whether any English families copied the idea at the time. Prince Albert, who is often wrongly credited with having brought the Christmas tree to Britain, certainly did more than any other man to encourage its general adoption. The Christmas tree at Windsor was the subject of a full-page illustration in the *Illustrated London News* in 1848 and this immediately captured the hearts and minds of the middle classes, already given to imitation of what was an essentially bourgeois Royal Family. Albert did more than merely provide an example, though, for he customarily presented large numbers of trees to schools and Army barracks each Christmas. In the USA, despite strong German influence, there is no record of the Christmas tree before 1855, while the French only adopted the idea after 1870.

CHRISTMAS TREE LIT WITH ELECTRIC LIGHT BULBS: the first was installed at his home in New York City by Edward H. Johnson, an associate of Thomas Edison, in December 1882.

The first commercially produced Christmas-tree lamps were manufactured in nine-socket string sets by the Edison General Electric Co of Harrison, N.J. and advertised for sale in the December 1901 issue of the *Ladies' Home Journal*. Each socket took a miniature 2-candlepower carbon-filament lamp operating on 32 volts.

COMMUNAL CHRISTMAS TREE: the first was instituted by the town of Pasadena, Calif., where an illuminated tree has been set up annually since 1909.

The first
CIGARETTES
commercially produced, were manufactured in France in 1843 by the State-run Manufacture Française des Tabacs. The first consignment of 20,000 cigarettes were sold at a charity bazaar organized by Queen Marie-Amélie in Paris that year. Production was entirely by hand and the output consequently limited. Only in 1872 did the consumption of cigarettes in France reach the 100 million mark.

The first factory to produce cigarettes by mass-production methods was established in Havana, Cuba, by Don Luis Susini, who abandoned hand-rolling for steam-driven machines in 1853. An alleged production figure of 2,580,000 cigarettes a day is thought to be exaggerated and may represent the monthly total.

GB: The first tobacconists known to have stocked cigarettes were Messrs H. Simmons of Piccadilly and Bacon

Bros of Cambridge, the records of both firms showing that they were pursuing this line of business by 1851. Simmons's are known to have made their own cigarettes to customer's order; Bacon Bros' may have been imported.

The first branded cigarettes manufactured in Britain were Sweet Threes, launched *c.* 1859 by Robert Peacock Gloag, the proprietor of a small factory in Deptford Lane. Gloag had served during the Crimean War of 1854–6 as Paymaster to the Turkish forces in the field and it was then that he first encountered cigarettes and learned the art of making them. It was the war also that created his market, for many British soldiers acquired the cigarette-smoking habit from their Turkish comrades-in-arms in the Crimea, as well as from Russian prisoners of war. An article that appeared in the trade journal *Tobacco* in 1890 described the nature of Gloag's early cigarettes:

The tobacco used was Latakia dust and the paper yellow tissue . . . the mouthpiece was of cane. The mode of manufacture was first to make the canes, into which the tobacco had been pressed. In order to keep the dust tobacco from escaping, the ends were turned in. The size of the Cigarettes was that which is now known as an Oxford, and they were put up in bundles of ten, to be retailed at 6d.

Gloag's Sweet Threes were about 5in long and twice as thick as the standard modern product. (King-size cigarettes today are about 3¼in long.) Manufacture was by hand throughout, a fast worker being able to fill about 1,250 cigarettes a day.

The oldest brand of cigarettes still made in Britain is Passing Clouds, which date from 1874. Other existing 19th-century brands are Three Castles (1878), Gold Flake (1883), Woodbines (1888), Weights (1891; originally sold unpacketed by weight), and Player's Navy Cut (1892).

The first brand of cigarettes to be sold in cardboard packets of the modern 'push-up' kind was Wills's Three Castles in 1892. Formerly cigarette packets were generally made of paper, which meant that the contents were easily crushed. Some firms began inserting cardboard stiffeners into their packets and it was the idea of printing pictures on these, a practice introduced by Wills's Globe Cigarettes *c.* 1883, that started the craze for cigarette-card collecting.

The first brand of cigarettes to be sold in cellophane-wrapped packets was Craven A in May 1931.

WOMAN KNOWN TO HAVE SMOKED CIGARETTES: the first in England was the widowed Lady Caroline Mordaunt of Walton Hall, Walton-Deivile, Warwickshire, who was being regularly supplied with her own special blend by Nicholas Contoupolis, tobacconist of Queen Victoria Street, in 1858.

The first woman of distinction to smoke in public in England was the Duchesse de Clermont-Tonnerre, who electrified fellow guests by lighting a cigarette in the dining-room of the Savoy Hotel in 1896. At this date women had already taken to smoking in the privacy of their boudoirs in some considerable numbers. In 1897 the *Home Companion*, a paper with a large following among suburban housewives, made the startling revelation that no less than six European Queens were given to the habit, though readers were doubtless relieved to learn that Queen Victoria was not among their number. It was in this year also that the *Southern Tobacco Journal* of Richmond, Va. made the daring experiment of publishing for the first time an advertisement featuring a woman cigarette-smoker – a blow for liberty which America evidently was not ready for, since no other advertiser was foolhardy enough to repeat the idea until 1919. Seemingly American women needed no such blandishments, for by 1908 the City Fathers of New York had been so outraged by the sight of women smoking in public that the practice was made an indictable offence. (As far as is known this by-law has never been repealed.) In Britain it remained comparatively rare until World War I and even as late as 1919 a waiter deliberately knocked a cigarette out of a young lady's mouth in a London restaurant.

For the first Cigarette Coupons *see* Gift Coupons.

The first
CINEMA
of any permanence was the 400-seat Vitascope Hall, opened at the corner of Canal Street and Exchange Place in New Orleans by William T. Rock on 26 June 1896. Admission was 10c and patrons were allowed to look in the projection room and see the Edison Vitascope projector for another 10c. Those possessed of a liberal supply of dimes could also purchase a single frame of discarded film for the same price.

The first projectionist was William Reed. Most of the films were short scenic items, including the first English film to be released in America, Robert Paul's *Waves off Dover*. A major attraction was the film *May Irwin Kiss*, which may be said to have introduced sex to the American screen. A typical programme shown during the autumn of 1896 consisted of the following:

The Pickaninnies Dance
The Carnival Scene
The Irish Way of Discussing Politics
Cissy Fitzgerald
The Lynching Scene

Doors were open from 10am to 3pm and from 6pm to 10pm.

The identity of the first purpose-built cinema has not been positively established, but an interesting claim comes from Japan, where the Denki-kan Electric Theatre was opened at Asakusa, Tokyo in 1903.

The first of the giant picture palaces was the 5,000-seat Gaumont-Palace which opened in Paris in 1910. Formerly the Hippodrome Theatre, back-projection had to be used as there was no room for a projection-booth behind the auditorium. It was one of the first cinemas to employ the use of two projectors for the continuous showing of multi-reel films. The extraordinary capacity of the Gaumont-Palace at this early date can best be understood by comparison with the largest cinema ever built, the Roxy Theater in New York, which had 6,200 seats, and the currently largest cinema in Britain, the 3,485-seat Odeon at Hammersmith.

GB: The Berners Hall, Upper Street, Islington opened as a cinema by the Royal Animated and Singing Picture Co on 6 August 1901 with a programme that included *The New Man*, starring De Voy Hirst, and synchronized-disc 'talkies' of Marie Lloyd, Vesta Tilley and others. There had, however, been an attempt to establish a permanent cinema in London even before the opening of Vitascope Hall. This was an establishment at 2 Piccadilly Mansions that Birt Acres [*see also* Film (Motion Picture)] started up under the management of T. C. Harward in May 1896. It came to an untimely end after only a few weeks operation when the building caught fire.

The first purpose-built cinema in Britain was the Balham Empire, opened by the British Cinema Co Ltd under the management of E. A. Dessant in July 1907. Two shows were given every evening, with matinées on Wednesdays and Saturdays. While the persistent claim of the Biograph in Wilton Road, Victoria to have been built in 1905 has been accepted by most reference books, recent research has revealed that it did not open until 1909.

The first cinema in Britain with sloping floor and projection-booth was the Picture Palace at St Albans, Hertfordshire, opened by Arthur Melbourne-Cooper of the Alpha Trading Co in 1908. It was also the first cinema to depart from the standard theatre practice of charging more to sit in the front stalls than at the back. The *Bioscope* reported:

This arrangement was somewhat resented at first by patrons of the higher priced seats, but when they found the specially-raised floor gave them a better view than could be got from the front, they appreciated the innovation.

The idea was suggested to Melbourne-Cooper by his usherette, whom he later had the good sense to marry.

Contrary to the popularly held view that the cinema was an infrequently encountered novelty prior to World War I, figures indicate that the growth of film entertainment was so spectacular from *c.* 1906 in the USA, and 1908 in most parts of Europe, that within three or four years it had achieved the status of a major industry. In Berlin alone 300 new cinemas were opened during 1908. The same year saw a rapid expansion throughout the industrial Midlands and the northern regions of Britain, with public halls, warehouses, shops and variety theatres being converted into cinemas in every major city. By 1912 it was estimated that there were 4,000 cinemas in the British Isles, a figure that had remained virtually unaltered when counts were made in 1921 and 1934. Many, it is true, had small seating capacity, and nearly all attracted an almost exclusively working-class clientele, which probably accounts for the lack of attention paid to the phenomenon at the time. Middle-class cinema-going came in with World War I, and was due to a combination of circumstances: the relaxation of chaperonage, the provision of better-appointed and more luxurious cinemas, the feverish desire for entertainment by officers home on leave, and not least, the vastly improved standards of film-making after 1914, which saw the widespread introduction of full-length features starring 'name' actors and actresses.
ARTS CINEMA: the first was the Studio des Ursulines, founded in Paris by Laurence Myrga and Armand Talliser on 14 January 1926.
DRIVE-IN CINEMA: the first was opened on a 10-acre site off Wilson Boulevard, Camden, N.J. by Richard Hollingshead on 6 June 1933. The screen, measuring 40×30ft, was erected against a scenario 60×150ft, and there was accommodation for 400 cars. The sound came from direction-speakers supplied by RCA-Victor.

The first
CINEMA: NEWS THEATRE
was the Embassy, Broadway and 46th Street, New York, which opened on 2 November 1929. It ceased showing newsreels and sports films in November 1949 owing to the competition from television – probably the first cinema to close for this reason.
GB. The Pavilion, Shaftesbury Avenue, opened 1930.

The first
CIRCUS
was established in 1769 by ex-Cavalry Sgt Maj. Philip Astley. He sold a diamond ring which he had found on Westminster Bridge, and with the £60 obtained, opened an equestrian ring on Halfpenny Hatch, Lambeth. No admission fee was charged, but in common with other equestrian shows of the time a collection was taken up after every performance. Evidently the audience responded generously, for the following year Astley moved to a better site close to Westminster Bridge. Here he constructed a roped-off enclosure with stands round the sides, and charged an entrance fee of 1s for a seat and 6d standing. At the same time a drummer-boy was hired to add musical effects.

The precise date at which Astley's became a circus in the modern sense rather than simply a trick-riding display is hard to establish. It is known that he had a strong man, one Signor Colpi, working for him in 1777, and that within the next three years he acquired a clown called Fortunelly, another called Burt (sometimes claimed as the first circus clown), a number of acrobats who performed rope-vaulting tricks 'in different attitudes', and an engaging performer known as 'The Little Military Learned Horse'. The equestrians, the real stars of the show, were three men named Griffin, Jones and Miller, who performed under the aegis of Astley himself, considered by many the greatest horseman of his age.

Apart from horses, few animals were displayed. A 'military monkey' named General Jackoo made his appearance in the ring at Astley's in 1768, but there is no record of any larger beasts making their circus début until 1816, when two elephants named Baba and Kiouny went through a routine at Franconi's Circus, Paris, that included catching apples with their trunks, uncorking bottles and drinking the contents, and playing the hurdy-gurdy. Only in 1828 did Astley's follow this lead when an elephant was hired from Cross's Exeter Change Menagerie. The animal was merely shown to the wondering spectators and was not required to perform. A lion, tiger and four zebras, all similarly inactive, appeared at Astley's in 1832. The first real wild-beast act took place at Astley's Amphitheatre in 1838, when the American Van Amburgh, otherwise known as 'Morok the Beast Tamer', presented a mixed group of lions, tigers and leopards (*see also* Lion Tamer).

As a popular medium of entertainment the circus spread rapidly. A Spaniard named Juan Porte established the first in Europe at Vienna in 1780. Two years later Astley himself introduced circus to Paris. In America, Rickett's Circus opened in Philadelphia in 1792 and was visited by President Washington the following year. Russia also had a circus by 1793. Philip Astley is reputed to have helped found no less than 19 circuses in various countries of Europe. The original Astley's Amphitheatre continued to function on the same site at the south side of Westminster Bridge until as late as 1893.
FLYING-TRAPEZE CIRCUS ACT: the first was performed by Jules Leotard at the Cirque Napoléon, Paris on 12 November 1859. Only 21 years of age at the time, Leotard had devised the act while practising on the ropes and rings suspended above the swimming-pool at his father's gymnasium in Toulouse. During the early 1860s he appeared at the Alhambra in London, causing a sensation by flying across the hall from trapeze to trapeze above the heads of the audience sitting at their supper-tables. Leotard was immortalized as 'That Daring Young Man on the Flying Trapeze' in a popular ditty sung by George Leybourne. He also lent his name to the tight-fitting costume still worn by acrobats and trapeze artistes.
SAFETY-NET FOR CIRCUS PERFORMANCES: the first was introduced by the Spanish acrobatic troupe, the Rizarellis, at the Holborn Empire in 1871. Leotard had relied on the less certain precaution of a pile of mattresses on the floor.
HUMAN CANNON-BALL CIRCUS ACT: the first was performed at West's Amphitheatre in London, on 2 April 1877, by Zazel, billed as 'the beautiful lady fired from a monstrous cannon'. The weapon was powered by elastic springs and gently pitched Zazel into a large safety-net every week-day for two years without mishap. Her salary for this was £120 a week.

The first
CITY IN THE WORLD TO EXCEED ONE MILLION IN POPULATION
was London, which according to the census of 1811 was inhabited by a total of 1,009,546 people. Seventy years later there were still only seven cities in the world with a population of a million, namely: London – 3,452,350; Paris – 2,269,023; Peking – 1,648,814; Canton – 1,500,000 (estimated); New York – 1,206,299; Vienna – 1,103,857; Nanking – 1,000,000 (estimated). London remained the largest city in the world until 1957, when it was overtaken by Tokyo. The

Japanese capital became the first city with a recorded population of 10 million in January 1962, a staggering rise since its wartime decline from 6,779,100 in 1940 to only 2,777,000 in 1945.

The first
CLOCK
mechanical, of which there is record is described with diagrams by the Chinese Imperial tutor Su Sung in his *Hsin I Hsiang Fa Yao* of 1088. Su Sung's clock was a massive machine, 30ft high, with a water-powered driving-wheel and an an escapement to control the gear-wheels regulating the time-keeping mechanism.
GB: The earliest recorded mechanical clock in Europe was made by the Austin Canons and set up against the rood-screen of Dunstable Priory, Bedfordshire in 1283. This probably had a verge and foliot escapement of the kind common to most medieval clocks.

The oldest surviving mechanical clock in working order in the world is the Salisbury Cathedral clock of 1386. It was found in derelict condition in the Cathedral tower by T.R. Robinson in 1929 and has since been restored to its original condition.

The earliest record of a clock with a dial in Britain is contained in the Sacrist's Rolls of Norwich Cathedral for 1325. This was an astronomical dial and was set up inside the Cathedral. The first clock dial known to have been fixed to the outside of a building was erected on the newly built tower of Magdalen College, Oxford in 1505.

The first illuminated clock dial was that of St Brides Church, Fleet Street, London, in 1826. It was lit by 12 gas-burners.
ALARM CLOCK: the earliest known is a small German timepiece from Würzburg dating from 1350 to 1380 and designed for hanging against a wall. It is now preserved at the Mainfränkisches Museum in Würzburg. Alarm clocks during the Middle Ages were confined almost exclusively to monasteries, where it was necessary to keep the canonical hours.
PENDULUM CLOCK: the first was made by the Dutch scientist Christiaan Huygens at The Hague in December 1656. It was based on the principle of oscillating motion expounded by Galileo some 70 years earlier. Commercial production was undertaken by Huygens's clockmaker, Samuel Coster, from *c.* 1658.
GB: Introduced by Ahasuerus Fromanteel in 1658.

The first
CLUB
founded for social intercourse in Britain was a London dining society called 'La Court de Bone Compagnie', which is known to have been in existence in 1413. Most of the members were drawn from among the gentlemen of the Temple, including the poet Hoecleve, two of whose ballads relate to the activities of the club. The first is in the form of a letter addressed from the brethren to their fellow member Henry Somer, congratulating him on his appointment as Sub-Treasurer of the Exchequer. The contents indicate that Somer has remonstrated with the company for over-lavish expenditure, to which the members reply that they are willing to reduce their expenditure whenever Somer chooses to set an example.

The Court de Bone Compagnie appears to be an isolated example of a medieval club. There are no further recorded examples of any similar association of like spirits until the advent of the 'Right Worshipfull Fraternity of Sireniacal Gentlemen', better though anachronistically known as the 'Mermaid Club', which began meeting at the Mermaid Tavern at the end of the 16th century. This was the club of which Raleigh, Shakespeare and Ben Jonson were supposed to be members, though on no very reliable authority.

The earliest-known use of the word 'club' in the sense employed here is contained in Ben Jonson's 'Vision on the Muses of his Friend Michael Drayton' of 1627, in which the dramatist declares that it is not his intention to 'raise a rhyming club about the town'. The first club definitely known to have used the word in its title was the Rota Club (*see also* Debating Society) of 1659.
SERVICE CLUB: the first was the Naval Club, founded under the Presidency of Admiral Sir John Kempthorne in 1674 'for the improvement of a mutuall Society, and an encrease of Love and Kindness amongst them'.
CLUB WITH ITS OWN PREMISES: the first and the earliest example of the genus 'West End Club' was White's, whose members took up residence at 38 St James's Street in 1755. Like many other 18th-century clubs, White's began life as an informal group of coffee-house frequenters, or in this case, patrons of White's Chocolate House. The earliest evidence of its existence as a formally constituted club is a rule book and list of members dated 30 October 1736. White's was also the first club to institute a smoking-room, in 1845. It is presently the oldest club of its kind in London, and possibly the most exclusive socially.
CLUB TO ADMIT MEMBERS OF BOTH SEXES: the first was Almack's, established at Almack's Assembly Rooms in King Street, St James's in 1770. The founders were six women of rank and fashion, including Lady Pembroke and Lady Molyneux. Candidates for election had to be nominated by members of the opposite sex, and likewise could only be blackballed by the opposite sex. The principal activity of the club was gaming for high stakes.
CLUB EXCLUSIVELY FOR WOMEN: the first was the Berners Club, founded in Berners Street in 1871.

See also Working Men's Club, Boys' Club.

The first
CLUB COLOURS
of which there is certain knowledge were adopted by the I Zingari Cricket Club and displayed for the first time on the occasion of their inaugural match at Newport Pagnell in August 1845. The colours – black, red and gold – were intended to symbolize 'Out of darkness, through fire, into light'.

One earlier claim deserves attention. Exeter College Boat Club, Oxford ordered a special boating handkerchief, which became available for sale to members of the crew on 1 June 1844. Although no colours are recorded in the Club's minutes, it seems likely that this would have been of a distinctively uniform pattern and probably designed to be worn round the neck.

The first
COCKTAIL
authentic reference to, is contained in the American periodical *The Balance* for 13 May 1806 in the following terms:

Cocktail is a kind of stimulating liquor, composed of spirits of any kind, sugar, water, and bitters – it is vulgarly called bittered sling and is supposed to be an excellent electioneering potion.

There are numerous stories accounting for the origin of the name. In the version favoured by Joseph Nathan Kane, the American author of *Famous First Facts*, the first so-called 'cocktail' was served by a barmaid called Betsy Flanagan at Halls Corners, Elmsford, N.Y. in 1776. The bar was decorated with tail feathers, and when a drunk called for a glass of 'those cocktails', Miss Flanagan responded by giving him a mixed drink decorated with a feather.
COCKTAIL BAR: the first in Britain was opened at Gore House, near Hyde Park, London on 1 May 1851 by Alexis Soyer, the celebrated chef of the Reform Club, as one of the attractions of his 'Gastronomic Symposium of All Nations'. The décor of the bar was designed by the novelist George Augustus Sala. A selection of 40 different cocktails was served, including Mint Julep, Sherry Cobbler and Brandy Smash. Although Soyer had

intended the establishment to be permanent, he was refused a renewal of his licence on the grounds that the Licensing Officer had never seen 'a more dissipated place, or a more dangerous place for the morals of young persons'. It closed on 14 October 1851.
DRY MARTINI: the first was concocted by bartender Jerry Thomas at the Occidental Hotel, San Francisco, Calif. in 1860. The original recipe was as follows: 1 dash of bitters, 2 dashes of Maraschino, 1 pony of sweet gin, 1 wine-glass of Vermouth, 2 small lumps of ice; shaken and stirred into a large cocktail-glass with ¼ slice of lemon.

The first
COCOA
was prepared by Coenraad van Houten of Amsterdam in 1828 by extracting excess cocoa butter from the crushed cacao bean. This process rendered a powder form of soluble cocoa, whereas drinking-chocolate (*q.v.*) at this time was sold in the form of cakes and had a disagreeably high fat content.
GB: Cadbury's Cocoa Essence was introduced by Cadbury Bros of Birmingham in December 1866. Previously potato starch and flour had been used to counteract the greasy effect of the cocoa butter in drinking-chocolate. Their Cocoa Essence was a pure cocoa powder.

The first
COEDUCATIONAL SCHOOL
in Britain was opened by Henry Morley at Marine Terrace, Liscard, Cheshire for boys and girls aged 8 to 15 in the spring of 1849. The school was unusual in several other respects, having carpeted classrooms, no corporal punishment, and lessons in the form of quizzes between two competing teams. It was also the first school known to have included current affairs in its formal curriculum, the whole of Monday morning being given over to the discussion of a topic in the news. Discipline was maintained by a system of rewards and deprivations, and the most marked sign of Morley's displeasure was the discontinuance of lessons as a punishment. 'Lessons were not to be regarded as their pain, but as their privilege, when they became too unmanageable the privilege was for a time withdrawn' he wrote in one of the earliest texts on progressive education. (School-keeping, *Household Words*, 21 January 1854.) The fees of the school were 10gns a year, but despite an increasing number of pupils, Morley was unable to pay his debts, and in June 1851 he accepted a position on Charles Dickens' *Household Words* and closed the first real venture into coeducation as a system.

For the first coeducational college, *see* Women's College.

The first
COFFEE
as a beverage is recorded *c.* AD 1000 by the Arabian philosopher and physician Avicenna, who called it *bunc*, a word still used in Ethiopia. For centuries its use was almost exclusively medicinal, and it was only in the 16th century that it began to be drunk socially in Arabia and Persia.
COFFEE-HOUSES: the first recorded were opened at Constantinople in 1554 by two merchants, Hakeem of Aleppo and Jems of Damascus. They were known as *Mekteb-i-irfan*, meaning 'schools of the cultured'.

The practice of serving coffee with sugar and milk was introduced by a Polish adventurer called Franz Georg Kolshitsky, who opened a coffee-house in Vienna's Domgasse in 1683. He was also the originator of the style of coffee known as 'Viennese', straining it in order to produce a clear liquid without grounds.
GB: John Evelyn, who was at Balliol College, Oxford from 1637 to 1640, recorded in the first volume of his celebrated *Diary*:

There came in my time to the College one Nathaniel Conopios, out of Greece. . . . He was the first I ever saw drink coffee; which custom came not into England till thirty years after.

INSTANT COFFEE: the first was Nescafé, introduced by Nestlé's of Vevey, Switzerland in 1938 after eight years of research. The task of reducing coffee beans to a soluble powder had been undertaken by the company following suggestions made by the Brazilian Institute of Coffee in 1930.

The first
COLLAPSIBLE TUBE
was patented by American artist John Rand on 11 September 1841 and first used commercially by the Devoe & Reynolds Co for packing oil-paints. In Britain, Rand's lead tubes were adopted by most of the London artists' colourmen soon afterwards.
TOOTHPASTE TUBE (collapsible metal): the first was devised in 1892 by Dr Washington Sheffield, a dentist of New London, Conn., and later manufactured by his Sheffield Tube Corp.
GB: Beecham's Tooth Paste was retailed in tubes the same year. Toothpaste was formerly packed in round pots, usually of Staffordshire ware.
COLLAPSIBLE POLYTHENE TUBE: the first was made by the Bradley Container Corp of Delaware in 1953 for Sea and Ski, a skin-tanning lotion.

The first
COLOURED MP
to sit in a European legislature was M. Mathieu Louisi, a print-worker of Pointe-à-Pitre, Guadeloupe, who was elected to the French National Assembly as representative for Guadeloupe on 22 August 1848. His maiden speech made in November, a moderate appeal for more harmonious relation between black and white in the colonies, was received with 'loud marks of disapprobation'. He lost his seat in the next election.
GB: The first coloured Member of Parliament was Dadabhai Naoraji, born the son of a Parsee priest in

Mathieu Louisi

Bombay, who was elected Liberal representative for Central Finsbury by a majority of three votes over his Unionist opponent on Wednesday, 6 July 1892. *The Times* reported a week later:

Telegrams of thanks to the electors of Central Finsbury, and of congratulations to Mr Naoraji, are received every day from India. Meetings are being held in various parts of India to express satisfaction with Mr Naoraji's return. . . . Mr Naoraji is also receiving telegrams and letters of congratulations every day from different parts of the United Kingdom.

Mr Naoraji had originally come to England in 1855 as a partner in the first Indian firm established in this country. He sat as Member for Central Finsbury until 1895, and continued to work vigorously for the rights of

Indians in British India and for the fostering of good relations between the races until his retirement from active public life.

The first
COLOURED PEER
was Lord Sinha of Raipur, who was created a Baron in 1919 in recognition of his services as the first Indian member of the Viceroy's Executive Council and as the Indian representative in the Imperial War Cabinet. He died in 1928. His son, the 2nd Lord Sinha, became the first coloured peer to actually take his seat in the Lords in 1946, after a protracted suit to establish his claim to the title in the absence of birth and marriage certificates. He spent nine months of each year in London in order to attend Parliament and sat on the Liberal benches.

The first
COMIC
was *Comic Cuts*, an eight-page weekly edited by Houghton Townley and issued by Alfred Harmsworth on 17 May 1890. The earliest issues contained more text than pictures, including a serial 'Confessions of a Ticket of Leave Man'. The humorous content was contained under whimsical headline titles, 'Comicalities', 'Tiny Chips', 'Jokelets', 'Funiosities' and 'Jestnuts'. A typical example reads: '"That was an arrow escape" growled an old bachelor as he dodged one of cupid's darts.' The remainder of the paper was taken up with cartoons, short features and odd facts. Circulation the first week was 118,864, rising after a month to 300,000. (Higher than some national newspapers of the time.) Although the 'extended cartoon' technique had been used since the first issue, the first true comic strip in *Comic Cuts*, entitled 'Those Cheap Excursions!', was featured in No. 4, 7 June 1890. This was tucked away at the back, but on 15 October 1890 a rival comic called *Funny Cuts* appeared with a full front-page strip cartoon drawn by Alfred Gray – an innovation that established the standard comic format of today.

The first
COMIC BOOK
in the current style and format was *Funnies on Parade*, published by the Eastern Color Co of Waterbury, Conn. in 1933. Its format, 7×9in, was determined by the size of a standard American newspaper page; four pages were printed to the sheet and folded twice. *Funnies on Parade* was produced in four colours and contained reprints of 'Joe Paloka', 'Mutt and Jeff', 'Hairbreadth Harry', 'Keeping Up with the Joneses' and 'Connie'. It was not sold direct to the public, but issued as a gift premium by such companies as Proctor & Gamble and Canada Dry.
COMIC BOOK TO BE SOLD REGULARLY: the first on the news-stands and the first to be issued as a periodical was *Famous Funnies*, published by the Dell Publishing Co at a price of 10c in May 1934.
COMIC BOOK TO CONTAIN ORIGINAL MATERIAL (standard format): the first was *New Comics*, issued by Major Malcolm Wheeler Nicholson in December 1935. The accent was on adventure serials, and the first 80-page issue introduced characters like Homer Fleming's 'Captain Jim of the Texas Rangers'. This led to a new trend in comic-book publishing, the creation of the comic-book heroes, characters who had not previously appeared in newspaper comic strips. Of the two most enduring figures in this genre, Joe Schuster's 'Superman' performed his first deeds of valour in the June 1938 issue of *Action Comics*, and Bob Kane's caped crusader, 'Batman', began his rise to comic-book immortality in the May 1939 issue of *Detective Comics*.

The first
COMIC STRIP
in a newspaper, was Richard Outcault's 'Yellow Kid', which first appeared in strip form in the Sunday colour supplement of the *New York Journal* on 24 October 1897. This initial episode was entitled 'The Yellow Kid takes a Hand at Golf' and depicted the erratic efforts of its hero to address the ball. The Yellow Kid had originally been featured as a single-panel cartoon in Joseph Pulitzer's *New York World* in February 1896. The central character was a flap-eared, bald-headed child clad only in a sack-like yellow robe whose pranks and antics were vigorously chronicled by Outcault against a background of New York slum tenements. The Kid's most distinctive feature, his curious saffron garment, was designed by the artist specially for an experiment in tint-laying. The experiment was successful, with two unexpected results – the entry into English usage of a new phrase, the 'Yellow Press', and the genesis of the newspaper comic strip.
DAILY COMIC STRIP: the first was 'A. Piker Clerk', drawn by Clare Briggs for the *Chicago American* in 1904. It was also the first of the 'funnies'. A. Piker Clerk was a chinless counter-jumper whose exploits on the race-track and efforts to raise loans for 'dead certs' enlivened the sports page of the *American* for about a fortnight before William Hearst, proprietor of the paper, decreed that Briggs's creation was vulgar and must be dropped forthwith.

The first successful daily cross-strip was Bud Fisher's 'Mr. A. Mutt', another luckless punter, who began to appear on the sports page of the *San Francisco Chronicle* on 15 November 1907. Mutt was joined by Jeff on 29 March 1908, and they have stayed

Popular journalism takes a stride forward – the arrival of the comic strip

8 NEW YORK JOURNAL, SUNDAY, OCTOBER 24, 1897.

THE YELLOW KID TAKES A HAND AT GOLF.

Forceful Repartee.
CHIMMY (proudly)—I've been taking quinine!
JOHNNIE (bitterly envious)—Well, yer needn't t'ink yerself a whole set o' chimes 'cos yer got a ringin' in yer ears.

Not Enough to Go Around.
SUNDAY SCHOOL TEACHER—How did the people come to go into the ark?
PROMISING PUPIL—I suppose they couldn't borrow umbrellas.

Fall.
The melancholy days have come,
The saddest of the year,
When we must now resume our thick
And woolen underge[illegible].

Somewhat In Doubt.
HER FATHER—I suppose, young man, your intentions are of the best?
HER SUITOR—Well—er—I intend to marry your daughter.

Wanted to Find Out.
MINISTER—Will you take this man for better or for worse?
BRIDE—How do I know? That's what I'm marrying him for, to find out.

together ever since.
GB: The first British newspaper comic strip was Charles Folkard's 'Adventures of Teddy Tail – Diary of the Mouse in Your House', which began appearing daily in the *Daily Mail* on 5 April 1915. The Mouse acquired the famous knot in his tail in the fourth episode (9 April), tying it himself to facilitate the rescue of a beetle who had fallen down a hole. Teddy Tail continued to amuse successive generations of children for over 40 years, beginning his adventures costumed in tweed coat and plus-fours, then apparently decreasing in age as the years advanced, and finally departing from the pages of the *Daily Mail* in short jacket and Eton collar.

The first
COMMEMORATIVE PLAQUES
on London buildings to record their association with distinguished persons were erected by the Royal Society of Arts in response to a suggestion, made by (Sir) George Bartley in May 1866, that London should follow the example of various French and German towns in this respect. In 1867 the first plaque was placed on the house in Holles Street, Cavendish Square, where the poet Byron was born. It remained in position until 1889, when the house was demolished. The circular pottery tablets closely resembled their modern counterparts except that they were brown instead of blue.

The first
COMMUNIST PARTY
(Marxist) was the Communist League, formerly a revolutionary secret society known as 'the League of the Just', which was reorganized under its new name at a Congress convened in London by Joseph Moll on 1 June 1847. The main purpose of the Congress was to secure the collaboration of Friedrich Engels and Karl Marx in formulating the Party programme. Though both the founders of modern Communist philosophy expressed their willingness to attend, Marx did not arrive because of the cost of the fare from Brussels. The aim of the Party was declared to be 'the downfall of the bourgeoisie, the rule of the proletariat, the overthrow of the old society of the middle class, based on class distinction, and the establishment of a new society without classes and without private property'.

At the 2nd Congress of the League, held in November 1847, the executive committee instructed Karl Marx, who was present on this occasion, to draft a Party manifesto. His *Manifest der Kommunistischen Partei* was published in German by J.E. Burghard of Bishopsgate, London in February 1848. A rather poor English translation under the title 'The Communist Manifesto' appeared in *The Red Republican* two years later. Despite the short life of the first Communist Party – it was dissolved in 1851 – its Manifesto, totally ignored in England at the time of publication, ultimately became the blueprint for world revolutionary Communism.

The founder of Russian Communism was Georgi Valentinovitch Plekhanov of Tambov, who established the Marxist Liberation of Labour movement at Geneva in 1883.

The first Communist Party in Russia was the Russian Social-Democratic Workers' Party, founded by nine delegates from local organizations representing workers' interests who met in Congress at Minsk on 1–3 March 1898. All nine were subsequently arrested by the police, and none played any important role in the subsequent history of the Party. The Party Manifesto was drafted by Peter Struve, who later became an active opponent of Communism. The Social-Democrats split into two factions – Mensheviks and Bolsheviks – at the 2nd Party Congress held in Brussels and London, July–August 1903.
COMMUNIST GOVERNMENT: the first was formed in Russia under Lenin (Vladimir Ilich Ulyanov) following the Bolshevik Revolution of 7 November (25 October by the Russian calendar) 1917. The composition of the new ministry, known as 'the Council of People's Commissars', was approved by the 2nd All-Russian Congress of Soviets on the evening of 8 November. The decision to rename the Bolshevik Party the Communist Party was taken at the 7th Party Congress of 6–8 March 1918.
GB: The present Communist Party was established at the Communist Unity Convention held at the Cannon Street Hotel, London, 31 July–1 August 1920. There was already in existence a party called the 'Communist Party' that had been formed by Sylvia Pankhurst six weeks earlier. It merged with the CPGB the following year.

The first Member of Parliament who was a member of the Communist Party was Lt-Col Cecil L'Estrange Malone, who had been returned for East Leyton as a Coalition Liberal in the 'Coupon Election' of 1918. Having been converted to Communism after a visit to Russia in 1919, he joined the CPGB on its formation and served on the original Joint Provisional Committee of the Party. On 7 November 1920 he made a 'Hands off Russia!' speech that earned him a sentence of six months' imprisonment for sedition. Col Malone left the CPGB in mid-1922, losing his seat in Parliament the same year.
MEMBER OF PARLIAMENT ELECTED AS A COMMUNIST: the first was J.T. Walton Newbold, returned for Motherwell in the General Election of 17 November 1922 with a vote of 8,262, a majority of 1,048 over his nearest rival (an Independent) in a four-cornered contest. He made his maiden speech on 'Rents and the Unemployed' on 9 December 1922 and on the following 22 February, earned the distinction of being the first Communist invited by the BBC to participate in a political broadcast. In the General Election of November 1923 Newbold increased the size of his vote but lost to the Labour candidate. The following year he joined the Labour Party but resigned in 1931, and ended his life as a devout Roman Catholic in Eire in 1943.

The first
COMPRESSION-IGNITION ENGINE
to be developed commercially was patented in England by Herbert Akroyd Stuart in 1890 and produced by Richard Hornsby & Sons of Grantham, Lincolnshire, in 1892. The first unit to be sold was acquired by the Newport Sanitary Authority the same year. The compression ratio of the original Akroyd-Hornsby engine was too low for it to be started from cold, and it was necessary to apply an extraneous heater to a chamber on the cylinder-head in order to effect initial combustion. Once the engine was running, the heating element could be removed and it was then self-sustaining. It is principally over the question of this starting method that engineering historians have long been in dispute with regard to the invention of the diesel engine. In fact Hornsby & Sons did operate an experimental high-pressure version of the Akroyd engine early in 1892. Although it was not developed further, this particular model was capable of being started without the use of any extraneous ignition device and preceded Dr Rudolf Diesel's first high-pressure compression-ignition (c.i.) engine by over a year. In another important respect the standard Hornsby c.i. engine came closer to the modern concept of a diesel than Diesel's prototype, since the fuel was injected into the combustion-chamber by means of a plunger-pump. Diesel's engines, on the other hand, employed a system of fuel-injection by high-pressure air jet. No purpose is served by denying Rudolf Diesel credit for the invention that bears his name, though seen in its historical perspective his idea, albeit more sophisticated than Akroyd and Hornsby's, was not completely original.
MOTOR VEHICLES POWERED BY C.I. ENGINES: the first were four delivery wagons fitted with imported

Akroyd-Hornsby engines in the summer of 1895 by Valentine, Lynn & Son, carriage-builders of Brooklyn, N.Y., and placed in service with the De La Vergne Refrigerating Co.
GB: A single model of the Hornsby-Akroyd Patent Safety Oil Traction Engine was sold to H.F. Locke-King of Weybridge in 1897. Hornsby's sales leaflet offered a range of four sizes with engines rating 16–30bhp, but no other sales are recorded.
HIGH-PRESSURE C.I. ENGINE: the first to be commercially developed was patented in Germany by Paris-born Dr Rudolf Diesel, Sales Manager of the Linde Ice-Making Machine Co, on 28 February 1892. The following year Diesel secured the co-operation of the Krupp and Maschinenfabrik Augsburg concerns in providing financial backing and workshop facilities, and his prototype engine sprang fitfully into life for the first time at the latter's Augsburg plant on 10 August 1893. Another four years of research and development ensued before the Diesel engine was ready for commercial exploitation, but by 1897 it was sufficiently advanced for him to dispose of the American rights to a German-American brewer, Adolphus Busch, for one million marks ($250,000). Although it was several years before he was able to instigate production in the USA, Busch did have a single Diesel engine built by the St Louis Iron & Marine Works, and this became the first high-pressure c.i. engine in commercial operation anywhere in the world when it was installed at the Anheuser Busch Brewery on 2nd Street, St Louis, Mo., in September 1898. Regular commercial production was begun at Augsburg in 1899.
GB: The first successful high-pressure Diesel engine was built by the Diesel Motor Co of Guide Bridge, near Manchester and demonstrated on 25 March 1901. This was also the first two-stroke Diesel engine in the world.

See also Bus; Crawler Tractor; Motor Lorry; Railcar, Diesel; Submarine; Tractor.

The first
COMPUTER
programmed, designed to receive instructions from punched cards, make calculations with the aid of a memory bank, and print out the solution to a problem, was the Analytical Engine, conceived by Charles Babbage and partially constructed by him in London between 1822 and 1871. Although Babbage lavished £6,000 of his own money and £17,000 of the Government's on this extraordinarily advanced machine, the precision work needed to engineer its many thousand moving parts was beyond the technology of the day. It is doubtful whether Babbage's brilliant concept could have been realized in his own century, using the available resources. If it had been, then it seems likely that the Analytical Engine could have performed the same functions as many of the early electronic computers.

The first practical programmed computer was built by George Scheutz of Stockholm, Sweden, and exhibited at the Paris Exposition of 1855. Based on the principles expounded by Babbage, but of simpler construction, Scheutz's 'calculating engine' could compute to four orders of difference, and print out answers accurate to eight places of decimals. The prototype was acquired by the Dudley Observatory of Albany, N.Y., where it was used for calculating astronomical tables. A second model, built to Scheutz's design by Bryan Donkin of London in 1858, was used by an insurance company in the compilation of actuarial tables for life-insurance purposes.
COMPUTER DESIGNED EXPRESSLY FOR DATA PROCESSING: the first was patented by Dr Herman Hollerith of New York on 8 January 1889. The prototype model of this electrically operated tabulator was built for the US Census Bureau and employed for computing results in the 1890 Census. Using punched cards containing information submitted by respondents to the Census questionnaire, the Hollerith machine was able to make instant tabulations by means of electrical impulses actuated by each hole and printed out the processed data on tape. Dr Hollerith left the Census Bureau in 1896 to establish the Tabulating Machine Co to manufacture and sell his equipment. This eventually became part of IBM, and the standard 80-column punched card used by the present company is still known as the 'Hollerith card'.
ELECTRONIC COMPUTER: the first was the Electronic Numerical Integrator and Computer (ENIAC), developed for the US Army Ordnance Dept by J. Presper Eckert and John W. Mauchly of the Moore School of Electrical Engineering at the University of Pennsylvania, Philadelphia and completed in 1946. Weighing some 30 tons, it contained 18,000 vacuum tubes and semiconductor diodes, and 1,500 relays. The Ordnance Dept installed it at the Ballistics Research Laboratory of the Aberdeen Proving Ground in Maryland, where it was employed to calculate firing tables for artillery, taking into account such variables as the velocity of the wind, type of shell and temperature of the air. ENIAC represented a major stage in a line of progress that can be directly traced to two earlier computers, the Z3 built by Konrad Zuse at the German Aircraft Research Institute in Berlin in 1941, and the Harvard Mark I developed by Prof. Howard Aiken at Harvard University between 1939 and 1944. Both these computers, though they marked an important advance on previous systems, were electro-mechanical devices, and not all-electronic as has often been claimed.
COMMERCIALLY MANUFACTURED ELECTRONIC COMPUTERS: the first in regular production were introduced simultaneously by Remington Rand of Philadelphia in the USA, and by Ferranti of Hollinwood, Lancashire in Britain. The first Ferranti Mark I machine in operation was installed at Manchester University and working during the first half of 1951, though only formally inaugurated on 9 July of that year. Remington Rand's first Univac I computer was installed at the US Census Bureau in Philadelphia during the same period and was the subject of an official dedication ceremony on 14 June 1951.
ELECTRONIC COMPUTER IN REGULAR BUSINESS USE: the first was the Lyons Electronic Office (LEO), which began full-scale operation at the headquarters of the J. Lyons & Co food and catering organization, Cadby Hall, London, in January 1954. LEO was used by Lyons for accounting and pay-roll preparation and also on a hire basis by the Inland Revenue and British Railways. In the USA the electronic computer entered the business world later the same year, when a Univac I was acquired by the General Electric Appliance Park at Louisville, Ky.

The first
CONCENTRATION CAMP
was Holmogor, established by the Bolsheviks at Archangel, Russia, in 1921. According to Milhaljo Mihajlov, this was the first camp 'whose sole purpose was the physical destruction of the prisoners'. Estimates of the numbers who died in Soviet concentration camps between 1921 and 1953 vary, but most authorities agree that it could not have been less than 10 million and one survey suggests 19 million. The Stalinist terror reached its peak in 1936, when there are believed to have been 16 million prisoners.

The idea that the British 'invented' concentration camps was fostered by Dr Goebbels during the 1930s. In 1938 Nazi propaganda picture postcards, formerly sold as 'genuine Russian concentration camp scenes', were relabelled for issue as 'genuine British concentration camp scenes in South Africa'. The camps of the Boer War, however, were designed for internment and were not intended to be punitive.

Dr Goebbels seems to have overlooked the fact that even the term itself was in use at an earlier date, having been coined by the Spanish to describe the internment camps they established in Cuba in 1895.

The first
CONCERT, PUBLIC
was held in London on 30 December 1672 at what the organizer, John Banister, described as 'the Musick-school', and his contemporary, the musicologist Roger North, as 'a publick room in a nasty hole in White Fryers'. Banister was in financial straits at this time, having been dismissed from his position as Leader of the Court Band for impertinence to the King. Accordingly he took a room above a public house behind the Temple and began a series of daily afternoon concerts for which an admission fee of 1s was charged. Seats and small tables were ranged round the side of the room and the patrons, mainly shopkeepers, were able to call for ale, cakes and tobacco during the course of the programme. The musicians sat on a raised dais and performed behind curtains. The reason for this is obscure. Roger North, to whom we are indebted for the only eye-witness account of Banister's concerts, said merely that modesty required it. Wrote North:

There was very good musick, for Banister found means to procure the best hands in town, and some voices to come and performe there, and there wanted no variety of humour, for Banister himself did wonders upon a flageolett to a thro-base, and the severall masters had their solos.

Banister's concerts continued at various locations in London, more or less regularly, until his death in 1678. During that year another impressario, Thomas Britton, the 'musical small-coal man', started a series of subscription concerts in a room over his coal depot in Clerkenwell. By the end of the century concert-going was already a popular London diversion, 25 years before the first public concerts to be held on the Continent were inaugurated in France.

The first
CONSERVATORY
was a viridarium erected by Daniel Barbaro in the Botanical Gardens at Padua, shortly after they were opened in 1545. The structure was probably brick or stone, without glass, and heated by a brazier or open hearth. Delicate plants were moved into this conservatory when winter set in and replanted outdoors in the spring.
GB: The first recorded conservatory was built by William Cecil, Queen Elizabeth I's Chief Secretary of State, at Burghley Court, Burghley, Northamptonshire in 1562, to protect his collection of orange, lemon, pomegranate and myrtle trees. There is still an extension to Burghley Court known as the 'Orange Court', and this is believed to be the original conservatory.
GREENHOUSE: the first in Britain (i.e. for plants other than citrus) was a stone building, 60ft long, with arched windows and a slate roof, constructed at the Oxford Physic Garden in 1621. No provision was made for heating the building, other than a charcoal brazier on wheels that was perambulated round by a gardener on particularly cold nights.

Early conservatories of this type cannot be regarded as forcing-houses, as the temperature given off by a brazier or from an open hearth would have been too uneven to generate growth. The hothouse as such can be said to date from the introduction of stove-heating from Holland and the first attempts to raise exotic plants *c.* 1690.

The first hothouse in Britain to be constructed almost entirely from glass, including a glass roof, was the Duke of Rutland's grapery at Belvoir Castle, Leicestershire. The glazing was completed under the direction of Stephen Switzer, an eminent horticulturist, in 1724.

Steam-heating of hothouses is recorded as early as 1788, when a Mr Wakefield of Liverpool installed the necessary apparatus in his conservatory. The earliest-recorded circulating hot-water system in a greenhouse was installed by Anthony Bacon on his estate at Aberaman, Glamorgan in 1822.

The glasshouse was generally confined to the gardens of the wealthy until the repeal of the tax on glass in 1845. By the later years of Victoria's reign, the glass conservatory had become a distinctive feature of every 'desirable' suburban villa.

The first
CO-OPERATIVE SOCIETY
was the Weavers' Society of Fenwick, Ayrshire, which began the co-operative distribution of groceries among its members according to a resolution signed by John Burns and 11 others on 9 November 1769. The Fenwick Weavers' Society had been established eight years prior to this date as a benevolent society dedicated to the maintenance of fair prices within the trade and the relief of the poor. To these worthy objects was added the pioneer exercise in distributive co-operation, the main commodity bought and sold being oatmeal. The Society undertook to sell to members at cost price after deducting the interest paid on any capital borrowed and also the wage paid to the storemen. No profit was aimed at, any surplus over costs being credited to the Society and any deficit being paid from the Society's exchequer.
CO-OPERATIVE SOCIETY PAYING A DIVIDEND ON PURCHASES: the first was the Lennoxtown Victualling Society, founded at Lennoxtown, Stirling in 1812. As no minute books of the Society survive earlier than 1826, it is not known whether the dividend system was introduced prior to the revised constitution of that year. Dividends were paid annually. For the first year's trading under the new constitution a profit of £397 was divided between 67 members.

The Rochdale Pioneers, who opened their Toad Lane Co-op on 21 December 1844, systematized the payment of dividends on purchases in such a way that this practice, rare hitherto, became standard for the whole co-operative movement.

The first
CORRESPONDENCE COURSE
was offered by Isaac Pitman of 5 Nelson Place, Bath, who issued an explanatory sheet detailing his system of shorthand on 10 January 1840 with an advertisement that 'Any Person may receive lessons from the Author by post at 1s each to be paid in advance, and enclosed in a paid letter.' This announcement coincided with the introduction of the Penny Post. Pitman suggested that for his first essay in shorthand the prospective pupil should transcribe about a dozen verses from the Bible, leaving spaces between the lines for corrections. Later impressions of the sheet issued the same year offered the lessons gratuitously, providing postage was prepaid. By 1843, the number of postal pupils had become so great that Pitman formed a panel of volunteer teachers into the Phonographic Correspondence Society to undertake the correction of the exercises.
CORRESPONDENCE SCHOOL: the first to be organized on a regular commercial basis was founded in Berlin in 1856 by Charles Toussaint and Gustav Langenscheidt to teach languages by post. The first course offered was in French, followed by English and other languages. The student received a monthly printed letter containing exercises in grammar and conversation and a passage of a story that was continued in serial form.

The foreign text was accompanied by a phonetic rendering line for line, as the aim of the school was to teach its students to speak the language fluently, not just to read it.

The first correspondence school to prepare candidates for professional examinations was Skerry's College, founded as a conventional adult school by C.E. Skerry at Edinburgh in 1878. The first postal tuition course was offered to candidates preparing for the Institute of Chartered Accountants examination in 1880. Courses were also offered for Civil Service candidates.

The first correspondence school to give technical education by post was the International Correspondence School of Scranton, Pa., founded by T.J. Foster in 1891. Courses were offered in mine engineering and surveying.

The first
CREASEPROOF FABRIC
was developed over a period of 14 years by a research team under Dr R.S. Willows at the Glossop, Derbyshire, laboratories of the Manchester textile manufacturers Tootal Broadhurst Lee. It was publicly announced for the first time on 9 August 1932. The answer to the problem of how to give cotton the crease-resistant properties of wool lay in the technique of impregnating fabric with synthetic resin solutions, not, as had been tried before, by laminating the fibres, but by inducing the resin to enter the body of each individual fibre. This gave the yarn an elasticity wanting in its natural state. The first commercially manufactured products in creaseproof fabric were Tootal ties, launched in the autumn of 1932. A full range of creaseproof dress fabrics reached the shops the following April.

The first recorded
CREMATION
in Britain, took place on 25 September 1769, when the body of Honoretta Pratt was burnt in her open grave at St George's Burial Ground, Hanover Square, London. Mrs Pratt was the daughter of Sir John Brooks of York and widow of the Hon. John Pratt, Treasurer of Ireland. Her monument recorded:

This worthy woman believing that the vapours arising from graves in the church yards of populous city's must prove hurtful to the inhabitants and resolving to extend to future times as far as she was able that charity and benevolence which distinguished her through life ordered that her body should be burnt in hope that others would follow her example, a thing too hastily censured by those who did not understand the motive.

Milan Crematorium established by Dr Pini in 1876

CREMATOR: the first, scientifically designed, was an open-furnace-type incinerator built by Dr L. Brunetti of Padua and used by him to cremate the body of a 35-year-old woman at Padua on 10 March 1869. Dr Brunetti displayed an improved model cremator and examples of cremated ashes at the Vienna Exhibition of 1873, attracting the attention of Sir Henry Thompson, Surgeon to HM the Queen, who returned to England resolved to propagate the idea. At a meeting held at his house on 13 January 1874 a declaration in favour of the adoption of cremation for the disposal of the dead was signed by 15 persons, including John Everett Millais, John Tenniel and Anthony Trollope. These signatories formed the nucleus of the Cremation Society founded on 29 April of the same year. On 9 October 1874 the first cremation of an English person in a modern cremator took place at Dresden, when the body of Lady Dilke, who had died at the age of 26, was immolated in a gas-fired regenerative furnace built by Siemens. The body had been embalmed before being transported from London.

The legality of cremation in Britain was established by Mr Justice Stephen in a judgement given at the trial of Dr William Price of Llantrisant, at the Crown Court, Cardiff in February 1884. Dr Price was charged with immolating the body of his five-month-old child in a 10-gal cask of petroleum. In his historic ruling Mr Justice Stephen stated that 'the great leading rule of criminal law is that nothing is a crime unless it is plainly forbidden by law . . . [and] that to burn a body decently and inoffensively is lawful'.

CREMATORIA: the first were established by Julius le Moyne in his own grounds at Washington, Pa., and by Dr Pini of the Milan Cremation Society at Milan, both in 1876. Le Moyne's crematorium, which was available to the public, had performed 42 cremations by 1900, and the Milan Crematorium a total of 1,355.

GB: Established by the Cremation Society at Woking, Surrey, on an acre of freehold land purchased in 1878. A Gorini furnace was installed the following year, but the crematorium could not be brought into operation until 1885 owing to opposition from the Home Office. The first cremation took place on 26 March, the name of the subject being withheld, though reported in *The Times* to be 'a lady well known in literary and scientific circles'.

The first
CROSSWORD PUZZLE
was compiled by Liverpool-born Arthur Wynne and published in the week-end supplement of the *New York World* on Sunday, 21 December 1913. Wynne was employed in what was familiarly known as the 'tricks and jokes department'; in the ceaseless quest for fresh and original material, he remembered how his grandfather had amused him as a child with a favourite Victorian parlour game known as the 'Magic Square, or Double Acrostic'. By separating the

words with black spaces, and adding a list of 32 clues, Wynne created the first crossword. There was little subtlety to the clues, which were mainly simple word definitions: 'What bargain hunters enjoy', five letters; 'A pigeon', four letters; 'A boy', three letters; 'An animal of prey', four letters. (Sales, dove, lad, lion.)

GB: Mr H. A. Marker of Edmonton, London, claims to have compiled crossword puzzles for distribution as an advertisement in a showroom in August 1924. A larger crossword was posted up in the window and crowds gathered in the street outside trying to solve it. The first crossword to appear in a newspaper was sold to the *Sunday Express* by C. W. Shepherd of Newspaper Features Ltd, and published on 2 November 1924. Shepherd had obtained the crossword from America, and he had overlooked the fact that one of the answers – the word 'honor' – was spelt the American way. The day before publication he received a call from the *Express* asking him to alter it to the English spelling. Thinking this was merely a matter of adding a 'u', he set blithely to work. By the time he had completed the drastic reconstruction necessary to make the word fit, he had become the first man to compile a newspaper crossword in Britain. The end result comprised 34 clues, listed as 'Horizontals' and 'Verticals', and the word 'honour' was omitted altogether.

CRYPTIC CROSSWORD PUZZLE: the first was pioneered by 'Torquemada' of the *Saturday Westminster* in 1925. Previously English crosswords had followed the American pattern and demanded no more than a reasonable vocabulary, but 'Torquemada', who borrowed the name of a particularly zealous Spanish Inquisitor, invented the kind of cryptic clue that contained, in the words of a bewildered American writer, 'puns, anagrams, rare literary allusions, out-of-the-way place names, all-but-forgotten cricket and soccer terminology, and downright unsporting tricks'. The style still remains peculiar to Britain. The first crossword to appear in *The Times* was compiled by Adrian Bell, and appeared on 1 February 1930. There were severe protests from the kind of subscriber who regarded *The Times* as an article of apparel, and the respectability of the venture had to be assured by printing a crossword in each of the Classical languages. The most cryptic puzzle of all appeared in *The Times* on 9 March 1940. It was compiled by Sir Max Beerbohm, and fulfilled an engaging dream which he described in his own words as: 'A crossword puzzle with clues signifying nothing – nothing whatsoever.'

The first
DEBATING SOCIETY
was the Rota Club, which met nightly at the Turk's Head in New Palace Yard, Westminster from the beginning of the Michaelmas Law Term of 1659. Founder-members included John Aubrey, John Milton and Andrew Marvell. The principal instigator of the society, James Harrington, described the form of debate in his *Censure of the Rota upon Mr Milton's Book* (1660):

it is our usuall custom to dispute every thing, how plain or obscure soever, by knocking Argument against Argument, and tilting at one another with our heads (as Rams fight) until we are out of breath, and then refer it to our wooden oracle the Box; and seldom any thing, how slight soever, without some Patron or other to defend it.

The 'wooden oracle' alluded to was a ballot-box, one of the first ever used in Britain, and the claim made for the Rota as the earliest debating society is based on the fact that it was the first such gathering to institute the practice of voting on the motion.

The Rota Club was ostensibly committed to the propagation of republican ideals, though it is doubtful whether all its members shared a devotion to the Cromwellian régime. Samuel Pepys became a member in January 1660, paying 1s 6d entrance fee, but obtained small value as the society was dissolved the following month when it became apparent that the Restoration was imminent.

The first recorded
DENTAL DRILL
was described in 1728 by the Parisian dental surgeon Pierre Fauchard in his book *Le Chirurgien-Dentiste*. This was a hand-drill specially designed for loosening decayed dental tissue and operated by twisting with the fingers in alternate directions.

POWER-OPERATED DENTAL DRILL: the first was a clockwork implement devised by George Fellows Harrington in June 1863 and subsequently manufactured at his own factory in Lind Street, Ryde, Isle of Wight. It retailed for 6gns.

ELECTRIC DENTAL DRILL: the first was a battery-operated device patented by George F. Green of Kalamazoo, Mich., on 26 January 1875. Dental drills powered from the main electricity supply were not introduced until 1908.

The first
DENTAL PRACTITIONER
in Britain to specialize exclusively in dentistry was Peter de la Roche, who is known to have had a practice in London in 1661. Samuel Pepys was numbered among his patients at that time. Prior to the 18th century – and in most countries well into the 19th – dentistry was a sideline undertaken by barbers, blacksmiths, farriers, horse doctors and fairground hucksters.

The first practitioner to win recognition for dentistry as a legitimate branch of medical science was Pierre Fauchard, who established a practice at Angers, France in 1696 and was the first to style himself a 'dental surgeon'. Originally trained as a naval surgeon under a specialist in dentistry, Surgeon-Major Alexandre Poteleret, Fauchard earned the title of 'Father of Modern Dentistry' by his substitution of sound medical techniques for the barbarities of those who customarily wielded pliers and chisel in the mouths of pain-distracted victims.

PROFESSIONAL QUALIFICATION FOR DENTAL PRACTITIONERS was first established by an Edict of Louis XIV in 1699, which entitled the College of Surgeons to conduct examinations in the art. A two-year course of study was prescribed and successful candidates were entitled to the designation 'Expert pour les Dents'. Nearly a century and a half elapsed before any other country followed suit, the Baltimore College of Dental Surgery conducting its first examinations for a Doctorate of Dentistry by the authority of the General Assembly of the State of Maryland in March 1841.

GB: Under the Medical Act 1858 the Queen was empowered to grant a Charter to the Royal College of Surgeons authorizing that body to institute dental examinations and award certificates of professional competency. Fifteen Licences in Dental Surgery were issued on 13 March 1860, the name of Thomas Bell heading the RCS list of the first qualified Dental Surgeons. Progress in raising dentistry from the level of a trade to that of a profession was anything but rapid in Britain; not until the Dentists Act 1921 did it become limited to those holding recognized qualifications.

The first
DENTURE
The earliest-known set of dentures embodying both upper and lower rows of false teeth was dug up from a field in

Switzerland, and is believed to date from the late 15th century. The teeth are carved from bone and attached to hinged side-pieces with gut. This denture would probably have been worn as an aid to beauty and would need to have been removed at mealtimes.

The first porcelain dentures were made *c.* 1770 by Alexis Duchâteau, an apothecary from Saint-Germain-en-Laye, nr Paris. After repeated failures – the porcelain contracted under firing, making it extremely difficult to judge how large a mould to use – he at last succeeded in making a pair that fitted so excellently that he was able to wear them for the rest of his life. A Parisian dentist, M. Dubois de Chemant, who had assisted Duchâteau in his experiments, began to manufacture the new dentures. The first really satisfactory false teeth to be made available to the toothless public at large, they united, said the Paris Faculty of Medicine in a testimonial, the 'qualities of beauty, solidity and comfort to the exigencies of hygiene'.

GB: De Chemant introduced his artificial teeth when he set up a London practice in 1792. The porcelain was supplied by the pottery firm of Wedgwood.

The first
DEPARTMENT STORE
was the Marble Dry Goods Palace opened on Broadway by Alexander Turney Stewart in 1848. Stewart had been a poorly paid schoolmaster in Ireland before he emigrated to New York in 1823 and set up his own business. At the time of its erection the Marble Dry Goods Palace was the largest shop in the world, extending the whole length of a city block. By 1876, the year of his death, Stewart's company had an annual turnover of $70 million a year, and his personal fortune was estimated at $80 million. A man of few personal attractions, he was never known to have given away any of his vast wealth.

GB: Both Kendal Milne of Manchester and Bainbridge's of Newcastle upon Tyne had been departmentalized by 1850, but sold only articles of wearing apparel. The true instigator of the modern department store in Britain was William Whiteley, who started the Bayswater, London, enterprise later to be known as the 'Universal Provider' in 1863 with a staff of three. He is said to have been inspired with the department-store idea by seeing so much merchandise under one roof at the Great Exhibition of 1851. In 1867 he opened a jewelry department, and thus became the first British retailer to break away from drapery and haberdashery in a departmentalized store. A 'foreign department' selling Oriental novelties followed three years later, an estate agency and a restaurant (the first in a store) in 1872, a cleaning and dyeing department in 1874 and a hairdressing salon in 1876. Whiteley's slogan 'Anything from a Pin to an Elephant' was borne out when he supplied the latter article to a Church of England clergyman. Like his American counterpart A.T. Stewart, Whiteley secured an unenviable reputation for personal meanness, matched only by his vanity. In 1879 he had several hundred cabinet-sized photographs of himself put on sale at 2s 6d each, a venture that resulted in only four purchases. He was eventually murdered in 1907 by a man who claimed to be his illegitimate son.

The first department store in Britain to be built as such was the Bon Marché at Brixton, which James Smith erected in 1877 with the £80,000 he had accrued the previous year when his horse Rosebery won both the Cesarewitch and the Cambridgeshire.

DEPARTMENT STORE WITH A SELF-SERVICE FOOD DEPARTMENT: the first was Woodward's of Vancouver, Canada in 1919.

The first
DETECTIVE STORY
was Edgar Allan Poe's 'The Murders in the Rue Morgue', published in *Graham's Magazine*, Philadelphia in April 1841. The story was set in Paris and Poe's detective was an impoverished and eccentric chevalier, Auguste Dupin. The hero was necessarily French, as France was the only country that had developed either private or police detection as a distinct profession by that date. It was reissued as a 12½ cents paperback in 1843, anticipating the form in which the majority of detective tales were to be issued in later years.

GB: The first detective story published in Britain was Edgar Allan Poe's 'The Purloined Letter'. It was originally contained in an American annual called *The Gift* (published September 1844), and appeared in abridged form in *Chambers's Edinburgh Journal* for 30 November 1844. In this story the detective Dupin makes his third and last appearance, having featured also in Poe's 1842 tale 'The Mystery of Marie Roget'.

DETECTIVE NOVEL: the first was *Recollections of a Detective Police Officer* by 'Waters', published by J. & C. Brown in June 1856. The story was entirely fictional, though it purported to be the autobiography of a real Metropolitan Police detective. The author was William Russell. *Recollections* also achieved the distinction of being the first detective novel to be translated into a foreign language, appearing in German (1857) and in French (1868).

'Waters' was not, however, the first fictional detective to make his appearance in an English novel. Charles Dickens, who early took an interest in the nascent detective force and published a series of articles about it in *Household Words* in 1850, created the character Inspector Bucket, whose investigations occupied 14 of the 66 chapters of *Bleak House* (London 1853). Bucket is believed to have been based on the real-life Inspector Field of the Metropolitan Police, who was personally known to the author.

The first detective novel by an author of repute and the first to break away from the 'autobiographical' form of

Britain's first department store as it was in the 1890s. The blank window represents the original Whiteley's of 1863.

Russell and his imitators, was Wilkie Collins's *The Moonstone*, published in three volumes by Tinsley of London in July 1868. This is also claimed to be the longest detective story ever written, totalling some 900 pages. The detective, Sergeant Cuff, was based on Superintendent Foley, who had figured prominently in the controversial Constance Kent or 'Road Murder' case of 1860, from which the plot of the book is derived.

The female detective made her appearance as early as 1862 in Wilkie Collins's *No Name*, though only as an incidental character. Probably the first detective novel to feature a woman in the role of investigator was *The Recollections of a Lady Detective*, Anon, London, 1864. Thus the fictional lady detective made her appearance some 60 years before her real-life counterpart.

WOMAN DETECTIVE WRITER: the first was Anna Katherine Green of Buffalo, N.Y., whose rotund and rheumatic detective Ebenezer Gryce made his début in *The Leavenworth Case* in 1878. This was also the first detective novel by an American writer of either sex. Miss Green, the wife of a furniture-manufacturer, explained her invasion of this male world by saying that she considered the writing of a detective novel to be a suitable preparation for a career as a poetess. The story concerned the death of a millionaire and had as its principal characters two very attractive female cousins who, with sighs and heaving bosoms, uttered such deathless lines as: 'My reputation is sullied for ever', and 'The finger of suspicion never forgets the direction in which it has once pointed.' Miss Green nevertheless understood her craft and the culprit proved to be one of the least suspected characters. By the time of her death in her 90th year in 1935 she had written over 30 detective novels.

The first
DICTIONARY, ENGLISH

was *A Table Alphabeticall, containing and teaching the true writing and understanding of hard usuall English words* compiled by Robert Cawdrey, a schoolmaster formerly employed at Oakham and Coventry, and published in London in 1604. It contained about 3,000 words. The only surviving copy is in the Bodleian Library, Oxford.

DICTIONARY OF THE ENGLISH LANGUAGE CONTAINING THE WORD IN ITS TITLE: the first was Henry Cockeram's *The English Dictionary*, London, 1623. The term had been used earlier in the titles of foreign-language dictionaries (*q.v.*) published in Britain. Cockeram's *Dictionary* was unusual in that it gave a guide to correct usage. 'Vulgar' words were given their 'refined' equivalent.

The first English dictionary to attempt the definition of words in common use, so-called 'easy words', was *The New English Dictionary* by J.K., London, 1702. J.K. has usually been identified as John Kersey. His work contained only 'such English words as are genuine and used by Persons of clear Judgment and good Style, . . . omitting such as are obsolete, barbarous, foreign or peculiar . . . and abstruse and uncouth Terms of Art'.

COMPLETE ENGLISH DICTIONARY (complete in the sense that the lexicographer included all the English words known to him): the first was the *Universal Etymological English Dictionary* of Nathaniel Bailey, London, 1721. It was also the first dictionary to give the derivation of words, and so justified the inclusion of such simple terms as 'man', 'woman', 'dog' and 'cat', which would have been superfluous in earlier compilations concerned only with definition. (Indeed Bailey's definition of 'cat' consisted of the curt phrase: 'A creature well known.') Used by Samuel Johnson as a basis for his own, better-known dictionary, Bailey's work remained the chief rival to that of the great Doctor during the latter half of the 18th century. It continued to be issued until 1802. Of the revised editions, the 1727 version of Bailey is notable as the first dictionary to contain illustrations, and that of 1731 as the first to give some guidance as to the correct pronunciation of words.

DICTIONARY CONTAINING ILLUSTRATIVE QUOTATIONS FROM LITERATURE: the first was *A Dictionary of the English Language*, compiled by Dr Samuel Johnson for a syndicate of London booksellers and published in two folio volumes on 15 April 1755.

The significance of Johnson's *Dictionary* reaches far beyond his introduction of quotations into lexicography, for it had an immeasurable effect on the standardization of the English language, particularly with regard to spelling. Dr James Murray pointed out in his Romanes Lecture of 1900, how the word 'dispatch', given by Johnson as 'despatch' in his Dictionary (the first time the alternative spelling is noted in print, and probably a slip on Johnson's part), came to be commonly spelt with an 'e' during the first half of the 19th century, and this on the *Dictionary*'s authority, though it was never spelt so by the Doctor's contemporaries.

DICTIONARY OF THE AMERICAN LANGUAGE: the first was compiled by Samuel Johnson Jr and published in New York in 1798. His father, Dr Samuel Johnson, sometime President of Columbia University, and author of the first text on American grammar (1756), was almost exactly contemporaneous with his celebrated namesake in England, though they were not related.

The first complete American dictionary was *An American Dictionary of the English Language*, by Noah Webster, New York, 1828. Its 70,000 words were some 12,000 in excess of the number contained in any dictionary hitherto, either British or American.

Dieting set to music – a song sheet

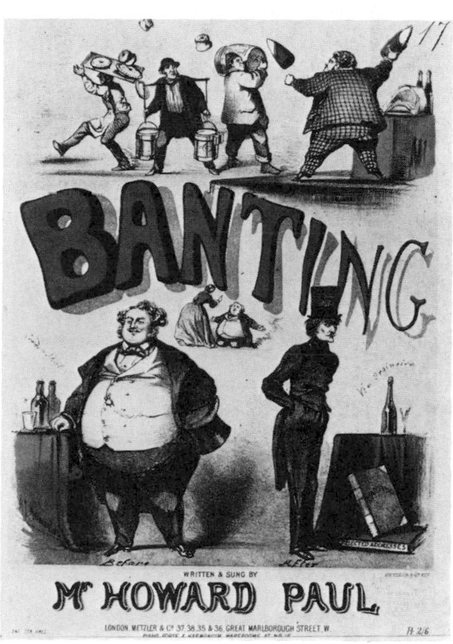

The first
DIET, SLIMMING

scientifically planned, was prescribed for a grossly overweight London undertaker called William Banting by Dr Harvey, an ear specialist, in 1862. The Banting diet, later enshrined in the verb 'to bant', was based on the reduction of carbohydrates, and was thus the precursor of most of the weight-reducing systems in use today. In Banting's case, it meant that the undertaker was obliged to forgo pastry, potatoes, pies and all sweetstuffs and restrict himself to lean meat, fish and fruit.

His new régime consisted of the following:

Breakfast
4 oz lean meat, fish or bacon; 1oz toast
Dinner
'A little more meat', vegetables (no potatoes); fruit; 1oz toast
Tea
Tea without milk; a rusk; fruit
Supper
4oz meat or fish

Within a year Banting had decreased his 203lb bulk to a svelte 153lb, and was encouraging others to follow his example in his 'Letter on Corpulence'. At first dieting tended to be a male preoccupation, but became a fashionable activity among women when they ceased to distort their figures with corsets and stays after 1914.

The first
DINNER-JACKET
was worn by Griswold Lorillard on the occasion of the Autumn Ball held at the Tuxedo Park Country Club, New York on 10 October 1886. Lorillard's 'tuxedo', as it came to be known in America, consisted of a short black coat with satin lapels, and was modelled on the English smoking-jacket then in vogue. His temerity in appearing before mixed company in such a garment doubtless raised some eyebrows, for prior to World War I, dinner-jackets were generally regarded as informal evening wear to be worn only in the absence of ladies.
GB: Introduced as the 'dress lounge' in 1888. The term 'dinner-jacket' did not come into currency till 10 years later.

The first
DISC JOCKEY
on British radio was to have been Compton Mackenzie, but as he disappeared on an island-hunting expedition shortly before he was due to appear, his place was taken instead by his brother-in-law Christopher Stone, who presented his first record round-up from the BBC's Studio 3 at Savoy Hill on 7 July 1927. Although record recitals had been given before, they had not been presented in quite this way. Stone earned the distinction of being the first DJ by presenting an individual selection of records and giving introductory comments to each title. At the outset he was not paid, but was allowed to mention the *Gramophone*, which he edited with Compton Mackenzie. This was one of the very few occasions on which the BBC allowed commercials. Later the arrangement was dropped and Stone was paid 3gns a session. On his death in 1965 *The Times* said: 'He endeared himself to the public by the whimsical, human touches with which he extricated himself when occasionally he put on a wrong record or forgot to start the turntable.' One of his whims was the making of his will on a gramophone record in 1931. Another was that he never ceased to object to the term 'disc jockey', particularly when applied to himself.

The first
DISH-WASHING MACHINE
(power model commercially produced) was developed over a period of 10 years by Mrs W. A. Cockran of Shelbyville, Ind., and finally completed in 1889. Mrs Cockran's husband had kept her short of money, and it was only after his death that she had been able to raise enough to perfect the invention from friends who believed in her work. She built various models, some for family and others for hotel use, the larger ones being driven by a steam-engine. A contemporary newspaper reported that the Cockran dish-washer was 'capable of washing, scalding, rinsing and drying from 5–20 dozen dishes of all shapes and sizes in two minutes . . .'. The manufacturing rights were acquired by a Chicago machine company.

The first
DIVORCE
civil, granted in England was enacted by Parliament in 1546 in order to make lawful the bigamous marriage of Lady Sadleir of Standon, Herts. She had formerly been Mrs Margaret Barr, but had married Sir Ralph Sadleir after her previous husband had disappeared and been presumed dead. Mr Barr having made an unwelcome reappearance, the Ecclesiastical Courts were powerless to confirm Lady Sadleir's second marriage, since they could only nullify a union where it could be proved to have been contracted unlawfully. Because in these peculiar circumstances the unfortunate Lady Sadleir had entered into her second, bigamous marriage in perfect good faith, a Private Bill was introduced into Parliament to dissolve the contract made with her first husband.

Lady Sadleir had been born Margaret Mitchell in humble circumstances, and was employed as a laundress at the time she married Barr. Her second marriage was exceptionally happy, despite the social gulf that separated her from Sir Ralph, one of Henry VIII's most trusted Ministers. They were not only blessed with seven children, but with ever-increasing wealth, for when he died in 1587, Sadleir had the reputation of being the richest commoner in England. Lady Sadleir was perhaps even more fortunate than she knew, for hers was the only civil divorce granted to a woman before 1801.
CIVIL DIVORCE ON THE GROUNDS OF ADULTERY was first granted by Act of Parliament to William Parr, Marquess of Northampton, in 1551 and dissolved his marriage to Anne, *née* Bourchier. The Act gave him the right to marry again while his first wife still lived, a measure that has been described by H. M. Luckcuck in his *History of Marriage*, as 'the first real inroad on the indissolubility of Christian matrimony, as a principle of English law'. The Marquess had in fact been too impatient to await any revocation of the principles of English law and had taken to himself a second wife, Elizabeth Brooke, some four years earlier. The divorce regularized this union, though the Marquess is probably unique in English history in actually having his divorce annulled – when he later fell into Royal disfavour – as well as his marriage.

The Northampton and Sadleir divorces are the only two civil cases on record prior to the Restoration. The only alternative form of decree enabling remarriage was an ecclesiastical divorce, *a vinculo matrimonii* (from the bonds of marriage), a recourse open to those who could satisfy the prelates that the original contract of marriage was invalid. In effect this meant that in the eyes of the Church the marriage had never taken place. On occasion the ecclesiastical judges found it expedient to employ the narrowest interpretation of the law on just impediments to marriage, as in the classic example of Henry VIII's divorce from Catherine of Aragon.
DIVORCE COURTS of the civil judiciary were first established under the Matrimonial Causes Act 1857, which came into effect on 1 January 1858. There were two immediate and interrelated effects. For the first time divorce was brought within the means of the middle classes; whereas the cost of obtaining a Private Act of Parliament to annul a marriage had been estimated at an average of £700 or £800, the judicial process involved expenditure of, perhaps, an eighth of this sum. Consequent on this change was a very marked increase in the number of divorce suits, so much so, that the Chairman of the Divorce Commissioners, Lord Campbell, was constrained to remark that in recommending the transfer from a legislative to a judicial procedure of divorce it had not occurred to him that the number of divorces would rise much above the average of three a year current before the Act. He was shocked beyond measure to find that only a few months after it became law, there were no less than 300 cases pending before the Courts.

Divorce for all cannot be said to have become an economic reality before the introduction of Legal Aid in 1949.

The first
DOG SHOW
was organized by a prominent Newcastle sportsman, Mr Shorthouse, and a local gunsmith, Mr Pape, and held at Newcastle upon Tyne Town Hall,

28–29 June 1859. There was a total of 60 entries in two classes, one for pointers and the other for setters, and the prizes consisted of guns manufactured and donated by Mr Pape. The prize for pointers went to R. Brailsford's liver-and-white dog, while the prize for setters went to J. Jobling's Dandy. Mr Brailsford, who had conceived the idea of the show, acted as a judge of the setter class and Mr Jobling as a judge for the pointer class.

The first
DRESSWEAR HIRE FIRM
was Moss Bros of Covent Garden, founded as a second-hand clothes shop by Moses Moss in 1860. The hiring service began almost by accident in 1897 to accommodate a single customer, one Charles Ponds, an ex-stockbroker and amateur vocalist who had come to the end of his monetary resources. Ponds had decided to turn his talent for comedy monologues to financial gain, but on obtaining his first professional engagement to entertain at an evening soirée, he found himself in need of a tail-coat, his own having been pawned long before. He approached Alfred Moss, who as Moses's eldest son had inherited the business, and asked for the loan of a dress suit. Moss obliged not only on this, but on several subsequent occasions when Ponds's services were in demand for an after-dinner diversion. At first no question of a fee was raised, certainly not by Ponds, but after a while his benefactor decided it was time to put the arrangement on a regular business footing and a hiring fee of 7s 6d was agreed. As Ponds prospered in his new profession, Alfred Moss suggested he might find it more economic to buy the suit of clothes he was wearing so regularly. The entertainer declined, saying that he saw no point in having to look after it himself when he could have it from Moss Bros in first-class condition, neatly cleaned and pressed, whenever he needed it. From this informal beginning, the Moss Bros clothes-hire service expanded to include not only morning dress and evening wear, but also wedding dresses, ball gowns, court dress, Coronation robes, ski clothes and theatrical costumes.

The first
DRIVING LESSONS
in Britain were offered by the Motor Carriage Supply Co of Balderton Street, London in June 1900. The Instructor was a Mr Hankinson, described by one appreciative lady pupil as 'patient, persevering and encouraging'. The Motor Carriage Supply Co gave tuition in driving only as a sideline to their main business, which was the first in England to be described as a garage (*see* Service Station).
DRIVING SCHOOL: the first in Britain, titled as such, was the Liver Motor Car Depot and School of Automobilism, Birkenhead, established by William Lea in May 1901. The Chief Instructor was Archibald Ford, who was later to claim that he had been the prime mover in opening the School. Towards the end of the summer it was moved to Berry Street, Liverpool and renamed The Lea School of Motoring. According to a report in the *Autocar* for 11 October 1902, the enterprise was 'most successful', two of the pupils travelling up specially from London for tuition.

See also Driving Test.

The first
DRIVING LICENCES
were issued to French motorists under the Paris Police Ordinance of 14 August 1893 (Rule I, Para 1), which stated: 'No motor vehicle . . . can be used without a regular authorization issued by us on the demand of the owner. This authorization can at all times be cancelled by us, at the instigation of the engineers.' Applicants were required to pass a driving test (*q.v.*) in order to secure authorization to drive.

Driving licences in card form were required to be carried and shown on demand by every motorist in France under a Decree of 10 March 1899 titled 'Circulation des Automobiles' and were issued by the Ministère des Travaux Publics as from that date. Licences had to bear the photograph of the holder and there was a space for insertion by the issuing officer of the type of vehicle the holder was authorized to drive. A total of 1,795 licences had been issued in the Paris area by 1 November 1899.
GB: Driving licences were introduced under the Motor Car Act of 14 August 1903, of which Section 3 stated: 'The (County or County Borough) Council . . . shall grant a licence to any person applying for it who resides in that county . . . on payment of a fee of five shillings.'

Licences were renewable annually. Under Section 4 of the Act provision was made for endorsing or suspending the licence after a second offence, and for the disqualification of a driver at the discretion of the courts.

The age limit for car-drivers was set at 17, and for motor cyclists 14. Prior to the Act no age limit had existed and the youngest owner-driver in the country was reported (January 1903) to be six-year-old Master Ernest Bond of Bishopston, Bristol, who rode a motor cycle specially built for him by his father.

The Motor Car Act became effective on 1 January 1904. The first 13 licences were issued by the London County Council in December for official purposes. The first member of the public to be issued with a driving licence was Mr Richard Cain of Bermondsey, chauffeur and bodyguard to Prince Hatzfeldt, a cousin of the Kaiser, on 28 December 1903.

The first
DRIVING TEST
was introduced under Rule III, Para 18, of the Paris Police Ordinance relating to the registration and licensing of motor vehicles of 14 August 1893. Tests were conducted under the supervision of the Chief Engineer of Mines, whose office included that of Inspector of Steam Motors in the Department of the Seine ('steam motors' was interpreted to include any self-propelled vehicle), and included an examination of the candidate's driving ability, his capacity to undertake running repairs, and his knowledge of the components of the engine. Candidates were required to be 21 years of age or over.

Driving tests were extended to the other departments of France under the 'Circulation des Automobiles' Decree of 10 March 1899, and were administered from that date by the Ministère des Travaux Publics.

The first Englishman to take a driving test was the Hon. Evelyn Ellis, who passed his examination as an 'autocar conductor' while on a visit to Paris, February–March 1896. The driving examiner was M. Michel Levy.
GB: Driving tests were introduced by Mr Leslie Hore Belisha, Minister of Transport, and came into effect on a voluntary basis on 13 March 1935; they were official from 1 April 1935 and compulsory from 1 June 1935. All those who had taken out their first driving licence since 1 April 1934 were obliged to take a test. Initially the fee was 7s 6d, but this was reduced to 5s on 1 June 1937 as it was found the Driving Test Organization had made an unintended profit of £16,000 the previous year. There were originally 200 examiners, including 16 supervisors, chosen from a total of 34,000 applicants. Women examiners were employed from the start, the first to receive her appointment being Miss Muriel Gillham, originally from Sydney, Australia, who was based at the Dartford Driving Test Centre in the Metropolitan Traffic Area.

Britain was one of the last countries in Europe to bring in the test; by 1934 it was already compulsory in Austria, Italy, Hungary, Czechoslovakia, Yugoslavia, Spain, Germany, Turkey, Switzerland, Portugal, Norway, Sweden, France, Holland and Denmark.

'L' Plates and Provisional Licences became compulsory in Britain on the same date as driving tests.

The first
DRY-CLEANING
process was discovered in 1849 by M. Jolly-Bellin of Paris, when he upset a lamp on a table-cloth newly laundered by his wife. Attempting to cover up the stain before his wife's return from shopping, he found that those parts which had been spattered with spirit had become cleaner than the rest. After careful experiment he proceeded to add to his tailoring business a new service – *Nettoyage à sec*. The garments brought for cleaning were unstitched and laid in sections in a pan of turpentine-oil mixture, which Bellin named 'camphene'. They were then brushed, re-dipped, dried and sewn up again.
GB: The first dry-cleaner was Pullar's of Perth, whose service was introduced in 1866. An improved spirit, prepared from benzine, petroleum and benzol, was used in preference to camphene, and garments were dipped without being taken to pieces as in France. Pullar's ran a postal service that covered the whole of Britain.

The first
DUPLICATING MACHINE
was invented by James Watt in order to expedite the large amount of copying involved in running his steam-engine business at Soho, Birmingham. It was first described in a letter he wrote to Dr Black on 24 July 1778: 'I have lately discovered a method of copying writing instantaneously, providing it has been written the same day, or within twenty-four hours. It enables me to copy all my business letters.' The apparatus consisted of a flat-bed press with either a side-arm lever or screw and horizontal bar. The manuscript or drawing to be copied was placed in the press against a piece of transparent tracing-paper or unsized drawing-paper which had first been moistened with a fixative of vinegar, borax, oyster-shells, bruised Aleppo galls and distilled water. The formula for this astringent was included in Watt's patent for 'a new method of copying letters' taken out on 14 February 1780. As the ink penetrated right through the unsized copying-paper, the reverse impression of the text on the topside could be employed as a master for reproducing a number of duplicates on ordinary sized paper. Thus Watt's apparatus can also be regarded as the first offset-printing press.

The firm of James Watt & Co was formed for the manufacture of duplicating machines on 20 March 1780. Watt's partner, Matthew Boulton, initiated an aggressive marketing policy, aiming to secure 1,000 subscriptions of £5 5s before the new product was launched. Circulars were distributed to Members of the Houses of Parliament, and there were practical demonstrations which attracted so much attention at Westminster that 'the Speaker . . . was often obliged to send his proper officer to fetch away from me the members to vote and sometimes to make a House'. Specimens of every kind of writing were displayed in all the principal coffee-houses together with their duplicates. An attempt was also made to secure Royal patronage, Boulton having heard that the King was a great letter-writer, and a demonstration was given at Court. The versatility of the process was constantly emphasized, attention being drawn to its ability to copy music for orchestras and military orders for distribution in the field. A special portable model was designed for travellers, and another for India with springs of best steel to withstand the changes of climate. Despite all these exertions, the innovation was not welcomed everywhere. The directors of the Bank of England were particularly unenthusiastic, thinking that it would facilitate forgery, and Boulton was constrained to say they had 'behaved foolish and rude', adding uncompromisingly: 'Some of the Directors are Hogs.'

David Gestetner demonstrating his Cyclostyle duplicating machine

In the first year, 150 machines were sold, 30 of them to overseas buyers. A special ink mixed with mucilage was supplied by the firm in powder form. Orders steadily increased, and within a few years the duplicating machine had become a standard fixture in most business concerns.

Letter-copiers very little different from Watt's original prototype continued in use in offices right up to World War I, when they were superseded by the use of carbon paper (*q.v.*) and, for multiple runs, Cyclostyle stencils.

MIMEOGRAPH: the first duplicating process to employ a wax stencil, was invented by Thomas Alva Edison in 1875, while experimenting with paraffin paper for possible use as telegraph tape. He was granted a patent for 'a method of preparing autographic stencils for printing' on 8 August 1876, and another patent for an improved method in 1880. Although he made no attempt to develop the process commercially, it was taken up by a Chicago lumberman, Albert Blake Dick, who bought the patent and constructed a flat-bed duplicator suitable for office use. The stencil was placed into a wooden frame and the text inscribed on the wax surface with a stylus. Then ink was applied to the stencil with a roller and squeezed through on to the copying sheet beneath. The A. B. Dick Co sold its first Diaphragm Mimeograph on 17 March 1887.

The first duplicating machine employing a wax stencil to be put on the market was the Cyclostyle, invented and manufactured in London in 1881 by a Hungarian immigrant, David Gestetner. The first typewriter stencil was introduced by Gestetner in 1888, A. B. Dick following with a Mimeograph version two years later. Both brand-names have become generic, and the processes differed little except in the method of applying the ink to the stencil.
The ROTARY DUPLICATOR was invented by an Austrian, A. D. Kleber, who brought his apparatus to London and commenced manufacture of the Neostyle Rotary in 1899. The firm became the Roneo Co in 1908.
See also Photocopier.

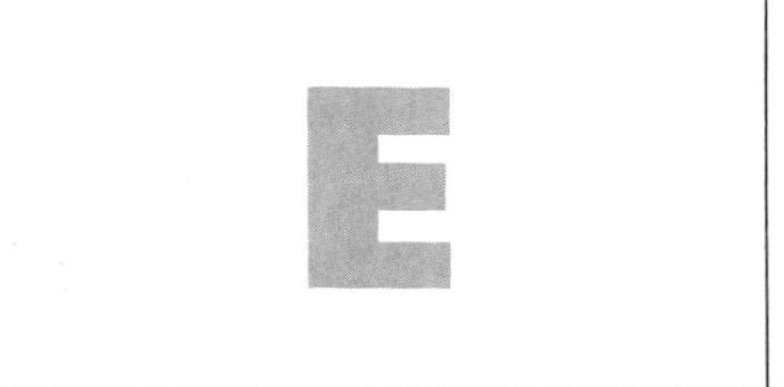

The first
ELASTIC
(woven) was manufactured in 1830 by Messrs Rattier et Guibal at their waterproof-cloth factory in Saint-Denis, a suburb of Paris. The pioneer British rubber-manufacturer, Thomas Hancock, who had supplied the firm with plant and workmen two years earlier, described in his memoirs the sequence of events that led to the successful production of elastic:

I have understood that a German, whose name I am not acquainted with, conceived the idea of introducing a thread of rubber into a woven web or fabric, so as to form the warp. . . . He was at a loss how to cut the thread . . . and went to Paris and communicated to my friends there [i.e. Messrs Rattier and Guibal] *his invention and his difficulty. Experiments were conducted at their works, and the person I took with me and left to superintend succeeded in producing a thread of rubber. Soon after this elastic web appeared in this country, I had some made. I entered into an agreement with an eminent house in Manchester, supplying them with the rubber thread (then called gut), which they soon manufactured into beautiful webs of different widths and different degrees of elasticity and strength.*

The new elastic web was apparently on sale in Britain by 1831, for an issue of *The World of Fashion* noted in that year:

Mrs Bell's house has long been unrivalled for the elegance of its corsets, which boast those advantages so rarely united, of strengthening and supporting the frame, and adding singular grace to the shape. A recent discovery enabled Mrs Bell to extend these advantages still farther by substituting India rubber for elastic wires.

Flat elastic braid or 'knicker elastic' was introduced in Britain in 1887.

The first
ELASTIC BANDS
made from vulcanized rubber were patented on 17 March 1845 by Stephen Perry of Messrs Perry & Co, rubber-manufacturers of London. Production of rubber bands 'for papers, letters, etc.' was inaugurated by the firm about the same time.

The first man to die in the
ELECTRIC CHAIR
was convicted murderer William Kemmler at Auburn Prison, N.Y. on 6 August 1890. The idea of inflicting capital punishment by electrocution was conceived by one Harold P. Brown, a strange and rather shadowy figure who conducted the initial experiments with equipment placed at his disposal by Thomas Alva Edison, the so-called 'wizard of Menlo Park'. Assisted by Dr A.E. Kennelly, Edison's Chief Electrician, Brown proceeded to electrocute a large number of animals. *The Electrical Engineer*, which thoroughly disapproved of the whole undertaking, reported in August 1889:

Many unfortunate dogs and other animals were tortured to death by Messrs Brown and Kennelly, such of them as could not be killed by electricity being, as one of the spectators testified, despatched by a blow on the head with a brick.

These allegations stirred up a storm of controversy, which became even more heated when it was suggested by certain leading members of the electrical industry that Brown's use of Westinghouse generators for the experiments without the authority of that company was a deliberate attempt on behalf of the Edison interests to discredit their rivals.

A week after Kemmler's execution, which by that time had become a national issue, *The Electrical Engineer* inveighed against the authorities for allowing him to be used as a guinea-pig in what turned out to be a horrifyingly mismanaged attempt to apply science to the judicial act of killing.

Making due allowance for the sensational reports of the daily press [said an angry but carefully composed leading article], *it is quite certain that the death of the victim at Auburn was not instantaneous, that respiration was resumed some minutes after the application and cessation of the current, that the current was turned on again, this time despatching the convict, but not without burning his flesh at the points of contact with the electrodes, and not till he had exhibited to the spectators meanwhile evidences of the vital struggle not less revolting than those usually seen upon the gallows.*

The *New York Times* described it as 'an awful spectacle, far worse than hanging'.

The official report on the execution stated that the death of William Kemmler had taken 8min from the time he entered the room.

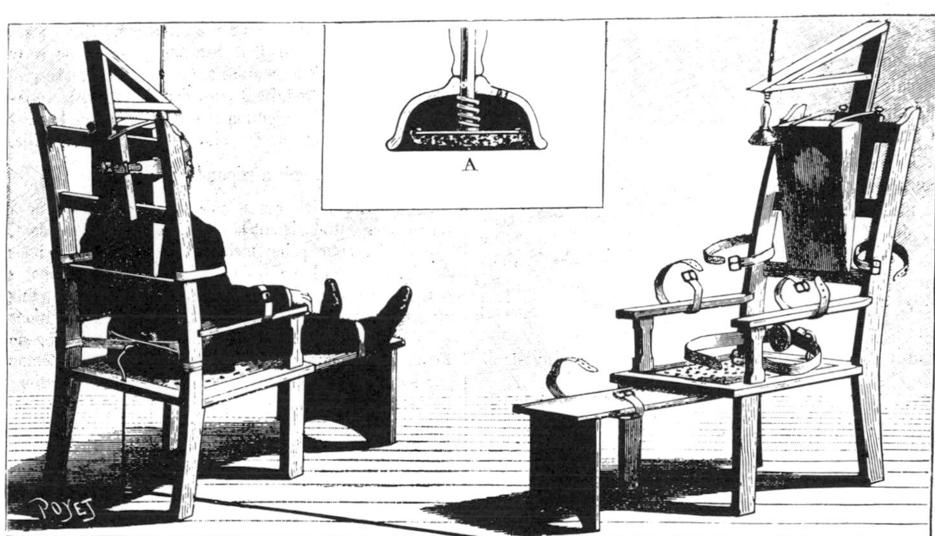

An instrument of humanity or an instrument of torture? It took William Kemmler 8min to die when he became the first man to go to the chair in 1890. A: *head electrode*

The first
ELECTRIC FAN
to be produced commercially was developed by Dr Schuyler Skaats Wheeler, Chief Engineer of the Crocker & Curtis Electric Motor Co, N.Y., in 1882. Manufacture commenced the following year, the Company's earliest models being two-bladed desk fans.

The first oscillating electric fan (gear-driven) was produced in the USA by the Eck Dynamo & Electric Co in 1908. This type of fan superseded the revolving models which had the disadvantage of blowing the breeze in unwanted directions.

GB: Commercial production of electric fans was started *c.* 1888 by B. Verity & Co of London for supply to GEC and other electrical concerns.

The first
ELECTRIC HEATING SYSTEM
was patented in the USA by Dr W. Leigh Burton in 1887 and introduced commercially two years later by the Burton Electric Co of Richmond, Va. A writer in *The Electrician* said:

The Burton Electric Heater consists of a cast-iron case, enclosing some resistance coils, which are covered with dry, powdered clay, for the purpose of absorbing the heat from the wires, and thus preventing them from burning out. The current supplied to the heaters has a potential of 80V, and each heater uses about 2½amp. It has been found that such a current raises the temperature of a heater to about 200 °F.

Shaped like a low table, the radiators were 27in long and 8in wide, and stood on iron legs raising them 4in from the floor. To begin with their use was confined to electric tramcars, though

they were advertised as suitable for household use. Towards the end of 1891, however, the Aspen Mining Co of Aspen, Colo., acquired a quantity of Burton Electric Heaters from the Electric Merchandise Co in Chicago, for use in their motor-stations. These are the first buildings known to have been heated by electricity.
GB: The first commercially produced heaters were designed for Crompton & Co of Chelmsford, electrical engineers, by H. J. Dowsing (*see also* Electric Oven; Motor Car: Electric Starter) and offered for sale in 1894. These consisted of portable wrought-iron screen radiators in various sizes, ranging in price from £2 7s 6d to £5; an electric wall radiator of 600W at £3; ship radiators and tramway heaters; and a number of rather bizarre ornamental heaters in Art Nouveau style, including one made to represent a sunflower.

The first public building in Britain to be heated electrically was the Vaudeville Theatre, London in January 1895. The order was received by Crompton & Co at 11am one Tuesday; by 6pm the complete system, comprising 22 wall-mounted radiators and 4 large, portable, screen radiators, was installed and ready for use. Running cost for 4hr each evening was 12s.

The first
ELECTRIC LAMP
of practical utility was developed by the self-taught Scottish scientist, James Bowman Lindsay, whose first successful experiment in electrical illumination was described by the *Dundee Advertiser* of 31 July 1835:

Mr Lindsay, a teacher in this town, formerly lecturer to Watt Institution, succeeded on the evening of the 25th July in obtaining a constant electric light. It is upwards of two years since he turned his attention to this subject, but much of that time has been devoted to other avocations. In beauty the light surpasses all others, has no smell, emits no smoke, is incapable of explosion, and not requiring air for combustion can be kept in sealed glass jars. It ignites without the aid of a taper, and seems peculiarly calculated for flax houses, spinning mills, and other places containing combustible materials. It may be sent to any convenient distance, and the apparatus for producing it is contained in a common chest.

It appears likely that Lindsay's lamps were incandescent, for in a letter to the *Dundee Advertiser* (30 October 1835) he refers to his use of 'a glass tube without air', though it must be conceded that nowhere does he describe a filament. That the lamp had practical utility is clear from the fact that this letter was written by its light, and he further claims that 'from the same apparatus I can get two or three lights, each of which is fit for reading with'. One lamp would give sufficient illumination for reading a book held 1½ft from it. The power source, according to his friend and contemporary, Alexander Maxwell, consisted of galvanic cells. Maxwell's unpublished 'Reminiscences' also reveal facets of Lindsay's character that explain to some extent the reason why he did not continue developing his invention to the point where it might have achieved commercial application. He was 'a man of profound learning and untiring scientific research, who, had he been more practical, less diffident, and possessed of greater worldly wisdom, would have gained for himself a good place amongst distinguished men. As it was . . . he went through life as a poor and modest schoolmaster.' Lindsay himself gave a perfectly straightforward reason for abandoning his experiments, and one fully in keeping with the disinterestedness of the man: 'Having satisfied myself on this subject [i.e. electric light], I returned to some glossological investigations that had been left unfinished. . . .'
INCANDESCENT ELECTRIC LAMPS (produced commercially): the first were developed independently, but at the same time, by Thomas Alva Edison of Menlo Park, N.J., and by (Sir) Joseph Swan of Newcastle upon Tyne. In view of the rival claims to priority that emanate from both sides of the Atlantic, the exact chronology assumes some importance. Edison began his experiments in September 1878, achieving a satisfactory result a little over 12 months later. The first Edison bulb to burn for a reasonable length of time was Model No. 9, which had a carbonized cotton filament. Under the date 21 October 1879 he wrote in his notebook:

No 9 on from 1.30 am till 3 pm – 13½ hours and was then raised to 3 gas jets for one hour then cracked glass and busted.

The lamp was patented on 1 November 1879, but it soon became apparent that the carbonized sewing-thread, which Edison was using for a filament, was not sufficiently durable for constant burning. Early in 1880, therefore, he switched to carbonized paper filaments, and these proved sufficiently long lasting to be used in the first commercially produced lamps, manufactured in October (*see below*).

Joseph Swan made the first public announcement of his incandescent electric lamp at a meeting of the Newcastle upon Tyne Chemical Society on 18 December 1878. In the course of his lecture he displayed a bulb containing a $\frac{1}{25}$in carbon conductor, but was unable to show it in operation, as it had already burned out through excessive current being applied in a laboratory test. A similar lamp was shown alight during another lecture that he gave at Sunderland on 18 January 1879. Although this demonstration took place some 10 months before Edison's successful laboratory experiment, it cannot be regarded as more than a preliminary stage in the progress towards the production of a marketable electric light bulb. Not until early in 1880 did Swan produce a true filament lamp, employing a carbonized cotton thread similar to that used by Edison, but rather longer lasting. This was the subject of a patent taken out on 27 November 1880, and under which Swan lamps were subsequently manufactured.

The first commercially produced electric light bulbs were manufactured at the Edison Lamp Works, established at Menlo Park on 1 October 1880. There were originally some 200 stages in the manufacturing process of each individual light bulb, and the fact that most of them had to be performed by hand partly accounts for the high retail cost of $2.50 per lamp. Prices were gradually reduced and demand increased accordingly, though the domestic market remained small before household electricity-supply became generally available in the larger cities during the 1890s.
GB: Commercial production of electric light bulbs was begun by the Swan Electric Light Co with the opening of a factory at Benwell, just outside Newcastle upon Tyne, early in 1881. Glassblowers were recruited from Germany, since men sufficiently skilled for the delicate process of blowing glass bulbs could not be found in England. The cost per bulb was originally 25s retail, but by 1883 this had been reduced to 5s.

See also Christmas Tree; Electric Sign; Electric Torch; Fluorescent Lighting; Motor car with Electric Lamps.

The first
ELECTRIC LAMPS: DOMESTIC INSTALLATION
permanent, was made by Moses G. Farmer, a professor at the Naval Training Station at Newport, R.I., who lighted the parlour of his home at 11 Pearl Street, Salem, Mass., with a platinum burner lamp of his own invention in July 1859. It was powered from a galvanic battery located in the cellar of the house.
GB: The distinction of being the first to light the home with electricity is

usually given to Col R.E.B. Crompton, who installed arc-lamps, powered from Grove cells, at his home in Porchester Gardens, London, in December 1879. According to a report in the trade journal *The Electrician* for 12 July 1879, however, Mr H.W. Tyler was then in process of having arc-lamps rigged up at his country-seat, Wyvenhoe Hall, nr Colchester, Essex.

The first house in Britain to be lighted with incandescent electric lamps was Mr W.G. Armstrong's country-mansion, Cragside, at Rothbury, Northumberland in December 1880. Those in the reception-rooms were protected by glass globes, taking the form of hanging ceiling-lights, wall-brackets and table-lamps. The last were converted kerosene lamps. Elsewhere the Swan bulbs hung naked, presenting, it was said, 'a very beautiful and star-like appearance'. The Cragside installation is also notable as the first hydro-electric plant in Britain, as the Siemens generator was driven by a small waterfall at the back of the house.

The first house in Britain lit with electricity throughout was Berechurch Hall, near Colchester, in 1882. Octavius Coope, for whom the house had just been built, made a careful calculation of the relative costs of installing gas or electricity. In an age before gas was piped into the country, and before any central electricity-supply, the country-house owner who was not content to rely on oil-lamps as his sole means of household illumination was faced with the choice of building either a private gasworks or his own power-station. The big advantage of electricity for those with their own generators was that it was much cheaper to produce than gas, for Coope estimated that Berechurch could be lit for just over £200 p.a., whereas the cost of gas would have been closer to £400.

High initial outlay was perhaps the principal factor militating against the widespread adoption of the new form of illumination, but not the only one. Lord Ernest Hamilton recalled in his memoirs that electric light was considered 'insufferably vulgar' in its early days. Even as late as 1921 scarcely 12% of the households in Britain were electrically lit, and not until the following decade had the majority of dwellings been wired, the proportion rising from 32% in 1931 to 65% in 1938. Complete changeover to electricity cannot be said to have been achieved before 1961, when 96% of households were on mains supply.

The first
ELECTRIC LAMPS USED FOR STREET LIGHTING

were arc-lamps installed experimentally in le quai Conti and la place de la Concorde, Paris, by Messrs Deleuil et Archereau in 1841.

GB: An arc-lamp was erected on the north tower of Hungerford Bridge by W.E. Staite in 1849, and burned for 3hr nightly over a two-week experimental period.

STREET LIT PERMANENTLY BY ELECTRICITY: the first was la rue Impériale in Lyons, where arc-lamps were installed by Messrs Lacassagne et Thiers in 1857. Little further progress appears to have been made in France until l'avenue de l'Opéra, Paris, was electrically lit in June 1878.

GB: The Société Générale d'Electricité de Paris received a contract from the Metropolitan Board of Works to light the Victoria Embankment in 1878, and 20 Jablochkoff Candles were switched on for the first time on 13 December of that year. Power was supplied from a Gramme dynamo located in a small shed near by, the current being carried by multi-core underground cable. This is believed to have been the first time that electric cables were laid below the surface of the street in Britain.

TOWN IN WHICH ELECTRIC LIGHTING ENTIRELY REPLACED GAS: the first was Wabash, Ind., which was illuminated by four 4,000-candle-power Brush arc-lights, each suspended 50ft above the business quarter, on 31 March 1880.

INCANDESCENT ELECTRIC STREET LAMPS were first installed at Newcastle upon Tyne by Messrs Mawson & Swan in 1881. The first five lamp-standards, three in Mosley Street, one in Pilgrim Street and another in Grey Street, were illuminated on 11 April. The *Newcastle Daily Chronicle* reported enthusiastically, noting that 'the shadows generally lurking around the ordinary street lamp-posts [were] palpably absent'.

The first
ELECTRIC MOTOR

capable of practical application was patented by Thomas Davenport of Rutlant, Vt. on 25 February 1837. Davenport put two 50lb motors of his own design to work the same year, one for drilling holes up to $\frac{1}{4}$in diameter in iron and steel, the other for turning hardwood. Each incorporated an electromagnet and operated at a speed of 450rpm. In 1839 he built a larger motor to drive a rotary printing-press, which he used to print the first electrical journal in the USA, *The Electro-Magnet and Mechanics Intelligencer*, published 18 January 1840.

GB: The first practical electric motors were built by Robert Davidson of Aberdeen in 1839. Prof. Forbes, also of Aberdeen, wrote an account of them in a letter to the *Philosophical Magazine* the same year:

> *. . . he has an arrangement by which with only two electro-magnets and less than one square foot of zinc surface, a lathe is driven with such velocity as to be capable of turning small articles. Second, he had another arrangement by which, with the same small extent of galvanic power, a small carriage is driven on which two persons were carried along a coarse wooden floor of a room.*

The industrial application of battery-powered electric motors was severely limited since, as the Editor of the *Philosophical Magazine* pointed out in 1850, electric power from this source was about 25 times more expensive than steam-power.

The first use of electricity to provide mechanical power on a considerable scale for industrial purposes was made at the Paris factory of the Société Gramme in, or shortly before, 1873. All the machinery was driven by a motor supplied with current from a Gramme dynamo.

Davenport's electric motor, 1837

The first miniature electric motors were made by Thomas Alva Edison at Menlo Park, N.J. in 1880 to drive an electric pen he had designed for producing punctured copying stencils. The motor measured approx. 1 × 1½in, and operated at approx. 4,000rpm to drive a vibrating needle in the pen-holder that would pick out letters in punctured dots. It was powered by a minute two-cell battery. Edison's electric pen provided a successful method of duplicating multiple copies of manuscripts before the typewriter stencil rendered it obsolete (*see* Duplicating Machine). Manufacture was undertaken by the Western Electric Co and at least 60,000 miniature motors and pens were sold for use in banks and offices.

The first
ELECTRIC MOTOR HORN
manufactured in Britain was the Wagner Electric Motor Horn, produced by United Motor Industries Ltd at Sherbourne Works, Coventry, and advertised for sale for the first time in *The Motor* for 28 August 1906. According to the company's own sales literature, the horn was an instantaneous success. 'It has taken the Town by storm,' they announced jubilantly in September. 'Sales are positively embarrassing.' The *Autocar*, in a test report published the same month, said that the Wagner Horn could be heard at a distance of 800yd, compared with the 400–500yd range of an ordinary bulb horn. Among the earliest users were Cecil Edge and S.F. Edge, who had electric horns fitted to their Napier cars.

The first
ELECTRIC OVEN
was installed at the Hotel Bernina in Samaden, Switzerland in 1889. No record survives of the inventor, but *The Electrician* reported, in August of that year, that it contained German silver resistance coils, and that it had been found capable of performing all the normal cooking operations. The Hotel Bernina had its own electric power-supply generated from a dynamo driven by a waterfall. As a good deal of power was going to waste during the day, the proprietor hit upon the idea of utilizing the current for cooking when it was not required for lighting.

The first electric oven produced for sale was manufactured by the Carpenter Electric Heating Manufacturing Co of St Paul, Minn., in 1891. It was described by the New York trade journal *The Electrical Engineer* as follows:

The baking oven is 18 ins long, 14 ins high, and 12 ins deep, made of well-seasoned white pine, lined with asbestos felt, and bright tin. There are two sheet-iron shelves in each oven, and also two resistance plates on the bottom and one on the top, connected with a switch on the outside of the oven, so that two temperatures may be obtained. These ovens have a small glass window in each door, so that the baking can be watched. Each resistance plate consumes about five amperes on 110 volts, and it has been found that it only requires from 12–15 minutes, at a maximum temperature, to heat the oven to 250 °F. The current can then be turned off and the baking continued.

GB: The first-recorded demonstration of electric cookery took place at the Eldon Dining Hall in Newcastle upon Tyne on 11 March 1892. It was about this time that a Mr Hammer arrived from the USA with a quantity of the Carpenter Co's apparatus, and so it is possible that this was the equipment used. The meal prepared consisted of cutlets.

The first electric oven manufactured in Britain was designed by H.J. Dowsing (*see also* Motor Car: Electric Starter) of Crompton & Co, electrical engineers of Chelmsford, and marketed in January 1893. The electrical system employed was based on the one used in the Carpenter ovens, which Dowsing had demonstrated at the Crystal Palace the previous April. The earliest surviving Crompton catalogue, dated 1897, lists three different models for general use at prices of £10–£16, and a small, circular table-model with a hot-plate for £5 10s. An accompanying note directs that 'the oven should be switched on full for half an hour before required for use'. The high cost of electricity at the time must have made this a serious drawback. Even *The Electrician*, which championed the idea of electric cooking, had to admit that it was two or three times cheaper to cook a meal by gas, and noted the fact that electric stoves cost a great deal more to buy and install than the gas equivalent. It was not until 1906 that electric cooking became economically competitive with gas, and then in certain areas of London only. From 1 January of that year, the Westminster Electric Supply Corp and the St James's and Pall Mall Electric Light Co both reduced their charges for electricity for cooking and heating, from 3d to 1d a unit. The real breakthrough for electricity in the kitchen came only with the massive housing campaign of the 1930s, sales of electric cookers rising from 75,000 in 1930, to 240,000 in 1935. By the outbreak of World War II, the total number of electric cookers in use in Britain numbered nearly 1½ million, compared with approximately 9 million gas ovens.

The first
ELECTRIC POWER-STATION
providing current for both public and domestic use was the Central Power Station at Godalming, Surrey, a hydro-electric installation built by Messrs Calder & Barrett at Pullman's Leather Mill on the River Wey and operated by them with effect from 1 October 1881. The generating equipment was supplied by Messrs Siemens Bros, who took over the running of the power-station the following year. The principal customer was the Godalming Town Council, the instigator of the project, which contracted with Calder & Barrett to light the town for 12 months for £195. Ordinary gas standards were converted for use with electricity, and the cables were laid along the gutters of the streets. Little information is available about the domestic power-supply, except that it was stated that it could be provided 'nearly as cheaply as gas'. The fact that electricity was admitted to be more expensive, combined with the high cost and relatively short life of Swan bulbs (about 1,200hr), probably discouraged all but the more progressively minded rich, or shopkeepers in search of an attractive novelty, from going over to electricity. Eventually Siemens conducted a survey in the town to ascertain whether there was likely to be any marked increase in private business; finding the results anything but encouraging, they closed down the world's pioneer power-station on 1 May 1884.

The first electric power-station in London was established at 57 Holborn Viaduct, by the Edison Electric Light Co. It began serving the area between Holborn Circus and the Old Bailey with public power-supply for street lighting on 12 January 1882, and domestic current as from 12 April. In contrast with the rather lukewarm attitude of Godalming consumers, response from commercial undertakings on the Holborn Viaduct was enthusiastic and immediate. No less than 30 buildings were lit up with Edison incandescent bulbs on the first day of supply, including the GPO at St Martin le Grand, and such famous business houses as Negretti & Zambra, the photographers, the Vaseline Co, W.D. & H.O. Wills and the Coventry Machine Co. The London, Chatham & Dover Railway Station also shone forth, as did the City Temple, the first church in Britain illuminated by electricity, and the first two hotels in London to be lit by incandescent bulbs, Spiers & Pond's and the Imperial. Notable also were the first electrically lit pub, the Viaduct Tavern, and the first electrically lit restaurant, Spiers & Pond's, next door to their hotel.

Having established an impressive world lead in the provision of public electricity supply, Britain then promptly lost it through one of the most short-sighted and retrogressive pieces of legislation to reach the Statute Book during the later 19th century – the Electric Lighting Act 1882. This empowered local authorities to take over privately run power-stations operating in their area after only 21 years, which meant that it was virtually impossible for an electric company to recoup its capital and development costs. During the six years that the Act remained in force, not a single electric-supply undertaking began generating under the powers conveyed by a Board of Trade licence. Although the 21-year period was extended to a more liberal

42 years under an amending Act of 1888, even in 1890 such major urban centres as Manchester, Leeds, Edinburgh, Hull and Nottingham were without power-stations to provide a service for domestic consumers.
PUBLICLY OWNED ELECTRIC POWER-STATION: the first in Britain was installed in Bolton Road, Bradford by Messrs Siemens Bros on behalf of Bradford Corporation and began generating current for public supply on 20 September 1889.

The first
ELECTRIC SIGNS
were advertised by Willing's Electric Signs of King's Cross, London, in *The Electrician* for 31 December 1881, as being 'Suitable for signs, facias, window decorations, novelties, advertisements, etc.' During the course of 1882 Maj. W. J. Hammer displayed the word EDISON, spelt out in Edison bulbs that flashed on and off, above the Great Organ in the Crystal Palace at Sydenham. Another illuminated sign appeared over the entrance arch to the International Hygiene Exhibition in Berlin. Meanwhile in New York, Miner's Theater became the first to put its name up in lights.

In 1890 the first electric advertising sign in Piccadilly Circus, believed to have been for Bovril, was erected on the north-east side. A year later, Broadway was lit up with the legend 'Buy Homes on Long Island Swept by Ocean Breezes', a persuasive electrical message spelt out by Oriental & Manhattan Hotels, who were presumably diversifying. By 1906 there were 3,000 electric signs in Manhattan, most of them bedazzling the denizens of Broadway. G.K. Chesterton commented on the 'Great White Way' after visiting New York: 'What a glorious garden of wonders this would be, to anyone who was lucky enough to be unable to read.'

The first strip lighting capable of being twisted into words was Moore Tubing, developed by D. McFarlan Moore of the Moore Electric Co, London, and originally used for advertising signs in 1905. The earliest practical electric-discharge lamps, Moore Tubes, were filled with carbon dioxide or nitrogen and gave a good quality of light, but suffered from being expensive both to install and maintain. They were eventually superseded by neon lighting (*q.v.*), which was brighter and more economic to run.

The first
ELECTRIC TORCH
was a square 2-candlepower bull's-eye lantern, manufactured by the Bristol Electric Lamp Co in 1891. It weighed 2lb with battery. The first large order was from the Bristol General Omnibus Co, which purchased 60 for the use of their ticket inspectors early in 1892.
TUBULAR TORCH: the first was manufactured in 1898 by the American Electric & Novelty Manufacturing Co of New York (later the American Eveready Co). The first model put on sale had a cardboard tube with metal fittings, a brass reflector and no lens.
GB: The 'Ever Ready' Electric Torch No. 1 was advertised for sale by the British Mutoscope & Biograph Co of Great Windmill Street, London, at 18s in August 1900. Batteries, said to give 5,000 flashes, cost 1s 6d. The advertisers assured prospective purchasers that it could be lighted in a keg of gunpowder without any danger.

The first
ELEVATOR
(passenger) was installed in King Louis XV's private apartments in the Petite Cour du Roy at the Palace of Versailles in 1743. The King had provided a suite on the second floor for his mistress, Mme de Châteauroux, and the elevator was designed to give him access to her from his own apartment on the floor below. It was on the outside of the building, though within the privacy of a courtyard, and was entered by the King via his balcony. The mechanism consisted of a carefully balanced arrangement of weights inside one of the chimneys, so that the 'Flying Chair', as it was known, could be raised or lowered by hand with the minimum of effort.
GB: The earliest-recorded passenger elevator was installed at the Coliseum, a panorama building designed by Decimus Burton, and erected in Regent's Park, London for a successful showman called William George Horner in 1829. Panoramas were a popular entertainment in which a vast concave scene, painted on a canvas extending beyond the angle of vision, was given an illusion of depth by the trick effects of light. Horner's establishment opened with a 'View of London from the Top of St Paul's'. Spectators had first to ascend into a replica of the dome of the Cathedral, from whence they were able to look down in wonder at the majestic city spread before them. That there was an alternative to an exhausting climb is known from a passage contained in the *Visitor's Guide to London* published by N. Whittock in 1835. The reader is informed:

Those that wish to ascend to the panorama without the trouble of walking up stairs, may, by paying sixpence, ascend by the moving apartment, which is a small circular room, in which six or eight persons are comfortably seated. . . .

A descriptive booklet of the Coliseum issued some years later gives a further account of the elevator, now enlarged, after the building had been 're-embellished' in 1848.

The Ascending Room, capable of containing 10 or 12 persons . . . is raised by secret machinery to the required elevation. This chamber is now entirely altered, being decorated in the Elizabethan style, and the light admitted through a stained glass ceiling.

Although nothing positive is known about the nature of this 'secret machinery', it seems probable that it was based on Horner's patent of 27 January 1818 for a 'Machine for acquiring a very high mechanical power in a small compass, with little friction, and without the possibility of running amain when employed in raising or lowering weights.' Harder to

The first office block with a group of elevators – the Boreel Building, New York, 1879

account for is the reason why his successful invention of the passenger elevator attracted so little attention, despite the fact that the model at the Coliseum appears to have continued in service until the building burned down in 1875.

PASSENGER ELEVATOR INSTALLED IN A DEPARTMENT STORE: the first was supplied by Elisha Graves Otis for the five-storey building of E.V. Haughwout & Co, Broadway, New York on 23 March 1857. Otis was the first manufacturer of passenger elevators, having previously been engaged in the production of freight hoists at his Yonkers, N.Y. elevator plant. The price quoted for the E.V. Haughwout elevator was $300.

HOTEL ELEVATOR: the first was a vertical screw-operated model installed at the six-storey Fifth Avenue Hotel, New York by O. Tuft of Boston on 23 August 1859.

OFFICE BLOCK EQUIPPED WITH A PASSENGER ELEVATOR: the first was the Equitable Life Assurance Society Building, New York in 1868.

GROUP OF HIGH-SPEED PASSENGER ELEVATORS: the first was installed at the Boreel Building, New York City by the Otis Elevator Co in September 1879 and consisted of four units designed to be operated simultaneously. The introduction of high-speed passenger elevators had a profound effect on town-planning in the USA and ultimately in most other industrialized nations, as it meant that cities could grow upwards rather than simply outwards. The building of skyscrapers, which would have been technically feasible many years earlier, was necessarily delayed until elevators could replace stairways.

ELECTRIC PASSENGER ELEVATOR: the first was built by Messrs Siemens & Halske for service in a 66ft-high observation tower at the Mannheim Industrial Exposition of 1880. The lift was designed to operate at a speed of ½ metre per second. It carried 8,000 passengers without incident during the month of the Exposition.

The first
EMPLOYMENT AGENCY

was the Bureau d'Adresse, opened by Théophraste Renaudot at the sign of the Grand-Coq in la rue de la Calandre, Paris on 4 July 1631. A registration fee of 3 sous was charged to employers seeking staff, and likewise to prospective employees seeking engagement, unless they were too poor to pay, in which case the service was free. Renaudot's intentions were principally philanthropic and he paid particular attention to the needs of clients up from the country for the first time. In 1639 the Paris Police issued an Ordinance to the effect that all unemployed strangers arriving in the capital must register with the Bureau d'Adresse within 24 hours on pains of being sent to the galleys for vagabondage. The employment section of the Bureau dealt chiefly in vacancies for domestic servants and shop assistants; in addition there were a number of other departments dealing in houses for sale and rent, furniture and effects, travelling arrangements, etc.

GB: The first employment agency was the Office of Entries, established in King Street, London, by newspaper-proprietor Henry Walker on 12 August 1649. Walker has been described as a former 'ironmonger, preacher and seditious libeller', but at the time when he opened his agency he was running a newspaper called *Perfect Occurrences*, which he used as a medium for advertising job opportunities. In this way he offered to accommodate the 'Many that desire to be entertained into gentlemen's services' and 'Those that are well affected and desire parochiall charges'. The fee was 4d to both employer and employee. Like Renaudot's agency, on which it was modelled, Walker's Office of Entries undertook a comprehensive range of agency business in addition to that of employment. It does not seem to have met with the same success as its French counterpart, however, since there is no record of its continued existence after *Perfect Occurrences* ceased publication in October 1649. A number of other 'Intelligence Offices' sprang up to replace it, but they soon earned a reputation for sharp practice and exploitation of the unwary in sad contrast to Renaudot's lofty ideals.

A notable exception to this low standard was the agency conducted by the apothecary John Houghton FRS (*see also* Weather Forecast) in the 1690s. His lists of vacancies, which happily survive, provide the only detailed evidence of the kind of jobs offered through a reputable employment agency during the 17th century. 'I want a negro man that is a good house carpenter and a good shoemaker' runs one entry, while another says: 'I want a pritty boy to wait on a gentleman who will take care of him. . . .' Others are for 'a good usher's place in a grammar school', 'a young man that can read and write, mow and roll a lawn garden, use a gun at a deer, and understand country sports' and for 'several curious women that would wait on ladies to be housekeepers'.

The first
ENCYCLOPEDIA

titled as such was Paul Scalich's *Encyclopaedia, seu Orbis disciplinarum*, Basle, 1559. The literal meaning of the term is 'learning within the circle'.

ENCYCLOPEDIA WITH ENTRIES ARRANGED IN ALPHABETICAL ORDER: the first was Antoine Furetière's *Dictionnaire Universel*, Paris, 1690.

ENGLISH ENCYCLOPEDIA: the first was John Harris's *Lexicon Technicum; or, An Universal English Dictionary of Arts and Sciences*, London, 1704.

ENCYCLOPEDIA CONTAINING ENTRIES FROM OUTSIDE CONTRIBUTORS: the first, compiled under the direction of specialist editors, was Johann Zelder's monumental 64-volume *Universal-Lexicon*, published in Leipzig from 1731 to 1750. Zelder was a bookseller by trade, without patronage or additional source of income. His vast work was only completed when a lottery was held in Leipzig to provide him with funds. Even then he remained in such straitened circumstances that he was unable to afford a complete set of his own encyclopedia, and was obliged to supervise the later volumes without reference to vols XIII and XIV.

ENCYCLOPAEDIA BRITANNICA: the first edition was produced by Andrew Bell, Colin Macfarquhar and William Smellie and published in 6d parts at Edinburgh from December 1768 to 1771. One notable entry read: 'WOMAN. The female of man. See HOMO.'

The first
ENVELOPE

known to have been used in Britain was used to enclose a letter addressed to Sir William Turnbull, Secretary of State, by Sir James Ogilvie on 16 May 1696. It measured only 4¼ × 3in, and is now preserved at the State-paper Office. Envelopes were very seldom used before the introduction of uniform postage, as they were charged as an extra sheet.

The first manufacturer was S.K. Brewer, a Brighton stationer who began producing envelopes in limited quantities *c.* 1830. These proved sufficiently popular with the modish Brighton visitors, who apparently did not object to paying double postage, for Brewer to place an order with the London firm of Dobbs and Co when he was no longer able to meet the demand by his own efforts. There is no evidence to suggest that the idea caught on elsewhere at this time.

PREPAID ENVELOPES were first issued by the New South Wales Post Office on 1 November 1838. The embossed stamp was an interesting forerunner of adhesive postage stamps, and was the first of the modern methods of indicating prepayment. The envelopes were sold for 1s 3d a

Stamp used on the first prepaid envelops, Sydney, 1838

dozen and were for use within the Sydney district post. The rate for pay-on-delivery letters not enclosed in envelopes was 2d.

GB: The first prepaid envelopes for the use of the general public were introduced to coincide with the issue of adhesive postage stamps on 6 May 1840. The face of the envelope bore a curious design executed by William Mulready RA. This depicted Britannia dispatching winged messengers to the various peoples of the earth, including Indians, Chinese, Negroes, Redskins and Pilgrim Fathers, as well as an Eskimo being drawn across the ice by a reindeer. This seemingly harmless allegory, though a trifle inappropriate for an envelope that was intended only for inland mail, could hardly have deserved the torrent of ridicule and abuse that rained down upon it. Criticism varied from that of Henry Cole, who stated that it was unsuitable 'for a dry commercial use in which sentiment has no part', to a waggish complaint that Mulready's four winged messengers could only muster seven legs between them. The ill-fated Mulready envelope was withdrawn after a brief and inglorious career, and as several million had been printed in expectancy of universal acclaim, a special machine had to be constructed by the Post Office for their destruction.

The first embossed envelopes were issued by the GPO on 29 January 1841. *GUMMED ENVELOPES* were introduced in Britain in 1844, and according to the testimony of a memoir written some 40 years later, provoked a number of affairs of honour precipitated by recipients who asserted that a man who sends his spittle through the post to another must expect to be called upon to give satisfaction in the traditional manner.

The first
EQUALS SIGN
denoted by = was used by Robert Record, Fellow of All Souls, Oxford, in his algebra text *The Whetstone of Witte*, London, 1557. He explained that he had chosen this particular symbol because 'noe 2 thynges can be moare equalle' than two parallel straight lines.

The first
ERASER OR INDIA-RUBBER
is first mentioned in English by Dr Joseph Priestley in his *Familiar Introduction to the Theory and Practice of Perspective*, London, 1770. In an addendum he wrote:

Since this work was printed off, I have seen a substance excellently adapted to the purpose of wiping from a paper the marks of a black-lead pencil. It must, therefore, be of singular use to those who practice drawing. It is sold by Mr Nairne, Mathematical Instrument Maker, opposite the Royal Exchange. He sells a cubical piece of about half an inch for three shillings, and he says it will last for several years.

Mr Nairne does not appear to have been in any way exceptional in his prices, for five years later stationers were reported to be charging a guinea an ounce for the rare substance. Although the French term *caoutchouc* persisted in Britain until the 1850s, an encyclopedia of 1778 notes that it 'is popularly called rubber or lead eater'.

The first
ESCALATOR
was the Reno Inclined Elevator, patented by Jesse W. Reno of New York on 15 March 1892, and first installed at the Old Iron Pier on Coney Island in the autumn of 1896. The Reno escalator consisted of an inclined endless-belt conveyor made up of wooden slats each 10cm wide and 60cm long. The grooved slats had rubber-covered cleats running in a forward direction to give the necessary grip and passed under combplates at either end of the belt, as in a modern escalator. An electric motor drove the conveyor and its plush-covered rubber handrails at a speed of about 1½mph.

The first practical moving staircase (i.e. with flat steps) was patented by an American inventor called Charles A. Wheeler on 2 August 1892. This did not have a comb-plate landing device, and passengers had to get on and off via a side entrance. Although Wheeler's escalator was never actually built, his patent was purchased in 1898 by Charles D. Seeberger, who incorporated its flat-step feature into an improved design of his own. Seeberger's prototype model was built by the Otis Elevator Co, with whom he made a manufacturing agreement, and brought into operation at their Yonkers, N.Y. factory on 9 June 1899.

The first Seeberger escalator in public use was installed at the Paris Exposition in 1900. It was brought back to America the following year and re-erected at Gimbel's Department Store on 8th Street, Philadelphia, where it continued to operate until 1939.

The first step-type escalator with a comb-plate landing device was the Otis 'L' which, embodying the salient features of both the Reno and Seeberger models, was introduced commercially in 1921. Since that date there have been no radical departures in fundamental escalator design.

GB: The first escalator in Britain was installed at Harrods in November 1898 at the instigation of the Manager, Richard Burbage, who had an unreasoning dislike of lifts. According to an entry made in his diary, this 40ft-long Reno Inclined Elevator could accommodate 4,000 passengers an hour. An attendant was positioned at the top ready to dispense brandy or sal volatile gratuitously to those ladies and gentlemen who were overcome by the experience. Many Londoners who would never aspire to shopping at Harrods had their first opportunity to ride on an escalator when another Reno Inclined Elevator was set up at the Crystal Palace, Sydenham the following year, carrying fare-paying passengers at a penny a time. It was celebrated in a popular music-hall song by W.P. Dempsey called 'Up the Sliding Stairs'.

The first moving staircases in Britain were two 40ft Seeberger escalators, connecting the District and Piccadilly

Earls Court Station escalator, 1911

platforms at Earls Court Underground Station, opened for public use on 4 October 1911. Notices on the wall requested passengers: 'Please do not sit on the stairs. Step off with the left foot first.' Evidently the District Railway was uncertain about the public's willingness to entrust itself to anything so novel, because they engaged a man with a wooden leg called 'Bumper' Harris to ride up and down the escalator all day to instil confidence into the faint hearted. In addition a porter was detailed to stand on the platform and announce in a loud voice on the arrival of each train: 'This way to the moving staircase! The only one of its kind in London! Now running!' Apparently these blandishments were unnecessary, for the *Illustrated London News* reported: 'Passengers on their way to the City have been seen to leave a train, go up with the stairs and down with the stairs – and catch the next train.'

The first
ESCORT AGENCY
was opened in London by Mrs Horace Farquharson in 1937. Rates varied according to conditions of hire, which were always of the utmost propriety, but the younger son of a peer could be obtained for £3 an evening. Mrs Farquharson's service included presentations at Court, for which the sum of £5,000 would secure the patronage of a Duchess, and £3,000 that of a Marchioness.

The first
ESPERANTO
textbook was *Lingvo Internacia*, published in Russian by Dr Ludovic Zamenhof, a Polish oculist, under the pseudonymn 'Dr Esperanto' (i.e. one who hopes) at Warsaw in 1887. Zamenhof was born in 1859 at Bielostock, a town populated by Russians, Poles, Germans and Jews. He himself was Jewish. At an early age he became concerned at the bad relations that existed between these language groups and determined to further the brotherhood of man by devising a universal tongue, to be learned as a second language by all who shared his ideal. This task he began while a 14-year-old schoolboy at the Classical Academy in Warsaw; by 1878, when he was 19 years of age, he had progressed far enough to start instructing some six or seven of his friends in its rudiments. A meeting was held at his home on 17 December of that year for the purpose of celebrating the birth of the new language in speech and song. This group of pioneer Esperantists soon fell away when its members found themselves exposed to the ridicule of their elders, and Zamenhof was left to continue the work alone.

After many set-backs his work was published in a slender 40-page volume, the result of nearly 15 years' labour. It contained a declaration that the author renounced all personal rights in his work, since 'an international language, like a national one, is common property'.

Early adherents of Esperanto were chiefly Germans, Swedes and Russians. Among the last was numbered Count Leo Tolstoy, who claimed that with the aid of Zamenhof's book he had learned to read Esperanto within the space of two hours. As the movement spread westward it found its strongest support in France, where the first national association was formed in 1898.

GB: The first exponent of Esperanto in Britain was an Irish-born career diplomat and linguist, Richard H. Geoghegan, who translated the Esperanto instruction book into English. It appeared in 1889, Polish, French and German versions having succeeded the original Russian edition in the interim.

The first organized group of Esperantists in Britain was the Society for the Learning and Propagation of Esperanto, founded by Yorkshire journalist Joseph Rhodes at Keighley on 7 November 1902. The British Esperanto Association was established in 1904.

The first
EXCLAMATION MARK
used in print appears in the *Catechism of Edward VI*, printed by J. Day, London, 1553. Day is more often remembered for the motto he used in conjunction with his printer's device: 'Arise, for it is Day.'

The first
FAN CLUB
was The Keen Order of Wallerites, founded in London by fans of the popular actor-manager Lewis Waller. It was in existence by 1902 and is thought to have been established a year, or possibly two years, earlier. Members wore a badge showing on one side Waller in powdered wig as Monsieur Beaucaire and, on the other, his favourite flower – somewhat inappropriately for so masculine an actor – a pansy. The club colours were blue and mauve, Waller's racing colours. The behaviour of adherents towards Mr Waller himself was strictly controlled by the regulations of the society, which forbade anyone but the Secretary to address him personally, but members were expected to gather in force to support their hero on every first night. A rival fan club, the True-to-Trees, was founded to pay honour to Beerbohm Tree.

Members of the Keen Order did not refer to themselves as 'fans', since the term was at that time unknown in England. In the USA, however, it had been used as early as 1889, the first recorded appearance in print being a reference to 'Kansas City baseball fans' in the 26 March issue of the *Kansas Times and Star*. Its earliest recorded use in Britain was by the *Daily Express* in 1914, referring to 'First League football fans'. The word came into general currency the following year, applied to film-goers.

The first
FASHION PHOTOGRAPHS
appeared in the Parisian fashion journal *La Mode Pratique* in December 1891. The photographs were tinted by hand and reproduced by a crude two-colour process. The following year a London edition of the magazine, titled *Fashions of Today*, carried the first fashion photographs to be published in Britain. Neither journal can be considered a leader in its field and there was little further development until the founding of *Les Modes* in 1901. Not only did the photography in this magazine show a marked improvement over earlier efforts, but the attitudes of the models, according to Doris Langley Moore in her *Fashions through Fashion Plates*, 'show a high degree of professionalism'.

The first fashion photographs taken by a photographer of international renown were a series of 13 studies of Paul Poiret creations by the Luxemburgeois-American, Edward Steichen. These were reproduced in the April 1911 issue of *Art et Décoration*. They mark the point at which fashion photography began to develop into an art in its own right and ceased to be a cheap substitute for drawings.

The first
FIELD-MARSHALS
were George, Earl of Orkney, Governor of Edinburgh Castle, and John, 2nd Duke of Argyll, destined, according to Pope, 'to shake alike the senate and the field'. They were elevated to the newly created rank by George II on 12 and 14 January 1736, respectively.

Prior to this date the most senior commanders in the British Army were known by the title of 'Captain-General'. The designation 'Field-Marshal' was borrowed from the State of Hanover, which had instituted the rank of *Feld-marschall* the previous year. *FIELD-MARSHAL TO RISE FROM THE RANKS:* the first was Sir William Robertson Bart, GCB, GCMB, KCVO, DSO, who took the Queen's Shilling at Worcester on 13 November 1877 and was posted to the 16th (Queen's) Lancers at Aldershot four days later.

Robertson was the youngest son of the village tailor at Wellbourn, Lincolnshire. He left school at the age of 12, and had become in turn a gardener's boy and a footman before enlisting. When his mother heard that he had joined the Army, she wrote: 'I will name it to no one. I would rather bury you than see you in a red coat.'

Having climbed to the rank of Troop Sergeant-Major, he was gazetted 2nd Lieutenant in the 3rd Dragoon Guards on 27 June 1888.

Robertson became the first officer from the ranks to enter the Staff College in January 1897, and after service in the Boer War was appointed head of the Foreign Section of Intelligence. Promoted General in June 1916, he served as Chief of the Imperial General Staff for the remainder of the war, and after the Armistice as Commander-in-Chief, British Army of the Rhine. On 29 March 1920, at the recommendation of the Secretary of State for War, he was elevated to the rank of Field-Marshal after 42 years' service in the Regular Army.

The first
FILM (MOTION PICTURE)
process was developed by the French-born inventor Louis Aimé Augustin Le Prince, who began experimenting with moving photographic images at the Institute for the Deaf, Washington Heights, New York, where his wife was employed as a teacher of art. His daughter, Miss M. Le Prince, claims to have seen the dim outlines of moving figures projected on a whitewashed wall at the Institute in 1885. In November 1886 Le Prince applied for an American patent for

The successive production by means of a photographic camera of a number of images of the same object or objects in motion and reproducing the same in the order of taking by means of a 'projector' . . . with one or more intermittently operated film drums.

Although the US patent in respect of an 'Apparatus for producing Animated Pictures' was granted on 10 January 1888, the part of the specification referring to cameras and projectors with a single lens was disallowed on the questionable grounds that it

The one-lens camera used by Le Prince, 1888

infringed Dumont's British patent of 1861. In fact this related only to an arrangement of glass plates to form the facets of a prismatic drum, and had nothing to do with the reproduction of moving images on a screen. As it stood, Le Prince's US patent covered only a more complex 16-lens device. Consequently, many film historians have discounted his claim to have developed a practical single-lens cinécamera despite the accumulation of evidence in his favour. The following is a summary of the points made by E. Kilburn Scott in an article published in the May 1931 issue of the *Photographic Journal*:

(*a*) Miss M. Le Prince stated that she had clear recollection of her father working with a single-lens camera-projector at the Institute for the Deaf between 1885 and 1887, when the family removed to Leeds, England. The individual frames of the films taken during this period were about 1½in square.

(*b*) Le Prince's British patent, issued on 16 November 1888, covered both a single-lens camera and a single-lens projector.

(*c*) In an affidavit sworn on 21 April 1931, Frederick Mason, a woodworker of Leeds, declared that he had assisted in the construction of a single-lens camera in the summer of 1888, which he described thus:

The camera has two lenses, one being for taking the photograph and the other for the view finder. The gate mechanism behind the lens is constructed to hold the film firmly in position during exposure, and then to momentarily release it while being drawn upward without it being scratched. The intermittent movement consists of a toothed cam which engages with a projection on the side of the top reel, the latter pulling the film through the gate and also winding it up.

The handle projecting from the side of the camera operates the mechanism through gear wheels. A brass shutter revolves in front of the lens which has in it an adjustable diaphragm. Turning the handle at the proper rate enables pictures to be taken at the desired speed.

(*d*) Two fragments of film taken with this camera survive, and afford the earliest existing evidence that Le Prince had succeeded in making motion pictures. The first was taken in the garden of Le Prince's father-in-law, Mr Joseph Whitley, at Roundhay, Leeds and was labelled at a later date by the inventor's son Adolphe:

Portion of a series taken early in October, 1888, by the second one-lens camera. Le Prince's mother-in-law in this picture died October 24, 1888. Le Prince's eldest son is also in the picture, as is his father-in-law. Taken from 10 to 12 a second. There was no trial of speed contemplated here.

The second fragment, taken from the window of Hicks Bros, ironmongers, at the south-east corner of Leeds Bridge, is labelled:

Portion of a series taken by Le Prince with his second one-lens camera in October, 1888. A view of the moving traffic on Leeds Bridge, England, taken at 20 pictures a second in poor light. His eldest son was with him when he took the picture..

(*e*) Commenting on the above film, Le Prince's mechanic James W. Longley indicated that a projector had already been completed at this time:

Leeds Bridge – where the tram horses were seen moving over it and all the other traffic as if you was on the bridge yourself. I could even see the smoke coming out of a man's pipe, who was lounging on the bridge. Mr Augustin Le Prince was ready for exhibiting the above mentioned machine in public. We had got the machine perfect for delivering the pictures on the screen.

According to the testimony of Adolphe Le Prince there were two projectors built, one with three lenses in 1888–9 and a single-lens apparatus in 1889. The former is known from a diagram of Longley's to have incorporated the use of a Maltese cross to secure intermittent picture shift.

The film used by Le Prince for the Roundhay and Leeds Bridge sequences was sensitized paper in rolls 2⅛in wide.

In the autumn of 1889 he began using Eastman celluloid roll film, which had just been introduced into Britain. This provided a far more suitable support material and it seems likely that Le Prince was ready to start the commercial development of his motion-picture film process by the beginning of 1890. A new projector was built so that a demonstration could be given before M. Mobisson, the Secretary of the Paris Opéra. On 16 September 1890 Le Prince boarded a train at Dijon bound for Paris with his apparatus and films. He never arrived. No trace of his body or his equipment was ever found and after exhaustive inquiries the police were able to offer no rational explanation of his disappearance. The mystery has never been solved.

At the same time as Le Prince was engaged on his experiments at Leeds, William Friese-Greene was conducting similar researches in London, but short lengths of his film that survive suggest that his camera was not capable of taking pictures at a speed sufficient to create an illusion of motion.

The first motion-picture film process to be developed commercially is generally attributed to Thomas Alva Edison, the American electrical engineer, who filed a caveat with the US Patent Office on 17 October 1888 for an optical phonograph. In this he proposed an apparatus for viewing in rapid succession a series of microphotographs wound round a glass cylinder. The idea was not a practical one. In January 1889 Edison assigned William Kennedy Laurie Dickson, an assistant at his laboratories in West Orange, N.J., to work on the development of what was to become the Kinetoscope, a film-viewing machine designed for use in amusement arcades. Dickson, the French-born son of English parents, had early training as a photographer and was better suited to this kind of research than his mentor, who knew little of optics. He abandoned the use of rectangular sheets of celluloid for camera-work, and tried the Eastman celluloid roll film. On finding this unsuitable, he substituted 50ft lengths of film produced by the firm of Merwin Hulbert. These long rolls were first purchased on 18 March 1891, which is the earliest date at which it seems likely that Dickson could have made successful films for viewing in the peep-show Kinetoscope apparatus. There is an oft-quoted claim that a film was projected on a screen in synchronization with a phonograph record for Edison's benefit on his return from visiting the Paris Exposition in October 1889. This, however, seems highly improbable in view of the lack of any references to the supposed projector in the very complete Edison archives for this period.

PUBLIC DISPLAY OF FILMS: the first showing took place at the Edison Laboratories in West Orange on 22 May 1891, when 147 representatives of the National Federation of Women's Clubs, having lunched with Mrs Edison at Glenmont, were taken over her husband's workshops and allowed to view the new Kinetoscope. The *Sun* newspaper reported:

The surprised and pleased clubwomen saw a small pine box standing on the floor. There were some wheels and belts near the box, and a workman who had them in charge. In the top of the box was a hole perhaps an inch in diameter. As they looked through the hole they saw the picture of a man. It was a most marvelous picture. It bowed and smiled and waved its hands and took off its hat with the most perfect naturalness and grace. Every motion was perfect . . .

The film used for this demonstration appears to have been taken with a horizontal-feed camera without sprockets. This would have been an imperfect apparatus at best, and it is not until October 1892 that there is evidence that Dickson had built an effective vertical-feed camera using perforated film. In that month the *Phonogram* published an illustration showing sequences from four films evidently taken with such a device. These included pictures of Dickson himself, together with his helper, William Heise, and also shots of fencers engaged in swordplay, and wrestlers. By this date, then, it can be positively asserted that Dickson had overcome all the obstacles that had stood in the way of making films suitable for commercial exhibition. He was to receive little thanks for his work. After Dickson had left West Orange in 1895, following a dispute with his employer, Edison steadfastly refused to concede that anyone but himself was responsible for bringing the invention to fruition. Most writers were content to accept Edison's own version of events until the appearance in 1961 of a painstaking work of scholarship titled *The Edison Motion Picture Myth*. The author, Gordon Hendricks, demonstrates by reference to the hitherto unpublished papers in the Edison archives that all the experimental work on the Kinetoscope was conducted by Dickson, or under his direction, and that Edison himself can be credited with little more than instigating the research programme and providing facilities for carrying it out.

COMMERCIAL PRESENTATION OF FILMS: the first showing took place at Holland Bros' Kinetoscope Parlor, 1155 Broadway, New York, which opened for business on 14 April 1894. The Kinetoscopes were arranged in two rows of five, and for 25c viewers were allowed to watch five films – to see all the films they had to pay double entrance money. The sum of $120 was taken the first day, which suggests that this first 'cinema audience' totalled nearly 500. The films, made in the Edison 'Black Maria' at West Orange (*see* Film Studio), were titled: *Sandow, Bertholdi (mouth support), Horse Shoeing, Bertholdi (table contortion), Barber Shop, Blacksmiths, Cock Fight, Highland Dance, Wrestling, Trapeze.*

The Edison Co had commenced the making of films for commercial exhibition the previous month, and was thus the first film production company in the world. The earliest subject that can be positively dated is the *Sandow* film, which, according to Gordon Hendricks, was made on 7 March 1894. Eugène Sandow was a professional strongman and may have been the first stage performer to appear before the film camera. Other celebrities who made films for Edison during 1894 were Annie Oakley, later to be immortalized by the musical based on her life, *Annie Get Your Gun*, and the legendary Buffalo Bill. The first English artistes to make their film début were two of George Edwardes's Gaiety Girls, Miss Murray and Miss Lucas, who were then appearing in a show at Daly's in New York, and consented to come out to West Orange to dance the *Pas Seul* before the camera.

The first catalogue of Edison films, issued by distributors Raff & Gammon at the end of 1894, listed 52 titles, at prices ranging from $10 for a *Marvellous Lady Contortionist*, to $100 for a five-round prize-fight shown in full.

GB: The first motion picture films presented commercially in Britain were shown at a converted store in Old Broad Street, London, where a Greek showman called George Trajedis installed six Kinetoscopes in October 1894. The films, obtained through Holland Bros in New York, included *Boxing Cats, The Barber Shop* and *A Shoeblack at Work*. The charge to viewers was 2d per film.

FILM PRESENTED PUBLICLY ON A SCREEN: the first was a short film titled *La Sortie des Ouvriers de l'Usine Lumière*, which was shown before the members of the Société d'Encouragement à l'Industrie Nationale by Auguste and Louis Lumière at 44 rue de Rennes, Paris, on 22 March 1895. The film, believed to have been taken by the Lumières in August or September 1894, showed workers leaving the Lumière factory at Lyons for their dinner-hour.

The first commercial presentation of a film on a screen took place in a converted store at 153 Broadway, New York on 20 May 1895, when a 4min film of a boxing-match, specially staged between 'Young Griffo' and 'Battling Charles Barnett', was shown before a paying audience by Maj. Woodville Latham, founder of the Lamda Co, the first film company in the world to be established as such. The projector was a primitive and imperfect machine called the 'Eidoloscope', designed for the Lamda Co by former Edison employee Eugène Lauste (*see also* Film, Sound). Although some authorities have cast doubt on whether the Eidoloscope was really capable of creating an illusion of movement on the screen, it seems that however imperfect these performances may have been, they must have attained sufficient technical competence for Latham to have gone on attracting an audience.

The first film performance before a paying audience in Europe was given by Max and Emil Skladanowsky with a projector of their own invention at the Berlin Wintergarten on 1 November 1895. The films were made up in endless bands and the action lasted only a few seconds before it was repeated. Taken at the rate of eight pictures a second, the films were flickering and jerky, but the fact that there was movement on the screen at all was sufficient for the Nazis to claim, some 40 years later, that Germany had given birth to the cinema industry ahead of any other country. In fact neither the work of Lauste and Latham in America, nor that of the Skladanowskys in Germany, was destined to have any lasting effect on the development of the cinema. It is generally agreed that the première of the Lumières' show, before a paying audience at the Grand Café, 14 boulevard des Capucines, Paris on 28 December 1895, marks the début of the motion picture as a regular entertainment medium. The Lumières were the first to build a completely satisfactory projector; they were also the first to license the manufacture of cinematograph equipment for sale, which was undertaken on their behalf by Jules Carpentier of Paris.

The Edison concern had failed meanwhile to produce an efficient projector. The Edison Vitascope, which made its début at Koster & Bial's Music Hall on Broadway on 23 April 1896, was the work of Thomas Armat, who was persuaded to allow his invention to be exploited under Thomas Edison's name.

GB: The practical development of the motion picture in Britain can be dated from the granting of a patent for a combined cinécamera and projector, with an appliance for loop-forming, to Birt Acres of the Northern Photographic Co, Hadley, Hertfordshire on 27 May 1895. Acres had been associated in this enterprise with another more celebrated film pioneer, Robert Paul, an optical-instrument maker of Hatton Garden. The claims later advanced by both men to have been the only inventor led to a certain amount of acrimony between them. Paul's interest in films was first aroused in October 1894, when he was approached by the Greek showman George Trajedis (*see above*) with a request to manufacture some Edison Kinetoscopes. This Paul agreed to do on learning that Edison had omitted to patent the machine in Britain. Since Edison's agents understandably refused to supply films for the pirated machines, Paul approached Acres with the suggestion that he should construct a camera so that they could make their own Kinetoscope subjects. Early in 1895 (probably February) Acres had the completed camera ready and, using film obtained from the American Celluloid Co of Newark, N.J., took some shots of the front of his house, Clovelly Cottage, Barnet, at the rate of 40 pictures a second. The original presentation of this film, at Paul's workshop in Hatton Garden, has often been described as the first occasion on which motion pictures were shown on a screen in Britain, but Acres has made it clear, in some manuscript notes now in the possession of the British Film Institute, that in fact it was displayed in a Kinetoscope viewer. For reasons unknown, it was not until August that Acres was able to use the Kineopticon projector for his first presentation of motion pictures on a screen, which took place in a coach-house at Wrotham Cottage, Barnet. By this time he had filmed the Oxford and Cambridge Boat-race and the Derby of 1895 (*see also* Film: Sporting Event), as well as the Kaiser opening the Kiel Canal (*see also* Film: Newsfilm), and it seems reasonable to assume that the programme was made up of these subjects.

The first public screening of motion pictures in Britain of which there is contemporary record was given before the Royal Photographic Society at its London headquarters by Birt Acres on 14 January 1896. The films shown consisted of the Epsom Derby and Kiel films noted above and in addition *The Serpentine Dance*, *Boxers*, *Breaking Waves*, *Three Skirt Dancers* and *The Boxing Kangaroo*.

Although this was the first public screening which can be definitely proved, Sidney Birt Acres has claimed that his father gave a 'semi-private performance' at the Assembly Rooms, New Barnet in August 1895, and a public performance before a paying audience at Barnet Town Hall later in the year. During the latter show Acres's assistant, Arthur Melbourne Cooper, is said to have blown a trumpet behind the screen during a film of the Barnet Militia – an early attempt at sound-effects. Melbourne Cooper himself is believed to have given a number of commercial film shows on his own account before the end of 1895. His wife Kate recalled that her first encounter with her future husband had been when as a child she attended a Christmas show which he gave at Welham Green Boys' School, North Mimms, supposedly in December 1895. The films included a man sawing wood, a harrow being driven across a field, a group of children coming out of school, a pillow-fight, the penny steamer at Westminster, Barnet Militia, the Changing of the Guard, a fire-engine answering a fire call, lady cyclists, a a comedy sequence showing two Chinamen on a park bench having their pigtails tied together, and another called *A Study in Black and White*, in which one man threw flour at another, who retaliated with soot. Mrs Melbourne Cooper recollected that her future husband instructed two of the boys in the audience to sit on the pressure bag through which gas was fed to the projector.

These claims apart, the earliest presentation before a paying audience of which contemporary record survives took place on 20 February 1896, when the French musician F. Trewey exhibited the Lumière Cinématographe at the Regent Street Polytechnic.

FILM PRODUCTION COMPANY: the first in Britain was established by Robert Paul, who issued his first catalogue of commercially made films for general distribution towards the end of 1896. This lists over 40 different films, though it omits *Rough Seas at Dover*, usually said to have been his first commercial production, and which Paul claimed had been made for him by Birt Acres as early as February 1895. The largest single category was of general-interest actualities, totalling 23 films, including two early examples of *cinéma-verité* – one of a child falling from a steam-launch and being rescued by a swimmer, and the other of a bookmaker's runner being arrested.

The only two acted films were comedies – one titled *2 a.m.*, and representing an erring husband (M. Paul Cierget) returning home at that hour to meet the displeasure of his wife (Mme Selwicke); the other called *The Soldier's Courtship* with Fred Storey in the name-part (*see* Film Actor).

See also Cinema.

The first
FILM ACTOR

The first motion picture film to involve the use of actors was a brief costume drama titled *The Execution of Mary Queen of Scots*, which was shot by Alfred Clark of Raff & Gammon, Kinetoscope proprietors, at West Orange, N.J. on 28 August 1895. The part of Mary was played by Mr R. L. Thomas, Secretary and Treasurer of the Kinetoscope Co. After approaching the block and laying his head upon it, Thomas removed himself, the camera was stopped, and a dummy was substituted. The camera was then started again for the decapitation scene. This was the first use of trick photography or special effect work in a film.

The first person employed to play a comedy role in a film was M. Clerc, a gardener employed by Mme Lumière at Lyons, France. He was cast in the part of the gardener in the Lumière brothers' production *L'Arroseur arrosé*, a film premièred at the Grand Café in Paris on 28 December 1895. Clerc is seen watering flower-beds with a hose. A mischievous boy, played by a 14-year-old Lumière apprentice called Duval, creeps up behind the gardener and places his foot on the hose to stop the flow of water. As the perplexed gardener holds the nozzle up to his eye to see whether there is a blockage, young Duval removes his foot and dances with joy as a burst of water gushes into M. Clerc's face. Clerc and Duval were the first performers to be seen on the screen, since *The Execution of Mary Queen of Scots* had been made for viewing in Edison's Kinetoscope 'peep-show' device.

PROFESSIONAL ACTOR TO PERFORM IN A FILM: the first was Fred Storey, who played the title-role in R. W. Paul's *The Soldier's Courtship*, a short comedy made on the roof of the Alhambra Music Hall, Leicester Square in April 1896 and premièred underneath the same month.

During the early years of the film industry it was customary for performers to remain anonymous, though an exception was made in the case of established stage stars. A notable example of well-known artists lending their talents to the screen during the cinema's infancy is the short scene from the Broadway comedy *The Widow Jones*, filmed by Raff & Gammon in April 1896, in which John Rice and May Irwin performed the world's first screen kiss.

The first British performer to make a regular career as a film actor was a comedian called Johnny Butt, who made his screen début in 1899 playing the part of a bear in a trick film produced by R. W. Paul at his New Southgate Studios. Paul paid him 5s a day, which in monetary terms put the film actor on about the same level as a tram-driver or a dock-labourer. Butt remained in films all his life, making his last appearance in *The Informer* shortly before his death in 1931.

The star system, usually thought of as an American invention, in fact had its earliest beginnings in Germany. Here, as in Britain and the USA, it was deliberate policy on behalf of film-makers not to give their lead players any star billing, lest they should over-value their services. From 1907 onwards, it was recognized that particular performers could draw the crowds, but they were identified only by such pseudonyms as the 'Imp Girl', the 'Biograph Girl' or, in the case of the German actress Henny Porten, who made her début in Oskar Messter's 1907 production of *Lophengrin*, the 'Messter Girl'. It was Henny Porten who eventually emerged as the first 'film star' – the first actress to establish a personal following among cinema-goers and have her name promoted as an attraction. This came about through the unprecedented success of a Messter film of 1909 that she had scripted herself and in which she played the romantic lead. Titled *Das Liebesglück der Blinden* (*The Love of the Blind Girl*), it was received with such acclaim that Messter was persuaded to reveal his star player's identity. With her name on the credits, Henny then proceeded to justify the film-makers' worst fears by demanding an increase in salary – from £10 to £11 5s a month. Messter refused and Henny walked out of the studio. Having failed to call what he thought was her bluff, the Director sent an assistant, Kurt Stark, to fetch the girl back with the promise that the rise would be paid. Henny returned to the studio, married Stark, and went on to become Germany's idol of the silent screen.

Britain's first film actor performing Britain's first screen kiss – Fred Storey in The Soldier's Courtship, *1896*

In the USA, the star system emerged soon after Germany had paved the way. Perhaps fittingly it began with an outrageous publicity stunt, establishing a tradition that has enlivened and bedevilled the American film industry ever since. Early in 1910 Carl Laemmle had succeeded in luring the still-anonymous Florence Lawrence away from Biograph to work for his own company, Imp. He then arranged for a story to break in the St Louis papers that the actress had been killed in a street-car accident. Public interest in the supposed tragedy having been thoroughly aroused, Laemmle placed the following advertisement in the same papers on 10 March 1910:

The blackest and at the same time the silliest lie yet circulated by the enemies of IMP was the story foisted on the public of St Louis last week to the effect that Miss Lawrence, 'The Imp Girl', formerly known as 'The Biograph Girl', had been killed by a street car. It was a black lie so cowardly. We now announce our next film The Broken Path.

Within a year her name was appearing on film posters in larger type than the title.

Having become America's first named star, Florence Lawrence won herself an international reputation on the silent screen, but with the advent of talkies she was no longer in demand and was forced to become an extra at the MGM Studios. She finally committed suicide in January 1939.

GB: The first recognized film star in Britain was Gladys Sylvani, who became the lead player at the Hepworth Studios at Walton-on-Thames in 1911. Her name was advertised in the billing of *Stolen Letters*, Hepworth's first 1,000ft story film, which was released on 24 December of that year. Generally, though, the star system failed to develop on English soil, where most leading film parts were taken by stage players.

An actor like Stewart Rome would be paid as little as £10 a week for playing leading roles even after World War I. Hollywood salaries, by comparison, reached astronomical heights – Pola Negri, by no means the highest-paid actress of 1920, was commanding £50,000 a year – exactly 100 times as much as Stewart Rome.

The first
FILM: ADVERTISING FILMS

were made in France, Britain and the USA in 1897. The single surviving American example of that year was copyrighted by the Edison Co of West

Orange, N.J. on 5 August 1897. The Library of Congress Catalog records:

The film shows a large, poster-type backdrop with the words 'Admiral Cigarettes'. Sitting in front of the backdrop are four people in costume: Uncle Sam, a clergyman, an Indian, and a businessman. To the left of the screen is an ash-can size box that breaks apart and a girl, attired in a striking costume, goes across the stage towards the seated men and hands them cigarettes. Then she unfolds a banner that reads, 'We all Smoke.'

Advertising films were also made by the New York firm of Kuhn & Webster in 1897 for Haig Whisky, Pabst's Milwaukee Beer and Maillard's Chocolate. These were shown by back projection on an open-air screen facing Broadway at 34th Street, Herald Square. The projectionist was Edwin S. Porter, later to achieve fame as director of *The Great Train Robbery* (*see also* Film: Westerns). On this occasion, however, the only celebrity he achieved was in the police court, where he was charged with being a public nuisance and causing obstruction to traffic by encouraging crowds to linger on the sidewalk.

The French advertising films were the work of Georges Méliès, and were first shown in the open air on the boulevard des Italiens, near the Paris Opéra, in 1898. However, it is probable that some of them were made the previous year, and may have predated the Admiral Cigarettes commercial. They were made at Méliès's studio at Montreuil-sous-Bois for clients who included Delion Hats, Mystère Corsets, Chocolat Menier, and Moritz Beer.

GB: The first advertising film was made in 1897 for Bird's Custard Powder by Arthur Melbourne Cooper of St Albans, Hertfordshire (*see also* Film: Public Performance; Film Close-up). The film brought to life a contemporary poster for Bird's Custard, showing an old man walking down stairs with a tray of eggs, slipping and, of course, breaking all the eggs. The message was that he had no cause to worry as he used Bird's Custard Powder. The company made an agreement with Melbourne Cooper that he should be paid £1 for every copy of the film distributed. In 1899 he made what is believed to be the earliest surviving British advertising film, an appeal by Bryant & May for donations to supply the troops in South Africa with matches, as it seems this was something the Army authorities had overlooked. The film is notable for its use of animated cartoon technique, the 'performers' being match-stick men who climb up a wall and form themselves into the legend: 'Send £1 and enough matches will be sent to supply a regiment of our fighting soldiers.'

The first
FILM SHOT FROM AN AEROPLANE

was taken by L. P. Bonvillain, a Pathé cinematographer, piloted by Wilbur Wright at Camp d'Auvours, France in September 1908. This was over a year before the first still photograph was taken from an aircraft in flight (*see also* Photograph: Aerial).

FILM OF A TOPICAL (NON-AERONAUTIC) EVENT TAKEN FROM THE AIR: the first was made by the Warwick Trading Co for its *Bioscope Chronicle* newsreel on 21 April 1913. The film showed the Royal Yacht *Victoria and Albert* bearing King George V across the Channel on a visit to Paris, and the arrival at Calais. The pilot, B. C. Hucks, flew the camera-operator straight back to Hendon, where a representative of the film company was waiting to rush the canister to the laboratories. The complete film of the King's journey from London to Paris, including the aerial sequences, was shown during the matinée performance at the Coliseum at 5.20pm the same day.

The first
FILM: ANIMAL STAR

to appear regularly in films was the dog Rover, hero of Cecil Hepworth's outstandingly successful low-budget (£7 13s 9d) box-office hit *Rescued by Rover*. It was originally released in the spring of 1905, but was twice remade to satisfy demand when the prints ran out. He subsequently starred in seven other films.

The first
FILM: ANIMATED CARTOONS

were made in the USA and Britain in 1906. The earliest American example was *Humorous Phases of Funny Faces*, produced by James Stuart Blackton for the Vitagraph Co of New York. Like nearly all early American film cartoonists, Blackton used the technique of showing an artist drawing a still picture which then magically came alive and moved. The film consisted of 8,000 drawings and showed simple animated scenes such as a man rolling his eyes and blowing smoke from his cigar at a girl, a dog jumping through a hoop, etc.

GB: The first British cartoon, released in April of the same year, was made by ex-conjurer Walter Booth for the Charles Urban Trading Co. Titled *The Hand of the Artist* it showed an artist (Booth) drawing a coster and his donna who then come to life and dance the cake-walk.

The first cartoon film to tell a story, albeit a very simple one, and the first to dispense with the live artist technique, was Emile Cohl's *Fantasmagorie*, a 2min film first shown at the Théâtre du Gymnase in Paris, on 17 August 1908. Cohl made the film for Léon Gaumont, by whom he was employed as a scenarist. The first regular cartoon character to appear in a series of animated films was Cohl's Fantôche, a kind of match-stick man combating the cruel world, who made his début in *Le Cauchemar du Fantôche* in September 1909. Robert Desnos has described Cohl as the first to 'cut the umbilical cord which still linked the life of the characters on the screen with the secretions of the fountain pen'. He made about a hundred cartoons between 1908 and 1918 and can thus be regarded as the first professional screen animator.

ANIMAL CARTOON CHARACTER: the first was Gertie the Trained Dinosaur, who made her first appearance in a film of the same name, made by the American animator Winsor McCay in 1910. It was the much-loved animal cartoon characters who eventually gave animated films a distinct appeal of their own as suitable entertainment for children. This development can best be dated from the advent of Pat Sullivan's Felix the Cat in 1917, an animal who 'kept on walking', and who has been described as the first to attain something of the celebrity of a human star.

The use of a celluloid overlay bearing the moving parts of a drawing against an opaque stationary background – the technique generally employed in cartooning today – was patented in the USA by Earl Hurd on 19 December 1914.

NATURAL COLOUR CARTOON FILM: the first was *The Début of Thomas Kat*, produced by the Bray Pictures Corp of New York in the Brewster colour process and released by Paramount in 1916. The drawings were made on transparent celluloid and painted on the reverse, then filmed with a colour camera. Thomas Kat was an unfortunate kitten taught by his mother to pursue mice, but who inadvertently mistook a rat for the smaller breed of rodent.

FULL-LENGTH FEATURE CARTOON: the first was *The Sinking of the Lusitania*, made by Winsor McCay and released by Jewell Productions in the USA on 15 August 1918. McCay used 25,000 drawings for this animated actuality and the film took 22 months to complete.

CARTOON TALKING PICTURE: the first was Walt Disney's *Steamboat Willie* featuring Mickey Mouse: made in Hollywood and premièred at the

Colony Theater, New York on 19 September 1928. Another Mickey Mouse talkie, *Plane Crazy*, had in fact been completed before *Steamboat Willie*, but was released later.

FULL-LENGTH COLOUR CARTOON TALKING PICTURE: the first was Walt Disney's *Snow White and the Seven Dwarfs*, which opened at the Cathay Circle Theater, Los Angeles on 21 December 1937. The colour was by Technicolor.

For the first colour Disney cartoon *see* Film: Colour Process.

The first
FILM ARCHIVE
was the Danish Statens Arkiv for historiske Film og Stemmer, which had its origins in the spring of 1910 when Anker Kirkeby of the Copenhagen newspaper *Politiken* approached Ole Olsen of Nordisk Films with the idea of preserving a selection of films likely to be of historic interest in the future. During the ensuing three years a collection of films was assembled, including a number, specially taken for the archive, which showed prominent Danish writers, scientists, politicians, etc. and shots of parts of old Copenhagen due for redevelopment. The archive was formally established at the Royal Library in Copenhagen on 9 April 1913.

The first National Film Archive formed as a record of the film industry, rather than as a record of public events, was set up by the British Film Institute in London in May 1935.

The first
FILM AWARDS
were made in connection with a special cinema competition held at the International Exhibition, Turin in 1912. The Grand Prix of 25,000 francs was awarded to the Ambrosio Film Co for the Italian feature *After Fifty Years*, an historical drama set in the Austro-Italian War of 1859.

ACADEMY AWARDS: the first were presented by the Academy of Motion Picture Arts and Sciences in Hollywood, Calif. on 16 May 1929 for films released between 1 August 1927 and 31 July 1928. The winner of the Best Actor Award was the German star Emil Jannings for his performances in *The Way of All Flesh* and *The Last Command*; the Best Actress Award went to Janet Gaynor for her roles in *The Last Command*, *Seventh Heaven*, *Street Angel* and *Sunrise*. The Award for Best Picture was made to William Wellman's *Wings*, starring Clara Bow.

The name 'Oscar' for the trophy presented to Award winners was first used in 1931, after Mrs Herrick, Secretary of the Academy, had remarked of the sculpted figure: 'He looks like my Uncle Oscar.' Formerly it had been known simply as 'The Statuette'.

The first
FILM CENSORSHIP BOARD
(National) was founded in the USA, in March 1909, as the National Board of Censorship of Motion Pictures. It was established by the People's Institute of New York City, a self-appointed guardian of public morals, but was accepted quite willingly by the film industry, production companies paying a fee of $3.50 per 1,000ft of film submitted to the Board. There was no system of classification, as in Britain (*see below*); a film was either passed for public exhibition or rejected unless cut.

GB: The British Board of Film Censors was inaugurated by the Kinematograph Manufacturers' Association in October 1912 with powers effective from 1 January 1913. The moving spirit behind the venture was the film producer Will Barker, who was concerned at the increase in the number of films being produced 'for the smoking-room' – 'blue movies' in modern parlance – which he considered would bring the whole industry into disrepute. Together with Col A.C. Bromhead and Cecil Hepworth, two leading figures of the film world since the 1890s, he persuaded the Kinematograph Manufacturers' Association that it was up to the trade to put its own house in order, and with the approval of the Home Secretary the Board was established under the Presidency of G.A. Redford, formerly a playreader for the Lord Chamberlain.

During the first year of operation the Board examined 7,510 films (average length just over 1,000ft), of which 6,861 were granted 'U' Certificates (Universal), 627 'A' Certificates (Adult), and 22 were rejected for such reasons as 'indelicate or suggestive sexual situations', 'holding up a Minister of Religion to ridicule', 'excessive drunkenness' and the portrayal of 'native customs in foreign lands abhorrent to British ideas'.

'X' CERTIFICATE (for exhibition before adult audiences only): the first was awarded to the French film *La Vie Commence Demain* (*Life Begins Tomorrow*), which opened in London on 9 January 1951. The reason for the 'X' rating was a sequence dealing with artificial insemination. Previously the film would either have to have been banned or cut.

The first
FILM: CLOSE-UP
was a scene of Fred Ott sneezing, filmed by William Dickson at the newly built Edison studio (*see also* Film Studio) at West Orange, N.J. on 2 February 1893. *Fred Ott's Sneeze* was also the first film to be copyrighted, on 7 January 1894.

The first use of close-ups inter-cut with medium shots was by Arthur Melbourne Cooper of St Albans, in his *Grandma's Reading Glass* of 1900. In this film a small boy is seen focusing a magnifying glass on various objects, including a watch, a newspaper, canary, kitten and Grandma's eye. The boy was played by Bert Massey and Grandma by Miss Bertha Melbourne Cooper. The film was distributed by G.A. Smith of Brighton, to whom it has generally been attributed.

The first
FILM: COLOUR PROCESS
commercially successful, was Kinemacolor, a two-colour system using panchromatic film stock developed in 1906 by George Albert Smith of Brighton, England, for the Charles Urban Trading Co, a leading production company of the day. The first colour film by this process was taken outside Smith's house at Southwick, Brighton, in July 1906 and showed his two children playing on the lawn, the boy dressed in blue and waving a Union Jack and the girl in white with a pink sash. Kinemacolor was patented in November 1906.

The first public presentation of Kinemacolor before a paying audience took place at the Palace Theatre, Shaftesbury Avenue on 26 February 1909 and consisted of 21 short films, including the Band of the Queen's Highlanders at Brighton, sailing at Southwick, various scenes taken at Aldershot, the Water Carnival at Villefranche and the Children's Battle of Flowers at Nice.

The Natural Color Kinematograph Co was established by Charles Urban in March 1909 for the production and distribution of films by the Kinemacolor process. The first commercial production in Kinemacolor for general release was *A Visit to the Seaside*, probably made in the summer of 1908. This was taken at Brighton and showed scenes of the Front, a boat party disembarking, pierrots (The White Coons), children eating ice-cream, paddling, etc., bathing belles emerging from bathing-machines, and the Band of the Cameron Highlanders. A speciality was made of news pictures, the first important news event to be filmed in colour being the funeral of King Edward VII on 20 May 1910, at which no less than nine kings were present.

The first full-length colour feature film was *The World, the Flesh and the Devil*, a 1hr 40min melodrama, produced by the Union Jack Co in Kinemacolor from the book by Laurence Cowen, and trade shown on 4 February

1914. Billed as 'A £10,000 Picture Play in Actual Colors' in 'four parts and 120 scenes', the film opened at the Holborn Empire on 9 April 1914. Like most of the Kinemacolor dramas, the acting and direction were execrable, the colour impressive.

A Kinemacolor version of Thomas Dixon's *The Clansman*, made in the USA in 1913, may have been a full-length feature, but the film was never released owing to a question of copyright and no copy has survived. It starred Linda Arvidson, the wife of D.W. Griffith, who was to make a highly successful black and white version of the story two years later as *Birth of a Nation*.

Kinemacolor brought Charles Urban an international success, for besides the 300 cinemas and halls which installed Kinemacolor equipment in Britain, he was able to dispose of foreign exhibition rights in most major countries of the world. However, the special projection equipment necessary put Kinemacolor beyond the range of the small exhibitor, and the Natural Color Kinematograph Co was never able to produce enough films to keep a cinema constantly supplied with colour programmes. Other limitations of the process included the necessity to film in strong sunlight, and the loss of light occasioned by projecting through filters, which meant using a smaller screen than customary for black and white films.

THE WORLD THE FLESH AND THE DEVIL
By LAURENCE COWEN.
Reproduced with Stereoscopic Relief — in Four Parts — 120 Scenes —
A 100 Minute Thrill — The Greatest Photo-Play in London —
Matinees only Daily, 2.30 to 5 p.m.
THE HOLBORN EMPIRE
Prices: 6d. to 5s.
The escape from the Mill.

The first full-length colour feature film, 1914

The Kelly Gang shoot it out in the first feature film, a 1906 Australian production

The first three-colour process to achieve practical results was Gaumont Chronochrome, exhibited before the French Photographic Society in Paris on 15 November 1912. The films shown were taken with a three-lens camera, each lens having a filter in one of the primary colours. Subjects exhibited at this first demonstration included scenes taken in the Vilmorin-Andrieux Gardens, butterflies, Deauville beach at the height of the social season, harvesters and other rural scenes. Chronochrome was shown in London on 16 January 1913, and in June of the same year was used as a medium for the first-ever colour talkies, a number of brief humorous sketches with synchronized dialogue from an Elgephone phonograph attachment, which were presented at the 39th Street Theater in New York City. Although Chronochrome cannot be described as a commercial success, demonstrations of the process were still being given as late as 1920.

TECHNICOLOR FILM: the first was *The Gulf Between*, starring Grace Darmond and Niles Welch and produced by the Technicolor Motion Picture Corp in a two-colour additive system in February 1917. The Technicolor Motion Picture Corp had been founded in Boston by Dr Herbert Kalmus of the Massachusetts Institute of Technology two years earlier. Kalmus took Technicolor to Hollywood in 1923. Although he had developed a subtractive process the previous year, the double-coated film was given to cupping, and scratched more easily than monochrome. To most producers the cost at 27c a foot was prohibitive in comparison with an average 8c a foot for monochrome stock. Technicolor's breakthrough came with the introduction of the three-colour process in 1932. The first film to be produced in three-colour Technicolor was the 1932 Disney cartoon *Flowers and Trees*.

THREE-COLOUR FULL-LENGTH TECHNICOLOR FEATURE: the first was *Becky Sharp*, directed by Rouben Mamoulian for Pioneer Films and released in the USA and Britain in 1935.

GB: The first full-length three-colour Technicolor feature made in Britain was *Wings of the Morning*, a race-track drama starring Henry Fonda and the French actress Annabella, which opened at the Gaumont, Haymarket in May 1937. Basil Wright of the *Spectator* remarked that though *Wings of the Morning* denied every canon of decent film-making, it had established colour, and that colour was here to stay.

See also Film, Animated Cartoon in Colour; Film, Sound in Colour.

The first
FILM, FEATURE

(over 1hr running-time) was the Australian production *The Story of the Kelly Gang*, made by the theatrical company of J. & N. Tait at Heidelberg, Victoria, and premièred at the Athenaeum Hall, Melbourne on 26 December 1906. The cast included Elizabeth Veitch as Kate Kelly and Charles Tait, who also directed, as Ned Kelly. Running-time was approximately 70min. The cost of production was estimated at £400 and gross takings, including receipts from its showings in England, at £25,000.

GB: The first British feature film was *Oliver Twist*, directed by Thomas Bentley at the Hepworth Studios in Walton-on-Thames, and released in September 1912. Oliver was played by a girl, Ivy Millais, and the part of Nancy by Alma Taylor. The producer, Cecil Hepworth, recalled in his autobiography that the 60min film had little artistic merit, but enjoyed considerable success at the box office.

The first
FILM FESTIVAL

was inaugurated in Venice in an attempt to revive the tourist trade, which had been badly hit by the Depression. It was held at the Hotel Excelsior in association with the International Art Exhibition, 6–21 August 1932. The nations represented were the USA, Great Britain, France, Germany, Italy and Soviet Russia. There were no awards, but judging took place by popular vote. The following won the

most acclaim in response to the questions posed:
Which actress did you like the best? – Helen Hayes.
Which actor did you like the best? – Fredric March.
Which director seemed the most convincing? – Nicolai Ekk (*Road to Life*).
Which film was the most entertaining? – *Nous la Liberté*.
Which film moved you most? – *The Sin of Madelon Claudet*.
Which film had the most original sense of fantasy? – *Dr Jekyll and Mr Hyde*.
GB: The International Festival of Documentary Films, Edinburgh, opened by the Lord Provost at the Playhouse Cinema on 31 August 1946.

The first
FILM, HORROR
was a one-reel production of R.L. Stevenson's *Dr Jekyll and Mr Hyde*, released in the spring of 1908 by the Selig Polyscope Co of Chicago. The name-part was played by Richard Mansfield, supported by the other members of the company then touring with Luella Forepaugh and George Fish's 1897 stage-version of the story. The film was faithful to the play, even to opening and closing with a curtain.
GB: The first British horror film was also a version of *Dr Jekyll and Mr Hyde*, made by Lucius Henderson in 1912, with James Cruze and Harry Benham in the lead roles. Of the 20 or so adaptations of the story made up to now (few of them owing much to Stevenson's original), this was the only one in which Jekyll and Hyde were played by two different actors.

The first
FILM, IN-FLIGHT MOVIE
was First National's production of Conan Doyle's *The Lost World*, shown during an Imperial Airways scheduled flight to the Continent in April 1925.

The first airline to introduce regular in-flight movies was TWA, commencing with the presentation of *By Love Possessed* (Lana Turner, Efrem Zimbalist Jr) in the first-class section during a scheduled internal flight from New York to Los Angeles on 19 July 1961.

The first
FILM, INSTRUCTIONAL
was a film of an operation at the Surgical Clinic of the University of Berlin, shot by Oskar Messter in 1898, and used for teaching purposes at the University of Kiel the following year.

The first
FILM MUSIC
was composed by the Australian musician R.N. McAnally to accompany the Salvation Army Bioscope Co's 50min documentary drama *Soldiers of the Cross*, premièred at the Melbourne Town Hall on 13 September 1900. McAnally's music was rendered by the Salvation Army's Silver Biorama Band, which accompanied the film on tour.

The first musical accompaniment to a narrative feature was composed by Camille Saint-Saëns for *L'Assassination de Duc de Guise* and played at the film's première in Paris on 17 November 1908.

The first
FILM: NEWSFILM
(other than sporting subjects) was made by photographer Birt Acres of High Barnet, Hertfordshire (*see also* Film (Motion Picture)) on the occasion of the opening of the Kiel Canal by Kaiser Wilhelm II on 20 June 1895. Besides the arrival of the Kaiser at Holtenau aboard his yacht *Hohenzollern*, Acres took films of the laying of a memorial stone, and of a number of other events held as part of the celebrations, including scenes of the Kaiser reviewing his troops at Hamburg and leading a procession through the streets of Berlin. He also filmed a charge of Uhlan Lancers at the Tempelhof Feld in Berlin, starting a cameraman's tradition of taking risks in the cause of newsfilm reportage by arranging with their commander that the horsemen should charge directly at the camera. Seized with the desire to run for his life as the troop thundered towards him with drawn lances, he nevertheless continued to grind the handle of his camera and was afterwards congratulated by the CO as 'the pluckiest fellow he had ever met'. The first public screening of the films took place before the Royal Photographic Society on 14 January 1896.
GB: The first newsfilm shot in Britain was taken by Birt Acres on 27 June 1896, and showed the Prince and Princess of Wales arriving at the Cardiff Exhibition. Acres secured special permission to film the Royal party, on the proviso that he himself was not seen. Accordingly a small aperture was cut in a canvas screen forming one side of a private walkway along which the Prince and Princess would approach the exhibition entrance. Since there was no corresponding hole for the viewfinder, Acres had to begin shooting on receipt of a signal from an official. He filmed the whole scene without being able to see anything of his subject. The film was premièred at a special Royal Command performance at Marlborough House on 21 July 1896.
NEWSFILM OF AN INDOOR EVENT: the first was made by Oskar Messter, who filmed the Berlin Press Club Ball by artificial light early in 1897. Illumination was provided by four Körting & Matthiessen 50amp arc-lamps on portable stands.
NEWSFILM OF AN UNSCHEDULED HAPPENING: the first was of a fire at the Windsor Hotel, New York, in which 45 people lost their lives, filmed by J. Stuart Blackton and Albert E. Smith on 17 March 1899.
NEWSREEL: the first regularly shown was the *Warwick Journal*, believed to have been started in 1900 by the American film-maker Charles Urban, proprietor of the Warwick Trading Co, London. As no copies are known to survive and the newsreels were not listed in the Warwick catalogues, practically nothing is known about them beyond their bare existence. The idea appears to have been successful enough to have inspired imitators, as two more newsreels made their appearance shortly after, *Williamson's Animated News* and the *Gaumont Graphic*. None of these early enterprises survived long and it was only with the founding of the French *Pathé-Journal* in 1908, and its English counterpart *Pathé Animated Gazette* two years later, that the newsreel be came an established weekly institution.
SOUND NEWSREEL: the first was *Fox Movietone News*, of which the first edition was shown at the Roxy Theater, New York on 27 October 1927. It became a regular weekly feature commencing 31 December 1927. A British version, originally known as *Fox Movietone* but later changed to *British Movietone*, was started in 1929.

See also Film, Sporting Event.

The first
FILM: NUDE SCENE
was played by Australian star Annette Kellerman in the Fox production of *Daughter of the Gods*, which was made on location at St Augusta, Jamaica in the summer of 1915. Miss Kellerman was a former professional swimmer and had been the centre of controversy five years earlier when she wore the first one-piece bathing-suit.

The first
FILM RENTAL COMPANY
was established in 1902 by Harry J. Miles in San Francisco. Previously exhibitors had been obliged to buy their films outright; the standard price was about $100 a reel. Miles hired out films at $50 a reel per week, a scheme that allowed him a 100% profit on the fourth rental
GB: The Wulterdaw Kinema Supply Co Ltd, founded in London by E.G. Turner in 1904.

The first
FILM REVIEWS
(critical) were written by Frank E.

Woods and published in the *New York Dramatic Mirror* commencing with the issue for June 1908. Woods used the pseudonym 'Spectator', which was to be adopted some 25 years later by the world's first television reviewer (*q.v.*).

NEWSPAPER TO INTRODUCE REGULAR FILM REVIEWS: the first was the *Chicago Tribune*, which appointed Jack Lawson as film critic in 1914. Lawson was killed in an accident soon after and his place was taken by Miss Audrie Alspaugh, who wrote under the by-line 'Kitty Kelly'. American film historian Terry Ramsaye recalled: 'Kitty Kelly could make or break a picture in the Middle West. . . . Her column was a large success, and she became the best disliked name in the world of the film studios.'

The first
FILM SCRIPTWRITER

was New York journalist Roy McCardell, who was hired in 1900 by Henry Marvin of the Biograph Co to write 10 scenarios a week at $15 each. Since most of the films made by Biograph at that time were 50–100ft in length, McCardell found he was able to complete his first week's assignment in a single afternoon.

GB: The first scriptwriter to be employed on a regular basis in Britain was Miss Blanche MacIntosh, who was engaged by the Hepworth Studios at Walton-on-Thames in 1912. In contrast to the liberality of the American film industry, Miss MacIntosh received 1gn for her first script, which was for a film titled *In Wolf's Clothing.* Previously it had been the custom of British film producers to shoot without a script or write their own scenarios, though occasionally a script might be specially commissioned for longer features.

The first
FILM: SLOW-MOTION SEQUENCE

was made by Oskar Messter of Berlin in 1898, with a specially constructed high-speed 60mm camera of his own design. Among the earliest sequences filmed with this camera was one that showed a cat falling off a wall beside a Hipp millisecond watch. This was filmed at 66 frames per second, though the camera was capable of filming at speeds of up to 100 frames per second.

The first
FILM, SOUND

The first films with synchronized sound accompaniment to be successfully shown before a paying audience were presented at three temporary cinemas operated at the Paris Exposition between 15 April and 31 October 1900. All three used a sound-on-disc system under separate but not totally dissimilar patents. The Phonorama, exhibited by the Compagnie Générale Transatlantique, showed coloured scenes of 'la vie Parisienne' and 'a series of tableaux of the cries of Paris', accompanied by music, singing and speech. In la rue de Paris, le Phono-Cinéma-Théâtre was bringing major stars to the talking screen for the first time. Presented by Clement Maurice, the programme of seven films included the celebrated comedy actor Coquclin in the role of Cyrano de Bergerac, and Mme Sarah Bernhardt playing the duel scene from *Hamlet.* Mme Bernhardt was thus first to speak the words of Shakespeare from the screen. The other exhibition of talking films, given by Henri Joly at le Théâtre de la Grande Rue, included a short film titled *Lolotte*, which was probably the first comedy film with dialogue, and also the first talkie to relate some kind of simple story. The scene takes place in an hotel bedroom and is played by three characters, a newly married couple and the *patron* of the hotel, the latter performed by Joly himself.

GB: The first sound films were presented by the French Ciné-Phono-Matograph system at the London Hippodrome in 1901 and included Vesta Tilley singing 'The Midnight Sun', Alec Hurley's 'Lambeth Cake-Walk', and Lib Hawthorne's 'Kitty Malone'. Most of the early sound-on-disc films made in Britain consisted of music-hall acts or short comedy sketches. The first real story film with spoken dialogue was a one-reel comedy titled *They Can't Diddle Me*, featuring Tom Graves, produced in 1907 by the Sheffield Photo Co.

SOUND-ON-FILM PROCESS: the first was patented by French-born Eugène Lauste of Brixton, London on 11 August 1906. Lauste's first successful experiment in recording and reproducing speech on film was made in 1910, with an electrodiamagnetic recorder and string galvanometer. He used a French gramophone record, selected at random, for the initial trial, and by coincidence the first words to be heard in the playback were 'J'entends très bien maintenant.' (I hear very well now.) A colleague in the film business, L. G. Egrot, recalled visiting Lauste at Brixton about this time:

He had already started building his camera to take pictures and sound together, the front part of the camera allowing to test the different systems he was experimenting with for sound recording. . . . Very often on a Sunday, a bandmaster friend of his, Mr Norris, would come along with his band and play in the garden of the house where, in 1911, Mr Lauste had had a wooden building erected as an experimenting studio. The machine was taken out, with all leads, some picture would be made and some sound recorded.

Lauste sound film, 1912

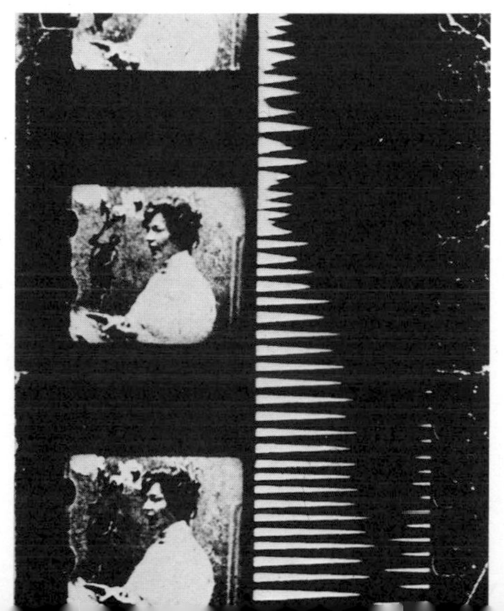

Lauste completed his sound-on-film projector and reproducing apparatus in 1913, and was about to embark on the commercial exploitation of the process when war broke out. In 1916 he went to the USA with the idea of obtaining financial backing, but the entry of America into the war the following year dashed his hopes again.

The first programme of sound-on-film productions to be presented in public was shown at the Alhambra cinema in Berlin on 17 September 1922 before an invited audience of 1,000 people. The films were made by the Tri-Ergon process developed by Joseph Engl, Joseph Massolle and Hans Vogt and included the first story film with dialogue recorded on the actual film band. Titled *Der Brandstifter* (*The Arsonist*), and taken from Von Heyermann's play of the same name, it had a cast of three with Erwin Baron playing seven of the nine parts. The other films were mainly orchestral with vocal accompaniment. Press reaction was mixed, criticism being levelled not so much against the level of technical achievement, but at the notion of talking films, which it was said would destroy the essential art of the motion picture – mime – and detract from the cinema's international appeal.

The first presentation of sound-on-film productions before a paying audience took place at the Rialto Theater, New York on 15 April 1923, when Lee De Forest (*see* Radio Broadcast; Radio Telephone) showed a number of singing and musical shorts made by his Phonofilm process. The sound films formed a supporting programme to the main (silent) feature, *Bella Donna* with Pola Negri. During the following 12 months, 34 cinemas in the eastern United States were wired for Phonofilm sound. The films made at the De Forest Studios between 1923 and 1927 included monologue numbers by Eddie Cantor, George Jessel and Chic Sale; dialogues between Gloria Swanson and Thomas Meighan and Weber and Fields; Folkina's 'Swan Dance'; play-lets with Raymond Hitchcock; and orchestral subjects featuring Ben Bernie, Paul Specht and Otto Wolf Kahn. The year 1924 saw three notable sound-on-film 'firsts' from Phonofilm – President Coolidge was filmed delivering a campaign speech on the White House lawn, the first time that a President of the USA had spoken from the screen; the first Technicolor film with a sound-track was made, the subject being Balieff's *Chauve Souris* danced in the open air; and the first story film to be released commercially, *Love's Old Sweet Song*, a two-reeler directed by J. Searle Dawley with Mary Mayo and Una Merkel in the leading roles. Although the first to exploit sound on film commercially, De Forest failed to establish talking pictures as a major entertainment medium and the Phonofilm patents were eventually taken over by William Fox together with those of the Tri-Ergon system.

GB: The first public demonstration of sound on film in Britain took place at the Finsbury Park Cinema on 14 June 1923, when a programme of Phonofilm shorts was trade shown. The *Bioscope* reported:

> *Several pictures were projected, including a vocalist rendering a song from* Carmen, *a dancer imitative of Pavlova with dying swan musical effects, and others. The synchronization was as near perfect as possible, but the articulation sounded to me somewhat throaty.*

The first sound-on-film production shown before a paying audience in Britain was the Technicolor dance subject *Chauve Souris* (*see above*), which was shown with musical sound-track at the Tivoli in London in the summer of 1925. The first sound-on-film talking pictures displayed to a paying audience were premièred at the Empire Cinema, Plumstead on 4 October 1926. The programme opened with a film of Sidney L. Bernstein explaining how Phonofilm worked, and this was followed by a number of shorts featuring vocalists Billy Merson, the Radio Franks and Dick Henderson; accordion-player Phil Baker; 'eccentric fiddler' Joseph Termini; and the Helen Lewis Ladies' Band. These films, the first British-made sound-on-film productions for general release, were shot at the Clapham Studios by the De Forest Phonofilm Co of Great Britain.

FULL-LENGTH FEATURE FILM WITH SOUND (in part): the first was D. W. Griffith's *Dream Street*, produced by United Artists in 1921. Described by one cinema historian as 'a dreadful hodgepodge of allegory and symbolism', it was a total failure when originally presented as an all-silent picture at the Central Theater, New York in April. After it had closed, Griffith was persuaded by Wendell McMahill of Kellum Talking Pictures to add a sound sequence. On 27 April the star, Ralph Graves, was brought to the Kellum Studios at West 40th Street to record a love-song on synchronized disc, and this was included when the film re-opened at the Town Hall civic centre on 1 May. A fortnight later a second sound sequence was added, consisting of the shouts and whoops of Porter Strong shooting craps together with other background noises.

The first feature film with dialogue, the first with a sound-track throughout, and the first made by a sound-on-film process, was *Das Mädchen mit den Schwefelhölzern* (*The Little Match-Girl*, from the story by Hans Andersen), which was produced by UFA at their Berlin Studios in association with the Swiss Tri-Ergon AG in 1925. The film was premièred in Berlin, but taken off after only two days owing to the poor quality of the sound.

The first successful talking feature was Warner Bros' *The Jazz Singer*, starring Al Jolson, which opened at New York on 6 October 1927. Made by Warners' sound-on-disc Vitaphone system, the dialogue and singing sequences were comparatively brief, but the phenomenal reception it received on both sides of the Atlantic marked the beginning of the end of the silent picture.

The first all-talking feature film was Warner Bros' Vitaphone production *Lights of New York*, which was premièred at the Strand Theater, New York on 6 July 1928. Starring Helene Costello, the picture was so determinedly all-talking that the dialogue continued non-stop from opening credits to End title.

GB: The first talking feature was Alfred Hitchcock's *Blackmail*, made by British International Pictures at Elstree with Anny Ondra and John Longden and premièred at the Regal, Marble Arch on 21 June 1929. The first reel had incidental sound and music only, but the characters began to speak in the second as the plot unfolded. It was billed as '99% talking', a slight exaggeration. The posters also carried the slogan 'See and Hear It – Our Mother Tongue as It should be Spoken' – a sideswipe at the American-English that had dominated the screen hitherto. Ironically the female lead, Czech actress Anny Ondra, spoke virtually no English and her voice was dubbed by Joan Barry – the first time that this technique had been used in talking pictures.

(*NB:* British International Pictures' *Kitty*, which is sometimes claimed as the first British talking feature, was made as a silent film before *Blackmail* and a sound-track added afterwards. The part-talkie version was not released until December 1929.)

The first all-talking feature made in Britain was *The Clue of the New Pin*, adapted from the Edgar Wallace novel of the same name and produced by British Lion in association with British Photophone. The film was directed by Arthur Maude, starred Donald Calthrop and Benita Hume, and was released on 16 December 1929. An undistinguished production, the film is chiefly memorable for the fact that a young unknown called John Gielgud played a small part in it.

FULL-LENGTH COLOUR TALKING FEATURE: the first was Warner Bros' *On With the Show*, directed by Alan Crosland with Ethel Waters and Joe E. Brown and premièred at the Winter Garden, New York on 28 May 1929. It was made in two-colour Technicolor with Vitaphone sound.

The talking picture arrived amid predictions of failure on almost every side; within three years of the first successful all-talkie, sound had all but ousted the silent picture – the last major silent, *The White Hell of Pitz Palu*, being made in Germany in 1931. By December 1930, 13,500 out of 21,700 cinemas in the USA had been wired for sound, and at the end of the following year there was scarcely any silent cinemas remaining. In Britain the figure rose from 500 out of 4,000 in December 1929 to 2,725 in December 1930. The last cinema in Britain to show silent films only was the Electra at Royton, Lancashire, run by the Progress Film Co. In contrast to their name the proprietors refused to countenance anything as new fangled as talkies, and only closed down in 1935 when the renters were no longer able to maintain a supply of silent films.

The first
FILM OF A SPORTING EVENT
was taken at the Edison Laboratories, West Orange, N.J., and depicted a six-round boxing-match fought between Mike Leonard and Jack Cushing on 14 June 1894. Leonard, the better-known fighter, was paid $150 for his services and his opponent $50. The ring was only 12ft square, in order that all the action might be followed by the immobile camera. Having knocked

Cushing out in the last round, Leonard summed up after the fight:

I hit him when I liked and where I liked. I'd hit him oftener, only Mr Edison treated me right and I didn't want to be too quick for his machine. I generally hit 'im in the face, because I felt sorry for his family and thought I would select the only place that couldn't be disfigured.

The film was premièred at a Kinetoscope parlour located at 83 Nassau Street, New York, probably at the beginning of August 1894. From a commercial point of view it was not a complete success, as each round was shown in a different Kinetoscope for which a separate charge was made. At 10c a round, it cost 60c to see the whole film, so most patrons preferred to pay a single dime to see the knock-out round only.

GB: The first sports film in Britain and the first anywhere in the world to be taken of a regularly scheduled sporting contest was made by Birt Acres of the Oxford and Cambridge Boat-race on 30 March 1895. It was primarily intended for viewing in the Kinetoscopes manufactured by Acres's partner Robert Paul, but was probably also seen on the screen when Acres became an exhibitor the following year.

The first FILM: STEREOPHONIC SOUND

process was patented by the Parisian film-makers Abel Gance and André Debrie in 1932. The first film with a stereophonic sound accompaniment was a re-edited version of Gance's 1927 8hr silent epic *Napoléon Bonaparte*, presented with added dialogue and sound-effects at the Paramount Cinema, Paris in 1935.

The first successful process of stereophonic musical accompaniment was Fantasound, developed by Walt Disney Studios in association with RCA, and first employed for the sound-track of Walt Disney's 1941 feature-length cartoon *Fantasia*, with music by the Philadelphia Orchestra under the direction of Leopold Stokowski.

GB: Stereophonic sound was first used for narration and effects in conjunction with the programme of 3-D shorts shown at the Festival of Britain Telecinema in 1951.

The first feature with a complete stereophonic dialogue was Warner Bros' *House of Wax*, released in 1953.

The first FILMSTRIPS

were produced by Underwood's of New York, who began putting their large photographic library on 55mm film in 1919. The subjects were mainly people and places and each frame had a brief identifying caption. Distribution to schools was undertaken by the Stillfilm Co, the filmstrips taking the place of the glass slides which previously had been the most widely used visual aid. Curiously the filmstrip did not come into use as an educational medium until some 15 years after the introduction of motion-picture films for teaching purposes.

The first FILM STUDIO

was Thomas Edison's 'Black Maria', a frame building covered in black roofing-paper, built at the Edison Laboratories in West Orange, N.J. and completed at a cost of $637.67 on 1 February 1893. Here Edison made short vaudeville-act films for use in his Kinetoscope, a peep-show machine designed for use in amusement arcades. The building was so constructed that it could be revolved to face the direction of the sun.

The first studio in which films were made by artificial light was opened by Oskar Messter at 94a Friedrich Strasse, Berlin, in November 1896. For illumination Messter used four Körting & Matthiessen 50amp arc-lamps on portable stands. Messter's earliest productions by artificial light included *From Tears to Laughter* and *Lightning Artist Zigg*.

The first artificially lit studio in the USA – the Biograph Studio at 11 East 14th St, N.Y. – was not opened until 1903.

GB: The first film studio in Britain was built at the back of the Tivoli Theatre in the Strand in 1897 by the Mutoscope & Biograph Co. Like Edison's Black Maria, the studio was mounted on a cup-and-ball fixture that enabled it to be revolved in the direction of the sun. It could also be rocked to and fro for 'storm at sea' sequences and similar effects. The glass panels that made up the sides of the studio could be dismantled for 'outdoor' scenes.

The first FILM STUNTMAN

employed as stand-in for an actor was Lt H. H. Arnold, who undertook the flying sequences in a film titled *The Military Air Scout* at Nassau Boulevard, N.Y. on 30 September 1911.

The first FILM MADE FOR TELEVISION

(narrative) was a short silent film titled *Morgenstunde hat Gold im Munde* (*The Early Bird catches the Worm*), produced by F. Banneitz of the Commerz-Film AG, Berlin, on behalf of the German Reichs-Rundfunkgesellschaft early in 1930. Intended specially for transmission by low-definition television, the actors' movements were exaggerated for visual emphasis and the costumes were designed for greater contrast than in a normal cinema film.

The first film drama made for high-definition television was *Wer fuhr IIA 2992?* (*Who was Driving Car Number IIA 2992?*), a thriller scripted by Gerhart W. Göbel of the Reichspost and produced by UFA in Berlin in the summer of 1939. Göbel devised the plot after watching a police announcement on television appealing for help in a murder case. The story centred round a hit-and-run driver, since the Nazi Propaganda Ministry would not allow murder as a theme of films to be shown abroad. The film was first shown during television demonstrations in Bucharest and Sofia in 1940 and was also used after the war when the German Post Office resumed experimental transmissions in 1950.

GB: The first film drama was *A Dinner Date with Death*, a pilot for a television series titled *The Man who walks by Night*, shot at Marylebone Studios by Vizio Films Ltd, 11–14 July 1949, and transmitted by BBC Television on 28 September 1950. Produced by Roy Plomley of *Desert Island Discs* fame, the film was directed by Eric Fawcett, scripted by Duncan Ross, and starred Patricia Jessel and James Cairncross. Designed for a half-hour programme with a break for commercials, it was also the first British television drama to be televised on American networks.

The first FILM SHOWN ON TELEVISION

(commercially made) was a short of George Robey performing a monologue, *The Bride*, transmitted from the Baird Studios, Long Acre, London on 19 August 1929.

The first television station to show films as part of the regular programme service was the De Forest Radio Corporation's W2XCD Passaic, N.J. commencing 1 March 1931. These were mainly documentary and travel shorts, two of the earliest to be aired being *People who Live in the Desert* and *Lumbering in British Columbia*.

GB: The first film to be transmitted as part of the regular programme service in Britain was a 5min test film of a boxing-match televised by the Baird Co on 6 March 1931. This was followed three days later by a Charlie Chaplin silent featuring the Keystone Cops.

FULL-LENGTH FEATURE FILM SHOWN ON TELEVISION: the first was a 1925 dramatic comedy titled *Police Patrol*, which was transmitted in six daily episodes by W2XCD Passaic, N.J., 6–11 April 1931. Directed by Burton King for Gotham Productions, it related the story of a New York

policeman (James Kirkwood) who arrests a girl thief (Edna Murphy) the exact double of his sweetheart (also Edna Murphy).
GB: The first feature film shown on the BBC's public high-definition programme service was *The Student of Prague*, a German production with English subtitles starring Anton Walbrook and Dorothea Wieck, transmitted on 14 August 1938.

The first
FILM, THREE-DIMENSIONAL
was *The Power of Love*, made in the USA by Perfect Pictures in 1922. Patrons were required to wear spectacles with one red and one green lens, in order to obtain the illusion of depth.

The first talking picture in colour and three dimensions was a Russian production of *Robinson Crusoe*, filmed on the Black Sea Coast in 1945–6 under the direction of A.N. Andreyevsky. It had its première in Moscow in February 1947. The most difficult technical problem encountered was persuading a wild cat to walk along a thin branch towards the camera. After five nights occupied with this one scene, the cameramen succeeded in getting a satisfactory shot. The effect, according to accounts, was riveting, the animal seeming to walk over the heads of the audience and disappear at the far end of the cinema.

The first
FILM: WESTERNS
were copyrighted by the American Mutoscope & Biograph Co on 21 September 1903. One was titled *Kit Carson* and related the story of its hero's capture by Indians and subsequent escape through the agency of a beautiful Indian maiden. There were 11 scenes and the film had a running-time of 21min. The other film, titled *The Pioneers*, showed the burning of a settler's homestead by Indians, who kill the homesteader and his wife and carry off his daughter. The film ends with the dramatic rescue of the child by frontiersmen who have found the bodies of her parents. Running-time was approximately 15min. Both films were released in August 1904.
(*NB:* The more celebrated *The Great Train Robbery*, generally described as the first Western and often as the first film to tell a story, was copyrighted by the Edison Co on 1 December 1903.)
The first film actor to establish himself as a cowboy star was 'Bronco Billy' Anderson, who made 376 Westerns for the Essany Film Co between 1908 and 1915. Anderson, whose real name was Max Aronson, appeared in more films during his relatively short career than any other performer before or since.
WESTERN TALKIE: the first was Fox Movietone's *In Old Arizona*, directed by Raoul Walsh and Irving Cummings, with Edmund Lowe, Warner Baxter and Dorothy Burgess, and presented at the Fox West Coast Criterion Theater, Los Angeles on 25 December 1928. Billed as 'The First All-Talking Outdoor Picture', it was shot on location in Zion National Park and Bryce Canyon in Utah, in the Mohave Desert and at the San Fernando Mission in California – almost anywhere except Old Arizona.

The first
FILM: WIDE-SCREEN PROCESS
was adopted by Enoch J. Rector of the Veriscope Co of New York for his 15min production of the Corbett-Fitzsimmons championship filmed at Reno, Nevada on 17 March 1897. The 70mm film gave a picture ratio of 2:1.

The first wide-screen feature film was *The Fox Movietone Follies of 1929*, filmed in the 70mm Fox Grandeur process and presented on a 28 × 14ft screen at the Gaiety Theater, Broadway in September 1929. A number of other wide-screen processes were introduced during 1930 and 1931, including Warner Bros' 65mm Vitascope, Paramount's 56mm Magnafilm and RKO's 60mm Spoor Berrgren development, but the effects of the Depression forced studios to curb these experiments with unorthodox film gauges. The principal drawback at the time was that 60% of the cinemas in the USA lacked space for a screen more than 24ft wide.
FILM PRODUCTION IN CINEMASCOPE: the first was Twentieth-Century Fox's *The Robe*, which was premièred at Grauman's Chinese Theater, Hollywood on 24 September 1953.
FILM PRODUCTION IN CINERAMA: the first was *This is Cinerama*, which opened in New York on 30 September 1952 and ran for 122 weeks. The first full-length Cinerama feature was Metro-Goldwyn Mayer's 1962 production *The Wonderful World of the Brothers Grimm*, directed by George Pal and Henry Levin. Cinerama was developed by self-taught inventor Frederick Waller of Huntingdon, New York, who had originated the idea as early as 1938 for an oil exhibit at the New York World's Fair. His intention had been to project moving pictures all over the interior surface of the exhibition building, but technical difficulties persuaded him to compromise with a half-dome, using 11 16mm projectors to cover the vast area of screen. After the war he resumed work on the process, reducing the number of projectors to three and adopting a wide-screen ratio of almost 3:1.

Waller's process is by no means the ultimate in wide-screen projection. The similarly named Cineorama, introduced by Raoul Grimoin-Sanson at the Paris Exposition of 1900, employed a battery of 10 projectors to show an elaborately hand-coloured film on the widest screen possible – a completely circular screen 330ft in circumference with the audience seated in the middle.

The first
FINGERPRINTS:
The systematic use of fingerprints as a means of identification was initiated by William Herschel of the Indian Civil Service at Jungipur in 1858. On 28 July of that year he took the palm-print of Rajyadhar Konai, a local contractor from the village of Nista, on the back of a contract for 2,000 maunds of road metalling. The impress was made with the home-made oil-ink used by Herschel for his official seal, and included clear prints of all the fingers of the right hand. Herschel admitted that his original intention in taking Konai's fingerprints was not so much for the purpose of positive identification as a means of frightening the Bengali out of all thoughts of repudiating the document at a later date, but so pleased was he with the success of the experiment that he determined to pursue it further. Accordingly he inaugurated the first register of fingerprints while serving as Magistrate at Arrah, Bengal in June 1859. At first he contented himself with collecting the prints of his friends and colleagues, but on being transferred to Nuddea the following year he found such an alarming incidence of fraud and forgery that he

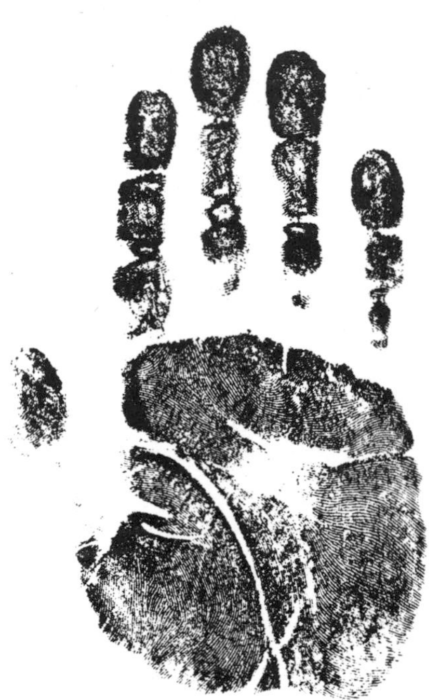

Konai's fingerprints, 1858

began to investigate the possibility of enforcing the statutary use of fingerprints on leases and contracts. His proposals, however, were rejected by the Calcutta Secretariat. It was not until his appointment to the magistracy of Hooghly in 1877, when he became responsible for both the criminal courts and the Department for the Registration of Deeds, that he was able to introduce the use of fingerprinting for official purposes. In order to prevent Army pensioners from drawing their pensions twice over, he maintained a record of their fingerprints and required them to make an imprint on receipt of the money due, for purposes of comparison. At the same time the system was adopted at Hooghly Gaol as a precaution against the hiring of substitutes to serve sentences – a fairly common practice at the time – and also for the registration of legal documents. Herschel regarded fingerprinting chiefly as a means of preventing impersonation, and did not foresee its use in criminal investigation.

FINGERPRINTS USED AS A MEANS OF CRIMINAL DETECTION were first advocated by Henry Faulds, a Scottish physician, who made a number of experiments while employed at the Tsukiji Hospital in Tokyo. He wrote in a letter to *Nature*, published in the issue for 28 October 1880:

When bloody finger-marks or impressions on clay, glass, etc., exist, they may lead to the scientific investigation of criminals. Already I have had experience in two such cases, and found useful evidence from these marks. In one case greasy finger-marks revealed who had been drinking some rectified spirit. The pattern was unique, and fortunately I had previously obtained a copy of it. They agreed with microscopic fidelity. In another case sooty finger-marks of a person climbing a white wall were of great use as negative evidence.

Fauld's letter brought little immediate result, except the revelation of Herschel's previous researches in the field. Failing to attract the notice of the Police Commissioners, he spent the rest of his life making vitriolic attacks on Herschel and anyone else who proved unwilling to accept his claim to be the sole pioneer of fingerprinting.

The first police force to adopt the use of fingerprints for criminal investigation was the La Plata Division of the Provincial Police of Buenos Aires. This was done more or less unofficially by Juan Vucetich, who had been deputed by the Chief of Police to set up an anthropometrical department, and used the opportunity to establish a fingerprint classification based on Francis Galton's system. His classification, which he called by the unwieldy name of 'Icnofalagometrico', came into regular use on 1 September 1891, and on 31 March 1892, he inaugurated the world's first Fingerprint Bureau at San Nicolas, Buenos Aires.

CONVICTION ON THE EVIDENCE OF FINGERPRINTS was first secured by the La Plata Police in July 1892. On 29 June at Necochea, Buenos Aires Province, a woman called Francisca Rojas had come running out of her house covered in blood, screaming that she had been attacked and her children murdered. She accused a neighbour called Velasquez, a ranch-worker who had been pestering her to marry him. He was arrested the same night, beaten up, and then bound and laid by the corpses of the two victims as an inducement to confess. When it was revealed that Rojas had a lover who had publicly declared he would marry her but for the children, the police began to entertain doubts, and on 8 July Inspector Eduardo Alvarez was sent from La Plata to search for incriminating evidence. He found it on a doorpost in the woman's hut – a number of bloody fingermarks. Alvarez cut the wood away and sent it to headquarters at La Plata. The prints were compared with those of the suspect, and those of the mother of the murdered children, and found to correspond exactly with the latter. Confronted with this evidence, she broke down and confessed to the crime. As there was no capital punishment for women in Argentina at that time, she was sentenced to life imprisonment.

GB: The first criminals in Britain to have their fingerprints recorded were inmates of Pentonville Prison, over 100 of whom were fingerprinted by Francis Galton in a demonstration before a Home Department committee in 1893. As a result of the recommendations of the committee, fingerprinting was officially adopted by the Convict Office in 1895, but was of little practical use since the indexing of the prints was done on the ill-conceived Bertillonage system. The first police officer to be trained in fingerprinting, Inspector C. Stockley Collins, received instruction at the Galton Laboratory the same year. The Metropolitan Police Fingerprint Bureau was established by Sir Edward Henry in July 1901.

The first conviction on the evidence of fingerprints was secured by the Metropolitan Police in the case against Harry Jackson, accused of stealing billiard-balls from a house at Denmark Hill in June 1902. Jackson had left an imprint of his thumb on a freshly painted window-sill, and it was on this evidence that he was convicted at the Old Bailey on 13 September following.

The first
FIRE-BRIGADE

in Britain was established by Nicholas Barbon to protect houses insured by his Phenix Fire Office (*see also* Fire Insurance). In 1684 he wrote that his firemen were like 'Old Disciplined Souldiers, that do greater things, then [*sic*] Ten times that Number of Raw and Unexperienced men.' This is the earliest reference to the employment of firemen, and although little else is known about the Phenix fire-brigade, it was probably composed of Thames watermen, who would be called out in the event of fire, and paid according to the amount of time required to quench the blaze. In the following century the rate was generally 1s for the first hour, 6d for succeeding hours, and unlimited beer. Other inducements included a colourful costume of decorated tunic and breeches and exemption from impressment for the Navy. The last brigade maintained by an insurance company was the Norwich Union Fire-Brigade, Worcester, disbanded 1929.

MUNICIPAL FIRE-BRIGADE: the first was founded at Beverley, Yorkshire, on 20 June 1726. The firemen were part-time and were paid 'according to their deserts' whenever they were called out. This was the earliest town brigade known to have been formed with members nominated by name; formerly it had been customary for parish engines to be maintained by an engine-keeper, who would call upon bystanders for assistance.

The first fire-brigade to maintain full-time firemen on a regular weekly wage was the London Fire Engine Establishment. It was brought into existence on 1 January 1833 by the united efforts of the 10 major fire insurance companies, led by Charles Bell Forde of the Sun Fire Office. There were 80 firemen under the command of Supt James Braidwood, 4 central districts and 19 sub-fire-stations. Wages began at 1gn a week, rising to 24s 6d after several years' service. No time off was allowed, except for occasional leaves, and firemen attended an average of three fire calls a day, in addition to drills and training. Not until 1891 did London firemen become entitled to 1 day off in 14. That firemen were able to enjoy some respite from their arduous duties, albeit illicitly, is indicated by frequent entries in the minute books to the effect that a fine of 5s had been imposed for 'entertaining a female in the watchbox of an escape station'.

The first recorded
FIRE-ENGINE

was built for the city of Augsburg by Anthony Blatner, a goldsmith, in 1518.

Although few details survive, it appears from the reference in the *Kunstgeschichte der Stadt Augsburg* that it consisted of a large lever-operated squirt mounted on a wheeled carriage. *GB:* The earliest reference to a fire-engine is contained in the minutes of the 'Company of Four and Twenty' (parish council) at Braintree, Essex for 1 October 1632: 'Fire Engyne. It is agreed that an engyne be procured for the common good of the parish to quench any starr fyers that may befall. Such an one as in use in London.' (Nothing is known about this engine.)

The first fire-engine to incorporate an air vessel (i.e. capable of discharging a continuous jet of water) was patented by Nicholas Mandell and John Grey of London in 1712. An advertisement in the *Post Boy* in 1715 asserted: 'This engine throws up water in a continued stream, which by a leather pipe may be directed to any room or part of a house.' *SELF-PROPELLED MOTOR FIRE-ENGINE* (petrol driven): the first was built by Cambier et Cie of Lille, and demonstrated at the French Heavy Autocar Trials held at Versailles in October 1898.
GB: Built by the Royal Carrying Co, Liverpool in 1901 and commissioned by the Liverpool Fire-Brigade, the fire-engine consisted of a tender mounted on a Daimler chassis, and was designed to carry six men and equipment, including a chemical engine removed from a horse-drawn appliance. When the first fire call came in August, to a blazing cotton-warehouse, driver George Bechtel's response was so instantaneous that he left his crew behind. The appliance moved sufficiently slowly, however, for them to run after it and jump aboard, and it arrived at the scene of the fire at precisely the same time as the accompanying horse-drawn engine. The self-propeller did not prove completely satisfactory, and its constant backfiring won it the nickname 'Farting Annie'.

The first
FIRE-EXTINGUISHER
was invented by German physician M. Fuches in 1734, and consisted of glass balls filled with a saline solution, designed to be hurled at the blaze. Advertisements depicting a whole family lobbing these balls at a blazing inferno in their drawing-room, with expressions of rapturous enjoyment on their faces, appeared in English journals up until World War I.

The modern automatic fire-extinguisher was devised by Yarmouth barrack-master Capt. George Manby after witnessing a disastrous fire in an Edinburgh tenement block in 1813. As the fire was on the fifth floor it was too high to reach with a hose, and nothing could be done to stop it spreading. Recording his impressions of this experience, he declared that he was 'fully persuaded that the application of even a small portion of water at a critical moment would often effect what, at a later period, a much larger power of water could not accomplish'. In 1816 he devised a cylindrical copper extinguisher, 24in high, with a capacity of 4gal. It was filled three-parts full with what Manby described as 'anti-phlogistic fluid', in fact plain water mixed with pearl-ash, and the remaining space charged with compressed air. They were manufactured by Messrs Hadley, Simpkin & Lott of Long Acre, and several hundred sold before the public lost interest in what was regarded then as hardly more than a modish novelty. It was not until half a century later that the idea was revived and, with a less fatalistic attitude towards fire, received the support it deserved.

The first
FIRE INSURANCE
originated in Hamburg as a municipal enterprise on 3 December 1591. On this date the earliest-known contract for insurance against loss by fire was signed by 101 persons, principally brewers, who were property-owners of the Free City. No premiums were required on the policy, but signatories to this and similar contracts – which continued to be drawn up for each 101 applicants – pledged themselves to pay a maximum of 10 thalers to any fellow member whose property was damaged by fire. At first responsibility for collecting the moneys due lay with the individual claimant, but evidently this system did not work out very satisfactorily in practice, for in 1637 the City Council accepted responsibility for receiving payments and disbursing them to insurers who had sustained fire loss.

These mutual insurance groups continued until 17 December 1676, when the Hamburg Ratsherren decided to terminate the existing contracts and institute a new system of individual policies with regular premiums at a fixed rate. This date marks the founding of the Hamburger General-Feur-Cassa as the first regularly constituted fire insurance company in the world. The maximum level of compensation was kept purposely low, as the burghers wished to discourage policy-holders from regarding fires as something that could realize a cash profit. Originally premiums amounted to $\frac{1}{4}$% of the value of the property per annum, but the company was forced to raise its rates to $\frac{1}{2}$% after a great fire in 1684 which destroyed over 300 houses in the city. At the same time fire insurance was made compulsory by the City Council. The Hamburger Feuerkasse is still run today as a municipal endeavour.
GB: The first fire insurance company in Britain began operating from an office in Threadneedle Street, London on 13 May 1680. The author of this venture rejoiced in the baptismal name of If-Jesus-Christ-had-not-died-for-thee-thou-hadst-been-damned Barebones and was the son of the noted Parliamentarian Praise-God Barebones. For business purposes he styled himself Nicholas Barbon. Trained as a physician, he had abandoned this calling to become a speculative builder after the Great Fire of London in 1667 and built up such a considerable fortune that he was able to afford the heavy risks involved in venturing into the untried field of fire insurance.

Barbon's policies were issued for periods of up to 31 years, and the premium rate was originally 6d per pound rental value of brick-built property, or 1s in the pound for timber-frame buildings. The name of the company was changed in 1705 from the Fire Office to the Phoenix (generally spelt 'Phenix'); the emblem adorned its policies and probably also its fire-marks, although no example of the latter has ever been found. It was finally wound up *c.* 1712.

The earliest fire insurance companies, the Phoenix (1680), the Friendly (1684), the General (1685) and the Amicable (1696), restricted their business to London and its environs. The first insurance company to insure property outside the capital was Charles Povey's Exchange House Fire Office in 1708. Two years earlier it had pioneered in another direction as the first to insure the contents of buildings against fire as well as the buildings themselves. The business was refounded in 1710 as the Sun Fire Office and continues today under that name as Britain's oldest insurance company. *See also* House Journal.

The first
FLAG-DAY
was held at Pontypool and Griffithstown, Monmouthshire in aid of the National Relief Fund on 21 August 1914. The idea of selling flags for charity originated with Mrs Harold George of Griffithstown, the wife of a Great Western Railway engine-driver. A few days after the outbreak of war, her twin sons, fired with martial ardour, came to her with a request for something with which they could play at soldiers. She secured some red, white and blue ribbon and, cutting it into small pieces, made it into miniature flags with the aid of match-sticks. The

milkman arrived while she was thus engaged and pointing out that it had been announced in the papers that day that the Prince of Wales was setting up a National Relief Fund in aid of the dependants of servicemen, suggested that the little flags could be sold to raise money for this worthy cause. Although the exact amount collected is not recorded, Mrs George's efforts were sufficiently successful to inspire immediate imitation and she later received a letter of commendation from Queen Mary.

The first national flag-day was held in aid of the Belgian Relief Fund on 3 October 1914.

The first
FLAG FLOWN AT HALF-MAST
was on board the *Heartsease* in July 1612, as a mark of respect to Capt. James Hall, leader of an expedition in quest of the North-West Passage. He had been murdered by Eskimoes on the west coast of Greenland. The log of the *Patience*, her sister ship, recorded: 'When the *Heartsease* joined the *Patience* her flag was hanging down and her ensign was over the poop which signified the death of someone on board.'

The first
FLUORESCENT LIGHTING
(hot-cathode) was developed by the General Electric Co at Nela Park, Ohio, and first shown publicly at the Annual Convention of the Illuminating Engineering Society in Cincinnati in September 1935. The tube, 2ft long, emitted a brilliant green light and was labelled: 'The fluorescent lumiline lamp – a laboratory experiment of great promise.'

The first practical application of fluorescent lighting was made at a dinner held in Washington, D.C. on 23 November 1936, to celebrate the centenary of the US Patent Office. The banqueting-hall was illuminated by GEC fluorescent lamps.

Commercial production of fluorescent lamps was inaugurated by GEC and Westinghouse, both companies launching their product on 1 April 1938. The GEC lamps came in three sizes – 15W, 20W and 30W – and in lengths of 18, 24 and 36in respectively. The price range was $1.50–$2.00 and the lamps were available in seven different colours.
GB: The first installation of fluorescent lighting was made on the west-bound platform of Piccadilly Circus Underground Station on 2 October 1945.

The first installation of fluorescent street lighting in Britain was made at Rugby by the British Thomson Houston Co on 1 August 1946; and another shortly afterwards in Old Bond Street, London.

The first
FOOTBALL POOL
was Pari-Mutual Pools, established in 1922 by ex-Coldstream Guards officer John Jervis Barnard in a one-room office at 28 Martineau Street, Birmingham. The first coupon contained a single pool with six teams to win and the number returned was insufficient to pay the postage bill. At the beginning of the next season, Barnard was on the point of abandoning the whole project when he decided to have one more try. For some reason that he was never able to explain the coupons suddenly began flooding back. Barnard continued to operate Jervis Pools, as the firm was renamed, until 1938, when he sold it to David Cope of Cope's Pools.

Although Barnard himself never made a great deal of money from the pools idea, others who copied it were more successful. Among their number was John Moores, founder of Littlewoods and ultimately the first pools millionaire. As a 26-year-old telegraphist at the Commercial Cable Co's Liverpool station in 1923, he and two other operators came across a Jervis coupon and tried to calculate how many the promoter would have to send out before he could expect to show a profit. Reckoning on 4,000 coupons as a viable figure, they made up their own coupon and had it printed under the pseudonym 'Littlewood' – a protective guise necessary if they wanted to remain telegraphists. The coupons were distributed outside Manchester United Football Stadium by boys specially hired for the job. Only 35 people decided to try their luck and the stakes totalled a modest £4 7s 6d, from which £2 12s was paid as a first dividend. Soon afterwards, Moores's two partners withdrew from the project, but he determined to go on alone. Seven years later he had made his first million.

The highest dividend paid out to a single winner before the war was the £30,780 received by R. Levy of London for four away wins in April 1937.

The first six-figure winner was Mrs Knowlson of Manchester, who won £104,990 on 7 November 1950.

The first person to receive half a million pounds as an individual British football-pool prize was Cyril Grimes of Liss in Hampshire, who won £512,683 on 4 March 1972.

The first
FOUNTAIN-PEN
was reported from Paris by two Dutch travellers, who saw what they described as a 'marvellous invention', a silver pen containing its own ink, on sale there for 10 francs in 1656.
GB: 'A silver reservoir pen which is very necessary' is how Samuel Pepys described the earliest-recorded example in Britain, presented to him by William Coventry in August 1663. The following Sunday he used the novel device for taking down a sermon, and he may have written portions of his diary with it.

The actual term 'fountain pen' is noted as early as 1710, and various rather primitive writing implements, of the kind that amazed the Dutchmen and delighted Pepys, made their appearance during the next two centuries, though never with sufficient impact to supersede the use of the traditional quill. Probaby the most successful was the Compound Fountain Pen patented by Joseph Bramah (*see also* Water-Closet) on 23 September 1809. This consisted of a thin silver tube, tapering to a quill nib. Ink was poured in at the top and sealed by an air-tight cork stopper. When writing, the flow of ink was activated by gently squeezing the barrel of the pen. The only significant advance made during the next 50 years was the introduction of the rubber ink-sac, patented by Walter Moseley in 1859.

The chief obstacle standing between the fountain-pen and the writing public at this stage of development was the lack of any suitable means of controlling the flow of ink. The problem began to occupy the attention of an American insurance salesman, Lewis Edson Waterman, when he had the misfortune to lose the sale of a large policy to a customer. At the critical moment, his fountain-pen had discharged its contents over the application form, a circumstance that determined Waterman to produce a practical pen suitable for business use. His lengthy and painstaking experiments eventually came to fruition in 1884 with the three-fissure feed, a system that allowed ink and air to pass in opposite directions at the same time. He began manufacture that year on a kitchen table at the rear of a small tobacconist's on the corner of Fulton and Nassau Streets in New York City.

The first
FROZEN FOOD
individual packaged products, were developed by Clarence Birdseye, and put on sale at 10 grocery stores in Springfield, Mass., on 6 March 1930. Birdseye had become interested in the possibility of preserving perishable foods by deep freezing while engaged in a US Government survey of fish and wildlife in Labrador between 1912 and 1915. 'That first winter', he wrote, 'I saw natives catching fish in fifty below zero weather, which froze stiff as soon as they were taken out of the water. Months later, when they were thawed out, some of these fish were still alive.' Birdseye learned to preserve fresh

vegetables while in Labrador, by putting them in a tub of water, and freezing them solid. In 1924 he established a company at Gloucester, Mass., called 'General Seafoods Corp', to develop the process commercially; he sold out to the Postum Co five years later for $22 million. It was agreed that Birdseye's name, split into two words, should be used for brand identification.

The initial range of products launched by the Postum Co at Springfield included peas, spinach, raspberries, loganberries, cherries, fish and various meats. Sales resistance was high at first, partly because the packets were kept in ice-cream cabinets and were not easily visible, and partly because of the relatively high price. One pioneer retailer recalled in later years that 'it took about five minutes to fast-talk a reluctant housewife into buying a package of peas at 35c'. By 1933, however, there were 516 frozen-food retail outlets in the USA.

The first pre-cooked frozen foods were chicken fricassée and criss-cross steak, introduced by Birds Eye in 1939. Other manufacturers marketed creamed chicken, beef stew and roast turkey with dressing the same year.

GB: The pioneer of frozen food in Britain was S. W. Smedley of Wisbech Produce Canners Ltd, Wisbech, Cambridgeshire. He began developing his own freezing process in 1936, after visiting the USA to study the freezing techniques in use there. Smedley's first frozen-food product was asparagus (retail price 2s 3d a pack) in May 1937, followed in June by strawberries (8oz pack 1s 2d; 16oz 2s), in July by garden peas (6oz pack 9d) and raspberries (price as for strawberries), and sliced green beans (6oz pack 1s 2d) in August.

The first
FRUIT MACHINE
was the 'Liberty Bell', designed and built by German immigrant Charles Frey at San Francisco in 1889. The pay-out ranged from 1 coin for two horseshoes to 10 coins for three bells. The original 'Liberty Bell' is preserved at the Reno casino of the same name.

The first
GARAGE
purpose-built to house motor cars, was erected in 1899 by Dr W. W. Barrett of Park Crescent, Hesketh Park, Southport. It was joined to his house by a passage for easy access and was equipped with engine-pits and facilities for cleaning his two cars, an 1898 Daimler and an 1898 Knitley Victoria. Dr Barrett was also distinguished as the first man in England to own a totally enclosed car, and as the inventor of the first practical jack for lifting cars.

Dr Zabriskie of 2103 Church Avenue, Brooklyn, N.Y., built a brick garage measuring 18 × 22ft for a cost of $1,500 the same year. He had purchased his Winton Road-Wagon in October 1898, but it is not known whether his garage was completed before or after Dr Barrett's.

By December 1899, commercially built wooden garages were being supplied to customer's requirements by Messrs F. Jackson & Co of the Soho Bazaar in Oxford Street.

Builders, too, were not slow to appreciate that the provision of a garage could enhance the value of a property. The *Autocar* reported in December 1901: 'In Hampstead a number of new houses have recently been erected, the appointments of which include a motor stable.'

The French word *garage* did not find immediate acceptance. Reporting in October 1901, the *Morning Leader* stated that the following terms were in current use by car-owners: 'motor shed', 'motable', 'motor den', 'motor barn', 'motorium'. The paper itself favoured 'the motory'. Correspondents to the *Autocar* suggested 'carhome', 'carrepose', 'carrest', 'cardomain', 'cardom', 'motories', 'motostore' and – the nearest anyone got to the word that was soon to supersede all the others – 'carage'. Even after 'garage' had passed into general currency on both sides of the Channel, it was not until 1925 that the august French Academy was prepared to accept it as a recognized word of the French language.

The first
GAS CHAMBER
was introduced by the State of Nevada, at the instigation of Maj. D. A. Turner, US Army Medical Corps, as being the 'quickest and most humane method of putting a human to death'. It was used for the first time at the Nevada State Prison, Carson City on 8 February 1924, when Gee Jon was executed for the assassination of a member of a rival Chinese tong. Death ensued some 6min after hydrocyanic gas had been admitted into the chamber.

The first
GAS FIRE
was a combined lamp and heating apparatus patented in France by Philippe Lebon of Bruchay, nr Joinville on 21 September 1799. The following year Lebon installed his Thermolampe at the Hotel Seignelay, Paris at his own expense in order to demonstrate its effectiveness. Apart from heating the apartments, the apparatus was also used to illuminate a fountain, but the unpleasant odour emitted from the gas discouraged potential customers. Although he continued to develop his invention, progress was abruptly terminated in 1804, when Lebon was stabbed to death in the Champs-Elysées on Napoleon's Coronation Day.

The modern gas fire depends on the principle of the bunsen-burner, oxygen being drawn in to mix with the gas and so produce a much hotter flame. Bunsen produced his burner in Germany in 1855, and within a year Messrs Pettit & Smith in England had adapted it for domestic heating and launched the first commercially practicable gas fire on to the market.

The first
GAS METER
was devised in 1815 by William Clegg, assistant to William Murdoch of Soho, Birmingham, pioneer of gas-lighting.

COIN-IN-THE-SLOT GAS METER: the first was patented by R. W. Brownhill of Birmingham in 1887. After every gas company in the country had refused to take it up, the South Metropolitan Gas Co finally agreed, in 1892, to install 100 meters as an experiment provided the patentee undertook to pay all costs if they proved unsuccessful. The South Metropolitan having expressed complete satisfaction at the end of the trial period, the rush to provide meters by other companies was so great that during the year 1896–7, the Mint was obliged to strike three times as many copper coins as in the previous 12 months. Other marked effects of the innovation were the general adoption of gas stoves (*q.v.*) in working-class homes, since the gas companies would supply these free with the meter, and a remarkable diminution of fires consequent on the replacement of oil lamps by gas lighting.

The first
GAS STOVE
commercially practicable, was designed by James Sharp, Assistant Manager of the Northampton Gas Co, and installed in the kitchen of his home in Northampton in 1826. The first commercially produced models were acquired by the Bath Hotel, Leamington and the Angel Inn, Northampton in 1834. At the former a special dinner was cooked for 100 people by gas alone. 'Everything was excellently done', said a contemporary

report, 'and notwithstanding that fish, pudding, fowl, bacon, greens had been steamed in the same steamer, no dish had contracted any unpleasant taste from its neighbour.' Despite this success, Sharp was chary about undertaking full-scale manufacture. One day, however, a magnificent four-horse carriage with liveried outriders drew up before his modest house and Earl Spencer descended to demand a gas-cooked lunch. This mark of approval convinced Sharp that a demand waited to be satisfied. In 1836 he opened a factory in Northampton employing 35 hands, and so established the gas-appliance industry.

Sharp's ovens were upright stoves, with hooks in the ceiling from which to suspend a joint of meat and a circle of burners in the base. The modern form of gas cooker, combining an insulated oven with shelves and cooking-top, emerged with the Bower's Registered Gas Cooking Stove in 1852. Thermostatic oven-regulators date from 1915.

The widespread adoption of gas stoves followed the decision of the gas companies to rent them out to their customers, an innovation pioneered by the Manchester Gas Committee with striking success in 1884.

The first
GIFT COUPONS

were introduced by Benjamin Talbert Babbit of New York in 1865 in order to discourage purchasers of his soap from the idea that they were paying for the wrapper. Each wrapper was overprinted with the word 'coupon', and 10 coupons entitled the customer to a 'beautiful lithograph picture'. Other gifts were added as the premium idea grew in popularity.

GB: The earliest reference to a premium gift scheme is contained in an advertisement placed by Herbert Smith in the *Peterborough Advertiser* of 25 November 1876:

Tea at 36, Narrow Street, Peterborough. H. Smith begs respectfully to inform his customers that he continues to give discount Tea Tickets to every purchaser of a ¼lb of Tea and upwards, quality very superior. A large number of useful and Ornamental Articles kept in stock, which are given in exchange for Tea Tickets.

CIGARETTE COUPONS were first given away with Kinnear's Handicap Cigarettes *c.* 1901, and entitled winners to a free week in Paris. The first firm to give merchandise in exchange for coupons was Ogden's, manufacturer's of the famous Guinea Gold Cigarettes, which introduced a range of gifts in 1902 that included table-tennis sets and bicycles. Another manufacturer, Goodbody's, offered a prize of £1 a week for life. Cigarette coupons ceased during World War I, were revived by Black Cat in 1926, banned in 1933, and brought back by Kensitas in 1956.

The first
GIRL GUIDE

companies began informally during the 18 months following the publication of Sir Robert Baden-Powell's *Scouting for Boys* (*see also* Boy Scout Troop) in January 1908. The earliest on record was the Cuckoo Patrol of Girl Scouts, which was founded by Glasgow schoolgirl Allison Cargill during the summer of 1908. At first the patrol was unsupervised except by Miss Cargill herself, who as instigator of the project had been elected Patrol Leader; but in the autumn of 1909 it was taken under the wing of the 1st Glasgow Troop of Boy Scouts, and William B. Heddow appointed Scoutmaster. The girls were allowed to wear the Scout belt and badges, and the khaki neckerchief of the 1st Glasgow Troop, and were often invited to accompany the Scouts on Saturday afternoon expeditions to Acre Wood at Maryhill, where they joined in the tracking games, fire-lighting exercises and other activities.

The idea of a female branch of the Scout movement first received official recognition with the publication of 'A Scheme for Girl Guides' in *Scout Headquarters Gazette* for November 1909. This had been prompted by the appearance of three members of the 1st Pinkney's Green Girl Scouts at the Crystal Palace Scout Rally in September of the same year, when B.-P. was reluctantly forced to take notice of their existence. Originally he had had no intention of extending the movement to include girls, lest it should be subjected to ridicule. By this time, however, there were already over 6,000 female 'Boy Scouts' registered in the UK (most of them having concealed their gender by giving initials instead of Christian name) and there was little choice, short of mass expulsion, but to form them into a separate section with a programme of activities suitable to the Edwardian young lady of gentle upbringing. This plan met with some resistance from the girls, who did not want to be relegated to the somewhat domestic role allotted them by B.-P. – in his own words, 'to give them the ability to be better mothers and Guides to the next generation'. They were nevertheless obliged to submit to the direction of a committee of ladies formed early in 1910 under the leadership of the founder's sister, Agnes Baden-Powell. The adventurous masculine pursuits described in *Scouting for Boys* had henceforth to be

Allison Cargill – the first Girl Guide?

abandoned in favour of learning to bandage patients and how to make tea (a novel skill to many girls accustomed to servants). At first camping under canvas was vetoed as indecorous, but this prohibition was later relaxed as Patrol Captains were often in favour of allowing their girls an opportunity of learning how to fend for themselves in the open.

The first
GLIDER

full-size man-carrying, was designed by Sir George Cayley of Brompton Hall, Brompton, Yorkshire and described in the *Mechanics Magazine* for 15 September 1852. The aircraft was a monoplane with a kite-shaped wing and an adjustable tail-plane and fin. The total wing area is estimated to have been 500 sq ft and the weight of the machine 300lb. The pilot was carried in a boat-shaped nacelle with tricycle undercarriage; by means of a tiller control, he could operate a second smaller tail-unit which served as both rudder and elevator.

Practical experiments with this glider are believed to have commenced the following year, when Sir George Cayley's coachman was persuaded to make the first true aeroplane flight in history by piloting the machine across a small valley at Brompton Hall. Mrs George Thompson, Cayley's granddaughter, a child of 10 in 1853, was able to recall the epoch-making event in an eyewitness account written nearly 70 years later:

Everyone was out on the high east side and I saw the start from close to. The coachman went in the machine and landed on the west side at about the same level. The coachman got himself clear, and when the watchers had got across, he shouted, 'Please, Sir George, I wish to give notice. I was hired to drive, not to fly.'

A modern reconstruction of Cayley's glider in flight

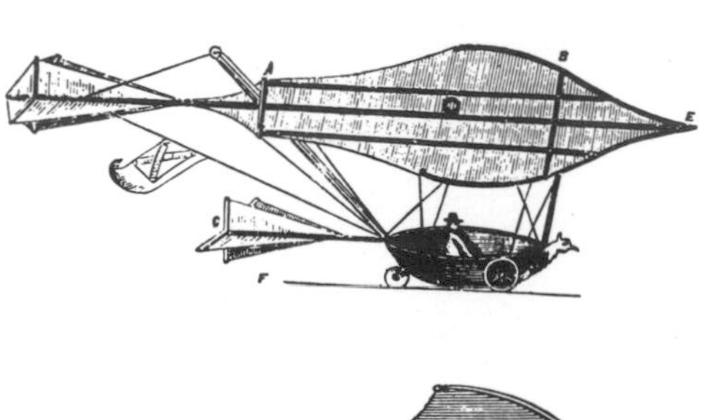

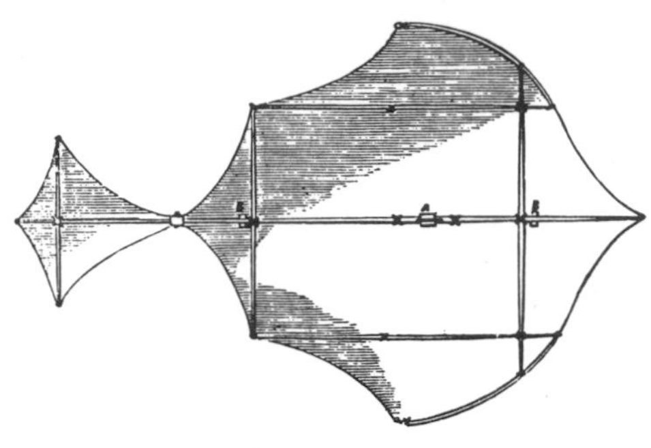

Cayley's designs for a man-carrying glider from the Mechanics Magazine

In a letter to J.E. Hodgson dated 2 November 1921, Mrs Thompson said that she thought the distance covered was about 500yd and that the coachman 'came down with a smash'. Although the name of the world's first aeroplane pilot is not known for certain, research among Sir George Cayley's household papers by Norris McWhirter has revealed that he was probably one John Appleby.

CONTROLLED GLIDER FLIGHT: the first was made by John Montgomery, who flew a distance of 200yd at about 18mph at Otay Mesa, Calif. in March 1884. This was an isolated achievement and he did not succeed in maintaining control in flight on any subsequent occasion.

The first series of controlled glider flights was made by Otto Lilienthal in a 44lb machine of his own design with wing area of 150 sq ft. In 1892 a canal was being cut through Grosskreuz, a suburb of Berlin, and the excavated earth was deposited on a level open space in the form of a conical hill. In the summer of the same year Lilienthal began using this mound to make the first of a series of over 2,000 jump-off flights, controlling the glider by shifting his body to alter the centre of gravity. He was killed on 10 August 1896 after losing control of the aircraft at a height of 25ft. According to an article by the Wright brothers in the September 1908 issue of the *Century Magazine*, it was the reports of Lilienthal's death that first inspired their interest in flight.

GB: The first controlled glider flights were made by Percy Sinclair Pilcher, a Lecturer at Glasgow University, who built a 45lb dihedral-winged monoplane with a surface area of 150 sq ft, in the early months of 1895. He made his first successful controlled flight at Wallacetown Farm, nr Cardross on 12 September, rising to an altitude of 12ft and remaining in the air for about 20sec.

SOARING FLIGHT: the first was made on 27 June 1909 in a Weiss glider piloted by Gordon England, who attained a lift of nearly 40ft over a distance of just under a mile at Amberley, near Arundel, Sussex.

The creation of the modern glider – separating the designer of the glider from that of the aeroplane – is generally credited to Frederick Harth, who built his first machine at Hildenstein in 1914. It was designed specifically to obtain lift and not merely to sustain flight. Two years later, Harth succeeded in remaining in the air for 3½min without losing height, during a flight in the Rhön Mountains.

GLIDING AS A SPORT began with the efforts of some enthusiastic German students, who formed the first gliding club in 1909 after a visit to the International Aeronautic Exhibition at Frankfurt. Under the leadership of Hans Gutermuth, the members of the Darmstadt High School Flying Sport Club built their own biplane and monoplane gliders, basing them initially on the designs of Otto Lilienthal. Their first flights were made from an elevation on the Darmstadt Parade Ground known as 'Chimborazo'. During the summer holidays of 1911 and 1912 the boys held a camp on the Wasserkuppe in the Rhön Mountains and built about 30 new gliders, in one of which Hans Gutermuth made a 1,000yd flight of 1min 52sec duration. Five of the 10 club members who took part in the Wasserkuppe trials 1911–12 were killed in action as Air Force pilots in World War I.

GB: The Amberley Aviation Society, Arundel, Sussex, founded by José Weiss, a French-born naturalized Englishman, and Gordon England in 1912.

GLIDING MEET: the first was organized by Oscar Ursinus, Editor of *Flugsport*, and held on the Wasserkuppe in August 1920. In mid September W. Klemperer, an engineer from Aachen, made the first rubber shock-cord catapult launch in his *Black Devil* and was able to sustain flight for 2min 32sec. The first flight-duration competition was held at the second Rhön Meet in 1921, but no award was made, and it was won for the first time by Arthur Maartens with a 66-min flight in his *Vampyr* on 18 August 1922. German aviation enthusiasts were given a particular incentive to take up gliding after World War I by the fact that powered flight was prohibited under the Treaty of Versailles. This helped Germany to maintain its commanding lead in glider development.

GB: The first gliding meet was held at Itford, Sussex, 16–21 October 1922. The main event, a flight-duration competition sponsored by the *Daily Mail* for a prize of £1,000, was won by M. Maneyrol in a Monopole tandem with a time of 3hr 21min 7sec.

WOMAN TO PILOT A GLIDER: the first was Mrs Florence Taylor, wife of Australian poet and amateur scientist George Augustus Taylor, who flew her husband's home-built aircraft at Narrabeen Beach, N.S.W. in December 1909.

GB: Lady Bailey made her maiden flight from a hill in Buckinghamshire in April 1930.

CROSS-CHANNEL FLIGHT BY GLIDER: the first was made by the

Canadian opera-singer Lissaint Beardmore, who flew from Lympne, Kent to Saint-Inglevert Aerodrome, nr Boulogne in a Professor Sailplane on 19 June 1931.

See also Pilot's Licence, Glider.

The first
GOLDEN DISC
awarded to a recording artiste in recognition of a million sales, was Glen Miller's 'Chattanooga Choo Choo', a novelty song originally heard in the 1941 film *Sun Valley Sérenade* and recorded by RCA Victor the same year. Sales having reached seven figures within a few months, RCA had a 'master' disc sprayed with gold and presented to Glen Miller during a Chesterfield broadcast on 10 February 1942.

It cannot be established with certainty which was the first recording to sell a million copies, since audited sales figures are a relatively recent innovation. The performance most often cited in this respect is Caruso's rendering of the aria 'Vesti la Giubba' ('On with the Motley'), from *Pagliacci*, which he originally recorded for the Gramophone Co of London on 12 November 1902 and remade for Victor with orchestral accompaniment in 1907. The latter version achieved cumulative sales of over a million during the next 40 years or so. In fact it has no claim as 'the first disc to sell a million', only a tentative claim to have been the first disc recorded that ultimately topped the million mark, and even that is arguable.

The most likely candidate for the first disc to achieve 'golden' status is Victor Talking Machine Co's record No. 17081, of Al Jolson singing 'Ragging the Baby to Sleep', which was made on 17 April 1912. An instantaneous success, it is believed to have sold a million copies within a year or two of issue, and was probably the only record to attain this distinction before World War I.

The first golden LP (33⅓rpm) was Decca's 1949 disc of the Rodgers and Hammerstein musical *Oklahoma!*, with the original theatre cast. It had reached 1,750,000 by 1956, which was before any other LP had made the million mark.

The first
GOLLIWOG
was created by Florence K. Upton, the New York-born daughter of British parents, in her *Adventures of Two Dutch Dolls and a Golliwog*, published by Longmans & Green, 1895. The character was based on a black-faced rag-doll of the kind sold at American country fairs in the mid 19th century, which had belonged to Miss Upton's grandmother in her childhood. Toymakers were quick to seize on the popularity of the story-book doll, though not everybody was equally enamoured of the newcomer. One critic deplored that 'anything so hideous should please and fascinate children'. Miss Upton replied: 'The Golliwogg is ugly, but he has a good heart, and he is a dear fellow, and are not children ahead of adults in reading character? They see his beautiful personality.' In 1917 the original Golliwog belonging to Miss Upton was auctioned at Christies for 450gns, the proceeds contributing to the cost of an ambulance for the Front. He was purchased by a Miss Faith Moore, who presented him to the Prime Minister, and he now lives in honourable retirement at Chequers. Florence Upton died in 1922 and lies buried in Hampstead Cemetery, where her gravestone bears the image of the character she created 'to the unfading delight of generations of children'.

The first
GREETINGS CARD
for birthdays and other occasions was designed by W. Harvey and engraved by John Thompson of London in 1829. The design was in the form of an elaborately decorated medallion surrounded by scrollwork and surmounted by the date, together with the words: 'To . . . on the ANNIVERSARIE of . . . day From . . .'

The first
GUIDE DOGS FOR THE BLIND
were trained in 1916 by the Austrian War Dog Institute and by the German Association for Serving Dogs. The original instigator of the project was Dr Gorlitz, Director of the Frauendorf Sanatorium nr Stettin. One of the doctor's patients was a young German officer, partially paralysed, whom he used to accompany for remedial walks in the grounds. On one occasion Dr Gorlitz was called away in the middle of their walk and the patient tried to continue on his own. His unsteady progress was watched by the Director's Alsatian dog, Excelsior, who then disappeared in the direction of the sanatorium building and returned with the officer's walking-stick. When Dr Gorlitz came back he saw the dog gently leading his patient over the lawn to the house. The idea that dogs of such superior intelligence and adaptability could be systematically trained to perform similar service for the blind led first to the experiments inaugurated in 1916, and at the end of the war to the setting up of a permanent training centre at Potsdam under Government auspices.

GB: The Guide Dog movement in Britain was begun at Wallasey, Cheshire in July 1931 by Miss M. E. Crooke, a local dog-breeder, and Mr Musgrave Frankland, himself blind and Secretary of the National Institute for the Blind in Liverpool. Initially the dogs were trained by G. W. Debetaz, who had been lent by L'Oeil qui Voit, the American-run Guide Dog organization in Switzerland. The recipient of Guide Dog No. 1, Meta, was G. W. Lamb, a war-blinded ex-soldier from St Dunstan's.

The first
GUNS
of which there is authentic reference are recorded in 1326. A manuscript titled De Officiis Regum (On the Duties of Kings), compiled by Walter de Milemete for the young Edward III, contains an illustration of a vase-shaped gun mounted on a table and being fired at the touch-hole with a red-hot iron. The projectile is a four-headed arrow and it is probable that the shafts would have been bound round with leather to the same diameter as the bore of the weapon. A manuscript from Holkham Hall in Norfolk dated 1326–7 depicts a much larger gun mounted on stone supports. Neither MS mentions the guns in the text.

The earliest written evidence of guns is a Decree passed by the City of Florence on 11 February 1326 which refers to 'pilas seu palloctas ferreas et canones de metallo' (iron bullets and metal cannon). Most of these early guns were designed to destroy masonry rather than men. The first anti-personnel gun was the ribauldequin, a kind of primitive machine-gun consisting of a line of small-bore barrels each loaded separately, of which the earliest known is recorded at Bruges in 1339.

There is no evidence in ancient Oriental literature to support the oft-quoted claim that the Chinese and Indians were familiar with firearms prior to their introduction in Europe. Guns were first introduced into China by the Portuguese in 1520. Such pyrotechnic missiles as existed at an earlier date were probably designed to be fired from catapults or dropped on assailants from a height. Similarly the claims advanced on behalf of Berthold Schwartz as inventor of the gun should be entertained with caution. This legendary figure may or may not have led an earthly existence. He is variously recorded as having been born in Freiburg, Goslar, Ghent, Mainz, Metz, Cologne, Brunswick and Prague, as well as having Danish, Greek, Negro and Welsh origins attributed to him. He is asserted to have been a Franciscan, Augustinian and Dominican monk

and not a monk at all and is variously supposed to have invented the gun in 1250, 1313, 1320, 1354, 1359 and 1380.
ARTILLERY IN WARFARE: the first recorded use occurred at the Siege of Cividale in Italy by German forces in 1331, when *vasi* and *sclopi* were employed by the defenders to repel the attack.

The first use of artillery by British forces took place at the Battle of Crécy on 26 August 1346. According to an anonymous Italian MS, 'The English knights, taking with them the Black Prince, a body of wild Welshmen and many bombards, advanced to meet the French army . . . they fired all the bombards at once and then the French began to flee.'

The earliest record of a 'hangone' is contained in a list of equipment carried on Edward I's ship *Christophe de la Tour* in 1338. They were first used in warfare by the Duke of Orleans, who equipped his army with 4,000 pieces, each handled by two men, in 1411. Indifferent marksmanship limited their effectiveness at first but by 1414 the Duke's men had learned to handle the new weapon and proved themselves at the Siege of Arras.

The first
GUY FAWKES DAY
The earliest recorded celebration took place two years after the Gunpowder Plot, when bonfires were lit by direction of the Corporation of Bristol, 5 November 1607.

The earliest record of fireworks on Guy Fawkes Day is contained in some lines of doggerel written in 1677:

Now boys with squibs and crackers play
And bonfires blaze turns night to day.

The first
GYM SLIP
was designed in October 1892 by Miss Margaret Tait, a student at Mme Bergman-Osterberg's Hampstead Physical Training College, and first worn by her fellow student Anna Pagan, who wrote home in a letter, dated 25 October:

Madame is wearing out my shoe-leather trotting me up and down the stairs to show my costume off, and the others are being altered. She wants it adopted in schools. A jersey and knickers, with a dress blouse, the jersey forming the yoke and sleeve.

Undeservedly derided, the gym slip was an important factor in enabling girls to participate in team games, since prior to its introduction there had been no 'acceptable' costume that gave them the necessary freedom of movement.

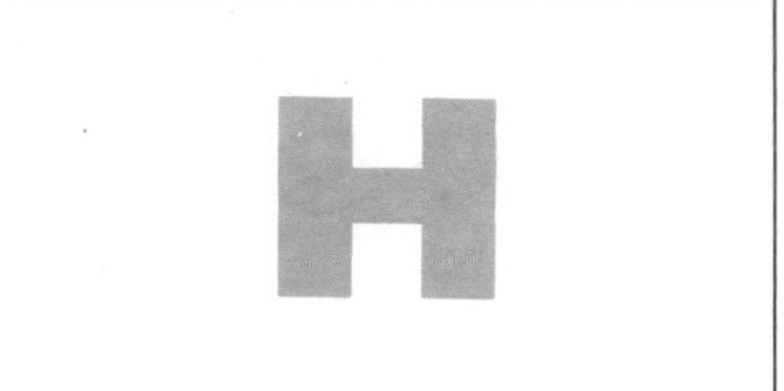

The first
HALFTONE PROCESS
of reproducing photographs in printer's ink was developed by the Swedish engraver Carl Gustaf Wilhelm Carleman, whose first successful single-line halftones were used to illustrate his *Photography by Typographic Printing Press*, published at Stockholm in May 1871. Its frontispiece, a study from nature of two women and a boy walking along a lakeside path, was one of 12 photographs similarly reproduced without the aid of manual engraving. Carleman used a mechanically lined screen to break up the image into lines of varying surface area, which, according to the distance they were separated, gave an accurate impression of light and shade. His was the earliest practical method by which process blocks could be used with high-speed letterpress; meaning, in effect, that for the first time it was possible to have photographic illustrations in magazines alongside the text. The only essential difference between Carleman's system and modern halftone engraving is that today the picture is generally composed of dots, allowing for sharper definition.

The first magazine in the world to contain a halftone illustration was the July 1871 issue of *Nordisk Boktryckeri-Tidning*, in which an article on Carleman's work was accompanied by a picture of an owl on a branch.

The first use of halftone for topical illustration dates also from 1871, when a book titled *Paris' Ruiner* was published in Stockholm by Iwar Haeggström with three studies of ruined Paris reproduced by the Carleman process.

In 1874 the French illustrated weeklies *Le Monde Illustré* and *L'Illustration* published the earliest halftone portrait photographs, showing Col Staaf (the Swedish Military Attaché) and the Arctic navigator Baron Nordenskjöld respectively. After this, interest in the Carleman process seems to have languished, and no further progress was made in halftone-work until the American Stephen Horgan pioneered the use of photomechanical methods for newspaper photographs (*q.v.*) in 1880. Generally the invention of the halftone has been credited to those who made a commercial success of it, such as Georg Meisenbach of Munich and Frederick Ives of Philadelphia. The wholly original contribution of Carl Carleman, despite the first-hand evidence of his published work, has been largely ignored by historians outside Sweden.
GB: The first halftone illustrations to be reproduced in a periodical were 15 studies by amateur photographer C.J. Hinxman of animals at London Zoo, published in the *Graphic* for 5 September 1885.
COLOUR HALFTONE: the first to be published in a periodical was a portrait of the 1890 Derby winner, which appeared in the February 1892 issue of *Land and Water*. The printing was executed by Messrs Waterlow & Son of London.

See also Newspaper Photograph; Advertisement, Photographically Illustrated.

The first
HEARING AID, ELECTRIC
was the Acousticon, patented by Miller Reese Hutchinson of New York on 15 November 1901, and manufactured by the newly formed Hutchinson Acoustic Co the following year. It consisted of a large housing for the batteries, about the size of a portable radio, and a telephone-type receiver to hold to the ear. One of the earliest users was Queen Alexandra, who had been partially deaf since infancy. The Queen used the Acousticon aid throughout the Coronation ceremony in 1902 and afterwards presented the 26-year-old inventor with a medal to mark her appreciation. Among the 90 or so patents granted to Hutchinson during his lifetime was one for the Klaxon, an innovation that caused his friend Mark Twain to remark to him: 'You invented the Klaxon horn to make people deaf, so they'd have to use your acoustic device in order to make them hear again!'
ELECTRIC HEARING AID DESIGNED TO BE WORN ON THE PERSON: the first was the Amplivox, weight 2½lb, which was marketed by A. Edwin Stevens of London in October 1935.
TRANSISTOR HEARING AID: the first was manufactured by the Sonotone Corp of Elmsford, N.Y. and marketed on 29 December 1952.

The first
HELICOPTER
capable of lifting a man off the ground in vertical flight was designed by E.R. Mumford to a specification titled 'The Solution to Aerial Flight' dated 6 January 1905, and built by William Denny & Bros, shipbuilders of Dumbarton, Scotland. The machine had six 25ft-diameter propellers and was originally powered by a 25hp Buchet

engine, replaced in 1909 by a 25hp N.E.C. and in 1911 by a more powerful 40hp N.E.C. Construction was originally of bamboo, but when this became waterlogged in a storm, it was replaced with metal. Denny's official history records that during trials 'the combined efforts of a squad of men were necessary to prevent its disappearing with an intrepid member of the staff as pilot'. By 1912 it had achieved tethered flights of up to 10ft from the ground.

The first helicopter to achieve free flight was a twin-rotor machine designed by French cycle-dealer Paul Cornu and test flown at Lisieux on 13 November 1907. Powered by a 24hp Antoinette engine, the machine attained a maximum of 20sec in the air at a height of 6ft.

GB: The first helicopter to achieve free flight was designed by Louis Brennan and test flown at the Royal Aircraft Establishment, Farnborough in 1925. Some 80 vertical take-offs were made before the machine crashed in October of the same year.

FORWARD FLIGHT: the first sustained flight was made by Etienne Oehmichen in a four-rotor helicopter powered by a 180hp Rhône rotary engine on 14 April 1924. The 1,181ft flight established the first helicopter distance record recognized by the Fédération Aéronautique Internationale.

The first practical helicopter capable of full take-off and forward flight control, as well as being able to maintain stability and fly at a reasonable speed, was the Gyroplane Laboratoire, designed by Louis Breguet and René Dorand and first flown on 26 June 1935. Powered by a powerful 420hp Hispano-Wright engine, the Gyroplane established a speed record of 67mph on 22 December 1935, an altitude record of 517ft on 22 September 1936, and a duration record of over 1hr on 24 November 1936. Development continued up to the outbreak of war, when it was stored at Villacoublay Air Base. The machine was destroyed in an Allied air raid in 1943.

The first helicopter to be registered as an 'Approved' aircraft and thus the first that can be regarded as truly out of the experimental stage was the Focke-Wulf FW 61, designed by Dr Heinrich Focke and test flown in free flight at Bremen on 6 June 1936. In June 1937 it broke the Breguet-Dorand records with a speed of 76mph, altitude 7,999ft and duration of 1hr 20·5min, as well as a distance record of 50 miles. Registration was secured the same year. The reality of practical helicopter flight was brought to general notice in 1938, when the German woman pilot Hanna Reitsch gave a brilliant display of the FW 61's control and manœuvrability before a large audience in the Deutschlandhalle, Berlin – one of the few occasions on which an aircraft has been flown indoors.

GB: The first practical, fully controllable helicopter was the Weir W.5, built by the Scottish firm of James Weir to the design by C.G. Pullin and test flown by his son Raymond Pullin in June 1938.

HELICOPTER IN SERIES PRODUCTION: the first was the 1,000hp Bramo-engined Focke-Achgelis Fa 223 six-passenger transport, which made its first free flight in August 1940. Although production began early in 1942, practically all the models built to order of the Luftwaffe were destroyed in Allied air attacks before delivery, and only eight were actually delivered to the Luftwaffe. One of these aircraft made the first helicopter crossing of the English Channel in September 1945 when its German crew flew it to the Airborn Forces Experimental Establishment in Britain.

The US Army had taken delivery of its first helicopter, the Sikorsky VS-300, at Wright Field, Dayton, Ohio in May 1942. Series production of the more powerful 180hp Sikorsky R.4 began at Bridgeport, Conn. in 1942 and deliveries commenced to the US Army and the Royal Navy the following year.

GB: Series production of the WS-51 was commenced by Westland Aircraft Ltd under licence from Sikorsky in January 1947.

Paul Cornu's helicopter, 1907

The first
HOLIDAY CAMP
run on modern lines (i.e. permanent and catering to families) was Dodd's Socialist Holiday Camp, Caister-on-Sea, Norfolk, founded by J. Fletcher-Dodd in 1906. The present Douglas Holiday Camp in the Isle of Man can claim an earlier date of foundation, having been established on a permanent basis in 1900, but it was run for men only until after World War II.

Caister's earliest surviving prospectus, for the season Easter–October 1914, describes the facilities of the Camp as a dining-hall for 200 (meals served outdoors in fine weather), a dark-room and cycle-shed, kitchen and flower gardens, a shop (selling bathing-costumes, tobacco, biscuits and confectionary, mineral waters, stationery, newspapers and picture postcards at 1s a dozen), a reading-room and a bathing beach with changing-sheds. The dining-hall was furnished with a piano, games and newspapers and was used after supper for amateur theatricals, lectures, debates and fancy-dress balls. Outdoor entertainments included lawn-tennis, croquet and cricket, picnics and rambles, and motor-car tours.

Accommodation consisted of green canvas bell-tents sleeping four, or square tents for two, equipped with spring-stretcher bedsteads and wool mattresses. 'House Tents', built of wood and canvas, could be hired for an extra 3s a week per person. The terms were 21s per week inclusive, or for periods of less than a week, 3s 6d a day.

The menu was somewhat frugal, in keeping with the homespun image of early 20th-century Socialism, but wholesome and probably rather more abundant than many working-class campers were accustomed to at home.

Breakfast: 8am

Porridge, Shredded Wheat or Grape Nuts with new milk; tea, coffee or cocoa; ham, fish or eggs; 'Camp-made' wholemeal and white bread; butter, marmalade and stewed fruits

Dinner: 1pm

Roast beef or mutton, two vegetables; fruit pies, milk or steamed puddings; bread

Tea: 5pm

Wholemeal and white bread, butter; jam; salad; cake; buns; fruit in season from camp gardens

Supper: 9pm

Milk, cocoa and lemonade; biscuits and cheese

Intoxicants were not allowed on the premises. Other rules stated that campers were to be punctual at meals (a bugle summoned them to the dining-hall) and that bathers must wear the regulation costume. Persons talking

The holiday camp at Caister-on-Sea as it was more than 50 years ago.

loudly after 11pm would be dismissed from the Camp. Campers were expected to help in some of the everyday tasks of the establishment.

Lest any potential guests should be anxious about their eligibility to stay at a 'Socialist Holiday Camp', Mr Fletcher-Dodd assured them that 'all schools of thought are represented'.

By 1920 the accommodation had been extended to cater to 300 guests. A new club-room had just been erected with a full-size billiard-table, and some ex-Army huts provided, suitable for parties of four, six or eight. The menu had changed little from pre-war except that shrimps and potted meats had been added for tea, and there was a dark hint of margarine 'when butter is not procurable'. The terms, though, had now risen to exactly double the rate in 1914.

Ten years later the facilities had again expanded to include a comfortably appointed lounge and three hard tennis-courts, in addition to the two existing grass ones. The rules do not appear to have diminished at all, and indeed leave the impression that as Mr Fletcher-Dodd grew older he felt obliged to impose a more stringent discipline on his guests. Persons neglecting to keep their tents clean and tidy were now to be fined 6d for each offence. There was also a new prohibition against 'rowdy conduct and improper language', which suggests that some members of the jazz generation may have been behaving themselves with less propriety than Mr Dodd had been accustomed to from his Edwardian campers.

During the 1930s the holiday camp became an established British institution, helped by the fact that the majority of workers were by then entitled to holidays with pay. The increased competition from the new Butlin's and Warner's camps had its effect on Caister as it had on all the older camps. By the final pre-war season of 1939 the renamed Caister-on-Sea Holiday Camp had undergone a transformation. There was now accommodation for 1,000 guests, a fully equipped sports ground and a putting-green, a car park with lock-up garages, a special Camp railway station (formerly campers had travelled 3 miles from Great Yarmouth station), a café, a large dance-hall with resident band, a table-tennis room and a bowls-lawn.

No mention is made in the brochure of the lectures and debates that so stimulated the minds of an earlier generation of campers. Some of the bell-tents were still in service, though even these were fitted with electric lights. Most campers opted for a chalet. Even the old bugle had been replaced with a siren, a sound that many 1939 campers were going to hear a lot more of in the years to come.

The first
HOME-MOVIE OUTFIT
was the Amateur-Kinetograph, a ciné-camera-cum-projector offered to amateur film-makers by Oskar Messter of Berlin in his October 1897 catalogue. The apparatus divided into two parts, the front portion being used for projection with an illuminant placed behind the gate. Standard 35mm film was supplied by Eastern Photographic Materials Co Ltd of London. The catalogue also listed a selection of 84 films produced at Messter's own studios in Berlin's Friedrich Strasse for professional use or for home viewing.
GB: Like Messter's home-movie outfit, the first apparatus for amateur film-makers marketed in Britain consisted of a combined camera and projector. Called the 'Birtac', it was produced by pioneer film maker Birt Acres (*see also* Film: Motion Picture) in 1898 at a price of 10gns, or 12gns including a developing and printing outfit. The film used was a 17·5mm gauge, chosen because it could be produced by simply slitting standard 35mm film down the middle. It was supplied in 20ft daylight-loading cartridges at 2s 6d a roll. For projection illumination an upright Welsbach mantle fed from the domestic gas-supply was used, the gas being pressurized in a bag with weights loaded on to it.

Although home-movie outfits were available in Britain, France and Germany before the end of the 19th century, there is no known surviving example of a Victorian home movie. In 1932 it was recorded that the earliest-known example of a film taken by an amateur was one made by E.W. Mellor, Treasurer of the Royal Photographic Society, during a trip to Egypt in 1909. The Editors would be interested to hear of any film of purely 'family interest' made by an amateur cinematographer before this date.

Home movies did not achieve widespread popularity until the introduction of non-inflammable film by Charles Pathé, who brought out his 28mm K.O.K. projector and cinécamera in 1912, backed by an extensive library of films for home entertainment. In the USA the 22mm Edison Home Kinetoscope appeared the same year, designed for use with Eastman Kodak safety film.

The first 16mm cinécamera was the Kodak Model A, produced in prototype form by J.G. Capstaff of the Eastman Kodak Co at Rochester, N.Y. in May 1920. After further developments it was announced for sale, together with the Model A motorized Kodascope projector, on 5 July 1923. The latter was of such robust construction that a number are still in use.
9·5MM HOME-CINEMA APPARATUS: the first was the Pathé Baby projector, introduced by Pathé Cinema of Paris in December 1922, and followed 12 months later by a camera. Designed by Pathé's Ferdinand Zecca, the 9·5mm Baby was intended to bring amateur movie-making within the reach of those who could not afford the larger, more expensive gauges.
8MM CAMERA AND PROJECTOR: the first was introduced in the USA by Eastman Kodak in August 1932. The camera used a special 16mm film which was run through twice, once in each direction, then slit down the middle after processing. This almost halved the cost of home movie-making in the USA, where 9·5mm was virtually unknown.
COLOUR FILM FOR AMATEUR USE: the first was Kodacolor, a two-colour additive process developed by the French inventor R. Berthon and marketed in the USA in July 1928. The Eastman Kodak Co had acquired the rights in Berthon's process from the Société du Film en Colours Keller-Dorian in 1925. A banded three-colour filter was used on a standard 16mm

camera and likewise on the projector.
GB: Kodacolor was demonstrated for the first time before the Royal Photographic Society on 18 October 1928. It was introduced commercially the following year.

The first three-colour film stock for amateur use was 16mm Dufaycolor, produced by Spicer-Dufay Ltd at their plant in Sawston, nr Cambridge and marketed in 1934 by Ilford Ltd. Sixteen-millimetre Kodachrome was launched in the USA in 1935 and 8 mm Kodachrome in 1936.

SOUND PROJECTOR FOR AMATEUR USE: the first was RCA's 16mm Model PG-30, introduced in the USA in 1930.
GB: Five 16mm sound projectors appeared on the market in Britain in 1931 – the RCA Portable Home-Talkie, the Talkiefone, the Gaumont Acoustic Portable, the Reylik and the Animatophone.

NATIONAL AWARD FOR AMATEUR FILM-MAKERS: the first in Britain was the Era Challenge Cup for the best amateur film of the year, presented for the first time in 1931. There were 50 entries.

The first
HORSE-BOX

purpose-built, was constructed by Messrs Herring, coachbuilders of Long Acre, to the order of the racehorse-owner Lord George Bentinck, and used for the first time on 18 September 1836, when it set out from Goodwood drawn by six post horses to carry the thoroughbred Elis to Doncaster for the St Leger.

Apart from one isolated instance 20 years earlier, when a specially sprung bullock caravan had been used to convey Mr Territt's horse Sovereign from Worcestershire to Newmarket for the Two Thousand Guineas, racehorses had always been walked to the courses where they were to compete. For big events, like the Derby, they were generally stabled in the neighbourhood for about a month before the race, to give them ample time to recover from the journey. This meant, of course, that if a horse was known to be entered at a particular meeting, it clearly could not be attending other meetings at any great distance immediately afterwards.

It was this simple principle that encouraged the sporting Lord George to design a van of a kind never seen before, with padded interior and accommodation for two horses. Sunday, 18 September 1836 was three days before the date of the St Leger. The distance between Goodwood and Doncaster was 224 miles. While the horse-box was trundling over the country roads from Sussex to Yorkshire at the astonishing rate of some 75 miles a day, Lord George was secretly backing Elis heavily through his commission agents, and securing uncommonly favourable odds from bookmakers who thought that with the three-year-old safely ensconced at Goodwood, there was little chance that he would be a starter. Elis not only arrived at Doncaster in time for the race but, ridden by J. Day, won the St Leger by two clear lengths.

MOTOR HORSEBOX: the first was a specially designed chain-driven van with a Napier petrol engine built by the Motor Power Co in 1901.

The first
HOTEL

was Low's Grand Hotel, Covent Garden, opened in January 1774 by David Low at 43 King Street, a house formerly occupied by the eccentric Lord Russell, who had redesigned its interior to resemble the between-decks of a warship. Before Low switched his avocation from hairdresser to hotelier, visitors arriving in London for anything more than an overnight stay would generally seek furnished lodgings, while those on short visits put up at inns. Low's venture, described by Horace Walpole in 1776 as a 'Hotel Garini', introduced the idea of a public place of residence designed primarily for the accommodation of families. In this it differed from the inns and taverns of the time, whose major business was the provision of refreshment, and to whom the letting of rooms was of secondary importance.

In order to publicize the Grand Hotel, Low had a series of gold, silver and copper medallions struck for distribution to princes, nobles and commoners respectively. Despite, or perhaps because of, such effusions of good will to his guests, Low failed to prosper in the hotel business and in 1780 he abandoned it for another trade, becoming the first chiropodist (*q.v.*) to style himself as such. In this too, he eventually failed, being forced to enter a workhouse, from which he was expelled for stabbing the Master.

The Grand Hotel continued under new management after Low's departure. In 1794 a Mrs Hudson was proprietress; an advertisement issued by her in that year quaintly informs the public that the establishment has 'stabling for one hundred noblemen and horses'. At the beginning of the 19th century the Hotel acquired celebrity for its cuisine, the dining-room acquiring the name of 'The Star' on account of the number of distinguished people to be seen eating there. In succeeding years it became known variously as 'Froome's', 'Joy's', 'Evans's' and 'The Falstaff', finally ceasing to be a hotel in the 1880s.

HOTEL EQUIPPED WITH BATHROOMS: the first was the Tremont House, Boston, Mass., which was opened on 16 October 1829. The eight bathrooms, all located in the basement, were approached by a separate entrance on to the street. Since the Tremont House could accommodate some 250 guests, possibly this helped to discourage long queues for their use.

The first hotel with private baths was the Mount Vernon Hotel, Cape May, N.J. in 1853. The first in GB was the Savoy Hotel, with 70 private bathrooms, opened by Richard D'Oyly Carte on 6 August 1889. Holloway, the builder, was frankly incredulous when D'Oyly Carte gave instructions as to the number of bathrooms required, and asked him whether he expected his guests to be amphibious. The novelty of the innovation can be gauged by the fact that the Savoy's closest rival, the newly opened Hotel Victoria in Northumberland Avenue, rejoiced in 4 bathrooms for 500 guests. The price of a double room with bath at the Savoy was 12s a night.

RAILWAY HOTELS: the first were the Victoria and the Euston, both four-storey buildings designed by Philip Hardwicke for the London & Birmingham Railway Co and opened simultaneously at Euston Station in September 1839. The Victoria, on the west side of the Station, was intended for the humbler class of traveller, being described in the Company's literature as a 'dormitory and coffee room'. It was unlicensed. Opposite it was the Euston, maintained in regal style by the Manager, Mr Bacon, a former steward of the Athenaeum, and catering to 1st-class passengers only.

HOTEL WITH A BRIDAL SUITE: the first was the Irving House, New York City, which offered this attraction in 1844.

CENTRALLY HEATED HOTEL: the first was the Eastern Exchange Hotel, Boston, Mass., where steam-radiators were installed in 1846.

HOTEL TO EMPLOY WAITRESSES: the first was the Delavan House, Albany, N.Y. in May 1853. The celebrated American feminist, Amelia Bloomer, promoter of the pantaloon garments named after her, recorded in a letter written a few months later:

Stopping over night at the Delavan House in Albany, we were agreeably surprised on entering the dining-room for supper to see about a dozen young women in attendance on the tables. This was something new. When we visited the house last winter the waiters were all men, as is usual in such places. Now not a man was to be seen in that capacity; but in place of their heavy tread, and awkward motions, was woman's light footfall and easy graceful movements. In a conversation with the proprietor we learned that the change was . . . entirely satisfactory . . . the only objectors being a few women preferring black men.

BIBLES IN HOTEL ROOMS were first distributed by the Gideons at Superior Hotel, Iron Mountain, Mont. in November 1908.
HOTEL TO INSTALL TELEVISION SETS IN ITS BEDROOMS: the first was the Hotel New Yorker, New York City in February 1932. The sets, supplied by the Freed Television & Radio Corp, were provided in all 'de luxe suites'. Guests were able to tune in to up to 5hrs of entertainment programmes daily from the CBS television station W2XAB.

For the first hotel to cook by electricity, *see* Electric Oven. For the first hotel to install an elevator, *see* Elevator.

The first *HOUSE JOURNAL*

was the *British Mercury*, instituted in 1710 by the Company of London Insurers (which later became the Sun Fire Office) and delivered three times a week to the houses of any policy-holders willing to subscribe. The earliest dated issue is No. 8 for 4–6 October 1710, though a Company minute of the previous April indicates that the journal was already in existence then.

Between 2 August 1712 and 2 May 1716 the *British Mercury* was published under the imprint of the Sun Fire Office, where 'Policies to the value of £500 each are delivered out . . . to any person who shall take them, paying the Stamp Duty, and the first Quarterly 2s if they desire no Mercury, or 2s 6d if they will have it.' In 1716 it was superseded by a quarterly publication called the *Historical Register* and this lasted until 1738.

No other commercial undertaking is known to have followed the Sun's example during the 18th century, and the next recorded house journals are the *London and Dover Railway Advertiser* of 1844–5 and *Thacker & Co's Monthly* of 1844–53. The first in the USA was *The Mechanic*, published by the H. B. Smith Machine Co of Vermont from 1847 to 1914.

The first *HOVERCRAFT*

was developed by (Sir) Christopher Cockerell, an electronics engineer and spare-time boat-builder of Somerleyton, Suffolk, who patented the idea on 12 December 1955. His initial experiments had been made the previous year with a Heath Robinson-type apparatus that has since become one of the classics of inventor's improvisation. An empty food can, open at one end, was inserted into a slightly larger Lyons Coffee tin with both ends removed. Screwed into this position, the cans were attached to the nozzle of a vacuum-cleaner clamped on to a stand and the switch reversed so that the cleaner would expel air, rather than draw it in. Placing a pair of kitchen scales directly beneath the aperture of the Lyons tin, Cockerell found that the thin film of air being thrust downwards between the inner and outer walls of the two cans was being discharged at a pressure of 3lb as registered by the scale, or three times the pressure expelled from the pipe of the vacuum-cleaner without the tin-can attachment. Thus he demonstrated the basic principle of all modern hovercraft, the 'annular jet'.

The first full-size experimental hovercraft was the 3½ton 30ft long SR-N1, built by Saunders-Roe and launched at Cowes, Isle of Wight on 30 May 1959. Powered by a 435hp Alvis Leonides air-cooled radial engine, it had a maximum speed of 25 knots and operated with a 9in clearance above the surface. Later modifications increased the maximum speed to 68 knots.
CHANNEL CROSSING BY HOVERCRAFT: the first was made by the Saunders-Roe SR-N1 from Dover to Calais on 25 July 1959.
HOVERCRAFT PASSENGER SERVICE (regular): the first was inaugurated on 20 July 1962 by British United Airways, who operated a 60-knot 24-seater Vickers-Armstrong VA-3 on the Dee Estuary between Wallasey, Cheshire and Rhyl, Flint. The service continued until September.
CHANNEL HOVERFERRY SERVICE: the first was inaugurated between Dover and Boulogne by the British Rail Seaspeed SR-N4 Mountbatten Class ACV *Princess Margaret* on 1 August 1968. The SR-N4 weighed 168 tons, was powered by four Bristol Siddeley Marine Proteus gas-turbine engines each developing 3,400shp, and had a carrying capacity of 609 passengers or 254 passengers and 30 cars.
TRACKED HOVERCRAFT (full-size): the first was the Vickers RTV 31 High Speed Passenger Train, built on behalf of the National Research Development Corp and delivered to the test track at Earith, Huntingdonshire on 2 August 1971.

The first *HUNGER STRIKE*

was staged by Russian prisoners during the reign of Tsar Alexander III (1881–94). The earliest definitive evidence of the practice dates from 1889, when it was reported that some women inmates of Kará Gaol had been forcibly fed.
GB: The first hunger strike was conducted in July 1909 by Miss Marion Wallace Dunlop of Ealing, a suffragette who had been sentenced to one month's imprisonment for painting a clause from the Bill of Rights on the walls of the House of Commons. She was committed to Holloway on 1 July and began refusing food on the 5th. The authorities left trays of the most appetizing and delectable food by her bedside all night, but she threw it out of the window next morning. After maintaining her fast for 91 hours she was released.

Forcible feeding was first employed in September of the same year, milk and meat juices being poured down a tube inserted down the gullet or through the nostrils. The longest hunger strike on record was one for 94 days by nine prisoners at Cork Gaol in Ireland, 11 August–12 November 1920.

The first *HYMN-BOOK*

in the vernacular was published at Prague by Severin for the Hussites of Bohemia on 13 January 1501. It contained 89 hymns in the Czech language, of which 21 were by the Bohemian divines Konvaldský, Taborský and Lucas Pragensis. The name of the hymnal is not known, as the only surviving copy lacks the title-page.
GB: The first English hymn-book was Miles Coverdale's *Goostly Psalmes and Spiritualle Songes*, London, 1539. Besides paraphrases of 9 Latin hymns, it contained 15 others, of which at least 13, and possibly all, were translations from the German. This hymnal was never employed in regular Church worship, as it was prohibited immediately upon publication.

The first hymnal containing original matter in English was George Wither's *Hymns and Songs of the Church*, for which Orlando Gibbons provided 16 of the tunes. On its publication in 1623 the King granted Wither a privilege by which a copy was to be bound up with every Bible printed. This aroused intense opposition from the Stationers' Company and they were able to obtain an Order from the Privy Council for the suppression of the hymnal. It is unlikely that Wither's hymn-book would have been employed in Anglican Church worship, as the singing of hymns at services was proscribed by an Act of Elizabeth I and remained so until the end of the 17th century.

The first religious body in England to

adopt the singing of hymns as part of its regular form of worship was the Baptist congregation of Benjamin Keach at Horsley Down, Southwark, which introduced the practice of singing a hymn at the Lord's Supper in 1673. Keach published the first Nonconformist hymnal, *Spiritual Melody*, in 1691. This collection of 300 hymns was the first to be adopted by an English Church. The Congregationalists began the use of hymns in worship the same year and published their first hymn-book in 1694. The first Methodist hymn-book was John and Charles Wesley's *Hymns and Sacred Poems* of 1739.

The first Church of England hymn-book published in Britain for general use was Martin Madan's *A Collection of Psalms and Hymns, Extracted from Various Authors*, London, 1760. Hymn-singing (as opposed to the rendering of Psalms and anthems) made little progress outside the cathedrals and more fashionable churches until the introduction of choirs into Anglican parish churches in the 1840s.

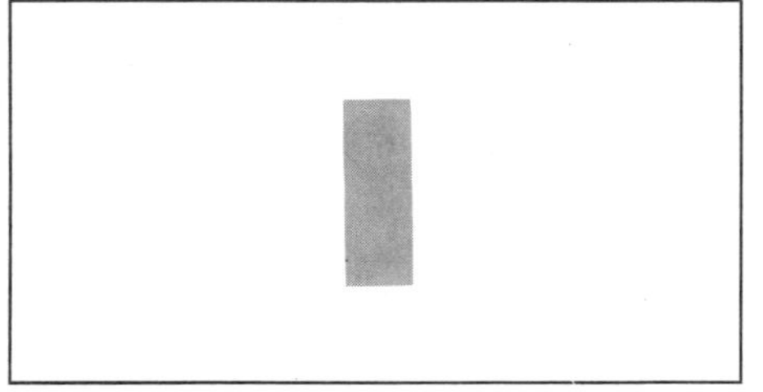

The first
ICE CREAM
authenticated reference to in Britain, appears in the accounts of the Lord Steward's Department for 1686, itemizing 12 dishes of ice cream at £1 per dish for James II and his officers, who were in camp at Hounslow Heath.

Much controversy surrounds the origins of ice cream, and its true history has been obscured by claims that it was eaten by Alexander the Great, Nero and the Egyptian Pharaohs. These, and others of the ancients, were fond of confections made with, or chilled by, snow, but this was not ice cream. It appears that the sorbet, or water-ice, was introduced in Florence in the 16th century, and travelled thence to France. In 1660 an Italian called Procopio Cultelli who was then working as a *limonadier* (lemonade vendor) in Paris, took the first step towards mechanization when he contrived a special churn for the manufacture of ices. This he employed for making a sorbet from chilled lemonade. Dairy ice cream was first introduced to France in the 18th century by the proprietor of the Parisian coffee-house Le Caveau, who had the arms of the Duke of Chartres, one of his most distinguished patrons, sculpted in ice cream in 1774. He popularized the dish under the name of 'iced butter'.

French ice-cream parlour, c. *1810*

The available evidence points towards Britain as the birthplace of dairy ice cream. Charles I had a French chef, Gerald Tissain, who prepared iced desserts which seem to have been made with milk or cream, and who was awarded an annual pension of £20 for life in recognition of his efforts.

Ice cream was popular with the wealthy throughout the 18th century, and there were a number of ice-cream parlours in Piccadilly and its environs. It continued to be expensive – George Washington spent $200 on ice cream in two months in 1790 – until the introduction of mass-production methods by Jacob Fussell, a Baltimore dairyman, in 1851. Fussell ran four milk routes in the city, and found that the irregular demand for cream caused severe wastage. The only person making ice cream in Baltimore at this date was producing a confection of doubtful wholesomeness with boiled milk and sugar, and retailing it at 60c a quart. Purchasing a quantity of freezers, Fussell set up as an ice-cream wholesaler and started what was in effect the world's first ice-cream factory. Bulk production enabled his ice cream to be retailed at 25c a quart, an unprecedentedly low price, and within a year of delivering his first consignment on 15 June 1851, he had launched similar businesses in Washington and New York.

In Britain the introduction of factory-made ice cream was delayed by the ready availability of cheap ices from hokey-pokey men, which began with the large influx of Italian immigrants after 1865. The street sale of ice cream had, however, started in a small way at a somewhat earlier date. Henry Mayhew, in his *London Labour and the London Poor*, which was published in 1851, notes the 'novel and aristocratic luxury of street-ices', which would indicate that the trade may have been in existence during the late 1840s. At this time there were estimated to be 30,000 adult street-vendors in London.

The Italian hokey-pokey men continued to hold their virtual monopoly of the low-priced ice-cream business until 1922, when Thomas Wall, a sausage-manufacturer, concerned at the cost of running his Acton factory on short-time during the summer off-season, embarked on the manufacture of the first wrapped brickettes. These were marketed through the traditional outlet for ice cream – the street – though the means was novel. Shopkeepers having refused to stock wrapped brickettes, a 20-year-old Walls's employee, Cecil Rodd, then a £3 a week odd-job man, suggested taking them direct to the public on tricycles. He himself rode the first 'Stop Me and Buy One'. Walls's venture into factory-made ice cream was an instantaneous success and in 1923 Lyons and Eldorado entered into competition. The latter were the first to introduce ice creams in cinemas.

ICE-CREAM CONES were first produced in 1896 by an Italian immigrant to New Jersey, Italo Marcioni, and a special mould was patented by him on 13 December 1903. The innovation attracted little attention and was not popularized until its reintroduction at the Louisiana Purchase Exposition at St Louis in 1904, when a Syrian penny-sugar-waffle concessionaire named E. A. Hamwi started rolling waffles into the shape of a cone for the benefit of the ice-cream vendor who occupied the adjoining booth.

GB: Ice-cream cones were introduced by Lawrence Askey, who walked from Italy in 1910 to set up as an ice-cream salesman in England.
WAFER ICE CREAMS were introduced to Britain by an ice-cream seller called Lewis from his pitch in Bolton Market Hall in 1905. He devised the rectangular brass slide used for making up the sandwich, designing it to fit the new thin wafer biscuits that had recently been marketed by Peak Frean & Co. The original name given to wafer ice-creams was 'sliders'.
CHOC-BARS were first marketed in the USA in 1921 by Christian K. Nelson of Onawa, Iowa, founder of the Eskimo Pie empire.

The first
IDENTIKIT
was used in the identification of a criminal by Sheriff Peter Pitchess of Los Angeles County Police in February 1959. The case involved the armed robbery of a liquor store, the owner of which was able to give the police a sufficiently clear description of the thief for them to build up an identikit likeness for circulation in the neighbourhood. This resulted in the naming of a suspect, who confessed to the crime on being apprehended.

The idea of Identikit was originally conceived by Hugh C. McDonald, a detective in the Los Angeles Identification Bureau, who began working on it shortly after the war. Some 50,000 photographs were dissected and reduced to 500 master foils – making up a kit comprising 37 noses, 52 chins, 102 pairs of eyes, 40 lips, 130 hairlines, and an assortment of eyebrows, beards, moustaches, spectacles, wrinkles and headgear.
GB: Identikit was introduced at Scotland Yard by Sir Richard Jackson of the CID. The first case in which it was employed led to the speedy arrest of murderer Edwin Albert Bush in March 1961 by a junior police constable on patrol in Soho.

The first
INCOME TAX
was the *Catastro* introduced in Florence under Lorenzo de' Medici in 1451. It was later replaced by the *Scala*, an income tax levied on a progressive basis, but this degenerated into a convenient means of political blackmail and, on the overthrow of the Medicis in 1492, it was repealed.
GB: Introduced by William Pitt the Younger as a war measure with effect from 9 January 1799, the new tax was levied at a standard rate of 10% on incomes over £200, and on a reduced scale for incomes between £60 and £199. There were allowances for children forming part of the taxpayer's family and also in respect of premiums for life insurance, repairs to property and tithes. Revenue the first year amounted to £6 million.

A pamphlet titled *A Plain, Short, and Easy Description of the Different Clauses in the Income Tax, so as to Render it familiar to the Meanest Capacity* was distributed to taxpayers, and this is believed to have been the first explanatory leaflet issued by a Government Department. Like some of its modern counterparts, its effect was to plunge the public into even greater confusion. A contemporary cartoon depicts John Bull scratching his head over the pamphlet and complaining: 'I have read many crabbed things in the course of my time but this for an easy piece of business is the toughest to understand I ever met with.'

The tax was repealed following the Peace of Amiens in 1802, by which time the public outcry was so great that Parliament ordered that all documents and records relating to it should be destroyed.

It was reimposed in 1803, repealed in 1816 at the conclusion of the Napoleonic Wars, and introduced for the first time as a peacetime measure by Robert Peel in 1842 at the rate of 7d in the £ for incomes in excess of £150 p.a. The lowest rate was 2d in 1875, and the highest 10s in 1941–6.

The first modern democratic State to impose an income tax on its citizens in time of peace was the Swiss Canton of Basle in 1840.
SUPER-TAX was introduced by David Lloyd George in his Budget of 1909 at the rate of 6d in the £ over £3,000 for persons whose income exceeded £5,000. Surtax replaced super-tax in 1927.
PAYE (Pay-as-you-earn) came into force on 6 April 1944.

INOCULATION
with human smallpox pustules was practised in India, China, Senegal, Tripoli, Tunis, Algiers, Turkey, Circassia and Persia for a considerable length of time before the earliest accounts were published by Europeans at the beginning of the 18th century. The first description in English was published by a Mr Kennedy, surgeon, in *An Essay on External Remedies*, London, 1715. Kennedy wrote of the method used by the Turks at Constantinople:

They first take a fresh and kindly pock from someone ill of this distemper, and having made scarifications upon the forehead, wrists, and legs, or extremities, the matter of the pock is laid upon the foresaid incision, being bound on there for eight or ten days together; at the end of which time, the usual symptoms begin to appear, and the distemper comes forward as if naturally taken ill, though in a more kindly manner and not near the number of pox. . . . I was credibly informed . . . that of the number of two thousand which had then lately undergone that method, there was not any more than two that died.

The author went on to say that just before his arrival in Constantinople a Greek physician, Dr Janoin, had experimented by inoculating his two sisters and was thus the first European doctor known to have conducted the operation.
GB: Inoculation is believed to have originated in South Wales, where it was also of ancient custom. The earliest instance of which details survive occurred in 1668, when one Margaret Brown, described as 12 or 13 years of age, was inoculated from the pustules of a midwife called Joan Jones at Haverford West. According to the testimony of William Allen of St Ishmaels, who was born *c.* 1642, inoculation had been a common practice when his mother was a child. It would seem likely, therefore, that variolous inoculation was known in Wales at the beginning of the 17th century.

The first inoculation by a qualified English medical practitioner was made on the son of Lady Mary Wortley Montagu, wife of the British Ambassador to the Ottoman Court, by the Embassy surgeon, Dr Charles Maitland, at Pera in March 1717. Lady Mary introduced the practice into England in April 1721, when her infant daughter was inoculated by Dr Maitland in London. The first adults to be inoculated were seven prisoners in Newgate, who were promised a free pardon if they survived. The operation was carried out by Maitland on 9 August 1721 and all seven lived to enjoy their liberty.

The principal danger of variolation was that the patient was liable to infect others with a more serious eruption of the disease, and there were a number of instances in which whole towns suffered epidemics spread from someone in the process of being inoculated. Variolous inoculation was banned by Act of Parliament in 1840.
VACCINATION (i.e. inoculation with non-variolous matter) is believed to have been performed for the first time in 1771 on Robert Fooks, a butcher of Bridport, Dorset, in order to induce cowpox as a prophylactic against smallpox. The vaccination was made with a needle in two or three places on the palm of his hand, which later began to inflame, leaving permanent scars afterwards. On recovering from

the cowpox he was inoculated with human smallpox pustules by Mr Downe, surgeon of Bridport, but without effect. Although in after years Fooks was often in contact with members of his own family suffering from smallpox, he never caught the disease himself.

The first physician to make a systematic practice of vaccination and publish the results of his experiments was Dr Edward Jenner, who had originally been inspired with an interest in the subject while an apprentice at Chipping Sodbury in 1770, when he had heard a dairymaid remark concerning smallpox: 'I cannot take that disease, for I have had cowpox.' He performed his first vaccination on an eight-year-old boy, James Phipps, at Berkeley, Gloucestershire on 14 May 1796, using virus from a cowpox pustule on the hand of Sarah Nelmes, a dairymaid who had been infected by her master's cows. On 1 July Jenner inoculated Phipps with variolous smallpox matter, which produced no result, thus establishing that the earlier experiment had been effective. He published his *Inquiry into the Causes and Effects of the Variolae Vaccinae* in June 1798, after it had been rejected by the Royal Society the previous year. By 1801 6,000 people had been vaccinated, and the number greatly increased after the opening of 13 vaccination clinics in London by the Royal Jennerian Society in 1803.

The first
INSULIN

was isolated by Dr Frederick Banting and his assistant Charles Best at the University of Toronto Medical School in Canada on 27 July 1921 and applied to a depancreatized dog the same day. Banting's discovery derived from his idea that a 'hypothetical hormone' necessary for the utilization of sugar might be extracted from a duct-litigated pancreas. This secretion, later known as 'insulin', was to prove the ultimate weapon against the scourge of diabetes.

DIABETIC PATIENT TREATED WITH INSULIN: the first was 14-year-old Leonard Thompson, to whom the drug was administered at Toronto General Hospital by Dr Walter A. Campbell and Dr Alma A. Fletcher on 11 January 1922. In an advanced stage of the disease, the boy had little prospect of survival when he was admitted to the hospital. With the aid of insulin he was afterwards able to lead a normal life.

The first
INTERNAL-COMBUSTION ENGINE

to be commercially developed was a

The first commercially produced internal-combustion engine – Italy, 1860

three-stroke gas-engine designed by Eugenio Barsanti and Felice Matteucci of Florence in 1853 and patented three years later. The first engine in actual operation was installed at the Maria Antonia Railway Station in Florence in 1856. On 19 October 1860 the Società Anonima del nuova motore Barsante e Matteucci was formed to manufacture the engines.

Etienne Lenoir of Paris (*see also* Motor Car) designed an engine powered by illuminating gas in 1859, receiving French Patent No. 43,624 on 24 January 1860. A company called the 'Société des Moteurs Lenoir' was formed the same year, the actual manufacture of the engines being undertaken by the firm of Gautier et Cie. By December 1864 there were 143 Lenoir gas-engines being used for industrial purposes in Paris.

GB: Lenoir gas-engines were manufactured in limited quantities for the Lenoir Gas Engine Co of London at the Reading Ironworks in 1861.

See also Compression-Ignition Engine.

The first
INVALID CARRIAGE

was a tricycle-chair used by the crippled Stephen Farfler of Nuremberg *c.* 1650. It was operated by hand-cranks driving an internally toothed front wheel, and is believed to have been built by Johann Haustach, who had already designed a 'manu-motive' chair for his own use some 10 years earlier. Farfler's invalid carriage was to be seen every Sunday morning standing outside the Lorenze Kirche, waiting for its legless owner to propel himself home after divine service.

PETROL-DRIVEN INVALID CARRIAGE: the first was the Coventry Chair, powered by a De Dion motor and manufactured by the Rudge Cycle Co of Coventry, England in 1899. Strangely enough this preceded the introduction of the first hand-propelled, chain-driven invalid carriage, which only appeared the following year.

The first
IQ TEST

for the measurement of intelligence, was developed by the Parisian psychologist Alfred Binet. He adapted methods which the English scientist Francis Galton had previously employed for the assessment of sensory perception. In 1896 Binet began his work by examining 80 children, asking them to describe a simple picture, and classifying the descriptions into four or five generic types. After considerable research he devised a scale for registering intelligence quotient and this was published in *L'Année Psychologique* in 1905. The Binet Scale was used by the Paris educational authority for examining children who had been recommended for transfer to a special school for mental defectives. This was not, however, the first use of IQ tests in schools, for as early as 1897 the German psychologist Ebbinghaus introduced his *Kombinations-Methode*, based on Binet's initial researches, for the examination of pupils in certain Silesian schools. Ebbinghaus's tests were mainly concerned with comprehension and imagination, for which he used sections of mutilated prose, the child being required to fill in the missing words.

GB: The first IQ tests were conducted at Oxford using the Binet Scale in 1908. The experiment was carried out under the direction of Sir Cyril Burt, using 30 elementary-school children aged 12½–13½ and 13 preparatory-school boys of the same age group. Exercises included sense of touch and weight tests, auditory and vision tests, card-dealing, tapping an irregular pattern of dots with a pencil (as a study of concentration), alphabet-finding, spot-pattern tests, tracing a pattern in a mirror, and memory tests. At a later date Burt aroused considerable controversy and personal opprobrium by publishing more detailed findings based on a lengthy series of tests, which, he claimed, provided proof of higher intelligence among middle-class children than among pupils from working-class backgrounds, even when cultural deprivation of the latter was taken into account.

The first use of IQ tests on a mass scale was by the Division of Psychology of the US Army Medical Department, which in October 1917 began using a group test devised originally by A. S. Otis of Leland Stanford University and adapted for military use by Robert M. Yerkes. The purpose of the tests was to classify men according to their mental capacity, and to assist in selecting men for responsible positions. By the end of World War I, the Army intelligence examination had been applied to 1,726,966 men, of whom 7,800 had been recommended for immediate discharge as being of subnormal mental calibre. Nearly 30% of the total were found to be illiterate.

The first
IRON BOAT
was a 12ft-long pleasure-craft launched on the River Foss in Yorkshire on 20 May 1777. Apart from the fact that she was able to carry 15 passengers and was light enough to be carried by two men, nothing is known about this boat or its builder. The foregoing facts were recorded in a contemporary issue of the *Gentleman's Magazine*, 10 years before John 'Iron-Mad' Wilkinson built his 70ft barge the *Trial*, which hitherto has been generally acknowledged as the world's first iron boat.
IRON PASSENGER BOAT IN REGULAR SERVICE: the first was the *Vulcan*, designed by Sir John Robinson and built at Airdrie, Lanarkshire in 1819. She originally plied as a fare-paying passenger vessel on the Forth and Clyde Canal and was still in use as a coal-barge as late as 1864.
See also Ocean Liner; Steamboat.

The first
IRON BRIDGE
incorporating iron girders in its structure was built over the Rhône at Lyons by the French engineer M. Garvin in 1755. Originally it was intended to build the whole bridge of iron, but owing to the high cost only one of the three arches, a 25m span, was forged in iron, the remainder being completed in wood.
GB: The first iron bridge in Britain, and the first wholly iron structure of this kind in the world, was a 100ft span built across the River Severn in 1779 between Benthall, Shropshire, and Madeley Wood (now the village of Ironbridge) and opened to traffic on 1 January 1781. The height from the base-line to the centre was 40ft. The bridge was designed by John 'Iron-Mad' Wilkinson and the 378 tons of iron used in its construction was cast at Coalbrookdale by Abraham Darby the third, grandson of the man who first smelted iron from coke. It took three months to erect and no screws, rivets, nuts or bolts were used; dovetail joints together with pegs and keys were employed throughout.

Owing to movement in the structure, the bridge had to be closed to vehicular traffic in 1934, but continued in service as a pedestrian toll-bridge. Restoration work begun in 1972 cost in the region of £150,000, or nearly 50 times the sum it cost to build.

The first
IRON LUNG
was the Drinker Respirator, manufactured by Warren E. Collins Inc of Boston, Mass., and used for the first time at Boston Children's Hospital on 12 October 1928 to treat a small girl suffering from respiratory failure due to infantile paralysis. The original experimental model, built the previous year by Prof. Philip Drinker of Harvard University, had been assembled from an assortment of cast-off machinery, including two domestic vacuum-cleaners to give alternative positive and negative pressure.
GB: The first patient to be successfully treated in an iron lung was a 17-year-old schoolboy called John M. Turner, who contracted polio in September 1932 and was taken to the Wingfield Morris Orthopaedic Hospital nr Oxford. Early on the morning of 6 October the night nurse noticed that he was not breathing properly. Paralysis had spread to the whole body, including his breathing muscles.

An American member of the staff, Dr T. C. Thompson, remembered having read a report that a Drinker Respirator had recently been sent over from the USA for experimental purposes, and felt that if it could be traced in time the patient might have some chance of survival. After many telephone calls the respirator was eventually located at University College Hospital in London. The hospital authorities were prepared to loan it, but warned that their own experiences had not been encouraging, both patients who had been treated with it having died. The machine was loaded on to a lorry and driven down to Oxford, the necessary voltage adjustments being made on the journey.

Meanwhile John Turner was kept alive by artificial respiration until 5.30pm, when he was placed in the iron lung. At first he was totally dependent on the machine, but after two or three weeks he was able to spend increasingly long periods out of it. The treatment continued for nine weeks. As a result of a letter written to *The Times* by the boy, Lord Nuffield was inspired to offer a respirator to every hospital in the Empire.

The first person to live permanently in an iron lung was Frederick B. Smite Jr, the son of an American railroad magnate. In 1936 he contracted polio in Peking and was brought back to the USA in the respirator, travelling most of the way in a private train with a special medical staff in attendance. Smite, who became known as 'The Man in the Iron Lung', did much to make respirator treatment available to persons less wealthy than himself. He died aged 44 on 12 November 1954.

The first
JAZZ BAND
is claimed to have been formed by Negro musician Buddy Bolden in New Orleans *c.* 1900. Besides Bolden on trumpet, it comprised a cornet, clarinet, trombone, violin, guitar, string bass and drums. According to the musician Bud Scott 'Bolden went to church, and that's where he got his idea of jazz music.'

In assessing Bolden's claim to have been the originator of jazz, historians can rely only on the testimony of those who knew him and heard him play. However, one very illuminating piece of evidence is a recorded demonstration of his style, made by Bunk Johnson in the 1930s. While owing something to march-tunes and ragtime, Bolden's music appears to have had a distinctive rhythm of the kind now associated with pure jazz. Bolden's playing must have been only a stage in an evolutionary form; but if it is possible to mark a progression from the earlier forms of Minstrel and traditional Negro music, and call it the beginnings of jazz, this was probably it. Bolden's band continued to play in New Orleans until 1907, when its leader went mad and was confined to an asylum.
JAZZ ORCHESTRATION: the first to be published was Ferdinand Joseph 'Jelly Roll' Morton's 'Jelly Roll Blues', Chicago, 1915. Morton, self-proclaimed 'inventor' of jazz, claimed to have composed his first jazz orchestration in 1902 – 'New Orleans Blues'. His 'Jelly Roll Blues' was composed in 1905.

The origin of the word 'jazz' itself is obscured by conflicting claims. Morton asserted that he coined the term in 1902 to differentiate his music from ragtime. This has been disputed by historians who believe that the new style of music remained without a distinctive name until its northern awakening in Chicago *c.* 1916. According to band-leader George Morrison, however, it was known in Colorado at least five years before this date. Recording his impressions of early jazz on tape for Gunther Schuller at his Denver Studio in June 1962, he recalled:

I first heard the word jazz back around 1911. Yes, when I married, that word was coming in then. I remember it well because in 1911 when I first got married and I played for the dances, it was jazz we played. I had a sign on my little Model T Ford with a clef sign and lines and notes and everything, in green and gold and black, and on each side of my car I had a sign on the running board: George Morrison and his Jazz Orchestra.

The word 'jass' made its first appearance in print in the *Chicago Herald* with reference to Johnny Stein's band on 1 May 1916. In a report of a raid on Schiller's Café by a vigilante group called the 'Anti-Saloon League', the paper stated that the 60 intrepid women who entered the night-club found that it was impossible to be heard. 'The shriek of women's drunken laughter rivalled the blatant scream of the imported New Orleans Jass Band.' The word continued to be spelt in this way until the *New York Times* featured an advertisement for 'The Jasz Band' in its issue of 15 January 1917. The remaining 's' was dropped in an advertisement that appeared in the same paper on 2 February 1917 announcing 'The First Eastern Appearance of the Famous Original Dixieland JAZZ BAND'. This band had been formed the previous June by the members of Stein's Dixie Jass Band after a dispute with their leader.

GB: The first jazz band to perform in Britain was the Original Dixieland Jazz Band, which arrived at Liverpool aboard the *Adriatic* on 1 April 1919 and opened at the London Hippodrome in the musical revue *Joy Bells* on 7 April. The five-man ensemble was made up of leader Nick LaRocca on cornet, Emile Christian on trombone, Larry Shields on clarinet, Russel Robinson at the piano, and Tony Sbarbaro playing drums. Their initial engagement in England lasted for exactly one performance, as the star of the show, George Robey, felt he was being upstaged and demanded their instant dismissal. They quickly re-engaged to play at the Palladium starting 12 April and subsequently performed at the Martan Club, Rector's Club, the Hammersmith Palais and in Glasgow. Reception from the Press was mixed – the *Star* said they were doing their best 'to murder music' and suggested that jazz was a musical joke 'that is hardly worth attempting' – but the public seemed to love them. Lord Donegall, a fervent admirer, arranged a Command Performance before King George V, and the band was further honoured by being invited to play at the Victory Ball. They also made nine records for Columbia while in Britain, having already achieved the distinction of making the world's first jazz recording two years earlier in the USA.

ENGLISH JAZZ MUSICIAN: the first was pianist Billy Jones, who made his début with the Original Dixieland Jazz Band at the Hammersmith Palais on 11 October 1919. He had previously led a four-piece tango band that had alternated with the Original Dixieland at Rector's Club. An English band called the Murray Club Jazz Band had been billed as such as early as 1917, but the music they played was ragtime, not jazz.

The Original Dixieland Jazz Band left England aboard the *Finland* on 8 July 1920, leaving behind them the beginning of a British jazz movement. Newsworthy to the end, they were pursued to Southampton by a vengeful Lord Harrington bearing a shotgun, the object of his fury being the leader of the band, Nick LaRocca, who was alleged to have compromised the Earl's débutante daughter.

The first *JEANS*

were made in 1850 by Levi Strauss, a Bavarian immigrant to the USA. He arrived in San Francisco during the Gold Rush with a number of bales of cloth which he intended making into tents and wagon coverings. It proved an over-competitive trade, but Strauss was given the idea of making his cloth into hard-wearing work trousers by a miner who complained that ordinary trousers quickly became frayed and tattered on the diggings. Rivets were added for the first time in 1874, the idea originating with a current joke about a prospector called Alkali whose trousers were taken by his tailor to be riveted by a blacksmith on account of his habit of carrying rock specimens in the pockets. The early riveted jeans were priced at $13.50 a dozen.

The first *JEEP*

was designed in July 1940 by Karl K. Pabst, Consulting Engineer of the Bantam Car Co, Butler, Pa. in response to an invitation by the US Army to tender for a lightweight four-wheel-drive general-purpose field vehicle. The prototype, completed in September 1940, was taken to Camp Holabird, Md. for acceptance trials. An order was then placed for 70 pre-production models. Powered by a 45bhp four-cylinder Continental engine, these jeeps were in service with the US Army by early 1941. The seventh model of the series, preserved at the Smithsonian Institution in Washington, D.C., is now the oldest surviving jeep in the world.

Both Ford of Detroit and Willys-Overland submitted prototype jeeps for trial in November 1940 and the following summer the Willys MB design was accepted as standard, orders being placed with both firms for its manufacture. The Ford vehicle had the code-letters GPW, representing 'General Purpose – Willys'. The term 'jeep' is claimed by Ford to have been derived from the initials 'GP'. The word had been used, however, in the late 1930s by a number of manufacturers of multipurpose vehicles, borrowed in turn from a Popeye cartoon character called 'Jeep' who 'could do almost everything'.

Nearly 649,000 jeeps were produced during the war. Peak production rate at the Willys-Overland plant in Toledo, Ohio was one completed jeep every 80sec.

GB: The first jeep to arrive in England was a Willys MB, imported from the USA by the US Military Attaché in November 1941, and lent to 1st Airborne Division at Ringway, near Manchester. The jeep was found to be eminently suitable for airborne assaults, fitting snugly into a Horsa glider transport with room to spare for a light field-howitzer up front.

JEEP REDESIGNED FOR CIVILIAN USE: the first was the Willys model CJ-2A or 'Universal Jeep', which went into production on 4 September 1945.

GB: The first jeep-style vehicle designed specifically for civilian use in Britain was the Land-Rover, introduced by the Rover Co of Solihull, Warwickshire at the Amsterdam Motor Show on 30 April 1948. Some 200,000 units were built during the first 10 years of production.

The first *JIGSAW PUZZLES*

earliest reference to, is contained in *The Universal Director, or the Nobleman's and Gentleman's True Guide to the Masters and Professors of the Liberal and Polite Arts and Sciences*, London, 1763, which lists John Spilsbury of Russell Court, Drury Lane as 'Engraver and Map Dissector in Wood, in order to facilitate the Teaching of Geography'.

The oldest dated jigsaw puzzle extant is a hand-coloured engraved map of 'England and Wales Divided into their Counties', published by John Spilsbury in 1767 and now in the Hannas Collection. Each county made up a separate

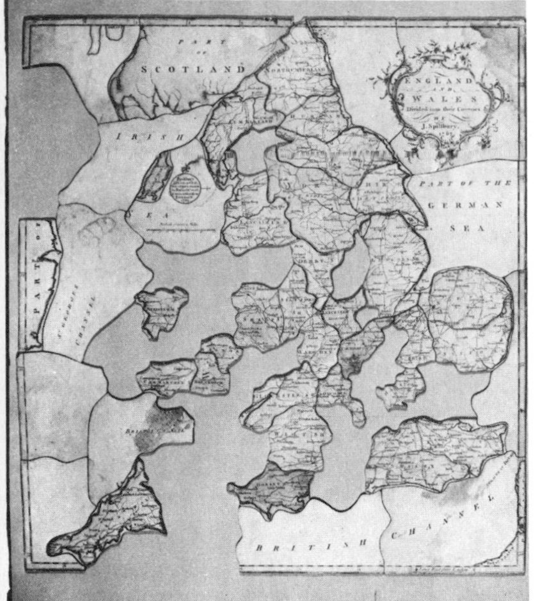

The earliest dated jigsaw puzzle – J. Spilsbury's dissected map of England and Wales, 1767

piece, so that none was interlocking. Spilsbury published a range of about 30 different dissected maps, the usual price being 10s 6d in a chip box, or 12s in a square box. He gave up the business on becoming drawing-master at Harrow School in 1782.

Although Spilsbury's puzzles were all of maps, pictorial jigsaws had made their appearance before the end of the century. Examples dating from the 1790s in the Hannas Collection include an oval engraving of John Gilpin's famous ride; a series of six woodcuts illustrating the fortunes of the Industrious Apprentice; views of the Bastille, exterior and interior, complete with rats; a hand-coloured engraving of soldiers drilling at Warley, Essex and another of a milkmaid offering a jug of fresh milk to her swain. Some of these puzzles had interlocking frames, but fully interlocking puzzles were not introduced until the beginning of the present century.

The first JUKEBOX

was installed at the Palais Royal Saloon, San Francisco, by Louis Glass, General Manager of the Pacific Phonograph Co, on 23 November 1889. It consisted of an electrically operated Edison phonograph with four listening-tubes, each controlled by a separate nickel-in-the-slot device.

PRE-SELECTIVE JUKEBOX: the first was the Multiphone, invented by John C. Dunton of Grand Rapids, Mich. in 1905. Standing 7ft high, it comprised a lyre-shaped, glass-fronted wooden cabinet embodying an Edison spring-motor phonograph and a hand-cranked rotary-selector mechanism that gave the listener a choice of 24 cylinder recordings. The cylinders, visible through the glass panel, were numbered, and an accompanying chart listed the titles.

The first disc-playing pre-selective jukebox was the John Gabel Automatic Entertainer, manufactured by the Automatic Machine & Tool Co of Chicago in 1906. The 5ft cabinet was glassed in on three sides, and a 3½ft horn protruded out of the top. It held 24 10in discs.

After going into a decline from about 1910, the industry revived with the introduction of the first all-electric jukeboxes by the Automatic Musical Instrument Co of Grand Rapids and by the Seeburg Co of Chicago in 1927. The addition of electrostatic speakers gave the jukebox the raucous effect that was to endear it to teenage patrons the world over. After a temporary set-back during the early Depression years, large-scale mass production began *c.* 1934, and by 1939 there were 350,000 jukeboxes in the USA.

GB: Manufacture of all-electric jukeboxes was begun by the Ditchburn Equipment Co of Lytham St Anne's in 1947.

The first JUVENILE COURT

was the Cook County Juvenile Court, Chicago, which sat for the first time on 1 July 1899. The judge on this occasion was Richard S. Tuthill.

GB: The first six juvenile courts were established under the Children Act 1908 at Bow Street, Clerkenwell, Tower Bridge, Westminster, Old Street and Greenwich and all opened their preliminary sittings simultaneously at 2pm on 4 January 1910. The 60 cases heard the first day (half of them at Clerkenwell) included charges of begging, gambling, playing football in the street, throwing missiles and fireworks, insulting behaviour, playing pitch-and-toss, malicious wounding, theft, trespass and the curious offence of 'shouting celery'.

The first KHAKI UNIFORM

was adopted by the Queen's Own Corps of Guides, an irregular corps of native cavalry and infantry Sepoys raised by Lt (later Lt-Gen Sir) Harry Burnett Lumsden at Peshawar on the North-West Frontier in December 1846. Lumsden was given authority to clothe the troops as he saw fit and chose a 'mud-coloured' uniform that would act as camouflage against the dusty soil of the country. The word 'khaki' is derived from the Persian *khak*, meaning 'dust' or 'ashes'. The Guides first went into action dressed in this style early in the New Year at Babuzai, a village on the Buneyr frontier whose inhabitants were refusing to pay taxes. The first occasion that the khaki-clad warriors fought side by side with British troops, at Sangao on 11 December 1849, they were very nearly fired upon by a Royal Artillery battery, an officer turning a gun on what he imagined must be enemy in such unconventional dress. Fortunately a keen-eyed gunner stayed his hand, crying out 'Lord! Sir, them is our mudlarks!'

REGIMENT OF THE BRITISH ARMY WEARING KHAKI: the first was the 52nd Regiment (Oxfordshire Light Infantry), who were outfitted with new uniforms of *Karkeerung* native cloth by their Commanding Officer, Col George Campbell, at Sealkote in the Punjab on 25 May 1857. The regimental history (1860) records:

The 52nd were the first British regiment thus clothed; for, being confident that if he applied in the usual formal manner and waited for authority, such authority would not be given until long after the time when this clothing would be of any service to the regiment, Colonel Campbell procured it entirely on his own responsibility.

On 12 July 1857 the 52nd engaged the Sealkote mutineers at Trimmoo Ghat, where it is said 'this very useful and novel dress deceived the enemy as to the character of the troops opposed to them'.

In 1882 the wearing of khaki was approved for all regiments on active service, though at first its general adoption was delayed by lack of a resistant dye. This problem was overcome two years later by the distinguished chemist Frederick Gatty. Previously a number of expedients had been tried, some owing more to ingenuity than science. Lumsden himself is claimed to have improvised the original khaki by soaking white cotton cloth in liquid mud and then ironing it dry. During the 2nd Afghan War of 1878–80, some officers dyed their uniforms by boiling them in tea-leaves, while in the Sudan campaign of 1882–5 the officers of the 19th Hussars decided to stain their toupees with stewed-tobacco juice.

The last British campaign to be fought in scarlet was the Ashanti War of 1895–6. The myth that the British lost a large number of men in the South African War of 1899–1902 because of the ease with which Boer snipers could pick off a red-coated enemy is probably due to confusion with the 1st Boer War of 1880–1 and the disaster at Majuba. The 2nd Boer War was the first major war in which all the British forces fought in khaki battledress. The innovation probably served to save many lives, though some stay-at-home critics found the colour too sombre and unappealing to be readily associated with martial glory. Among them was Queen Victoria, who described Boer War khaki as 'a sort of *café-au-lait* shade quite unsuitable for uniform'. Khaki was introduced for general service wear in 1902.

The first
LABOUR REPRESENTATION
The first political party dedicated to the purpose of securing Parliamentary representation of the working class was the Political Labor League of Victoria, which was founded at Melbourne under the chairmanship of Ben Douglas, a plasterer, on 22 March 1859. It marked a completely new departure in working-class politics, for it was intended as a Labour party that would seek the election of nominated Labour candidates, not simply as a pressure group supporting the candidate most likely to reflect its own interests. The party's platform included the payment of MPs, the 'immediate repeal of the Master and Servants Act and all class laws', the legal enforcement of an 8hr day, and, as a guiding principle, 'equality of all citizens'. In fact the Labor League had little effect on mainstream Victorian politics; after an existence of little over a year, it was merged with the Land Convention, having enjoyed a single triumph at the polls.
LABOUR MP: the first was Charles Jardine Don, a stonemason and former Chartist, who had emigrated to Victoria from Glasgow in 1853. He stood as Political Labor League candidate for Collingwood and was elected to the Legislative Assembly on 26 August 1859, continuing to sit, after the Labor League had been merged with the Land Convention, until 1864. According to a letter addressed to Sir Henry Barkly by the Duke of Newcastle, 24 December 1861, Don's maiden speech in the Legislature was made amid 'the stares and stillness of intense curiosity. The incarnation of our democracy was before our statesmen, and that was no joke. . . . He introduced himself as a new fact in the British Empire – an actual working artisan in a Legislative Assembly to speak and vote for his class.' Don accorded to the description of 'working artisan' in the fullest sense, for he used to work at his trade of stonemason by day and attend Parliament only at night. At one time he was actually one of the workmen employed on repairs to the Parliament Building, leaving the scaffolding at the end of the day to go down and sit in the Chamber.
LABOUR PRIME MINISTER: the first was Anderson Dawson, Member for Charters Towers in the Queensland Parliament, who was sent for by the Lt-Gov. of the Colony on 28 November 1899 and formed the first-ever constitutionally appointed socialist government three days later. On the same date, 1 December, the House refused to adjourn on Dawson's motion, and his short-lived Ministry resigned forthwith. Born the child of poor Scottish parents, Dawson was a mining amalgamator by trade. Though possessed of only the most rudimentary education, he was noted for a natural gift of expression and the economy of his speech.

The first effective Labour Government in the world was formed by John Christian Watson, Prime Minister of the Commonwealth of Australia from 27 April to 17 August 1904.
GB: The first working-class candidates to secure election to Parliament were Alexander Macdonald of Holytown, Lanark (also the reputed birthplace of Keir Hardie), and Thomas Burt of Muston Row, Tyneside. Both miners, they were returned for Stafford and Morpeth respectively in the General Election of 1874. Macdonald stood as a Liberal, but Burt campaigned as a Radical-Labour candidate, and was therefore the first MP to designate himself as 'Labour'. Initially they were paid by their unions while they sat in the House. Macdonald died in 1881, but Burt retained his seat for 44 years, becoming a Privy Councillor and eventually 'Father' of the Commons.

The first working-class Member to become a Minister was Henry Broadhurst, formerly an Oxfordshire stonemason, who became Under-Secretary at the Home Office under Gladstone in February 1886.
SOCIALIST PARTY: the first in GB was the Democratic (later the Social Democratic) Federation, founded 8 June 1881 by H.M. Hyndman, an Old Etonian and ex-Conservative MP who had been converted to Marxism. At first it concentrated on the Irish question, but adopted an avowedly Socialist policy at the Annual Conference of 1883. The manifesto included adult suffrage, the abolition of the House of Lords, and public ownership of the land. William Morris was an early and enthusiastic member, but later broke away to found a splinter group of his own. The SDF put up its first candidates for election in the General Election of 1885, campaign funds of £340 being donated by the Conservative Party, who hoped to split the Liberal vote thereby. J.E. Williams polled 27 votes in Hampstead and John Fielding 32 votes in Kennington. John Burns, an unemployed mechanic, secured 598 votes in Nottingham.
SOCIALIST MP: the first was R.B. Cunninghame Graham, a Scottish aristocrat who was converted to Socialism in 1887, while sitting as a Radical Member for North-West Lanarkshire. He became first President of the Scottish Labour Party, founded in Glasgow on 25 August 1888, and subsequently lost his seat campaigning as a Socialist in the General Election of 1892.

The first Socialist MP to secure election was James Keir Hardie of Holytown, Lanarkshire, who had been adopted by the Radical Association of West Ham South in 1890, and fought a straight fight against a Conservative in the General Election of 4 July 1892. Keir Hardie's majority was 1,232 over his opponent. Although he is generally described as 'the first Labour MP', two other candidates, J.H. Wilson, Middlesbrough, and John Burns, Battersea, were also returned as Independent Labour. The three Members represented no political party, and it would probably be fair to describe Keir Hardie as the only Socialist among them, despite John Burns's earlier flirtation with the SDF.

The first Socialist Party to secure representation in Parliament was the Independent Labour Party, founded at Bradford, 13 January 1893, for whom Keir Hardie fought both Preston and Merthyr Tydfil in the General Election of 2 October 1900. Although Keir Hardie concentrated his campaign in Preston, regarding his chances in Wales as slender, it was for Merthyr that he was elected. Richard Bell was elected for Derby at the same time, but later seceded to the Liberal ranks. Both Hardie and Bell were endorsed by the Labour Representation Committee (*see below*) and so can be regarded as the first candidates to be elected under the auspices of the present Parliamentary Labour Party.

The present Labour Party was founded as the Labour Representation Committee at a meeting attended by 129 delegates at the Memorial Hall, Farringdon Street, London on 27 February 1900. Originally an offshoot of the Trade Union movement, it was intended to promote candidates of any party who supported the Labour cause, but at the 6th Conference, held at the Memorial Hall on 15 February 1906, the title 'Labour Party' was adopted. At the General Election of the previous month, 29 Labour Members had been returned, and the Party had become a political reality.

The first Labour MP to become a member of the Cabinet was the Secretary of the Labour Party, Arthur Henderson, who was appointed President of the Board of Education in Asquith's Coalition Government on 25 May 1915.

LABOUR GOVERNMENT: the first was formed when King George V sent for James Ramsay MacDonald on 22 January 1924, following the defeat of the Conservative Government on a censure motion in the Commons the previous day. The state of the Parties was Conservative 259, Labour 191, Liberal 159.

Labour secured its first majority in the General Election of 30 May 1929, with a total of 288 seats against the Conservatives' 266, but was still outvoted by the combined Opposition, which included 59 Liberals. The Party won its first overall majority in the General Election of 26 July 1945, with 412 seats against Conservatives' 213 and Liberals' 12.

See also Woman MP; Woman Minister.

The first
LANGUAGE TUITION COURSE ON RECORDS

was Dr Rosenthal's Original Language Course, produced on 50 wax cylinders in 1893 by the International Institute of Languages, London and New York, in association with the Columbia Phonograph Co. The records were accompanied by a set of written texts and explanatory notes, and the fee for the course included the right to correspond with Dr Richard Rosenthal himself.

The first
LAUNDERETTE

was the Washateria opened at Fort Worth, Tex., by J.F. Cantrell on 18 April 1934. It contained four electric washing-machines that were charged for by the hour.

GB: The first self-service launderette was opened by Bendix Home Appliances Ltd at 184 Queensway, London on 9 May 1949. This was equipped with Bendix coin-operated automatic washing-machines and was thus also the first 'laundromat' in Britain, as well as the first in Europe.

The first
LAWN MOWER

was invented by Edwin Budding of Stroud, Gloucestershire, who on 18 May 1830 signed an agreement with John Ferrabee of the Phoenix Iron Works, Thrupp, nr Stroud for the manufacture of 'machinery for the purpose of cropping or shearing the vegetable surface of lawns'. Budding was employed at Mr Lister's textile factory, and is said to have been inspired with the idea of the lawn mower from using a machine designed to shear the nap off cloth. The first recorded customer was Mr Curtis, Head Gardener of Regent's Park Zoo, who bought a Ferrabee machine in 1831, paying 10gns for the large model. A smaller mower at 7gns was available for the use of country gentlemen, who, said Budding, 'will find in my machine an amusing, useful and healthful exercise'. Just how amusing the country gentlemen found the heavy and inefficiently geared machine is open to doubt, but it was clearly an improvement on cutting the lawn with scythes, which could only be done effectively when the grass was wet. The growth of the new industry was slow, only two firms exhibiting at the Great Exhibition in 1851, but the advent of lawn tennis in the 1870s brought a big influx of light side-wheel models into suburban back-gardens all over games-loving Victorian England.

PETROL-DRIVEN MOTOR MOWERS: the first were built experimentally by the Benz Co of Stuttgart and by the Coldwell Lawn Mower Co of Newbury, N.Y. in 1897. There is no evidence that either model was put into regular production.

GB: An experimental motor mower powered by a 6hp two-cylinder engine was built by Messrs Grimsley & Son of Halford Street, Leicester in May 1899.

The first commercially produced motor mower was designed by James Edward Ransome and manufactured by Ransomes, Sims & Jefferies Ltd at Ipswich in 1902. The first model sold, a 42in machine with a 6hp Simms petrol motor and passenger seat, went to a Mr Prescott Westcar of Strode Park, Herne Bay.

The first
LETTER BOXES

were erected in Paris by François Velayer for his Petite Poste in 1653. Nothing is known about the appearance of the boxes, but they probably consisted of no more than a locked wooden box with an aperture in the top fixed to the walls of buildings. Although it is recorded that they were sufficiently plentiful for no house in Paris to be far distant from one, they did not remain in service for very long as the *savoyards* (messengers), fearful for their livelihood, put mice in the boxes to destroy the mail. No further attempt to install letter boxes in the French capital was made until 1758, by which time they had been in use in Germany for over half a century.

GB: Before the introduction of pillar-boxes (*see below*) letters were commonly collected by a bellman, who perambulated the streets carrying a large leather bag with an aperture for posting and ringing a bell to announce his approach. There is, however, a casual reference to letter boxes in a work entitled *The Picture of London for 1805*:

Houses or boxes for receiving letters before four o'clock at the west end of the town and five o'clock in the City are open in every part of the metropolis: after that hour bellmen collect the letters during another hour, receiving a fee of one penny for every letter.

The earliest-known post-office letter box in Britain was a cast-iron box with a horizontal aperture and the inscription '1809' which was let into the wall of the post office in Wood Street, Wakefield. It is thought to have been designed and erected by the Postmaster's Clerk, one Jonas Ward.

The first official order relating to letter-boxes was issued by the General Post Office to all letter-receivers in London on 1 May 1814. It stated:

Every Office, or Receiving-House, must have a letter box in the Front for Unpaid Letters. It must be fixed in a part convenient for Public access; be large and strong, and kept locked, with the Key out, till the proper time of emptying for each dispatch. The words 'Unpaid Letter Box' to be painted on it. . . .

PILLAR BOXES were introduced in Belgium and were certainly in use by 1850, the year that the Parisian postal authorities adopted what was known as the 'Brussels-style box'. Although the date 1848 has been assigned to them by some postal historians, it is more probable that they made their first appearance on the streets of Brussels after the introduction of adhesive postage stamps in Belgium on 1 July 1849. Made of cast iron, these first pillar boxes resembled an up-ended cannon with a decorated top. The horizontal aperture was protected from the rain by a projecting capital and the whole was richly ornamented.

GB: The first four pillar boxes were erected at St Helier, Jersey and brought into public use on 23 November 1852.

One of the original Belgian pillar boxes of 1849

They were situated in David Place, New Street, Cheapside and St Clement's Road. The *Jersey Times* for 26 November 1852 described their appearance:

They are made of cast metal, are about four feet high and are sexagonal. On three of the sides, near the top, are the Royal Arms; on two sides the words Post Office; on the other the words Letter-Box; with a protected receiver. A sliding cover allows the collector to unlock the receiver and remove its contents. They are painted red and fitted in solid granite blocks two feet deep and raised four inches from the ground.

Although in after years credit for the innovation was claimed by Rowland Hill, then Secretary to the Postmaster-General, there can be little doubt from the evidence of surviving records that whatever encouragement Hill may have lent to the project, the real instigator was Anthony Trollope, later to secure a far greater celebrity as a novelist. In 1851 Trollope was employed as a Surveyor's Clerk and was sent over to the Channel Islands to inspect the postal services. His report to George Creswell, Surveyor of the Western District of England, in November of the same year, contained the following passage:

There is, at present, no receiving office in St. Heliers, and persons living in the distant parts of the town have to send nearly a mile to the principal office. I believe that a plan has obtained in France of fitting up letter boxes in posts fixed at the road side, and it may be thought advisable to try the operation of this system in St. Heliers – postage stamps are sold in every street and, therefore, all that is wanted is a safe receptacle for letters. . . . Iron posts suited for the purpose may be erected at the corners of the streets in such situations as may be desirable. . . .

Creswell forwarded the idea to the Postmaster-General, who approved it. The contract for manufacturing the boxes was awarded to John Vaudin of St Helier and it is believed that they were cast at Le Feuvre's Foundry in Bath Street. Three more boxes of a similar design were erected at St Peter Port, Guernsey, on 8 February 1853 and one of these, the oldest pillar box in use in Britain, still stands on its original site in Union Street.

The first pillar box in England was installed at Botchergate, Carlisle in September 1853 and the first six in London on 11 April 1855.

Early English pillar boxes were commonly painted green. Red was adopted as a standard colour in London in 1874 and for all provincial boxes from 1884.

The first
LIFE INSURANCE POLICY
recorded, was taken out on 18 June 1583 by London Alderman Richard Martin, who paid a group of merchant underwriters a premium of £30 13s 4d to insure the life of one William Gibbons for the sum of £383 6s 8d. The contract stipulated that this benefit should only be paid if the insured died within a year and ended hopefully 'God send William Gibbons health and long life.' Eleven months later Gibbons was gathered to the arms of his Maker. The underwriters then sought to evade payment by the dubious argument that he had not died within 'the full twelve months accounting 28 days to each month'. The case having been brought to court, it was ruled that 'the month is to be accounted according to the Kalendar' and Martin received the money due to him.

LIFE INSURANCE COMPANY: the first was the Amicable Society for a Perpetual Assurance Office, established in London by Sir Thomas Allen and the Bishop of Oxford in 1706. Insurers paid an annual fixed-rate premium in multiples of £6 4s (maximum £18 12s) and the company put £5 of each share towards a fund that was divided annually among the nominees of deceased insurers. The insured person had to be between the ages of 15 and 45, though no account was taken of his or her state of health. A limit of 2,000 was put on the number of £6 4s shares issued. This was reached by 1770, when the company claimed that it had already paid out a total of £378,184 to 3,643 claimants and boasted capital assets of £33,000

An earlier venture, dating from 1699, known as the 'Society for Assurance of Widows and Orphans', has sometimes been claimed as the first life insurance company, but as this did not involve the payment of regular premiums, but only a payment every time a member died, it is probably better described as a kind of modified tontine.

A remarkable feature of early life insurance was the propensity of speculators to take out insurance on the lives of well-known persons, particularly those with hazardous occupations, such as highwaymen. Among those who were the object of this form of gambling – it was little else – were the Prime Minister, Sir Robert Walpole, King George II (when he fought at Dettingen), and the Young Pretender during the Rebellion of 1745. This practice continued until made illegal by the Life Assurance Act 1774.

The first life insurance company to base its premiums upon a scientific calculation of life expectancy and grade them according to age at entry – the fundamental principles of modern life insurance – was the Society for Equitable Assurances on Lives and Survivorships. It was established in London on 7 September 1762 according to a plan proposed some six years earlier by James Dodson, Master of the Royal Mathematical School at Christ's Hospital, who had died in the meantime. The Society's actuary, the first employed by a life insurance company, was Mr William Mosdell (d. 1764). The term 'actuary' (from the Latin *actuarius*, a recorder of State papers) was coined by one of the founders of the Equitable, Edward Rowe Mores, to denote one who interprets bills of mortality, population figures and other relevant figures in terms of insurance risk.

The first
LIGHTNING-CONDUCTOR
designed for the protection of buildings

was attached by Benjamin Franklin to his house on the north side of Market Street, Philadelphia in September 1752. The upper end of the steel-pointed iron rod projected 7 or 8ft above the roof, while the lower end was thrust 5ft into the ground. Less than a year and a half earlier Franklin had been the first to publicly propound the theory that lightning was composed of electricity. The ideas expounded in his *New Experiments and Observations in Electricity* were put to the test by a French amateur scientist, M. Dalibard, who had an experimental lightning-rod erected in the grounds of his country-house at Marly-la-Ville, 18 miles out of Paris. On 10 May 1752 lightning struck the 80ft-high iron rod, and phenomena were observed that established beyond doubt that Franklin's hypothesis was correct. Before the results could be communicated to America, Franklin had made his famous kite experiment (4 July 1752) and proved the soundness of the theory for himself.

After fixing a lightning-conductor on his own house, Franklin arranged for similar rods to be erected on the State House (Independence Hall) and the Academy Building in Philadelphia, also in September 1752. These were the first public buildings in the world to be so protected. He made no attempt to patent his invention, but gave it freely to the world, publishing a full description in his own *Poor Richard's Almanac* in November of the same year. The idea spread rapidly through the American colonies, except in parts of New England, where it was denounced as a means of obstructing the will of God. In Europe its development was retarded by the equally short-sighted pronouncements of a celebrated French scientist, the Abbé Noller, who began by declaring that Franklin himself was a fiction, and on the worthy American's existence being proved, went on to assert that lightning-conductors would suck the lightning down from the clouds and so cause the destruction of the very buildings they were supposed to preserve. Unfortunately he was widely believed, with the result that no lightning-conductor was erected on a public building in Europe until 1769, when one was fixed to the steeple of the Church of St Jacob in Hamburg.
GB: The first lightning-conductor was erected by Dr William Watson, Vice-President of the Royal Society, on his cottage at Payneshill, near London, in 1762. The first public building to be protected by a lightning-rod was St Paul's Cathedral in 1770.

The first
LION TAMER
was 'Manchester Jack', lion keeper at Wombwell's Menagerie, a travelling show that toured England during the first half of the 19th century. His first act, performed in 1835, consisted of sitting on the back of an aged lion called Nero and prising open its mouth.

'Morok the Beast Tamer'

The first tamer to perform with a mixed group of animals was the American, Van Amburgh, who was billed at Astley's Amphitheatre in London as 'Morok the Beast Tamer' in 1838. His act, which included lions, tigers and leopards, was the first circus wild-beast act.

The first fatality occurred in January 1850 at Chatham, when Helen Bright of Wombwell's was attacked by a tiger which she had repeatedly flicked in the face with a whip. It crushed her head in its jaws and she died soon after being rescued from the cage.

The first
LIP READING
The first deaf mute to learn to lip read was Luis de Velasco, younger brother of the Constable of Castile, who was taught the art by the Constable's Secretary, Juan Pablo Bonet, *c.* 1615–20. Sir Kenelm Digby, who accompanied the Prince of Wales (later Charles I) on a visit to Madrid in 1623, described an encounter with Velasco in his book *On the Nature of Bodies*:

This Spanish lord was born deaf – so deaf that if a gun were shot off close to his ear he could not hear it – and consequently he was dumb. To remedy this unhappy accident physicians and surgeons had long employed their skill, but all in vain. At last there was a priest who undertook the teaching him to understand others when they spoke, and to speak himself that others might understand him; for which attempt at first he was laughed at, yet after some years he was looked upon as if he had wrought a miracle.

GB: The first person in Britain to learn to lip read was Daniel Whalley of Northampton, who had been deaf and dumb since the age of five. His mentor was the celebrated Dr John Wallis, Professor of Geometry at Oxford, who, according to the Rev. John Lewis's unpublished biography, succeeded in teaching Whalley to speak in just over one year, beginning the experiment in January 1662. It appears from contemporary accounts that Wallis's pupil learned to lip read perfectly, for he was able to repeat words of the Polish language spoken to him by a Polish aristocrat who was visiting Oxford at the time.

The first
LITERARY AGENCY
was founded in London by A.P. Watt of Aberdeen. He started as an agent by helping his friends Walter Besant and George Macdonald in dealings with their publishers, and finding that there was a demand for such a service, established himself in regular practice in 1875. Subsequent clients of A.P. Watt & Son have included John Buchan, G.K. Chesterton, Marie Corelli, Rider Haggard, Rudyard Kipling, Edgar Wallace, H.G. Wells, W.B. Yeats, Somerset Maugham, Dennis Wheatley, Field-Marshal Montgomery, A.P. Herbert, P.G. Wodehouse and John le Carré.

The first
LONG-PLAYING GRAMOPHONE RECORDS
were produced by the Neophone Co of Finsbury Square, London from 1904 to 1906, and consisted of 20in discs with a playing time of up to 12min. Early recordings included the 'Light Cavalry', 'Poet and Peasant', and 'Bohemian Girl' overtures, price 10s 6d each. They were generally held to offer an appalling standard of reproduction.
MICROGROOVE LONG-PLAYING RECORDS: the first were 10 and 12in 80rpm phenolic discs with 450 grooves to the inch, issued by the Edison Co in the USA in 1926. These lasted 12 or 20min each side and cost $1.75 and $2.50 respectively. The first two to be released were a 24min record of selections from *Carmen* and *Aida* played by the American Concert Orchestra, and a 40min record labelled 'Dinner Music', made up of eight different melodies rendered by the Hotel Commodore Ensemble under Bernhard Levitow. The Edison LPs were all made up from previously recorded singles, and this probably accounts for their lack of success. Forty minutes of one symphony or one opera would most likely have had a greater appeal to music-lovers than short

snatches of various composers thrown together in a rather arbitrary mixture. Some purists may have jibbed at seeing Gilbert and Sullivan described in the catalogue as 'popular American composers'. From a material point of view, the Edison records suffered from an over-dense crowding of the grooves, the walls of which proved too fragile to stand up to continued use. On the other hand, they could be played on a standard gramophone, adapted for long play by fitting a special diamond stylus reproducer. The records weighed 1lb and 1½lb each, and were ¼in thick.

33⅓RPM LONG-PLAYING RECORDS and *LONG-PLAYING GRAMOPHONES* were first launched by RCA-Victor with a demonstration held at the Savoy Plaza Hotel in New York on 17 September 1931. Their first release, in November 1931, was of Beethoven's Fifth Symphony performed by the Stokowski-Philadelphia Orchestra under Leopold Stokowski, and this was the first time a complete orchestral piece had been issued on a standard-size long-playing record. The 33⅓rpm record-players were all radiograms and ranged from $247.50 to $995, a high price bracket that doubtless contributed to the ultimate failure of the venture.

The 'long-player revolution' that was finally to oust the 78rpm record for ever began at a sales convention for Columbia representatives held at Atlantic City on 21 June 1948. Here Columbia unveiled the first really successful 33⅓rpm microgroove records, made by a process developed by Dr Peter Goldmark. These were vinylite discs with a 23min playing time each side, and 224–300 grooves to the inch. The initial releases included Mendelssohn's Violin Concerto, Tchaikovsky's Fourth Symphony, and the Broadway show *South Pacific*, average price $4.85. The success of Columbia's 1948 venture in comparison to RCA-Victor's attempt of 1931 can be attributed to an improved recording technique and longer-lasting records, cheaper record-players (an attachment for a standard player could be bought for as little as $29.95), and not least – a healthier economic climate in which to launch the enterprise.

GB: Decca began producing LPs under their London label in August 1949 for export to the USA only. The first 33⅓rpm LPs for home consumption, and also the first issues in Europe, were recordings of *Trial by Jury* and Munchinger's rendering of Bach's Brandenburg Concertos, released by Decca in August 1950.

The first
LOUDSPEAKER
was the Auxetophone, patented by Horace Short of London in 1898, and first used publicly at the Paris Exposition of 1900 to broadcast phonograph records of operatic arias from the top of the Eiffel Tower. The machine was operated by compressed air and, according to contemporary accounts, could be heard all over Paris. Short sold his Auxetophone patent to Charles Parsons in 1903. He himself later achieved distinction as one of the founders of the aircraft-manufacturing concern of Short Bros.

The first electrically operated loudspeaker, prototype of most modern systems, was developed in 1906 by Miller Reece Hutchinson (*see also* Hearing Aid) and Kelly Turner of the Hutchinson Acoustic Co of New York. Their Dictograph loudspeaker was marketed the following year as part of the first internal office communications system.

The first public use of electrical loudspeakers took place in September 1912, when the Bell Telephone Co co-operated with Western Electric in installing two water-cooled loudspeaking transmitters, an induction coil and 10 loudspeaker receivers at the Olympic Theater in Chicago. They were used not to amplify speech from the stage, but to transmit sound-effects from backstage to the auditorium, including cheers and applause from a supposedly near-by baseball stadium.

PUBLIC ADDRESS SYSTEM: the first occasion that loudspeakers were used as part of a PA system was early in 1913, when the Governor of the State of Oklahoma spoke over a 122-mile open-wire circuit from Oklahoma City to an audience of 345 people assembled in an hotel in Tulsa. The first open-air public address demonstration was conducted by Bell Telephone on Staten Island on 30 June 1916. Following these experiments, public address by loudspeaker was used to reach a large audience (i.e. beyond range of the unamplified human voice) for the first time on the occasion of the National Educational Association Convention at Madison Square Garden in New York from 3 to 8 July 1916.

The first
MAGAZINE
in the sense of a general-interest miscellany was the *Mercure Galant*, established by Jean Donneau de Vise, and first published in Paris in March 1672. Concerned principally with the gossip of the town, it enjoyed a considerable success in fashionable circles.

GB: The Gentleman's Journal: or, the Monthly Miscellany, by way of a letter to a gentleman in the Country, consisting of News, History, Philosophy, Poetry, Musick, Translations, Etc, was an octavo, published monthly for the first time in January 1692 by R. Baldwin 'near the Oxford Arms in Warwick Lane'. The editor was Peter Anthony Motteux, a Huguenot refugee, who seems to have written most of each 64-page issue himself, though there were verses contributed by Matthew Prior, Sir Charles Sedley and other poets of repute. Perhaps the most notable feature was an original composition by Henry Purcell (*see also* Opera) every month. Another interesting innovation was the magazine short story, which made its first appearance in the issue for March 1692. *The Gentleman's Journal* continued for 33 numbers, ceasing publication in 1694.

The term 'magazine' was first employed to signify a periodical miscellany by Edward Cave, who, as 'Sylvanus Urban, Gent.', started the *Gentleman's Magazine* – the first to use the word in its title – in January 1731. The word rapidly entered general currency, and was used in the title of the first magazine to be published in North America, Andrew Bradford's *The American Magazine*, which made its appearance on 13 February 1741 in Philadelphia, Pa.

ILLUSTRATED MAGAZINE: the first was *Memoirs for the Curious; or an account of what occurs that's rare, secret, extraordinary, prodigious and miraculous through the world, whether in Nature, Art, Learning*, an undated monthly printed by R. Janeway for A. Baldwin, London, 1701. Although 18th-century miscellanies carried occasional plates, illustrations in the text remained exceptional until the advent of *The Penny Magazine* in 1832.

The first magazine to publish a photograph was the *Art Union* for June 1846. Some 7,000 Calotype positive prints were supplied by William Henry Fox Talbot (*see also* Photography, etc.), the specimens being used to illustrate an article on the Calotype process. The photographic historian Helmut Gernsheim says that of the eight copies of this issue of the *Art Union* in his collection, each accompanying photograph depicts a different subject.

The first magazine to be regularly illustrated with photographs was the *Stereoscopic Magazine*, monthly, 1 July 1858–February 1865. Each number contained three stereoscopic studies.

For the first use of halftones in magazine illustration, *see* Halftone Process.

See also Children's Magazine; House Journal; Women's Magazine.

The first
MAGNETIC RECORDER
was the Telegraphone, patented by Valdemar Poulsen, a Danish engineer employed by the Copenhagen Telephone Co, in 1898. It was demonstrated publicly for the first time at the Paris Exposition of 1900. The Telegraphone used magnetized piano-wire running between spools at 7ft a second, and recordings could be erased at will. Commercial production was undertaken by the American Telegraphone Co of Springfield, Mass. in 1903, the machine being promoted as an office dictation apparatus and also as an automatic telephone-message recorder. An improved model with DC bias was employed by Prof. Lee De Forrest in 1913 for talking-film experiments he made at the Biograph Studios in New York. The Telegraphone suffered from a number of drawbacks that made its appearance as a commercial product somewhat premature, chiefly poor amplification – reception was via earphones – and its unwieldy bulk, which made it unsuitable for home or office use. Its failure, though, had to do more with inept company management than anything radically wrong with Poulsen's recording system, which was not only sound in principle, but provided the basis on which later inventors in the field developed commercially successful apparatus.

Ancestor of the tape recorder – Poulsen's Telegraphone, 1898

TAPE RECORDER (i.e. a magnetic recorder using tape instead of wire): the first was the Blattnerphone, originally employed in 1929 for adding synchronized sound to the films made at the Blattner Colour and Sound Studios, Elstree. Designed by film producer Louis Blattner, it was based on the patents of German sound engineer Dr Kurt Stille and was also the first successful magnetic recorder with electronic amplification. The first commercially produced Blattnerphone was acquired by the BBC in 1931. Possibly the first radio programme made up entirely of taped items was *Pieces of Tape*, recorded in 1932. King George V's Christmas speech was recorded on the Blattnerphone the same year, and early in 1933 the BBC set up a special Recorded Programmes Section. The Blattnerphone used steel tape on large reels and was extremely bulky, so that it was generally necessary to carry the voice to the machine (via wire relay) rather than the machine to the voice.

TAPE RECORDER USING PLASTIC TAPE: the first was the Magnetophon, produced by AEG of Berlin in 1935. The tape speed was 30in a second, and though the earlier models had a performance inferior to the Blattnerphone, the running cost of only 1s a minute compared favourably with the latter's 7s 6d a minute. While magnetic-recording technology remained relatively static in Britain and the USA during the war years, in Germany it made a number of major advances, of which the most important was the application of a high-frequency bias to the oxide-coated tape of the Magnetophon by H. J. von Braunmühl and W. Weber in 1940. At the end of the war 18 complete Magnetophons were recovered by the Allies from the AEG plant in Berlin and portioned out between the British, French and US occupation authorities. Every tape-recorder developed since 1945 can be regarded as a lineal descendant of the captured German Magnetophons, which resembled currently produced monaural machines in all essentials.

GB: The Duo-Trac Cell-o-Phone, introduced by British Ozaphone in 1937.

TAPE RECORDER PRODUCED FOR HOME USE: the first was the Soundmirror, marketed by the Brush Development Co of Cleveland, Ohio in 1947. The tapes used with this machine had ½hr playing time and cost $2.50 each.

PRE-RECORDED TAPES were first offered for sale by Recording Associates of New York in 1950. Their first catalogue listed eight recordings on plastic tape, of which Reel No. 001 was titled 'Cocktail Time' and featured 11 popular songs.

STEREOPHONIC TAPE RECORDER: the first, commercially produced, was the Magnecord, which was demonstrated at the US Audio Fair of 1949 by Magnecord Co of Chicago. It was developed in response to a request from General Motors for a binaural recorder suitable for analysing engine noise, monaural machines having failed to give the sound perspective required. The first home stereo outfit was produced by Livingston Electronics of New York in 1954 and the same company issued the first catalogue of pre-recorded stereophonic tapes in May of the same year. The first of these Audiosphere recordings, No. BN701, was of Schubert's 'Unfinished' Symphony together with Sibelius's *Finlandia* and was issued on a 7in reel at $10. Stereophonic tapes preceded stereo discs (*see also* Sound Recording: Stereophonic Discs) by nearly four years.

The first
MAIL-ORDER BUSINESS
was incorporated on 15 September 1871 as the Army & Navy Co-operative Society Ltd, at 117 Victoria Street, London. Established principally at the instigation of Maj. F.B. McCrea, who became its first Managing Director, the 'Stores' was founded with the object of supplying goods of the highest quality at the lowest economic price to its members, chiefly officers and NCOs of the Services, and their families. The Society issued its first mail-order catalogue in February 1872. The wide range of goods offered in its 112 pages included Gunpowder Tea at 4s 6d per lb; tinned lobster at 8d; hare soup at 1s 6d a quart; cigarettes (still smacking a little of the *demi-monde* in 1872) price 1s 4d for 25; Virginia Rob Tobacco at 4s 9d per lb; champagne or gin at 28s a dozen bottles; a quill-pen machine from 4s; Blair's Gout Pills at 2s 3d a box; Areca Nut Tooth Paste at 1s 6d a pot; table croquet; Ladies' Merino Drawers at 5s 9d a pair; a Ladies' Cheltenham Costume in Dark or Light Grey, or Brown Tweed at 56s 6d; and an Admiral's cocked hat for 124s.

As no parcel post existed at this time, goods were forwarded within the London area by Carter Paterson's parcels delivery service at rates of 14lb for 3d, rising to 1s for 112lb. Outside London, mail-order customers were asked to 'particularise the railway or other conveyance on the back of the order'. Orders from India or the colonies might contain such exotic particulars as 'Cobb & Co's Stage Coach' (in Australia and New Zealand), river-steamer or bullock wagon.

Army & Navy mail-order catalogues were generally issued quarterly, the largest being the March 1887 edition, which had 1,954 pages. The 109th and last catalogue was published in 1939. Since that date the Army & Navy Stores has continued to do business as an ordinary department store and it is no longer run as a co-operative society.

The first miscellaneous retail business to be run exclusively by mail order (i.e. unconnected with a shop) was established in a single room at 825 North

Clark Street, Chicago by Aaron Montgomery Ward in 1872, the same year that the Army & Navy Co-operative Society issued its first catalogue. The first Montgomery Ward price-list consisted of a single sheet of paper measuring 12×8in. By contrast, the 1904 catalogue, of which over 3 million were sent out, weighed 4lb.

The first
MAN-MADE FIBRE
was produced experimentally in 1883 in the form of cellulose-based artificial silk by (Sir) Joseph Swan (*see also* Electric Lamp) at Newcastle upon Tyne. Swan was then engaged in developing his incandescent electric light bulb and wanted to find a substitute for the fragile cotton filaments used in its manufacture. He succeeded in producing an improved light-bulb filament by squirting nitro-cellulose through an orifice into a coagulating fluid to make a single thread. Employing an even finer hole for the jet of nitro-cellulose, he was able to create a thread fine enough to be woven into fabric. A number of small mats and doilies were crocheted in this material by Mrs Swan and displayed at the Inventions Exhibition of 1885, but Swan did not develop the process commercially.

A similar method of producing artificial silk was patented in France in 1885 by Comte Hilaire de Chardonnet, who established the world's first factory for the manufacture of man-made fibre at Besançon in 1892. Chardonnet's *soie artificielle* was satisfactory for braids, tassels, fringes and the like, but inadequate for woven goods.

MAN-MADE TEXTILE YARN: the first capable of being woven and dyed, was viscose rayon, developed by C.H. Stearn and C.S. Cross at a pilot plant set up at Kew, Surrey in 1898. Viscose filament had been patented in that year by Stearn, while viscose itself, a substance obtained by treating wood-pulp with caustic soda and other chemicals, was the subject of a master patent taken out by Cross in 1892. British rights to the process were acquired by Samuel Courtauld & Co for £25,000, and commercial production began at a specially built factory outside Coventry in July 1905. Manufacture of rayon by the purchasers of the French and German patent rights was started in their respective countries the same year. It was in Germany that the first stockings made from synthetic fibre were produced at the Bamberg rayon factory in 1910.

The first
MARGARINE
was patented in France by Hippolyte Mège-Mouriès of Paris, on 15 July 1869, and was the only entry in a prize competition organized by Napoleon III for 'a suitable substance to replace butter for the Navy and the less prosperous classes'.

Mège-Mouriès had begun his experiments at the Ferme Impériale de la Faisanderie, Vincennes two years earlier, and is said to have outraged the villagers by underfeeding his cows in the cause of science. The conclusion he drew from this exercise was that the natural fat in a cow's body is the agency that produces milk, and that it could also provide a substitute for butter. The final result of his researches took the form of a compound of suet, skim milk, pig's stomach, cow's udder and bicarbonate of soda. At one stage of the process it had the appearance of 'a cascade of pearls', so the inventor called it 'margarine' – from the Greek *margarites*, meaning 'a pearl'.

Although a factory was established at Poissy to undertake manufacture of margarine, the Franco-Prussian War broke out before production was under way. Two enterprising Dutch butter-merchants, Jan and Anton Jurgens, acquired the rights for 60,000 francs a year and in 1871 opened the world's first fully operative margarine factory at Oss in Holland.

In England, where all margarine was imported in the early years, the new food was advertised as 'Butterine' until this name was prohibited by Act of Parliament in 1887. Austria, where a factory was set up in 1874, knew it as *Wiener Sparbutter*. The Americans were prepared to call it margarine as long as they did not have to eat it – demand remained very low while a law against adding colouring matter was enforced. No one wanted to spread their bread with something that looked like lard.

The first
MARRIAGE BUREAU
was the Office of Addresses and Encounters, established in Threadneedle Street, London, next to the Castle Tavern, by Henry Robinson on 29 September 1650. Paragraph 20 of his prospectus announced: 'Such as desire to dispose of themselves or friends in marriage, may here likewise be informed what encounters there are to be had, both of Persons and Portions.'

The first marriage partners to be selected by computer were Shirley Sanders and Robert Kardell, both 26, who were brought together by this means on Art Linklater's television show *People are Funny* and married at the First Presbyterian Church in Hollywood on 18 October 1958. They were given a honeymoon in Honolulu by the sponsors of the show.

The first
MATCH
friction, was invented in 1826 by John Walker, a chemist of 59 High Street, Stockton-on-Tees, Co Durham. The discovery was accidental, as Walker's original intention was to produce a readily combustible material for fowling-pieces. His first match was a stick which he had been using to stir a mixture of potash and antimony; it burst into flame when he scraped it against the stone floor to remove the blob on the end. The earliest-recorded purchaser of a box of matches was a Mr Hixon, a Stockton solicitor, and the transaction is entered in Walker's day-book for 7 April 1827. The price was 1s for 100 matches plus 2d for the tin tube in which they were packed. Walker's matches were originally made of cardboard, like modern book-matches, but he soon adopted flat wooden splints, which were cut by hand by the inmates of the Stockton almshouses. He attempted to tap another source of cheap labour by employing boys from the local grammar school, paying them 6d for 100, but the arrangement was terminated after one enterprising youth had tried his hand at mass production by using a jack-plane to cut the splints. Although this brought a sharp rise in productivity, the matches were curved and would not lie flat in the box, with the result that Walker lost his temper and the boys lost their job. By this time he had abandoned the tube in favour of a pasteboard box, supplied to him by local bookbinder John Ellis at 1½d each. A strip of sandpaper was enclosed inside the box. Most of Walker's sales were to local people, but the fame of his matches spread far wider, and soon after he began production other chemists started to manufacture friction matches on their own account. Walker failed to patent his invention and match-making always remained a sideline to his pharmacy business.

SAFETY-MATCH was invented by Johan Edvard Lundström of Jönköping, Sweden, in 1855 and manufactured by the Jönköpings Tandstricksfabrik the same year. British rights to the Lundström process were acquired by Francis May of Bryant & May on 15 August 1855.

BOOK-MATCHES were patented by American attorney Joshua Pusey of Lima, Pa. in 1892 and manufactured by the Diamond Match Co of Barberton, Ohio in 1896. The first advertising match-book was produced by the Diamond Match Co for the Mendelson Opera Company to advertise one of its shows, *c.* 1898.

GB: Manufactured by the English factory of the Diamond Match Co in 1899.

The first
MATRIMONIAL ADVERTISEMENT
appeared in John Houghton's *Collection for the Improvement of Husbandry and Trade* on 19 July 1695. It read:

A Gentleman about 30 Years of Age, that says he has a Very Good Estate, would willingly Match Himself to some young Gentlewoman that has a fortune of £3000 or thereabouts, And he will make Settlement to Content.

Initially this method of seeking a marriage partner remained a strictly male preserve. When an audacious spinster called Helen Morison advertised for a husband in the columns of the *Manchester Weekly Journal* in 1727, the outraged citizens demanded that an example should be made and the Lord Mayor had her committed to a lunatic asylum for four weeks.

The first
MIDDLE NAME
The first Englishman known to have borne two Christian names was Henry Frederick, Earl of Arundel, baptized 1608. A contemporary was Sir Henry Frederick Thynne, created a Baronet 1641, died 1680. His date of birth is not recorded.

The first
MILK BOTTLES
were introduced by the Echo Farms Dairy Co of New York in 1879.
GB: A bottle with a wired-on cap was devised by George Barham of the Express Dairy in 1884, but did not prove successful. A further attempt was made by a North Country dairyman, Arthur Hailwood, who exhibited bottles of 'filtered' and 'medicated' milk at the Jubilee Exhibition in Manchester in 1887. Hailwood marketed sterilized milk in swing-stoppered bottles in 1894. It was not until 1906 that fresh milk, untreated except for pasteurization, began to be sold in bottles in Britain, the pioneer in this case being Ernest Lane of the Manor Farm Dairy, East Finchley.
ALUMINIUM-FOIL BOTTLE CAPS
were first produced by Josef Jonsson of Linköping, Sweden in 1914. They were introduced to Britain in 1929.

The first
MONARCH, BRITISH, TO ATTEND A PUBLIC THEATRE
was Charles II, who accompanied the King and Queen of Bohemia to see Davenant's opera *The Siege of Rhodes*, performed at the Lincoln's Inn Theatre on 2 July 1661. Samuel Pepys, who was a member of the audience, recorded in his *Diary*:

We stayed a great while for the King and Queen of Bohemia; and by the breaking of a board over our heads, we had a great deal of dust fell into the ladies' necks and men's necks, which made good sport. The King being come, the scene opened; which indeed is very fine and magnificent and well acted, all but the Eunuch, who was so much out that he was hissed off the stage.

The first
MONARCH, BRITISH, TO BE FILMED
was Queen Victoria during her autumn holiday at Balmoral in 1896. She recorded the event in her diary for 3 October:

At twelve went down to below the terrace, near the ballroom, and we were all photographed by Downey by the new cinematograph process, – which makes moving pictures by winding off a reel of film. We were walking up and down, and the children jumping about. Then took a turn in the pony chair, and not far from the garden cottage Nicky and Alicky planted a tree.

Downey was the Royal Photographer. The children who jumped about included the late Duke of Windsor, then aged two, who must consequently have had one of the longest records of film appearances when he died in 1972. 'Nicky and Alicky' were the Emperor Nicholas II and the Empress Alexandra Feodorovna of Russia, who had arrived at Balmoral for an informal visit 10 days earlier. The film was 'premièred' in the Red Drawing Room at Windsor on 23 November 1896.

The first
MONARCH, BRITISH, TO TRAVEL BY RAIL
was Queen Victoria, who travelled from Slough to Paddington on the Great Western Railway accompanied by her husband, Prince Albert, on 13 June 1842. The Royal Saloon, a 21ft-long four-wheeler, had been built by the GWR at Swindon two years earlier in anticipation of the Queen's desire to be conveyed on the company's track. The hangings were of crimson and white silk and the walls were decorated with oil-paintings. The wheels of the carriage were shod with wooden tyres to deaden the noise. It was drawn by the locomotive *Phlegethon*, which was driven by Daniel Gooch, the GWR Locomotive Superintendent, assisted by the celebrated engineer Isambard Kingdom Brunel.

Queen Victoria had a great aversion to speed and although a frequent rail-traveller over long distances – particularly to Balmoral Castle in Scotland – she would never allow the train to be driven at more than 40mph. The only occasion she was carried at a speed substantially in excess of this limit was on her last rail journey of all, following her death at Osborne, Isle of Wight in 1901. King Edward VII gave orders that the funeral train should make up a 10min delay – which it did by making the run from Gosport to Victoria at speeds of up to 80mph.

The first
MONARCH, BRITISH, TO VISIT A COMMONWEALTH COUNTRY
was King George V, who landed at Gibraltar accompanied by Queen Mary on 14–15 November 1911 *en route* to the Coronation Durbar in India.

The idea that the sovereign should regularly visit his or her overseas subjects is of comparatively recent origin. The first visit of a reigning monarch to Canada was made by King George VI in 1939, and the first to Australia and New Zealand by Queen Elizabeth II in 1953–4.

The first
MONARCH, BRITISH, TO VISIT A COMMUNIST COUNTRY
was Queen Elizabeth II, who arrived in Belgrade on 17 October 1972, at the start of a five-day official visit to Yugoslavia. Accompanied by Prince Philip and Princess Anne, the Queen was greeted by President Tito. She spent her first day in the Yugoslavian capital receiving the freedom of Belgrade at the City Assembly and laid a wreath on the tomb of the Unknown Warrior.

The first
MONARCH, BRITISH, TO VISIT THE USA
was King George VI, who crossed the border from Canada at Suspension Bridge Station, Niagara Falls, N.Y., accompanied by Queen Elizabeth, on 7 June 1939. From Niagara they travelled to Washington, D.C., where they lunched with President Roosevelt, and then continued to New York to visit the World's Fair.

The first
MONOPOLY
(board-game) was invented by unemployed heating-engineer Charles Darrow of Philadelphia, between 1931 and 1933. On completing the game Mr Darrow offered it to America's leading games-manufacturers, Parker Bros of Salem, Mass., but they rejected it on the grounds that it was too complicated to sell well. In 1934 he had 5,000 sets privately printed in Philadelphia and the game caught on sufficiently with local people for Parker Bros to reconsider. They launched it nationally for Christmas 1935 and at first it

showed no signs of having any unusual attraction. Not until Christmas was over did Monopoly-mania suddenly sweep America. 'In January 1936', the head of the company is on record as saying, 'it became the hottest fad that the game field has ever known.' It went on to become the largest-selling board-game of all time, with current figures standing at nearly 70 million sets sold. The annual issue of Monopoly money exceeds – dollar for dollar – the total output of the US Treasury.

The first
MOTEL
was the Motel Inn, San Luis Obispo, Calif., opened under the management of Harry Elliott by Hamilton Hotels on 12 December 1925. It was designed in the California Spanish Revival style by Arthur Heinman, who originated the name 'motel' in 1924, though the word did not enter any dictionary until 1950. The Motel Inn had accommodation for 160 guests, and each chalet had its own bathroom, telephone and garage. A number were equipped with kitchenettes and there was also a central dining-room. The Hamilton chain of hotels stretched from San Diego to San Francisco on one of the busiest motor routes in the USA, and this undoubtedly contributed to the success of the venture.

The first
MOTOR AGENT
was Emile Roger of 52 rue des Dames, Paris, who was appointed sole agent in France for German-built Benz vehicles in 1888. Roger later began manufacturing Benz cars under licence.
GB: Gascoigne l'Hollier, later the Anglo-French Motor Co, of Birmingham secured the British agency for Roger-Benz cars early in 1895.

The first agent for a British-manufactured car was James Edward Tuke of Burleigh Villa, Harrogate and Aldermanbury, Bradford, who became agent for Arnold Motor Carriages (*see also* Motor Car: Manufacture) in October 1896. Tuke's firm, which became the Yorkshire Motor Car Co the following year, was the first to sell motor cars on the hire-purchase system, a service they were advertising in December 1897.

The first
MOTOR BOAT
powered by an internal-combustion engine was a small gas-driven 2hp craft built in Paris by J. J. Etienne Lenoir (*see also* Internal-combustion Engine; Motor Car), consulting engineer to the firm of Gautier et Cie, and launched on the Seine in 1864. By Lenoir's own account this boat performed in-

Daimler motor boat, 1886, demonstrated for the first time on the Neckar

differently, but the following year he built a larger 12m launch with a 6hp motor for M. Dalloz, Editor of the Parisian newspaper *Le Moniteur Universel.* The inventor complained that it was too slow and used up too much fuel, but his customer seems to have been better satisfied, for he continued to use it on the Seine for two years.
MOTOR BOAT IN SERIES PRODUCTION: the first was a 20ft naphtha expansion-engined launch designed by F. W. Ofeldt in 1885 and manufactured by the Gas Engine & Power Co of New York.
GB: Naphtha launches built by the Gas Engine & Power Co of New York were imported by Rowland Wood, a prominent zoologist, from 1888.
PETROL-DRIVEN MOTOR BOAT: the first was built by Gottlieb Daimler (*see also* Motor Car; Motor Cycle) at Cannstatt, Germany and launched on the River Neckar in August 1886. Since petrol engines at this date were thought likely to explode, Daimler adopted the subterfuge of festooning the vessel with insulators and wires, in order to give the impression that it was powered by electricity. Commercial production began at Hamburg in 1890, and Daimler launches were in use by the Hamburg Harbour Police before the end of the year. Another early customer was the former Chancellor of Germany, Prince von Bismarck.
GB: The first petrol-driven motor boat in Britain was a 2hp Daimler model, imported from Germany by Frederick Richard Simms (*see also* Motor Car Fitted With Bumpers) in May 1891. This he operated from a mooring at Putney Bridge, having been refused permission to take it on any English waterway other than the Thames. The following year he bought a 10hp Daimler engine and installed it in a 38ft pinnace, which he sold to Mr G. Leake. The distinction of having launched the first British-built motor boat can be credited either to Simms for this venture or, more properly, to Frederick Lanchester, father of the Lanchester cars (*see also* Pneumatic Tyres), who produced the first motor boat with a British-built engine, designed by himself, in 1894.

Regular commercial production of motor boats in Britain was inaugurated in 1893 by the Daimler Motor Syndicate Ltd, established under the direction of F. R. Simms, his cousin Robert Gray and a wine-merchant called Theo Vasmer. The fitting of Cannstatt Daimler engines to British-built boats was commenced in a workshop hired from the District Railway Co at Putney Bridge Station. It was in connection with this enterprise that the petrol industry in Britain began, Simms making arrangements with Messrs Carless, Capel & Leonard of Hackney Wick to make supplies regularly available to the purchasers of his motor launches.
MOTOR-BOAT RACE: the first was the Harmsworth Cup Competition, held over an 8½-mile course from the headquarters of the Royal Cork Yacht Club to Glanmire, Co Cork, Ireland on 11 July 1903. The Cup was won by Campbell Muir in S. F. Edge's 75hp Napier launch, a 40ft vessel with steel hull.
MOTOR BOAT IN SCHEDULED COMMERCIAL SERVICE: the first was a petrol-driven passenger and cargo vessel which began operating on the River Niger between Timbuktu and and Kulikoro in the French Sudan at the end of 1904.

See also Outboard Motor.

The first
MOTOR CAR
with an internal-combustion engine was built by the Belgian engineer J. J. Etienne Lenoir at the factory of the Société des Moteurs Lenoir (*see also* Internal-combustion Engine) in la rue de la Roquette, Paris in May 1862. Lenoir had originally trained as an enameller, but later turned his attention to railways, inventing electric brakes and a new kind of railway

The world's first motor car – the 1863 Lenoir

signalling system. While employed as consulting engineer to the Paris engineering firm of Gautier et Cie, he began experimenting with internal-combustion engines fuelled with illuminating gas. His first essays in this direction were of immense size, but by 1862 he had produced an engine small enough to fit to a carriage. The 1½hp engine ran on liquid hydrocarbon fuel at 100rpm.

It was some time before Lenoir felt sufficient confidence in his new vehicle to take it out on the public highway, but in September 1863 he summoned up the courage to drive from la rue de la Roquette through the bois de Vincennes to Joinville-le-Pont, a distance of about six miles. The journey there and back took a driving time of 3hr, an average speed of 4mph.

The following year Lenoir received the world's first order for a motor car from no less a person than Tsar Alexander II of Russia. How the Tsar heard about Lenoir's car is not known, for it received comparatively little publicity at the time. He is remembered, though, for the interest he took in technical progress, and many of the innovations he made in Russia were based on French example. The car was built and set out for the railway station at Vincennes under its own power. There it was entrained for St Petersburg. What happened to it on arrival is an unsolved mystery. There is no record whether the Tsar ever rode in his motor carriage and it is quite possible that there was no one attached to the Imperial Court with sufficient engineering skill to make it start. Nor is it known whether any arrangements were made for a supply of fuel. Indeed, nobody seems to have known about the sale until 1906, when a set of papers detailing the transaction were found in Paris. A hunt for the car was then set on foot in Russia, but with negative results. It had vanished without trace, and if it was still in existence at that time, hidden away in a barn or store-room, it seems unlikely that it would have long survived the chaos of the Bolshevik Revolution. Lenoir himself abandoned the motor car to concentrate his energies on developing a practical motor boat (*q.v.*).

PETROL-DRIVEN MOTOR CAR: the first was built in 1883 by 27-year-old Edouard Delamare-Deboutteville, the son of a cotton-mill proprietor, who was inspired with the idea of seeking an alternative to horse transport for carrying cotton goods from his father's factories at Montgrimont and Fontaine-le-Bourg to the railhead at Rouen. With the help of his mechanic, Charles Malandin, Delamare-Deboutteville modified an 8hp stationary gas-engine for use with petrol as a fuel, and fitted it to a four-wheeled hunting-brake. Road tests were carried out between Deboutteville's home at Fontaine-le-Bourg and near-by Cailly. The effect of the brake's iron-tyred wheels on the rough stone *pavé* was too much for it, and the vehicle was eventually abandoned as too fragile for the power of the motor. Deboutteville subsequently built a rubber-tyred tricycle, but the motor was too heavy and the frame collapsed. After this set-back the inventor abandoned the idea of self-propelled carriages and concentrated his attention on stationary engines, winning a number of awards for his improvements and receiving the Légion d'honneur in 1896.

The first successful petrol-engined car, representing the beginning of the continuous development of commercially practicable motor vehicles, was built by the Rheinische-Gasmotorenfabrik Karl Benz of Mannheim, Germany in the autumn of 1885. The three-wheeled single-cylinder vehicle weighed about 560lb and was powered by a ¾hp water-cooled engine with electric ignition and a mechanically operated inlet valve. The engine drove the two rear wheels. An advanced feature of the car was its remarkably sophisticated differential gear. Benz was granted a patent on the design of the car on 29 January 1886.

The first public demonstration of Benz's three-wheeler took place on 3 July 1886, when it was driven for about a kilometre in Mannheim at a speed of 15kph. This historic event was reported the next day in the *Neue Badische Landeszeitung* under the heading 'Miscellaneous'.

During the winter of 1886–7 Benz built a more powerful 1½hp car, and this was followed by a 2hp model which won a Gold Medal at the Munich Industrial Exhibition in September 1888. Meanwhile Gottlieb Daimler of Cannstatt had produced the first successful four-wheeled petrol-engined car at the Esslinger Maschinenfabrik in August 1886. The single-cylinder engine was mounted on to an ordinary horse-drawn carriage, but Daimler soon realized that if motor transport was to have a future, it was essential for the vehicle to be designed as an entity. His *Stahlradwagen* (Steel-wheeled carriage) of 1889 marked this departure and is also notable as the first car with a two-cylinder high-revving V-engine. It had a respectable maximum speed of 17·5 kph, and was remarkably reliable for its time.

The motor-manufacturing concerns founded by Karl Benz and Gottlieb Daimler (*see also* Motor Car: Manufacture) were eventually united in 1926 as Daimler-Benz, but during their life-times the two fathers of the industry worked quite independently and never met each other.

NB: A monument erected to the Austrian inventor Siegfried Marcus in Vienna bears the inscription: 'Inventor of the Petrol Automobile – 1864.' Since the end of the last century, the claim of Siegfried Marcus to have built the first petrol-engined vehicles – a motorized hand-cart allegedly of 1864 and a full-size car allegedly in 1875 – has been generally accepted by motor historians as legitimate and factually accurate.

The legend began in 1898, when Prof. Czischek exhibited the Marcus car at a trade motor show in Vienna, as an historic relic of 1875. This date was subsequently written into innumerable motoring histories and it was not until 1961 that the Austrian historian Dr Seper was able to prove, from documents found in the Vienna Technical Museum, that the car was in fact built in 1888 by the firm of Märky, Bromowsky & Schulz at Adamsthal (Adamov), in what is now Czechoslovakia, and that Marcus himself, the designer of the engine, never saw the vehicle until it was exhibited by Czischek. The handcart dated from 1870.

GB: The first British petrol-engined motor car was built by a young gas-fitter and plumber called Frederick William Bremer, in his workshop at the back of his mother's house in Connaught Road, Walthamstow. His original idea was to fit a gas-engine to a bicycle to reduce the effort of pedalling, but he abandoned this idea in favour of a four-wheeled motor car, which he began work on in 1892 when he was 20 years of age. Bremer's father was a Berliner by birth, and is known to have made a number of trips back to his home country. Certain design features of the Bremer car suggest that it may have been inspired by the Benz, and it is possible that Frederick Bremer may have accompanied his father to Germany and actually seen a Benz in operation.

The car was a very small two-seater with a single-cylinder water-cooled engine driving the rear wheels by means of crossed belts from flywheel pulleys to fast and loose pulleys on the counter-shaft, then by endless chain. Ignition was by trembler-coil and wipe-contact, and was variable. The sparking-plug was improvised from glass, clay-pipe stems, mica and fibre.

Bremer's car first ran on the public highway in December 1894, a month after the first imported car braved the Locomotives on Highways Act (*see below*). The body at this date was incomplete but was finished in January 1895. Its speed was claimed to be between 15 and 20mph, but this may be a slightly exaggerated estimate.

Bremer himself is an anomaly among motoring pioneers. With no influential connections, no monetary backing, and only the most basic training in mechanical engineering, he succeeded in building a successful car and taking to the road as England's first working-class motorist. Having achieved so much, he was satisfied to go on plumbing, and after effecting a number of improvements to his car, it was relegated to a shed. When the Motor Registration Act was passed in 1903, Bremer did not bother to register the car – an omission that was to lead to an extraordinary Parliamentary precedent being established many years later, when its restorers sought to run it on the highway. No attempt had been made to restore the Bremer when it was presented to the Walthamstow Museum in 1931, and over the years its condition deteriorated. It was not until 1961 that it was noticed by two local car enthusiasts, who applied to the Museum for permission to undertake its complete restoration. The painstaking work – even the paint was made up according to a formula of the 1890s – took them nearly two years, but at the end of that time it was ready to run again. It was then found that as the car had never been registered, it was not exempt from any of the stringent construction-and-use regulations that apply to modern cars.

In 1964 Parliamentary history was made when special amending legislation was introduced to permit the Bremer to run on the public highway, and in November of the same year it was able to take part in the annual London to Brighton Rally with John Trott, one of the two restorers, at the tiller. The car was examined before the run by the Veteran Car Club Dating Committee, and officially warranted as having been built in 1894.

MOTOR CAR TO RUN ON THE PUBLIC HIGHWAY: the first in Britain was a 2hp Benz Velo purchased by coffee-dealer Henry Hewetson of Catford in Mannheim for £80, and brought to England in November 1894. For six weeks he drove the car in and around Catford without interference, but was then warned by an Inspector of Police that he would be prosecuted unless he complied with the provisions of the Locomotives on Highways Act 1865, including the requirement that the car should be preceded by a man on foot bearing a red flag.

Hewetson secured the services of two youths, one of whom he employed to ride ahead of the car at some distance on a bicycle and give warning if he sighted a policeman. The other rode in the car, but dismounted on receiving a signal from the first boy, and proceeded to stroll leisurely in front of the vehicle holding aloft a derisory 2 sq in of red linen on a pencil until the law was safely out of sight.

Hewetson and Bremer were the only two motorists in Britain in 1894. Others known to have imported cars during 1895 include the following: The Hon. Evelyn Ellis of Datchet, Panhard, 3 July 1895; Sir David Salomons of Tunbridge Wells, Peugeot, October 1895; Leon L'Hollier of Birmingham, Roger-Benz, November 1895; J.A. Koosen of Southsea, Lutzmann, 21 November 1895; Walter Arnold of East Peckham, Benz, November 1895; T.R.B. Elliott of Clifton Park, Kelso (first car in Scotland), Daimler, 27 December 1895; Dr T. Pritchard Roberts of Harrogate, Benz, late 1895.

Petrol-driven cars were built in England during 1895 by J.H. Knight, Herbert Austin, Frederick Lanchester, and J.D. Roots. It seems, then, that at the end of 'motoring's first year' there were about 14 or 15 petrol vehicles on the roads of Britain, and a few steam and electric cars may have brought the total up to 20. No official figures exist prior to 1904, but it has been estimated that there may have been 700–800 cars in Britain by the turn of the century, compared with 5,000 in France. Most were concentrated in London and the Home Counties. In July 1902 the *Autocar* reported as a remarkable fact: 'Last week a member of our staff, whilst in the West End, counted 23 cars within three-quarters of an hour.' Ten years later there were 9,000 private cars within the London area and 8,000 taxis, while the number of private cars in the country as a whole totalled 88,265.

The phrase 'motoring for the million' first became a reality in 1930, when there were 1,056,214 private cars and vans currently licensed. The 10 million figure was passed in 1967. The USA had become the first country with a million cars in 1913.

The first
MOTOR CAR FITTED WITH BUMPERS

in Britain was a 20hp Simms-Welbeck car to which pneumatic bumpers were attached by the Simms Manufacturing Co of Kilburn in the summer of 1905.

Although the idea was patented by F.R. Simms the same year, it was not entirely original. The first car in the world to have a bumper, mounted on the front of the vehicle only, was the prototype model of the Czech-built Präsident, constructed at the Imperial Nesseldorf wagon factory in Moravia in 1897. In this case, however, the design innovation was short-lived, as the bumper fell off within the first 10 miles of the car's initial test run to Vienna on 21 May 1898 and was not replaced.

The first
MOTOR CAR, DOCTOR TO USE

for visiting patients was Dr Carlos C. Booth of Youngstown, Ohio, who employed a vehicle of his own design for doing his rounds in 1895. He abandoned it after some 18 months due to 'commotion among the horses' of Youngstown.

GB: Dr T. Pritchard Roberts of Harrogate acquired a belt-driven Benz for doing his rounds the same year. The horses of Harrogate evidently proved less fractious than those of Youngstown, for by 1925 Dr Roberts had been owner of no less than 64 different cars.

The first
MOTOR CAR USED FOR ELECTIONEERING
was a Mueller-Benz lent by the H. Mueller Co of Decatur, Ill., to the Democratic candidate for the Presidency, William Jennings Bryan, who employed it to tour round Decatur, and as a platform for meetings, during his visit to the city on 23 October 1896. The Mueller car had run second in America's first automobile race, held at Chicago the previous November. Bryan likewise ran second, being defeated by the Republican candidate, William McKinley.
GB: The first election car was an Arnold-Benz belonging to J.E. Tuke of Harrogate, a motor agent, who ferried the Liberal candidate for the South Ward of Bradford, J. Dawson, round the district on 31 October 1896, and allowed him to use it as a platform for open-air meetings. On polling day, 2 November, the car was used to take voters to the polls, but, said Tuke darkly, 'many got their first ride in a motor car under false pretences'.

The first
MOTOR CAR FITTED WITH ELECTRIC LAMPS
recorded in GB, was described by a correspondent to the *Autocar* of 26 November 1906, who claimed that in November 1904 he had fitted his car with an electric lamp powered by a six-cell 48amp 12V accumulator.

The first manufacturer to produce and market an electrical lighting system for cars was the Polkey Automobile Electric Lighting Syndicate Ltd of Hockley Lamp Works, Birmingham, in the summer of 1908. The set comprised two headlights, two side-lights and a tail-lamp, together with a 60amp 8V Vandervell accumulator. The headlamps, fitted with Osram bulbs, afforded a light described by the *Autocar* as of 'so powerful and penetrating a character that the rays obtain for a distance of some 150 yards'.

The first
MOTOR CAR FITTED WITH AN ELECTRIC STARTER
was the prototype Arnold Sociable, the first petrol-driven car in series production in Britain, built by W. Arnold & Son Ltd of East Peckham (*see also* Motor Car: Manufacture) in November 1896, and sold to a Mr H.J. Dowsing of Ealing the following month. Dowsing, an electrical engineer by profession, added an electric self-starter of his own design (Patent No. 10781 of 1896) to the car. This consisted of a dynamotor, coupled to a flywheel, which would act as a dynamo to charge the battery and as a motor when required to start the engine.

The first self-starter system manufactured in Britain was produced by Messrs Hayward & Fox of 23 King Street, Norwich in February 1901.

The first production car to be sold with an electric self-starter system as a standard fitting was the Belgian-made 1902 Dechamps, manufactured by Atelier H.P. Dechamps of 31 rue Frère Orban, Brussels. Three different models were available, a 9hp and a 14hp tonneau, and a smaller 7hp vehicle, all of them fitted with Dumont self-starters.

The Delco self-starter, designed by Charles Kettering of Cadillac, and first demonstrated on 27 February 1911, has often been described erroneously as the first self-starter on a standard production model car. Though this is patently not true, the Delco did have a special significance as part of the first completely self-contained electrical system performing the three functions of ignition, starting and lighting. It was offered as a standard fitting on the 1912 Cadillac.

The first
MOTOR CAR WITH A FULLY ENCLOSED BODY
was the French-built two-seater 2½hp Renault, manufactured at Billancourt in 1898. Remarkably robust for such a small car, one model drove from Paris to Rambouillet in 2hr 49min in 1899, covering the 65 miles at an average speed of nearly 24mph. The enclosed Renault (there was also an open version) was intended principally for the use of doctors on their rounds, and with its very short wheel-base has been described as having 'a silhouette like a top hat on a roller skate'.
GB: Prior to the introduction of an enclosed production model, there were a number of attempts by individual owners and experimenters to provide weather protection for the driver as well as the passengers. The first on record was Dr W.W. Barrett of Hesketh Park, Southport (*see also* Garage), who acquired a six-seater Daimler in December 1898 and had a special enclosed body built for it. There were three windows on either side and three doors, one at the rear of the vehicle.

The following year Messrs Mulliner, coachbuilders, offered a detachable enclosed body designed by V. Friswell of Friswell Ltd, Holburn Viaduct, London as an optional extra to the Benz Ideal, a popular car in the lower price bracket.
SALOON CAR: the first full-sized was a four-seater motor brougham produced by the Duryea Co of Coventry, and exhibited for the first time at the Stanley Motor Show on 16 January 1903. It was followed in 1904 by the 12hp Argyll, the first all-British saloon car (the Duryea Co was an American concern), which had a brougham body with two side-doors and a rear entrance, and a remarkably elegant curved windscreen.

The first
MOTOR-CAR HIRE SERVICE
was instituted by the Paris Automobile Club in January 1896. Six vehicles were stationed outside the clubhouse and were available for immediate hire at 3 francs an hour, or 30 francs a day, with driver.

The Automobile Club's service was instituted principally with the idea of winning converts to the cause of motoring. A strictly commercial car-hire service was started the following month by the Société Anonyme Française de Fiacres Automobiles of 52 rue des Dames, Paris. The brain behind this enterprise was Emile Roger, the agent for Benz cars in France, who in 1888 had been the first man to purchase a commercially manufactured petrol-driven car (*see also* Motor Car: Manufacture). He undercut the Automobile Club's rates, offering Benz cars on hire for 2 francs an hour.
GB: James Edward Tuke, motor agent of Harrogate and Bradford, began a hire service of Arnold Sociables and Victorias in December 1896. Hire charges ranged from 3s an hour for a two-seater Sociable to £10 a month for a six-seater Victoria.

The first
MOTOR CAR: MANUFACTURE
of petrol-driven vehicles was begun by the Rheinische Gasmotorenfabrik Karl Benz of Mannheim, Germany in 1888. Benz had produced the first efficient and commercially practicable motor car three years earlier (*see also* Motor Car), but the first recorded sale was made to Emile Roger of Paris, the invoice being dated 16 March 1888. The 2hp single-cylinder car, a three-wheeled two-seater, was forwarded to Paris in four packing-cases, and when it arrived Roger found he was unable to assemble the parts. He took the vehicle in pieces to the Panhard et Levassor factory to consult with their engineers, but the car remained immobile until May, when Benz himself paid a visit to the firm.

Benz issued their first catalogue the same year. Initially the cars were all three-wheelers, but in 1893 two basic four-wheeled models were produced, the Victoria and the *vis-à-vis*. Neither of these was standardized, being built according to the customer's specifications. Total sales of Benz vehicles at the end of that year stood at 69. The first standard model in series production was the Benz Velo, produced in April 1894. Powered by a 1½hp engine, it had a maximum speed of 12mph and was priced at 2,200 marks.

Benz und Cie amalgamated with the Daimler Motoren-Gesellschaft in 1926 to become the Daimler-Benz AG, manufacturers of the distinguished Mercedes marque that had been introduced by Daimler in 1901.

GB: In Britain there were no less than five manufacturers with some claim to have fathered the industry; the most probable in the light of existing evidence was the Arnold Motor Carriage Co of East Peckham, an offshoot of W. Arnold & Son Ltd, a firm of agricultural engineers founded in 1844. Walter Arnold was associated with Henry Hewetson in importing the first Benz car to England in November 1894, and together they secured the agency for the sale of Benz cars in this country. He then applied to Benz for a licence to manufacture cars under the Benz patents and this was granted. The first Arnold-Benz engine was completed in the summer of 1896 and it was decided to proceed with the manufacture of a pilot series of 12 cars. The engine employed in the prototype, although based on the Benz patents, differed considerably in detail. The bore and stroke dimensions of the cylinder were altered to give an improved power output, and the cylinder-barrel and water-jacket were separate castings ('wet-liner' construction), instead of a single integral casting as on the Benz engine.

The prototype Arnold, the first petrol-driven car known definitely to have been manufactured for sale in England, made what is believed to have been its first extended road trial from East Peckham to Bromley on 13 November 1896, the eve of the Emancipation Run to Brighton. Having proved its road-worthiness, it was taken back to the works and the Benz transmission system replaced by a similar Arnold-designed belt-drive.

Although it is beyond dispute that the first customer was H.J. Dowsing of Ealing, the date he took delivery of the car is less certain. It is likely, though, that Dowsing was in possession of his Arnold before the end of 1896 and that – if the claims outlined below are discounted – the car represented the total output of the British motor industry (in terms of deliveries) for that year.

The prototype Arnold, named 'Adam' by its owner, earned further distinction as the first car in the world to have an electric self-starter (*q.v.*). Dowsing was an electrical engineer of considerable repute, his other achievements in this field including the introduction of the electric oven (*q.v.*) and electric heating (*q.v.*) to Britain.

1893 Benz Victoria

It is fortunate that Dowsing felt a sufficient affection for the car never to part with it during his lifetime. Although stored away for many years and allowed to decay, Adam was brought out in 1927 to participate in the early 'Old Crocks Runs'. Less fortunately it was taken for repair to a number of garages who had no regard for its antiquity and replaced worn-out original parts with the nearest modern equivalent to hand. The coachwork in particular suffered, painted an unsuitable green with a tar-brush, though all this was in keeping with the idea of the 'Old Crocks Runs', which was for the cars to look as funny as possible, in striking contrast to the reverence with which veterans are regarded today. After Dowsing's death, the car was bought in 1930 by Capt. E. de W.S. Colver, a pioneer of the Veteran movement and one of the first to insist that historic cars were not laughable 'old crocks', but industrial artefacts to be preserved as nearly as possible in their original condition. He had no idea what make of car it was when he bought it, but returning home after the 1930 Brighton Run was amazed to hear an old countryman who looked like a jobbing gardener remark in broad dialect: 'Ee, that's one o' them there Arnolds.' On discovering that the Arnold firm was still in existence, Capt. Colver was delighted to find that they still retained a stock of all the original parts that were missing, and he was able to restore the car to its original condition. He continued to run it until his death in 1971, when the car was purchased by a member of the Arnold family.

The other 11 cars of the series, each of which bore a nameplate inscribed 'Arnold Petroleum Carriage, Benz's System', were completed during 1897 and 1898. According to the Arnold catalogue the single-cylinder, rear-mounted horizontal engine was rated at 'about 1½hp' and it was stated that 'these carriages . . . will ascend hills of 1 in 10'. Capt. Colver is on record as saying that while this statement may have been literally true, it would perhaps have been fairer to mention that they were capable of climbing such a gradient providing both driver and passenger were out in the road pushing from the rear. The coachwork was a cruder version of the Benz Sociable and the price 'delivered in London, complete with lamps', was £130.

Having accomplished what they had set out to do, and finding that manufacture of the 12 cars had incurred a loss of £2,000, the proprietors of the Arnold Motor Carriage Co decided against further production. They continued in business as motor agents until the turn of the century, before disposing of their interest in the imported Benz to Henry Hewetson. The firm of W. Arnold & Son Ltd meanwhile continued in the engineering business, as it still does today.

The other firms engaged in motor manufacture in Britain in 1896 and which may or may not have proceeded beyond the purely experimental stage to actual sales are Messrs Lister & Co of Keighley, Yorkshire; Messrs Petter, Hill & Boll of Yeovil, who registered on 5 November 1896 as the Yeovil Motor Car & Cycle Co; and Roots & Venables of Westminster Bridge Road, London.

Referring to Lister & Co, the *Autocar* recorded in its issue for 11 April 1896:

We understand that the firm have already commenced delivery, having just completed their first order for the East Indies of a two-passenger gig, whilst they have on order for Malta a new departure in autocars, in the shape of a sanitary cart, to carry about 25 cwt of night soil. They are now prepared to book orders for fairly early delivery, and in the case of two-passenger gigs can execute within a month or six weeks from receipt of order.

Inquiries made in Malta have elicited no record of the delivery of a motorized sanitary cart. There is no mention of the firm in contemporary Keighley directories. The only other known references are contained in the *Keighley News* for 2 May 1896, in which a Mr Frank Lister is reported to have filed a patent 'for improvements appertaining to road vehicles propelled by steam, oil, electric or like motor mechanism', and in the *Autocar* for 14 January 1899, which carries a description of the new Lister car, a four-seat three-wheeler with a two-cylinder oil engine.

Roots & Venables and Petter's of Yeovil both claimed to be fulfilling orders for oil-engined motor carriages as early as July 1896. In its issue for 21 November 1896 the *Autocar* reported that the Petter cars 'which have been delivered have proved so satisfactory in work' that it had been decided to continue manufacture of an expanded range. The same paper reported in June 1898: 'We understand that the firm have relinquished the manufacture of motor cars driven by heavy oils, as they found that its odour and other objections more than counterbalanced its advantages.'

The evidence of Roots & Venables' manufacturing activities is similarly inconclusive. J. D. Roots, who had started experimenting with internal-combustion engines in 1884, claimed to have built a four-wheeled oil-engined car prior to November 1895. The Roots Oil Motor & Motor Car Co Ltd was registered on 7 July 1897 and continued in business until 1902. During this period a vehicle called the 'Petrocar' was advertised for sale at £165, but whether it was in production in 1896 cannot be substantiated.

The fifth claimant, and undoubtedly the first successful manufacturer of cars in Britain, was the Daimler Motor Car Co, which was founded at the instigation of Henry Lawson and registered on 14 January 1896. The intention of the Company was to produce motor vehicles under patents acquired the previous year from the German Daimler concern in Cannstatt by the British Motor Syndicate Ltd. Although a factory, the Motor Mills, was acquired in Coventry in April 1896, it was not until the spring of the following year that actual production started.

The first Coventry-built Daimler car purchased by anyone unconnected with the Company was delivered to Maj.-Gen Montgomery of Winchester in the last week of August 1897. This important event, which signalled the start of a continuously developing British motor industry, was recorded in the *Hampshire Chronicle* for 28 August, which described the two-day drive from Coventry to Winchester. 'The riding', according to the Major-General, 'was simply delightful, the swift, gliding, noiseless motion along the level roads being particularly exhilarating.' Apparently not all the gallant gentleman's friends and acquaintances were in agreement with him. A youthful female neighbour wrote in a letter to a friend: 'We never go to see the general now because he always wants us to go for a ride in his horrid motor car.'

The first production model Daimlers rated 4hp with a two-cylinder engine, tiller-steering and an average speed of 10–12mph. A prospectus handed out by Henry Sturmey, Editor of the *Autocar* and a Director of the Company, during a run from John o' Groats to Land's End in the autumn of 1897, contained the following selling points:

No! It can't explode – there is no boiler.
It can be started in two minutes.
It can be stopped in ten feet when travelling at full speed.
It costs less than ¾d a mile to run.
The car can carry five people.
It can get up any ordinary hill.
It was built by the Daimler Motor Company of Coventry and cost £370.

Output at this time was running at four cars a week, manufacture of a single vehicle taking about three months.

Despite the early lead in motor manufacture taken by the German Benz and Daimler enterprises, restrictive traffic laws in Germany hindered the progress of the industry and the French soon became recognized as world leaders in the development of the automobile. Production in France had been begun by the Paris firm of Panhard et Levassor in 1892, closely followed by Peugeot, and both these firms were aided by the distinction they won in the earliest motor races (*q.v.*). Total output in 1900 was in excess of 1,500 vehicles, most of them produced by six companies:

De Dion	400
Peugeot	350
Panhard	300
Georges Richard	150
De Dietrich	150
Mors	100

As in most other countries, motorcycle production considerably outstripped car production, with 4,000 manufactured during the year. The total value of the motor industry's exports was £330,000.

The first reliable world figures, for 1903, show France as producing nearly three times as many motor vehicles as her nearest competitor, and half of the total world output of 61,927 vehicles:

France	30,204
USA	11,235
GB	9,437
Germany	6,904
Belgium	2,839
Italy	1,308

MASS-PRODUCED PETROL-DRIVEN MOTOR CAR: the first in the world came not from France but from the USA, and this was symptomatic of the growing importance of American cars in the world market. The car in question was the curved-dash Olds, the first to be manufactured in a quantity exceeding 10 a week, which made its appearance in April 1901. By the end of the year a total of 433 had been produced, and this figure rose from 2,500 in 1902 to an unprecedented 5,508 in 1904. Manufactured in Detroit by Ransom E. Olds, the extreme simplicity of the car enabled it to be retailed at only $650, a price much lower than any other car of comparable performance. Its speed barely exceeded 20mph, but its extreme lightness – the car only weighed 800lb – gave it remarkable hill-climbing powers.

GB: The first motor-manufacturer to produce 10 cars a week was the Hozier Engineering Co of Bridgetown, Scotland, which began manufacturing the Argyll car in 1900. Production for the first year was 100 cars and reached 500 for the first time in 1904.

The first
MOTOR-CAR RADIO

on record was fitted to the passenger door of a Ford Model T by 18-year-old George Frost, President of Lane High School Radio Club, Chicago, and was in use by May 1922.

GB: The first car radio was fitted to a Daimler limousine by the Marconi-

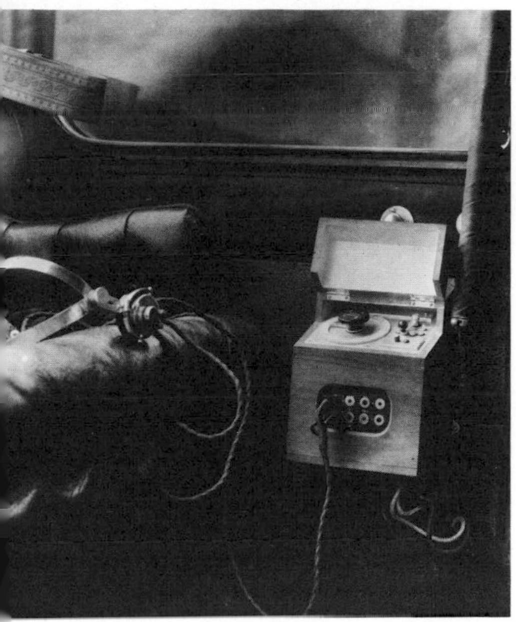

Marconi car radio, 1923

phone Co, and exhibited at the Olympia Motor Show in November 1922. Subsequent demonstrations were given at the Scottish Motor Show in Glasgow the following January. Since reception from London proved inadequate the Post Office generously licensed a special transmitting station, 2BP, which Marconi's were permitted to operate for the duration of the Show. Although it was intended to exploit car radio commercially, the Daimler-Marconi experiments proved to be premature and the development programme was dropped. A number of portable radio sets for use in cars were demonstrated at the 1925 Radio Show at the Albert Hall. Although these were designed principally for use while the car was stationary, reception was possible with the car in motion given favourable atmospheric conditions and within reasonable distance of the transmitter.

Probably the first private car in Britain to be fitted with built-in radio was Capt. Leonard F. Plugge's 14hp Standard Park Lane saloon, which had a Standard Telephones seven-valve supersonic heterodyne set installed in 1926. The receiver and its two-valve low-frequency amplifier were concealed behind the dashboard on the left-hand side of the steering-column, and there was a pleated disc loudspeaker on the roof that doubled as a lampshade. The volume could be controlled either from the steering-wheel or from the back of the car. A row of batteries was slung in cradles underneath the chassis, so the only part of the 'works' that showed was a frame aerial encased in celluloid and mounted on the off-side front wing. The total weight of this unobtrusive wireless installation was reported to be 100lb.

COMMERCIALLY PRODUCED CAR RADIO: the first was the Philco Transitone, introduced by the Philadelphia Storage Battery Co in 1927. By 1933 there were claimed to be 100,000 cars fitted with radio in the USA.

GB: The Philco Transitone was offered for sale at 33gns in the autumn of 1932. The *Autocar* reported in November that 'several high grade coach builders are now fitting them in bodies for Rolls-Royces'.

The first
MOTOR CAR WITH A SUPER-CHARGED ENGINE

was the Great Chadwick Six, which was fitted with three compressors driven by leather belts at six times engine speed by Lee S. Chadwick and his assistant J.T. Nichols at Pottstown, Pa., in the winter of 1907–8. The supercharged Chadwick was first used in competition by works driver Willie Haupt in the Giant's Despair Hill-climb at Wilkes-Barre, Pa. on 30 May 1908. On this occasion Haupt beat the previous record of 1min 59sec for a petrol-engined car by a clear 21sec. At the end of the season, Chadwick revealed the secret behind his many successes in hill-climbs and sprints. He announced that he was prepared to offer the 'blower', as it was called, as an optional extra to his Runabout and Tourabout models for $375, guaranteeing that they would attain a speed of 100mph. About half a dozen Chadwicks were adapted in this way.

The first production-model car designed with a supercharged engine as standard fitment was the Mercedes 10/45/65 of 1922. The figure 45 indicated the engine power unsupercharged (advisable at speeds under 35mph) and the 65 its horsepower supercharged.

The first supercharged racing-car to win a Grand Prix event was a Fiat in the Grand Prix of Europe and Italy held at Monza on 9 September 1923. From this date onwards nearly all cars used in major competition events employed forced induction.

The first
MOTOR-CAR THEFT

occurred in Paris in June 1896, when the Baron de Zuylen's Peugeot was stolen by his mechanic from the maker's, where it was undergoing repairs. Thief and vehicle were apprehended later at Asnières.

The first
MOTOR-COACH

service (inter-urban) was inaugurated between Clacton and London by the London Motor Van & Wagon Co at the beginning of August 1898. The Company ran four vehicles every Friday from Clacton to London and back to Clacton, taking 5½hr in each direction to cover the 70-mile distance. The service does not appear to have been sustained for more than a few weeks.

In the USA the first service was established by the Nassau County Motor Coach Co, founded early in 1899 to run coaches between suburban points on Long Island. This enterprise also occasioned the earliest use of the term 'motor coach'.

LONG-DISTANCE MOTOR-COACH SERVICE: the first was inaugurated between London and Leeds by A.E. Wynn of Knaresborough, Yorkshire on 27 August 1900. The vehicle ran once a week in each direction, taking two days on the road for the 200-mile journey. Return fare was 2gns.

The first
MOTOR-COACH EXCURSIONS

were run by the Blackpool Motor Car Co, formed with a capital of £25,000 in the first week of August 1897. Within a month the Company had six vehicles operating in the Blackpool area, and takings were said to be £40 a day. The drivers were paid 25s a week, which was the same as the average weekly wage of a London horse-bus driver at that time.

The first company to run whole-day motor-coach excursions was the South African Motor Car Co, which began running regular Sunday trips from Cape Town to Somerset West Strand on 13 March 1898. The 16s fare for the 75-mile round trip included lunch at Somerset Strand, a small coastal town lying across False Bay from the Cape of Good Hope. The 'beautiful and comfortable cars' described in the Company's advertisements are believed to have been German-built Daimlers.

GB: The first whole-day motor-coach excursion, advertised by the Llandudno Motor Touring Co as its 'Grand Tour', was run on 2 August 1898, with tickets at 12s single and 20s double. The Benz wagonette left the North Western Hotel in Llandudno at 9.30am and proceeded via Penmaenmawr to Bethesda, where lunch could be had at the Douglas Arms with 'ample time for . . . visiting the huge Penrhyn Slate Quarries, the largest in the world'. Capel Curig was reached by 3.15pm, affording a 'fine view of the Snowdon Range', and the coach stopped at the Victoria Hotel, Llanrwst an hour later for tea. The party arrived back at Llandudno at 6.45pm. The total round trip was nearly 60 miles.

The first
MOTOR-COACH TOUR

was a six-day continental excursion

from Paris to Aix-le-Bains which began on 11 July 1898. Organized jointly by Thomas Cook & Son and the Compagnie Nationale d'Automobiles, the tour cost 180 francs (about £9) and took the coach party on a route that passed through Fontainebleau, Sens, Auxerre, Avallon, Semur, Dijon, Dôle, Salins, Saint-Laurent, Geneva and Annecy. The vehicle was a De Dion steam omnibus with seats arranged in six tiers, four facing forward and two backward. The sides of the coach were open, but there was a glazed partition separating the passengers from the driver and also a glass window at the rear. Average speed on a level surface was 16kph, and the schedule allowed for 6hr a day to be spent 'in actual autocaring'. There was a baggage limit of 20kilos per passenger, as this had to be carried on the roof.

Cook's pioneer continental coach tour appears to have been exceptional, and there is no evidence that it was repeated. The real beginning of the coach-touring business dates from 1910, when Messrs Chapman of Eastbourne (later to become the Southdown Motor Co) operated a six-day tour of North Wales in a 22-seater petrol-driven Dennis motor coach. A number of other bus companies entered the holiday field in the years immediately preceding World War I, generally, but not always, carrying their passengers in open charabancs. One exception was Sussex Tourist Coaches, who were proud to announce in 1914 that their Daimler Silent Knight coach had a 'cover over the top' and 'glass windows all round'.

CONTINENTAL COACH TOURS: the first regular were six-day excursions to the battlefields of France and Flanders, operated by Chapman's of Eastbourne in 1919. The following year saw the start of luxury coach touring when Motorways Ltd of London started running a pair of specially fitted vehicles between Calais and the Riviera. Built on ex-US Army-truck chassis, these remarkable coaches were each furnished with a dozen swivel armchairs, a buffet kitchen and a WC. By 1924, Motorways were offering coach holidays to North Africa, and in 1935 they were the first to open up the coach route to Soviet Russia.

The first *MOTOR CYCLE*

was built by Gottlieb Daimler at Cannstatt, Germany and patented on 29 August 1885. It was powered by a single-cylinder four-stroke engine developing 700rpm, and incorporated internal flywheels, fan-cooling, a mechanically operated exhaust valve and an automatically operated inlet valve.

MOTOR-CYCLIST: the first was Paul Daimler, Gottlieb's son, who drove the machine from Cannstatt to Untertürkheim and back, a round trip of six miles, on 10 November 1885. Daimler did not intend the vehicle as a commercial proposition, but as a test-bed for his newly developed petrol engine.

GB: The Petro-Cycle was designed by Edward Butler of Erith, Kent, and built by F. B. Shuttleworth Ltd, marine engineers, in 1887–8. It was powered by a two-stroke engine developing 100rpm (increased to 600rpm after modification) and had three wheels, a sub-clutch control, water-cooling and a jet-carburettor. After running the Petro-Cycle for six months, Butler was constrained to write: 'The authorities do not countenance its use on roads, and I have therefore abandoned in consequence any further development of it.' It had, however, already been ridden by Mrs Butler, who thus became the world's first woman motorist.

The first motor bicycle in Britain was built by H. Taylor, a Kettering cycle agent, in mid 1892, and was powered by a $1\frac{1}{4}$hp water-cooled engine with spray-carburettor and tube ignition. Unlike most early motor cycles, Taylor's belt-drive machine had no pedals and to start it the rider had to run alongside.

COMMERCIALLY PRODUCED MOTOR CYCLE: the first was the $2\frac{1}{2}$hp Motorrad, manufactured at the Munich works of Heinrich and Wilhelm Hildebrand and Alois Wolfmüller in 1894. It was powered by a water-cooled 760cc single-cylinder engine developing 600rpm, and was capable of 24mph. The first batch of 50 was delivered in November 1894 and over 1,000 were produced during the next two years. Alexandre Darracq commenced manufacture of the Millet motor cycle in France the same year.

GB: The Beeston Tricycle, a De Dion design, was manufactured under licence by the New Beeston Cycle Co, Coventry in August 1896.

The first *MOTOR CYCLE USED FOR MILITARY PURPOSES*

was a $1\frac{1}{4}$hp Cyclometer tricycle supplied to the 26th Middlesex (Cyclist) RV and driven from Corps Headquarters at Chelsea to the camp of the South London Volunteer Brigade at Woking on 30 March 1899. The tricycle was ridden by C. H. E. Rush of the London Autocar Co, the suppliers, and used for towing a Maxim machine-gun during the Brigade's Easter manœuvres at Aldershot.

MOTOR-CYCLE DESPATCH-RIDERS: the first were four motor tricyclists of the French Army, described as *éstafettes militaire motoristées*, who took part in the Army manœuvres of 6–18 September 1899 in the Verdun–Sainte-Menehould region.

MOTOR CYCLE USED IN WARFARE: the first was carried on the armoured train *Spitfire* during the South African War and employed by Lt F. R. S. Bircham for scouting purposes round Mafeking in 1900.

The first *MOTOR-CYCLE RACE*

was organized by the Automobile Club de France in association with the Paris–Marseilles Race for cars and held over a 152km course from Paris to Nantes and back on 20 September 1896. There were eight competitors, three mounted on De Dion motor tricycles; three on Michelin-Dion tricycles; one on a Bollée tricycle; and one on a Hildebrand-Wolfmüller motor cycle. The winner was M. Chevalier on a Michelin-Dion in 4hr 10min 37sec.

Motor funeral – Buffalo, N.Y., 1900. The hearse was the vehicle in front.

GB: The first motor-cycling meet was organized by Charles Jarrott of the Motor-Car Club as part of the events held at Sheen House, Richmond on 29 November 1897, to celebrate the first anniversary of the Emancipation Run to Brighton (*see also* Motor Race). There were two classes, one for tricycles and the other for motor bicycles. Jarrott, an enthusiast who bought nearly every motor vehicle he could lay his hands on, was able to compete in both, as he owned a motor tricycle and a motor bicycle. In the first race, riding a De Dion tricycle, he was beaten by F.T. Bidlake on a Clement. In the second, held over a mile distance on a hard-surface oval track, he was an easy victor on his powerful Fournier racing motor bicycle in a time of 2min 8sec.

The first
MOTOR-CYCLING FATALITY
happened on 11 February 1899, when George Morgan, a 37-year-old clerk employed by St Thomas's District Council, Exeter, fell from his newly acquired motor tricycle and sustained a severe haemorrhage. He died 12 days later.

The first
MOTOR HEARSE
was an electric vehicle used for a funeral in Buffalo, N.Y. in May 1900. Fourteen other electric cars made up the funeral procession.
GB: The first motor hearse made its appearance in Coventry on 15 April 1901. The *Motor-Car Journal* reported:

The funeral was that of William Drakeford, who had been in the employ of the Daimler Motor Co Ltd, at the Motor Mills as caretaker, and previous to that firm occupying the premises he had been engaged by the old Cotton Company for a long period, his terms of service in connection with the mills extending over forty years. The motor-vehicles used for the funeral comprised three cars, that upon which the coffin was carried being a specially arranged 6hp Daimler carriage. It was painted black, and the body of the car was draped with black cloth on either side, which gave it a very sombre appearance.

The first purpose-built motor hearse was a 24hp De Dion which made its appearance in Paris towards the end of 1905. No others are recorded until the spring of 1907, when an electric hearse was introduced in Berlin. Its owner declared with satisfaction that he was now able to perform burials 'in one-third the usual time'.
GB: Produced by Messrs Pergetter of City Mews, Coventry in 1909, the vehicle had a specially designed body mounted on a Lotis chassis and was driven by a four-cylinder White & Poppe engine. A special gear arrangement allowed it to be driven at the pace of the bearers walking on either side.

The first
MOTORING ASSOCIATION
was the American Motor League, founded on 1 November 1895 at Chicago, Ill. as a result of a letter addressed to the *Chicago Times-Herald* by Charles Brady King the previous month. Chicago had recently become the automobile centre of the USA by virtue of the fact that the *Times-Herald* was organizing a major racing event scheduled for the end of November, and this had attracted pioneer motorists from all over the country. Sixty members attended the inaugural meeting, which was followed by a second on 29 November for the election of officers and the adoption of a constitution. According to the latter:

The purpose of this association shall be the advancement of the interests and the use of motor vehicles. This shall be done by reports and discussions of the mechanical features, by education and agitation, by directing and correcting legislation, by mutual defense of rights of said vehicles when threatened by adverse judicial decisions, by assisting in the work of constructing better roads, better sanitary and humane conditions, and in any other proper way which will assist to hasten the use and add to the value of motor vehicles as a means of transit.

Eleven days after the inception of the American body, and prior to its being constituted as a regular society with elected officers, the first motoring association in Europe was established. This was the Automobile Club de France, which came into being on 12 November 1895 with premises at 4 place de l'Opéra, Paris.
GB: The Self Propelled Traffic Association, founded at the instigation of Sir David Salomans (*see also* Motor Show) at a meeting held at the Cannon Street Hotel in London, on 10 December 1895. The principal aim of the Association was to seek repeal of the notorious Locomotives on Highways Act, which restricted motor cars to a maximum speed of 4mph in the country and 2mph in towns. After intensive lobbying, this was achieved in November 1896, and from then on the Self Propelled Traffic Association ceased to play an important part in motoring affairs. It amalgamated with the Automobile Club of Great Britain in July 1898.

The oldest of the existing motoring associations is the Royal Automobile Club (RAC), which was founded as the Automobile Club of Great Britain on 10 August 1897. The Automobile Association (AA) was established on 26 June 1905.

The first
MOTORING FATALITY
occurred on 17 August 1896 at the Crystal Palace, London, when Mrs Bridget Driscoll of Old Town, Croydon was run over and her skull fractured by a wheel of the car. The driver was Arthur Edsell, who was employed by the Anglo-French Motor Co to give joy-rides in a Roger-Benz on the terrace of the Crystal Palace. Edsell's vision was obstructed by two other cars in front and Mrs Driscoll, in a state of panic, stood still in the path of the approaching vehicle. At the inquest it was stated that Edsell was driving at 4mph at the time of the accident. The verdict was Accidental Death.
MOTORING FATALITY ON THE PUBLIC HIGHWAY: the first took place in Stockmar Road, Hackney on 23 September 1897, when nine-year-old Stephen Kempton of 106 Chalgrove Road, Hackney was crushed to death by a taxi belonging to the Electric Cab Co. The boy was stealing a ride on one of the springs of the cab when his coat became entangled in the chain-drive, dragging him between a rear wheel and the body of the vehicle.
CAR-DRIVER KILLED IN A MOTORING ACCIDENT: the first was Henry Lindfield of Brighton, who sustained fatal injuries in a crash that occurred on 12 February 1898 while he was journeying from London to Brighton in his Imperial electric carriage accompanied by his 18-year-old son Bernard. Lindfield was the Brighton agent for International Cars. At the inquest his son testified that:

after reaching Purley Corner they were descending the hill with the motor cut out and the brakes on. Half-way down the incline the witness's bag fell out of the carriage, and his father endeavoured to stop the machine, which then began to run from one side of the road to the other, the steering gear failing, and the car eventually turned completely round, running through a wire fence and striking an iron post. This turned the car partly over against a tree, catching the deceased's leg between the carriage and the tree. The witness was thrown clear over his father, who was unable to move until help was got to push the car back. The deceased had only driven the car two or three times.

Lindfield was taken to hospital, where his leg was amputated, but he died from the effects of shock the following day. Despite Bernard Lindfield's evidence that the motor was cut out at the time of the accident, it appeared from a subsequent examination of the gears that his father had the car regulated at full speed.

In February 1969 the Mayor of Harrow unveiled a plaque on Grove Hill, Harrow which bears the words: 'Take Heed. The first recorded motor accident in Great Britain involving the death of the driver occurred on Grove Hill on 25th February 1899.' The accident in question involved an eight-seater Daimler wagonette driven by E.R. Sewell of the Daimler Motor Car Co, who was demonstrating its capabilities to a prospective purchaser. Although this unhappy episode has generally been accepted by motoring historians as the first occasion of a driver fatality, it would seem clear from the surviving records of the Lindfield inquest that this is not so, though it may be claimed as the first motor accident involving the death of the driver of a petrol-driven car. The crash was also the first to cause the death of a passenger, 63-year-old Maj. James Richer, a Department Head at the Army & Navy Auxiliary Stores (the intending purchasers of the vehicle), sustaining a fractured skull from which he died four days later without regaining consciousness.

The first
MOTORING JOURNAL
was *La Locomotion Automobile*, a monthly founded by Raoul Vuillemont and first published at 2 place du Caire, Paris on 1 December 1894.
GB: The *Autocar*, edited by Henry Sturmey, was published weekly, price 3d, by Iliffe & Son of Coventry commencing Saturday, 2 November 1895. In his opening leader the Editor assured the equine interest that there was little prospect of cars ever driving horses from the roads, adding benignly that the only likely effect would be that in future 'he will exist under improved conditions'. There were at this time probably less than a dozen cars on the roads of England and predictions tended to be optimistic rather than coolly rational. 'In the present congested state of many of the streets in large towns', wrote Sturmey blandly, 'it will be of incalculable benefit when horseless carriages become common.'

In the age before motor cars became general, the motoring Press was remarkable chiefly for its proliferation. No less than 11 titles had been registered before the end of the century and a total of 74 by 1914. Two of these were attempts to produce daily newspapers for motorists – *Daily Motoring Illustrated*, which survived for eight issues in November 1905; and the *Daily Auto* of 1908, which failed after the first issue. A similar fate attended a paper started the same year in the interest of the majority who did not own cars, and which bore the striking title *The Non-Motorist*. Of the general motoring journals founded during this period only two survive today – *Autocar* (1895) and *Motor* (1903).

The first
MOTORING OFFENCE
in GB resulting in a summons was committed on 17 October 1895 by John Henry Knight of Barfield, Farnham, who was charged with permitting a 'locomotive' to be 'at work' in Castle Street, Farnham without a licence, and James Pullinger, charged with 'working the same during prohibited hours'. The case was heard before R.H. Combe at Farnham Petty Sessions on 31 October, the prosecution submitting that the summons had been brought under a Surrey County Council by-law. This required that all locomotives other than those used in road maintenance or agriculture should be licensed by the Council, and that locomotives might be driven on the public highway only during prescribed hours. The locomotive in question was in fact a three-wheeled, tiller-steered, petrol-driven motor vehicle designed and owned by Knight, who at the time of the offence was watching from the pavement while Pullinger drove. Both defendants were found guilty and fined 2s 6d each and costs.
MOTORIST TO BE CONVICTED OF DRUNKEN DRIVING: the first was London taxi-driver George Smith, 25, of 192 Portnall Road, who was charged at Marlborough Street Police Court on 10 September 1897 with being drunk-in-charge of an electric cab in Bond Street, at 12.45 the same morning. According to the evidence of PC Russell 247C, the defendant had driven his cab on to the pavement and into the front corridor of 165 Bond Street. 'The prisoner', it was reported, 'admitted having had two or three glasses of beer.' He was found guilty and fined 20s.

Drunken driving had been made an offence under the Licensing Act 1872, which imposed penalties for being 'drunk in charge on any highway or other public place of any carriage, horse, cattle or steam engine'. Although the term 'carriage' was interpreted by the courts as covering motor carriages, it was not until 1925 that Section 40 of the Criminal Justice Act extended the provisions to cover 'any mechanically powered vehicle'.
MOTORIST CONVICTED OF SPEEDING: the first was Walter Arnold, miller, of East Peckham, Kent, who was charged before C.W. Powell at Tonbridge Police Court on 28 January 1896 with exceeding the speed limit of 2mph in a built-up area while driving through Paddock Wood eight days previously. It transpired that Arnold had happened to pass the local police constable's house just as that worthy was having his dinner. The constable left his food, grabbed his helmet, and gave chase on a bicycle. After a five-mile sprint he caught up with the motor car and booked Arnold for speeding. According to the principal prosecution witness 'the carriage was proceeding at about eight miles an hour'. The defendant, who was fined 1s and costs, later became the first man in Britain to manufacture petrol-engined motor cars (*See* Motor Car: Manufacture).

The first
MOTOR INSURANCE
was introduced in Britain by the General Accident Co on 2 November 1896. According to Sir Francis Norie-Miller, a few motor policies were issued 'almost simultaneously' with the minute of that date approving 'the Manager's recommendation to issue a prospectus to insure motor cars'. These were effected under special terms arranged between the Company and the insured.

The first general quotation for motor insurance was made by the Scottish Employers' Insurance Co about a week later, offering coverage at 30s per car (£2 in London) plus 30s per cent (£2 in London) on the sum assured. Damage caused by frightened horses was specifically excluded.

The first country to introduce compulsory third party insurance was Norway in 1912.
GB: Introduced 1 January 1931 under the Road Traffic Act 1930.

The first
MOTOR LORRY
the first practical self-propelled goods wagon capable of carrying (as opposed to drawing) freight was built by John Yule in 1870 for transporting large marine boilers from his works at Rutherglen Loan, Glasgow to the Glasgow Docks, a distance of two miles. The vehicle was powered by a 250rpm twin-cylinder steam-engine mounted on a 26ft chassis of red pine, and fully loaded was capable of moving at ¾mph.

Even at this slow speed Yule considered his six-wheeled steam-wagon an economic proposition. The cost of employing 400 men to drag a 40-ton marine boiler to the docks worked out at about £60; a single journey by the wagon incurred a fuel bill of £10 – a carriage rate of 2s 6d per ton mile.
PETROL LORRY: the first was a chain-driven Panhard et Levassor Chariot à plateforme, which was built

1896 Daimler – the first motor lorry in regular commercial production

at the Panhard works at 19 avenue d'Ivory, Paris, from a design dated 13 October 1894. The over-all length of the vehicle was 2·98m and it had an open platform at the rear 1·5m long. The Panhard lorry was driven for the first time by M. Mayade, the Chief Engineer of the firm, on 10 February 1895.

The first commercially manufactured petrol lorry was produced by the Daimler Co of Cannstatt in 1896. Development had begun as early as 1891, but it is not clear whether a prototype had been built in the intervening period. A catalogue of September 1896 offered the Daimler-Güterwagen in four models – 4hp designed to carry a 1,500-kilo load; 6hp with 2,500-kilo capacity; 8hp with 3,750-kilo capacity; 10hp with 5,000-kilo capacity. The vehicles were powered by twin-cylinder Phoenix engines mounted at the rear and were capable of speeds of up to 12kph. The catalogue offered as an optional extra a heating arrangement, consisting of hot water circulating in tubes, that could be mounted on the driver's box. This may have afforded some comfort in cold weather as the driver's box was unenclosed.

The first Daimler petrol lorry to be sold was acquired by the Speditionsfirma Paul von Maur of Stuttgart in the spring of 1897. The second, the first mechanized brewer's dray, went to the Böhmisches Brauhaus in Berlin.

GB: The first petrol-driven motor lorry was built for the Western Australian Freight & Express Co Ltd by Messrs T. Coulthard & Co of Preston and completed in January 1897. It was powered by a 16hp four-cylinder vertical Pennington engine mounted on a platform next to the driver and was capable of 12mph. The vehicle was a combined omnibus and freight-carrier, with a seating capacity of 10 and a platform to take a load of 1 ton. It was intended that it should run between Fremantle, Western Australia and the mines at Kalgoorlie, but though photographs exist of the lorry on test in England, there is no record of it ever having arrived in Australia.

The first motor lorries manufactured for use on English roads were two corporation dust-carts built for the Chiswick Vestry by Thornycroft & Co in the spring of 1897. These were powered by compound steam-engines with opposed cylinders, vertical launch-type water-tube boilers and chain-drive with a differential gear. They were of steel construction, 15ft long by $6\frac{1}{2}$ft broad and could carry up to 4 tons of refuse at a time. The first man employed to drive them was the former driver of the Chiswick Vestry's steam-roller.

The first petrol-engined lorry in use in Britain was built by the Anglo-French Motor Carriage Co of Birmingham to the special order of a Scottish firm for carrying bales of jute and was exhibited at Manchester in July 1897 prior to delivery. As the Anglo-French Co were principally importers of Roger-Benz cars and did not manufacture on their own account, it seems likely that the engine was brought from Paris.

The first petrol-driven motor lorry in regular series production in Britain was the Milnes-Daimler, a 10hp vehicle with a two-cylinder engine built by Messrs G. F. Milnes, and publicly demonstrated for the first time at the Liverpool Trials of June 1901. It was 17ft long with an 11ft wheel-base and designed to carry a load of $1\frac{1}{2}$–2 tons at an average speed of 6mph. The first purchaser was H. Seal of Albany Nurseries at Enfield, who was using his Milnes-Daimler to carry $2\frac{1}{2}$ tons of tomatoes into London twice daily by early July 1901.

ARTICULATED LORRY: the first was built in 1898 by Thornycroft. The vehicle was a 4-ton steam-wagon with a four-wheeled tractor unit and a two-wheeled trailer attachment fitting on to a turntable behind the cab. It was entered for the Liverpool Trials of Motor Vehicles for Heavy Traffic, organized by the Self Propelled Traffic Association 24–27 May 1898, and won the premier award.

DIESEL-ENGINED LORRY: the first was a 5-ton vehicle with a 50hp pre-combustion chamber engine, produced by Benz at Stuttgart in August 1923.

GB: Six different designs of diesel truck, ranging from $1\frac{1}{2}$ to 5 tons, were produced by the Caledon Motor Co of Glasgow early in 1927. The firm appears to have overreached itself and went into liquidation a few months later, the diesel-wagon plant being acquired by Garrett's of Leiston, Suffolk, an old-established agricultural engineers. Garrett's then proceeded to build two more lorries to Caledon designs, 4 and 5 tons in weight, both with Dorman engines in Thompson frames. In September 1927 the smaller of these two vehicles became the first diesel lorry in regular operation when it was purchased by Scottish Commercial Cars Ltd. The first production models, Garrett four- and six-wheelers fitted with McLaren engines, were marketed the following year.

See also Motor Van; Road Haulage.

The first
MOTOR MAIL VAN

was a Daimler Motor Van supplied to the Post Office for trials by the British Motor Syndicate Ltd. A service began operating between St Martin's-le-Grand and the South Western District Post Office, Howick Place, a distance of $2\frac{3}{4}$ miles, during the week ending 23 October 1897. A load of up to 900lb of letter mail was carried and the journey performed in both directions five times a day. A time of 23min was allowed for the distance, the same as for horse-drawn vans, but according to a contemporary report the motor van 'not only kept better time than they usually do, but as a rule reached its destination at each end before it was due'. The motor van was also used for carrying parcels between Howick Place and Kingston-upon-Thames the following week, making the 30-mile return journey in 5hr, including six stops for deliveries and a $\frac{1}{2}$hr break at Kingston.

The first regular service commenced on 17 June 1898, when a Daimler wagonette supplied by the West of Scotland Motor Co began running between Inverary and Ardrishaig, Argyllshire, a distance of $26\frac{1}{2}$ miles which it performed in about 3hr at an average speed of $8\frac{1}{2}$mph. The service continued until bad roads and mechanical failures during the winter led to a reversion to horse-working.

The first
MOTOR MUSEUM
was founded by Edmund Dangerfield, proprietor of the magazine *Motor*, and opened at the Waring Galleries, 175 Oxford Street, London on 31 May 1912. The idea was not a new one. As early as January 1902 the *Motor-Car Journal* had remarked: 'It would be rather interesting to start an inquiry as to where the oldest car in England is, of the petrol type. One day we may come to regard it as a precious relic.' A few years later the Automobile Club convened a meeting to discuss a proposal that a motor museum should be established, but as nobody attended, the matter was dropped. The first car to be purchased for its historic value alone was an 1894 Panhard, bought for £100 by public subscription in 1910 and presented to the Science Museum in South Kensington. The following year Edmund Dangerfield was fired with the idea of forming a national collection of historic motor vehicles, and approached the South Kensington Museum with the suggestion that it should be housed there. The reply he received stated that the Museum had accommodation for no more than three vehicles. Realizing that he was unlikely to obtain any official backing for the project, the proprietor of *Motor* determined to act independently.

The Motor Museum opened with 40 exhibits, including an 1861 Crompton steam car, the 1894 Bremer (*see* Motor Car: GB), J.H. Knight's three-wheeler of 1895, the first Wolseley of 1895, an 1897 Arnold-Benz (*see* Motor Car: Manufacture) and the 1895 Holden motor cycle. One exhibit that attracted particular interest was a black and yellow Bersey electric cab (*see* Taxi) in which the Prince of Wales, later Edward VII, had ridden from Marlborough House to Buckingham Palace in November 1897. The Museum was obliged to move after only two months in its Oxford Street premises, but by March 1914 it had reopened at the Crystal Palace. With the outbreak of war the space was needed for storage purposes and the collection was dispersed. Some of the vehicles were returned to their donors, while others, no less valuable, were dumped on a piece of waste ground near Charing Cross Station without any cover and left to disintegrate.

The first
MOTOR RACE
was organized by M. Fossier, Editor of the French cycling magazine *La Vélocipède*, and held on 20 April 1887 over a course from Saint-James in Paris, along the Seine to the bridge at Neuilly. The race resulted in a walk-over for Georges Bouton, the only competitor, who completed the course in his four-seater steam quadricycle. The first race in which there was more than one competitor was organized by *La Vélocipède* the following year, when Bouton drove a three-wheeled De Dion to victory over his only rival – driving a Serpollet steamer – in a time of 30min for the 20km course between Neuilly and Versailles.

The first motor race which included petrol-driven cars and the first long-distance race was arranged by the Automobile Club de France and the French newspaper *Le Petit Journal* over a course from Paris to Bordeaux and return on 11–14 June 1895. Although Emile Levassor was the first to complete the 732-mile run – in a time of 48¾hr and at an average speed of 15·25mph – he was disqualified because his 3½hp Phoenix-engined Panhard et Levassor car was a two-seater, proscribed under the rules of the race. His nearest rival, Koechlin, driving a much slower Peugeot, was declared the winner. Of the 23 starters, 8 petrol vehicles and a steamer arrived back in Paris.

TRACK RACING EVENT: the first was held over a five-lap course of a dirt-track, 1 mile in circumference, at Narragansett Park, Cranston, R.I. on 7 September 1896, as one of the attractions of the Rhode Island State Fair. The winner was A.H. Whiting, who drove an electric Riker to victory over seven other competitors (six of them driving petrol cars) in a time of 15min 1·75sec, and at an average speed of 24mph.

GB: The famous Emancipation Run from London to Brighton on 14 November 1896 (to celebrate repeal of the so-called 'Red Flag Act'), was described by its sponsors, the Motor-Car Club, as a 'tour', and entrants were asked to wait for each other at various stages of the route so that they could all enter Brighton in procession. It is apparent from contemporary accounts, however, that the 33 competitors themselves regarded the event as a race, and this impression is reinforced by the fact that the Motor-Car Club issued an official list of arrivals with their times, of which the first three were:

1. Léon Bollée driving a Bollée tricycle
   Time: 3hr 44min 35sec
2. Camille Bollée driving a Bollée tricycle
   Time: 4hr 0min 20sec
3. Earl of Winchilsea driving a Panhard Wagonette
   Time: 5hr 1min 10sec

The first track event in Britain and the first motor race since the Emancipation Day Run (apart from informal events at fêtes) was a mile handicap held at the Crystal Palace cycle track under the auspices of the English Motor Club on Monday, 8 April 1901. The competitors were Charles Jarrott in an 8hp Panhard; H.J. Lawson Jr in a 5hp Panhard; and F.F. Wellington in a Mors dog-cart. The winner was Jarrott in a time of 2min 16sec.

WOMAN MOTOR-RACING DRIVER: the first on record was Mme Labrousse of Paris, who competed in the Paris–Spa Race of 1–2 July 1899 and was classed 5th in the first division for cars carrying at least three persons.

GB: The first woman to win a motor-race in Britain was a Miss Wemblyn, who drove her 6hp Parisian Daimler to victory over three other entrants in a special Ladies' Race held at Ranelagh on 14 July 1900.

INTERNATIONAL CHAMPIONSHIP MOTOR RACE: the first was the Gordon Bennett Cup, first competed for by representatives of France, Belgium, the USA and Germany over a course from Paris to Lyons on 14 June 1900. There were five entries, of which two finished. All ran over dogs. The winner was M.F. Charron of France, driving a Panhard at an average speed of 38·5mph.

GRAND PRIX: the first was organized by the Automobile Club de France and held over 12 laps of a 65-mile triangular circuit at Le Mans on 26–27 June 1906. The 770-mile race, consisting of six laps of the circuit on each of the two days, was won by the Hungarian professional racing-driver Ferenc Szisz driving a 90hp 13-litre Renault at an average speed of 63mph.

GB: The first British Grand Prix was held at Brooklands over 110 laps (287 miles) on 7 August 1926 and won by Robert Sénéchal and Louis Wagner, driving a Delage in 4hr 56sec at an average speed of 71·61mph. The fastest lap was achieved by (Sir) Henry Segrave in a Talbot at 85·99mph. The event was held again in 1927 but then discontinued. The present series of GP races was inaugurated with the first British GP to be held at Silverstone, 28 September 1948.

24-HOUR RACE: the first was the Endurance Derby held at Point Breeze, Philadelphia, on 25 May 1907 and won by Messrs Brown and Moyes in an Autocar, which covered 791 miles at an average speed of 33mph.

The first
MOTOR SCOOTER
was the Auto-Ped, produced by the Auto-Ped Co of New York in 1915. In appearance it resembled a child's scooter as there was no seat, the rider standing on a low platform to drive the

machine. It was powered by a 2hp engine and had a top speed of 35mph.
GB: The Kingsbury was produced by the Kingsbury Aviation Co in 1919, in association with the Storey Machine Tool Co at the Storey works in Pomeroy Street, Peckham. Powered by a 216cc two-stroke engine, the Kingsbury had an attractive finish in black, dark grey and gold line. Like the Auto-Ped, they were mainly of the stand-up-to-ride variety, though a limited number were made with a bicycle saddle on a tall shaft. A large range of different makes of scooter became available during the course of 1919, not only in Britain but also in Germany, where a model was brought out by Krupp, and in France, where the Monet-Goyon enjoyed a brief success.

After disappearing almost completely after 1924, the motor scooter was revived in Italy at the end of the war by Dr Enrico Piaggio, who saw it as a means of restarting production following the destruction of his aircraft works at Pontedera by enemy bombing. A prototype designed by his Chief Engineer, Corradino d'Ascanio, was ready for trials by August 1945, and it was decided to call it the 'Wasp', which in Italian is *Vespa*. Full-scale manufacture by Piaggio & Co began in April 1946; the response was so immediate that Vespas began to be manufactured under licence in Germany in 1950, and in France the following year. In Britain they were introduced by Claude McCormack of the Douglas Co, who began production under licence at Bristol in 1951. A total of 1 million Vespas had taken to the roads in Europe by 1955.

The first
MOTOR SHOW
was the Éxposition Internationale de Vélocipédie et de Locomotion Automobile (2nd Salon Cycle), held at the Palais de l'Industrie in the Champs-Elysées, Paris from 11 to 25 December 1894. There were nine exhibitors. The Compagnie de Voitures sans Chevaux showed a two-seater motor tricycle and a four-seater *vis-à-vis* car with a Klaus engine; the Decauville Co a Filtz steam car; De Dion-Bouton a steam-tractor and two steam cars; Duncan, Superbie et Cie a Hildebrand-Wolfmüller motor bicycle; Blant et David two Serpollet steam cars; Panhard et Levassor a number of Daimler-engined vehicles; Peugeot a number of Daimler-engined vehicles; Emile Roger a Roger-Benz car; Tenting a four-seater car with an engine of their own design.
GB: The first motor show was organized by Sir David Salomans and held at the Agricultural Show Ground, Tunbridge Wells on 15 October 1895. Advertised as a 'Horseless Carriage Exhibition', the show comprised five exhibits, listed in the official catalogue: a Panhard et Levassor vehicle with Daimler engine; a Daimler fire-engine lent by the Hon. Evelyn Ellis; a De Dion-Bouton tricycle: a steam-horse attached to a carriage, De Dion Bouton; Gladiator tricycle (this was not shown on the day); a Peugeot *vis-à-vis* with Daimler engine.

The first trade show was the International Horseless Carriage Exhibition, organized by the Motor-Car Club (principally a trade federation) and held at the Imperial Institute in London on 9 May 1896. The 10 exhibitors included Daimler, Humber and the Arnold Motor Carriage Co. Most were showing imported cars, the only British-made vehicles being electric carriages manufactured by the Offord Co and the Bersey Co, and Humber motor cycles.

Since 1903 the Motor Show has been held under the auspices of the Society of Motor Manufacturers and Traders, originally at the Crystal Palace, but from 1905 to 1936 at Olympia. It has been staged at Earls Court since 1937.

The first
MOTOR TOUR
of any distance in a petrol-driven car was made in August 1888 by the wife of the inventor Karl Benz, with her two sons, Eugen, aged 15, and Richard, aged 13, from their home at Mannheim to Pforzheim, a distance of 180km. Although the two boys had been taught to drive, neither was allowed to take the tiller of any of their father's cars except under his supervision or that of the shop foreman. Their mother having occasion to visit relatives in Pforzheim, Eugen suggested this would be an ideal opportunity to make an extended motor journey on their own. Frau Benz entered into the conspiracy with a readiness not usually associated with Victorian matrons, and the three set off from Mannheim early one morning in the 2hp three-wheeler car. Karl Benz was unaware of their intentions, though a note was left for him, explaining that they would be coming back and had not deserted him.

Eugen drove, with Frau Benz occupying the seat next to him, and Richard perched on the rear over the engine. The first stop was made at Heidelberg, where they ate a meal, and the motorists then continued to Wiesloch. From there the road became steeper, and Frau Benz and Eugen were obliged to dismount and push the vehicle up the hills, while Richard took the tiller. Progress downhill afforded unforeseen hazards owing to the inadequacy of the leather brake-linings, which soon wore away with pressure. Periodic stops had to be made at cobblers' on the way, to obtain more leather for the brake-blocks.

Further trouble was experienced when the driving-chains became loose. A little later the fuel pipe to the carburettor was found to be blocked, but this was remedied with one of Frau Benz's hatpins. When an ignition wire short-circuited after rubbing against another part of the engine, Frau Benz once more rose to the occasion by taking off her garter and using it to insulate the wire.

Throughout the journey the Benz family were the object of incredulous amazement, and this nearly provoked a fight at an inn in the Black Forest, when two peasants began a violent dispute about whether the car was driven by clockwork or by a supernatural agency. They arrived safely at Pforzheim, and after a five-day stay, the two boys and their mother motored back to Mannheim.

The lovely Bertha Benz, who took her husband's car without his knowledge to make the first motor tour

A practical outcome of the trip was that Benz accepted his sons' judgement that the vehicle was underpowered for hill-climbing and added an additional gear.
GB: The first motor journey of any length was made by the Hon. Evelyn Ellis and Frederick Simms. They left Micheldever, Hampshire at 9.26am on 12 July 1895 in Ellis's French-built Panhard car, and arrived at his home in Datchet, Buckinghamshire at 5.40pm. The 56-mile journey was made by way of Basingstoke, Blackwater, Bagshot and Virginia Water, in a total driving time of 5hr 32min, and at an average

speed of 9·84mph, in contravention of the 4mph speed limit then in force.

Simms remarked that during their whole drive they were the objects of most intense curiosity, 'whole villages turning out to behold, open-mouthed, the new marvel of locomotion'. At this time, there were only three or four other petrol-driven cars in the whole of England. 'The departure of coaches', Simms wrote in a letter to the *Saturday Review*, 'was delayed to enable their passengers to have a look at our horseless vehicle. . . .'

Both these motoring pioneers won considerable celebrity in the early automobile movement. The Hon. Evelyn Ellis became the first Englishman to take an official driving test (*q.v.*) the following year, while F.R. Simms was one of the principal founders of the Royal Automobile Club in 1897. His work with the Daimler Co of Coventry from its creation in 1896 was later to earn him the title of 'Father of the British Motor Industry'.

The first
MOTOR VAN
was a steam-driven delivery van with a Serpollet engine, built by M. Le Blanc of 19 rue Lord Byron, Paris, in 1892 for the celebrated Paris department store La Belle Jardinière. The bodywork by Châtelet David was finished in the store's livery and bore the inscription 'Livraison à Domicile' (Deliveries to the Home). The van remained in service for about three years.

The first motor company to undertake the manufacture of petrol-driven motor vans was the French firm of Peugeot Frères, which completed its first production model in December 1895. Powered by a 4hp Daimler motor, the van was claimed to be able to carry about 1,000lb load at 9½mph, and about 650lb load at 12mph. The Grands Magasins du Louvre put in an order for 18 Peugeot vans for carrying parcels, the first of which was delivered on Christmas Day.

GB: There is some doubt as to which was the first firm in Britain to use a motor van for deliveries. In the November 1896 issue of the *Automotor and Horseless Carriage Journal* it was reported that a motor van was already in use by Messrs Thornton, Varley & Co, drapers of Hull, but the make is not specified. The same paper also carried a news item saying that two Lutzman Patent Motor-Vans had been imported from Paris the previous month by Messrs Julius Harvey, one for their own use and the other for Lever Bros, the soap-manufacturers. Shortly afterwards Lever Bros acquired another van through Arnolds of East Peckham, who were agents for Benz vehicles in England. This vehicle, which was decked out in Sunlight Soap livery, took part in the historic Emancipation Run from London to Brighton on 14 November 1896. It was by no means the only commercial vehicle to participate in the celebration of the right to motor on the public highway, for there were also two Daimler petrol vans, one belonging to Peter Robinson and the other to Harrod's, and a Panhard with bodywork by Offord that acted as a breakdown van to assist other vehicles in distress. The Peter Robinson van actually carried parcels for delivery in Brighton, and must have been the first goods vehicle in Britain to have made a run of this distance carrying a pay-load.

The first motor van manufactured in Britain was a chain-driven 1½-ton steam van with a Strickland vertical twin-tandem compound engine, built by Thornycroft at Hogarth Lane, Chiswick, in 1896, and sold to the South Wales Motor Car & Cycle Co of Cardiff. It was delivered on 2 January 1897, having completed the 150-mile journey under its own steam in just 25hr.

The first petrol-driven motor van manufactured in Britain was a Daimler parcels van built at Coventry in December 1896 and exhibited at the Birmingham Show the following month. On 2 February 1897 it carried a payload for the first time, making the 70-mile round trip between Coventry and Birmingham on 3s worth of petrol.

The first customer to take delivery of a Coventry-built Daimler parcels van was Sutton & Co of Manchester on 6 June 1897.

MOTOR VAN WITH A TOTALLY ENCLOSED CAB offering all-weather protection to the driver was first manufactured by the Star Engineering Co of Wolverhampton in 1902. Available in 7, 10 and 15mph models, it was designed to be convertible into a private car when not in use for the carriage of goods. The side-panels of the van were fitted with wide-view windows measuring about 30 × 15in.

This is believed to have been the first production model of any full-sized motor vehicle to be totally enclosed; previous attempts at weather protection (*see* Motor Car with a Fully Enclosed Body) were confined to landaulettes and detachable bodies of the brougham kind as an optional extra.

The Peter Robinson van – first in Britain to carry merchandise, November 1896

The first
MOTOR VEHICLE REGISTRATION PLATES
were introduced in the Department of the Seine under the Paris Police Ordinance of 14 August 1893, which stated: 'Each motor vehicle shall bear on a metal plate and in legible writing the name and address of its owner, also the distinctive number used in the application for authorisation. This plate shall be placed at the left-hand side of the vehicle – it shall never be hidden.'

The requirement for motor vehicles to carry number plates was extended to the rest of France under a Decree of 30 September 1901 and applied to any vehicle capable of exceeding 30kph. By this date registration plates were already mandatory in Belgium. The *Motor-Car Journal* reported from Brussels in May 1901:

Every car is numbered and registered by the police and carries an enamelled iron plate, generally on the front axle. The plate measures about 9 ins by 5 ins with the number in black letters on a white ground. At the back of the car there is a lamp with the number painted on the glass in such a manner that when the lamp is lighted the number can be seen. The numbers are very disfiguring, and give one the impression that the cars are not private carriages, but are for hire.

The owner of a Daimler interviewed by the *Motor-Car Journal*'s Belgian Correspondent said that the system 'gave rise to all kinds of petty interference with the rights of the subject'. The Correspondent was of the opinion that any such step in England would have 'a disastrous effect on the development of the industry'.

He was not alone. In 1899 Britain's leading motoring journal, the *Autocar*, had come out firmly against proposals to introduce a scheme similar to the French one. An article in October stated: 'The fact that an autocar had to carry a numbered plaque like a common cab prowling for hire would be quite enough to prevent many people from using such vehicles. . . .' The County Councils and other local authorities, supported by the equine interest and others who had no love for motor cars, insisted that Parliament should legislate to make number plates mandatory. The motorists fought back, some even declaring that they would abandon their cars altogether if plates were introduced. The Commons, however, despite a fair number of motoring members, was determined that cars should be brought under stricter control, and the Motor Car Act 1903 provided not only for the licensing of drivers but also for the registration of vehicles. The Act became effective on 1 January 1904.

The first registration number was A1, secured by Earl Russell (the elder brother of Bertrand Russell) for his Napier just before Christmas 1903. The Earl sat up all night to ensure he would be first in the queue, but still only beat his nearest rival by five seconds. In 1907 the plate was purchased by George V. Pettyt of the Maudes Motor Mart in Halifax. On one occasion Pettyt was stopped in Yorkshire by a policeman who doubted the existence of such a number; he was detained until confirmation could be secured from the licensing authority in London. On his death in 1950 he bequeathed the plate to Trevor Laker, a Director of the John Bull Rubber Co, with the proviso that he should have the use of it during his lifetime and it should then be sold, and the proceeds donated to the Guide Dogs for the Blind Association. Mr Laker arranged a more immediate benefit for the Association by selling the inheritance of the plate for £2,500, which he donated to them in August 1959. The only plate to fetch a higher sum of money was RR1, which was purchased by Rolls-Royce for £4,600 in the 1960s.

Although Britain was preceded in the introduction of number plates by France (1893), Bavaria (1899), Belgium (*c.* 1900), Spain (Mallorca) (1900), New York State (1901), Berlin (1901), Newfoundland (1901), Switzerland (1902), Ontario (1903), Denmark (1903), Italy (1903) and New Zealand (*c.* 1903), the numbering sequence still employed by the British licensing authorities is believed to be the longest running in the world.

The world's earliest-known surviving number plate, notable also as the first in Germany, was issued by the Munich Police Department to a Herr Beissbarth in respect of his Wartburg car on 14 April 1899. The rectangular metal plate bears the single figure '1'. It is now in the possession of Herr Beissbarth's son.

INTERNATIONAL IDENTIFICATION CODES (i.e. GB plates, etc.) were introduced under an agreement made at the International Convention on the Regulation of Traffic in 1926.

The first
MOTORWAY
designed for the exclusive use of motor traffic and with controlled access was the Avus Autobahn in Berlin. The dual-carriageway urban motorway, 6¼ miles long, ran from the Grunewald to the suburb of Wannsee, and was opened to traffic on 10 September 1921. It had been originally planned in 1909 and was nearly complete when the outbreak of World War I halted building operations. The instigator of the project was Karl Friedrich Fritsch, a motor-racing enthusiast, who proposed that the motorway should double as a race-track and proving-ground. For this reason it was designed with a loop at either end, so that in its sporting capacity the road would provide the means of racing back and forth without stopping. At the end of the war the scheme was taken over by the industrialist Hugo Stinnes. On completion it had two carriageways 26ft wide with a tarred surface, and a central reservation 26ft wide, planted with grass. Ten ferro-concrete flyovers spanned the motorway at irregular intervals. The Avus Autobahn is still in use as a public highway and as a manufacturers' test-track, although motor-racing has now been abandoned on amenity grounds.

INTER-URBAN MOTORWAY: the first was the Milano–Varese Autostrada, started by the Motor Roads from Milan to the Lombardy Lakes Co on 26 March 1923, and formally opened by the King of Italy on 21 September 1924. This initial 30-mile section was part of a larger network linking the Lombardy Lakes, completed a few months later. The total cost of the three sections was 76 million lire, and the scheme involved the construction of 33 viaducts, 56 tunnels and 60 miles of link roads. The 54-mile network was single carriageway throughout, mainly 36ft wide and surfaced in concrete.

The Italian autostrade of the inter-war period were based on a plan originally put forward by the Milanese financier and engineer Signor P. Puricelli and backed officially by Mussolini. The companies that built them derived their revenue from tolls and roadside poster hoardings. Despite the fact that they were constructed without central reservations, and sometimes with only three lanes, the autostrade were motorways in a modern sense, as they were designed for high-speed traffic and had controlled access and grade-separated interchanges. Their use was confined to motor vehicles with three or more wheels, which excluded motor cycles. By 1932, the year that Germany opened her first inter-urban motorway (the Bonn–Köln Autobahn), Italy already had 330 miles of autostrade open to traffic in eight sections, of which the longest was the 80-mile Milano–Torino Autostrada.

Although the building of the Autobahns was not, as is sometimes suggested, actually instigated by Hitler, it was under his direction that the programme was given such major priority. The first thousand miles of motorway in Germany had been completed by early 1938, and when World War II broke out there was a total of 2,300 miles. All were dual carriageway throughout, with hard shoulders on either side for emergency parking, and were designed to accommodate vehicles travelling at speeds of up to 100mph.

Other than Germany and Italy, the only other countries with completed motorways open prior to World War II were the USA (starting with the 15½-mile Bronx River Parkway in 1925), Canada (the 60-mile Queen Elizabeth Way, Toronto–Hamilton, 1939), and the Netherlands, where 70 miles of motorway were open to traffic by 1939.

GB: The first motorway was the 8½-mile Preston By-pass section of the M6 Birmingham–Carlisle, built by Lancashire County Council as agents for the Ministry of Transport under the direction of the County Surveyor and Bridgemaster, James Drake, and opened by the then Prime Minister, Harold Macmillan, on 5 December 1958. It was completed in two years three months at a cost of £3,750,000 by

Tarmac Civil Engineering Ltd of Wolverhampton. The motorway had dual two-lane carriageways with a central reservation and a minimum overall width of 112ft. It was surfaced with coated macadam and asphalt.

The first section of the M1, which is sometimes incorrectly described as Britain's first motorway, was not opened until 2 November 1959.

Though she entered the field so late, it would appear that it was in Britain that motorways were first seriously advocated. As early as 1900 the First Lord of the Treasury urged the coming need of 'great highways constructed for rapid motor traffic and *confined* to motor traffic'. This happened to be the very same year that the world's first motor road, designed for, but not restricted to, motor traffic, was opened in Madagascar. In 1920 Lord Montagu of Beaulieu produced a design for a London–Birmingham motorway that bore a most prophetic resemblance to that ultimately adopted for the M1. Despite considerable lobbying between the wars, no real progress was made until the passing of the Special Roads Act 1949, which gave powers for the construction of roads limited to certain classes of motor traffic. This legislation was necessitated by the fact that it was a recognized principle in law that the Queen's Highway was open to all subjects of the Crown without restriction, subject only to regulations relating to safety and licensing.

The first
MULTIPLE RETAILER

was W. H. Smith & Son, who negotiated a contract with the London & North Western Railway Co in October 1848 which allowed them the bookstall concession on all L & NWR stations for an annual rental of £1,500. Smith's first railway bookstall was opened at Euston on 1 November 1848. A fortnight later, a second contract was signed with the Midland Railway Co, and by 1862 Smith's had made further agreements with five other major railway companies. Although dealing chiefly in books and periodicals, the bookstalls also sold rugs, candles and other travelling comforts. Proprietors of some 800 retail outlets by the turn of the century, the firm did not branch out into conventional 'High Street' shop trading until 1905, the year they lost the GWR contract to Wyman & Sons Ltd.

The first multiple retailer to operate through conventional shops was the Singer Manufacturing Co, which opened its original branch for the sale and service of sewing-machines in Buchanan Street, Glasgow in 1856.

The first multiple retailer to deal in a range of different goods via conventional outlets, and pioneer of the modern concept of multiple retailing, was George Mence Smith, oil and colourman, who in 1860 was trading from 18 Beresford Square, Woolwich. In 1868 he was proprietor of nine oil and colourman's shops in Woolwich, Bexley, Erith and Plumstead, and by 1884 had added branches in Eltham, Greenwich and Croydon, making a total of 25. Most of these shops also dealt in groceries, though this was only a sideline; the real pioneer of multiple grocery stores was the firm of Walton, Hassell & Port, which had some 30 branches by 1870.

The development of multiple retailing in America was contemporary with the movement in Britain, though it is doubtful whether it began any earlier. The oldest surviving American multiple firm is the Great Atlantic & Pacific Tea Co, which started opening provision stores in 1864. Other extinct multiples may have existed in embryonic form at this date.

VARIETY CHAIN STORES originated at Utica, N.Y. on 22 February 1879, when Frank Winfield Woolworth established his first shop on the principle of 'nothing over 5c'. The public was not attracted by the idea, and with sales down to as low as $2.50 a day, Woolworth decided to move to Lancaster, Pa. in June. His new 5c store proving a resounding success, he was enabled to make a rapid expansion to other towns of the East Coast.

GB: The Penny Bazaar, Cheetham Hill, Manchester, was opened by Michael Marks and Tom Spencer under a deed of partnership signed on 28 September 1894, the latter paying £300 for his half-share in the enterprise. Marks was a Jewish immigrant from Bialystock, then part of Poland, who had arrived in Leeds in 1884, penniless, illiterate and unable to speak English. He had been started in business as an itinerant pedlar by a loan of £5 from Spencer's employer, a wholesaler named Isaac Dewhirst, whom he had stopped in the street to ask the way. With his first fixed retail outlet, a stall in Kirkgate Market, Leeds, which was opened the same year, Marks made a fundamental innovation by arranging the items for sale according to price. He went on to establish stalls in six other Lancashire street-markets before venturing to institute the variety chain-store business with Tom Spencer in Manchester. By 1900 there were 12 Penny Bazaar stores, three of them in London, and all selling a wide range of haberdashery, earthenware, hardware, toys, stationery and household goods at the one fixed price of a penny. During the next 15 years the number increased to 140, covering the entire country.

The first of the modern Marks and Spencer stores to break away from the old Penny Bazaar concept was opened at Darlington in 1922. Double-glazed windows replaced the previous open frontage, the horseshoe-shaped counter gave way to wall-counters, and for the first time the fascia bore the name Marks & Spencer.

The first
MULTI-STOREY CAR PARK

was opened in May 1901 by the City & Suburban Electric Carriage Co at 6 Denman Street, just off Piccadilly Circus, for the benefit of the owners of vehicles supplied by the Company. The garage had seven floors and was equipped with an electric elevator capable of raising a 3-ton lorry to the top storey. With a total floor space of 19,000 sq ft, it was claimed as the largest garage in the world at that date.

The first
MUNICIPAL HOUSING

was provided by the City of Liverpool

under the provisions of the Liverpool Sanitary Amendment Act 1864 and comprised four four-storey blocks containing 88 flats, and two three-storey blocks with 36 flats. Misleadingly named St Martin's Cottages, the buildings were erected in Silvester Street at a cost of £17,928 16s, including the purchase of the land, and completed in 1869. The flats had no bathrooms, larders or fuel stores and WCs were communal. The total rent-roll for the first full year of tenancy, 1870, was £1,365 17s 1d. No records of individual rents survive for that year, but comparison with figures for 1912, the earliest full breakdown available, suggests that weekly rents had altered little, except that there may have been a slight decrease. Rents in 1912 were 2s 6d–3s 6d for two rooms, 3s 6d–4s 6d for three rooms and 4s 9d–5s 6d for four rooms.

The four-storey blocks, which are still occupied, were fully modernized by the Corporation in the early 1950s, and the three-storey blocks demolished to increase the amount of daylight and air for the remainder.

Apart from the isolated initiatives taken by a few local authorities under special Acts, the provision of 'model dwellings' for the working classes remained entirely in the hands of housing trusts and private companies founded by philanthropists until the passing of the 1890 Housing Act, which enabled any local authority to build council houses subject to certain conditions.

The first
MUNICIPAL PARK
in the UK was Moor Park, Preston, formerly rough common-ground, but enclosed by the Corporation in 1834. According to a plan drawn up by the appropriately named surveyor P. Park in February 1835, an avenue was planted on the south side of the park and the new Serpentine Road constructed to form a boundary on the north side. An artificial lake, the Serpentine, was dug and two lodges erected at the western and southern entrances. A third lodge was added on the northern side in 1836. Apart from these embellishments, the rest of the park was left as 'ornamental grassland' until the 1860s, when gardens were laid out.
CHILDREN'S PLAYGROUNDS: the first in a municipal park were opened in 1859, when horizontal bars and swings were erected in Queen's Park and Philips Park, Manchester.

◀ *St Martin's Cottages, Liverpool – Britain's first council flats as they appear today*

The first
MUSEUM
in Britain run as a corporate institution open to the public was the Ashmolean Museum at Oxford, opened in a purpose-designed building in Broad Street on 6 June 1683. The nucleus of the Ashmolean's collection was John Tradescant's 'cabinet of rarities', which had been formed earlier in the century at South Lambeth, and which the younger Tradescant had willed to the antiquary Elias Ashmole. He in turn presented the collection to the University of Oxford. The exhibits, dispatched to Oxford in 12 carts, fell into two basic categories, 'Natural' and 'Artificial'. The former comprised stuffed animals and birds (including a specimen of the Dodo), shellfish, insects, minerals and plants; the latter a caseful of weapons from all nations, armour, costumes, household goods, coins and general curiosities. The first Curator of the Museum was Robert Plot. Admission charges seem to have been in the form of an exit rather than an entrance fee, since the amount was calculated acording to the length of time a visitor had spent in looking at the exhibits.
NATIONAL MUSEUM: the first in Britain was the British Museum, founded by Act of Parliament in 1753 and opened to the public on 15 January 1759. Although ostensibly there was free access to the collections, admission during the 18th century was by no means automatic. According to the German historian Wendeborn, writing in 1785, prospective visitors had to present their credentials at the Museum office, and if these were approved, an admission ticket would be issued after a lapse of 14 days. Even then the seeker after knowledge was not free to wander about the galleries looking at what interested him most, but was obliged to join a conducted tour, described by one visitor as 'rapid'.
MUNICIPAL MUSEUM: the first was Sunderland Corporation Museum, previously the museum of the local Natural History and Antiquarian Society, for which the Town Council accepted formal responsibility with effect from 9 November 1846. This was possible under the provisions of the Museums Act passed the previous year, which permitted municipalities of over 10,000 population to raise a ½d rate for the maintenance of a public museum. The collection was originally housed in rooms at the Sunderland Athenaeum that the Corporation rented for £10 p.a. Canterbury has also been claimed as the first municipality in Britain to establish a museum, but it would appear to have been marginally behind Sunderland, since the Canterbury Museum Committee did not authorize the opening of the institution to the public until 14 January 1847.

See also Motor Museum.

The first
MUSTARD
in paste form was produced commercially by Mrs Clements of Durham and retailed in London in 1720. It was sold in earthenware pots covered with parchment cut from legal documents – hence the dry legal joke about deeds and contracts 'fit only to cover mustard-pots'. Mustard had been known in Britain since the Middle Ages, but had been used only in seed form.

The first
NEON LIGHTING
was developed by the French physicist, Georges Claude, and displayed for the first time at the Paris Motor Show on 3 December 1910. Two 45mm diameter neon tubes, each 35m long, were used to illuminate the peristyle of the Grand Palais where it was held. The main drawback of neon lighting at this stage of its development was its colour – red – and although Claude had originally intended it for ordinary lighting purposes, he was persuaded by an advertising-man, Jacques Fonseque, that it could be better utilized for illuminated signs. The rights were acquired by the agency Paz et Silva, for whom Fonseque worked, and in 1912 the first neon sign was erected over a barber-shop at 14 boulevard Montmartre. The sign announced LE PALACE COIFFEUR in large red letters. In the same year the first neon advertising sign, consisting of the single word CINZANO, was displayed on the front of 72 boulevard Haussmann. Claude himself joined the firm of Paz et Silva to continue developments, and soon produced a tube giving a blue light. Other colours were added to the range by introducing powders of the appropriate hue into the glass tube. By 1914 some 150 neon signs had been installed on buildings in Paris.
GB: The West End Cinema in Coventry Street, London became the first public building in Britain to have its name emblazoned in neon in 1913. No other installations are known before 1923, when neon tubes were used to illuminate the tower of the Coliseum Theatre.

The first neon advertising sign, erected on a 35 × 20ft display site in Piccadilly Circus in 1924, announced that ANY TIME IS ARMY CLUB TIME. Army Club was a popular brand of cigarettes.

The first
NEWSPAPERS
in the sense of printed journals of news appearing at frequent intervals under the same imprint were two German publications that began life more or less simultaneously in the middle of January 1609.

Aviso Relation oder Zeitung was published weekly, commencing 15 January. Recently it has been proved beyond doubt that the paper was published at Wolfenbüttel in Lower Saxony, and it is now believed that the printer and publisher was Julius Adolph von Söhne, Keeper of the Royal Press. The *Aviso* continued to be issued until 1616, when there was a gap of four years before it was restarted by Elias Holwein. It was still in existence in 1624, but no copies are known after that date.

The other paper, *Relation: Aller Fürnemmen und Gedenckwürdigen Historien*, was published weekly at Strasbourg, numbered but not dated. The publisher was Johann Carolus and the paper lasted until at least 1622. The 37th number, issued in September 1609, contains a report of Galileo's telescope.

ENGLISH NEWSPAPER: the first was the *Corrant out of Italy, Germany, Etc.*, of which 11 numbers survive bearing dates from 2 December 1620 to 18 September 1621. It was printed at Amsterdam by George Veseler and 'soulde by Petrus Keerius, dwelling in the Calverstreete, in the uncertaine time'. The first issue bears no title at all, while some of the later numbers have a slightly varying title, no unusual thing in the early days of newspaper publishing. The lead story in the first issue, dateline 'Weenen, the 6 November', relates: 'The French ambassadour hath caused the Earle of Dampier to be buried stately at Presburg.'

Aviso Relation oder Zeitung – Wolfenküttel, Lower Saxony, January 1609

Avisa
Relation oder Zeitung.
Was sich begeben vnd
zugetragen hat / in Deutsch: vnd Welsch/land/Spannien/Niederlandt/Engellandt/Franckreich/Vngern/Osterreich/Schweden/Polen/vnnd in allen Provintzen/ in Ost: vnnd West Indien etc.
So alhie den 15. Januarij angelangt.

Gedruckt im Jahr/1609.

Pieter van den Keere, the publisher, was a map-engraver who had lived and worked in England. The political climate of the time made it safer for any printed news for English consumption to be printed abroad, and a number of other English-language corantos were produced at Amsterdam and The Hague during 1621, much to the annoyance of King James I, who took vigorous action to have them suppressed.

The first newspaper published in Britain was issued some time during the summer of 1621 by Thomas Archer of Pope's Head Alley, Cornhill, who was imprisoned in September 'for making, or adding to, his corantos'. No issues of this have been located. Apart from some irregular corantos of 1621–2 translated from the Dutch, the earliest newspaper published in Britain of which copies survive was the *Weekley Newes*, which was first issued by Nathaniel Butler on 2 August 1622 and continued, with variations of title, until 1625. This was undoubtedly the first newspaper in England to achieve regular and sustained publication over a period of years. It was generally 24 pages quarto and cost 1 groat. In common with other news-books of the time, the *Weekley Newes* confined itself exclusively to the reporting of foreign news, lest it should attract the unwelcome attentions of the Star Chamber.

The first newspaper in Britain to contain domestic news was *The Heads of Severall Proceedings of the Present Parliament*, published by John Thomas of Smithfield weekly from 29 November 1641 to 3 January 1642.

DAILY NEWSPAPER: the first was *Einkommenden Zeitungen*, published by Timotheus Ritzsch at Leipzig between July and September 1650. The paper was numbered but not dated, although there are grounds for believing it was first issued on 1 July. The only surviving examples are 68 issues from No. 6 to 83 (some are missing), preserved at Uppsala University in Sweden.

GB: The *Perfect Diurnall* published at the Office of Intelligence in London from 21 February to 16 March 1660, Sundays excepted.

The first successful English daily was the *Daily Courant*, published by E. Mallet 'next door to the King's Arms Tavern at Fleet Bridge', and launched on Wednesday, 11 March 1702. Instead of the usual folded sheet of four pages, the *Courant* boasted only a single sheet. The Editor explained that it was 'confin'd to half the compass, to save the Public at least half the Impertinences, of ordinary News-Papers'. Publication continued until issue No. 6002 in June 1735.

See also Newspaper, Colour Supplement; Newspaper, Evening; Newspaper, Provincial.

The first
NEWSPAPER ADVERTISEMENTS
appeared in the *Journal Général d'Affiches*, better known as the *Petites Affiches*, which commenced publication in Paris on 14 October 1612. Although no early issues of the paper survive, it is reasonable to suppose from its title, and from the nature of its contents during the succeeding three centuries of continued publication, that it was intended as an advertising medium from its inception.

The first conventional news-sheet (i.e. in the sense of a paper devoted chiefly to news-reporting) to contain an advertisement was an untitled Dutch coranto published in Amsterdam on 21 November 1626, which had a notice inserted beneath the editorial matter announcing that an auction sale was to be held for the disposal of a cargo of sugar, ivory, pepper, tobacco and wood taken from a prize-ship.

GB: Samuel Pecke's *Perfect Diurnall* (1643) began carrying regular book advertisements from 23 November 1646. The rate was 6d per insertion. Although there are earlier examples of book announcements in the journals of the day, these generally appeared as items of news, and there is no evidence that they were paid for by the publishers.

ILLUSTRATED ADVERTISEMENT: the first to appear in an English newspaper was inserted in the *Faithfull Scout* for 2–9 April 1652 by Hugh Clough, goldsmith of Lombard Street, and showed two jewels that had been stolen from his premises.

The first illustrated trade advertisement showing the product advertised appeared in the *Daily Courant* for 17 March 1703 and pictured a patent chocolate-maker offered for sale by the manufacturer, Robert Inwood of Whitefriars. Illustrated advertising remained the exception rather than the rule for the next century and a half, and it was not until 1849 that Cadbury's began running the first advertisements for a branded product that showed the advertiser's package, in this case their 'Homoeopathic or Dietic Coffee especially suited for invalids'.

CLASSIFIED ADVERTISING first appeared in Thomas Newcome's *Publick Adviser*, which ran from 19 May to 28 September 1657 and was also the first English paper devoted solely to advertising. The advertisements were classified under headings that included Shipping, Properties for Sale and To Let, Physicians, Artificers, Lost and Stolen (which embraced people as well as less mobile property), Stage Coaches and Carriers. There were eight receiving stations for advertisements and the charge per insertion depended on the nature of the announcement, ranging from 3s for 'Common Seamen desiring employ' to 1d in the £ for house properties.

The first newspaper to charge for classified advertising according to length was E. Everingham's *Generous Advertiser*, which began publication on Tuesday, 28 January 1707. The rate was 3d for 50 letters and the paper, a 'give-away', claimed a circulation of 4,000 in the Cities of London and Westminster.

The first newspaper to institute a 'personal column' on its classified page was *The Times* on 22 February 1886.

BOX NUMBERS were first introduced in the classified advertisement columns by the *Daily Telegraph* on 6 July 1882.

THEATRICAL ANNOUNCEMENT: the first appeared in the *Flying Post* for 4 July 1700 and announced a benefit performance of *The Comical History of Don Quixote* at the New Theatre, Lincoln's Inn Fields, for 'a gentleman in great distress, and for the relief of his wife and children'.

Later in the 18th century the announcements of the London theatres came to be regarded as an important circulation booster, and in 1767 the *Monitor* declared that its competitor, the *Gazeteer*, was paying £200 p.a. to the managers of Drury Lane and Covent Garden for the privilege of carrying their advertisements.

UNSOLICITED TESTIMONIAL: the earliest known appeared in the *General Advertiser* for 19 January 1752. Elizabeth Gardiner, the headmistress of a girls' boarding-school, recommended the use of Mr Parson's stays, which she declared were compulsory items of apparel for her charges.

FULL-PAGE ADVERTISEMENT: the first, for Edmund Lodge's *Portraits and Memoirs of the most illustrious Personages of British History*, appeared in *The Times* on 1 January 1829.

The first full-page illustrated advertisement, for British Cornflour, appeared in the *Courier* and *West End Advertiser* for 10 July 1842 and showed a woodcut reproduction of a bull's head. This can be regarded as the precursor of display advertising, which made little impact on newspapers before the turn of the century, though increasingly used for magazine advertising from the 1870s.

COLOURED ADVERTISEMENT: the first to appear in a British newspaper was a whole-page display advertisement for Dewar's White Label Whisky, illustrated with a photograph in Dufaycolor, which appeared in the *Glasgow Daily Record* on 7 October 1936.

The first *NEWSPAPER CARTOON*

was a political caricature on the subject of President James Madison's repeal of the Embargo Act in America, which appeared in the Washington paper the *Federal Republican* early in 1814. It was drawn by John Wesley Jarvis, better known as a portrait-painter than a cartoonist, and showed a terrapin floating on its back and grasping the body of the President, who had cut off its head with a knife – the severed head having Madison's ear clamped in its jaws. The Embargo Act, readers would have been aware, was commonly known as a 'terrapin policy'. No other cartoons are known to have been published in American newspapers during the next 50 years, and it was not until the 1870s that the *New York Evening Telegram* and the *New York Daily Graphic* started carrying them at all regularly.

GB: The earliest-known cartoon to have appeared in an English newspaper was a large unsigned $7\frac{1}{2} \times 10$in satirical drawing titled 'The Unknown Tongue', which was printed in *Bell's New Weekly Messenger* for 8 January 1832. This was on the theme of the Reform Bill and showed the House of Lords in shocked disarray at the prospect of being swamped by 50 newly created peers. Several noble lords have collapsed, while others call out 'Treason', 'Death', 'Murder', 'Sacrilege', 'Horror', the Duke of Wellington adding 'O fie fie'.

The newspaper cartoon in Britain might have developed as a regular feature but for the advent of several satirical weekly magazines during the Reform Bill crisis. In the event there was little further progress before 1888, when the newly established London evening the *Star* became the first English newspaper to make frequent and continuous use of the political cartoon. This practice began with the publication on 2 February of a cartoon by Francis Carruthers Gould on the visit of Lord Ripon and Mr Morley to Ireland with the heading 'Wouldn't He Like to Arrest Them!' Gould worked for the *Star* on a freelance basis until he joined the *Pall Mall Gazette* in 1890. It has often been claimed, on the basis of this appointment, that he was the first newspaper staff cartoonist in Britain. The credit has been given to the right man but the wrong newspaper. Although he was a staff artist on the *Pall Mall Gazette*, he was employed as a straightforward illustrator, mainly doing portraits of people in the news, and contributed cartoons on no more than two occasions in three years. Not until he moved to the *Westminster Gazette* in 1893 did Gould truly become a staff cartoonist, creating a new force in journalism by his trenchant 'picture politics'. In 1906 he became the first member of his profession to be honoured with a knighthood.

The first *NEWSPAPER COLOUR SUPPLEMENT*

was a four-page section of the *New York World* instituted on Sunday, 19 November 1893. The first issue had two half-page illustrations printed in five colours, one showing 'A Scene in Atlantic Gardens, Saturday Night' and the other 'The Cathedral at Eleven O'Clock Mass.'

The colour supplement of the kind that has now become familiar to British newspaper-readers, i.e. a rotogravure section issued in magazine format, was also a product of American inventiveness, making its first appearance as a syndicated eight-page section given away by seven US newspapers, among them the *New York Times* and the *Philadelphia Public Ledger*, with their issues of 29 March 1914. The gravure colour supplement early established its role as a disseminator of 'instant culture', this first number consisting of a descriptive article on the Altman Collection in the Metropolitan Museum of Art, New York, with reproductions of 13 paintings.

GB: The first gravure colour supplement was the *Sunday Times Colour Section* (later renamed *Sunday Times Magazine*), which began publication on 4 February 1962. The cover showed 11 photographs by David Bailey of Jean Shrimpton in a Mary Quant dress and one of footballer Jimmy McIlroy. The contents comprised an article on Peter Blake and Pop Art, a feature about a young lecturer at the London School of Economics, Alan Little, who was the son of a Liverpool milkman, and a recipe for stewed oysters by the hitherto unknown Robert Carrier. Edited by Mark Boxer, the first issue of the *Sunday Times Colour Section* – derided and abused as it was by the rest of Fleet Street and most of its readers – had already found a formula of classless but competitive pace-setting that was to ensure an increasing success throughout the style-conscious, acquisitive, affluent 1960s.

The first
NEWSPAPER COLUMNIST
was Dr John Hill of Peterborough, who began contributing a daily column to the *London Advertiser* and *Literary Gazette* under the signature of 'The Inspector' on 11 March 1751. This was the first regular signed newspaper feature. During the two years that the column appeared Hill was estimated to be earning £1,500 a year from journalism, a figure probably unequalled at the time. It would appear that Hill's column was not unlike its present-day counterparts, for the elder D'Israeli described it as 'a light scandalous chronicle all the week with a seventh day sermon'. It was also libellous, and on one occasion Hill was publicly caned by an outraged Irishman.

The first
NEWSPAPER, EVENING
was *Dawks's News-Letter*, published in London by Ichabod Dawks commencing Tuesday, 23 June 1696. It was printed in a special italic script to resemble handwriting, and space was left at the bottom of each issue for subscribers to add their own messages if they were sending it on to a friend in the country. Referring to the novel typeface, Dawks expressed the hope that it would 'be useful to improve the younger sort in writing a curious hand'. However, he was probably motivated more by the fact that older readers in the shires hankered after a form of paper resembling the more intimate handwritten news-letters that had preceded printed newspapers. It was published three times a week on Tuesdays, Thursdays and Saturdays between 4pm and 5pm and was sold by subscription only for 10s a quarter. The last-known issues were published in 1716 and throughout this period the *News-Letter* was published at Wardrobe Court in Great Carter Lane.

The first
NEWSPAPER, FIELD
issued by or for troops on active service was *The American Flag*, published at Matamoros, Mexico for General Scott's Army commencing 6 June 1846. Some 20 similar papers were issued during the course of the Mexican-American War (1846–8).
GB: News of the Camp, A Journal of Fancies, Notifications, Gossip and General Chit Chat, Published in the Military Camp of Her Majesty's Forces Defending the Beleaguered Inhabitants of Pretoria, price 6d, three times weekly from 25 December 1880 to 9 April 1881. The paper was edited by Charles Du Val, an English actor travelling in South Africa with a touring show at the outbreak of the 1st Boer War, and C.W. Deecker, former proprietor of the Transvaal *Argus*. At the beginning of the siege, Du Val had been appointed Attaché to the Garrison Commandant and so was able to issue the paper with semi-official recognition, the military authorities reserving the privilege of using its columns for the publication of notices and district orders. Circulation amounted to 500 copies per issue.

The first
NEWSPAPER HEADLINE
carried on the front page of an English newspaper appeared in the London evening the *Star* on Wednesday, 16 July 1890 and read MANY HAPPY RETURNS OF THE DAY – WEDDING OF PROFESSOR STUART MP. This remained an isolated example until 1894, when both the *Star* and the *Evening News* began using horizontal display headlines over two columns. Not until 9 July 1896 did an item of major news receive banner headline treatment, the *Evening News* for that day proclaiming across its front page: MATTERS IN RHODESIA GROW WORSE INSTEAD OF BETTER. The story below reported that Salisbury was 'a mass of seething discontent', the officers could not agree on the best method of defence against the insurgent black population, and that the official members of the Salisbury Town Committee had resigned in protest at the state of affairs.

The first
NEWSPAPER PHOTOGRAPH
was a halftone illustration executed by Stephen H. Horgan, from Henry J. Newton's photograph of New York's Shantytown, which appeared in the *New York Daily Graphic* on 4 March 1880.
GB: A halftone portrait of George Lambert, Liberal candidate for South Molton, from a photograph by J. Browning of Exeter, was featured in the *Daily Graphic* on 4 November 1891.

The first newspaper in the world to employ its own staff photographers was the *Daily Illustrated Mirror* (London) in February 1904. It was also the first newspaper to publish genuine news photographs (as opposed to portraits and 'studies'), and the first to print a photograph on its front page (22 March 1904).

The first
NEWSPAPER, PROVINCIAL
published in England was the *Norwich Post*, founded by Francis Burgess in 1701. Scholars differ as to the exact date the first number was issued, but a count back from the earliest surviving copy, No. 287, would indicate that it was published on 8 November, providing the paper appeared subsequently at regular weekly intervals. In 1706 Dr Thomas Tanner, Rector of Thorpe Bishop's, Norwich, wrote to a friend: 'The Norwich newspapers are the principal support of our poor printer here, by which, with the advertisements, he clears nearly 50s every week, selling vast numbers to the country people.' The price of the *Norwich Post* was 1d, so that if Tanner's estimate of the paper's revenue is reliable, and allowing a margin for advertising, it would appear that the circulation was about 400 to 500. Certainly the venture was successful enough for two rival papers to make their appearance that year – the *Norwich Gazette* and the *Norwich Post-Man* – giving Norwich the added distinction of being the first city in England to offer its citizens a choice of newspapers. With a population estimated at about 30,000, Norwich was then the second largest city.

The first newspaper photograph – New York Daily Graphic, *4 March 1880*

The claim of *Berrow's Worcester Journal* to descend from a newspaper allegedly published in 1690 or 1691 remains unproven, and it seems improbable that any regular publication would have been issued outside London at that date. It is, however, the oldest provincial newspaper in England, as it certainly existed under the title of the *Worcester Post-Man* as early as 1709. The present title was adopted in 1808.

The provincial Press of the 18th century did not concern itself much with local news, and most reports were copied from the London papers or the manuscript news-letter circulating at the time. As in London, the emphasis was on foreign happenings, particularly military and diplomatic. There were, however, occasional exceptions, and

G.A. Cranfield quotes the two-column description of the Lord Chancellor's visit to Exeter published in *Brice's Weekly Journal* in 1726 as one of the earliest instances of purely local reporting. It was not until the Industrial Revolution upset the equilibrium of country life that the affairs of local government became of sufficiently pressing interest to warrant extensive and regular coverage in the provincial papers.

The first
NEWSPAPER TO CONTAIN A REGULAR WOMEN'S FEATURE
was the *Star*, a London evening paper, which instituted a weekly Saturday column titled 'What Women are Doing' on 2 August 1890. The opening feature dwelt on the need to teach working-class housewives about good taste in interior decoration; the problems of ladies' maids and the experiences of one who was beaten by her mistress with a hairbrush; the inferiority of fashions in Islington compared to those of Newington Causeway; and the progress of the Women's Printing Society.

The first
NISSEN HUT
was designed by Canadian-born Capt. Peter Norman Nissen, Officer Commanding 29 Company RE, and the prototype erected at Hesdin, France in 1916. The bow-shaped hut had a ground measurement of 27 × 15ft and was roofed with bent corrugated-iron sheets. It was lined inside with matchboarding and lighted by windows on either side of the door at one end, and a single centrally placed window at the other. Nissen's invention, for which he was awarded the DSO, answered an urgent need for temporary structures to house the large numbers of troops being drafted into the Army following the introduction of conscription that year. Nissen was not entirely alone in the field. There were also Aylwin Huts, Armstrong Huts, Tarrant's Portable Huts, Forest Huts, Liddell Huts and Weblee Huts during World War I, all named after RE officers. World War II saw the advent of Iris Huts, Romney Huts, Tufton Huts and Abbey Huts (named after Westminster Abbey). None of these designs, however, was as ubiquitous as the Nissen, which has continued to be used in both peace and war without alteration to its basic shape. One recent variant, though, may emulate its success. This is a new type of Nissen Hut made of heavy duty cardboard, designed in 1971 by 22-year-old Richard Nissen, grandson of Peter Nissen, for use in disaster areas. The temporary hut can be erected in 90min and will last for about a year.

The first
NUMBERING OF HOUSES
was introduced on the Pont Notre-Dame, Paris in 1463.
GB: The practice is first noted in *A New View of London* of 1708, which records that the houses in Prescot Street, Whitechapel had been numbered by the people living there, a group of refugees from Europe.

By 1763 there were about a dozen numbered thoroughfares in London, and two years later an Act of Parliament enjoined on the Court of Common Council the task of numbering all the houses of the metropolis, excepting only those that had names. One immediate effect of numbering was the disappearance of the hanging signs by which traders had formerly indicated their address.

The first
NYLON
was developed at the laboratories of the American chemical company E.I. du Pont de Nemours by a research team under the direction of Dr Wallace Carothers and patented on 16 February 1937. The first commercially produced nylon product was toothbrush bristles, manufactured at du Pont's Arlington, N.J. plant on 24 February 1938. Nylon yarn was produced commercially for the first time at du Pont's factory in Seaford, Delaware on 15 December 1939, and made up into stockings by various hosiery-manufacturers. By mutual agreement among traders, the competing brands of nylon stockings were launched throughout the USA simultaneously on 15 May 1940.
GB: Nylon was first produced in Britain in the form of yarn by British Nylon Spinners in a converted weaving-shed in Lockhurst Lane, Coventry on 23 January 1941. Wartime output at Coventry and a second BNS plant at Stowmarket was confined to Government and Services supply needs, particularly parachute fabric.

The first British-made nylon products to go on public sale were nylon stockings in December 1946.

The first
OCEAN CRUISE
of which details survive was a four-month voyage round the Mediterranean organized by the Peninsular & Oriental Steam Navigation Co, starting from Southampton on 26 July 1844. Three ships were employed, the *Lady Mary Wood* (553 tons) taking passengers to Vigo, Lisbon, Cadiz and Gibraltar, the larger *Tagus* (782 tons) taking them on to Constantinople via Athens, and the *Iberia* (516 tons) completing the outward trip as far as Jerusalem and Cairo. The return journey was made by the same ships and by the same route. This particular excursion was chronicled by William Makepeace Thackeray, who was offered a free passage by the company in order to popularize the idea of cruising as a pastime. The P & O had inaugurated this service to the Mediterranean ports two years earlier, but it is not clear from the records whether any attempt had been made to attract cruise passengers before Thackeray and his fellow excursionists embarked on the *Lady Mary Wood* in 1844.

Thackeray published a full account of his cruise as *Notes of a Journey from Cornhill to Grand Cairo* in 1846. In the preface to this work he makes it clearly apparent that he was one of a party of cruise passengers, even though the ship did carry a number of other people with more orthodox reasons for travelling. Despite the fact that he was prodigiously seasick for much of the cruise, Thackeray seems to have enjoyed the novelty of voyaging for pleasure and entered into shipboard life with nautical gusto. His published description tends to concentrate on the shore excursions, but he does give some account of impromptu saloon concerts and the joy of sitting on deck beneath a star-studded sky at night, as well as the feeding arrangements. These varied according to the ship. In the *Lady Mary Wood,* Thackeray and his fellow passengers suffered the ministrations of a 'cook, with tattooed arms, sweating away among the saucepans in the galley, who used (with a touching affection) to send us locks of his hair in the soup'. Aboard the *Iberia*, however, the dinners were so excellent that he reproduces the Bill of Fare for 12 October as they approached Alexandria:

Mulligatawny Soup

Salt Fish and Egg Sauce

Roast Haunch of Mutton
Boiled Shoulder and Onion Sauce
Boiled Beef
Roast Fowls
Pillow ditto
Ham
Curry and Rice

Cabbage; French Beans;
Boiled Potatoes; Baked ditto

Damson Tart
Currant ditto
Rice Puddings
Currant Fritters

The first ocean cruise by a ship chartered solely for this purpose was organized in 1867 by Capt. Charles C. Duncan of New York and advertised as 'An excursion to the Holy Land, Egypt, the Crimea, Greece and intermediate points of interest.' The original instigator of the scheme was the noted divine, Henry Ward Beecher, who was planning to write a biography of Jesus Christ and wanted to do some field-study in Palestine. Why he should have considered it necessary to take several hundred companions with him remains obscure, but in the event he decided not to go. Those who did paid $1,200 for the trip, excluding the $5 a day in gold that they were advised to take for shore expenses, and were only accepted as passengers after a careful screening by a selection committee. Not only were they expected to be of an acceptable social standing, but also to display a fitting degree of moral earnestness. The humorist Mark Twain applied for a berth so that he could write a series of articles for the *Daily Alta Californian*. However, he prejudiced his chances by presenting himself before Capt. Duncan exuding 'fumes of bad whisky', but scraped by as the organizer was under the mistaken impression that he was a Baptist minister. Twain had high hopes of 'a royal holiday beyond the broad ocean' and the chance to 'dance, and promenade, and smoke, and sing, and make love, and search the skies for constellations. . . .' He was doomed to disappointment. Although his book, *Innocents Abroad*, gives a light-hearted account of this first large influx of American tourists to Europe, he expressed his true feelings in a critical letter to the *New York Herald*:

Three fourths of the Quaker City's passengers were between forty and seventy years of age. The pleasure ship was a synagogue, and the pleasure trip was a funeral excursion without a corpse. . . . Such was our daily life on board ship – solemnity, decorum, dinner, dominoes, devotions, slander.

The first shipping company to inaugurate regular cruises on ships confined to round-trip passengers only was the North of Scotland & Orkney & Shetland Steam Ship Co, whose purpose-built cruise ship SS *St Sunniva* began making summer-holiday excursions to the Norwegian fjords in 1887.

The first *OCEAN LINER*

operated on a fixed schedule was the 424-ton sailing-packet *James Monroe*, owned by the American company, the Black Ball Line. She sailed for her maiden voyage from Pier 23 in New York's East River on 5 January 1818 and arrived at Liverpool on 2 February after a 'downhill' transatlantic run of 28 days. She carried eight passengers. The appointments of the ship far surpassed those of any other passenger-carrying vessels of the time, including a commodious saloon richly furnished in mahogany, and satinwood-panelled staterooms with marble pillars flanking the doors. A small 'farm' of cows, pigs, sheep and hens was maintained on deck so that the voyagers could be supplied with fresh meat, milk and eggs. Bread was baked daily.

STEAMSHIP IN REGULAR TRANSATLANTIC PASSENGER SERVICE: the first was the *Great Western*, designed by Isambard Kingdom Brunel for the Great Western Steamship Co and launched at Patterson's Yard, Bristol on 19 July 1837. Leaving Bristol under the command of Capt. James Hosken on 8 April 1838, she made her maiden voyage to New York in 15 days 5hr at an average speed of 8·8 knots, just failing to beat the smaller *Sirius* for the accolade of first British steamship to cross the Atlantic. Like the *James Monroe* before her, the 1,320-ton *Great Western* set new standards of passenger comfort, her magnificent 75ft saloon eclipsing any that had ever been seen on a sailing-vessel. Accommodation was provided for 120 1st-Class passengers, 20 2nd-Class and 100 Steerage.

IRON STEAMSHIP OPERATED AS AN ATLANTIC LINER and the first *LINER FITTED WITH A SCREW PROPELLER*, was the *Great Britain*, built by Patterson's to Brunel's design for the Great Western Steamship Co and launched by the Prince Consort at Bristol on 19 July 1843. She left Liverpool for her maiden voyage on 26 July 1845 with 60 passengers and 600 tons of cargo, and arrived in New York after a voyage of 14 days 21hr.

The first *OLD AGE PENSIONS*

were introduced in Germany by Bismarck under the Old Age Insurance Act of June 1889, which came into operation on 1 January 1891. The contributory scheme was compulsory for persons over 16 years of age who were in full employment and earning less than 2,000 marks (then equivalent to approx. £100 or $500) p.a. The pension became payable to persons at the age of 70 after premiums had been paid for a minimum of 30 years. Contributions were graduated according to income, starting at 7 pfennigs a week for those whose annual wage did not exceed 300 marks. The employer contributed an equal amount. As in West Germany today, the amount of the pension depended on the rate of the contributions. During 1891, the first year of the scheme, the sum of 15,299,004 marks was paid out to 132,926 pensioners.

Britain's first OAP's drawing their pensions, 1 January 1909

The first country of the British Commonwealth to introduce old age pensions was New Zealand under the Old Age Pensions Act passed on 1 November 1898. The scheme was non-contributory and provided for an annual pension of £18 for those with an income of £34 or less, diminishing by £1 for every £1 of income in excess of this sum. Applicants had to be 65 years of age if male, and 60 if female, of good moral character, and at least 25 years' resident in the colony. The first payments were made in March 1899 and were made retrospective to 1 January of that year. A total of 4,699 pensions were granted during the first full year of operation, including one of only £1 p.a. to an applicant in Otago.

The New Zealand scheme differed from its German forerunner in that it was intended to provide an income sufficient for the necessities of life. The German pension was kept deliberately below this level, as it was paid only to those still capable of working after the age of 70 and was in the nature of a subsidy to their earnings; those incapable of further labour (at any age) were entitled to an 'infirmity pension', amounting to roughly half as much again. Thus the New Zealand system can be regarded as the progenitor of most modern schemes.

GB: A non-contributory old age pension scheme, allowing payment of 5s a week to persons over 70 years of age with an income of under £21 p.a., was introduced by the Chancellor of the Exchequer, Lloyd George, in his 1908 Budget. The original Bill contained provision to exclude anyone who had been in prison or on Poor Relief in the last 20 years, and also to deprive pensioners of their vote, but these clauses were struck out before it became law.

The first payments of old age pensions were made on 1 January 1909, and were marked by displays of rejoicing and euphoria up and down the country. Peter Wilsher (*The Pound in your Pocket*, London, 1970) has described some of the events of that historic day:

A huge bonfire was lit on the White Horse Hills. In Bromsgrove the streets were hung with bunting, and bands paraded the streets. In Walworth an old woman offered the postmaster two rashers of bacon in gratitude for his help in filling up the forms. In Spalding people said that they would keep the money as a memento for their grandchildren, and in Bishop's Stortford a seventy-five-year-old farmhand died as he signed the receipt. The National Society of Amalgamated Brassworkers sent a congratulatory New Year's telegram to the Prime Minister and the Chancellor of the Exchequer in gratitude for 'Glorious Pensions Day'. And the Lord Provost of Glasgow, echoing the sentiments of the House of Lords, the Charity Organization Society, and most leading figures in the City, told a savings-bank meeting that such pensions could only tend to encourage the thriftless, and to dissipate the proud spirit of Scottish independence.

The scheme was made contributory in 1925.

The first
OLD-SCHOOL TIE

was the Old Etonian tie, whose colours – narrow blue and broad black stripes – were decided at a meeting of the Old Etonian Association on 7 July 1900. The idea had first been mooted some three years earlier and the intervening time occupied in arguing about the most suitable colour combination. Eventually it was agreed that light blue was appropriate since it had been the official Eton colour for upwards of a century, and that black would lend the tie sufficient dignity for it to be worn in London.

The first
OMBUDSMAN

was Lars August Mannerheim, who was appointed as Swedish Justitieombudsman on 1 March 1810 and held office until 1823, when he resigned the post. Mannerheim was the only Justitieombudsman to date without legal training. The office was created as an institution of the Swedish Estates under the Constitution of 1809 to serve as a bulwark between the State and the individual. During the first century of the office in Sweden, the ombudsman's activities were principally directed towards the law officers, police and prison administration. Investigations of Government malpractice became more usual in the present century as the Civil Service became centralized and more distant from those it served.

The first Parliamentary Commissioner was Sir Guy Powles, formerly NZ High Commissioner to India, appointed by the New Zealand Government at a salary of £4,100 p.a. with effect from 1 October 1962.

GB: The first Parliamentary Commissioner was Sir Edmund Compton, formerly Comptroller and Auditor-General, who took office under the Parliamentary Commissioner Act 1967 on 1 April 1967.

The first
OPERA

was *Dafne*, with libretto by Ottavio Rinuccini and music by Jacopo Peri, originally performed at the Palazzo Corsi in Florence during the Carnival early in 1597 (exact date unrecorded). None of the music survives except for some brief passages interpolated by Corsi himself. The story was founded on the legend of Daphne and Apollo.

The earliest opera of which both text and music survives is Rinuccini and Peri's *Euridice*, which was performed for the first time at the Palazzo Pitti in Florence on 6 October 1600. The orchestra on this occasion consisted of a clavecin, a chitarone, viol and great lute.

GB: The first English opera, and the first opera performed in England, was Sir William Davenant's *The Siege of Rhodes*, presented in five acts with music by Henry Lawes, Matthew Locke and the Royalist Capt. Cooke at Rutland House, Charterhouse Yard in Aldersgate Street, London in September 1656. One of the very few theatrical performances countenanced during the Commonwealth, it took as its theme the siege of the city of Rhodes by Solyman the Magnificent in 1522, when 600 knights of the Order of St John held out for nearly six months against a quarter of a million Turks. In treating what was then comparatively recent history it owed nothing to Italian opera, which concentrated exclusively on Classical themes. Davenant's *Siege of Rhodes* was notable in other respects, for it was the first time movable scenery had been used on the public stage in England, and the first dramatic performance to feature an English actress, Mrs Edward Coleman, who sang the part of Ianthe to her husband's Alphonso.

ITALIAN OPERA PERFORMED IN ENGLAND: the first in the original was Giovanni Bonocini's *Almahide*, presented at the Haymarket Theatre in January 1710.

COVENT GARDEN OPERA COMPANY was formed in the summer of 1946 and staged its first full-scale production, Bizet's *Carmen*, on 14 January 1947 under the direction of Karl Rankl.

See also Radio Broadcast: Opera; Television: Opera.

The first
OUTBOARD MOTOR

was a four-stroke air-cooled Daimler Marine Engine produced by the American Motor Co of New York in 1896. Due to lack of demand only 25 units were manufactured.

The term 'outboard motor' was originally coined by Cameron B. Waterman, who was also the first to produce this type of engine on a large scale. His Waterman Porto Outboard Motor was first manufactured at Detroit in 1906.

GB: The 3hp Fafnir was manufactured by the Stirling Motor Construction Co of Edinburgh and Twickenham in 1904. A contemporary report spoke of 'the celerity with which the motor can be detached when desired'.

The first
PACKAGE HOLIDAY

was a 'Whitsuntide Working Men's Excursion' to Paris, organized by the Committee of Working Men under the Presidency of Sir Joseph Paxton, MP, with travel arrangements made by Thomas Cook. The first party of tourists left London Bridge Station at 10.15am on Friday, 17 May 1861.

Cook departed from his normal tour arrangements (*see* Travel Agency) in that he was prepared to issue coupons for pre-paid hotel accommodation at a cost of 5s–6s a day, inclusive

The first package holiday tourists arriving in Paris, 1861

of meals. Formerly his tourists could pay only their fares in advance and were expected to meet all other expenses on the way as they arose. The innovation meant that the thrifty working man could pay his 20s for the journey in a 3rd-Class covered carriage, 25s for board and lodging at 'a good second-class hotel' and 1s registration fee all at once, in effect a 46s package deal for his six-day holiday.

A choice of 13 hotels was offered, including Austin's Railway Hotel in la rue d'Amsterdam, where those venturing forth from their native shores for the first time (the majority) were assured of a 'substantial English dinner'. A total of 1,700 working men and their families crossed the Channel on this great adventure, though only a minority took advantage of the 'package' system of pre-payment. The hotel arrangements were reported to be excellent and several ladies were seen departing on the last day laden with bouquets of flowers presented to them by the proprietors.

The idea of letting loose such a large number of the humbler classes on a foreign capital all at once was disconcerting for some. 'To many the title of the excursion is offensive,' it was reported, 'especially as it conveys the idea of some great attempt at fraternization of English workmen with French ouvriers.' However, these fears proved groundless, and Mr Cook was able to write with satisfaction afterwards:

I heard . . . that at a dinner party at which several of the [*French*] *Ministers were present, the Excursion was the subject of conversation, and great pleasure was expressed at the behaviour of the visitors. Up to the latest period it was reported by the police authorities, that not a single case of misbehaviour had come under the argus eyes of one of the most vigilant police systems ever established.*

By 1866 Thomas Cook was advertising regular all-in package holidays in Paris throughout the season at an inclusive charge of £3 13s for seven days with 3rd-Class travel, £4 1s 2nd Class and £4 15s 1st Class. Cook's early package tours ranged in price to embrace most income levels of Victorian middle-class society, and on occasion were priced to suit the pockets of the better-paid workers. At one end of the scale was the four-day trip to Paris for the 1867 Exposition for 36s inclusive; at the other a 12-week tour with 1st-Class hotels and travel to Egypt, Syria, Palestine, Turkey, Greece, the Ionian Islands, Austria, Italy, Switzerland and France, offered at 103gns in 1868.

WINTER SPORTS PACKAGE HOLIDAYS were first organized in 1902 by (Sir) Henry Lunn, and to begin with were restricted to Old Etonians and Old Harrovians. A total of 440 winter sportsmen were accommodated in two hotels at Adelboden, a Swiss resort that offered virgin ski slopes as it had hitherto been known only as a summer-holiday centre. Looking back in a speech made many years later, Sir Arnold Lunn (son of Sir Henry) remembered:

We were very unsophisticated. That first winter at Adelboden we all sat down to dinner at two long tables. Evening amusements were more varied. We danced three or four times a week and devoted the remaining days either to indoor gymkhanas or to amateur theatricals. The polka and the lancers were only just dying out. Reversing was still considered a trifle fast, and to dance more than twice with the same partner was distinctly compromising; skating still retained pride of place among winter sports, and the skaters were the aristocrats of Adelboden. . . . Very few people skied that first season, and of those still fewer ventured beyond the practice slopes.

The first
PAPERBACK BOOK
series was the 'Collection of British Authors' published by Christian Bernhard Tauchnitz in Leipzig in 1841. The first title in the series was *Pelham* by Edward Bulwer-Lytton. Other early Tauchnitz authors included Dickens, Scott, Thackeray, Capt. Marryat, Thomas Carlyle and George Eliot. The books were all printed in English and were intended for the use of the English and American tourists who were travelling on the Continent in ever-increasing numbers with the advent of rail networks. Tauchnitz secured the rights to publish English works in all non-English-speaking countries, one of the terms of his contracts being that the purchasers would be instructed that the books must be discarded when finished, and not brought into an English-speaking country. Hence Tauchnitz introduced a new formula into publishing that still appertains to paperbacks today – the idea of the disposable book. He was also a pioneer in another respect, for his scrupulously drafted agreements between author and publisher were the precursor of modern international copyright. Hitherto authors had seldom been paid royalties on books published abroad. In 1860 Tauchnitz was raised to the rank of Freiherr with the title of Baron for his services to publishing, and he was elevated to the Saxon First Chamber (equivalent to the House of Lords). England made him an honorary Consul-General and he became a close personal friend of Queen Victoria. Tauchnitz died in 1895, but the series was continued by his heirs until 1933, by which time it comprised 5,097 titles by 525 different authors. It was subsequently taken over by another firm of Leipzig publishers, and since 1960 has been published in Stuttgart.

GB: 'Clarke's Cabinet Series', published by H.G. Clarke, 66 Old Bailey, London, 1844–5. The series consisted of 67 titles, fiction and non-fiction, of which the first was *Psyche* by Mrs Tighe, bound in illuminated paper wrappers printed in colour. Only two examples from the series survive, including a copy of *Psyche*.

The modern 'Paperback Revolution' can be dated from the publication of the first Penguin book by Sir Allen Lane in 1935. Lane's idea of 'A whole book for the equivalent of 10 cigarettes' was realized on a nominal capital of £100, and the chief retail outlet was Woolworth's. The first batch of 10 titles was issued from a disused crypt in Holy Trinity Church, Euston Road on 30 July. Penguin No. 1 was *Ariel*, a life of Shelley by André Maurois. According to Sir Allen Lane the Penguin device was chosen because it 'had an air of dignified flippancy and was easy to draw in black and white'. The original price of the books was 6d.

The first
PARACHUTE
descent by an aeronaut was made over the Parc Monceau, Paris on 22 October 1797 by André-Jacques Garnerin, who was released from a balloon at the height of 2,230ft. Garnerin rode in a gondola fixed to the lines of the 23ft diameter parachute, which was supported by a rigid pole and had its 32 white canvas gores folded like a closed umbrella. Above the parachute his brother rode in another gondola, suspended beneath the balloon, and cut the holding rope with a knife to precipitate descent. Since there was no vent in the apex of the parachute, Garnerin came down to earth with the most violent oscillations, earning the added distinction of becoming the first man ever to suffer from airsickness. For his second jump he had a hole made in the top of the canvas hemisphere.
GB: The first descent was made by Garnerin from a height of 3,000ft, over London on 21 September 1802. He landed near St Pancras Church and was immediately seized by a powerful fit of vomiting, having injudiciously abandoned the centre vent for this his fifth parachute 'jump'.

The first successful parachute descent by an English aeronaut was performed by John Hampton over Cheltenham on 3 October 1838. The authorities, mindful of a parachute fatality that had occurred the previous year, made every effort to prevent Hampton's venture, but found that they had no legal means of restraining him. The gas company was equally reluctant to supply gas for the balloon, but Hampton assured them he intended only to make a tethered ascent by way of experiment. Accordingly when balloon and parachute rose from Montpellier Gardens on the appointed day they were anchored to the ground by a long rope, but as soon as the end of the line was reached, Hampton slashed at it with a knife and proceeded to ascend to a height of several thousand feet. The parachute descent lasted 13min, the whole of which time he was in a state of stark terror, as he readily admitted afterwards, but terminated in a safe and uneventful landing.
EMERGENCY PARACHUTE JUMP: the first was made by Jordaki Kurapento when his Montgolfier balloon caught fire over Warsaw, Poland in 1808. This is the only recorded instance of an aeronaut 'bailing out' prior to the advent of powered aircraft.
PARACHUTE DESCENT FROM AN AEROPLANE was first made by 'Captain' Albert Berry from a Benoist biplane flying at 1,500ft over Jefferson Barracks, Mo., on 1 March 1912. The parachute was stowed in a conical container fixed beneath the mainplane. Piloted by Anthony Jannus, the aircraft took off from the Benoist Flying School at Kinloch Park at 2.30pm and arrived at the jump zone ½hr later. According to the report in *Flight*, Berry fell some 400ft before his canopy opened. He landed safely on the parade ground and immediately reported to the office of the Commandant, Col W.T. Wood, where he delivered a dispatch warning that 'the enemy has routed the left flank of the Kinloch Army, wounding the commanding officer, and is rapidly closing in on the remaining forces'. Despite the military nature of his exploit, 'Captain' Berry's rank was an assumed one, used in his professional role as a stunt parachute jumper. As far as aviators were concerned, the chief importance of his achievement lay in the fact that it proved the ability of an aircraft to remain stable after dropping a passenger. Its military implications were ignored.
GB: The first descent was made by William Newall over Hendon from a five-seater Grahame-White Charabanc piloted by R.H. Carr on 9 May 1914. Newall crouched between the port undercarriage struts with his feet braced on the skid below and held the parachute on his lap. At 2,000ft F.W. Gooden, positioned just behind the parachutist, prised him from his perch with his foot and Newall made a safe descent in 2min 22sec, landing in the centre of the aerodrome.
WOMAN TO MAKE A PARACHUTE DESCENT FROM AN AEROPLANE: the first was Mrs Georgia Thompson of Henderson, N.C., who had joined the Charles Broadwick stunt parachute team as a 15-year-old wife and mother in 1908 and made her first aircraft jump from Glenn Martin's home-built biplane over Griffith Park, Los Angeles on 21 June 1913. At San Diego on 4 July 1914 'Tiny' Broadwick, as she was known professionally, made the first descent from an aircraft using a manually operated parachute with a rip-cord. It is claimed that another American parachutist, H. Leo Stevens, had introduced a rip-cord the previous year, but this was intended as a secondary safety device for use in cases where the static line failed to open the parachute, and there is no evidence of its actual use in the air earlier.
SERVICE PILOTS ISSUED WITH PARACHUTES: the first were members of the German Army Air Service, some of whom are known to have been flying with Heinecke cushion-type parachutes by the spring of 1918. On 1 April of that year Vzfw. Weimer of Jasta 56 became the first pilot to bail out in an emergency when his Albatross DVa was shot down over the British lines. He landed safely and was taken prisoner.
GB: The first Service flier to make a parachute descent was Capt. C.F. Collett, RFC, who used a Calthrop 'Guardian Angel' for an experimental jump from a height of 600ft on 13 January 1917. A limited number of Guardian Angels were issued to the RAF shortly before the end of the war, but too late to be of much practical service to combat fliers.
PARACHUTIST TO MAKE A FREEFALL DESCENT: the first was Staff Sergeant Randall Bose of the US Army, who jumped from a height of 4,500ft over Mitchell Field, Long Island, in 1924 and delayed pulling his rip-cord until he had fallen for 1,500ft. The experiment was made to win a bet from a friend that he would not be able to drop for 1,000ft and still open his parachute.

The first freefall parachutist to use the spreadeagle skydiving position to control his descent was American Spud Manning, who pioneered the technique in 1931 with a jump from 15,000ft. The following year he performed aerobatics in the course of a descent. Modern skydiving as a sport originated in France c. 1946.
SPORT PARACHUTING CLUB: the first was formed at Tushiro Aerodrome, Moscow in 1933. Russia had pioneered sport parachuting three years earlier with the holding of the first Soviet Parachute Sport Festival. During the course of the 1930s hundreds of local clubs were formed and practice-jump

platforms erected in most of the public parks, a development that enabled Russia to maintain a world lead in the training of parachutists.

The first
PARISH MAGAZINE
was the *St Michael's, Derby Parish Magazine*, a monthly founded by the Rev. John Erskine Clarke in January 1859. The first number cost 1d and had an illustrated cover showing the Church, various houses and cottages, and a school with boys playing football outside. The contents were lively with stories, poems, children's features, thrilling tales of missionary life and extracts from recent books, as well as general news of the parish and church activities. An 'Answers to Correspondents' column was started in the third issue for those 'who do not exactly understand statements or allusions made in the Services and Sermons and who yet from fear to trench on our time or dislike to acknowledge their own ignorance, refrain from seeking that information we would be too glad to give. . . .'

The first
PARKING METER
was devised by Carlton Magee, the Editor of a leading Oklahoma City newspaper, who was appointed Chairman of a Businessmen's Traffic Committee set up in 1933 to inquire into methods of imposing stricter parking controls in the town. Magee established the Dual Parking Meter Co, so called because the meters were designed to serve the dual purpose of regulation and revenue. The Oklahoma City Traffic Authority gave the Company an initial order of 150 units and the first parking meters came into service on 16 July 1935.
GB: Six hundred and twenty-five meters were installed in north-west Mayfair by Westminster City Council and came into operation on 10 July 1958. The charge was 6d for 1hr, 1s for 2hr, with an excess payment of 10s for a further 2hr or part thereof, and a £2 penalty for any waiting time exceeding 4hr.

The first
PEDESTRIAN CROSSING
in GB was established in Parliament Square, London at the instigation of the London Traffic Advisory Committee in December 1926. The crossing was indicated by a square white sign on a metal post bearing a cross, a directional arrow, and the words PLEASE CROSS HERE. Others were erected at 16 points in Piccadilly Circus, the Haymarket and neighbouring streets the following August. Principal crossings were marked with two parallel white lines

The installation of Britain's first pedestrian crossing, Parliament Square, 1926

painted across the road. In 1933–4 these were replaced with a herring-bone pattern of white lines, and the square board gave way to a large circular sign marked with the letter 'C'.

In 1934, a new type of standardized crossing marked by studs on the road and yellow beacons on the pavement was introduced at the behest of the Minister of Transport, Sir Leslie Hore-Belisha. The name 'Belisha Beacon' for the pavement signs, which were first erected in Kensington Road in September, was suggested in a letter to *The Times* of 13 October 1934 from Mr H. Lang Jones of West Dulwich in response to an earlier correspondent who had favoured 'Beleacon'. The original beacons were made of glass and were the constant prey of small boys with stones, so that it soon became necessary to replace them with painted aluminium globes. Plastic beacons with winking lights were introduced in July 1952.
ZEBRA CROSSINGS were introduced in 1951, with regulations effective from 31 October.

The first
PENICILLIN
was discovered by Dr Alexander Fleming at St Mary's Hospital, Paddington, London in September 1928. Having been absent on holiday since the previous month, Fleming had left a pile of culture plates in a corner of the laboratory beyond the reach of the sun. These were about to be submerged in antiseptic when he took a number of plates from off the pile in order to demonstrate a point to Research Scholar D.M. Pryce. One of the plates displayed unusual characteristics, as there was an absence of staphylococcal colonies in the vicinity of the mould. Following an intensive study of the phenomenon, Fleming made his initial findings known when he read a paper, 'Cultures of a Penicillium', to the Medical Research Club on 13 February 1929. Audience reaction was nil, no questions being asked at the end as was customary when a theory or new discovery had excited the members' interest.
CLINICAL APPLICATION OF CRUDE PENICILLIN was first made at St Mary's on 9 January 1929, when Fleming treated his assistant, Stuart Craddock, for an infected antrum by washing out the sinus with diluted penicillin broth and succeeded in destroying most of the staphylococci. Rather more effective use of the drug was made in 1931 at the Royal Infirmary, Sheffield. Here Dr C.G. Paine successfully relieved two cases of gonococcal ophthalmitis in children (gonorrhoea contracted from their mothers at birth) and one of an adult suffering from severe pneumococcal infection of the eye. The latter was a Colliery Manager who had been injured down the pit when a small piece of stone had lodged behind the pupil of his right eye. Penicillin cleared the infection, enabling an operation to be carried out to remove the chipping. The patient subsequently recovered his normal vision. These were probably the first cases in which ordinary hospital patients were successfully treated with penicillin, though all these applications were local and no attempt was made to establish the possibility of effective chemotherapy of the common bacterial infections. There was little further development during the remainder of the decade.
PURIFIED PENICILLIN was first prepared at the Sir William Dunn School of Pathology during the summer of 1940 by Prof. Howard Florey of Adelaide, South Australia, and Prof. Ernest Chain, a German-born Jewish refugee. Florey announced the results of their research in a paper titled 'Penicillin as a Chemotherapeutic Agent', which appeared in the *Lancet* for 24 August 1940.
CLINICAL APPLICATION OF PURIFIED PENICILLIN first took place at the Radcliffe Infirmary, Oxford on 12 February 1941, the patient being a policeman suffering from generalized blood poisoning from a small sore at the corner of his mouth. A striking improvement was made in his condition after 800mg of penicillin had been administered in 24hr, but within five days Florey's team had exhausted the entire world supply of the drug and on 15 March the patient died.

The first completely successful treatment with penicillin began at the Radcliffe Infirmary on 3 May 1941, when a patient suffering from a 4in carbuncle was administered the drug intravenously. Within four days the infected area was already healing and on 15 May the patient was discharged from hospital.

The first large-scale plant for the regular production of penicillin was constructed at the Sir William Dunn School of Pathology at Oxford under the direction of Prof. Chain in the summer of 1941. The first commercial firm to undertake production of penicillin was Kemball, Bishop & Co of Bromley-by-Bow, which delivered its initial consignment of twenty 10-gal churns of penicillin brew to the School of Pathology 'as a free gift in the interest of science' on 11 September 1942.

Sir Alexander Fleming, Sir Howard Florey and Dr E.B. Chain were jointly awarded the Nobel Prize in October 1945 for their work on penicillin.

The first known
PERAMBULATOR
was a miniature carriage built at Chatsworth *c.* 1733 by William Kent on behalf of the 3rd Duke of Devonshire. This elegant little vehicle was fitted with 21in wheels at the rear and 16in wheels in front and had a body in the shape of a scallop shell with folding hood. Its most bizarre feature was the undercarriage, a framework made up of bronze snakes imitative of the Cavendish snakes that form part of the Devonshire family crest. Shafts and a small collar indicate that it was intended to be drawn by a dog.

The only surviving perambulator that might possibly be contemporary with the Chatsworth example is a *voiture d'enfant* in the collection of the French Musée National de la Voiture at the Château de Compiègne. This has been claimed by some historians to have been built for Louis XV's infant Dauphin (b. 1729), but the Director of the Museum is of the opinion that it is of German rather than French origin and most likely to date from the second half of the 18th century.

William Kent's pram of the 1730s does not appear to have inspired any imitators in England until a second, Surrey-style baby carriage was built at Chatsworth in 1780. This was fitted with a long curved handle so that it could be drawn by a footman. None of the many 18th-century portraits of children provide evidence of perambulators being used by other aristocratic families between these dates, though the *Autobiography of Francis Place* contains a passage which suggests that in a rude form they were already known at the other end of the social scale. Francis Place, pioneer birth-controller and radical agitator, was born in Holborn in 1771, the son of a failed baker. Writing about his early childhood, he recalled that it was one of his father's customary amusements to

take all the children and my mother on an excursion to the Cock on Clapham Common, or to Hornsey Wood, or to Wimbledon common or to a Public House at Winchmore Hill. The smaller children were dragged along in a child's chaise. A bottle of wine was always put into the seat of the chaise as was also a convex glass now in my possession with which to light his pipe, sometimes provision for the day was also taken. These journeys were to me excessively fatiguing, as every one who was able was compelled to share the labour of dragging the chaise.

The children who rode in the chaise were Place's younger brother George, born in 1773, and his youngest sister Ann, born in 1775. The date of these excursions, then, seems likely to have been 1777 or 1778. The chaise was evidently quite large, since it was able to accommodate not only two sitting children but also a miscellany of refreshments and belongings. It is not surprising that at the age of about seven young Francis Place found it fatiguing to walk, and sometimes drag a heavy perambulator, the 18 miles to Wimbledon and back. The fact that the chaise is described as having a seat makes it clear that this was not a stick-wagon, a kind of miniature tumbril that originated among the Kentish hop-pickers and is known to have been used fairly extensively by working-class mothers for trundling their children about during the early years of the 19th century. Unlike the Place children, accustomed to sharing a seat with a bottle of wine, juvenile stick-wagon passengers were obliged to ride standing up, unless they chose to squat on the floor.

The Cavendish permabulator, believed to date from 1733. Note the snakes

REGULAR MANUFACTURE OF PERAMBULATORS began in 1850, when rival concerns were established by John Allen in the Hackney Road and by A. Babin of New Street in the City of London. Both produced similar models that owed nothing to the scaled-down road carriages built previously by individual craftsmen for the aristocracy or the stick-wagons of the peasantry, but broke new ground with a push-chair body mounted on three wheels. Hitherto all perambulators had been dragged, not pushed.

DOLL'S PRAM: the first was made in 1862 by the employees of perambulator-manufacturer J.R. Frampton of Trinity Street for his small daughter. Frampton himself was not particularly impressed and dismissed a suggestion that a lucrative trade might be done in toy prams. They were, he declared, just 'nonsense'. Other manufacturers were quick to see the potentiality of the idea and reaped considerable profits from it.

Prior to 1876 nearly all perambulators were of the push-chair type, designed for children old enough to sit up. In that year a number of firms introduced basinette models in which a small baby could lie full length. Like a miniature brougham in appearance, they were really the prototype of the modern pram. It must remain one of the mysteries of the pram trade why such a seemingly obvious development took so long to come to fruition. A parallel advance took place in the USA, though generally the American models were cruder and lacked the elegance of their English counterpart. 'An inartistic, uncomfortable vehicle, its body made of cane or other vegetable product' is how the Editor of the *Pram Gazette* described the American basinette, adding sententiously: 'That class of pram scarcely suits British tastes.'

It is unlikely that any other invention based on so simple a concept as the perambulator has ever been the subject of so many patents, well over 3,000 having been granted since the first in 1853. Some represented genuine advances in design, the majority, however, leaving little imprint on perambulator history. The petrol-engined pram of 1921, which accommodated its driver standing up on a rear platform, has passed into the same limbo as the perambulator which turned into a bath, the garden-roller that turned into a perambulator, and the floating pram shaped like a canoe. Other flights of fancy included a carriage propelled by the baby itself, who was expected to keep the mechanism in motion by alternately rising and sitting.

The first
PERMANENT WAVING

was introduced by Karl Ludwig Nessler, who was born at Todtnau in the Black Forest in 1872, the same year as Paris stylist Marcel Grateau devised his Marcel Wave. The son of a poor shoemaker, Nessler would have been apprenticed to his father's trade but for defective eyesight. Instead he became a hairdresser, first in Switzerland, then in Paris, where he learned the art of Marcel waving. By the time he arrived in London in 1901 he was already experimenting with a device of his own designed to make Marcel's *Ondulations* longer lasting. One day he tried it out on a client, but was detected by his employer and instantly dismissed. Fortunately he had sufficient savings to open a salon of his own in Great Castle Street and to develop his machine. On the evening of 8 October 1906, the permanent wave was publicly demonstrated for the first time before an audience of hairstylists invited by Nessler to his latest salon at 245 Oxford Street. There was no doubt that the system was effective, but the trade was not enthusiastic. The machine was large and cumbersome, the client was obliged to wear a dozen brass curlers each weighing 1¾lb, and the whole difficult process took over 6hr to complete. It was also expensive, and it is not surprising that at 10gns per application Nessler's customers for his Nestlé permanent waving averaged scarcely 70 a year. With the outbreak of World War I he emigrated to the USA rather than face internment as an alien. It was a fortuitous move, for in 1915 the celebrated exhibition ballroom-dancer Irene Castle introduced the 'bobbed' hairstyle to America and permanent waving became the rage.

The first
PETROL PUMP

was made by Sylvanus F. Bowser of Fort Wayne, Ind. and delivered to local store-keeper Jake Gumper on 5 September 1885. Despite the date, which coincided almost exactly with Karl Benz's first attempts to fit an internal-combustion engine to a horseless carriage, this ancestor of all petrol pumps had nothing to do with motoring or the motorist. Jake Gumper had drawn Bowser's attention to a problem concerned with the retailing of kerosene, and more particularly of butter, that was bringing his name into poor repute with his more fastidious customers. The kerosene barrel, which leaked, stood next to the butter cask and complaints had been received that the butter tasted of paraffin. The simplest solution would have been to remove one of the casks to another part of the store; fortunately for posterity neither Gumper nor Bowser appear to have thought of this. Instead Bowser set to work in a barn next to the store, and devoted his mind to devising a means of dispensing lamp oil in given quantities. The result was a round tank with a cylinder soldered inside and an outlet pipe coming from the top of the tank. A hand-operated piston controlling two marble valves and wooden plungers was fitted inside the cylinder. When the wooden handle was raised, a gallon of kerosene flowed from the tank into the cylinder; when lowered the kerosene was discharged.

Although Bowser established a flourishing manufacturing concern to undertake production of his brainchild, the marriage of the petrol pump to the motor car did not come about for another 20 years. The first self-measuring pump designed specifically for motor spirit was introduced by S.F. Bowser & Co Inc at Fort Wayne in 1905.

Two other major developments of the Company included the first petrol pump to register quantity on a clock dial, the Bowser Red Sentry of 1925, and the first pump to incorporate an automatic price-indicator, marketed on 1 November 1932.

GB: Hand-operated petrol pumps were installed at a number of petrol-filling stations (*see also* Service Station) in Britain in 1920. The first automatic pump, by Bowser, was put into operation by a Manchester garage in 1921.

The first
PHOTOCOPIER

was marketed by the Rectigraph Co of Rochester, N.Y. in 1907. The patentee of the Rectigraph machine was George C. Beidler, who conceived the idea four years earlier while working in an Oklahoma City land-claim office. The need for constant duplication of legal documents led him to search for a better means than retyping or laborious copying by hand, his initial experiments being made with an ordinary dry-plate camera. The prototype Rectigraph photocopier followed and was patented in 1906.

The first
PHOTOGRAPH

from nature, permanently fixed, was taken by Nicéphore Niepce from an upper-storey window at his house at Gras, near Chalon-sur-Saône, France, probably in the summer of 1826, and represents a view of the courtyard with a pigeon-house on the left, a pear tree, bakehouse and barn in the centre, and another wing of the house to the right of the picture. It was made in a camera obscura obtained from the Paris firm of opticians Chevalier et fils in January of the same year. A metal plate was rendered light sensitive with a solution of bitumen of Judea and exposed in the camera for about 8hr. The latent image was then developed by washing the plate with a mixture of oil of lavender and white petroleum, a process that dissolved away those parts of the bitumen that had not been hardened by light. The resulting picture was a permanent direct positive.

During the following year, while on a visit to his brother at Kew, Niepce presented this photograph to the English naturalist Francis Bauer. It was lost in 1898 and only recovered in 1952, when it was discovered in a trunk that had been stored unopened in an English country-house since 1917. The pewter plate was then presented by the owner to the photographic historian Helmut Gernsheim, who had been instrumental in locating it. A halftone of the original made by the Kodak research laboratory was reproduced in *The Times* for 15 April 1952, the first occasion the photograph had been seen publicly since it was taken 126 years earlier. The world's first true photograph is now in the Gernsheim Collection at the University of Texas. Niepce died in 1833 before his process was sufficiently developed for commercial exploitation (*see below*). Most of his energies during the 19 years he spent in research were concentrated on photographic art reproduction, and only one other fixed image from nature is known. This was a still-life made on glass in 1829, which shows a table laid for a meal. The original plate was smashed by a madman in 1909, but a rather poor halftone made in 1891 indicates the progress made by Niepce in three years. In contrast with the impressionistic 1826 view at Gras, every object in the still-life study is almost perfectly defined.

GB: The earliest surviving photograph is a paper negative made by William Henry Fox Talbot of a central leaded window in the South Gallery of Lacock Abbey, his Wiltshire home, and labelled by him on the back: 'Latticed window (with camera obscura), August 1835. When first made the squares of glass, about 200 in number, could be counted with the help of a lens.' Talbot used ordinary writing-paper sensitized with silver chloride, which he exposed for ½hr in the miniature camera obscuras made for him by the local carpenter at Lacock. He wrote in *The Pencil of Nature* (1844):

With these I obtained very perfect but extremely small pictures, such as . . . might be supposed to be the work of some Lilliputian artist. . . . In the summer of 1835 I made in this way a great number of representations of my house in the country, which is well suited to the purpose, from its ancient and remarkable architecture.

Talbot had been inspired to invent a means of fixing the camera's image by his own inability to draw accurately. The original latticed-window negative is preserved in the Science Museum Collection. This and other studies of Lacock he exhibited for the first time at the Royal Institution on 25 January 1839 – two and a half weeks after the Frenchman Daguerre (*see below*) had announced success in the same field. Up until this time Talbot had been working solely with negatives. His major contribution to photography, the negative-positive process, was described in the 2 February 1839 issue of the *Literary Gazette*. Helmut Gernsheim has written that in this single brief paragraph Talbot 'laid the foundations of modern photography; a negative which can be used for the production of an unlimited number of positive copies'.

COMMERCIALLY SUCCESSFUL PHOTOGRAPHIC PROCESS: the first was introduced in September 1839 by Louis J. M. Daguerre, proprietor of the Diorama in Paris, who had formed a partnership with Nicéphore Niepce 10 years earlier for the improvement of the latter's system of 'heliography'. Daguerre's advances in technique enabled the exposure time for a photograph to be reduced from about 8hr to only 15–30min. His results were published for the first time in a report made by the distinguished astronomer Dominique-François Arago to the French Academy of Sciences on 7 January 1839. In response to Arago's urging, the Government acquired the rights from Daguerre and Isidore Niepce, Nicéphore's heir, and made the method public property for all the world to use on 19 August 1839. (It was not known then that Daguerre had patented the process in England five days earlier.) Details of the process were announced at the same time and caused an immediate sensation in Paris. 'An hour later', wrote Ludwig Pfau, a German living in Paris at the time, 'all the opticians' shops were besieged, but could not rake together enough instruments to satisfy the onrushing army of would-be daguerreotypists; a few days later you could see in all the squares of Paris three-legged dark-boxes planted in front of churches and palaces.' Cameras manufactured to Daguerre's specifications (*see* Photographic Camera) went on sale the following month.

PHOTOGRAPH OF A LIVING PERSON: the first was a study made on paper by the Rev. Joseph Bancroft Reade in 1838 of his gardener leaning against the greenhouse in the grounds of the Vicarage at Stone, Buckinghamshire.

The first studio portrait was a daguerreotype of John Johnson taken by his partner Alexander Wolcott, instrument-maker, in New York on 7 October 1839. Wolcott and Johnson opened the world's first commercially run photographic portrait studio (*q.v.*) the following March.

The first
PHOTOGRAPH, AERIAL
(successful) was taken by the French aeronaut 'Nadar' (Gaspard Felix Tournachon) from a balloon 262ft above the Val de Bièrre on the outskirts of Paris during the last week of 1858.

GB: The first aerial photograph was made on a wet collodion plate by Henry Negretti from a balloon 4,000ft above the Valley of the Medway in 1863.

STILL PHOTOGRAPHS TAKEN FROM AN AEROPLANE: the first

Charles Shaw and the pilot M. Beau before take-off, and below, the first photograph taken from an aeroplane over Britain – Burton-on-Trent, 1910

were shots of the Camp de Châlons Airfield, near Rheims, taken in December 1909 by M. Meurisse of the Beranger Picture Agency while flying in an Antoinette monoplane piloted by Hubert Latham. Curiously this was over a year after the first cinematograph film had been made from an aeroplane. The four pictures, one of which showed another aircraft in flight, were reproduced in the Christmas issue of *l'Illustration*.
GB: The first photograph taken from an aeroplane was the work of Charles Shaw, Staff Photographer of the *Nottingham Guardian*, who photographed the river at Burton-on-Trent from an altitude of 400ft on 30 September 1910. The picture appeared in the *Guardian* the next day. Shaw had travelled to Burton after hearing that there were three French pilots giving a display there. He managed to persuade one of them, M. Beau, to take him up in a Farman biplane and though remarking on the absence of any sense of danger, found that changing plates while trying to hold on to the camera and his life was a formidable business. 'More than once the picture machine was all but blown away', he commented afterwards. 'Combining flight and photography is attempting almost too much to be pleasant as a regular pursuit.'

The first
PHOTOGRAPHIC CAMERA
manufactured for sale was marketed by Alphonse Giroux of Paris in September 1839, price 400 francs. A manufacturing agreement between Giroux and the inventor, Louis Daguerre (*see also* Photograph), had been signed on 22 June of the same year. The wooden camera measured $10\frac{1}{2} \times 12\frac{1}{4} \times 14\frac{1}{2}$in closed, and was fitted with an achromatic lens by Charles Chevalier of Paris. The firm of Giroux et Cie were the first photographic dealers in the world, supplying all the equipment necessary for daguerreotypy from their shop at 7 rue de Coq, Saint-Honoré.
GB: Giroux cameras were advertised for sale in the April 1841 issue of the *Art Union* by Britain's first photographic dealers, Claudet & Houghton of 89 High Holborn, London.

The first
PHOTOGRAPHIC CAMERA FILM
(flexible) was patented by Alfred Pumphrey of Birmingham in April 1881 and manufactured by his own factory the following year. Formed of collodion and hardened gelatine coated with gelatine emulsion, Pumphrey's films were retailed in packets of 12 and were obtainable in various sizes from $3\frac{1}{4} \times 4\frac{1}{4}$in to 8×10in. They could be used in any kind of standard plate camera or with his own patent 100-Fold Filmograph magazine camera, which took up to 100 photographs at one loading.
CELLULOID FILM: the first was Carbutt's Flexible Negative Film, developed by John Carbutt of Philadelphia and announced before a meeting of the Photographic Society of Philadelphia on 7 November 1888. It was manufactured from sheets of celluloid $\frac{1}{100}$in thick, which Carbutt obtained from the Celluloid Manufacturing Co. On 21 November of the same year he exhibited the first flexible transparencies to be made into slides at a demonstration held for members of the Franklin Institute. Regular production of Carbutt Eclipse film was under way by the following July.
CELLULOID ROLL FILM: the first to be manufactured commercially was marketed by the Eastman Dry Plate Co of Rochester, N.Y. on 27 August 1889 for use in their new Kodak camera. Although they secured a patent in December of the same year, the Eastman Co had been pre-empted by an application for a patent on transparent nitrocellulose roll film filed by the Rev. Hannibal Goodwin of Newark, N.J. on 2 May 1887. The specification being inadequate, his patent was not granted until 1898, and the Goodwin Film & Camera Co only started manufacture in 1902, two years after his death.

The first
PHOTOGRAPHIC PORTRAIT STUDIO
was opened at 52 1st Street, New York by Alexander Wolcott and John Johnson and announced as 'the first daguerreotype gallery for portraits' in the *New York Sun* for 4 March 1840. Exposure time was 3–5min, and the fee for a single portrait was $3.
GB: Established by ex-coal-merchant Richard Beard at the Royal Polytechnic Institution, London on 23 March 1841. The cameramen were J.F. Goddard and J.T. Cooper, both experienced operators. Beard himself knew little about photography, but a lot about making money. Before the end of the year the studio was taking an average of £60 a day. Owing to the long exposure necessary, sitters had to have their heads clamped into what one reporter described as 'a kind of neck-iron' to keep them from moving. In compensation for this rather uncomfortable ordeal, the customer was able to take away his neatly framed and glazed $2 \times 1\frac{1}{2}$in likeness only 5min or so after being released from restraint. The immediacy of the process has scarcely been bettered by present-day passport-photographers.
PHOTOGRAPHIC STUDIO TO OFFER PORTRAITS IN NATURAL COLOUR: the first was the St James's Studio, 45 Old Bond Street, London, established by the Rotary Photographic Co in 1906. The portraits were made by a three-colour process developed by the proprietors, enabling a carbon print to be taken from three separate negatives representing each of the primary colours.

For the first woman to open a portrait studio, *see* Woman Photographer.

The first
PHOTOGRAPHIC SOCIETY
was the Friends of Daguerreotypy, formed at Vienna in 1840 by Karl Schuh, a daguerreotypist from Berlin who one year later became Austria's first professional portrait-photographer. Regular meetings were held at which members displayed their work.
GB: The Edinburgh Calotype Club is believed to have been founded in 1842 shortly after William Henry Fox Talbot (*see also* Photograph) had communicated news of his discovery of the calotype process to the noted Scottish scientist Sir David Brewster. The members, nearly all of whom practised as advocates or were otherwise connected with the Parliament House, included Prof. Cosmo Innes, John Stewart of Napier Hall, and David Octavius Hill. The Calotype Club was almost certainly the world's first exclusively amateur photographic society. Meetings were held over breakfast at each of the members' houses alternately, except when some particularly notable advance had been achieved, when a formal dinner was arranged in recognition. The Club maintained two large photographic albums to which members contributed copies of their best work. From these it is apparent that they began by photographing scenes in and around Edinburgh itself, then moved farther afield, making studies of ancient buildings and views at Elgin and Dunblane, Melrose, Dunrobin, Traquair, Stirling and Glamis. A number of foreign scenes were contributed from Antwerp, Rouen and Rome, and one member travelled as far as Lima, Peru with his camera.

According to a 'Reminiscence of the Calotype Club' published in the *British Journal of Photography* in 1874, one difficulty encountered by members in the early days was the implacable opposition of their wives. 'They could not be taught', said the writer, 'to admire the dirty messes which were everywhere made, or to look with favour on the illustration of the effect of organic matter on nitrate of silver, as shown by their husbands' shirt sleeves and waistbands.' This problem was overcome, however, with the introduction of the albumen (white-of-egg) process in 1848, as the wives were delighted to have so many egg-yolks with which to make puddings.

The first
PHOTOGRAPH IN COLOUR
was a transparency of a tartan ribbon bow taken against a black velvet background by Thomas Sutton of Jersey, under the direction of the Scottish physicist James Clerk Maxwell and shown for the first time at the Royal Institution on 17 May 1861. Clerk Maxwell had the ribbon photographed three times, using colour filters consisting of bottles of red, green and blue liquids which were placed between the camera and the subject. Glass positives from the collodion negatives were then projected in register on a screen by three separate lanterns, each lantern being fitted with a filter to correspond with its transparency. Although the process was only of scientific value, in 1939 modern techniques were employed to make a colour print from the original negatives and a reproduction in the following year's *Penrose Annual* indicates that Clerk Maxwell had obtained an amazingly naturalistic effect.
COLOUR PRINT: the first was a picture of the spectrum, displayed before the Société Française de Photographie by Louis Ducos du Hauron on 7 May 1869. The inventor had patented his subtractive method of colour photography on 23 February of the same year. Du Hauron's earliest surviving colour print is a view of Angoulême taken in 1877, showing the red-roofed Romanesque Cathedral rising above honey-coloured houses and the greenish waters of the Charente river in the foreground.
SYSTEM OF COLOUR PHOTOGRAPHY TO BE DEVELOPED COMMERCIALLY: the first was patented by F.E. Ives of Philadelphia on 23 February 1890. Ives's Kromskop camera was fitted with two reflective mirrors by which three negatives of the same image might be obtained simultaneously through orange, green and blue-violet filters. The positive transparencies were combined in a special viewer, the Photochromoscope, and illuminated by red, green and blue-violet light respectively. The resulting single image appeared in natural colour. In 1896 Ives organized the Photochromoscope Syndicate Ltd of Clapham Common, London to produce viewers and lanterns for use with his Kromogram colour slides.

The first single-plate colour process and the first suitable for use by amateur photographers was introduced commercially by Sanger-Shepherd & Co of Red Lion Street, London in 1904. Within the next two years some four or five competing systems of colour photography came on the market, but it was not until the introduction of the Lumière Bros' Autochrome colour plates in 1907 that photography in natural colours can be said to have moved beyond the experimental stage.
COLOUR ROLL FILM: the first was Lignose, introduced in Germany in 1924. The first in Britain was Colorsnap Roll Film, marketed by Colour Snapshots Ltd in 1929. The Lignose concern was soon absorbed by Agfa and the film withdrawn from the market; Colorsnap likewise disappeared without making much impact. Amateurs had to wait until 1935 for a successful three-colour roll film in the form of Kodachrome. This was only really suitable for making transparencies, but was followed in 1942 by Kodacolour negative/positive film for colour prints.

The earliest surviving view card, 1872

The first
PICTURE POSTCARD
was engraved by 21-year-old Franz Rorich of Nuremberg and published at Zürich by J.H. Locher in 1872. It showed six small views of Zürich and was followed by two other cards each with three views of the city. During the same year Rorich and Locher produced view cards of Geneva, Basle, Schaffhausen, Rorschach and Neuchâtel, all Swiss towns, and of Lindau and Nuremberg in Germany. Rorich's 1872 Nuremberg card, which shows the city from the Mohrentor Gate, is the oldest surviving view card in the world. Collectors have identified earlier examples of official post-office cards bearing pictorial advertisements and decorated field postcards of the Franco-Prussian War, but these cannot be regarded as picture postcards in the accepted modern sense.
GB: Prior to 1894 there was a Post Office prohibition on the issue of any but official postcards (i.e. with a printed stamp). The relaxation of this rule on 1 September of that year enabled stationers and art-publishers to produce true picture postcards for the first time. The role of pioneer publisher is claimed by both George Stewart's of Edinburgh and F.T. Corkett's of Leicester, who produced views of their respective cities on $4\frac{1}{2} \times 3\frac{1}{2}$in court cards soon after the new regulation had come into force. However, the earliest surviving English view-card of authenticated date is postmarked Scarborough, 15 September 1894. This card, presently in the Collection of P.F. Hinton, bears a line-drawing of Scarborough Head and the Pier, but gives no indication of the publisher.

Picture-postcard sending and collecting had already become a mania in Europe by the mid 1890s. Growth in Britain was markedly slow, partly on account of poor standards of reproduction and unimaginative designs, but more so because of the singularly short-sighted policy of only selling them in packets of six. A general improvement in these respects coincided with a further relaxation in Post Office rules that allowed Britain to become the first country to issue picture postcards with a divided back, so that the message could be written on the same side as the address. In all other countries during the early years of the century the address side had to be left clear of extraneous matter, which meant in effect that the picture could never occupy the whole of the front if space was to be left for greetings. The change came about at the instigation of a German printer, F. Hartmann, who wanted to set up as a picture-postcard manufacturer in Britain, but was unwilling to do so under the existing restrictive regulations. Accordingly he submitted specimens of his divided-back postcards to the Postmaster-General, who not only approved his plan but requested the Editor of the *Picture Postcard Magazine* to publish a statement to this effect in the January 1902 issue. Curiously no formal amendment appears to have been made in the

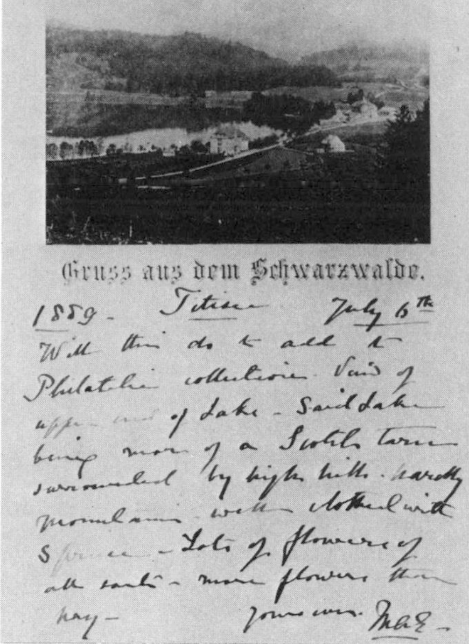

The first-known picture postcard (left) published in Great Britain, 1894; the first-known example with a photograph, 1889 (above)

regulations, only to their interpretation. The innovation heralded the emergence of the picture postcard in its modern form and was soon copied elsewhere, divided backs being introduced in France in 1904, Germany in 1905 and the USA in 1907.

COMIC PICTURE POSTCARDS were first published in Germany in 1880. In Britain the comic subject remained rare before 1902, but secured a permanent place in the canon of popular art with the introduction of what is generally known as the 'seaside postcard', a robustly vulgar genre originated by the fertile pen of Donald McGill. A naval architect by training, this prolific Scots-Canadian artist was not, as George Orwell suggested, a trade-name, but the richly inventive creator of 12,000 different postcards, the earliest-known example of which is No. 1140 in the Woodbury series, postmarked 7 December 1904. A sample of McGill's early humour in the pre-permissive society is a 1905 card showing a boy in bandsman's uniform sitting with his girl on a park bench, she with his swagger stick held in a suggestively erect position on her lap.

She: What are you thinking about, Tommy?
He: Same as you.
She: Oh, you naughty man!

For this and similar work he was paid a flat rate of 6s. By the time of his death in 1962 it was estimated that 350 million copies of his postcards had been sold; he died worth £735 gross.

PHOTOGRAPHICALLY ILLUSTRATED PICTURE POSTCARD: the earliest-known is a German *Gruss aus* (Greetings from) view of the lake at Schwarzwalde, posted on 6 July 1889. The monochrome photograph measures 3 × 2in, and is reproduced by the half-tone process. In Britain the first photographic cards were produced by Blum & Degan of London and Messrs Valentine of Dundee, *c.* 1898.

PHOTOGRAPHIC POSTCARDS IN NATURAL COLOURS were first issued in Germany by the Rotophot Co in Prof. Miethe's *Naturfarbenphotographie* process. The earliest-known example is a view of an unidentified village and is postmarked Hamburg, 16 October 1904.

PICTURE-POSTCARD ART REPRODUCTIONS are believed to have been issued first in Italy *c.* 1889. The earliest surviving dated example is a card published in Florence in 1891, showing Raphael's *Madonna della Seggiola*. The earliest-known British examples are a set of Turner paintings re-produced in full colour by Raphael Tuck & Sons of London in 1898–9.

The first *PILOTS' LICENCES*

(powered aircraft) were issued by the Aéro Club de France, without formal examination, to those pilots who had actually flown up to the end of December 1909. A list of 16 licence-holders was published on 1 January 1910, the names being arranged alphabetically to avoid any suggestion of precedence. By an unfortunate oversight it omitted the name of Charles Voisin, the first Frenchman to have made an officially recognized powered flight, while including, so it was claimed, a number of 'pilots' who had never flown at all. Thereafter licences were issued to pilots passing the Club's flying test, the first to qualify in this manner being the holder of brevet No. 17, Alfred Leblanc. Henry Farman's brevet, one of the original 16 and the first to be issued to a British subject, was back-dated to 7 January 1909.

GB: Royal Aero Club licence No. 1 was issued to J.T.C. Moore Brabazon (later Lord Brabazon of Tara) on 8 March 1910. The first four licences were granted automatically to pilots of proven experience. Licence No. 5 was granted to G.B. Cockburn on 26 April on the basis of his having satisfied the requirements of the Aéro Club de France in a test taken at Mourmelon on a Henry Farman biplane. The first pilot to pass the Royal Aero Club test was Alec Ogilvie, who was granted licence No. 7 on 24 May 1910 after qualifying at Camber Sands, Rye on his Short-built Wright Flier. The conditions of the test required that:

Three separate flights must be made, each of three miles round a circular course without coming to the ground. These flights need not necessarily be made on the same day. On the completion of each flight the engine must be stopped in the air, and a landing effected within 150yd of a given spot previously designated by the candidate to the official observers.

WOMAN TO BE GRANTED A LICENCE: the first was Mlle Elise Deroche, better known by her assumed title of Baroness de Laroche, who qualified for the brevet on 8 March 1910, though she had in fact flown solo the previous year (*see also* Woman Pilot).

GB: Hilda B. Hewlett, wife of the best-selling novelist Maurice Hewlett, took the Royal Aero Club test at

Brooklands on a Henry Farman biplane and was issued licence No. 122 on 29 August 1911.
GLIDER PILOT'S LICENCE (Royal Aero Club): the first was issued to C.H. Lowe-Wilde on 30 March 1930.
HELICOPTER PILOT'S LICENCE (Royal Aero Club): the first was issued to Wing-Cdr Reginald Brie, former Chief Test Pilot of the Cierva Autogiro Co, on 14 March 1947.

The first
PLASTIC
was Parkesine, a thermoplastic material produced from nitrocellulose, camphor and alcohol by Alexander Parkes of Birmingham and originally manufactured by the Parkesine Co at Hackney Wick, London in 1866. It was, the inventor said, a 'beautiful substance for the Arts, suitable for the production of medallions, salvers, holloware, cubes, buttons, combs, knife handles, pierced and fretwork, inlaid work, book binding, card cases, boxes and pen holders'. A number of these articles, and also plastic door-knobs and hand-mirrors, had been exhibited at the International Exhibition of 1862. An almost exactly similar thermoplastic was patented by John Wesley Hyatt of Albany, N.Y. on 15 June 1869, and given the name 'Celluloid'.

The first
PLASTIC SURGERY OPERATION
in Britain was performed at York Hospital, Chelsea on 23 October 1814, when Joseph Constantine Carpue built up a new nose from the integuments of the forehead for an Army officer who had lost his real nose through mercury poisoning. Carpue's method was based on information derived from an article published in the *Gentleman's Magazine* for October 1794 which described an operation undergone by one Cowasjee, a bullock-driver with the British Army in India whose nose had been cut off when he was taken prisoner. This involved drawing an outline of the new nose on the skin of the forehead, cutting about its edge, and drawing the flap of skin down and over to build up the required shape. Plastic surgery of this kind had been known in India since at least the 5th century AD, and was a particular skill of the Coomas, a caste of brickmakers in Hindustan. Carpue improved on their technique by creating a septum (the cartilage which divides the nostrils) and using sutures for grafting.

Plastic surgery was first practised on an extensive scale during World War I, when 11,000 maimed and disfigured British soldiers were effectively treated. The first special ward for plastic surgery was established under Sir William Arbuthnot-Lane at Cambridge Military Hospital, Aldershot in 1916. The first hospital devoted entirely to plastic surgery, Queen's Hospital at Sidcup, Kent, was founded under the direction of the New Zealand surgeon (Sir) Harold Gillies the following year. At the end of the war Gillies and T.P. Kilner became the first full-time civilian plastic surgeons.

The first
PLAYING-CARDS
were Chinese sheet dice, believed to have originated in the 10th Century AD, made to reproduce the notation of dice on paper. Others were derived from Chinese paper money, and it is thought that some of the earliest card games were played with actual bank-notes. The *T'u-shu-chi-ch'êng Encyclopaedia*, Book 807, folio 6, contains the following passage:

According to the History of the Liao Dynasty, the Emperor Mu Tsung, in the 19th year of the period Ying-li [AD 969] . . . made reference to the game of cards when he said to his ministers, 'Games of cards were played in the house of Duke Ch'ien, and in that very year in the second month he was killed by Siao-ho, ruler and subjects became victims of barbarity, and misfortune followed misfortune. Yet such unlucky objects are now held in the hand daily by scholars and officials. Is that not the following of an evil example?'

A Chinese playing-card believed to be the oldest surviving example in the world was found in 1905 by Dr A. von Le Coq together with fragments of manuscript dating from the Uigur period in the Sangim Valley nr Turfan, Chinese Turkestan. This card, which corresponds to the Red Flower of the modern Chinese pack, probably dates from the 11th century. It forms a narrow rectangle in shape, about three times as long as it is broad, and bears the figure of a man bordered by a thick black line. Characters inscribed at the top and bottom of the card denote the name of the maker.

The origin of playing-cards in Europe is obscure. The earliest reference in literature appears in an Italian manuscript by Pipozzo di Sandro titled 'Trattato del governo della famiglia', believed to date from 1299. This work contains a sentence that reads in translation: 'If he play for money in this manner, or at cards, you must facilitate the means of his doing so.' ('Se guichera di denari o cosi o alle carte, gli apparuchierai la vie.')

The earliest-known surviving examples of European playing-cards come from France. Charles Poupart, Treasurer to Charles VI, made the following entry in the accounts of the Royal Household for 1392: 'Paid to Jacquemin Gringonneur, painter, for three packs of cards [ieux de cartes] in gold and colours of divers devices, to present to the said lord the king for his amusement, 60 sols parisis.' These cards were intended to humour the monarch during his recurrent bouts of madness. Seventeen cards of this period from a Tarot pack, almost certainly dating from the last quarter of the 14th century, are preserved at the Bibliothèque Nationale in Paris and are thought to be examples of the actual cards painted by Gringonneur.

The earliest-known playing-cards printed in Europe, and the earliest to bear the four suits of the modern pack, were found in 1841 by the French antiquarian M. Henin in the cover of an old book he purchased in Lyons. These 10 cards had been used as stiffeners in the binding. All are court cards and the pictures on them are wood-engravings printed with a pale ink of brownish tint and afterwards coloured with a stencil. They are thought to date from *c.* 1440, and to have been made in Provence. They would doubtless have been used for playing Piquet, the earliest-known game played with the conventional (as opposed to Tarot) pack. Eight of the cards are preserved in the British Museum and two, the knave of clubs and the knave of spades, in the collection of the United States Playing Card Co, Cincinnati.
GB: The earliest written evidence of playing-cards in England is an Act of 1463 prohibiting the import of 'dyces, tenys balles, cardes for pleiying'. The earliest-known surviving examples of playing-cards believed to be of English manufacture were found in the cover of an undated volume of *c.* 1490 belonging to the Cathedral Library of Peterborough. From the costume designs they are thought to predate the 1463 Ordinance.
PLAYING-CARDS BEARING AN ADVERTISEMENT on the back were first issued by Thomas Tuttle, scientific- and mathematical-instrument maker of London, in 1700.
DOUBLE-HEAD COURT CARDS: the earliest known belong to a German pack issued in 1813 to celebrate the Battle of Leipzig. The kings are represented as the monarchs of the four allied countries on the victorious side; the knaves by portraits of the marshals commanding the armies in the battle; and the queens are personified as Pomona, Flora, Diana and Ceres. Double-head court cards remained rare until the middle of the 19th century.
JOKER: the earliest known is contained in a London Club pack issued by

Samuel Hart & Co of 222–228 West 14th Street, New York in 1857.

The first
PNEUMATIC TYRES
were patented by civil engineer R. W. Thompson of London on 10 December 1845 as an 'Improvement in Carriage Wheels which is also applicable to other rolling bodies'. The specification read in part:

The belt [viz. *inner tube*] *may be made of a single thickness of india rubber or gutta percha in a sheet state and suphurised . . . and then enclosed in a canvas cover. A strong outer casing in which to hold the elastic belt is then built up (so to speak) around the tyre by riveting together a series of circular segments of leather and bolting them to the tyre. . . .*

Thompson's pneumatic tyres were demonstrated publicly for the first time the following summer. The *Mechanic's Magazine* for 22 August 1846 reported:

The interest of the visitors to the parks this week has been much excited by the appearance among the crowd of gay equipages of a brougham with silent wheels, so silent as to suggest a practical inconsistency of a most startling character between the name and quality of the thing. The tyres of the wheels consist of elastic tubular rings, made, we believe, of caoutchouc enclosed in leather cases and inflated with air to any degree of tightness desired.

The motion of the carriage is exceedingly easy. We are informed that it is now gone about a hundred miles over roads of all sorts, even some which are newly macadamized, and that the outer leather casing is (contrary to what might have been expected) as sound and entire as at first, not exhibiting in any part of it the slightest tendency to rupture.

The tyres were subsequently tested on a number of heavy wagons and demonstrated an improvement in tractive effort of 60% over iron tyres when used on smooth roads and over 30% on rough roads.

In the spring of 1847 the *Mechanic's Magazine* announced that Messrs Whitehurst & Co had secured a licence to fit Thompson's Ariel wheels to any type of carriage and that a demonstration model was on view at their Oxford Street showroom. The first recorded sale of pneumatic tyres was made to Lord Loraine of Albury Park, Guildford, who had them fitted to his brougham by a local firm, Messrs May & Jacobs, on 1 October 1847. The price paid was £44 2s for a set of four. In 1895 these same tyres were found rotting in a barn and sold to the Dunlop Co for £500.

Demand however was limited and as the tyres had to be made by hand they were correspondingly expensive. Over 70 bolts were used to fasten them to the wheel, so they were not easily detachable.

PNEUMATIC BICYCLE TYRE: the first was made by John Boyd Dunlop, a prosperous Belfast veterinary surgeon who had gained experience in working with rubber while devising various appliances for use in connection with his profession. At the time that he 'reinvented' the pneumatic tyre he had never ridden a bicycle in his life.

Dunlop's attention was originally drawn to the need for an improved cycle tyre one day in October 1887 as he stood watching his 10-year-old son Johnnie riding his tricycle round the garden and leaving deep tracks in the turf. The precursor of all Dunlop tyres was fashioned from a length of garden hose and filled not with air, but with water. Happily the Dunlops' family doctor, Sir John Fagan, was looking on and he, having had considerable experience of inflatable cushions and mattresses for the sick, suggested blowing the tyre up with air. This time Dunlop used sheet-rubber for the tube, which he attached to a wooden disc with a linen cover tacked on to the sides and inflated with a football pump.

Dunlop's first pair of cycle tyres were fitted to the rear wheels of Johnnie's Edlin Quadrant tricycle on the night of 28 February 1888 and ridden on by the boy that same evening.

In June 1888 Dunlop purchased a bicycle from Edlin & Co and fitted it with pneumatic tyres covered with finest Gents' Yacht sail-cloth from Arbroath. The success of this full-size machine encouraged Edlin's to enter into an agreement with the veterinary surgeon for the manufacture of racing safeties fitted with his tyres and on 19 December 1888 this historic advertisement in the *Irish Cyclist* announced the birth of a new industry:

Look out for the new Pneumatic Safety. Vibration impossible. Sole makers – W. Edlin and Co, Garfield Street, Belfast.

The front forks of the Pneumatic Safety were specially widened to a breadth of 2in to allow for the swollen girth of Dunlop's tyre, which was covered by two layers of canvas stuck together with rubber solution, the overlapping ends of the outer layer being bound round the rim of the wheel. Only cycles equipped with pneumatics were sold – about 50 during the first year of manufacture – and the tyres could not be purchased separately. The success of his tyre on the race-track encouraged Dunlop to undertake manufacture on his own account. The Pneumatic Tyre and Booth's Cycle Agency Ltd issued its first prospectus on 18 November 1889 and a small manufacturing plant was established in Dublin early in the New Year.

Dunlop's patent for 'an improvement in Tyres for the wheels of bicycles, tricycles and other road cars' had been taken out on 31 October 1888. Robert Thompson's earlier patent did not come to light until early in 1890 and the unwelcome knowledge was kept secret by the Pneumatic Tyre Co. Details, however, were published in the magazine *Sport and Play* on 30 September of that year. Replying in a later issue Dunlop wrote:

When I made my first tyre I was not aware of the registration of such a patent, and indeed it was not until long afterwards that I heard of it. Had I known that such a thing was in existence I would never have taken the trouble to get mine registered, but would have kept it for my son's amusement.

Although Dunlop's master patent had been invalidated, leaving the field wide open to other manufacturers, the Pneumatic Tyre Co continued to prosper and by April 1891 was turning out some 3,000 tyres a week. With the development of detachable pneumatics the solid cycle tyre was virtually a relic of the past.

PNEUMATIC MOTOR-CAR TYRES: the first were fitted to a 4hp Daimler by the Paris cycle-tyre manufacturer Edouard Michelin, who drove the car in the Paris–Bordeaux Race of 11 June 1895. Although 22 tyre-changes were necessary over the 1,200km route, Michelin succeeded in finishing 9th out of 19 entrants, achieving speeds of up to 25kph on the level. Each tyre was screwed to the wheel with 20 nuts and bolts.

GB: The first motor vehicle in Britain to be fitted with pneumatic tyres was built by Frederick Lanchester at Saltley, nr Birmingham, and test run in February or early March of 1896. The tyres were specially made for him by the Dunlop Co and were the first car pneumatics the Company had attempted. Since they had no pattern tools available for this kind of work, the tyres had to be made entirely by hand. Dunlop started to manufacture pneumatic motor tyres on a regular basis in 1900, but as they wore out after an average distance of 400 miles they took some while to find general acceptance among motorists.

BUS WITH PNEUMATIC TYRES: the first was a $2\frac{1}{4}$-ton De Dion-Bouton steam omnibus built in Paris and fitted with $4\frac{1}{2}$in Michelin tyres late in 1900.

This was the first motor vehicle of substantial weight to be run on pneumatics.

GOODS VEHICLE TO BE FITTED WITH PNEUMATIC TYRES: the first was a 1½-ton 8hp Daimler petrol lorry of German manufacture, supplied to the Dunlop Pneumatic Tyre Co in July 1902 and used daily for delivering stocks of tyres from Dunlop's Clerkenwell Road depot in London. Few heavy goods vehicles were driven on pneumatic tyres until the 1920s.

AIRCRAFT TO BE FITTED WITH PNEUMATIC TYRES: the first was the Vuia I built by the Rumanian-born aviator Trajan Vuia, and first tested at Montesson, France on 3 March 1906. The tyres were of some practical service, as the Vuia I covered a greater distance on the ground than it ever did in the air. Although five 'flights' were made in this aircraft, the longest, and last, was for a length of only 24m, terminating in a crash-landing.

TUBELESS TYRES: the first to prove commercially successful were manufactured by the B.F. Goodrich Co of Akron, Ohio, who began test marketing the puncture-proof tyres in Indiana, Ohio, Kentucky and West Virginia on 11 May 1947.

The first POLICE CAR

The first occasion on which a motor car was used for police-work in Britain occurred in April 1899, when Sgt McLeod of the Northamptonshire County Police borrowed a Benz vehicle, belonging to Jack Harrison, to pursue a man who was selling forged tickets for the Barnum & Bailey Circus in Northampton. The chase continued up the Weedon Road until the fugitive was apprehended between Harpole and Flore. Referring to the mandatory speed limit, the *Autocar* drily commented: 'We are not told if twelve miles an hour was exceeded at any part of the chase.'

The 'Flying Bedstead' with roof-mounted wireless aerials – Britain's first radio police car

The first motor car regularly employed on police-work was a Stanley Steamer acquired by the Boston (Mass.) Police Department in the summer of 1903. It replaced four horses formerly used for patrol duties in the Back Bay area. A traffic squad was already in operation at St Louis, Mo. by June 1905, when it was reported in the *Automobile* that the force was in need of faster and more powerful machines in order to overtake speed-limit violators.

GB: The first police cars were four open tourers and 12 two-seater Fords, purchased by the Metropolitan Police in 1919, the former for the use of the Assistant Commissioners and the latter for Superintendents.

The first cars used by the police in combating crime were two ex-RDF Crossley tenders appropriated to the Flying Squad in September 1920 (*see also* Police Detectives: Flying Squad). The following year these vehicles became the first police cars equipped with radio, being fitted with large roof-top aerials mounted on adjustable arms. Known among the criminal fraternity as the 'Flying Bedsteads', the Flying Squad took elaborate measures to disguise their conspicuous outline. The vehicles would appear in a different disguise daily, sometimes as milk trucks or railway lorries, at others as newspaper wagons or GPO vans. A house code for street names and districts was devised in case of the interception of messages by similarly up-to-date radio-equipped criminals.

The first police force to be equipped with radio in their patrol cars was the Lancashire Constabulary in 1932. In 1935–6 the Force introduced the first full-scale mobile VHF radio system in the world.

A 24hr radio patrol system was introduced by the Metropolitan Police in June 1934. London was divided up into 52 areas, each of which had at least one car on patrol throughout the day and night.

The first Panda cars were brought into use by the Lancashire Constabulary in 1965.

The first POLICE DETECTIVE

was Eugène François Vidocq, who became the first head of the French Sûreté in 1812. His early years held little promise of their later fulfilment. Born at Arras in 1775, he was apprehended for stealing his father's plate while still a schoolboy and suffered his first spell of imprisonment in a wretched prison called the 'Banders', which also served as a madhouse. Subsequently he joined the French Army, deserted, and enlisted in the enemy Austrian forces. After deserting again he found himself arrested on a charge of forging a release for a prisoner in Lille Gaol, and was sentenced to the galleys at Brest.

Vidocq escaped from Brest three times; twice he was brought back in chains. The third time that he was caught, he approached M. Henry, the Chief of the 2nd Division of the Paris Police, with an offer to serve as an informer provided he was not returned to the galleys. Henry recognized the advantages of this proposal, for few men could equal Vidocq's intimate knowledge of the criminal underworld. Accordingly he gave orders for the prisoner to be removed to La Force Gaol, and it was here that Vidocq served the remainder of his sentence, reporting incriminating conversations and plans for further villainy. On his release he continued to work clandestinely for the police, though unlike most police spies of the time, who rendered their services in exchange for a blind eye to their own illegal activities, Vidocq was scrupulously careful to maintain a clean record and established an unusual reputation for personal integrity.

At last Vidocq was suspected by his underworld associates as a spy and could no longer go among them with impunity. M. Henry was not prepared to lose such a valuable lieutenant, and in 1812 he took the bold step of forming a special branch devoted to crime detection and prevention, notwithstanding the bitter opposition of those who considered the only requirement for an effective policeman was brute force. The new department was called the Sûreté and Vidocq was appointed to its command. Enrolled as a bona fide member of the Paris Police, the ex-galley-slave now became the first full-time, salaried member of a regular police force to be engaged solely on detective-work.

The four men who comprised the original staff of the Sûreté were all chosen by Vidocq from among the prisoners he had known in La Force. Their base was a discreet building in la petite rue Sainte-Anne. The immediate reduction in the crime-rate effected by so small a force can be attributed partly to the scientific methods of detection that Vidocq pioneered. These included an elaborate classification of varying patterns of crime and a central registry containing files on all known criminals. Like many a good detective after him, he also relied on his own intuition. 'I do not need to see the whole of a criminal's face,' Vidocq once claimed. 'It is sufficient for me to catch his eye.'

During the time that Vidocq was head of the Sûreté, he was its only member who belonged on the Police Force. Those who assisted him were employed as agents only. Detectives were recruited from inside the Force for the first time with the appointment of Pierre Allard to succeed Vidocq in 1833. The reorganized Sûreté consisted at that date of 4 Brigadiers (Detective-Sergeants), 21 Inspecteurs de Police (Detective-Constables) and 4 clerks, all of whom were regular policemen.

Vidocq himself made another notable contribution to the history of detection after his retirement from the Sûreté by establishing the world's first private detective agency (*q.v.*). In his later years he declined into obscurity and died a pauper in 1855.

GB: The first police officer to be assigned to special duties outside his own division was Sgt James Otway of the Metropolitan Police, who was sent to Uxbridge on detachment from 'A' Division in February 1837 to investigate the murder of a boy called James Brill, whose body had been found in a wood. In June 1839 Sgt Otway and Insp. Nicholas Pearce, an ex-Bow Street Runner, were employed on the case of a clockmaker called Westwood, murdered in Soho. From this time Pearce remained more or less permanently on detachment for special inquiry duties. Otway was returned to his Division a year later for his irregular handling of an investigation.

The first regularly constituted detective force in Britain was formed on 15 August 1842 under the joint command of Insp. Pearce and Insp. John Haynes. One of the original six Detective-Sergeants was Sgt Whicher, believed to have been the model for Wilkie Collins's Sergeant Cuff in *The Moonstone*, the first of the great detectives of English fiction. *Punch* showed its customary disrespect for authority by dubbing them the 'Defectives'.

SPECIAL BRANCH originated in 1883 as the Special Irish Branch of the CID, its members consisting of specially selected detectives who were detailed to keep suspected Fenians under surveillance. Its first head was Chief Insp. Littlechild. When the Fenian outrages ceased in 1885 the Branch remained in being to keep track of all subversive activity, dropping the word 'Irish' from its title.

FLYING SQUAD of the CID was formed as a small mobile detachment of 12 detective officers under the command of Detective Insp. Walter Hambrook in October 1918. Their original transport consisted of a single horse-drawn covered wagon hired from the Great Western Railway, but this was replaced in 1920 by two ex-RAF Crossley tenders (*see also* Police Cars). Within a few days of their first appearance in these vehicles in September, the men of the 'mobile patrol experiment' had been given their more romantic title of the 'Flying Squad' by W. G. T. Crook, Chief Crime Reporter of the *Daily Mail*.

The first *POLICE DOGS*

The earliest recorded instance of a specially trained dog being used for law enforcement in Britain occurred at Midmar Lodge, Aberdeenshire on 8 February 1816, when a bull-terrier employed for detection work by Revenue Officer Malcolm Gillespie took part in the arrest of a party of whisky-smugglers. The dog had been taught to seize suspects' horses by the nose, making them rear up and drop their loads. The Midmar Lodge episode resulted in the capture of four ankers of illicit spirit, and another four staved in. The bull-terrier was shot dead in another engagement near Kintore on 30 July of the same year.

The regular use of trained dogs for police work was first recognized officially by the police authorities of Ghent, Belgium in 1899. For some time prior to this date the Ghent Police had been using dogs experimentally on night duty.

The first dog used for criminal detection by a police force in Britain was a bloodhound lent to Blackburn Police in April 1876 to aid them in tracking down the murderer of seven-year-old Emily Holland, a child who had been sexually assaulted and then had her throat cut. The dog was first taken to a field at Bastwell, where the mutilated body had been found, but it failed to pick up a scent. It was then taken to the house of two suspects. In the first of these the dog betrayed no excitement, but in the second, a barbershop in Moss Street, it led the police to a fireplace where the head of the child was found concealed in the chimney. The occupier of the house, William Fish, was arrested and subsequently confessed to the crime.

The regular use of police dogs in Britain was introduced for the first time by the North Eastern Railway Police Force early in 1908 at the instigation of the Chief Goods Manager, E. C. Geddes. Concerned at the number of thefts of goods in transit, he had arranged the previous November for a deputation of the NER Police to visit the Canine Police Force in Ghent (*see above*) to watch their dog-handlers at work. On their return the General Manager agreed to the purchase of three young Airedale terriers for use at Hull Docks. The experiment proving a success, permanent kennels were built at the dockside and by 1912 there were police kennels at Hartlepool, Tyne Dock and Middlesbrough.

The first of the City and County Police Forces of Britain (i.e. other than railway police) to use dogs was the Wiltshire Constabulary, whose Chief Constable, Col Hoël Llewellyn, began using a bloodhound for tracking in 1910. This dog was not on the official strength of the Force, but in 1912 they acquired a number of Labradors for night-patrol work.

The first *POLICE FORCE*

functioning independently of the judiciary was established in Paris by a Royal Edict of March 1667, separating the judicial and police responsibilities of the Royal Watch. For the first time a Lieutenant of Police was appointed and charged with the security of the city. This post was filled for the next 30 years by Gabriel-Nicholas de la Reynie, who commanded a para-military force of 554 policemen, of whom 144 were mounted.

Originally the Paris Police Force was operated exclusively from the Châtelet, but in 1698 la Reynie's successor, the Marquis d'Argenson, established a police post at the Pont-Neuf, the first office to correspond with what today would be termed a 'police station'.

The Paris Police became a uniformed force by an Ordinance of the Prefect, Louis-Marie Debelleyme, dated 12 March 1829. This stated:

The purpose of uniform will be to constantly keep in the public's mind the presence of policemen at points where they will be of service; at the same time to compel them to intervene and restore order instead of vanishing into the crowd for fear of being noticed as often happens.

GB: The first statutory police force was the Marine Police Establishment, which was given the authority of law under the Thames River Police Act of July 1800. The Force had been founded two years earlier as a private venture similar to the various 18th-century police enterprises instigated by the Justices and others. Comprised of 60 full-time paid officers, this was the first effective regular professional force to operate in London. It was absorbed into the Metropolitan Police as the Thames Division in 1838.

By 1828 the policing of the metropolis was in the hands of four Bow Street patrols, seven police offices under the direction of the Middlesex Magistrates, each with 12 constables, and the Thames River Police – in all about 450 men under the over-all control of the Home Secretary. There were also about 4,500 of the derided old watchmen commonly known as 'Charlies'.

This was the extent to which the citizens of London were afforded civil protection when Sir Robert Peel's newly created Metropolitan Police, the first uniformed statutory force in the country, went on parade in front of the Foundling Hospital in Bloomsbury to be sworn in on Saturday, 26 September 1829. The uniforms distributed to them on this occasion, made by Charles Hebbert, tailor of Pall Mall East, consisted of a blue frock-coat with eight large brass buttons and a brass-buckled leather belt. The metal-framed tall top hat was designed to serve a twofold purpose – to protect the wearer from assault and for use as a platform to see over walls or reach high windows. A number of men arrived on parade carrying umbrellas, it being a wet day. A prohibitive order was issued the same evening that still remains in force.

The first patrols of the Metropolitan Police went on duty at 6pm on Tuesday, 29 September 1829. Their hours of duty were 12 per day, seven days a week, and for this a constable received 21s a week, from which 2s was deducted for quarters. The type of man attracted was far from the later ideal of the incorruptible policeman. Already several men who had paraded at the Foundling Hospital in an intoxicated condition had been summarily ejected, and of the first 2,800 men recruited, no less than 2,238 were subsequently dismissed, 1,790 for being drunk on duty.

The original headquarters of the Metropolitan Police was at 4 Whitehall Place, overlooking Great Scotland Yard. In addition there were five police stations located in former watch-houses. The area patrolled by the 3,300 men who were on the strength by May 1830 extended seven miles outwards from Charing Cross in every direction, and was divided into 17 districts, each under the command of a superintendent.

The first police force to adopt helmets in place of top hats was the Metropolitan Police in 1864. At the same time tunics replaced swallowtail coats; embroidered numerals on the collar gave way to metal ones; and sergeants were given chevrons on their sleeves. Whistles superseded rattles in London in 1884.

The first
POLICEMAN TO BE MURDERED ON DUTY
in Britain was Constable William Grantham of the Metropolitan Police, who was patrolling in Somers Town on the night of 29 June 1830 when he came across two drunken Irishmen fighting over a woman. Attempting to intervene, he was knocked to the ground and kicked to death by all three, including the woman he had sought to protect.

The first
POLICE MOTOR-CYCLE PATROL
was instituted by New York City Police Department with the acquisition of three machines in 1905. The experiment was sufficiently successful for the Department's budget for 1906 to include allocation for the purchase of 20 more motor cycles. *Motor World* signified its approval of the decision in these words:

The means of rapid locomotion obviously should be in the hands of the police as well as of the citizens, whether they be honest or dishonest. The fact that there are some 23,000 automobiles in New York State alone at the present time renders such considerations of the greatest importance.

A special six-man Motorcycle Speed Squad was established at Los Angeles in 1911.
GB: The Metropolitan Police inaugurated motor-cycle patrols in 1930.
POLICE MOTOR-CYCLE PATROL EQUIPPED WITH RADIO TELEPHONE: the first was instituted by the Metropolitan Police Force of the District of Columbia at Washington in 1937.

The first
POLICEWOMAN
uniformed and with full powers of arrest, was former social worker Mrs Alice Stebbins Wells, who was appointed to the Los Angeles Police Department on 12 September 1910. On her first day Mrs Wells was given a Gamewell key, a book of rules, a first-aid book, and a policeman's badge. At that time members of the police force were entitled to use their badges as free passes on street-cars when on duty or riding to work. Finding that she was invariably accused by the conductor of misusing her husband's badge, Mrs Wells drew this to the attention of her superiors and was subsequently issued with 'Policewoman's Badge No. 1'. The general disbelief that she was really invested with the powers of a police officer – the idea of policewomen had been a staple joke in the comic weeklies since at least the 1850s – was considerably lessened when she began to wear an official uniform she had been allowed to design herself.

Mrs Wells's chief duties included the supervision and enforcement of laws concerning 'dance halls, skating rinks, penny arcades, picture shows and other similar places of public recreation'. Also numbered among her activities were 'the suppression of unwholesome billboard displays, searches for missing persons, and the maintenance of a general information bureau for women seeking advice within the scope of police departments'. Soon after her appointment an order was issued to the effect that: 'No young girl can be questioned by a male officer. Such work is delegated solely to policewomen, who, by their womanly sympathy and intuition, are able to gain the confidence of their younger sisters.'

Besides the efficient discharge of these duties, Mrs Wells was notable for her active work in propagating the need for policewomen elsewhere. As a result of her efforts in this respect, 17 police departments in the USA were employing policewomen by 1916.
NB: A number of reference books have stated that the world's first policewoman was a Mrs Marie Owen, allegedly appointed to the Detroit Police Department by Supt Morgan A. Collins in 1893. It should be noted that this is disclaimed by the Police Department in question, who have no record of ever having had a Mrs Owen on their regular strength. Nor was there ever a Superintendent by the name of Morgan A. Collins.
GB: The first woman to wear police uniform in Britain was Mrs Henrietta Robley-Browne, who went on unofficial patrol in Shaftesbury Avenue in July 1914 wearing a costume of her own design. Mrs Robley-Browne was one of the original recruits to a volunteer organization of policewomen, formed by feminist leader Miss Nina Boyle as a result of revelations that girl witnesses in cases of indecent and criminal assault were being mistreated. Immediately after the outbreak of war in August 1914, Miss Margaret Damer Dawson was inspired with a similar idea and gathered a nucleus of volunteers. On learning of Miss Boyle's proposed force, the two amalgamated under the title 'Women Police Volunteers' (changed to 'Women's Police Service' the following year) and Miss Damer Dawson assumed active command. Recruits were instructed in drill, giving and taking evidence, police-court procedure, general police laws, first aid, the law relating to women and children, signalling, patrolling and ju-jitsu. One of their number later recalled: 'The attribute of a good officer which we found most difficulty in acquiring was the slow, easy-looking, correct police step.'

At first there appears to have been some variation between the uniforms worn, but on 16 November 1914 two designs were submitted to HM Queen Mary, one by Edith Watson and the other by Henrietta Robley-Browne. The Queen chose the latter, which consisted of a dark blue tunic with shoulder-straps bearing the letters 'WPV' in silver, a flat cap with silver braid for officers and a hard hat in blue felt for other ranks. This costume was sanctioned by the Metropolitan Police Commissioner, Sir Edward Henry.

The first two policewomen to assume active duty on completion of their training were Miss Mary Allen and Miss E.F. Harburn, who reported to the Provost-Marshal at Grantham, Lincolnshire on 27 November 1914. Their principal task lay in controlling the effects on the local population of a new Army camp just outside the town containing 18,000 men, the population of the town itself being only 20,000. Hitherto the WPV had operated with the blessing of the Metropolitan Police Commissioner, but had enjoyed no official standing. The date that Miss Allen and Miss Harburn arrived at Grantham, in response to a formal request by the military authorities, can thus be regarded as marking the real entry of women into police-work.

In May 1915 Miss Allen and Miss Harburn were posted to Hull and in December of that year became the first women to be sworn in as Police Constables. Working directly under the orders of the Chief Constable, they were now invested with the full power of arrest and subject to the rules and discipline of the Force. In becoming the first Police Force in the country to employ women on the official strength, Hull recognized their new status – no longer a purely voluntary one – by making provision for a regular wage to be paid to them from police funds. This amounted to £2 2s 6d weekly. The innovation is particularly significant in view of frequent allegations that the members of the Women's Police Service (as it had then become) were never more than self-appointed guardians of moral order, functioning without official authorization.

From April 1916 the Women's Police Service was considerably expanded in response to a request from the Minister of Munitions to Sir Edward Henry for a force of trained policewomen to place in the factory areas with dense concentrations of women employees. A total of 985 women police were supplied for duty in the munitions factories during the remainder of the war.

At the end of the war, most members of the WPS (then numbering 500) returned to civilian life, though some who chose to stay on were drafted to Borough Police Forces and County Constabularies. There were also 40 working in London in 1919 independently of the Metropolitan Police, mainly on factory premises. All those serving with provincial forces had full powers of arrest.

On the death of Miss Damer Dawson in 1919, Miss Mary Allen succeeded to the post of Commandant. She had the unusual distinction for a police officer of having served two terms of imprisonment in her younger days; as a militant suffragette she had on one occasion tried to force her way into the House of Commons, and on another smashed the windows of the Home Office. She travelled widely during the period between the wars, advising foreign Governments on the introduction of women police, and was also instrumental in establishing the first female police detachments in Germany (1923) and Egypt (1930). In the later 1930s her admiration for Mussolini and Hitler provoked controversy, and after questions had been asked in the House of Commons in 1940 the renamed Women's Auxiliary Service lost much of its official support.

WOMEN TAKEN ON THE STRENGTH OF THE METROPOLITAN POLICE: the first were members of the Metropolitan Police Women Patrols, inaugurated by the Commissioner of Police, Sir Nevil Macready, by a Police Order dated 23 December 1918. One hundred recruits were placed under the command of Mrs F. Stanley, the first batch of trained policewomen leaving Peel House Training School to take up regular duties in February 1919. This force was totally independent of the Women's Police Service, for which Sir Nevil had an ill-concealed disfavour, describing it as a 'militant organization . . . dressing in uniform of a rather masculine type'.

Sir Nevil Macready had justified his creation of the new Women Patrols with the words: 'It is not the thing for a full-blown constable to go and stir up ladies and gentlemen lying about in the parks. It had far better be done by women.' This rather narrow view of the policewoman's role – he suggested little else to keep them occupied – may account for the rather unhappy start to the experiment. In 1922 the *Geddes Report* commented on the women members of the Force: 'Their powers are very limited, and their utility, from a police point of view, is, on the evidence submitted to us, negligible.' In accordance with the Geddes Committee's recommendations, the size of the Force was cut to 20, but for the first time its members were sworn in as constables, with full powers of arrest. Women officers of the Metropolitan Police now began to assume an important and necessary function and by the outbreak of World War II numbers reached 200.

The first
POLYTHENE
was produced in March 1933 at the Northwich, Cheshire laboratories of ICI by R.O. Gibson, who reacted ethylene and benzaldehyde at a temperature of 170 °C and noted that the effect of the experiment was to leave a 'white waxy solid' adhering to the inner surface of the reaction vessel. The first practical use to which polythene was put was as insulating material in a mile length of submarine cable manufactured by the Telegraph Construction & Maintenance Co in July 1939 and subsequently laid between the Isle of Wight and the mainland. Regular production was instituted by ICI on 1 September 1939, most of the wartime output being devoted to cable insulation and components for airborne radar systems. The first household articles to be manufactured in polythene were washing-up basins in 1948.

The first
POODLE PARLOUR
in Britain was The Dogs' Toilet Club, opened at 120 New Bond Street, London in 1896. The idea of catering to the special wants of pampered pets was introduced from Paris, where Mme Ledouble had opened a Maison de Haute Couture for dogs a few years previously. The cost of a shampoo at the Dogs' Toilet Club was 5s, yolks of egg being used instead of soap to prevent irritation of the client's skin. Chiropody came at 2s 6d, and a special assistant was available to clean canine teeth with table salt, though some owners insisted on a perfumed dentifrice being used. Poodles could be adorned with their owner's crest or monogram – clipped in the fur – for a fee of 2gns.

Madame Ledouble's business card

The first
POP GROUP
of the current vocal and instrumental genre was The Bluecaps, a five-man

group from Nashville, Tenn., comprising Dickie Harrell (drums), Jack Neal (string bass), Willie Williams (rhythm guitar), Cliff Gallup and lead singer Gene Vincent. Their first recordings, 'Be-Bop-a-Lula' and 'Woman Love', were released by Capitol Records in June 1956. While the former climbed rapidly into the American charts, 'Woman Love' achieved almost equal distinction by being banned by the BBC. An LP album, *Bluejean Bob*, was released later the same year. The group finally split up in 1959.

The first
POP MUSIC CHART
based on record sales was published in *The Billboard* (New York) for 4 January 1936. There were separate listings for the 10 best-sellers of the three leading record companies. Chart toppers for the week ended 30 December 1935 were 'Stop, Look and Listen', Joe Venuti and Orchestra (Columbia); 'Quicker Than You Can Say', Ozzie Nelson and Orchestra (Brunswick); 'The Music Goes Round', Tommy Dorsey and Orchestra (RCA-Victor).
GB: The first Top Ten record sales chart was published in the *New Musical Express* for 14 November 1952.

1 'Here in My Heart', Al Martino
2 'You Belong to My Heart', Jo Stafford
3 'Somewhere Along the Way', Nat King Cole
4 'Isle of Innisfree', Bing Crosby
5 'Feet Up', Guy Mitchell
6 'Half As Much', Rosemary Clooney
7 { 'High Noon', Frankie Laine / 'Forget Me Not', Vera Lynn }
8 { 'Sugar Bush', Doris Day and Frankie Laine / 'Blue Tango', Ray Martin }
9 'Homing Waltz', Vera Lynn
10 'Auf Wiedersehen', Vera Lynn

The first
POSTAGE METER
authorized for the franking of business mail, etc. was devised by Norwegian inventor Karl Uchermann and manufactured in 1903 by Krag Maskinfabrik of Kristiania (now Oslo). The frank-dies were supplied to licensed users of the machines by the Norwegan postal authorities and covered the value, town of origin and date. The first machines came into use on 15 June 1903 and the system continued in operation until January 1905.

The first country to adopt metered mail on a permanent basis was New Zealand, where the postal authorities accepted for public use a machine patented in 1904 by Ernest Moss of Christchurch, founder of the Automatic Stamping Co Ltd.
GB: The first licence to use a postage meter was issued by the GPO to the Prudential Assurance Co, Holborn on 16 August 1922. The machine was supplied by Postage Meters & Machines Co, the London subsidiary of the American Pitney-Bowes Co.

The first
POSTAGE STAMPS
were struck on the Billets de Port Payé used by François de Villayer's Petite Poste that operated in Paris in 1653. No examples of the Billets survive, but they are believed to have consisted of bands of paper bearing a printed device indicating postage paid. At this time prepayment was exceptional for general posts, the more usual practice being for the receiver of the letter to pay the postage fee.
GB: The first stamps indicative of prepayment were introduced by William Dockwra for his London Penny Post on 1 April 1680. These were triangular in shape and bore the words 'Penny Post Paid' surrounding a letter that denoted the sorting office. Ten examples of Dockwra's hand-struck stamps survive, five struck at the Westminster Office, four at Lime Street and one at the Temple. After the termination of Dockwra's service, the London District Post continued to use the same stamps until 1794. The first hand-struck postage stamp used by the GPO was introduced in 1715 and consisted simply of a circle containing the letters 'PD'.

For the first Embossed postage stamps (1838) *see* Envelopes.
ADHESIVE POSTAGE STAMP: the first was printed by James Chalmers at his printing-works in Dundee in August 1834 as a sample to illustrate his idea for standardizing the prepayment of postage. He failed to arouse any interest at first, but on 4 December 1837 he was able to submit a number of examples to the Parliamentary Select Committee set up to consider Rowland Hill's proposals for postal reform. Hill's original suggestion for prepayment was an envelope with the stamp printed on it. Surviving proofs of Chalmers's essay dated 10 February 1838 show a square stamp printed in sepia bearing the legend 'General Postage – NOT EXCEEDING HALF AN OUNCE – One Penny' enclosed in a decorative surround.

Chalmers actually used one of his essay 2d stamps on a letter posted to Lt-Col Moberly, Secretary of the GPO, on 2 October 1839 – the first time an envelope bearing an adhesive postage stamp ever went through the post.

After the introduction of adhesive postage stamps by the Post Office, a lengthy dispute arose between those who believed Chalmers to be the inventor, and those who favoured the claim of Rowland Hill. Though this has never been resolved to the satisfaction of all parties, it would seem that Chalmers was the first to produce an actual sample of an adhesive postage stamp (August 1834), and Hill the first to suggest the idea in print (1837), though only as a limited alternative to stamped envelopes.

The first adhesive postage stamps for general use were the Penny Blacks and Twopenny Blues officially issued by the GPO on 6 May 1840. A few had been sent through the post during the preceding days, and the earliest surviving example of a used Penny Black is on a letter addressed to Peckham and postmarked Bath, 2 May 1840. The stamps were designed by William Wyon and Henry Corbould, engraved by Charles and Frederick Heath, and printed by Perkins, Bacon & Co.
PICTORIAL POSTAGE STAMPS: the first stamps to illustrate something other than portraits were the 1d, 2d and 3d 'Sydney Views' issued by the New South Wales Post Office on 1 January 1850.

Sydney View, 1850

GB: No stamp has yet been issued without the Sovereign's portrait. The first to bear additional pictorial matter was the 'Wembley Commemorative' issued on 23 April 1924.
PERFORATED STAMP the first was the Penny Red issued in February 1854. The originator of the idea, Henry Archer, had constructed his first perforating apparatus in 1847, but this only made slits along the sides of the stamps. By the end of the following year, however, he had adapted it so that a succession of small holes were punched in the paper.

COMMEMORATIVE STAMP: the first was the 2 pfennig green and carmine pictorial, issued by the Frankfurt-am-Main Privat-Brief-Verkehr (District Post) to commemorate the 25th Anniversary of the German Federal and Jubilee Shooting Contest, Frankfurt, July 1887.

The first commemorative stamp in the British Empire and the first issued by any national postal service was the New South Wales 1s Centenary Issue of January 1888.

GB: The 1d and 1½d pictorials bearing the King's head, the Wembley Lion and the words 'British Empire Exhibition', issued at a special post office in the Exhibition grounds on 23 April 1924.

PICTORIAL SERIES OF POSTAGE STAMPS: the first was issued by North Borneo in 1894 and depicted various indigenous animals.

CHRISTMAS STAMP: the first was a 2 cent pictorial bearing a map of the world, issued by the Canadian Post Office in December 1898, and originally designed only to mark the advent of Imperial Penny Postage. According to Sir John Henniker Heaton, then Post-master-General, it had been intended to introduce Imperial Penny Postage on 9 November, the Prince of Wales's birthday. When Sir John explained the new scheme to the Queen, she inquired when it was to come into force. 'We think of introducing it on the Prince's birthday', he replied. The Queen, considering this encroached on her own position, asked coldly, 'And what Prince?' The PMG responded without hesitation, 'The Prince of Peace, Your Majesty.' The Canadian stamp, which had already been designed to include the date, was thereupon changed to read 'Xmas 1898'.

GB: 3d and 1s 6d pictorials bearing designs by the winners of a nation-wide competition for children organized by the GPO, one a picture of a snowman and the other of the Three Kings of the Orient, were issued on 1 December 1966.

STAMP MACHINES were devised by the Stamp Distribution Syndicate and fixed on pillar boxes in London by special arrangement with the GPO in May 1891. The machines supplied penny postage stamps (the ordinary rate for an inland letter), which were slotted into the back of a memo book containing 64 pages of notes, a number of full-page advertisements and a calendar for 1891. There was no charge for the book, the cost of which was covered by advertising revenue. The stamps had the initials SDS punctured through Queen Victoria's neck.

In 1906 the GPO began making permanent installations inside London post offices. Outside GPO machines were introduced in 1921.

STAMP BOOKS were first issued by the US Post Office in denominations of 12×2c, 24×2c and 48×2c at a price of 1c over face value on 16 April 1900.

GB: Books containing 24×1d stamps in panels of six were issued by the GPO at a price of 2s 0½d on 16 March 1904. They were printed by Thos de la Rue & Co Ltd, who had pioneered the idea of stamp books nearly 20 years earlier when they produced a dummy specimen with a pink cover in exactly the same format as the one still used by the GPO today. The legend on the front read: '2/- Post Office of Africa 2/-. This book contains 12 Penny Stamps and 24 Half-penny Stamps.' The stamps inside carried the standard Queen Victoria profile in green ink surrounded by the name of the Company. It is believed to have been submitted to the Inland Revenue in 1885 in connection with a scheme for issuing penny revenue stamps in books.

AIRMAIL STAMPS: the first official ones were issued by the Italian Post Office in 1917, when 200,000 25c Express Letter stamps were overprinted with the words 'Esperimento Posta Aerea – Maggio 1917 – Torino–Roma Roma–Torino' for the experimental airmail service operated between Rome and Turin in May of that year. No airmail stamps have been issued in GB.

The first *POSTCARD*

was copyrighted by John P. Charlton of Philadelphia in 1861. The rights were acquired by Philadelphia stationer Hyman L. Lipman, who issued the cards printed with a decorative border pattern and the words 'Lipman's Postal Card, Patent Applied For'. They remained on sale until the introduction of the first US Post Office official postcard issue of 1873.

The first official prepaid postcards were issued by the Austrian Post Office on 1 October 1869, following a suggestion by Dr Emmanuel Herrmann of the Wiener Neustadt Military Academy which had been published in the *Neue Freie Presse* the previous January. The straw-coloured cards bore a 2 kreuzer stamp. During the first two months of issue no less than 2,930,000 cards were sold, part of the attraction being that no extra charge was made beyond the cost of the stamp.

GB: The first official issue was made by the Post Office on 1 October 1870. As in Austria, the cards were sold for the cost of the stamp, in this case a ½d Lilac, and a million were sent the first week. Initially their popularity seems to have been chiefly with the lower orders, as there was a feeling among the better educated that to expose one's thoughts to the gaze of the postman was neither seemly nor discreet. This prejudice was overcome largely due to the example of Mr Gladstone, who was an inveterate postcard-writer. Privately printed postcards were permitted from June 1872, provided they were submitted to the Inland Revenue Department to have a ½d stamp impressed upon them. The use of adhesive stamps on privately issued postcards was authorized in 1894.

Although the official Post Office issue of 1870 is generally recognized as representing the introduction of postcards in Britain, a Leith colour-manufacturer called Mr Lundy later claimed to have sold cards of his own design prior to this date.

See also Picture Postcard.

The first *POTATO CRISPS*

were prepared in 1853 at the Moon Lake House Hotel, Saratoga Springs, N.Y., by Red Indian chef George Crum in response to the request of a diner for 'thinner than normal French fried potatoes'. The idea was immediately successful and became a regular feature of the Moon Lake House menu as 'Saratoga Chips'. The commercial production of potato crisps followed within a few years, beginning as a back-kitchen industry with whole families cooking, packing and selling the crisps from their own homes.

GB: Introduced by Carter's Crisps of London in 1913. Mr Carter had encountered crisps in France and decided to launch them commercially in Britain. Among his employees was one Frank Smith, who left to start his own business, Smith's Crisps, in 1920. Smith's took over Carter's a few years later.

The first *PREPARATORY SCHOOL*

to be founded as such (i.e. to prepare boys for the public schools) was Temple Grove, established in 1810 by the Rev. Dr Pearson at a country-mansion formerly owned by Viscount Palmerston, which lay in 20 acres of grounds between Mortlake and Richmond Park. The 'Young Gentlemen of the Seminary at Temple Grove', as an early speech-day programme described them, entered the school at 7 plus and left by the time they were 14, most of them destined for Eton. An engraving dated 1818 shows that the boys wore a uniform comprising top hat, long-tailed jacket and white pantaloons. The curriculum, almost exclusively Classical, was designed, in the words of the Headmaster, that they might 'daily experience those advantages which distinguish the polished gentleman from the rustic clown'. These advantages, it was believed, could be derived only from a hard regimen, outside as well as inside the classroom. The austere conditions that governed life at Temple Grove in the 1830s were forbiddingly described by H. J. Coke, of the famous Norfolk family:

We began our day with two large spoonfuls of sulphur and treacle. After an hour's lessons, we breakfasted on one bowl of milk – 'sky-blue' we called it – and one hunk of buttered bread, unbuttered at discretion. Our dinner began with pudding, generally rice – to save the butcher's bill. As to cleanliness, I never had a bath, never bathed (at the school) during the two years I was there. On Saturday nights, before bed, our feet were washed by the housemaids, in tubs round which half a dozen of us sat at a time. Woe to the last comers! For the water was never changed.

Although Temple Grove was the first school to be founded specifically to fulfil a preparatory function, there are at least two other schools that can claim to have been in existence at a considerably earlier date. Cheam was established under George Aldrich at Cheam, Surrey in 1647. Like most private Classical schools of the 17th and 18th centuries, Cheam prepared boys for the universities as well as the major public schools, and there was no upper age limit. It cannot be said to have become a preparatory school in the modern sense until the headmastership of Robert Tabor (1855–91), when the age range was restricted to under-14s in line with other rival institutions.

Twyford, founded originally as a rectory school in the latter half of the 17th century, has an equal claim with Temple Grove to be regarded as the earliest preparatory school, since by the time of its removal to its present premises near Winchester in 1809 it had already begun to assume some of the characteristics of a modern prep school. Boys between the ages of 8 and 13 were prepared for Eton, Rugby, Winchester and other public schools. Its most famous alumnus, albeit a fictitious one, was Tom Brown, whose experiences at Twyford in the mid 1830s, as related by Thomas Hughes (an old boy) in the opening chapters of *Tom Brown's Schooldays*, make an interesting comparison with those of Master Coke at Temple Grove.

The first *PRINTED BOOK*

known, is a copy of the *Diamond Sutra*, a Buddhist scripture concerned with the non-existence of all things and presented in the form of discourses by the Buddha to his disciple Subhuti. It consists of a 16ft scroll made up of six sheets of text and one sheet of woodcut illustration pasted together, each sheet measuring 12×30in. The text, printed from wood blocks, ends with a colophon stating that it was 'printed on May 11, 868, by Wang Chieh, for free general distribution, in order in deep reverence to perpetuate the memory of his parents'. The illustration depicts the Buddha surrounded by both male and female disciples and a pair of fat smiling cats. The book was found together with some 1,130 bundles of manuscript walled up in one of the Caves of the Thousand Buddhas, nr Tunhuang in Turkestan by a mendicant Taoist priest in 1900.

BOOK PRINTED FROM MOVABLE TYPE: the first known was the *Sun-tzu-shi-chia-chu*, published in Korea in 1409. There is some evidence to support a claim that *The Family Sayings of Confucius* was printed from movable type, partly in 1317 and partly in 1324.

The earliest tangible evidence of a book printed from movable type in Europe is two leaves of a 27-line *Donatus Latin Grammar* which were found in the binding of an account-book dated 1451. The type is believed to be the same as that used by Johann Gensfleisch zum Gutenberg for the printing of his 36-line Bible at Mainz five years later.

The earliest dated book printed from movable type in Europe and the first in a vernacular tongue is *Eyn manung der Christenheit widder die durken* (*Appeal of Christianity against the Turks*), believed to have been printed by Gutenberg at Mainz in 1454. The only existing copy contains six leaves, with nine pages of German text, including a calendar.

PRINTED BIBLE: the first, and the earliest-known full-length work printed from movable type in Europe, was Gutenberg's 42-line Bible believed to have been printed at Mainz between 1451 and 1456. Of the 48 copies known to survive, 36 are on paper and 12 on vellum. The copy preserved at the Bibliothèque Nationale, which is in two folio volumes with a total of 643 leaves, contains a manuscript colophon at the end which reads in translation: 'This book was illuminated, bound and perfected by Henry Cremer, vicar of the Collegiate Church of St Stephen in Mainz, on the Feast of the Assumption of the Blessed Virgin [15 August], in the year of Our Lord 1456. Thanks be to God. Hallelujah.' Gutenberg's undated Bible of 36 lines to the page is held by some authorities to have been printed prior to 1456.

The first book printed by an Englishman was *The Recuyell of the Histories of Troye*, a translation from the original French published in English by William Caxton at Bruges in 1474. Caxton prefaced the work with the explanation: 'It is not wreton with penne and ynke as other bokes ben . . . for all bokes of this storye . . . were begonne in oon day, and also fynysshid in oon day.'

The first book printed in Britain was *The Dictes or Sayengis of the Philosophres*, a folio work of 78 leaves 'drawen out of frensche into our Englisshe tonge' by 'Lord Antone Erle of Ryuyers lord of Scales of the Ile of

A page from the first printed book – the Diamond Sutra of AD 868

Wyght' and published by William Caxton at Westminster on 18 November 1477.

The first
PRISONER-OF-WAR CAMP
purpose-built in Britain, was Norman Cross Depot, near Stilton in Huntingdonshire, erected by HM Transport Commissioners for the reception of French POWs and occupied for the first time on 7 April 1797. Previously it had been customary to confine POWs in civil prisons, fortresses or floating hulks, but by the end of 1796 the number of prisoners entering Britain had grown so large that it became necessary to take immediate steps to provide special accommodation. The 40-acre camp, designed for 8,000 prisoners, was constructed in less than four months by a team of 500 carpenters and other tradesmen, all of whom were required to work seven days a week on pain of dismissal.

The prisoners' living quarters comprised 16 two-storey wooden barracks, each group of four being surrounded by a wooden stockade within the main outer fence of the camp. In the centre, commanding a view of the four enclosures, was an octagonal blockhouse with a gun-port in each of its sides. The first batch of prisoners to arrive at the camp were some 300 sailors from the warships *Réunion* and *Révolutionnaire*. They were followed by other crews from French vessels and in November 1797 by the first Dutch prisoners, captured at the Battle of Camperdown the previous month.

Attempts to escape, which were relatively frequent, though seldom successful, were punished by so many days in the 'Black Hole', which approximated to what was known to latter-day British POWs as 'the cooler'. Any reward payable to his captors had to be defrayed by the prisoner himself, who was put on half rations till the debt was paid off.

The diet of the prisoners consisted of beer, beef, bread and salt daily, green vegetables every other day, and butter and cheese once a week. This could be supplemented by provisions bought at the market held outside the camp gates each day, purchases being made through the agency of certain nominated prisoners who were allowed out under guard for the purpose. The inmates of the camp earned money for these and other comforts by the manufacture of wood and bone models and marquetry-work.

Apart from model-making, gambling appears to have been the principal avocation of the captives, though as in the POW camps of World Wars I and II, sports and amateur theatricals helped to occupy the time. A plan of the camp in 1809 shows that by then the prisoners had their own theatre.

Although peace was declared in 1802, resulting in the closure of Norman Cross Depot, it was reopened the following year with the renewal of hostilities and continued in operation until 1814. Some POWs remained in captivity during the whole of this period, an unenviable record only surpassed by the last German POWs of World War II, who remained captive in Soviet Russia nearly 20 years after the end of the war. The camp was finally demolished in 1816.

The first
PRIVATE DETECTIVE AGENCY
was the Bureau des Reseignments au Service des Intérêts Privés, established in Paris by the ex-Chief of the Sûreté, Eugène François Vidocq (*see also* Police Detective) in 1833. The agency suffered a set-back when Vidocq was charged with assaulting one of his employees and fined 50 francs, plus 60 francs damages. After a few years it was closed down under Government pressure, some of Vidocq's more spectacular successes having proved embarrassing in high places.

The first
PUBLIC LAVATORY
(containing water-closets) was a 'gents' opened at 95 Fleet Street, London by the Society of Arts on 2 February 1852. One for ladies, situated at 51 Bedford Street, Strand, was opened on 11 February. The two principal instigators of the scheme were (Sir) Samuel Morton Peto, a building contractor who had been responsible for the erection of Nelson's Column in Trafalgar Square, and (Sir) Henry Cole, father of the Christmas card (*q.v.*) as well as being one of the principal promoters of the Great Exhibition the previous year. It was the success of the lavatories provided at the Crystal Palace that inspired the Society of Arts to promote the idea of installing public conveniences in the principal thoroughfares of London. Not only would this high-minded endeavour answer an urgent public need, argued Cole and Peto, but it was also likely to be profitable. The Crystal Palace lavatories had reaped a net profit of £1,790 in only 23 weeks.

The arrangements made for fitting out and operating what the Society of Arts euphemistically dubbed 'Public Waiting Rooms' were admirable. Peto personally supervised the installation of handsome water-closets set in box-frames of polished wood and each convenience was placed in the charge of a superintendent and two attendants. That these facilities were intended for the benefit of the middle classes is evidenced by the price charged – 2d for the use of the basic amenities and another 2d or 3d for 'washing hands, clothes brushes, etc.'. It evidently occurred to the Society, though, that not all the bourgeoisie were as respectable in their habits as one might wish, for a request was made to the Metropolitan Police Commissioners that their men on the beat should make periodic visits.

The Society was equally attentive to publicity. The two public lavatories were advertised in *The Times* three times a week for a month and no less than 50,000 handbills explaining their purpose were distributed. Unhappily the public remained deaf to these blandishments. During the whole of February 1852, only 58 people used the Fleet Street gents, while the record for the ladies in Bedford Street was even worse – a total of 24 patrons between the opening date of the 11th and the end of the month. With reluctance the Society of Arts abandoned their experiment.

The idea was revived by William Haywood, the City of London Corporation Engineer, who instituted the first municipal public lavatory, as well as the first underground public lavatory, outside the Royal Exchange in 1855. The contractors were Jennings' of Brighton, later to be noted for their introduction of the pedestal water-closet and picture-frame seat. Haywood's was also the first gents to charge 1d, a price that remained standard for nearly all public conveniences until the introduction of decimal currency in 1971. It is believed that this constitutes a record in price maintenance.

Prior to this first flush of 19th-century sanitary enlightenment, people had a choice either of not venturing too far from home or recourse to a common privy. The latter expedient could be hazardous. According to Lawrence Wright in his *Clean and Decent* (Routledge, 1960), one John de Abydon was set on by rogues and killed in 1291 just as he was coming out of a common privy in London Wall within Cripplegate Ward. Another privy on London Bridge in the 14th century was built on struts over the Thames, discharging directly into the water. The supports eventually became so rotten that it collapsed, while occupied, into the river below.

In an age of robust manners, however, the general absence of conveniences presented few problems to the base majority, and hardly more to their betters. John Aubrey writes of Sir William Fleetwood in his *Brief Lives*:

One day going on foote to Guild-hall with his Clarke behind him, he was surprised in Cheapside with a sudden and violent Loosenesse, near the Standard. He turned up his breech against the Standard and bade his man hide his face; For they shall never see my Arse again, sayd he.

It is recorded that in 17th-century Edinburgh there was an itinerant street trader who perambulated the city with a bucket, crying 'Wha wants me for a bawbee?' Extortionate as this may sound for the convenience of a pail and the protection of the trader's cloak, it should be remembered that at this time the Scots coin, worth 6d, was equivalent to an English halfpenny.

The first
PUBLIC LIBRARY
municipal, in Britain was established by the civic authorities of Norwich in 1608. The books were housed in three rooms in the house of Jerrom Goodwyn as 'a lybrary for the use of preachers'. Like the parochial and cathedral libraries that preceded it, the Norwich Library principally contained theological works, and an early membership-list indicates that most, though not all, of its patrons were clergy. The Norwich City Library Collection was eventually taken over by Norwich Public Library (founded 1857), and consequently these 1,772 volumes represent the oldest collection of books in the country to have been preserved intact for public use.
PUBLIC LIBRARY WITH SERVICES OF A FULL-TIME LIBRARIAN: the first was Chetham's Library, Manchester, founded with the bequest of £1,000 to buy books, and a liberal endowment for maintenance made by linen-merchant Humphrey Chetham in 1653.

The first Librarian, appointed in 1656, was the Rev. Richard Johnson, who was paid £10 p.a. in addition to free board and lodging. Chetham's was unique for its time in that it not only catered for a lay readership, but was freely open to anybody who wished to take advantage of the facilities offered. The building was open for six hours a day in winter, and seven in summer. Although at the outset most of the books were of a theological nature, as indeed were the majority of the books published in the 17th century, the number of secular works grew rapidly, and by 1684 there were sections devoted to history, travel, law, medicine, topography and science. In 1849 the Select Committee on Public Libraries reported that Chetham's Library was the only important library in Britain fully and freely accessible to the public. It then held some 20,000 volumes and was used by about 25 people a day, including a number of working-class readers who borrowed foreign-language books.
RATE-SUPPORTED PUBLIC LIBRARY and the first *MUNICIPAL LENDING LIBRARY* was opened on 14 January 1847 by Canterbury Corporation, which had taken advantage of the Museums Act 1845 to purchase the museum and library of the Canterbury Philosophical and Literary Institution. The Museums Act empowered municipalities with a population exceeding 10,000 to raise a ½d rate towards the maintenance of a museum and though it made no mention of libraries, Canterbury succeeded in remaining marginally within the law by establishing a museum and library on the same premises. There was a combined admission charge of 1d for entry to both institutions and an additional fee of 1d for every book borrowed.
FREE PUBLIC LENDING LIBRARY: the first was Manchester Free Library, opened in the former Owenite Hall of Science at Campfield on 6 September 1852. Instituted under the terms of the Public Libraries Act 1850, its promoters emphasized that it was intended as much for the working people of the town as for the 'educated classes' and this was reflected in the fact that no less than 22,000 factory operatives responded to the appeal for capital funds. The vigorous direction of Manchester's first Librarian, Edward Edwards, rendered the undertaking an instant success, 77,232 books being lent during the year 1852–3.
PUBLIC LIBRARY WITH OPEN ACCESS SHELVES: the first was Clerkenwell Library, where this innovation was made by the Librarian, James Duff Brown, in 1893. Previous practice in all public libraries had been for the borrower to consult the catalogue and then ask a library assistant to fetch the book required.

See also Children's Library; Record Library.

The first
PUBLIC OPINION POLL
was conducted at Wilmington, Del. to determine voters' intentions in the 1824 US Presidential election. The result of the poll, based on a random sample of 532 electors, was published in the *Harrisburg Pennsylvanian* on 24 July 1824. It showed a clear lead for Andrew Jackson over John Quincy Adams and two other candidates.

The first opinion poll on an issue (as opposed to voting intentions) was carried out by the *Chicago Journal* between 18 and 29 March 1907, and put the question whether the privately run Chicago tramways should be taken over by the municipality. The poll indicated that 59% of the people were in favour of the proposal. In the official referendum held to vote on the Ordinance the corresponding figure was 55%.

The first nation-wide public opinion poll was organized by *Farm Journal* in an attempt to predict the result of the 1912 US Presidential election.

The modern representative sampling method of conducting public opinion polls was developed independently by Dr George H. Gallup of the American Institute of Public Opinion, Elmo Roper of the Fortune Survey, and Archibald Crossley of the Crossley Poll. All three began publishing results in 1935, though Roper's July poll on automobile-ownership is believed to have been the first in print. This included the question: 'Do you regard an automobile as a luxury or a necessity?' – 75·5% of male respondents said it was a necessity. Representative sampling was the first scientifically calculated method of polling, since it ensured that respondents were selected from age, sex, class and other interest groups in correct proportion.
GB: The first poll was conducted according to Dr Gallup's sampling method by Dr Henry Durrant of the British Institute of Public Opinion on 14 January 1937. Two questions were asked: 'Do you consider that Franco's Junta should be recognized as a legal Spanish government?' (No 86%); 'Do you favour compulsory military training?' (No 75%). In April 1938 Dr Durrant carried out the first election poll in Britain, correctly forecasting that the Labour candidate, Edith Summerskill, would win the West Fulham by-election.

PUBLIC RELATIONS
as a recognized technique of business management originated with Ivy Ledbetter Lee, a former financial journalist who set himself up as a public relations consultant in New York in 1903. Early clients included a number of politicians, a circus, a group of bankers, and the unpopular Thomas Fortune Ryan. At first Lee's approach to the art of public persuasion differed little from that of other press agents, one of whom wrote in 1905 that his business was 'not the dissemination of truth, but the avoidance of its inopportune discovery'. The emergence of modern public relations can really be dated from 1906, when Ivy Lee was called in by the anthracite-coal proprietors during the major strike of that year. Their leader, George F. Baer, had refused to talk to either the press or the President of the United States, the latter having attempted to arbitrate in

the dispute. In contrast, the miners' leader, John Mitchell, had won over both by his charm, forthrightness and evident desire to supply all the facts for which he was asked. While the miners' cause was acclaimed by the press, Baer and his colleagues were almost universally condemned.

Lee's first act was to issue a press notice signed by Baer and the other leading proprietors. It began: 'The anthracite coal operators, realizing the general public interest in conditions in the mining regions, have arranged to supply the press with all possible information . . .'. This was followed by a notice setting out Lee's own 'Declaration of Principles', which was in the nature of a charter for public relations as a business activity separate from press agentry on the one hand and advertising on the other.

Following the coal strike, Lee was retained by the Pennsylvania Railroad Co to handle press relations after a major rail disaster. Reversing the usual practice of suppression of facts when accidents were likely to tarnish the reputation of a railway company, Lee gave full facilities to the press to view the disaster scene for themselves and released all available information. The result justified what seemed to the more conservatively minded railway directors to be reckless indiscretion. The Pennsylvania Railroad received fairer press comment than had ever been its experience previously after a serious accident.

One of Lee's most notable successes was as Public Relations Adviser to John D. Rockefeller, who had an unenviable reputation as a hard-faced capitalist oppressor. Lee succeeded in transforming this image by a skilful projection of the more attractive traits of his client's personality. One device used by him to effect this was to fill the old man's pockets with dimes for distribution among urchins in the street, an activity that provided press and public with practical evidence of what was in fact a genuinely kindly nature.

GB: The earliest practitioner of public relations in a modern sense in Britain was the Marconi Co of London and Chelmsford, which established a special department, the Marconi News Agency, in October 1910 for the dissemination of news items and feature articles about the Company and its achievements in the field of wireless telegraphy. Another pioneer public relations exercise, the first Government PR campaign, was carried out at the behest of Lloyd George the following year by the Insurance Commission to explain the benefits of the National Insurance Act, an unpopular measure that had attracted a considerable volume of adverse publicity. Apart from war propaganda, the continuous development of Government public relations activity dates from 1919, when the first Press Officer was appointed by the Air Ministry. The Ministry of Health followed suit the following year with the appointment of Sir Basil Clarke, a former Reuters Correspondent, as Director of Public Information.

PUBLIC RELATIONS CONSULTANCY: the first in Britain was Editorial Services Ltd, established in Bedford Street, London, by Sir Basil Clarke in 1924 following his resignation from the Ministry of Health the previous year. Somewhat appropriately his first campaign was conducted on behalf of a dairy group to promote the idea of milk pasteurization, an innovation that had met with some resistance from the public. On the strength of this success Editorial Services was retained on a three-month renewable contract by the National Milk Publicity Council. The minutes of the Council's Advertising and Publicity Committee for 1924–5 record that the agency charged 100gns a month and achieved a monthly average of 135 cuttings favourable to milk-drinking.

PUBLIC RELATIONS OFFICER: the first to be so styled in Britain was Sir John Elliot, appointed by Southern Railway in 1925.

The first
RADAR

working apparatus, was developed by Dr Rudolph Kühnold, Chief of the German Navy's Signals Research Department, during the summer and autumn of 1933 and consisted of a 700W transmitter, working on a frequency of 600 megacycles, a receiver and disc reflectors. The first practical tests with this equipment were conducted at Kiel Harbour on 20 March 1934, when Kühnold succeeded in receiving echo signals from the battleship *Hesse* as she lay at anchor 600yd distant from the transmitter. An experimental installation was then made at the Naval Research Establishment at Pelzerhaken, near Lübeck, and in a demonstration before high-ranking naval officers in October 1934, echoes were picked up from a ship seven miles away. By chance, signals were also received from a seaplane flying through the beam, the first time an aircraft had been detected by radar. Following this achievement the German authorities allocated the sum of 70,000 Reichsmarks (then equivalent to approx. £11,500 or $57,500) for the setting up of a continuous development programme.

GB: In January 1935 (Sir) Robert Watson-Watt, Superintendent of the Radio Research Laboratory at Ditton Park, was asked by the newly formed Committee for the Scientific Survey of Air Defence to investigate the possibility of devising a 'death-ray'. He replied that in the present state of scientific knowledge death-rays were out of the question, but presented instead a paper titled 'Detection and Location of Aircraft by Radio Methods'. The first practical demonstration of aircraft detection by electromagnetic waves was held by Watson-Watt and his junior colleague A.F. Wilkins at Daventry before the Secretary of the Committee on 26 February 1935. A Heyford bomber, flying through the short-wave radiations of the BBC's Empire Station at Daventry at a height of 6,000ft, was identified at a distance of eight miles on a cathode-ray oscilloscope display housed in the back of a Morris van.

This initial experiment, using only readily available laboratory equipment, was followed by the setting up of a purpose-built installation at Orfordness, Suffolk, where in mid June an aircraft was tracked by radar for a distance of 17 miles, a performance improved to 40 miles the following month. These tests were particularly significant for the fact that the observers were able to take continuous measurements of the range of the aircraft.

The encouraging results achieved at Orfordness, and later at Bawdsey Manor, nr Felixstowe, prompted a Government decision in December 1935 to build five permanent air-defence radar stations covering the approach to London via the Thames Estuary. The first of these, at Bawdsey Manor, was handed over to the RAF in May 1937. By August a further decision had been taken to provide an apron of radar stations protecting the whole east coast of England. The complete chain of 20 stations, stretching from Ventnor to the Firth of Tay, went on continuous watch starting on Good Friday 1939.

At the outbreak of World War II, Germany had eight similar coastal radar stations guarding the narrow approach between the Dutch and Danish borders. Bearing in mind how conspicuous high-masted radar stations are, it is an extraordinary fact that neither country was aware that the other had discovered radio detection and developed it for air defence.

It is clear that Britain derived greater benefit from radar during the early part of the war than her opponent. Prof. P. M. S. Blackett, one of the original members of the Air Defence Committee, is on record as saying that without radar 'the Battle of Britain in 1940 – a near thing at best – might have been lost, with incalculable historic consequences'.

Radar is not, strictly speaking, an invention and nor can any one nation claim credit for originality, since the technique used by Watson-Watt and others for measuring the distances of electrically charged layers in the upper atmosphere was known several years before its inception. For this reason it is not surprising that radar was evolved independently by a number of other countries – France, Japan and the USA – concurrently with developments in Britain and Germany. In assessing relative achievements, however, it is worthy to note that although Germany was the first country to produce a working radar-detection system, only in September 1935 did her scientists adopt the use of pulse transmissions for calculating range, some three months after this essential prerequisite to the effective use of radar had been accomplished in Britain.

While work on radar was begun in the USA by the Naval Research Laboratory as early as January 1934, progress by a nation not under the immediate threat of war was inevitably slower than in an unsettled Europe. Successful demonstrations of aircraft detection were first held in June 1936. One contribution the Americans did make was the name 'radar', coined by Comdr S. M. Tucker, USN, *c.* 1940, and adopted officially by the British in 1943. Previously, radar had been known in Britain as RDF (Radio Direction Finding), a cover name to disguise its true function.

SHIP TO BE FITTED WITH RADAR: the first was the 500-ton German naval trials vessel *Welle* at Pelzerhaken in September 1935. Transmitting pulses on 600 megacycles, the radar installation was capable of detecting and ranging coastlines at a distance of 12 miles and other ships at 5 miles.

The first warship to carry radar as part of her regular equipment was the German pocket-battleship *Graf Spee*, which was fitted with a 355-megacycles Seetakt gun-ranging set during the summer of 1936.

GB: A 1½m wavelength installation was made aboard the Royal Navy's minesweeper *Saltburn* at the end of 1936, but tests were not satisfactory and development subsequently concentrated on 7m wavelength radar. This resulted in the Type 79Y set, fitted to the cruiser *Sheffield* in August 1938.

AIRBORNE RADAR: work was begun at Bawdsey Manor, Felixstowe by the newly formed Airborne Research Group of the Telecommunications Research Establishment in the autumn of 1936 and the first aircraft equipped with radar, an RAF Heyford based at Martlesham, was flying as part of the test programme with a 7m set by the following March. Practical success with ASV (Air-to-Surface Vessel) equipment was first achieved on 3 September 1937 with the location of two battleships, HMS *Rodney* and HMS *Courageous*, at a range of five miles as they lay in the Channel south-west of Beachy Head.

The first operational ASV radar equipped aircraft, belonging to flights of Squadrons 217 and 270, RAF, were fitted with Mark I sets in September 1939.

Concurrently with research into ASV radar, an Airborne Interception (AI) set was developed for the location of enemy bombers and installed in 30 Blenheim aircraft during August and September 1939.

Night fighters of the RAF's Fighter Interception Unit at Middle Wallop went into action during the early summer of 1940 with Mark III AI sets and scored their first kill in July, when Flt Sgt Ashfield identified a Ju 88 beyond the range of visibility. Sir Robert Watson-Watt has stated that 'Nowhere else in the world did there exist in 1940 any airborne radar', a circumstance that gave Britain an inestimable advantage over her foe.

The first *RADIO*

system of signalling by, was described by Mahlon Loomis of Washington, D.C. in a paper dated 21 July 1866. During October of the same year Loomis succeeded in conveying messages over a distance of 14 miles between Catochin Ridge and Bear's Den in Loudoun County, Va. The experiment was witnessed by US Senator Samuel C. Pomeroy of Kansas and US Representative John A. Bingham of Ohio. The inventor gave the following account of the method by which he achieved radio telegraphy:

From two mountain peaks of the Blue Ridge in Virginia which are only about two thousand feet above tide water, two kites were let up – one from each summit. . . . These kites had each a small piece of fine copper-wire gauze about fifteen inches square attached to their underside and connected also with the wire six hundred feet in length which held the kites when they were up. . . . Good connection was made with the ground by laying in a wet place a coil of wire one end of which was secured to the binding post of a galvanometer. The equipments and apparatus at both stations are exactly alike. The time pieces of both parties having been set exactly alike, it was arranged that at precisely such an hour and minute the galvanometer at one station should be attached, or be in circuit with the ground and kite wires. At the opposite station the ground wire being already fast to the galvanometer, three separate and deliberate half-minute connections were made with the kite wire and instruments. This deflected, or moved, the needle at the other station with the same vigour and precision as if it had been attached to an ordinary battery.

After this initial demonstration, Loomis continued his experimental work, and, according to a number of reports, he erected a pair of permanent steel radio masts. On 20 July 1872 he was granted the world's first wireless patent for an 'Improvement in Telegraphing'. In January of the following year Congress passed a Bill incorporating the Loomis Aerial Telegraph Co with the right to sell stock to the value of $2 million, but in a period of severe financial blight the necessary funds were not forthcoming and Loomis was obliged to struggle on with his research without capital until his death in 1886.

GB: The first system of radio communication was devised by David Edward Hughes, who discovered in 1879 that a microphone connected to a telephone receiver would emit a sound whenever the circuit in his induction balance was broken. Further experiments conducted at his house at 40 Langham Street in London – about a minute's walk from the present Broadcasting House – proved that a feeble electric spark in any circuit gave out such intense currents that they could be detected by a microphonic joint with a telephone ear-piece in any part of the building. As the maximum distance between the farthermost rooms of his house was only 60ft, Hughes obtained greater range by setting the transmitter in operation and walking up and down Great Portland Street with the receiver in his hand and the telephone to his ear. The signals increased in strength until he had progressed some 60yd from the transmitter, then diminished until at 500yd they could no longer be heard with certainty.

Hughes exhibited his method to Sir W. H. Preece and Sir William Crookes in December 1879, and again to Prof. Huxley and Sir George Stokes on 20 February 1880. The last named was sceptical. Hughes wrote many years later:

The experiments shown were most successful, and at first they seemed astonished at the results; but towards the close of three hours' experiments, Professor Stokes said that all the results could be explained by known electro-magnetic induction effects, and therefore he could not accept my view of actual aerial electric waves unknown up to that time, but thought that I had quite enough original material matter to form a paper on the subject to be read at the Royal Society.

I was so discouraged at being unable to convince them of the truth of these aerial electric waves that I actually refused to write a paper on the subject until I was better prepared to demonstrate the existence of these waves.

Hughes continued his researches, but never published the results, which did not become known until Sir William Crookes alluded to them in an article published in the *Fortnightly* in 1899. Invited to establish his claim to priority of discovery, Hughes refused, saying that it would be 'unfair to later workers in the same field to spring an unforeseen claimant to the experiments which they have certainly made without knowledge of my work'. Credit for making known the existence of radio waves must therefore be accorded to the German electrical scientist Heinrich Hertz, whose brilliant researches on the subject in 1887–9 paved the way for practical radio telegraphy and broadcasting.

COMMERCIALLY PRACTICABLE METHOD OF RADIO COMMUNICATION: the first was devised by Guglielmo Marconi of Bologna, Italy, who conducted his initial laboratory experiments to this end at his father's country-house, the Villa Grifone at Pontecchio, 11 miles from Bologna, in 1894. He began experimenting out of doors towards the end of September 1895, his brother Alfonso carrying the receiving set while Guglielmo himself worked the Morse key of the transmitter. Successful transmission across an open space was acknowledged by Alfonso with a white flag, but Guglielmo considered that the real test of the effectiveness of his apparatus was whether he could transmit signals over such natural obstacles as hills and mountains. Accordingly Alfonso discarded the flag and took the receiving set and a hunting-rifle to the far side of the hill behind the Villa Grifone. After a while Guglielmo began to signal from a room in the house, and a few minutes later a shot from the rifle announced that he had achieved what Sir William Preece was later to describe as 'a new system of telegraphy that will reach places hitherto inaccessible . . .'.

Marconi giving a private demonstration of radio before naval and military observers on Salisbury Plain, September 1896 – an artist's impression

Following his successful demonstrations at the Villa Grifone, Guglielmo Marconi offered his invention to the Italian Ministry of Posts and Telegraphs. On receiving a letter of rejection, he decided to bring his apparatus to England which was then the foremost Naval Power in the world and the most likely to appreciate the potentiality of radio-signalling. Arriving in February 1896, he received an initial set-back when his radio equipment was broken beyond repair by aggressive Customs Inspectors, who suspected that it was some 'infernal machine', and its owner, being Italian, an anarchist. Guglielmo took rooms at 71 Hereford Road, Bayswater, together with his mother who had accompanied him, and on 2 June 1896, applied for a patent for a method by which 'electrical actions or manifestations are transmitted through the air, earth or water by means of electrical oscillations of high frequency'. Shortly afterwards, he secured an introduction to Sir William Preece, Chief Engineer of the Post Office, who took an immediate interest in the 21-year-old Italian and his remarkable achievement, and did much to further his cause in scientific circles. On 12 December 1896 the first public demonstration of wireless was given under his auspices at Toynbee Hall in London. The following July Marconi formed the Wireless Telegraph & Signal Co Ltd for the manufacture of radio equipment and maintenance of radio stations.

PERMANENT RADIO INSTALLATION: the first was the Needles Hotel Wireless Station, at Alum Bay, Isle of Wight, established by the Wireless Telegraph & Signal Co Ltd in November 1897.

COMMERCIAL APPLICATION OF RADIO was first made by the Wireless Telegraph & Signal Co Ltd on behalf of Lloyd's, who ordered transmitters and receivers for the Rathlin Island Lighthouse and a shore station at Ballycastle, Co Antrim. The first messages from the lighthouse, reporting 10 ships, were received on 26 August 1898. Subsequently all Lloyd's signal stations were equipped with radio.

The first
RADIO BROADCAST

was presented by Canadian-born Prof. Reginald Aubrey Fessenden (*see also* Radio Telephone) via the 420ft-high radio mast of the National Electric Signalling Co's radio station at Brant Rock, Mass. on 24 December 1906. The programme opened with Fessenden himself playing Gounod's 'O, Holy Night' on the violin, after which he sang and then recited some verses from the Gospel of St Luke. The next item was Handel's 'Largo' played on a gramophone record, and the transmission concluded with a Christmas greeting from Fessenden to his listeners. The broadcast was picked up by a number of ships' radio operators within a five-mile range of the radio station. A second broadcast was made on New Year's Eve with much more favourable atmospheric conditions; reception was reported from as far away as the West Indies.

GB: The first broadcast in Britain was made the following year, when Lt Quentin Crauford RN obtained Admiralty permission to air a concert from the radio-room of HMS *Andromeda* for the benefit of other ships at Chatham. Crauford had himself adapted the *Andromeda*'s radio telegraphy system to enable the transmission of speech. Over 20 years later his memories of the occasion were recorded in the *Daily Mail*:

In 1907 I had several signalmen to help me. I chose the most musical of them to sing the first song, 'God Save the King'. This was the first song ever broadcast. We followed it up with 'Rule Britannia', 'Trafalgar Day', 'On the Mississippi Shore', 'There is a Tavern in the Town', 'Three Blind Mice' and others. The Admiralty did not want the general public to know of the invention. I was not allowed to say a word about it. They thought it could be adapted with great profit for use in submarines.

The first regular experimental broadcasts were transmitted from a studio on the top floor of the Parker Building on Fourth Avenue, New York in February 1907 by the De Forest Radio Telephone Co (*see* Radio Telephone). Lee De Forest wrote in his diary: 'My present task (happy one) is to distribute sweet melody broadcast over the city and sea so that in time even the mariner far out across the silent waves may hear the music of his homeland. . . .' To start with the programmes consisted solely of Columbia gramophone records; the first live performer was the Swedish soprano Eugenia Farrar, who sang 'I Love You Truly' and 'Just a wearyin' for You' in a broadcast from the USS *Connecticut* at Brooklyn Navy Yard in September.

Although he concentrated on musical presentations, in 1909 De Forest brought his well-known mother-in-law, Harriet Stanton Black, to the studio to give the world's first broadcast talk, her subject being the topical one of women's suffrage. Other notable 'firsts' included the first 'outside broadcast' in January 1910, when listeners were able to hear Caruso live from the Metropolitan Opera House (*see* Radio Broadcast: Opera), and the first studio broadcast by an artiste of international repute, given by the *prima donna* Mme Mariette Mazarin, the following month.

The De Forest transmissions are believed to have ceased in 1911, when the fortunes of the Radio Telephone Co were at a low ebb. Other early broadcasting services were offered by Thomas E. Clark of the Clark Wireless Telegraph & Telephone Co, Detroit, who began transmitting record programmes in 1907 for the benefit of the Great Lakes steamers, and by Charles D. Herrold, who began broadcasting from his School of Radio at the Garden City Bank Building at San José, Calif. in January 1909. The latter began transmitting records, live vocalists and – according to one claim – news, on a once-weekly basis. Within two years it had become the first broadcasting station in the world to establish a daily scheduled service. The exact date when daily broadcasting was initiated is not known, but a number of pioneer amateur radio operators in the San José area have signed affidavits to the effect that they were listening in to the Herrold station every week-day as early as 1910. The Herrold station was assigned the call letters SJN in 1912, was reclassified as KQW in 1921, and became KCBS in 1949. As such, it is generally acknowledged to be the oldest broadcasting station in the world. A plaque, now adorning the American Trust Co Building in San José, asserts that this was where the 'World's First Regular Broadcasting Station' had its beginning, a claim that must rest on whatever definition of 'regular' is accepted in this context.

Rival claimants to the honour are far from few, though all American. De Forest's 1907 station had been 'regular' in the sense that it continued broadcasting for four years without any long intervals off the air. The station started up again in 1916 with the installation of a transmitter on the roof of his laboratories at High Beach in the Bronx, and broadcast record concerts five nights a week until America's entry into the war put a stop to all non-essential use of radio telephony. It reopened as Station 2XG in 1919, taking an important step towards the realization of radio as a real entertainment medium by the appointment of announcers (Bill Gowen and Bill Garity), as well as the first programme director known to history, Richard Klein.

Early in 1920, 2XG came to a premature end when De Forest decided to move the station from High Bridge to the World's Tower Building on 46th Street and Broadway. In doing so, however, he unwittingly broke the law by transferring his transmitter from the Bronx, where it was licensed, to Manhattan, where it was not. The New York Federal Radio Inspector not only notified De Forest that he must cease broadcasting forthwith, but at the same time ruled that 'there is no room on the ether for entertainment'.

Thus 2XG represented the half-way stage between purely experimental broadcasting and fully fledged entertainment service. De Forest himself credited Station WWJ Detroit with the honour of having initiated the modern era of broadcasting, describing it as 'the first commercial radio station in America to broadcast regular daily programmes'. Originating as 8MK Detroit, the station began transmitting experimentally from the *Detroit News* office early in 1920. Regular scheduled broadcasts, consisting of record concerts, were advertised in the *News* from 20 August 1920 – the first time that daily programme announcements had appeared in any newspaper.

The other principal contender to the title of 'first full-service broadcasting station' (i.e. not experimental) is KDKA Pittsburgh. A comparison between the claims of WWJ and KDKA is made below.

KDKA owes its origin to an advertisement placed in the *Pittsburgh Sun* by the Joseph Horne Department Store on 29 September 1920. Headed 'Air Concert Picked up by Radio Here', it described how programmes broadcast by Dr Frank Conrad's amateur station 8XK could be heard 'on the wireless receiving station which was recently installed here for patrons interested in wireless experiments'. Similar receivers, stated the advertisement, were on sale now in the West Basement at prices of $10 upwards.

Dr Conrad was a radio engineer employed by the Westinghouse Co, whose Vice-President, H. P. Davis, was among those who saw the Joseph Horne advertisement. The next day Davis suggested that Westinghouse should erect a station at East Pittsburgh and operate it on a daily schedule 'so that people would acquire the habit of listening to it just as they do of reading a newspaper'.

The station was licensed by the Department of Commerce and assigned the call letters KDKA on 27 October 1920. Westinghouse had already begun manufacturing a special home receiver which was produced in sufficient quantity to ensure that everyone who wanted one would be able to listen in to the opening broadcast on 2 November. These can reasonably be regarded as the first sets designed solely for listening to broadcasts rather than for conducting radio experiments.

At the time that KDKA came on the air under the direction of Frank Conrad, Detroit's 8MK was still being run as an amateur experimental station

personally financed by William Scripps, publisher of the *Detroit News*. It was not owned by the newspaper, and despite De Forest's generous tribute, it was not at this stage in any sense commercially operated. KDKA's claim to priority, as the earliest non-experimental broadcasting station, is based on the fact that it was founded as a commercial enterprise whose only object would be to provide a programme service sufficiently entertaining and informative to induce prospective listeners to buy radio sets. In this important respect it differed from all previous broadcasting stations, whose interest had been primarily in the technical development of radio. Detroit referred to its listeners as 'radio operators', seeing them as fellow experimenters; Westinghouse aimed to reach the family circle rather than simply the radio ham.
GB: The first broadcasting service in Britain was inaugurated on an informal and spasmodic basis by the Marconi Co, which began transmitting speech and music from a 15kW transmitter at its Chelmsford works in January 1920. For a brief period, 23 February–6 March, a series of 30min programmes were aired on a twice-daily basis. The entertainment, arranged under the direction of H. J. Round and W. T. Mitcham, was made up of readings from newspapers, gramophone records and live musical performances. The instrumentalists who provided these first live 'radio concerts' were drawn from the Marconi engineering staff, and included G. W. White on piano, A. V. Beeton on oboe and W. Higby on the cornet. Vocal numbers were rendered by Edward Cooper, a tenor otherwise employed in the Marconi mounting shop. The first paid artiste ever to broadcast in Britain (probably in February 1920) was Winifred Sayer, an amateur soprano who worked for the Hoffman Manufacturing Co in Chelmsford. She was paid a fee of 5s for her services and told by the Managing Director of Marconi's, Godfrey Isaacs, that she had helped to make history. Miss Sayer, who took a less lofty view of her pioneering role, insisted on referring to the new medium of broadcasting as 'this Punch and Judy show'.

The first professional artiste to broadcast in Britain was Dame Nellie Melba, who gave a 30min concert from Chelmsford on 15 June 1920. This was commissioned by Lord Northcliffe, the proprietor of the *Daily Mail*, and included 'Home Sweet Home', 'Nymphs et Sylvains', the 'Addio' from *La Bohème*, and 'Chant Venitien'. Melba described the broadcast as 'the most wonderful experience of my career'. Her fee was £1,000.

The experimental transmissions from Chelmsford were suspended in November 1920, as they were held to be interfering with radio communication to aircraft and ships. After representations to the Post Office by the radio societies, whose members made up the bulk of the listening public, broadcasting was resumed from Marconi's Station 2MT at Writtle on 14 February 1922. Headed by P. P. Eckersley, Head of the Experimental Section and later the first Chief Engineer of the BBC, the Writtle pioneers launched Britain's first sustained and regular scheduled broadcasting service with a ½hr programme at 8pm every Tuesday. Writtle was remote from any centre of population, and though the occasional professional artiste was inveigled into making the trip down from London in return for a £1 fee, most of the entertainment was improvised by the staff. One of their number, R. T. B. Wynn, recollected the light-hearted approach of Writtle broadcasting in an article he wrote for *London Calling* in 1946:

Some time on Tuesday afternoon the piano would be trundled into the hut, and we would receive a bunch of records – most of which were usually rejected as too highbrow! Programme planning was done at the 'Cock and Bull' up the road, about half an hour beforehand. We had artistic ambitions – for example we put on Cyrano de Bergerac, *the first play ever to be broadcast in this country. . . . But our star was Eckersley. He'd go up to the microphone, and apparently without effort, be spontaneously funny for ten minutes at a time. He talked to our listeners as if he'd lived next door to them for years, and they loved it.*

'Our listeners' in the spring of 1922 numbered some 8,000 licensed radio operators and their families. Most were listeners-in to the only other two European broadcasting stations operating at that date, the Paris Eiffel Tower Station, which transmitted a daily afternoon 'recital', and the Nederlandsche Radio-Industrie service from The Hague, consisting of a Thursday evening programme, and the weekly 'Dutch Concert', as it was known, from 3 to 5pm on Sundays.

Three other broadcasting stations were established in Britain during 1922, Marconi's 2LO at Marconi House in the Strand (11 May), Metropolitan Vickers' 2ZY Manchester (16 May), and Western Electric's 2WP at Oswaldestre House, Norfolk Street in London (October). While these stations were all merged into the British Broadcasting Company in November, Writtle maintained its independence, and for the two months until close-down on 17 January 1923, it offered the only British alternative to the BBC until the advent of 'Pirate Radio' in the 60s.

Listening-in required an intense expression in the spring of 1922! The BBC was yet to come.

BBC PROGRAMME: the first was a news bulletin, broadcast from 2LO at 6pm on 14 November 1922 and repeated at 9pm. These two items, together with a weather report, made up the full schedule for the opening of Britain's first daily sustained broadcasting service (*see also* Radio Broadcast: News). The following day, when the two regional stations at Birmingham and Manchester came on the air, broadcasting was devoted to the announcement of election results. The first entertainment programme, an hour-length selection of vocal and instrumental items, was broadcast from 2LO at 7pm on the 16th. The opening number, 'Drake Goes West', was sung by Leonard Hawke, baritone, who thus became the BBC's first performer.
CHOICE OF BBC PROGRAMMES: the first was offered on 8 January 1925. At 7.30pm the new high-powered long-wave transmitter at Chelmsford broadcast Acts I and II of *Maritana*, in a direct relay from the Old Vic. Five minutes later less highbrow listeners were able to tune in to *US* on the National Programme, a pierrot show featuring George Lamb and Amy Dennett. Most of the time, however, Chelmsford was used for transmitting the National service after 7pm. The BBC's first alternative channel was 5XX Daventry, which opened on 27 July 1925.

The present Radio 2 began as the

Light Programme on 29 July 1945. Radio 3 was instituted as the Third Programme on 29 September 1946.

Radio 1 came on the air for the first time at 7am on 30 September 1967, with disc jockey Tony Blackburn introducing *The Breakfast Show*. The first record played on the BBC's new Pop channel was 'Flowers in the Rain' by The Move. *LOCAL RADIO STATION:* the first was Radio Leicester, opened by the Rt Hon. Edward Short, MP, Postmaster-General, on 8 November 1967.

The first
RADIO BROADCAST: CHILDREN'S PROGRAMME
(regular) was *The Man in the Moon Stories for Children*, which were broadcast twice weekly from Westinghouse's WJZ Station at Newark, N.J. commencing in the autumn of 1921. The reader was Miss Josephine Lawrence. *GB: Children's Corner*, transmitted from the BBC's Birmingham Station 5IT with A.E. Thompson, Engineer-in-Charge, as 'Uncle Tom', from 5 December 1922. *Children's Hour* began from the BBC's London Station on 23 December 1922.

The first
RADIO BROADCAST: COMEDY PROGRAMME (GB)
was a ½hr show titled *Listening In*, which was broadcast from 2LO London on 29 July 1922, in a special transmission to the Monotype Athletic Club Garden Fête at Horley. Featuring music-hall comedian Will Hay as 'Professor Broadcaster', this 'musical burlesque in fifteen radio calls' consisted of excerpts from a forthcoming production at the Apollo Theatre.

The first comedy programme written specially for radio and the first original radio script of any kind was Helena Millais's *A Cockney Fragment from Life*, in which she herself portrayed 'Our Lizzie', a Cockney char, in a broadcast from 2LO's Marconi House on 20 October 1922. Reappearing on the air shortly after the BBC began broadcasting in November, 'Our Lizzie' subsequently established herself as radio's first comic character and her creator as one of radio's earliest stars.

The first regular broadcast comedy series was the BBC's *Band Waggon*, starting 5 January 1938, in which Arthur Askey and Richard 'Stinker' Murdoch rented an imaginary flat above Broadcasting House, with a camel and a goat, and occupied themselves polishing the six time-pips.

The first
RADIO BROADCAST: COMMERCIAL
was a 10min talk on Hawthorne Hall, a new co-operative apartment house at Jackson Heights, N.Y., transmitted by Station WEAF New York on behalf of the Queensboro Corp at 5.15pm on 28 August 1922. The commercial was read by a Mr Blackwell of the Queensboro Corp. The sponsor paid $500 for five successive daily 'spots', and was later able to report that two apartments had been sold in response to the advertisement. WEAF's service was described by the owners of the station, A. T. & T., as 'toll broadcasting'. The station itself provided no programme material at all, but anyone could come in and give his or her message to the world, commercial or otherwise, or demonstrate his own particular talents, for a set fee of so much a minute air time. Other early sponsors to broadcast commercials on WEAF during 1922 were Tidewater Oil, American Express, Macy's, Metropolitan Life, Colgate's, and I. Miller Shoes.
GB: The first advertiser to broadcast a radio commercial to a British audience was Selfridge's, which sponsored a fashion talk from the Eiffel Tower Radio Station in Paris in 1925. Three listeners reported hearing the broadcast, which was arranged by Capt. Leonard F. Plugge (*see also* Motor-car Radio). Although this particular experiment was not repeated, between 1928 and 1930 Radio Hilversum broadcast a fortnightly series of concerts by de Groot's Orchestra which were sponsored by a British radio manufacturer. The French commercial station Radio Toulouse began catering to British advertisers in 1929. Radio Normandie, which could reach a larger British audience than French, followed suit in 1931. Radio Luxembourg began transmissions in the spring of 1933, though at first it broadcast in English on Sundays only.

The first commercial radio station on the British mainland was London Broadcasting, which began transmitting on 8 October 1973. The first commercial, a 60sec spot at 6.08, advertised Birds Eye Fish Fingers.

The first
RADIO BROADCAST: DISCUSSION PROGRAMME
in Britain was transmitted by the BBC on 22 February 1923, when Sir Ernest Benn, a right-wing publisher, propounded that 'Communism would be a danger to the good of the people', and was answered by the Communist MP (*q.v.*) for Motherwell, J.T. Walton Newbold. This programme was notable as the first BBC programme to take notice of party politics, the first on a controversial topic, and the first in which a Member of Parliament participated.

The first
RADIO BROADCAST: ELECTION ADDRESS (GB)
was made on behalf of the Labour Party by the Rt Hon. J. Ramsay MacDonald, speaking from Glasgow on 13 October 1924. The *Illustrated London News* reported: 'Mr MacDonald did not "broadcast" well, owing to his oratorical devices of raising and lowering his voice, turning from side to side, and striding about the platform at various distances from the microphone.'

The first
RADIO BROADCASTING: EXTERNAL SERVICE
was inaugurated with a short-wave transmission from the Netherlands to the Dutch East Indies by the Philips Electrical Works Station PCJJ on 11 March 1927. The first programme consisted of gramophone records. On 1 June 1927 Queen Wilhelmina made her first broadcast to the Empire.
GB: An experimental Empire Service was inaugurated by the BBC from the Marconi Station G5SW Chelmsford on 11 November 1927. Following protracted and unsuccessful negotiations with the Government, the BBC decided to 'go it alone' without financial aid, and began its official Empire Broadcasting Service from Daventry on 19 December 1932. At first there was no special appropriation of funds for the new service and the first week's programmes were produced at a cost of 10gns. Soon after the King's Christmas Message to the Peoples of the Empire had been broadcast for the first time in 1932, a sum of £100 a week was allocated to Empire programmes.

The first external broadcasts of the BBC in a foreign language were made with the inauguration of the Arabic Service on 3 January 1938. Although there had been some discussion whether these broadcasts should be tailored to present Britain in the best light by omitting 'unwelcome facts of news', the BBC took a stand on this that was to characterize its overseas propaganda henceforward and particularly during the war. On the first day of the Arabic Service, an item was included in the news reporting the execution that morning of a Palestinian Arab on the orders of a British Military Court. It was this refusal to compromise with truth in order to serve short-term interests that helped to give the BBC External Service the credibility lacking in the heavily censored German and Italian overseas broadcasts.

The first
RADIO BROADCAST: NEWS BULLETINS
were broadcast from Station 8MK

Detroit commencing 20 August 1920. The bulletins were compiled from news agency wire service reports supplied by the *Detroit News*.
GB: The first news bulletin was broadcast by the BBC as its first-ever programme item on 14 November 1922. The *Daily News* reported:

Two budgets of news were sent out by wireless telephony – one at 6.00pm and the other at 9.00pm. The call sign was 2LO and the news came over in a clear voice which first announced the sending station – the London Broadcasting Station. Mr Bonar Law was announced as having made his final election speech at Glasgow, his policy being 'quietness and stability'. Mr Churchill was said to be none the worse for his rowdy meeting the previous night, and there were to be no police court charges, said the wireless. The skeleton story of a train robbery, the sale of a Shakespearian first folio, and the fog in London were other news items. This first budget of news concluded with the latest billiards scores.

The name of the newsreader has not been identified, though the likeliest candidate would have been the BBC's newly appointed Director of Programmes, Arthur Burrows.

The first
RADIO BROADCAST: OPERA
presentation was transmitted from the Metropolitan Opera House, New York on 13 January 1910, by the De Forest Radio Telephone Co. This occasion was also notable as the first 'outside broadcast' in history. The operas heard were *Cavalleria Rusticana* and *Pagliacci*, with Caruso singing the role of Canio in the latter. The female leads were sung by Mme Destinn and Bella Alten respectively. The acoustical microphone was placed in the footlights, though for the first aria – 'La Siciliana' from *Cavalleria Rusticana*, sung by Ricardo Martin from behind the curtain – a microphone was placed on a table in front of him. Receiving sets were installed at the Opera House itself, the Park Avenue Laboratory of the De Forest Radio Telephone Co, the De Forest factory at Newark, N.J., the Metropolitan Life Building, and the Hotel Breslin near Times Square. In addition, the broadcast was picked up by radio operators at the Brooklyn Navy Yard and by a number of ships in New York Harbour, including RMS *Avon*, whose Captain had invited 260 guests on board to listen.
GB: The first opera presentation was Act I of Mozart's *The Magic Flute* by the British National Opera Co, transmitted by the BBC direct from the Royal Opera House, Covent Garden on 8 January 1923.

The first
RADIO BROADCAST: ORCHESTRAL CONCERT
was an hour-long performance of the California Theater Orchestra of San Francisco under Herman Heller, transmitted by Lee De Forest (*see also* Radio Telephone; Radio Broadcast) via a transmitter on the Humboldt Bank Building adjoining the theatre in April 1920. These Heller concerts were continued on a regular basis for some months and attracted an appreciative audience of music-lovers as well as radio hams. 'In one isolated community far back in the Coast Range', wrote De Forest in his *Autobiography*, 'an opulent rancher installed a receiver and loud-speaker, and for miles around, his neighbours would journey each Sunday to hear that marvel coming out of the air from "Frisco".'
GB: Transmitted by the BBC on 23 December 1922. The programme records do not name the orchestra, revealing only that the leader was J. Pennington, and that one of the pieces played was Quilter's *Children's Overture*.

The first
RADIO BROADCAST: PLAY
was Eugene Walter's melodrama *The Wolf*, presented by WGY Schenectady (N.Y.) in a 2½hr adaptation with H. Edward Smith and Rosaline Greene in the leading roles on 3 August 1922. Smith also produced the play. Regular Friday-night productions by the WGY Players – radio's first repertory company – began the following month. The scripts were typed on paper 'especially selected for its freedom from crackling sound'. At first the Players gave their services gratuitously, but by 1924 Rosaline Greene, America's 'first leading lady of radio', was being paid $5 a performance.
GB: An abbreviated version of Rostand's *Cyrano de Bergerac* was presented by the engineering staff of the Marconi experimental station 2MT Writtle on 17 October 1922. The cast included R.T.B. Wynn, later Chief Engineer of the BBC, and Capt. P.P. Eckersley, Head of Marconi's Experimental Section.
PLAY WRITTEN FOR RADIO: the first was *The Truth about Father Christmas*, a Christmas play for children by Phyllis M. Twigg, broadcast by the BBC on 24 December 1922.

The first
RADIO BROADCAST: RECEIVING SETS
were produced in kit form by the Radio Telephone Co of New York in 1910, and sold to amateur radio enthusiasts at the demonstration-room in the Metropolitan Life Building. Lee De Forest, founder of the enterprise, wrote in his *Autobiography*: 'This was the first office or store in the world devoted wholly to the sale of radio apparatus to the public. A recent Harvard graduate, Quincy R. Brackett, was placed in charge of this rapidly expanding end of our business. Brackett thus became the first radio salesman in the world.' Purchasers of radio receivers could check the times of experimental broadcasts in the pages of the *Wireless Experimenter*.

Ready-made radio sets for home reception of broadcast programmes were first produced by the Westinghouse Co for listeners to Dr Frank Conrad's experimental Pittsburgh Station 8XK (later to become KDKA) and advertised for sale from $10 upwards by the Joseph Horne Department Store in the *Pittsburgh Sun* for 29 September 1920. These sets did not differ substantially from the receiving sets used by radio hams, but they were the first to be advertised in conjunction with a broadcasting service, rather than for personal experimentation. The first specially designed receiving sets were manufactured by Westinghouse in October 1920 at their East Springfield plant, in anticipation of the opening of the first regular broadcasting station, KDKA Pittsburgh, on 2 November 1920.
GB: A broadcast receiving set capable of picking up all the European experimental broadcasting stations was demonstrated before the Wireless Society of London by the British Thomson-Houston Co Ltd in 1920, but there is no evidence it was ever offered for sale.

The first home receiving sets were manufactured by the Marconi Co at Chelmsford in the summer of 1922 in preparation for the commencement of regular broadcasting by the BBC in the autumn. Three models were available: the Marconiphone Crystal Junior,

Marconiphone V.2 home radio set 1922

designed by C.S. Franklin; the Marconiphone V.1, designed by P.W. Willans; and the Marconiphone V.2, also by Franklin. The two latter were both single-valve sets.
PORTABLE RADIO SET: the first produced in Britain was the Burndept Ethophone V Portable, which was advertised for sale in July 1923. It was designed to look like a suitcase when closed and access to the controls was via two panels in the front that opened outwards.

The first
RADIO BROADCAST: REQUEST PROGRAMME
was *You Ask – We Play*, compèred by Heinz Goedecke of Deutschlandsender, Berlin and broadcast irregularly from 25 October 1936 until 26 March 1939. Six bands participated live in the opening programme, including the Musikkorps of Hitler's personal bodyguard, the Leibstandarte SS.

The idea had originated the previous Christmas Day, when a listener in Weimar had called Deutschlandsender during a performance by Barnabas von Geczy and asked for a special request number. He offered to pay but Heinz Goedecke, who took the call, said it would be improper. The listener then proposed that he should make a donation of 20 Reichsmarks to the Nazi Winter Help Fund instead. This was accepted and radio's first request number, 'Weinende Geige', was played over the air by von Geczy's Violin Orchestra. Goedecke's request programme proved enormously popular all over Germany and raised considerable sums for the Winter Help Fund.
GB: From My Post-bag, with Sandy Macpherson at the BBC Theatre Organ, first presented on the London Regional Programme on Friday, 19 May 1939. At first the name of the listener requesting the tune was not broadcast over the air, but in October 1939 Sandy Macpherson received a letter from Pte F. Dunnington of the RASC suggesting a new type of programme that would put families separated by war in touch with each other. From this idea developed the first modern request programme in which correspondents asked for particular selections to be played for relatives or loved ones. *Sandy's Half-Hour* began on 28 February 1940 with a request by A/C Rolfe of the RAF for 'Shanty Town Moon' to be played for his wife. At the end of the month Sandy was receiving over 5,000 letters a week, many accompanied by cheques and postal orders for charity, as in the original German programme. These unsolicited inducements were, however, returned to their senders. The most popular requests during the initial season were 'We'll Meet Again', 'Faithful For Ever', and 'I Shall be Waiting'.

The first
RADIO BROADCAST: SPORTS COMMENTARY
was transmitted by KDKA Pittsburgh on the occasion of Johnny Ray's fight against Johnny Dundee at the Motor Square, Pittsburgh on 11 April 1921. The commentator was Florent Gibson of the *Pittsburgh Star*.

The first professional radio sports commentator in the world was Australia's Mick Ferry, who began his career with a broadcast for 2FC Sydney from Randwick Racecourse on 11 April 1925.
GB: The first commentary was broadcast via Station 2LO by Arthur Burrows, who described the fight between Ted Kid Lewis and Georges Carpentier at Olympia on 11 May 1922. The broadcast, which was sponsored by the *Daily Mail*, was the only sports commentary given before 1927, restrictions having been put on the BBC in this respect so that the newspapers should not face 'unfair competition' from the new medium.
• The first commentary of a team game in Britain, as well as the first BBC sports commentary, was given by Capt. H.B.T. Wakelam on the occasion of the England *v.* Wales Rugby International played at Twickenham on 15 January 1927. The only instruction he received in the new art from the BBC was a small notice posted up just below eye-level bearing the simple command 'Don't Swear'. Although he obeyed this injunction, he did not come through the experience entirely without criticism. The wife of an ex-International in South Wales wrote to Wakelam telling him he was a plague and a menace, for her husband had been so excited by the commentary that he imagined he was out on the field again and smashed up most of the living-room furniture. Capt. Wakelam became the BBC's first regular sports commentator, pioneering in soccer, cricket and tennis transmissions as well as rugby.

The first
RADIO BROADCAST: TIME SIGNALS
(regular) were transmitted from the Eiffel Tower Radio Station in Paris in 1913. The *Illustrated London News* advised: 'With the aid of a cheap and simple apparatus, consisting of short aerial wires in one's garden, a running-coil conduct detector, and telephone, one may listen, in the comfort of one's own home, to the signals flashed from Paris at certain intervals during each day.' Some readers may have found it easier to look at the clock.
GB: The GMT time signal and its preceding 'pips' were broadcast by the BBC regularly from 5 February 1924. The Pips idea had originated with Frank Hope-Jones, Chairman of the Wireless Society of London and an authority on electric clocks. In a broadcast talk on time measurement that he gave on 21 April 1923, he concluded with a count-down of the five seconds leading up to 10pm. He afterwards suggested that a permanent service of accurate time-pips, one per second, from five seconds to the hour to the exact hour, should be provided directly from the Royal Observatory at Greenwich to the broadcasting studio at Savoy Hill. This was implemented by connecting two highly accurate, if rather vintage, 1874 Dent chronometers at the Observatory to the BBC control-room by Post Office telephone lines. The pips were delivered in the form of short bursts of 1,000c/s tone by means of an electrical oscillator in the control-room.

The first
RADIO BROADCAST: VOX POP INTERVIEWS
were conducted on 27 June 1932 by Ted Husing of CBS, who carried a lapel microphone round the lobby of the Congress Hotel, Chicago where the delegates to the Democratic Convention were gathered. Husing asked bystanders spot questions about the prospect of Franklin D. Roosevelt's nomination for the Presidency. The first regular interview programme of this nature was *Vox Pop*, which began with broadcasts from the lobby of the Hotel New Yorker, New York by Parks Johnson in June 1935.
GB: The first Vox Pop interviews in either medium of broadcasting were conducted by Freddie Grisewood during the BBC Television transmission of the Coronation procession on 12 May 1937. A number of people in the crowd were asked how far they had travelled and how long they had been waiting to see the procession. The idea was completely spontaneous, and intended by the commentator only to fill a lengthy delay before the head of the procession came within camera range.

The first
RADIO DISTRESS SIGNAL
was transmitted from the East Goodwin Lightship on 17 March 1899 when the merchant vessel *Elbe* ran aground on the Goodwin Sands. The message was received by the radio operator on duty at the South Foreland Lighthouse, who was able to summon the aid of the Ramsgate lifeboat. The East Goodwin

Lightship became the first vessel to send a radio signal of its own distress on 28 April 1899 when it was rammed by the SS *R.F. Matthews*.

Prior to the introduction of SOS, the recognized call sign for ships in distress was CQD. The signal, devised by the Marconi Co and effective from 1 February 1904, was intended to mean: 'All Stations – Urgent', but was popularly misinterpreted as 'Come quick – danger'. SOS was established as an international distress signal by an agreement made between the British Marconi Society and the German Telefunk organization at the Berlin Radio Conference, 3 October 1906. It was formally introduced on 1 July 1908.

The first occasion on which the SOS signal was transmitted in an emergency occurred on 10 June 1909, when the Cunard liner SS *Slavonia* was wrecked off the Azores. Two steamers received her signals and went to the rescue.

The first
RADIO: INTERNATIONAL TRANSMISSION

was made across the English Channel by Guglielmo Marconi on 27 March 1899. The next day *The Times* carried the following report from its Boulogne Correspondent, the first Press message ever sent from one country to another by radio:

Communication between England and the Continent was set up yesterday morning by the Marconi system of wireless telegraphy. The points between which the experiments are being conducted are South Foreland and Wimereux, a village on the French coast two miles north of Boulogne, where a vertical standard wire, 150 ft in height, has been set up. The distance is 32 miles. The experiments are being carried on in the Morse code. Signor Marconi is here conducting the trials, and is very well satisfied with the results obtained. This message has been transmitted by the Marconi system from Wimereux to the Foreland.

The first
RADIO, MILITARY

was employed by the British Army during the South African War of 1899–1902. A special RE Wireless Section under the command of Capt. J.N.C. Kennedy arrived at Cape Town on 24 November 1899, accompanied by a number of civilian radio engineers seconded to the War Office by the Marconi Co. Five radio sets were built into horse-drawn Australian-type sprung wagons and dispatched to Modder, Belmont, Enslin, Orange River and De Aar. The accumulators were first boosted on 1 December 1899 and attempts to establish regular communication continued until 31 March 1900, when the equipment was handed over to the Royal Navy for use with the Delgoa Bay Squadron.

From the beginning the experiment was bedevilled with unforeseen problems. The antennae masts supplied by Marconi's proved too large and heavy for easy mobility and were replaced by 30ft bamboo poles; these failed to withstand the weather conditions and split beyond repair. Attempts to raise the aerials on kites were no more successful, as there was seldom sufficient wind at the receiving and transmitting stations at the same time. The loose soil of the veld and rock beneath failed to provide a proper earth, and though Signor Marconi himself claimed that the sets were actually put into operation for a time, reports from the field suggest that the Wireless Section never succeeded in maintaining an effective signalling system.

The first effective use of radio for ground communications in warfare took place during the Somaliland campaign of 1903, when the Royal Navy Land Force set up radio stations using kite-supported aerials.

The first portable-pack radio set designed for military use was developed by the Marconi Co and issued to the Westmorland and Cumberland Yeomanry in 1911. Similar sets were supplied to the Italian Army the same year for use in the Libyan Campaign.

MILITARY USE OF RADIO TELEPHONE: the first was made by the US Army Signal Corps, which conducted a series of experiments in 1908 over the 18-mile distance between Sandy Hook and Bedloes Island, off Bridgeport, Conn. The German-made Telefunken set was fitted with carbon microphones and worked on a 550V direct current supplied from 10 electric arcs.

The first radio telephone sets used in warfare were issued to German forces on the Western Front in 1917.

GB: Radio telephone sets for general issue were first produced in 1929. No. 1 Set was designed for use by infantry and artillery brigades, No. 2 for divisions, and No. 3 for corps. All three types were mounted on motor vehicles and could be operated on the move.

WALKIE-TALKIE: the first set for military use (i.e. a portable wireless telephone pack-set) was produced at the US Signal Corps Engineering Laboratories at Fort Monmouth, N.J. in 1933.

GB: A 25lb one-man portable set demonstrated by the Royal Corps of Signals at Aldershot on 21 June 1937.

The first
RADIO TELEPHONE

capable of reproducing articulate speech was the Radiophone, devised by Charles Sumner Tainter and Alexander Graham Bell and successfully demonstrated for the first time on 15 February 1880. The transmitter was located on top of the Franklin School in 13th Street, Washington, D.C., and Tainter spoke into it the words: 'Mr Bell! Mr Bell! If you hear me, come to the window and wave your hat!' A moment later Bell appeared at the window of his laboratory on 14th Street, hat in hand.

Marconi portable pack set issued to the Westmorland and Cumberland Yeomanry 1911

The great telephone pioneer gave credit for the invention to A.C. Brown of the Eastern Telegraph Co, who had come to him two years earlier with a plan for telephony without wires. This was based on the action of a ray of light falling on selenium connected to a battery, with a telephone receiver in the circuit. The variations in the beam of light, actuated by the voice, were picked up at the receiving end by a wafer-thin mirror in the shape of a telephone diaphragm. The method was only effective across an open space with no obstructions to the light beam, and so its practical application was limited, though successful tests were carried out over a distance of 1½ miles between the Franklin School and the Virginia Hills. It was subsequently developed by the American Telephone & Telegraph Co, and was employed under the trade-name 'Photophone' during the early 1900s by the German Government for lighthouse-shore communication and also by the US Signal Corps. The system had one remarkable advantage over conventional methods of radio telephony in that the conversation could not be tapped.

The first conventional system of radio telephony (i.e. capable of relaying speech through the ether regardless of any barriers between transmitter and receiver) was developed by the Canadian electrical scientist Prof. Reginald Aubrey Fessenden, and demonstrated for the first time over a distance of approximately one mile at

Cob Point, Md. in December 1900.
TRANSATLANTIC SPEECH TRANSMISSION BY RADIO TELEPHONY was first made unintentionally by Prof. Fessenden in November 1906, when a conversation being transmitted between the National Electric Signalling Co's station at Brant Rock, Mass. and Plymouth, Mass. was picked up by radio operators at Michrihanish, Scotland.

The first direct transatlantic speech relay by radio telephone was made by the American Telephone & Telegraph Co from Arlinton, Va. to Paris on 21 October 1915. Mr B.B. Webb spoke to Lt-Col Ferrie, representing the French Government, who was operating the receiver installed at the Eiffel Tower Radio Station by the Bell Telephone System.

GB: The voice of Marconi engineer W.T. Ditcham was heard at Louisberg, Nova Scotia on 19 March 1919. Speaking on a wavelength of 3,800m from a $2\frac{1}{2}$kW transmitter installed at Ballybunion, Ireland, his opening words were 'Hullo America!' The first recording of broadcast speech was made on this occasion, the signals received at the Eiffel Tower being made into a gramophone record.

COMMERCIAL RADIO TELEPHONE INSTALLATION: the first was made in the spring of 1907 by Lee De Forest of the De Forest Radio Telephone Co on behalf of the Lackawanna Railroad Co. Two land stations were erected, one on the banks of the Hudson River at Hoboken, and the other at the Company's offices on 23rd Street, New York. A third transmitter, and the first radio-telephone apparatus to be operated from a ship, was installed on the Lackawanna ferryboat *Bergen*.

NAVAL VESSELS TO BE EQUIPPED WITH RADIO-TELEPHONE APPARATUS: the first were the USS *Virginia* and *Connecticut*, in which installations were made by the De Forest Radio Telephone Co in September 1907. Tests were conducted off Cape Cod the same month and articulate speech was received at distances of up to 21 miles. As a result of the experiments De Forest was commissioned by the US Navy to install radio-telephone equipment in all 24 vessels of Admiral Evans's fleet, which was then about to start on a round-the-world voyage.

GB: HMS *Vernon* and HMS *Furious* were equipped with radio-telephone apparatus by the De Forest Co in September 1908, and tests were conducted between the *Vernon* in Portsmouth Harbour and the *Furious* out in the English Channel at distances of up to 60 miles.

PUBLIC RADIO-TELEPHONE SERVICE: the first available to telephone subscribers was inaugurated between Long Beach, Calif. and Avalon, Santa Catalina Island, off the California mainland, by the Southern California Telephone Co on 16 July 1920. The distance was 30 miles, and Avalon subscribers could be connected to callers anywhere else in the USA via the land-lines that terminated at Long Beach. The project was engineered by the American Telephone and Telegraph Co and by the Western Electric Co. It was abandoned after three years of operation owing to tapping by other radio operators.

See also Aeroplane Equipped with Radio.

The first
RAILCAR
was the *Fairfield*, a six-wheeled steam railcar with vertical boiler, designed by Bridges Adams and built at Adams's works in Fairfield Road, Bow in 1848. It was put into service on the Tiverton Branch of the Bristol & Exeter Railway during the winter of 1848–9. The *Fairfield* had a cruising speed of 40mph and carried 16 passengers 1st Class, 32 2nd Class. The 1st-Class compartment had large panoramic windows of the modern type and was a pioneer in this respect.

DIESEL-ELECTRIC RAILCAR: the first was an eight-wheeled non-bogie railcar with a 75bhp engine and accommodation for 51 passengers, which began operation on the Mellersta–Sodermanlands Railway, Sweden in 1913.

GB: The first diesel-electric railcars in regular service were three Armstrong-Whitworth railcars of 95, 140 and 250hp named the 'Tyneside Venturers' and introduced by the London & North Eastern Railway on Tyneside routes in December 1931.

The first
RAILWAY ACCIDENT: FATALITY
occurred at the foot of Simpasture on the Stockton & Darlington Railway on 19 March 1828, when driver John Gillespie was killed as the result of a boiler explosion. A second accident of a similar nature took place at Aycliffe watering station on 1 July, resulting in the death of driver John Cree. Both fatalities were due to the carelessness of the men involved in not allowing the weights of the safety-valves, fixed down during the journey, to remain down while their engines were stationary.

The first accident caused by a moving train, and the first involving a passenger took place at the opening of the Liverpool & Manchester Railway on 15 September 1830, when the Rt Hon. William Huskisson, MP was run down by the *Rocket* as he stood on the track at Parkside. According to Samuel Smiles:

> *The 'Northumbrian' engine with the carriage containing the Duke of Wellington was drawn up on one line in order that the whole of the train might pass in review before him and his party on the other. Mr Huskisson had alighted from the carriage, and was standing on the road, along which the 'Rocket' engine was observed rapidly coming up. At this moment the Duke of Wellington, between whom and Mr Huskisson some coolness had existed, made a sign of recognition and held out his hand. A hurried and friendly grasp was given, and before it was loosed, there was a general cry from the bystanders, 'Get in! get in!' Flurried and confused, Mr Huskisson endeavoured to get round the open door of the carriage, which projected over the opposite rail, but in so doing he was struck down by the 'Rocket'. His first words on being raised were, 'I have met my death'*

Huskisson was conveyed to Eccles in a critical condition by the *Northumbrian*, which in the emergency covered the 15-mile distance in a record 25min, but he died at the Rectory the same night.

The first
RAILWAY CARRIAGE: CORRIDOR COACH
was built for the Hudson River Railroad by Messrs Eaton & Gilbert of Troy, N.Y. in 1853. The car was 45ft long and divided into five compartments and a washroom with an 18in-wide side corridor.

GB: Designed by E.F. Howlden for the Great Northern Railway in 1882. Each carriage was divided into four 1st-Class compartments connected by a side corrdior and had a lavatory at each end, one for ladies, the other for gentlemen.

The first complete corridor train with connecting passages (bellows) between coaches was put into service on the London–Birkenhead run by the Great Western Railway on 7 March 1892.

The first
RAILWAY CARRIAGE: DINING-CAR
The first Buffet-Cars (self-service) were put into service on the Philadelphia, Wilmington & Baltimore Railroad in 1863. Two day-coaches were divided in the centre, one side being designated a 'smoker' and the other a 'buffet'. The food was cooked at the terminus and kept hot in steam-boxes. There were no seats in the buffet section, and passengers ate either standing up at the counter or took their food back into the smoker.

The first dining-car to serve full-

Britain's first railway buffet car, introduced by the LMS on Euston–Nottingham route, 2 June 1932

course meals prepared by a chef on the train was the *President*, a sleeping-car-cum-diner designed by George Pullman put into service by the Great Western Railroad of Canada in 1867. W.F. Rae, who travelled on the Great Central route in September 1869, recorded an impression of Pullman's innovation in his *Westward by Rail*:

The choice is by no means small. Five different kinds of bread, four sorts of cold meat, six hot dishes, to say nothing of eggs cooked in seven different ways and all the seasonable vegetables and fruits. . . . The meal is served on a table temporarily fixed to the side of the car and removed when no longer required. To breakfast, dine and sup in this style while the train is speeding at the rate of nearly thirty miles an hour is a sensation of which the novelty is not greater than the comfort.

GB: The *Prince of Wales*, placed in service on the London–Leeds run by the Great Northern Railway on 26 September 1879. No provision for 3rd-Class diners was made on any line till 1893.
BUFFET-CAR: (self-service) the first in GB was introduced by the London, Midland & Scottish Railway on the London–Nottingham run on 2 June 1932.

The first
RAILWAY CARRIAGE: SLEEPING-CAR
was the *Chambersburg*, introduced by the Cumberland Valley Railroad on its Harrisburg–Chambersburg, Pa. route in 1836. The carriage was divided into four sleeping-sections each containing three bunks. No bedding was provided and travellers wrapped themselves in shawls and slept with their boots on.
GB: 'Bed-carriages' were introduced on the Grand Junction and London & Birmingham Railways in 1838. The end compartment of what was otherwise a day-car-cum-mail-van could be converted into a sleeper for two people by placing a padded stretcher between the seats and opening a partition in the end wall that let into a boot to give additional leg room.

The first complete sleeping-carriage in GB was built at the North British Railway workshops, Cowlairs, in 1873 and put into service between Glasgow and King's Cross on 2 April the same year. It comprised two 1st-Class compartments with lavatories in between, a 2nd-Class compartment for two servants and a luggage-compartment. Passengers paid a 10s supplement over the normal fare and had to supply their own bedding.

The first
RAILWAY: DIESEL LOCOMOTIVE
was built for the Prussian–Hessian State Railways in 1912. The chassis and superstructure were by Borsig AG of Berlin, and the four-cylinder V-type two-stroke engine and auxiliary machinery by Gebr. Sulzer AG of Winterthur, Switzerland. Its performance proved disappointing and it was never put into regular scheduled service.

The first diesel locomotive to go into regular service was a Swedish-built metre-gauge Bo-Bo-type diesel-electric put into operation by Tunisian Railways in 1921.
GB: The first diesel-electric locomotive in service was built by W. Beardmore & Co of Dalmuir in 1928 and introduced on the Blackpool–Lytham route by LMS the same year.

The first
RAILWAY, ELECTRIC
the first experimental electric locomotive to run on standard-gauge track was designed by Prof. Charles Page of Washington, D.C. and operated by the Baltimore & Ohio Railroad in 1839 between Washington and Bladensburg.
GB: An experimental locomotive was constructed in 1842 by the Scottish engineer Robert Davidson, who equipped a car with an electric motor consisting of eight coils on cylinders of wood with sliding cores of soft iron acting like engine pistons and connected to cranks on the car axles. It was run for a short time on the Edinburgh & Glasgow Railway, and was able to make 4mph drawing a 5-ton load. It came to an untimely end in an engine-house at Perth at the hands of railway-workers who saw in the silent, smokeless locomotive a threat to their livelihood.
MAINLINE ELECTRIFICATION: the first in the world was carried out by the Baltimore & Ohio Railroad in 1894 over a 3·6-mile stretch of track, above and below ground, passing through the City of Baltimore. The innovation was made at the direction of the city authorities in order to obviate the smoke nuisance of steam-trains, the locomotives used being 1,080hp GEC Bo-Bos each capable of drawing a 1,870-ton load. Current was drawn from a rigid overhead conductor-line. Electric working for freight trains was inaugurated on 4 August 1894, and for passenger trains on 1 May 1895.
GB: The first electric trains in regular passenger service over existing standard-gauge track commenced operation at 12.50pm on 29 March 1904, when a three-coach train of the North Eastern Railway with a carrying capacity of 186 passengers left Newcastle Bridge Street for Benton on the Riverside Branch line. By 1 July of the same year the NER had completed its Tyneside scheme with the electrification of the 37-mile coastal loop.

The first mainline electrification in GB was carried out by Southern Railway on the route from London to Brighton and Worthing, and was opened to passenger traffic on 1 January 1933.

The first
RAILWAY EXCURSION TRAINS
were instituted by the Garnhirk & Glasgow Railway in 1831. A contem porary advertisement reads: 'Steam passenger carriages leave Townhead four times a day for Gartsherrie and enable trippers at a cost of 9d. for the closed and 6d. for the open carriages to make within the space of about two hours a pleasant, healthful and cheap excursion of about 16 miles.'

The first railway excursion for a specific event was arranged by the Whitby & Pickering Railway to carry passengers to a bazaar at Gromont being held in aid of the local church building fund, 7–8 August 1839. The fare from Whitby to Gromont was reduced from 9d to 6d, and the fare from Pickering from 2s 3d to 1s 6d.
RAILWAY EXCURSION AT GROUP-RATE: the first was organized by the Newcastle & Carlisle Railway Co on 14 June 1840, when 320 employees of Messrs R. & W. Hawthorn & Co and their families were carried from Newcastle to Carlisle at half the normal fare.

By 1841, the year in which Thomas Cook organized his first day-trip, railway excursions were an established and well-patronized system of travel at reduced rates, though the benefits accrued by both passenger and operator were not acclaimed by all. When the Newcastle & Carlisle Railway had the temerity to run an excursion on 29 August of that year – a Sunday – the Rev. W.C. Burns of Kilsyth placarded the streets with the following warning:

A REWARD FOR SABBATH BREAKING
People taken safely and swiftly to Hell!
Next Lord's Day, by the Carlisle Railway, for 7s 6d.
It is a Pleasure Trip!

The first
RAILWAY LOCOMOTIVE
was built by Richard Trevithick, the Cornish engineer, and ran for the first time on the Penydarren Railway, near Merthyr Tydfil in Wales on 6 February 1804. The engine had been constructed as a stationary unit for driving a steam-hammer; it was converted into a locomotive by mounting on a wagon chassis. The first passengers to travel in a train drawn by steam locomotion were Samuel Homfray and Richard Crawshay, ironmasters, and a visiting Government Engineer, Anthony Hill, who were drawn over the 9¾-mile line from Penydarren to Abercynon Wharf on 20 February 1804. Their coach was an ordinary road vehicle, having axles the same width as those of the locomotive; the rails were flanged. Two days later Homfray won a 500gn wager from Anthony Hill when Trevithick's locomotive succeeded in drawing a 10 ton load of bar-iron in five wagons over the full length of the track. On this occasion the general public also availed itself of rail passenger transport for the first time, 70 of the spectators climbing unbidden on to the wagons to enjoy the ride.

The first
RAILWAY, PASSENGER
was the Oystermouth Railway, established under an Act of Parliament of 29 June 1804. Horse-drawn goods traffic was inaugurated on the 7½-mile route from Swansea to Oystermouth in April 1806. The passenger service was arranged by contract between the railway company and Benjamin French, who undertook to run 'a wagon for the conveyance of passengers' for a year commencing 25 March 1807 and to pay £20 in tolls for the privilege. (In fact the service continued, with some interruptions and by various means of traction, until 1960.) The train ran twice a day in summer and the fare was 1s single. There were no stations as such, but check-gates were erected at the Brewery Yard and at Hughes's Forge.

Richard Ayton, writing in 1813, described the passenger wagon thus:

It is a very long carriage, supported on four low iron wheels, carries sixteen persons, exclusive of the driver, is drawn by one horse, and rolls along over an iron railroad, at the rate of five miles an hour, and with the noise of twenty sledge hammers in full play. The passage is only four miles, but it is quite sufficient to make one reel from the car at the journey's end, in a state of dizziness and confusion of the senses that it is well if he recovers in a week.

The first regular passenger service by steam-traction was inaugurated by the Canterbury & Whitstable Railway on 6 May 1830, the day after the opening of the line. Trains were hauled by a stationary engine over 4 miles of the route, owing to steep gradients, and by George Stephenson's 0–4–0 *Invicta* locomotive for the other two miles. The fare was 9d (later reduced to 6d), the duration of the journey was 35–40min, and there were 10 trains a day. Passengers rode in open wagons until the introduction of closed carriages in 1834.

The first passenger railway operated solely by steam locomotives, and the first to introduce 1st- and 2nd-Class carriages, was the Liverpool & Manchester Railway, which opened on 15 September 1830. Regular scheduled passenger service began on 4 October with four trains of 1st-Class carriages a day and two of 2nd Class. Fares for the 31-mile journey were 7s 1st Class, 4s 2nd Class. The 1st-Class carriages comprised three compartments constructed on the stage-coach principle, except that they had side windows in addition to those set in the doors. Thus the current style of railway compartment has survived, with few structural changes, from the first year of locomotive-drawn passenger railway traffic. The 2nd-Class accommodation

Opening of the first steam passenger railway – Canterbury–Whitstable, 6 May 1830

consisted of open wagons with awnings.

The first railway carriages with centre aisle and transverse seating were designed by Ross Winans for the Baltimore & Ohio Railroad in 1838. These double-truck cars had a door at either end leading out on to an open platform, so that it was possible, though hazardous, to walk the length of the train.

In the USA, where smoking was originally permitted in all passenger cars, the first non-smoking compartments (for ladies only) were provided by the Philadelphia, Wilmington & Baltimore Railroad in August 1838. In Britain, where all railways maintained strict non-smoking rules, the first smoker was provided by the Eastern Counties Railway on the Cambridge–Newmarket line in 1846.

The first
RAILWAY, PUBLIC
was opened in June 1789 by the Loughborough & Nanpanton Railway Co, established by William Jessop, civil engineer, at Loughborough, Leicestershire. Little is recorded about its operation.

The first public railway in London and the earliest to have attracted any considerable attention was the Surrey Iron Railway, opened for goods traffic on 26 July 1803. An inscription on the wall of the Ram Brewery, York Road, Wandsworth reads:

Set below are stone sleepers from the Surrey Iron Railway, the first railway established by Act of Parliament. This railway, constructed in 1802–3 by William Jessop, famous engineer and canal-builder, to the order of local industrialists and other subscribers who regularly met at the Spread Eagle Inn nearby, ran past this spot and carried in horse-drawn trains of up to 15 wagons, coal, raw materials and manufactured goods between Croydon and Jessop's Basin, a Thames-side wharf at Wandsworth.

Freight rates were 3d a mile per chaldron of coal (about 2,500lb); 3d a ton for general merchandise; 2d a ton for lime, manure, chalk, clay, sand, bricks, etc.; and 1d a ton for dung. According to one 19th-century writer the trains were drawn by 'a miserable team of lean mules or donkeys', which may be one reason why the company never prospered. After a number of changes of ownership the line was finally abandoned on 31 August 1846.

The first public railway worked by steam locomotives was the Stockton & Darlington Railway, opened on 27 September 1825. The first train to travel over the 27-mile track consisted of George Stephenson's 15-ton Locomotive No. 1, a tender, 6 goods wagons, the directors' coach, 6 passenger coaches and 14 wagons of workmen. Freight charge for coal was 1d a ton per mile; very little else was carried in the early days.

The first
RAILWAY, TROOP TRAIN
ran on the Baltimore & Ohio Railroad on 30 June 1831 to carry the 1st Division of the Maryland Guards under Brig.-Gen. George H. Steuart from Mount Clare Station, Baltimore, to Ellicott's Mills, a distance of 14 miles. There the troops quelled a riot of railway navvies, who were striking for back-pay due to them.

GB: The first strategic movement of troops by rail took place on 24 May 1839, when the 10th Regiment, having been brought from Ireland by sea, was transported from Liverpool to Manchester by troop train to suppress disorders arising from the Chartist demonstration scheduled to take place on Kersal Moor. The regiment was conveyed by two separate trains, one in the morning and the other in the evening, and marched from the station headed by different bands in order to give the Chartists the impression that two regiments had arrived. The 10th was a solely Irish regiment, and was specially chosen for this confrontation with the demonstrators as it was thought they would be less likely to fraternize with those of different race and religion.

During the turbulent period that followed, the railways contributed significantly to the maintenance of law and order in Britain, and possibly to the avoidance of a major upheaval in 1848, the 'year of revolutions'. Whereas formerly it had been necessary to station troops in areas subject to rioting or violence, thus fragmenting the available strength, the strategic use of railways enabled commanders to retain troops on garrison duty and send them out speedily for police action as and when required.

The first use of rail transport for the strategic deployment of a large fighting force occurred in March 1846, when the Prussian Sixth Army Corps was moved by the Upper Silesian and Freiburg/Schweidnitz-Breslau lines to the frontier of the Cracow Free State, then in a state of revolt. A total of over 12,000 men, 300 horses, 16 heavy guns, 15 ammunition trucks and 30 supply wagons were transported in trains carrying up to 766 men, the whole operation being carried out without interrupting normal civilian traffic on those parts of the railway affected.

Rail troop transport was first employed by British forces in the field during the Abyssinian campaign of 1868. A special military railway was constructed by the Royal Engineers from Zoulla, the port of disembarkation in Annesley Bay, 12 miles inland to Koomayleh at the entrance of the Soroo Pass. Although designed primarily for the carriage of stores and ammunition, Lt Willand, RE, states in his paper 'The Abyssinian Railway' (1870) that it was used at the end of the campaign to convey Sir Robert Napier's expeditionary force back to the port of Zoulla.

The first
RAINCOAT
was made by François Fresnau, Chief Engineer at Cayenne, French Guiana, who discovered rubber trees growing at Aprouage in 1747, and waterproofed an old overcoat by smearing it all over with latex.

The first raincoat regularly manufactured for sale was Fox's Aquatic Gambroon Cloak, marketed by G. Fox of 28 King Street, Covent Garden in 1821, and 'warranted never to get wet when properly made up'. Gambroon was a type of twill material containing mohair, but nothing is known about the waterproofing process.

At about the same time, Charles Macintosh of Glasgow was producing a waterproof fabric which consisted of two lengths of cloth stuck together with a solution of indiarubber dissolved in naphtha. Although this was perfectly weatherproof, it was impossible to tailor such a sandwich. It was not until James Syme, a young medical student from Edinburgh University, discovered a more practical way of dissolving rubber, using a property extracted from coal-tar, that Macintosh, obtaining the rights and patenting the process in 1823, began to produce the waterproofs that were to make his name a generic word. The first important commission won by the firm of Charles Macintosh & Co was the outfitting of Sir John Franklin's expedition to the Arctic in 1824. Macintosh continued to sell only the patent cloth, to be made up by individual tailors, until his amalgamation with the Manchester rubber goods manufacturer Thomas Hancock in 1830. Their initial success in producing ready-to-wear raincoats was offset by the coming of the railways, for travellers who had previously braved the elements on top of a stage-coach now rode enclosed. There was a growing prejudice too against the ungainly appearance of the garments, and also the peculiar smell they emitted, a fact commented on by the *Gentleman's Magazine of Fashion* in 1839: 'A Macintosh is now become a troublesome thing in town from the difficulty of their being admitted into an omnibus on account of the offensive smell. . . .' Another disadvantage, the tendency of the rubber to melt in hot weather, was overcome by Hancock's discovery of the vulcanization process in 1843. The problem of the smell was eliminated c. 1850 by a Lancashire manufacturer called Joseph Mandelberg, who produced a garment advertised as 'F.F.O.' – 'Free from Odour'.

For the first 30 years of their existence, waterproofs were something to be donned only in extremity. 'Some resemble a sack – others an ill made smock-coat', remarked one critic. The first showerproof material capable of being styled according to the prevailing mode was patented in 1851 by the Regent Street firm of Bax & Co, who dispensed with impregnated rubber altogether and produced a chemically treated wool fabric they called by the name of 'Aquascutum' – compounded from two Latin words meaning 'water-shield'. The Aquascutum raincoat won a considerable reputation during the winter campaign in the Crimea, and at least one distinguished soldier, Gen. Goodlake, owed not only his comfort but his liberty to the coat. During a skirmish with the Russians, he and a British Sergeant found themselves cut off. Having disposed of the nearest enemy in hand-to-hand combat, they took refuge in a ravine, only to find themselves completely surrounded. To their surprise, the enemy paid them no attention; because of their grey Aquascutums, the General and the Sergeant had been mistaken for Russians. When the Russian troops formed up to march back to the lines, the two Englishmen fell in with them, finally making a dash for freedom when they came within sight of the British encampment. The original raincoat worn by Gen. Goodlake on this occasion is preserved at Newstead Abbey.

The first
RECORD LIBRARY
for public use was inaugurated in 1914 with the gift of 25 phonograph records to the St Paul City Library, Minn. from a local women's club. By 1919 the Library had a stock of nearly 600 records and circulation for that year totalled 3,505. The Fine Arts Librarian, Miss Edah Flower Burnett, reported about this time: 'The collection was made simply for educational purposes. It is, therefore, limited to reproductions of the musical classics, both vocal and instrumental, patriotic music, and folk songs. And its use is limited to schools and clubs, six records being allowed a borrower for one week.'
GB: The first Record Library for public use was opened at Walsall, Staffordshire, by Alan Brockhurst in 1918. It began with 500 records and 40–50 members. Membership was 5s a year and the hiring fee was 3d a week per record. The venture failed after a year owing to the fact that most subscribers felt they were not getting full value unless they had worn out the record within a week.

The first public library in Britain to incorporate a record section was Middlesex County Library in 1935, but the service was only open to schools. The first record section open to the general public was inaugurated by Chingford Library in 1945.

The first
REFLECTING ROAD STUDS
were Follsain Gloworm studs, patented by Jean Neuhaus and first laid in England by Market Harborough Urban District Council in March 1934. Gloworm studs were also laid in Bedford Avenue, London later the same year.

Catseye studs were invented by Percy Shaw of Halifax, who is reputed to have been inspired with the idea in 1933 when driving along the Queensbury Road between Halifax and Bradford in a dense fog. He was prevented from crashing through a fence and down a sheer drop by the light of a cat's eyes warning him that he was driving off the road. After a year of experiments the first 50 studs were laid at his own expense at Drighlington crossroads, a notorious accident blackspot near Bradford, in April 1934. The following year he formed Reflecting Road Studs Ltd, and received his first order for 36 studs for a pedestrian crossing at Baldon, Yorkshire. Then as now the Catseye consisted of a cast-iron well weighing about 10lb which is sunk into the surface of the road. The rubber pad set in the centre of the well would be depressed as a car's wheel passed over it and automatically polished the glass reflectors. In 1937 the Ministry of Transport laid a 5-mile stretch of road with 10 different varieties of reflecting road studs. Within two years all had fractured or ceased to reflect except Catseyes, which remained in perfect condition.

Percy Shaw was the son of a dyer's labourer, who raised a family of 14 on wages of £1 a week. He remains a bachelor and has never left Yorkshire, living in a house with four television sets, no curtains, which he said obscured his view, and no carpets, which he believed harboured offensive smells and cigarette ash. He was awarded the OBE in 1965 for his contribution to road safety. Unlike many benefactors of humanity he has also made a considerable fortune from his invention, and when interviewed by Yorkshire Television in 1968, admitted to paying income tax on his royalties at the rate of £37,000 a year.

The first
REFRIGERATION PROCESS
by chemical action was developed in Rome during the 1540s and consisted basically of dissolving saltpetre in water. An account of this method of cooling was published by Blasius Villafranca under the title of *Methodus refrigerandi* (Rome 1550). The author claimed that all the wine and water drunk at the tables of the nobility in Rome was cooled in this way, and he claimed to have been the first to make the discovery public. Levinus Lemnius, writing in 1559, said that wine cooled by Villafranca's process was so cold 'that the teeth can scarcely endure it'.
COMMERCIALLY OPERATED REFRIGERATION PLANTS were developed simultaneously in Australia and the USA in 1850. America's pioneer of chemical freezing was Alexander Catlin Twining, who began experimenting in 1848 to determine whether ether vapour could be condensed rapidly enough to produce refrigeration. Two years later he had achieved sufficient success to install a commercial refrigeration plant at the Cuyahonga Locomotive Works in Cleveland, Ohio. The plant consisted of 10 freezing cisterns of cast iron, using ethyl ether, with a production capacity of up to 2,000lb of ice a day.

In Australia a former Editor of the *Melbourne Age*, James Harrison, established his first mechanical ice-making plant at Rodey Point on the Barwon River in Victoria at a cost of £1,000. This operated on the absorption system of refrigeration by the evaporation of ammonia. The following year, in 1851, Harrison made his first sale of refrigerating equipment to a Bendigo brewery, Messrs Glasgow & Co. Regular manufacture of Harrison freezers was undertaken by P. N. Russell of Sydney in 1859.
GB: The first commercial refrigeration plant was built under the Harrison patents by Siebe & Gorman of London in 1861 for Messrs Young, Meldrum & Binney, paraffin-refiners of Bathgate in West Lothian, Scotland. A second machine was delivered to a brewery the same year.

See also Frozen Food.

The first
REFRIGERATOR
for domestic use was the Domelre, an electrically powered machine manufactured in Chicago in 1913. It had a wooden cabinet with a compression-

The first domestic refrigerator, 1913

type refrigerating unit mounted in the top.
GB: The first household in Britain equipped with a refrigerator was Lord Leconfield's London home in Chesterfield Gardens in 1921. Lord Leconfield had brought the machine back with him from a visit to France. The first refrigerator marketed in Britain was the Frigidaire in 1924.

The first
REGISTER OFFICE MARRIAGES
were introduced under the Marriage Act 1836, which enabled persons wishing to dispense with a religious ceremony to have their marriage solemnized before a Registrar of Marriages. The Act came into effect on 1 July 1837, when some 600 District Register Offices were opened to serve areas having common boundaries with the existing Poor Law Unions.

The first
REGISTRATION OF BIRTHS, DEATHS AND MARRIAGES
on a regular and systematic basis was introduced in Canada in 1621. Canada is the only country in the world with a continuous series of birth records for more than three centuries. The first European nation to introduce compulsory registration was Sweden in 1686.
GB: The Registration Act, introduced by Lord John Russell, was passed on 17 August 1836, and came into effect on 1 July 1837. The first name entered in the Birth Registers at Somerset House is that of Mary Ann Aaron of Dewsbury, Yorkshire.

The first
RESTAURANT
to be described as such was the Champ d'Oiseau, established in la rue des Poulies, Paris by M. Boulanger in 1765. The fascia was adórned with a legend in Latin: 'Venite ad me, omnes qui stomacho laboratis, et ego restaurabo vos' (Come to me, anybody whose stomach groans, and I will restore you). Inside it was furnished with marble-topped tables and the speciality of the house was *Volailles au Gros Sel*. Previous to Boulanger's innovation, meals were served only at taverns, cookshops and occasionally in coffee-houses, though in London there were also 'ordinaries', such as Simpson's Fish Ordinary, opened in 1723, and chop-houses. Boulanger's venture was an instantaneous success and soon had scores of imitators. By the time of the Revolution in 1789 there were 100 restaurants in Paris. Fifteen years later the first restaurant guide, the *Almanach des Gourmands*, was able to list 500.

See also Department Store; Hotel; Staff Canteen.

The first
RICKSHAW
was invented in 1869 by an American Baptist minister, the Rev. Jonathan Scobie, to transport his invalid wife about the streets of Yokohama. Subsequent models were built to provide employment for the minister's converts.

The first
ROAD HAULAGE
operations in Britain, according to Stow, originated in 1564 or thereabouts. In his *Summarie of Englyshe Chronicles* he writes: 'And about that time began long wagons to come into use, such as are now come to London from Canterbury, Norwich, Ipswich, Gloucester, Etc., with passengers and commodities.' Previously the only method of conveying goods on land had been by pack-horse, or for heavier objects over short distances, by sled or rollers. These cumbersome great stage-wagons, with their broad, inclined wheels, also provided the first public passenger-transport services. Although extremely slow, on account of their weight and the condition of the roads, they remained in use for the carriage of freight until the coming of the railways. The wagons averaged about 20–30 miles a day; even in the early 1840s a goods train could accomplish the same distance in an hour.

The first successful mechanically propelled vehicles designed for road haulage over long distances were R. W. Thompson's steam-tractors *Chenab* and *Ravee*, built for Lt R. E. B. Crompton's Government Steam Train by Ransome, Sims & Head of Ipswich in 1871. The *Ravee* was test run between Ipswich and Edinburgh in October of the same year. These vehicles, together with another similar tractor, the *Indus*, were shipped out to the Punjab and arrived in parts at Rawalpindi in March 1872. There they were assembled for use by the Indian Transport Service. Hauling both freight and passengers, the steam trains were put in service over a 70-mile stretch of the Grand Trunk Road between Jhelum and Rawalpindi. Refuelling stations were positioned every 14 miles of the route and water-tanks at intervals of 7 miles. With an average speed of 5–8mph, the trains could cover the distance in a day providing there were no mishaps. Freight capacity was considerable – the *Indus* drew 64·3 tons up a gradient of 1 in 33 on test – but Crompton was handicapped by a shortage of rolling-stock. The only goods trailers available were four 6-ton wagons and two smaller ones. An early photograph of a Government Steam Train in operation shows it to be made up of tractor, tender, four large four-wheeled wagons and a passenger omnibus.

Thompson steamers were built for road haulage in those parts of the world without railways in fairly considerable numbers between 1871 and 1891. One firm alone, Robey's of Lincoln, made nearly 60 such engines in that period. They were also used in Britain, though generally for shorter runs to or from a railhead. In 1879 Capt. Losada, Manager of the Glasgow Tramways, stated that Thompson steamers were considered of such value in Glasgow that 'no single article weighing over 10 tons is ever moved except by one of them'.
ROAD-HAULAGE CONTRACTOR: the first to employ motor lorries for freight-work was M. Felix Dubois, who inaugurated a long-distance service over a 400km route between Kayes and Bamako in the French Sudan (now the Sudanese Republic) in the autumn of 1899. The vehicles were 9½hp De Dietrich petrol-driven lorries built to the design of Amédée Bollée at Lunéville, France; Dubois employed Chinese coolies to drive them. There were said to be 60 lorries and omnibuses at work by the early part of 1900, but this figure was probably exaggerated. The service lasted only a few months. Owing to the absence of made-up roads, the working parts soon became choked with sand and the enterprise had to be abandoned.

GB: The first experimental long-distance run undertaken in Britain was by a Clarkson & Capel No. 6 3-ton steam-lorry. The load of 2 tons of crystal carbonate of soda, and another ton of sundry goods, was carried 184 miles from Messrs Gaskell & Deacon's works at Widnes to Messrs Anderson, Tulloh & Co at 9 Great Tower Street, London on 8–15 August 1899. The lorry accomplished a respectable 49 miles the first day, but thereafter progress declined to an average 25 miles a day.

The first road-haulage contractor in Britain to inaugurate a regular trucking service was J. Stewart, of the Speedwell Motor Car Co, 71 Woolmanhill, Aberdeen. A daily service to and from Banchory, a distance of 18 miles, began on Monday, 11 March 1901. The vehicle used was a 2 ton 16cwt (6,272lb) lorry hauling a 17cwt (1,904lb) trailer.

Three factors distinguish the Speedwell Co's service from that of the motorized parcel-carriers already operating in the London area. Firstly, the vehicle used was a lorry, not a light delivery van. Secondly, an advertisement appearing in the *Aberdeen Daily Free Press* for 11 April 1901 clearly states that not only parcels are carried but also 'heavy goods'. Thirdly, the service was inter-urban.

Both the Speedwell Co and the London & Counties Distributing Co, a motorized fruit-hauliers founded the same year, ran to a schedule on a single fixed route. The real beginnings of successful motor road-haulage operation in Britain date from 1902, when the Road Carrying Co was formed by E. Shrapnell Smith to carry cotton and other bulk commodities between Liverpool and the various Lancashire cotton towns. The vehicles, supplied by Coulthard & Co and the Lancashire Steam Motor Co, consisted of 4-ton 25bhp steam-wagons each 17ft 6in long and capable of drawing a 2-ton trailer. These began making a nightly run from Liverpool to Blackburn in August, taking 12hr for the 40-mile journey. Operations were later expanded to take in most of south-west Lancashire. The loads carried were generally 6 tons, with freight rates varying between 2½d and 6d per ton mile. Drivers were paid 33s a week, a rate that compared favourably with a London bus-driver's wage of 25s a week, but driver's mates only received half as much. A day's run was usually about 45 miles, at an average speed of 5mph. At the end of the first year's operations Shrapnell Smith was able to report that no less than 59 varieties of goods had been handled, ranging from cotton to pickles.

It is doubtful whether any road-haulage contractor was able to compete on level terms with the railways prior to World War I, though there were obvious advantages in a door-to-door service, and the more enterprising were not slow to exploit this. Occasional long hauls are recorded, such as the 300-mile Bristol–Tunbridge Wells round trip made by a Western Road Carrying Co wagon in October 1903, but such ventures were exceptional. Most early contractors concentrated on local traffic, and the greater reliability of vehicles after 1905, concurrent with the change-over from steam to petrol, helped to establish short-haul freight working as a relatively efficient and economic system of transport. Long-distance road haulage developed soon after World War I, the disposal of 20,000 ex-WD vehicles to private hauliers stimulating the rapid growth of the industry.

See also Motor Lorry; Motor Van.

The first
ROLLER SKATES

were worn by Joseph Merlin, a musical-instrument maker from Huy, near Liège, Belgium, on the occasion of the celebrated Mrs Cornelly's masquerade at Carlisle House, Soho Square in 1760. Mounted on his skates, Merlin came sailing into the ballroom playing a violin. Being quite unable to change direction or retard his velocity, he impelled himself against a large mirror valued at over £500, smashed it to atoms, broke his instrument, and wounded himself severely.

After this inauspicious introduction nothing further is heard of roller skates until 1823, when Robert John Tyers, a Piccadilly fruiterer, demonstrated his Volitos at the tennis-court in Windmill Street. These had five small wheels arranged in a single line and were patented on 22 April of that year as an 'apparatus to be attached to boots . . . for the purpose of travelling or pleasure'. A somewhat similar skate was used for a simulated ice-skating scene in Meyerbeer's opera *Le Prophète* when it was performed in Paris on 16 April 1849.

The first four-wheeled roller skates, prototype of the modern kind, were patented by James L. Plimpton of New York in 1863. These had small boxwood wheels arranged in pairs and cushioned by rubber pads. With these skates it was possible not only to maintain a proper balance, but also to execute quite intricate figures. Their introduction heralded the craze for roller skating that swept first America and then Europe in the late 1860s and 1870s.

The first
ROYAL BROADCAST

was made by HRH the Prince of Wales, who made an address to the Boy Scouts of Britain from York House via the Marconi Co Station 2LO on the evening of 7 October 1922. The occasion was a National Scout Rally at Alexandra Palace and the broadcast was intended to bring the voice of their royal patron to all the Scouts unable to attend.

BROADCAST BY A REIGNING MONARCH: the first was made by HM King George V on the occasion of the opening of the Empire Exhibition, Wembley on 23 April 1924. The audience was estimated at 10 million, the *Daily Mail* having arranged for loudspeakers to relay the broadcast in a number of large towns. Although the BBC did not record the King's address, in 1955 a Croydon listener, Mrs Dorothy Jones, presented the Corporation with a recording made privately by her husband at the time. This is now one of the earliest broadcast recordings in the BBC Sound Archives.

The first
ROYAL COMMAND FILM PERFORMANCE

was held at Marlborough House on 21 July 1896 before 40 royal guests who had assembled for the marriage of Princess Maud the following day. The show was occasioned by a request from pioneer cinematographer Birt Acres of New Barnet, Hertfordshire to be allowed to exhibit publicly a film he had taken the previous month of the Prince and Princess of Wales attending the Cardiff Exhibition (*see also* Film: Newsfilm). Before giving his permission, the Prince of Wales commanded Acres to bring the film to Marlborough House for inspection. It was screened in a specially erected marquee together with 20 other short films, including Tom Merry the Lightning Artist drawing Mr Gladstone and Lord Salisbury, the Derby Races of 1895 and 1896, Henley Regatta, and scenes showing a boxing kangaroo, a Great Northern Railway express train and the pursuit of a pickpocket. The royal film was shown twice by popular demand.

ROYAL COMMAND FILM PERFORMANCE BEFORE THE SOVEREIGN: the first was given at Windsor Castle by command of HM Queen Victoria on 23 November 1897, when H. J. Hitchins presented a selection of Diamond Jubilee and other films taken for the Lumière Cinematographe. They were accompanied by a full orchestra under the baton of Leopold Wenzel.

This was not the first occasion on which Queen Victoria had witnessed moving pictures, though the previous showing had been by the Court Photographer of a film he had made of the Royal Family (*see* Monarch to be Filmed) and cannot strictly speaking be called a Command Performance. Nor was it the last, for the ageing monarch commanded a number of subsequent film performances and appears to have become something of a cinema addict.

FEATURE FILM PRESENTED BY ROYAL COMMAND: the first was Cecil Hepworth's production of *Comin' Through the Rye*, starring Alma Taylor, which was shown before Queen Alexandra in the State Dining-Room of Marlborough House on 4 August 1916. Hepworth was no stranger to Command Performances, having been present at the very first one when he had acted as assistant to Birt Acres.

The first feature film to be presented by command of the Sovereign was *Tom Brown's Schooldays*, which Lew Warren exhibited for King George V and Queen Mary at Buckingham Palace on 24 February 1917.

ROYAL COMMAND PERFORMANCE AT A PUBLIC CINEMA: the first was held at the Empire, Leicester Square on 1 November 1946, when King George VI and Queen Elizabeth, accompanied by Princess Elizabeth and Princess Margaret, saw David Niven and Marius Goring in *A Matter of Life and Death* – a deservedly forgotten film. The story was centred round a World War II pilot, but it was interwoven with fantasy sequences intended to illustrate the transitory nature of national and historical prejudice. The novelty of seeing the King 'going to the pictures' caused crowds to gather 10 hours before his arrival.

The first
ROYAL FAMILY, MEMBER OF, TO ENTER COMMERCE

as a regular employee was Prince William of Gloucester, who joined the City banking-house of Lazard Bros on 5 January 1965.

The first
ROYAL FAMILY, MEMBER OF, TO BE PORTRAYED ON THE STAGE

during his or her lifetime was HRH Queen Elizabeth the Queen Mother, played as Duchess of York by Miss Amanda Reiss in Royce Ryton's *Crown Matrimonial*, which opened at the Haymarket Theatre on 19 October 1972. The action of the play centred round the Abdication crisis of 1936. Impersonation of living members of the Royal Family was prohibited by the Lord Chamberlain prior to the lifting of stage censorship in 1968.

The first
ROYAL FAMILY, MEMBER OF, TO APPEAR ON TELEVISION

was the Duchess of Kent, who was seen purchasing a hat in a London store during a Baird experimental high-definition transmission made in 1935.

MONARCH TO APPEAR LIVE ON TELEVISION: the first was HM King George VI on 12 May 1937, when the return of the Coronation procession was televised from a BBC Television control van at Hyde Park Corner. There were about 2,100 sets in operation at this time.

CHRISTMAS BROADCAST ON TELEVISION BY THE SOVEREIGN: the first to the Peoples of the Commonwealth was made by HM Queen Elizabeth II on 25 December 1957.

MEMBER OF THE ROYAL FAMILY TO BE INTERVIEWED ON TELEVISION: the first was Prince Philip, who appeared on the BBC programme *Panorama* on 29 May 1961. The interviewer was Richard Dimbleby, who talked to the Prince about Commonwealth Training Week.

The first
ROYAL MOTORIST

was HIM the Sultan of Turkey, who on reading an account of Magnus Volk's experimental electric car in the *Leipsic Zeitung* in 1888, decided he must own one. Accordingly the following telegram was dispatched from Constantinople on 4 July of that year:

The Director of the Brighton Electric Railway, Brighton, England.
Seen in the Leipsic illustrated newspaper description of your electric dogcart. Please give me details of its price, and where to get one.
(Signed) First Chamberlain of His Majesty the Sultan, Osman.

Two days after receiving the first, Volk was delivered of another, more urgent wire:

Please send speedily to my address one electric carriage. The price mentioned in your despatch will be paid by myself to the Ottoman Bank first. Osman.

After sending his order, the Sultan evidently became worried at the possibility of delay, because his next telegram read:

No need for discussing price. Send dogcart earliest possible.

This car, the first ever manufactured for sale in Britain, was described in an article published in the *Brighton Herald* nearly 20 years later.

The body . . . was made in Messrs Peck's works [in Brighton] and Mr Volk installed the motive power. The car had four wheels, the two front ones being close together in order to allow the carriage to turn on its own length. The finish of the carriage, which was made of walnut wood, was exquisite, the upholstery being emblazoned with the Turkish Imperial Crest. There was room for four persons, and the car could do 10mph and could run 6hr on one charge. Its total weight was only just over a ½ ton. The electricity was stored in accumulators under the two seats. The motor was set in operation by means of a small switch, while a powerful brake on the hind wheel was worked by the driver's foot.

Rhys Jenkins, in his *Motor Cars* (London 1902), records that the vehicle was chain-driven to the rear wheels and that it was powered by a battery of 24 cells weighing 800lb. The engine was 1hp.

The first monarch to own a petrol-driven car was the Sultan of Morocco, who acquired a four-wheeled Canstatt Daimler motor carriage in August 1892. This vehicle, a two-seater, was specially fitted with a tasselled canopy and side curtains as protection against the sun, and had side panels decorated with an elaborate Moorish design.

The first member of a European Royal Family to own a motor car, and one of the first women in the world to do so, was Queen Christiana of Spain (consort of the last King of Spain, Alfonso XIII), who ordered an electric Victoria from Messrs Thrupp & Maberly of 425 Oxford Street, London in July 1896. The engine of the vehicle was designed by the Spanish engineer Julien.

The first European monarch to own a motor car was King Leopold of Belgium, who was reported in March 1898 to have recently acquired a car specially built for him at the Small Arms Factory, Herstal, near Liège. In April 1901 King Leopold became the first royal motorist to drive his car himself. His example was followed by the King of Italy, who in January 1902 became the first monarch to pass the driving test.

GB: It is regrettable not to be able to record that Queen Victoria was a motorist, particularly as she very nearly became one. In 1896 Prince Henry of Battenberg placed an order for a Jeantaud electric carriage, which he proposed to present to his mother-in-law, the Queen. Before the order could be executed, however, Prince Henry died of the effects of fever contracted while serving in the 4th Ashanti campaign. The bodywork of the car, which was then half-built, was notable for being made from aluminium on a tubular steel frame.

The first member of the British Royal Family to ride in a motor car was the Prince of Wales (Edward VII), who was driven by the Hon. Evelyn Ellis along a gallery of the Imperial Institute during an exhibition of motor cars on 14 February 1896. He first travelled by car on the public highway in April 1897, when he was driven from Cannes to Grasse in a car belonging to the Princesse de Sagon. The Prince was not seen in a motor car on the public highway in England until the following year. On the occasion of a visit to the Earl of Warwick at Warwick Castle, the Daimler Motor Co of Coventry lent five cars for the use of the royal party, and on 25 June 1898 the Prince was driven by J.S. Critchley to Compton Verney, the home of Lord Willoughby de Broke. Accompanying him was Lady Randolph Churchill, mother of Sir Winston.

By this time, however, the Prince had already acquired the rudiments of the art of driving. In 1900 the General Manager of the Daimler Motor Co, A.H.D. Altree, revealed that in the autumn of 1897 he had secretly taken a driving lesson on a 6hp Daimler phaeton in the grounds of Buckingham Palace.

As King, Edward remained faithful to the Daimler cars in which he had enjoyed his first motoring experiences, and when he came to the throne in 1901 was already the owner of three of the Coventry concern's vehicles, including a 14-seater brake for use as a 'beaters' car'.

The King's first car, purchased the previous year while he was still Prince of Wales, was a 6hp twin-cylinder Daimler Model A, ordered shortly after the highly successful Thousand Miles Trial, in which he had shown a great interest. The bodywork, by Hoopers of St James's, was finished in the royal livery of black and chocolate, picked out in red. The *Motor-Car Journal* reported: 'Beyond the painting, the only indication that the car belongs to Royalty is His Royal Highness's small crest affixed to one of the panels behind the lamp on the left side.'

The royal Daimler was delivered to the Royal Stables at Ascot Heath House, where the Prince was entertaining a large party of guests, on Monday, 11 June 1900. The *Motor-Car Journal* commented unctuously: 'It is satisfactory to be able to record that the motor car has been graciously received at the Royal Stables, not one of those who have had charge of the Prince's horses for many years showing the slightest antipathy to the newcomer.'

The Prince rode in his new car for the first time two days later, when he was driven over to Cumberland Lodge by his chauffeur, Sydney Letzman, who had entered the royal employ from the Daimler Motor Co. On this occasion the vehicle was preceded by a groom on horseback, as Letzman was unfamiliar with the roads round Ascot, but being unable to keep up with the car, even though it was being driven in bottom gear, this representative of the old order, rather symbolically perhaps, had to be sent home again. During the ensuing weeks the Prince received driving instruction from Mr Oliver Stanton, an American who had previously taught him how to ride a bicycle.

The original royal Daimler was kept by Edward's successor, George V, until 1930, when it was returned to the maker's. In 1938 King George VI visited the works and took the car out for what was described at the time as 'a bit of a bumpy ride'. At that time the car was considered little more than a joke; by 1968 it had become recognized as one of the most valuable historic vehicles in the country and in that year Daimler presented it to Queen Elizabeth II. Three years later it took to the road again when she entered her great-grandfather's first car for the 1971 London to Brighton Rally.

The first *ROYAL PILOT*

was HRH the Infante Don Alfonso of Orleans and Bourbon, cousin of King Alfonso of Spain, who learned to fly on an Antoinette monoplane at Mourmelon, France while a lieutenant in the Spanish Army and was granted his brevet on 23 October 1910. Prince Alfonso was Spain's second qualified pilot and her first military aviator. In 1913 he saw active service in the Spanish-Moroccan War as commander of a flight of Lohner biplanes and in 1921 became Chief Instructor of the Spanish Air Force. The Prince was still flying his own aircraft when well into his 80s.

GB: The first member of the British Royal Family to learn to fly was HRH the Duke of York, later King George VI, who was given instruction on an Avro 504 at Waddon Aerodrome by Lt Coryton during May 1919. The Duke was serving with the RAF at this time, but displayed little aptitude as a pilot. His elder brother, the Prince of Wales, though later renowned for his flying exploits, did not learn to fly until 1929.

The earliest reference to *RUBBER*

is made by the Spanish writer Pietro Martyre d'Anhiera in his *De Orbo Novo* (Alcala 1530). The author describes an Aztec game played with balls 'made of the juice of a certain herbe . . . [which] being stricken upon the ground but softly' rebounded 'incredibly into the ayer'. A more detailed description of rubber balls as used by the Arawaks of the Greater Antilles for the game of Batey is given by the Spanish historian Gonzalo Fernandez de Oviedo in his *Historia General y Natural de las Indias* (Seville 1535). These balls weighed about 12lb and were made from a mixture of grass, tree roots and other fibrous substances, bound together with a rubber paste and smoked hard. According to Tordesillas, writing at the beginning of the 17th century, Columbus saw the natives of Haiti playing games with rubber balls during his second Atlantic voyage of 1493–6.

The first satisfactory solvent for rubber was discovered by François Fresnau, who succeeded in dissolving raw rubber in turpentine at his home in Marennes, France in 1762 and thus laid the foundations of the modern rubber industry.

Manufacture of rubber goods on a small scale was begun by J.N. Reithoffer at Vienna in 1811, but the range of products remained severely limited until a means could be found of rendering the raw rubber sufficiently pliable to be rolled or beaten into the required shape. This problem was overcome in 1820, when Thomas Hancock of London developed a machine which he called the 'pickle', consisting of a revolving drum containing numerous sharp prongs. These prongs masticated the rubber and reduced it to a workable plastic mass. Hancock took out a patent on 29 April 1820 for 'application of a certain material to render various parts of dress and other articles more elastic'. The following year he established a factory at Goswell Mews, Goswell Street, London, and installed several large-scale masticators and iron rollers, which were driven by a horse-mill.

The first rubber products manufactured by Hancock were made by cutting strips of rubber from a prepared block. These were used for garters, braces, trouser-straps (trousers were just coming into fashion and were worn strapped under the instep), waist-bands, knee-caps, etc. and 'for a variety of surgical and other purposes'. Generally the application was made by coating cloth or other material with rubber solution and sticking on the strip of rubber. In the case of garters, braces and similar elastic goods the rubber was enveloped in a linen sheath. Another of the early products was rubber gloves, but as they were made with a leather lining, proved suitable only for heavy outdoor or industrial work requiring little manual dexterity. Probably the only one of Hancock's manufactures that was not a 'first' as far as rubber was concerned was the eraser (*q.v.*), which had already been in use in Britain for half a century.

SHEET RUBBER was first made by Thomas Hancock in 1822, using an ingenious process of his own devising to overcome the limitations of his iron rollers. Thin layers of rubber were sliced from a block measuring 8×4×2in, the largest Hancock could make at that time. The strips were then heat-welded together to form a sheet 'so thin as to be semi-transparent'. The first commercial application of sheet rubber was as a covering for corks to make stoppers for bottles. Why it was necessary to cover the corks at all remains something of a mystery.

The first rubber sheets for hospital use, etc. were manufactured by Thomas Hancock's brother John at his Fulham factory in 1824.

See also Foam Rubber.

The first
RUBBER BALLOONS
were made by Prof. Michael Faraday in 1824 for use in his experiments with hydrogen made at the Royal Institution in London. 'The caoutchouc is exceedingly elastic', he wrote in the *Quarterly Journal of Science* the same year. 'Bags made of it . . . have been expanded by having air forced into them, until the caoutchouc was quite transparent, and when expanded by hydrogen they were so light as to form balloons with considerable ascending power. . . .' Faraday made his balloons by cutting round two sheets of rubber laid together and pressing the edges together. The tacky rubber welded automatically, and the inside of the balloon was rubbed with flour to prevent the opposing surfaces joining together.

Toy balloons were introduced by pioneer rubber manufacturer Thomas Hancock the following year in the form of a do-it-yourself kit consisting of a bottle of rubber solution and a condensing syringe.

Vulcanized toy balloons, which unlike the earlier kind were unaffected by changes in temperature, were first manufactured by J.G. Ingram of London in 1847 and can be regarded as the prototype of modern toy balloons.

The first
RUBBER, FOAM
was produced in an electric mixer of the ordinary domestic variety at the Dunlop Latex Development Laboratories, Fort Dunlop, Birmingham in 1929. The idea of beating latex into a foam with an egg-whisk originated with E.A. Murphy. Using a gelling process perfected by another member of the team, W.H. Chapman, the Dunlop scientists succeeded in producing a rubber foam capable of being set in moulds.

The first foam-rubber products to be marketed were Dunlopillo motor-cycle pillion-seats, produced in limited quantities in 1931. The following year Dunlop provided foam rubber as an upholstery for 300 London buses and for the seats of the new Shakespeare Memorial Theatre at Stratford on Avon. Manufacture of Dunlopillo mattresses began in 1935 and of foam-rubber carpet underlays in 1937.

The food mixer used to make the first foam rubber, 1929

The first
SAFETY-RAZOR
designed for use with disposable blades was patented by King Camp Gillette on 2 December 1901. The original inspiration had come from his employer, William Painter, inventor of the disposable crown cork, who suggested: 'Why don't you invent something which will be used once and thrown away? Then the customer will come back for more.' Gillette was unable to act on this good advice until 1895; the idea came to him as he stood before the shaving-mirror one day and considered how little of his cut-throat razor was actually used for the business of shaving – no more than the edge. His plan was to produce a sharp edge with as little superfluous steel backing as possible.

The problem of producing a blade thin enough, flat enough, sharp enough and cheap enough, which steel-manufacturers told him was impossible, was finally solved by an inventive mechanic called William Nickerson, the only employee – on a half-time basis – of the nascent American Safety Razor Co, which Gillette had formed in Boston on 28 September 1901. Production began in 1903, though by the end of the year the sales figures were hardly indicative of the death of the cut-throat razor, the 51 purchasers of a Gillette Safety Razor having disposed of a nation-wide total of exactly 168 blades. Gillette's great idea may have seemed an ill-timed disaster; in fact he was on the threshold of triumph. A year later no less than 90,000 Americans had taken to the safety-razor habit and consumed between them nearly 12½ million disposable razor-blades.

GB: The Gillette Safety Razor was introduced in 1905.

LONG-LIFE STAINLESS-STEEL RAZOR-BLADES – a contradiction of Gillette's 'use-once-and-throw-away' principle – were first introduced by the British firm of Wilkinson Sword in 1956.

The first
SCHOOL EXAMINATIONS AND MARKS SYSTEM
reference to, is contained in a letter written by Dr Samuel Butler, Headmaster of Shrewsbury School, to one of his assistant masters on 10 October 1818:

I feel myself . . . under the necessity of requesting that you will be more particular with regard to your marks. I lay great stress upon them, being the only clue I have to understand the merits of the different boys, except what I can pick up from the monthly examinations, and I observe that your marks are greatly at variance with mine on these occasions.

The marks system referred to in the above passage was explained by the Headmaster's grandson, the celebrated author of *The Way of All Flesh*, Samuel Butler, who was himself a pupil at the school, in his biography of the Doctor:

There were two sets of marks, one for viva-voce lessons, and the other for exercises – the object being to show at a glance which class of work the marks referred to. For lessons the marks were V (very good), W (well), w (pretty well), t (tolerable), i (idle), and b (bad).

Dr Welldon of Tonbridge, who had been an assistant master under Butler, stated that the custom of holding half-yearly examinations had first been introduced at Shrewsbury, and that hitherto the only method of assessing the boys' progress was for visiting dignitaries to come at set periods to hear them at their lessons. In this respect Shrewsbury resembled most other schools of the pre-examination era. Promotion from one form to another was by seniority and unaffected by academic merit; once in the Sixth Form the principal stimulus to scholarship provided at lower levels – fear of the birch – was removed, and there was little incentive for the boy who lacked the love of learning for its own sake.

It is not known whether the monthly and half-yearly examinations instituted at Shrewsbury were written tests or viva voce, but as early as July 1830 the Sixth Form at Harrow was enjoying the privilege of printed examination papers.

EXTERNAL SCHOOL EXAMINATIONS (i.e. examinations conducted by an outside and independent examining body) were first held on 23–24 December 1850, when pupils of Mr Goodacre's School at Nottingham sat for the Certificate of the College of Preceptors. The Examiner on this occasion was the Dean of the College, Dr Richard Wilson. Three Higher Certificates and two Lower Certificates were awarded, while 12 other candidates received honourable mentions. During the following summer the College of Preceptors held examinations at schools in St Heliers, Kelvedon, Seacombe and Brighton and in December 1851, 35 girl pupils of a school whose name is regrettably unrecorded became the first members of their sex to undergo the ordeal by examination. Seven of their number gained Certificates. Until 1853 the papers were generally set by the teachers of the individual schools concerned, with the College of Preceptors' Examiners adding their own questions and acting in a supervisory capacity. Thereafter the Certificate Examination was placed on a more formal basis, being held twice-yearly at local examination centres with uniform papers for all candidates.

SCHOOL CERTIFICATE EXAMINATION CONDUCTED BY A UNIVERSITY EXAMINATIONS BOARD: the first was the Oxford Local, instituted by Oxford University in 1858 at the instigation of T. D. Acland, an enthusiastic agricultural reformer and former MP who sought to tempt farmers' sons into the universities by providing an examination of recognized status for the pupils of middle-class schools. The College of Preceptors' examination failed to fulfil his aims owing to the lack of *rapport* between the College and the universities. According to Acland's plan there were to be certificates awarded at two different age-levels, a system that has been followed by the university boards down to the present day. The examination for the Junior Certificate was open to candidates under the age of 15 and for the Senior Certificate to those under 18.

The first examination for the Oxford Local was conducted at 11 centres in the spring of 1858. There were 750 junior candidates, of whom 280 passed, and 401 seniors, 150 of whom were successful. The Local Examination Delegacy reported: 'There was often a tolerably wide range of information, and sometimes no small amount of original thought: but candidates who showed both these, frequently showed little power of putting their information together, and still less of expressing it in clear language.' The high percentage of failures provoked anxious comment in both the educational and the lay Press, many expressing the thought that if these results represented the attainments of the most advanced pupils, what was the standard of the majority? The *Educational Times*, however, put the blame fairly and squarely on the university, saying that boys of 14 had been subjected to an inquisition 'which twenty years ago would not have been required for a BA degree in Oxford itself'.

Similarly disappointing results attended the first experiment in allowing girls to sit for a university Local, a concession made with some misgivings in December 1863 by the Cambridge Local Examinations Syndicate. They had been goaded into this display of sexual equality by the redoubtable Miss Emily Davies, the founder of Girton College, Cambridge. Eighty-three candidates sat the examination in London, the papers being the same as the boys'. Despite the poor showing of the female candidates, the arrangement was continued on an experimental basis for three years and formally approved in May 1867. Oxford followed suit in 1870. The innovation aroused considerable controversy, and found the two most distinguished headmistresses of the period, whose names were generally spoken in the same breath, taking directly opposing stands on the subject. Miss Beale of Cheltenham Ladies College asserted that to enter her pupils for an examination taken by boy candidates of a generally inferior social status would lower the tone of her school; while Miss Buss, of the less socially exclusive North London Collegiate School, was an active supporter from the outset, entering no less than 25 of her pupils for the inaugural examination in 1863.

ELEVEN-PLUS EXAMINATION was initiated by Sidney Webb and Sir Herbert Llewellyn Smith of the London School Board with the introduction of the Junior County Scholarship Scheme in 1893. A total of 2,167 scholarships to grammar schools were awarded annually to the successful competitors from some 75,000 London schoolchildren. The age of 11 was chosen since the school leaving-age was then 12 (for those passing the Seventh Standard examination), and it was thought wiser to give the children this opportunity of continuing their education before they began making job arrangements.

The first Local Education Authority to abandon the Eleven-Plus Examination completely was Anglesey Education Committee on deciding to go 100% comprehensive in 1952.

GENERAL CERTIFICATE OF EDUCATION 'O' AND 'A' LEVEL EXAMINATIONS were introduced in 1950 to replace the examinations formerly held for the School Certificate and Higher School Certificate. These latter had been introduced under Board of Education Circular 1002 of June 1917, which stated that henceforth the Board would recognize only the certificates granted by approved examining boards under the control of a Secondary Schools Examination Council, in order to achieve some uniformity of academic standards. The basic difference between the School Certificate and the GCE was that whereas the former was a grouped examination, candidates having to pass a minimum of five subjects within one of four groups, the GCE was taken in individual subjects. In addition the GCE could be sat by a single pupil; the School Certificate was open only to whole classes.

The first
SCHOOL MAGAZINE
was a handwritten sheet edited by George Foster and Caspar Wistar, pupils of the Philadelphia Latin School (now the William Penn Charter School), and first published on 27 July 1774. Its title is not recorded and no copies are known to survive. The *Gentleman's Magazine*, described as 'a half sheet published every ten days by Robinson', succeeded it and ran for

three issues. In the next three years, six more titles made their appearance. The last of these, *The Students Gazette* (1777), resembled some modern underground high-school papers, its handwritten columns often containing scurrilous remarks about the masters and school governors. No other school magazine in America is known before 1822 and at the Philadelphia Latin School the pupils' journalistic aspirations lay dormant for 110 years before another, ninth paper was started in 1888.

GB: The first school magazine published in Britain and the first printed example on record was *The Microcosm, A Periodical Work by Gregory Griffin of the College of Eton*, published weekly by C. Knight of Castle Street, Windsor from 6 November 1786 to 30 July 1787. The name 'Gregory Griffin' cloaked the identity of an editorial collective comprising George Canning, John and Robert 'Bobus' Smith, and John Hookham Frere. In the opening number they stated an editorial objective fitting to the time and place: '. . . he, who hereafter may sing the glories of Britain, must first celebrate at Eton the smaller glories of his college'. This they did in a compilation of essays, letters and poems, one of the most notable contributions being an article by Canning, 'The Slavery of Greece' – an early intimation of the interest that was to influence his policy as Minister for Foreign Affairs (1820–27) and assist the liberation of Greece. Prime Minister for six months prior to his death in 1827, Canning was the first of many British premiers whose earliest experience of 'public affairs' has been in editing a school magazine. *The Microcosm* enjoyed a wide circulation outside the school, one of its readers being the Queen, who was sent copies by Fanny Burney. It lasted for 40 issues.

Only three other school magazines of the eighteenth century are recorded in Britain, all of them published at Westminster. One of these, Robert Southey's *Flagellant* (1792), enjoys the unique distinction for a school paper of being confined to the closed case of the British Museum, on account of its supposedly erotic nature.

See also University Magazine.

The first
SCOOTER

was invented in 1897 by 15-year-old London schoolboy Walter Lines, later to become the founder of Triang Toys. No patent was taken out, as Walter's father did not think it would be worth while. Among the ranks of schoolboy inventors, he was probably the youngest ever to produce in a commercially practicable form what was to become a mass-production item of merchandise. In his maturer years Walter Lines introduced another well-loved children's toy, the Fairy Cycle, which he launched in 1920.

The first
SECOND-HAND CAR DEALER

in Britain was the Motor Car Co of 15 Red Lion Square, London, established in September 1897. The *Autocar* reported that their first list included 17 second-hand vehicles, principally French, ranging in price from £30 for a Hildebrand motor cycle to £335 for a Peugeot phaeton. Pending sale, cars could be hired for £5 per week.

The first
SECURITY GUARDS

in Britain were employed by Night Watch Services of London, an organization founded in 1935 by the Marquess of Willingdon and merchant-banker Henry F. Tiarks. Fifteen uniformed guards, each equipped with truncheon, police whistle and torch, patrolled the Park Lane area on bicycles to guard the flats and houses of wealthy residents who subscribed to the service. Then, as now, the concept of security guards aroused some disquiet and the Labour Party leader George Lansbury described Night Watch Services as 'a first halting step to Fascism'.

The first
SERVICE STATION or *GARAGE*

for motor cars was established by A. Borol at 41 rue Sainte-Claire, Bordeaux in December 1895. The French motoring journal *La Locomotion Automobile* reported that Borol's garage had facilities for travellers to park their cars overnight. 'Additionally there is a workshop for the maintenance, repair and cleaning of all automobiles', the paper continued. 'One can be sure of always finding 680° motor spirit and special oil for motors at this depot. Also, of considerable advantage to tourists, A. Borol sends off on to the road motor spirit, oil and spare parts to whoever asks him for them.' As Borol was also the Bordeaux agent for Peugeot cars, he appears to have fulfilled every important function of a modern garage-proprietor.

GB: The earliest recorded service station was advertised in the *Autocar* for 10 April 1897: 'Autocarists visiting Brighton will find storage for car and supply of petrol at Brighton Cycle and Motor Co, Marine Parade (opposite Royal Aquarium). Staff of competent drivers and mechanics.'

The word 'garage' was first used in English in the sense of a repair and service station with reference to the Motor Carriage Supply Co of Balderton Street, London, in the *Autocar* for 23 June 1900.

BULK-STORAGE PETROL FILLING-STATION: the first was operated by the Automobile Gasoline Co, founded by Harry Grenner and Clem Laessing at St Louis, Mo. in 1905. Petrol was dispensed through a garden hose connected to a gravity-feed tank.

The first petrol filling-station with a forecourt and projecting canopy in the modern form was opened by Standard Oil of California at Seattle, Wash. in 1907. Generally, however, the layout of early American filling-stations was rudimentary in the extreme. A notable exception was a 13-pump garage with ladies' rest-room and a female attendant to dispense iced water opened at Memphis, Tenn. in 1912.

GB: The first bulk-storage petrol filling-station in Britain was opened at

Britain's first filling station – Aldermaston, 1919

Aldermaston, Berkshire in March 1920 by the Automobile Association (AA). The Treasurer of the AA had been on a winter motoring tour of California the previous year and had been struck by the comparative ease with which petrol could be obtained in the USA. The Aldermaston garage was equipped with a hand-pump dispensing National Benzole petrol, water for radiators, a compressor for inflating tyres, a fire-extinguisher and a telephone. It was manned by AA patrols and was for the use of members only.

See also Petrol Pump.

The first
SEWING-MACHINE
was patented by Thomas Saint, cabinet-maker of Greenhill Rents, in the parish of St Sepulchre, London on 17 July 1790. The specification, which lay buried among other patents of Saint relating to boots and shoes until discovered by Newton Wilson in 1874, was remarkable for its anticipation of so many features which later became basic in commercially developed machines. These included the perpendicular action, patented later by Isaac Singer, the eye-pierced needle and the pressing surfaces designed to hold the cloth taut, patented by Elias Howe, and the overhanging arm that constitutes a basic characteristic of most modern sewing-machines. The apparatus was apparently intended for sewing leather, but there is no record of whether it was built.

The first sewing-machine to be produced commercially was constructed in prototype form by Barthélemy Thimmonier, a poor tailor of Amplepuis, a Rhône village, in 1829. Two years later he received an order for 80 machines from a Paris clothing factory making military uniforms, and was taken on the staff as supervisor and mechanic. The experiment seems to have been only too successful, for the tailors, seeing Thimmonier's machines as a threat to their livelihood, incited a mob to destroy them. One model survived, and this Thimmonier carried back to Amplepuis, walking all the way and exhibiting the machine as a side-show curiosity to earn a few sous.

For the next few years Thimmonier eked out a precarious existence by selling handmade wooden sewing-machines for the equivalent of £2 each. In 1845 success seemed within his grasp again, a M. Magnin offering to put his latest model into regular series production. Built entirely of metal, the machines turned out by the Magnin workshops were capable of 200 stitches a minute and had every prospect of finding a secure market, given time to overcome innate French conservatism.

Mechanization invades the home – Singer sewing-machine, 1851

Three years later, though, the mob intervened again, this time on a larger scale, and the infant sewing-machine industry was swept away in the Revolution of 1848.

GB: Elias Howe of Spencer, Mass., who patented a lock-stitch machine in 1846, disposed of his British rights the same year to William Thomas, a corset-manufacturer of Cheapside, for the sum of £250. At the same time Howe went to work for Thomas, manufacturing the first British-built sewing-machines for use in his employer's own business.

DOMESTIC SEWING-MACHINE: the first was manufactured by Isaac Merritt Singer at Harvard Place, Boston in 1851. This was to become the first universally accepted labour-saving device for the home, invading virtually every middle-class household in Europe and America within the following two or three decades. In 1889 the Singer Manufacturing Co produced the first electrically driven sewing-machine at their plant at Elizabethport, N.J.

The first
SEX EDUCATION
course as part of a school curriculum was introduced in England at Abbotsholme School by its first Headmaster, Cecil Reddie, during the term beginning 1 October 1889. Reddie gave two main reasons for his innovation: 'to prevent mental illusions due to false ideas from within; to prevent false teaching from other fellows.' He had drawn up a memorandum on the subject dated 30 December 1888, as a guide for the future work of sex education at Abbotsholme. In it he grouped the boys according to three age classifications. The first group, labelled 'Pre-Pubity', were boys from 10 to 13 years old, who were to be taught 'the true facts of their origin, of their life development, and of the dangers that surround them . . .'. 'During Pubity' (age 13–16) the boys were to be taught 'the laws of the feelings they now experience . . . it is best at this period that they should think as little as possible about these matters'. The 'After Pubity' group (16–20) were to be instructed in 'the laws of later life, so that they will enter the world equipped on this point'. Reddie was a lone voice in the wilderness as far as England was concerned. He had few, if any, imitators at the time, though curiously he seems to have attracted little active opposition from professional moralists.

OFFICIALLY BACKED SCHEME FOR INTRODUCING SEX EDUCATION into the curriculum of State Schools was introduced *c.* 1900 at Breslau, Prussia, when the central school authorities requested Dr Martin Chotzen to deliver a course of lectures on sexual hygiene in education to 150 teachers. The lectures covered the anatomy of the sexual organs, the development of the sexual instinct, its chief perversions, venereal diseases, and 'the importance of the cultivation of self-control'.

The first
SHIPPING VESSEL BUILT OF STEEL
was the steam-launch *Ma Robert*, constructed in John Laird's shipyard at Birkenhead for the use of David Livingstone on his expedition up the Zambezi, and delivered on 6 March 1858. The vessel was taken out to Africa in sections aboard the sloop *Pearl*, and assembled and launched on the Kongone tributary in May of that year. By the time the expedition had reached the Kebrabasa Rapids the unfortunate *Ma Robert* had already been renamed the *Asthmatic*, 'from the puffing and groaning with which she managed her six or seven miles an hour, being easily passed by the native canoes'. Her steel plates constantly leaked, but with continuous repairs she was kept afloat until 20 December 1860 when she met her end on a sandbank above Senna.

For the first Atlantic Iron Steamship *see* Ocean Liner.

The first
SHOP WITH PLATE-GLASS WINDOWS
in Britain was 16 Charing Cross, London, a former print-shop converted into a tailoring establishment by Francis Place (*see* Perambulator) and

reopened on 8 April 1801. Although this innovation was condemned on all sides as reckless extravagance, Place wrote in his memoirs that he 'sold from the windows more goods . . . than paid journeymen's wages and the expenses of housekeeping'.

The first
SHORTHAND
system known to the modern world was published by Dr Timothy Bright under the title *Characterie; the art of short, swift, and secret writing* (London 1588). Unlike most of the pre-Pitman systems succeeding it, which were alphabetical in construction, Bright's employed arbitrary characters to denote particular groups of words. Despite the author's claim that his method could be learned in one month and completely mastered in two, it is highly improbable that it could ever have been used for taking down verbatim reports at normal speed of delivery. James Lewis, a later exponent of shorthand, remarked that it was as difficult to acquire as any foreign language.
TEACHER OF SHORTHAND: the earliest known was Jeremiah Rich, who instructed pupils in a system of his own making that he published in 1646. At that date he was holding classes at the house of 'Mrs Williams, a midwife' in St Olave's parish, Southwark. Rich's system was the first to attract any widespread attention, and it endured long enough for a reporter on the *Oxford University Herald* to be using a modified version as late as 1847. Pitman estimated that in Rich's day there were probably 1,000 shorthand-writers in England.
NEWSPAPER TO EMPLOY SHORTHAND REPORTERS: the first was the *Morning Chronicle*, whose proprietor, a Mr Perry, recruited a corps of stenographers for the transcription of Parliamentary debates in 1785. Although the *Morning Chronicle* was by no means the earliest newspaper to introduce Parliamentary reports, it was probably the first to give an accurate account of what was said in debate. Previously reporters of Parliamentary proceedings had tended to follow the example of Dr Johnson, a pioneer in the field, who condensed what he had heard spoken on the floor of the House in such a manner that 'the Whig rascals should not have the best of the argument'.
PHONOGRAPHIC SHORTHAND: the first practical system was devised by Isaac Pitman in May 1837 while employed as a schoolmaster at Wotton-under-Edge, Gloucestershire, and published on 15 November of the same year by Samuel Bagster under the title *Stenographic Sound-hand*, London, price 4d. The world-wide dissemination of Pitman's Shorthand began a few days later, when Isaac's brother Jacob left for Adelaide, South Australia, taking with him 100 copies of the book.

The first class in Pitman's Shorthand was inaugurated at the Mechanics' Institute, 3 Bath Street, Bath in the summer of 1839. Pitman began teaching his shorthand by post (*see also* Correspondence Course) the following year.

Between the publication of Bright's shorthand in 1588 and Pitman's in 1837, no less than 200 systems were formulated for general use. Few of these attained any widespread application, partly on account of their complexity, but also because they were usually published in very limited editions at a price far beyond the means of anyone wanting to learn shorthand in order to make a living. One aspiring shorthand student of the mid 18th century recorded how he had rented a 5gn manual for 1gn and transcribed the whole of it by hand. This was exceptional – generally the shorthand-writer of this period was a leisured gentleman of parts who liked to amaze his friends by quoting verbatim the vicar's Sunday sermon. The first text to be issued in a popular edition was Samuel Taylor's, published by William Harding at 3s 6d in 1823. Prior to this date, however, Taylor's *Universal Stenography* (1783) had won world-wide renown, providing the basis of the first shorthand systems to be published in Italy (1796), Spain (1800), Sweden (*c.* 1800), Hungary (1802), Portugal (1802), USA (1819) and Poland (1838).

Not until the present century did Pitman's Shorthand become standard in the UK for most official and commercial use. Even as late as 1882, the 168 newspaper, court and Parliamentary shorthand-reporters in London were employing as many as 13 different systems, of which the two most popular, Pitman's and Taylor's, could boast 94 and 45 adherents respectively. The Law Courts still used Taylor exclusively, while Hansard's five reporters divided 3–2 in favour of Pitman. The only major competitor to Pitman's Shorthand in the last half century has been the American system, Speedwriting, introduced to Britain in 1927.

The first
SIGNATURE TUNE
was 'The Jolly Brothers Waltz', adopted by the Australian artiste Albert Whelan when he made his English début at the Empire, Leicester Square in 1901. He always began his act by whistling the tune as he came on to the stage, removing his hat, stick and gloves as he did so. Shortly before leaving Australia for England, Whelan had been standing in the foyer of a Melbourne theatre, when he happened to overhear a theatre-goer whistling this old German tune as he handed his coat and hat to a cloakroom attendant. He thereupon decided to make it his own.

The first game of
SNOOKER
was devised by Sir Neville Chamberlain as a variation of Black Pool while he was serving as a subaltern with the Devonshire Regiment at Jubbulpore, India in 1875. The word 'snooker' was the customary sobriquet for a new cadet at the Royal Military Academy, Woolwich, one of whose alumni, a member of the Field Battery at Jubbulpore, happened to impart this information to Lt Chamberlain when he was being entertained in the Devons' mess. In a conversation with Compton Mackenzie nearly 65 years later, Sir Neville explained how it came to be applied to the game he had just invented:

The term was a new one to me, but I soon had an opportunity of exploiting it when one of our party failed to hole a coloured ball which was close to a corner pocket. I called out to him: 'Why, you're a regular snooker!' I had to explain to the company the definition of the word, and, to soothe the feelings of the culprit, I added that we were all, so to speak, snookers at the game, so it would be very appropriate to call the game snooker. The suggestion was adopted with enthusiasm and the game has been called snooker ever since.

The first rules of snooker were drawn up by Sir Neville and posted in the billiard-room of the Ootacumund Club, probably in the summer of 1882. He was then serving on the staff of General Sir Frederick Roberts, C-in-C Madras Army, and the opportunity of meeting and playing with officers of many different regiments undoubtedly helped to spread the game through India. News of it reached England, for when the professional billiard-player John Roberts came out to Calcutta in 1885 to coach the Maharajah of Cooch Behar, he told his patron that he had been asked to find out the rules. The Maharajah happened to be a friend of Sir Neville's, and he told the professional that he need seek no further, as he could introduce him to the only begetter. This was effected over dinner, with the result that John Roberts was able to launch the game in England on his return home.

The first
SOUND-RECORDING
apparatus was the Phonograph, designed by Thomas Alva Edison in

1877. The prototype was completed by John Kruesi, Edison's mechanic, at West Orange, N.J. on 6 December, and the first recording – Edison reciting 'Mary had a little lamb' – was made the same day. An account of this latest miracle of science appeared in the *Scientific American* for 22 December 1877.

Mr. Thomas A. Edison recently came into this office, placed a little machine on our desk, turned a crank, and the machine inquired as to our health, asked us how we liked the phonograph, informed us that it was very well, and bid us a cordial goodnight. These remarks were not only perfectly audible to ourselves, but to a dozen or more persons gathered around.

Commercial production was commenced by the Edison Speaking Phonograph Co, 203 Broadway, N.Y., formed 24 April 1878. The machines were leased out with a quantity of blank tin-foil cylinders to travelling showmen, who exhibited them to paying audiences and returned a percentage of the receipts to the Company. It was at one of these demonstrations in New York during the early months of the enterprise that the first known musical recording was made by Jules Levy, playing 'Yankee Doodle' on a cornet. The first instrument for domestic use, and the first to be sold outright, was the Edison Parlor Speaking Phonograph, marketed at $10 in 1878. After the initial novelty of the phonograph had faded, its obvious deficiencies – poor reproduction, the brevity of the tin-foil cylinder, and difficulty of operation – became apparent, and the public lost interest. Edison himself was busily engaged on the development of his incandescent lamp, and it was not until Bell and Tainter produced their improved Graphophone (*see below*) that he returned to the problem of sound reproduction.

GB: The first Edison-type Phonograph was constructed for William Preece, Chief Engineer of the GPO, by his assistant A. Stroh, and demonstrated before the Royal Institution on 1 February 1878. The correspondent of the *Graphic* reported:

Mr. Preece explained how he had, with great difficulty, obtained this instrument, which was, he believed, the first exhibited in London. A gentleman returned only a week before from America had kindly furnished him with drawings, and he had fortunately been able to enlist the services of the greatest mechanic of the day, who had, by working day and night, completed that afternoon the phonograph which stood before the audience. After remarking on the difficulty of knowing what to say in the circumstances, Mr. Preece spoke into the phonograph 'Hey, diddle, diddle, the cat and the fiddle' very distinctly, and after waiting a minute or so the instrument was caused to repeat what he had said. The words were distinctly heard but the voice was very faint and an unearthly caricature. Professor Tyndall then made his way to the table and gave the phonograph a well-known quotation from the works of Tennyson, who was present, 'Come into the Garden, Maud', which was afterwards echoed to the satisfaction of the audience.

Manufacture of the Edison tin-foil phonograph in Britain was begun by the London Stereoscopic Co, Cheapside and Regent Street, towards the end of 1878. The earliest-known advertisement appeared in Vol. I, No. 1 of the *Boy's Own Paper*, 18 January 1879, and offered Edison Speaking Machines for 10gns each.

SOUND-RECORDING APPARATUS CAPABLE OF REPRODUCING MUSIC: the first with any degree of fidelity (the 1878 experiment recorded above can have been little more than a cacophony of sound) was the wax-cylinder Graphophone, developed by Chichester Bell and Charles Sumner Tainter at the Volta Laboratory, Washington, D.C. between 1881 and 1885 and granted a US patent on 4 May 1886. Manufacture was commenced by the Columbia Phonograph Co in 1888, the same year that Edison, spurred on by his rivals' progress, brought out his own wax-cylinder Improved Phonograph. Both Edison and Columbia tried to promote their apparatus as office dictating-machines, but the price of phonographs compared unfavourably with the low wages of stenographers, and there was little response except by some Government Departments in Washington and a few blind typists. The real future of the phonograph lay in entertainment, and this was demonstrated when the first recording by a recognized musician was made by the boy pianist Josef Hofman at the Edison Laboratories in West Orange, N.J. during the course of 1888. The following year Edison recorded an orchestral concert at the Metropolitan Opera House, New York conducted by Hans von Bülow. Four phonographs were employed for the experiment, and the works recorded were Beethoven's 'Eroica', Haydn's B flat major Symphony, and the Prelude to Wagner's *Die Meistersinger*.

GB: The first musical recording was made on 29 June 1888, when Edison recording equipment was set up in the Press Gallery of the Crystal Palace on the occasion of the Handel Festival. The *Illustrated London News* reporter wrote:

The phonograph reported with perfect accuracy the sublime strains, vocal and instrumental, of the 'Israel in Egypt', received by a large horn projecting over the balustrade in the vast concert-room in the north transept. The machine was worked by Mr. De Courcy Hamilton, one of Mr. Edison's assistants, who had brought it from America. The 'phonograms' being sent to Mr. Edison, all the Handel choruses, as sung here by four thousand voices, will be heard in New York and other American cities.

COMMERCIALLY PRODUCED CYLINDER RECORDINGS for the retail trade were probably produced either late in 1889 or early in 1890. The earliest evidence that has come to light is a circular letter dated 19 June 1890 sent by the North American Phonograph Co to its agents, reducing the price of records to $1. There is no indication of the titles available at that time. *See also* Disc Recordings, below.

RECORD CATALOGUE: the first, a 10-page listing of 194 items, was issued by the Columbia Phonograph Co of Washington, D.C. in 1891. It included 27 marches, 13 polkas, 10 waltzes, 36 recordings by Whistling John Atlee (the first 'recording star'), 13 selections for clarinet and piano, 32 vocal (divided into 'Topical', 'Sentimental', 'Irish', 'Comic' and 'Negro'), 20 spoken records (principally comic monologues), 9 cornet and piano selections, and 34 miscellaneous, including an operatic arrangement from *Il Trovatore*. Most records were sold by mail order, and worn recordings could be returned in part exchange for new. Worn cylinders were consigned to the proprietors of nickelodeons, the jukeboxes (*q.v.*) of the day.

GB: The first commercially made British recordings of which any evidence survives were made by the London Phonograph Co, *c.* 1892. The cylinders were recorded by J.E. Hough, who enlisted the services of his assistant, Harry Bluff, to perform comic songs and sentimental ballads, with Edward Hesse, then pianist at the Royal Aquarium, as accompanist. Albert Chevalier, the 'Coster King of Comedy', described in his autobiography a visit he made in about 1892 to a funfair, where he heard a recording on a penny 'plug in and listen' phonograph of an artiste purported, erroneously, to be himself. This could quite probably have been one of the records made by Harry Bluff, who, apart from his other performing talents, was known among his friends as an excellent mimic and impersonator of music-hall stars.

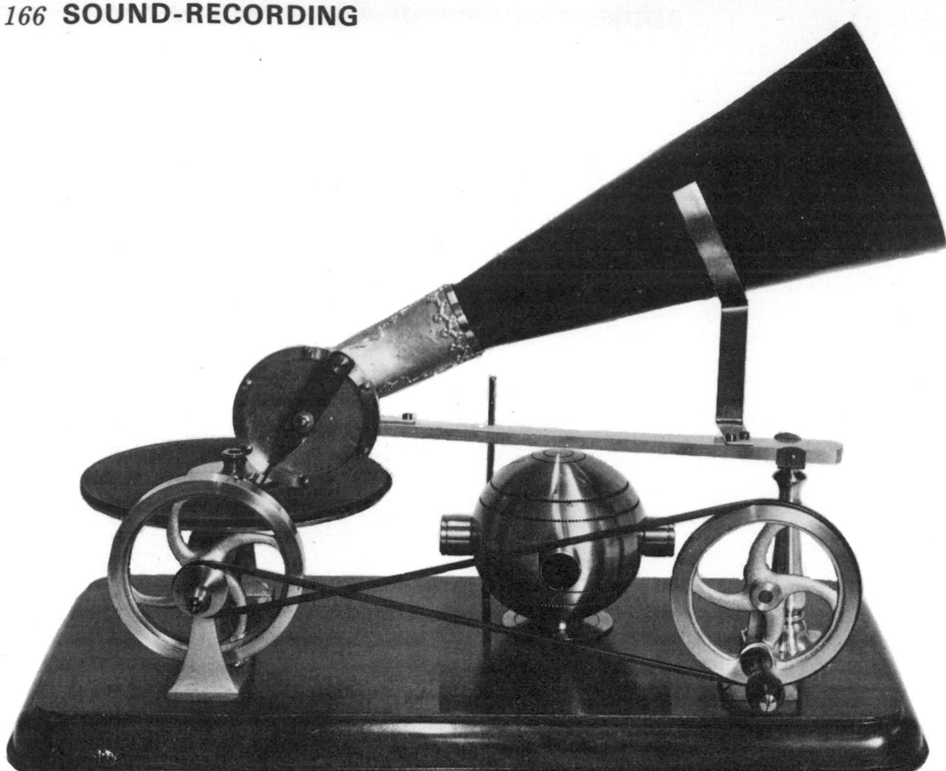

Berliner gramophone 1888. Discs not cylinders

GRAMOPHONE OR DISC RECORD-PLAYER: the first was invented by Emile Berliner, a German immigrant living in Washington, D.C., who applied for a patent on 26 September 1887, and demonstrated his apparatus before the Franklin Institute, Philadelphia on 16 May 1888.

Following a visit by Berliner to Germany, commercial manufacture of the Gramophone was begun by Kämmerer & Rheinhardt of Waltershausen in 1889. These hand-cranked machines were intended chiefly as toys, and played a 5in vulcanized-rubber disc at a speed of approximately 70rpm. The first full-size, electrically operated machines were produced by the United States Gramophone Co, Washington in 1894. These played 7in records; 10in records were introduced in 1900, and 12in in 1903. The first shellac records were made by the Berliner Gramophone Co of Philadelphia in 1897 from a composition prepared by the Durinoid Co of Newark, N.J. The first commercial studio for disc recording and the first record-shop were opened in adjoining buildings in Philadelphia by the Berliner Gramophone Co in 1897.

GB: The Kämmerer & Rheinhardt Gramophone was advertised for the Christmas market at 2gns by Messrs Perkins & Gotto of 60 Oxford Street, London in December 1891. It was accompanied by a selection of records that included 'Twinkle Twinkle Little Star', 'Sing a Song of Sixpence', 'Who Killed Cock Robin?', The Lord's Prayer, and 'Deutschland über Alles'.

Manufacture and commercial recording in Britain began with the establishment of the Gramophone Co (Berliner Patent) in Maiden Lane by W.B. Owen in 1898. The first disc to be issued was a rendering of a piece called 'Happy Darkies' by Percy Honri on concertina and Fred Gaisberg at the piano. The artistes were obliged to improvise the tune on the spot, having been told on arrival at the studio that they were prohibited from recording any copyright music.

The first factory to be operated solely for the manufacture of gramophone records was established by the Gramophone Co at Hanover, Germany in 1898 to produce disc recordings for the English market. The factory was equipped with 14 record presses for the mass production of 7in shellac records – an innovation that proved a turning-point in the record industry. Previously the only method of duplication had been to set up a bank of six or more recording-machines in front of the artiste, who performed into six or more horns, and was required to repeat the song over and over again until a sufficient number of multiples of six had been made to satisfy consumer demand. The new presses worked with a copper matrix made from a wax master, and could reproduce a limitless number of recordings at a correspondingly cheaper price.

PAPER LABELS ON DISC RECORDS: Berliner discs had their titles engraved on a blank space in the centre of the record. The first gramophone records with circular paper title-label were devised by Eldridge Johnson and issued by the Consolidated Talking Machine Co (later the Victor Co) of Camden, N.J. in 1900. The trade-mark depicted on these labels was adapted from Francis Barraud's painting of a fox terrier listening attentively to a horn gramophone – *His Master's Voice* – for which the Consolidated Co, an associate company of HMV's predecessor, the Gramophone Co (*see above*), held the US copyright. Barraud's painting had originally shown the dog Nipper listening to his master's voice (Barraud's recently deceased brother) on a cylinder machine, but having failed to sell the picture to a phonograph-manufacturer, he was persuaded by the Gramophone Co to paint out the phonograph and substitute a gramophone.

OPERATIC RECORDINGS: the first commercial releases on cylinder were made by Gustavello Affre, Adolphe Maréchal, Leon Melchissédec, Albert Vaguet and Maximilien-Nicolas Bouret for Pathé Frères of France in 1896. The first operatic discs were made by Ferruccio Giannini, who recorded 'La Donna è Mobile' and 'Questa o Quella' from *Rigoletto* for the United States Gramophone Co of Philadelphia the same year.

OPERA ON DISCS: the first complete was *Pagliacci*, conducted by the composer, Ruggiero Leoncavallo and recorded in Milan by Fred Gaisberg of the Gramophone Co, London in 1903.

DOUBLE-SIDED DISCS: the first were manufactured in 1904 by the International Talking Machine Co, Weissensee, nr Berlin, under the name 'Odeon' records. They were introduced into Britain the same year.

PORTABLE GRAMOPHONE: the first was the Decca Portable, manufactured by Barnett Samuel & Co,

Decca Portable, 1913

London in 1913. Earlier makes had been described as portable, but required assembly before playing. The Decca Portable became almost standard equipment in the dug-outs of World War I, rivalled as a morale booster only by whisky and *La Vie Parisienne*.
JAZZ RECORD: the first was 'The Dixie Jazz Band One Step', backed by 'Livery Stable Blues', recorded by Nick LaRocca's Original Dixieland Jazz Band for the Victor Co, Camden, N.J., and released on 7 March 1917.
GB: 'At the Jazz Band Ball' and 'Barnyard Blues', were recorded for Columbia Graphaphone Co by the Original Dixieland Jazz Band on 16 April 1919. The latter was an alternative for 'Livery Stable Blues' (*See also* Jazz Band).
ELECTRICAL RECORDING PROCESS: the first was developed by Lionel Guest and H.O. Merriman of London, who made a full-length experimental recording of the burial service of the Unknown Warrior at Westminster Abbey on 11 November 1920. Although not commercially practicable at this stage, the Abbey recording demonstrated that it was possible to substitute a microphone for the studio horn, and so record on location and at any reasonable distance from the sound source.

A commercial process was developed independently by J.P. Masefield and H.C. Harrison at the Bell Telephone Laboratories in the USA, and this was adopted by Victor and Columbia in America and HMV and Columbia in Britain. The first commercially produced electrical recording was a 10in disc of two songs from the University of Pennsylvania's annual performance by the Mask and Wig Club, released by Victor to Philadelphia dealers only in April 1925.
ALL-ELECTRIC GRAMOPHONE: electrical recording was accompanied by a corresponding advance in electrical reproduction. The first all-electric gramophone, with loudspeaker amplification in place of the traditional horn, was the Brunswick Panatrope, manufactured by the Brunswick Co of Dubuque, Iowa in 1925.
GB: The Model 600 Concert Gramophone, with an electro-magnetic pick-up taking the place of the sound-box and valve-amplifying circuit, was manufactured by HMV at Hayes, Middlesex in 1927.
AUTOMATIC-CHANGE GRAMOPHONE: the first was the HMV Automatic Gramophone, introduced in April 1928 at £125. To operate the machine a maximum of 20 records were stacked on a sprung base to the left of the turntable; the topmost disc was gripped by a feed-arm and transferred into the playing position. On release the sound-box arm swung into position and the turntable began to revolve. At the end of play an ejecting spindle lifted the record off the turntable and pitched it sideways into a rubber-lined box set vertically into the cabinet, and the feed-arm repeated the original process.
RADIOGRAM: the first (GB) was the HMV Radio-Gramophone Model 520, produced in 1929. The first table model was the HMV 501 of 1931.
HIGH-FIDELITY RECORDINGS: the first were issued by English Decca in December 1944. The first Hi-Fi record-player was the Decca Piccadilly, with a frequency range of 50–14,000cps, introduced the following year.
RECORDING ISSUED ON VINYLITE: the first was *Till Eulenspiegel* from RCA-Victor in October 1946. This was the first really practical unbreakable record since Berliner had ceased using vulcanized rubber half a century earlier. Vinylite began to oust shellac with the introduction of long-playing records (*q.v.*) two years later.
STEREOPHONIC DISC RECORDINGS: the first for commercial release were marketed by Audio Fidelity in the USA in April 1958.
GB: The first six stereo discs were released by Pye in May 1958. These included a selection of popular melodies performed by Larry Adler on the harmonica; Gilbert and Sullivan overtures by the Pro Arte Orchestra under Stanford Robinson; Tony Osborne playing a medley of tunes from various countries under the title 'Where in the World' (piano and orchestra); Vivaldi and Scarlatti concertos by the London Baroque Ensemble; Dvořák's Eighth Symphony and his Scherzo Capriccioso, by the Hallé Orchestra under Sir John Barbirolli; and a Bach recital by Ralph Downes on the Royal Festival Hall organ.

See also Long-Playing Gramophone Records; Magnetic Recorder.

The first
SPACE FLIGHT BY LIVING CREATURES

is believed to have taken place at the end of 1951, when four monkeys with the code-names Albert 1, 2, 3 and 4 were launched 85 miles into the stratosphere from White Sands, N. Mexico in a V2 rocket. The test, known as 'Operation Albert', was kept secret for fear of objections from animal-lovers. All four monkeys returned safely to Earth, though one subsequently died of heat prostration.

The first animal to go into orbit round the Earth was the dog Laika, launched in the Russian *Sputnik II* satellite on 3 November 1957. The satellite disintegrated in space on 14 April 1958.
MANNED SPACE FLIGHT: the first is alleged to have been made by a Russian named Alexis Ledovski in 1957. According to reports of the US House of Representatives Space Committee and the USAF Air Research and Development Command, Ledovski was launched from the Soviet missile test centre 60 miles south-east of Stalingrad and reached a height of over 200 miles before all communication with him ceased. The spacecraft could either have been carried beyond the pull of the Earth's gravity into outer space, or could have been burnt up on re-entering the Earth's atmosphere. Other astronauts reputed to have lost their lives in unsuccessful space-shots prior to 1961 have been named as Serentsy Schiborin (1958), Andrei Mitkov (1959) and Ivan Kachur (1960). The first space fatality admitted by the Russians occurred on 24 April 1967, when Col Vladamir Mikhailovich Komarov died during the descent of *Soyuz I*.
SUCCESSFUL, MANNED SPACE FLIGHT was first made by 27-year-old Flt Maj. Yuri Alexeyvich Gagarin, who was launched from Baikonur, Western Siberia, in the Russian spacecraft *Vostok I* at 09·07hr Moscow time on 12 April 1961, and landed 108min later at the village of Smelovka, near Engels in the Saratov region of the USSR. The 6·17-ton carrier-rocket contained a 2·4-ton capsule which was released when the speed of the spacecraft reached orbital velocity, about 7·8km a sec. Gagarin then made a single orbit of the Earth at a maximum height of 203 miles and a maximum speed of 28,000kph (17,398mph). The first astronaut to return safely to Earth, Maj. Gagarin was killed in an aircraft crash near Moscow on 27 March 1968.
WOMAN ASTRONAUT: the first was Valentina Nikolayeva Tereshkova, who made 48 orbits of the Earth in *Vostok VI* during a period of 71hr from 16 to 19 June 1963.
SPACE WALK: the first was made by Lt-Col Aleksey Arkhipovich Leonov, who left the Soviet spacecraft *Voshkod II* at approximately 08.30hr GMT on 18 March 1965 and spent 12min 9sec floating in space connected to the satellite by a nylon cord 16ft long. During this time he travelled a distance of about 3,000 miles at a speed of 17,500mph.

The first
SPACE-SHOT, INTERPLANETARY

was made by the US spacecraft *Mariner II*, which was launched on 27 August 1962 and after travelling a distance of 180 million miles, flew within 21,594 miles of the planet Venus on 14 December 1962. The most significant items of information transmitted back to the Earth receiving station at Goldstone, Calif., were that the surface temperature of Venus is some 800 °F, and that the Venusian 'day' lasts an estimated eight months.

The first spacecraft to land on another planet was the Russian *Venus III*, which was launched on 16 November 1965 and made a hard landing on Venus on 1 March 1966.

The first
SPACE-SHOT, LUNAR
was made by the Russian artificial satellite, *Luna I*, which was launched from Tyuratam, USSR on 2 January 1959 and flew to within 4,660 miles of the Moon's surface.
SPACECRAFT TO LAND ON THE MOON: the first was *Luna II*, which was launched on 12 September 1959 and crashed between the craters Archimedes and Autolycus in the Mare Imbrium two days later.
SOFT LANDING ON THE MOON: the first was made by *Luna IX* on 3 February 1966. A series of close-up pictures were transmitted back to Earth. The experiment demonstrated that the Moon's surface was hard enough to withstand the weight of a spacecraft.
MEN TO LAND ON THE SURFACE OF THE MOON: the first were Neil Armstrong, mission commander of the American *Apollo XI*, and Col Edwin Aldrin, pilot of the lunar-module *Eagle*, who touched down on the Sea of Tranquillity at 9.18pm BST on 20 July 1969.

Neil Armstrong stepped on to the lunar surface at 3.56am BST the following day. As he did so he said: 'That's one small step for man, one giant leap for mankind.' Aldrin followed him out of the module 20min later, and the two astronauts spent a further 1hr 44min carrying out their assigned tasks, which included collecting soil and rock samples, installing a special laser-beam reflector, planting the US flag, and unveiling a plaque. The words on the plaque were read out aloud by Armstrong, and heard by an estimated radio and television audience of 500 million people:

Here men from the planet Earth first set foot upon the Moon July 1969 AD. We came in peace for all mankind.

'... one giant leap for mankind' – Neil Armstrong, 21 July 1969

The first
SPECTACLES
earliest authentic reference to, dates from 1289 and is contained in Sandro di Popozo's manuscript work 'Traité de Conduite de la Famille'. He wrote:

I am so debilitated by age that without the glasses known as spectacles, I would no longer be able to read or write. These have recently been invented for the benefit of poor old people whose sight has become weak.

Richard Corson in his *Fashions in Eyeglasses* (London 1967) gives Italy 1287 as the probable place and date of the invention. There are various claims as to the identity of the inventor, but none has been substantiated.
GB: Spectacles are first mentioned in an inventory of the effects of Bishop Walter de Stapledon made at Exeter Palace in 1326. They were described as having silver frames and were valued at 2s.

Spectacles with concave lenses for myopia are first depicted in a portrait of Pope Leo X painted by Raphael in 1517. He is said to have used them most frequently when out hunting.

Until the 17th century, lenses were generally selected at random from the spectacle-maker's stock according to the whim of the customer. The first attempt to grade spectacle lenses systematically was made in 1623 by Valdés in Seville.

The first spectacles with rigid side pieces (temple spectacles) were manufactured by the London optician Edward Scarlett in 1727. The side pieces terminated in a scroll. Temple spectacles were known in French as 'lunettes à tempes permettant de respirer à l'aise' – since it was possible to breathe without the spectacles falling off one's nose. Previously the only method of retaining the spectacles against the head had been by thin cords that looped round the ears.

The first
SPIRITUALIST MEDIUMS
were Margaretta and Kate Fox, aged 14 and 11 respectively, who made what has been claimed as the first direct communication with the spirit world at their parents' homestead in Hydesville, New York on the night of 31 March 1848. For some weeks previous to this date the Fox family had been troubled by inexplicable rapping noises coming from all parts of the house, until on the evening in question Kate Fox challenged the unseen instigator of the sounds to repeat the snapping of her fingers. This being instantly responded to, Mrs Fox began to direct questions to the supposed spirit in such a way that they could be answered either by a rap, signifying 'Yes', a silence for 'No', or for more complex replies, a rap in answer to particular letters as the alphabet was called over. In this manner the spirit was identified as one Charles B. Rosma, a pedlar who had been allegedly murdered in the house some five years earlier and whose body was said to be buried beneath the floor of the cellar. The following day the Fox family and their neighbours dug up the cellar and found fragments of bone and human hair; the remainder of the skeleton was not recovered until 56 years later, when it was found behind the cellar wall.

In April 1850 Kate and Margaretta Fox were placed under contract by the great American showman Phineas T. Barnum and became the first professional mediums, giving public seances at Barnum's Hotel and Barnum's Museum, as well as private sittings at the homes of rich and eminent persons. The sisters continued their career for the next 30 years, during which time both became incurable alcoholics. Margaretta confessed in 1888 that the whole business of the raps had been artificially contrived and actually gave a demonstration of how she could make loud cracking noises with the bones of her foot. She later retracted this statement, claiming she had been paid to make it by enemies of the spiritualist movement.
GB: The first medium to practise in Britain was Mrs W.R. Hayden, the wife of a Boston newspaper-proprietor, who arrived in London in October 1852, and took up residence at 22 Queen Anne Street, Cavendish Square. Her first seance was held with Lady Combermere, Maj. Cotton, and Mr Henry

Thompson of York. Mrs Hayden evoked widespread interest by her psychic powers, as for instance when she was able to tell Mr Galla, the African explorer, the names of 'persons and places in Africa which nobody but himself knew'. Seances rapidly became a fashionable diversion and during the years 1853–4 invitations to 'Tea and Table Rapping' enjoyed a considerable vogue among the more forward-looking inhabitants of suburbia.

The first
STAFF CANTEEN
was provided at the New Lanark Cotton Mills according to a plan proposed in 1812 by the Manager, Robert Owen. 'The kitchen and eating-room', he wrote, 'will enable the proprietors to support the population of the village, not exceeding 2,200 individuals, at 1s 6d per week less than the expense at which they now feed themselves.'

Although some historians have cast doubt on whether the plan was ever carried into effect, it would appear from the testimony of Dr Henry Grey MacNab, author of *The New Views of Mr Owen of Lanark Impartially Examined*, that the canteen was in operation by 1819. The following passage is contained in his description of the Mills:

The building lately erected for a public kitchen: it is of considerable dimensions, being 150 ft in length by 45 ft broad, and three stories in height. The ground floor comprises two spacious kitchens, a bakehouse, storerooms and superintendent's department. The upper stories are divided each into equal apartments, those on the first being designed for eating-rooms and the two above for lecture and reading rooms, etc. . . .

Robert Owen was a visionary far ahead of his time in his regard for the welfare of his employees, and a considerable number of years were to elapse before any other factory-owners sought to emulate his ideas on mass catering. It was only in the 1850s that some employers began to set a room apart for eating and even then it was general for the workers to supply their own food to cook on the premises. One of the earliest firms to provide cooked meals was Colman's of Norwich, mustard-makers, who inaugurated a canteen in 1868 to supply their workmen with a pint of coffee for 1d when work started at 5.45am, and a hot meat dinner at midday for 3d or 4d.

The provision of industrial catering remained the province of a few philanthropic and enlightened industrialists until World War I, when a changing pattern of employment, and the vast influx of women into industries essential to the war effort, brought about a new attitude to factory welfare. Whereas less than 100 canteens existed in 1914, by the time of the Armistice there were approximately 1,000.

The first
STAMP-COLLECTOR
is believed to have been John Tomlynson, who began his collection on 7 May 1840 with a Mulready envelope posted to him the previous day. Inside the envelope, which survives, is an unused Penny Black and an accompanying note describing it as the first adhesive postage stamp. Tomlynson continued the collection for a number of years and parts of it have been preserved.

Victor Wetzel of Lille claimed to have started collecting stamps on the day the Penny Black was first issued – 6 May 1840. Doubts have been cast on this assertion, since it is unlikely that any British postage stamps would have been available in Lille on that date.

The first advertisement relating to stamp-collecting was inserted in the *Family Herald* for 22 March 1851 by T. H. S. Smith, a bookshop-proprietor.

The earliest record of schoolboy stamp-collecting is contained in a letter from the Rev. S.F. Creswell, a master at Tonbridge School, in the June 1860 issue of *Notes and Queries*.

STAMP-COLLECTORS' CLUB: the first was founded by the Rev. F. J. Stainforth, Rector of All Hallows, Staining, City of London in the early 1860s. Members met regularly at the Rectory to discuss and swop stamps. A more formal association of stamp-collectors came into being with the forming of the Société de la Timbrologie in Paris in 1865.

See also Postage Stamp.

The first
STAMP-DEALER
was the Brussels bookseller Jean-Baptiste Constant Moëns, who is believed to have begun dealing in stamps at his shop in the Galerie Bortier, Marche de la Madeleine in 1855. Moëns issued his first catalogue (without values) in 1862. Shortly afterwards he published the world's first philatelic handbook, titled *De la Falsification des Timbres-Poste*.

GB: E. Stanley Gibbons, who began collecting stamps as a schoolboy, arranged a display of stamps for sale in the window of his father's chemist shop at 15 Treville Street, Plymouth in 1856. By 1858 or 1859 the 'firm' of E. S. Gibbons had expanded into a room above the shop and engaged a lady clerk. On the death of his father in 1863, Gibbons abandoned the pharmaceutical part of the business and dealt exclusively in stamps. Shortly after taking this decision – undeterred by predictions of certain ruin – two sailors came into the shop and offered to sell him a sack of Cape Triangulars they had won in a raffle at Cape Town. Gibbons bought the sack for £5 and sold the contents for a profit of about £500. His first catalogue came out in November 1865 and he moved the business from Plymouth to London in 1874.

The first
STATELY HOME OPENED TO THE PUBLIC
was Wilton House nr Salisbury, home of the Earl of Pembroke, in 1776. The 2,424 visitors shown round in the first year did not have to pay an entrance fee, but were expected to tip the housekeeper at least half a crown. The following year the Earl of Leicester opened Holkham Hall, his seat in Norfolk, which could be viewed 'every day of the week except Sunday by Noblemen and foreigners, but on Tuesdays only by other people'.

The first organized excursion to see a stately home was arranged in 1848 by Thomas Cook, founder of the travel firm of the same name, who conducted parties of Midland workers by horse-drawn coach from Leicester to Belvoir Castle, seat of the Duke of Rutland. Shortly afterwards Cook arranged with the Duke of Devonshire to bring excursionists by train to Chatsworth. On one of these occasions, when 1,200 trippers had been let loose on the noble acres, Cook recounted proudly: 'I stood at the gates and saw almost every one of them enter, and I remarked their conduct returning home. There was no rudeness, no damage done to house or gardens, nor a drunken passenger to be seen as the party returned home.'

The first stately home to be opened out of necessity rather than *noblesse oblige*, and the first to be run as a regular commercial enterprise, was the Marquis of Bath's Longleat, nr Warminster, Wiltshire in 1947.

The first
STATUE TO A WOMAN
(other than royalty) in Britain was erected at Walsall, Staffordshire in memory of Dorothy Pattison, and unveiled on 11 October 1886. Sister Dora, as she was better known, was loved by the poor of Walsall for the devoted service she gave at the Cottage Hospital and as a District Nurse from 1865 until her death from cancer in 1878. The statue was sculpted by F. J. Williamson.

The first
STEAMBOAT
practical, was the 138ft-long paddle-wheeler *Pyroscaphe*, a 182-ton wooden

craft built at Écully, near Lyons by the Marquis Claude François Dorothée de Jouffroy d'Abbans. The trial run took place on the River Saône from Lyons to the Isle Barbe on 15 July 1783. This was the first occasion a vessel had moved against the current under its own power. The engine, constructed by Frèrejean et Cie of Lyons, had a horizontal double-acting 25·6in diameter cylinder enclosed within the boiler, rotary motion being transmitted by a double-ratchet mechanism connected to the piston-rod.
GB: A small 25ft-long 5-ton steamboat, apparently without a name, was built by William Symington for the Scottish landowner and amateur technician Patrick Miller of Dalswinton, nr Dumfries and underwent its first trial on Loch Dalswinton on 14 October 1788. Besides Miller and Symington, those on board included James Taylor, tutor to the Miller children, Alexander Nasmyth and the poet Robert Burns, who was a tenant on the estate. According to Taylor 'it answered Mr Miller's expectation fully and afforded great pleasure to the spectators present'. The speed attained was about 5mph. Symington's atmospheric twin-cylinder engine drove two paddle-wheels set one behind the other between the hulls of the catamaran-style boat.
COMMERCIAL STEAMBOAT SERVICE: the first was inaugurated on the Delaware River by John Fitch following an announcement in the *Federal Gazette and Philadelphia Daily Advertiser* for 26 July 1790:

The Steamboat is now ready to take passengers and is intended to set off from Arch Street Ferry in Philadelphia every Monday, Wednesday and Friday for Burlington, Bristol, Bordentown and Trenton and to return on the following days. Price 2s 6d to Burlington and Bristol, 3s 9d to Bordentown, 5s to Trenton.

As 26 July was a Monday, it is possible that the service actually started on that day. The vessel, designed by Fitch, was a stern paddle-wheeler driven by a beam-engine with a single 18in diameter cylinder. He was joined in the venture by a German watchmaker, Johann Voigt, who was responsible for the working of the engine and boiler, and can thus be regarded as the first ship's engineer. Although the service continued till the end of the summer, Fitch had chosen a route already well serviced with stage-coaches and passenger receipts were correspondingly low. While the average speed of the boat was 7mph, the coaches were evidently faster, as they could accomplish the journey from Philadelphia to Burlington in 1½hr less time. After the discontinuance of Fitch's service, there were no other ventures of this kind, either in America or elsewhere, until Robert Fulton began running his famous *Clermont* on the Hudson between New York and Albany in 1807. This has often been wrongly described as the first commercially operated passenger steamboat, though it would be fair to say that it was the first to maintain a successful regular service.
GB: A service three times a week from Broomielaw Quay, Glasgow to Greenock and Helensburgh was inaugurated by Henry Bell's 28-ton *Comet* in August 1812. The boat was built by John Wood & Sons of Port Glasgow and fitted with a 4hp single-cylinder engine constructed by John Robertson. The journey from Glasgow to Greenock took approximately 3½hr at an average speed of 6 knots.
STEAMBOAT SUCCESSFULLY FITTED WITH SCREW-PROPELLERS: the first was the 5-ton 25ft-long *Little Juliana*, demonstrated at Hoboken, N.J. by Col John Stevens in May 1804. She had twin four-bladed propellers of 18in diameter and achieved speeds of up to 8mph.
GB: The first screw-driven steamboat was the *Francis Smith*, a small wooden launch built at Wapping, Essex by Francis Pettit Smith, a farmer from Hendon, in 1836. His prototype wooden screw was in fact too large to be effective, but by a fortunate accident the blades broke and the vessel immediately increased its speed. Fitted with a smaller screw, she made a number of successful trips along the coast of Kent between Ramsgate, Dover and Hythe and was able to maintain an average speed of 5½ knots.

The first large sea-going steam-vessel driven by a screw-propeller was the 237-ton *Archimedes*, built at Poplar by H. Wimshurst for the Ship Propeller Co, a company formed to exploit Pettit Smith's patent, and launched in November 1838. (*See also* Ocean Liner).
STEAMBOAT NAVIGATED IN OPEN SEA: the first was Col John Stevens's 95-ton *Phoenix*, which made the voyage from New York to Philadelphia in 13 days under the command of Capt. Moses Rogers, 10–23 June 1809.

The first sea-going steamship in regular commercial service anywhere in the world (other than coastal steamers) was the 88-ton *Rob Roy*, which was built by Messrs Archibald MacLachlan & Co of Dumbarton with engines by David Napier and made her maiden voyage from Greenock to Dublin in June 1818. She was operated on a regular route from Greenock to Belfast by David Napier until 1821 and then went south to become the first Channel steamer (*see below*).
STEAMBOAT TO CROSS THE ENGLISH CHANNEL: the first was the 38-ton *Elise*, which left Newhaven under the command of Capt. Pierre Andriel on 17 March 1816 and made a stormy 17hr passage to Le Havre. The vessel had been purchased from Messrs Anthony Cortis & Co of London by Andriel, Pajol et Cie of Paris for service as a packet-boat on the Seine.

The first Channel steamer in regular commercial service was the *Rob Roy*, operated on the Dover–Calais route under British ownership (a Mr Boyd of Dover) from 1821 until 1823, when she was purchased by the French Government. Her average crossing time was 2hr 45min. The present average of 50min for the Channel crossing (short route) was regularly achieved for the first time when the SS *Empress* was put into service in 1887.
STEAMSHIP TO CROSS THE ATLANTIC: the first was the 320-ton paddle-wheeler *Savannah*, which left Savannah, Ga. under the command of Capt. Moses Rogers on 24 May 1819 and arrived at Liverpool under sail after a voyage of 27 days 11hr on 20 June, having run out of fuel off the coast of Ireland. She carried no passengers, as no one could be persuaded to buy a ticket for what promised to be such a hazardous voyage. In fact the danger of a boiler explosion – not uncommon at this stage of steamship development – was minimized by the fact that the *Savannah* spent only about 85 out of her 663hr at sea under steam.
GB: The first British steamship to cross the Atlantic was the 428-ton *Rising Star*, built as a warship for use in the Chilean Revolution by Daniel Brent of Rotherhithe and dispatched for Valparaiso from Gravesend on 22 October 1821. To what extent her powerful Maudslay engines were used on the six-month voyage is not recorded, though clearly much of it must have been made under sail.

The first steamship to cross the Atlantic wholly under power (with brief intervals for boiler-scraping) was the Canadian vessel *Royal William*, built in 1831 by Messrs Black & Campbell of Quebec with twin side-lever engines by Messrs Bennet & Henderson of Montreal. She sailed from Pictou, Nova Scotia with eight passengers on 17 August 1833 and arrived at Cowes, Isle of Wight on 4 September.
GB: The first British steamship to cross the Atlantic solely under steam was the *Sirius*, a London–Cork ferry-boat belonging to the St George Steam Packet Co, which the British & American Steam Navigation Co of London chartered in 1838 in an attempt to beat the *Great Western* to New York.

The 703-ton *Sirius* left Cork under the command of Lt Roberts, RN on 4 April 1838 and arrived in New York with her 49 passengers 18 days and 10hr later, with only 15 tons of coal left in her bunkers. The *Great Western* entered harbour only a few hours behind her, having made shorter time by over three days but just failing to overhaul her smaller rival. The latter's voyage probably has a greater significance in maritime history, as it marked the beginning of regular transatlantic steamship services (*see* Ocean Liner: Transatlantic).

IRON STEAMSHIP: the first was the 116-ton *Aaron Manby*, laid down in 1821 by Aaron Manby, proprietor of the Horsley Ironworks at Tipton, Staffordshire. The hull was cast at Tipton from ¼in thick plates and transported in sections for assembly at Rotherhithe, where the vessel was completed on 30 April 1822. Following trials on the Thames in May, she made her maiden voyage across the Channel with a cargo of linseed and, appropriately, iron, arriving in Paris on 10 June 1822.

The first STRIPTEASE

originated as the result of an incident that occurred at the Four Arts Ball, held at the Moulin Rouge, Paris on 9 February 1893, when an artist's model called Mona stripped for the edification of the Paris students. Her subsequent prosecution and fine of 100 francs provoked a riot in the Latin Quarter, and troops had to be called out when the students laid siege to the Prefecture of Police.

The publicity attracted by Mona's action and its consequences inspired the world's first theatrical striptease act, which took place at the Divan Fayouau Music Hall, rue des Martyrs, Paris, on 13 March 1894. The act was titled 'Le Coucher d'Yvette' and consisted of a girl stripping to go to bed. Variations on this theme were presented under such titles as 'Liane chez le Medecin' – a girl undressing for the doctor – 'Le Bain de Maid' – a girl undressing for her bath – 'Suzanne et la Grande Chaleur' – a girl undressing in a heat-wave – and 'La Puce' – in which the girl removed her garments one by one to rid herself of a flea.

The first SUBMARINE

was built in London by the Dutch physicist Cornelius Drebbel in 1624. The craft was constructed from a wooden framework covered in a greased-leather skin, and was manned by 12 rowers whose oars protruded through sealed ports. Drebbel and his crew are reported to have navigated under the surface of the Thames for 2hr during a demonstration before King James I. One of the most remarkable aspects of his achievement was the breathing arrangement that made such a feat possible, described by Robert Boyle as 'a composition of a liquid that would speedily restore to the troubled air such a proportion of vital parts as would make it again for a good while fit for respiration'. It is now believed that Drebbel had devised a means of producing oxygen, a century and a half before its official discovery by Joseph Priestley. Though intended as a naval craft, the Admiralty advised against its adoption.

The first submersible vessel to be used as an offensive weapon in warfare was the *American Turtle*, designed by David Bushnell of Saybrook, Conn. as a colonial answer to the might of the British Navy during the American War of Independence. Manned by Sgt Ezra Lee, the one-man midget submarine launched an attack on Admiral Howe's flagship, HMS *Eagle*, as she lay at anchor in New York Harbour on 7 September 1776. The attempt to blow her up failed as the mine that Lee attached to the *Eagle*'s hull drifted away before exploding harmlessly. Nevertheless, the *Turtle* has another claim to distinction as the world's first screw-propeller-driven vessel, the motive power being supplied by hand.

The first effective attack by submarine took place on 17 February 1864, when the Confederate vessel *H.L. Hunley*, armed with a ram torpedo, slipped into Charleston Harbor and sank the newly commissioned Federal corvette *Housatonic*. The force of the explosion was such that both vessels were blown up together, killing the submarine's crew of eight and her commander, Lt George Dixon. The *H.L. Hunley* was one of a number of submersibles built by the firm of Hunley, McClintock & Watson at Mobile, Ala. for the Confederate States' Navy during 1863–4. These small hand-propelled screw-driven craft were known as 'Davids', as they were designed to do battle with 'Goliath' – the Union Navy.

SELF-PROPELLED SUBMARINE: the first was *Le Plongeur*, a 420-ton vessel driven by compressed air and launched at Rochefort in 1863. Its range and speed proved too limited for naval use.

SUBMARINES IN REGULAR NAVAL SERVICE: the first in peacetime were 50 Drzweiki submersibles ordered by the Russian Government in 1879. They were intended for coastal defence only and could hardly be described as sea-going.

The first full-size, self-propelled seagoing submarine in naval service was the Swedish-built *Nordenfelt*, based on a design by Liverpool clergyman Samuel Garratt, and built at Landskrona in 1883. Acquired by the Greek Government in 1886, the *Nordenfelt* was a steam-driven vessel of 60 tons displacement and had a surface speed of 9 knots. It was also the first submarine to be armed with locomotive torpedoes.

GB: The first British-built submarines were two 160-ton steam-driven Garratt submersibles constructed at Chertsey for the Turkish Navy in 1887. They remained in service until 1910.

The first submarines commissioned by the Royal Navy were five Holland-type vessels built by Vickers at Barrow, where the launching of Submarine No. 1 took place on 2 October 1901. The 120-ton vessels were powered by a four-cylinder petrol engine on the surface and a 75hp electric motor under water. Each carried a complement of two officers and five ratings.

The Holland submarine had originally been conceived by Irish Fenian John P. Holland, as a weapon to be employed against the British in the cause of Home Rule for Ireland. His early experimental models were built in the USA but the work was financed by the revolutionary Fenian movement. In 1898 he produced his celebrated Holland No. 9, which proved far superior to any other existing submarine in rapid diving and general mobility; it was this model that was acquired by the US Navy in 1900 and by the Royal Navy a year later.

NUCLEAR SUBMARINE: the first was the US submarine *Nautilus*, built by the Electric Boat Co at Groton, Conn. and launched on the River Thames on 21 January 1954. The vessel, 324ft long, was designed by Admiral Hyman George Rickover and was powered by one Westinghouse S2W Reactor. The vessel had a maximum speed of 20 knots, and a displacement of 3,747 tons submerged. She carried a crew of 11 officers and 85 ratings. Under the command of Eugene Parks Wilkinson, USN, *Nautilus* sent the signal 'under way on nuclear power' on the occasion of her first sea trial on 17 January 1955. She was refuelled for the first time over two years later, after voyaging 69,138 miles.

The first SUPERMARKET

The earliest recorded self-service grocery stores were two independent enterprises established in California in 1912, the Alpha Beta Food Market at Pomona, and Ward's Grocetaria in Ocean Park. At approximately the same period a chain of self-service groceries

Winch suspension bridge – first in the Western World

known as 'Humpty Dumpty Stores' was started in California by the Bay Cities Mercantile Co. It is doubtful whether these ventures were large enough to be described as supermarkets, and as far as is known the customer still paid for her goods at a counter. The next significant advance towards the supermarket concept was made by Clarence Saunders, who introduced a turnstile entrance and regular check-out system at his Piggly Wiggly self-service grocery that he opened at 79 Jefferson Street, Memphis, Tenn. in 1916. This development proved so successful that within seven years he had built up a chain of 2,800 Piggly Wigglies throughout the USA.

The first supermarkets that had a shopping area large enough to satisfy the modern definition of the term 'supermarket' (i.e. at least 12,000 sq ft) were the King Kullen food stores, started by Michael Cullen on Long Island in 1930. Cullen took advantage of the Depression's low housekeeping budgets to offer the ultimate in cut-price merchandising; up to 300 separate items were sold at cost price only.

The term 'supermarket' was already in use by this date, though at first it appears to have been employed to connote any large cut-price grocery store, not necessarily self-service. The first grocery operators to adopt the word 'supermarket' as part of their trade-name were Albers Super Markets Inc, who opened their first store in November 1933.

GB: The first self-service grocery was a screened-off section of Romford Co-operative Society, opened on 5 June 1942.

The first full-size supermarket in Britain was opened by the London Co-operative Society at Manor Park on 12 January 1948.

The first
SUSPENSION BRIDGE

recorded, was a footbridge across the Indus which the Chinese monk Fa Hsien described in AD 399, saying that he thought it was then 'very old'. A suspension bridge over the Indus using iron-link suspension chains was reported by the Buddhist scholar Hsuan-Tsang in AD 630.

GB: The first suspension bridge in the Western world was the Wynch Bridge spanning the Tees about 2 miles above Middleton, Co Durham. It was a flimsy construction 70ft long and only 2ft wide, erected for the use of local miners in 1742. There was no further development of the technique, in Britain or elsewhere, until James Finlay built the first suspension road bridge in 1796 to carry the Unionstown–Greensburg (Pa.) turnpike across Jacob's Creek.

The first suspension road bridge in Britain was the 360ft span Union Chain Bridge across the River Tweed, built by Sir Samuel Brown in 1820.

The first
SWIMMING-POOL, INDOOR

was opened in London on 28 May 1742. The *Daily Advertiser* announced:

This Day is opened, At the Bagnio in Lemon St., Goodman's Fields:
The Pleasure or Swimming Bath which is more than forty-three feet in length, it will be kept warm and fresh every Day and is convenient to swim or learn to swim in. There are Waiters attend daily to teach or assist Gentlemen in the said Swimming Bath if required. There is also a good Cold Bath.
Subscribers may have the use of both for a Guinea.

The first municipal swimming-pool, and the first indoor pool anywhere in the provinces was opened by Liverpool Corporation at St George's Pier Head on 8 June 1829.

OPEN-AIR SWIMMING-POOL: the first designed as such was Peerless (originally Perilous) Pool, which was converted from an existing pond at Old Street, London in 1743. It measured 170 × 108ft, and was equipped with an arcade and boxes for dressing, as well as a screen of trees to protect bathers from the gaze of vulgar persons. Subscribers paid an annual subscription of £1 10s, and casual patrons 1s. The proprietor, William Kent, also had an artificial stream cut from the pool, and this was stocked with fish for anglers who cared to pay a small fee.

The first
TABLE-TENNIS

sets were manufactured by John Jaques & Son Ltd and marketed in 1898 by Hamley Bros of Regent Street under the name 'Gossima'. The inventor of the game was a Croydon engineer called James Gibb, a distinguished athlete who had won the 4-mile English Championship while a Cambridge undergraduate in the 1870s, and who was one of the founders of the Amateur Athletic Association (1880). The date at which he originally devised Gossima is uncertain, though 1889 is sometimes quoted. It began as an impromptu wet-weather pastime played on the Gibb family's dining-room table with cigar-box lids for bats and balls fashioned from champagne corks. The latter were too irregular and Mr Gibb next tried using small indiarubber balls covered with cigarette-paper to make them white. These proved too heavy for fast play and he decided to try hollow celluloid balls, sending to America to have them specially made. Celluloid answered admirably and Gibb felt ready to launch the game commercially. The manufacturer he approached first, Messrs Jeffries, turned it down, but Jaques were enthusiastic. As Gossima the game was slow to catch on, and John Jaques decided to change the name to 'Ping Pong'. It immediately became immensely popular, sweeping the country during the course of 1901 to become the first of a succession of Edwardian crazes. In other countries, including the USA, the game enjoyed a similar phenomenal success. The French, however, held aloof, one Parisian newspaper asserting it to be a proof of England's moral degradation that so much attention could be paid to Ping Pong while her soldiers were dying in South Africa.

Table-tennis bats were originally either of plain wood or in the form of vellum-covered battledores. The first with a studded rubber surface was Bryan's Atropos Patent Ping Pong Bat, announced in the September 1902 Army and Navy Stores catalogue price 2s 8d.
TABLE-TENNIS CLUB: the first was established in Moorgate Street in the City of London early in 1901.
TABLE-TENNIS TOURNAMENT (open): the first was the Championship of London, held at the Royal Aquarium on 14 December 1901. The winner of the men's event was R.D. Ayling and of the women's Miss V. Eames of Streatham.

The first
TAXI-CABS
to ply for hire were two Benz-Kraftdroschkes purchased for 8,000 marks each in the spring of 1896 by 'Droschkenbesitzer' Dütz of Stuttgart, and operated by him in that city. Stuttgart had the distinction of having two cab companies running petrol-driven taxis before any other city, with the exception of Paris, had even one. In May 1897 Friedrich Greiner started a rival service, and according to a contemporary report in *Der Motorwagen* his cabs averaged a creditable 70km a day. In a literal sense Greiner's were the first true 'taxis', as they were the first motor cabs fitted with taximeters. The Paris taxi-cab service – a single Roger-Benz operated by the Société Anglo-Française – had been started in November 1896 but does not appear to have survived more than a few months.
GB: The London Electric Cab Co of Juxon Street, Lambeth began operating 12 accumulator-driven 3½hp Bersey electric cabs in the City and West End of London on 19 August 1897. They had an average speed of 9mph and a range of up to 30 miles. A number of other cabs were retained by the Company for hiring out at 25s a day with driver, and by the end of the year there were a total of 25 in use. This was increased by a further 50 the following year. The cabs were painted in a livery of yellow and black and attracted considerable attention from the non-motoring public, who nicknamed them 'humming-birds'. *Punch,* always responsive to new ideas, featured a cartoon in which a ragged urchin is seen enjoying an illicit ride on the back of one. A bystander calls out the traditional 'Whip behind!' to the cabbie, to which the youngster rejoins: 'Yah! 'E ain't got no whip.'

Although at first the innovation seemed likely to be successful, at the end of two years the cabs were proving hopelessly uneconomic and were withdrawn from service. The attitude of the public towards them had not been enhanced by an accident in Hackney that resulted in the death of a child (*see* Motoring Fatality). The reliability of the drivers was also called into question when one of their number was convicted of being drunk in charge of his cab in Bond Street (*see* Motoring Offence). Early in 1900 the Electric Cab Co disposed of its vehicles, selling off 36 complete and 41 incomplete cabs.

The Metropolitan Police refused to license any further motor cabs until May 1904, when the first petrol-driven taxi to ply for hire in Britain, a Prunel Hansom operated by the London Express Motor Service, was issued with Hackney Carriage Plate No. 15831. This curious vehicle was built as a motorized replica of the familiar hansom cab, engine and driver occupying the place of the shafts. The bodywork was by Henry Whitlock Ltd of Holland Park, and the cab was powered with a twin-cylinder 12hp Aster engine.

By the end of the year there were three petrol-driven taxis in service, and the drivers were reputed to be taking as much as £5 a day, considerably in excess of the £10 a week required of them by the company. Fares were 8d a mile, which was also the price of a gallon of petrol; horse-cab fares in comparison were only 6d a mile. It was reported that officers returning to Aldershot after a late night in town were their most regular patrons.

The number of taxis plying for hire in London rose from 19 at the end of 1905 to 5,070 in 1910. Unlike the horse-bus, which had virtually disappeared from the streets within a year of being outnumbered by its mechanical rival, the hansom cab and the four-wheeler died a lingering death. As late as 1928 there were still 200 licensed horse-cabs, and it was not until 1947 that the last remaining horse-cab driver turned his licence in, having survived the first onslaught of the taxi by exactly 50 years.

The first introduction of
TEA
into Europe was from China, imported by the Dutch East India Co in 1609.
GB: The earliest reference to tea is contained in a letter signed by a man called Wickham in the employ of the East India Company and dated 27 June 1615. A shop bill issued about half a century later by Thomas Garraway (or Garway) of Change Alley, off Cornhill, describes how tea first became available for general consumption:

Tea in England hath been sold in the leaf for six pounds, and sometimes for ten pounds the pound weight, and in respect of its former scarceness and dearness, it hath been only used as a regalia in high treatments and entertainments, and presents made thereof to princes and grandees till the year 1651. The said Thomas Garway did purchase a quantity thereof, and first publicly sold the said tea in leaf and drink, made according to the directions of the most knowing merchants and travellers into those Eastern Countries . . . the said Thomas Garway hath tea to sell from sixteen to fifty shillings per pound.

Prior to 1839 all the tea drunk in Britain was imported from China. On 10 January of that year the first 8 cases of Indian tea, 5 of Assam pekoe and 3 of Assam souchong, were put up for auction by the East India Company at the tea sale-rooms in Mincing Lane. All 8 lots were bought by a Capt. Pidding at the vastly inflated price of 16s to 34s per lb.
TEA IN PACKETS was first sold by John Horniman of Ryde, Isle of Wight in 1826. The packets came in ¼lb and ½lb sizes and were guaranteed to contain only pure and unadulterated tea.
TEA-BAGS were first produced by Joseph Krieger of San Francisco c. 1920. Originally they were used almost exclusively by caterers, but by 1935 it was reported that the majority of tea-bags in the USA were being bought by housewives for use at home.
GB: The first tea-bags for home retail consumption were marketed by the Tetley Tea Co of Bletchley, Buckinghamshire in 1952. Tea-bags for export only had been manufactured in Jersey prior to World War II.

The first
TEDDY BEAR
is claimed to have been originated by

two separate and existing manufacturers, one in the USA and one in Germany, both quoting the same year, 1902, for the innovation, each asserting precedence over the other, and neither being able to provide documentary evidence in support of its claim.

The only proven fact in either version is that on 18 November 1902 the *Washington Evening Star* carried a cartoon by Clifford Berryman titled 'Drawing the Line in Mississippi', showing the President of the USA, Theodore, or 'Teddy', Roosevelt, refusing to shoot a captive bear cub. At that time the President was visiting Mississippi to intervene in a border dispute between this State and its neighbour Louisiana. Berryman's cartoon is alleged to have been founded on an actual incident during a Presidential bear-hunt. It was reproduced in a number of other newspapers and among those struck by the artist's engaging, cuddly little bear was a Russian immigrant called Morris Mitchom, proprietor of a small sweetshop in Brooklyn that also sold toys, many of them handmade by himself and his wife.

At this point oral tradition takes over. According to his son Benjamin, Morris Mitchom immediately conceived the idea of re-creating the Berryman bear cub in three-dimensional form. Cut out of brown plush, and with movable arms and legs, the prototype toy animal was placed in the sweetshop window next to a clipping of the cartoon and with a label proclaiming 'Teddy's Bear'.

Having come from an authoritarian country, Morris Mitchom was concerned about the propriety of using the President's name to promote the sale of his new toy. He plucked up courage to write to the White House asking Mr Roosevelt if he minded. The reply, in the President's own hand, granted permission in these words: 'I don't think my name is worth much to the toy bear cub business, but you are welcome to use it.'

This document, which if it could be produced would establish the Mitchom claim beyond doubt, was supposed to be in the possession of Morris's eldest son, Mr Joseph Mitchom, but could not be found among his effects when he died in 1951.

In 1903, according to Benjamin Mitchom, the wholesale firm of Butler Bros took his father's entire output of Teddy Bears, guaranteeing him credit with the suppliers of plush. Between that year and 1938 the business was styled the 'Ideal Novelty and Toy Company'; under its present title, the 'Ideal Toy Co', it is the largest doll-manufacturer in the world.

Germany credits the invention of the Teddy Bear to the Steiff Co, which was begun at Giengen in Swabia in 1880 by a crippled seamstress, Margarete Steiff, as a home workshop producing felt elephants. By 1902 the business was manufacturing a wide range of soft toys, including cats, dogs, pink porkers, donkeys, horses and camels, but not, until then, a bear. During that year Frl. Steiff's nephew Richard, who had often spent his art-student days sketching bears at the Stuttgart Zoo, is said to have produced a design for a plush bear with jointed limbs and a movable head. His aunt was unenthusiastic. The buyers at the Leipzig Fair the following year were equally indifferent; until, according to Steiff legend, the representative of an unnamed American firm appeared on the last day, was captivated by the furry animal, and ordered 3,000.

Although the Steiff concern was undoubtedly one of the earliest to enter the plush-bear business, they have undermined belief in their claims by propagating a wholly unfounded story to explain the acquisition of the name 'Teddy'. This was to the effect that the table decorations at Alice Roosevelt's wedding in 1906 consisted of Steiff bear-ware, and that when her father, the President, was asked what variety they were, he responded 'a new species called Teddy bears'. The use of Steiff products on this occasion has been categorically denied by the Roosevelt Association and by Archibald Roosevelt, the bride's brother.

The actor Peter Bull, doyen of Teddy Bear *aficionados*, believes that the Mitchom version of the naming is probably accurate, while allowing the possibility that the Steiff prototype could have been made at a marginally earlier date. Finally it should be said that nowhere has the term 'Teddy Bear' been found in print before September 1906, when it was reported in the American trade journal *Playthings* that there was a new craze for having them as car mascots. Bears were already sweeping America at this date, under a variety of different names, and soon became such a cult that one Michigan clergyman roundly declared that the Teddy was destroying all instincts of motherhood and leading the nation to race suicide.

GB: The oldest identified surviving Teddy in the country, providing conjectural evidence of the date that imports began, is a Steiff bear owned by Col J.R. Henderson, which, he claims, was bought for his elder brother in Edinburgh in 1903.

The earliest-known reference to the little creatures by name in Britain is an advertisement issued by Morrells of Oxford Street in London for Christmas 1909:

Old Mistress Teddy that lived in a shoe. Morrells unique Christmas Novelty consisting of one large and twelve Baby Bears, sledge, ladder, bottles, bowls, etc., contained in a large Crimson shoe 15 ins in length. Price complete 21s.

The first TELEGRAM

The first public telegraph service was opened on the completion of the Great Western Railway telegraph line from Paddington to Slough in May 1843. It was agreed at a GWR Board Meeting held on 10 January 1843 that William Cooke, the patentee of the system, should provide the Company with a free telegraph service and that in return, he or his licensee should be permitted to open the telegraph line to the public as a commercial undertaking.

The licence was acquired from Cooke by Thomas Home for an annual rental of £170 and on 16 May 1843 the first paid telegrams in the world were dispatched by Cooke's double-needle electro-magnetic telegraph over the 20-mile-long wire from Paddington to Slough. The fee per telegram was 1s, irrespective of the number of words, and messengers were kept in constant attendance at both ends for delivering the telegrams to any address in London, Windsor, Eton, Slough or neighbouring districts. Patrons who wanted to try out the new means of communication, but knew nobody in the Slough area, were able to dispatch questions to be answered by the operator at the other end, or alternatively a bell could be rung in the dispatch office to demonstrate that the message had been received. The telegraph office at Paddington was on the arrival platform, while the one at Slough was a separate building called 'Telegraph Cottage'. The public were admitted to both offices between the hours of 9am and 8pm on week-days, also for the payment of 1s. Home claimed that 'in the list of visitors are the illustrious names of several of the Crowned Heads of Europe, and nearly the whole of the Nobility of England'. He eventually surrendered his licence to the Electric Telegraph Co (*see below*) after operating the service for $4\frac{1}{2}$ years, and the line was finally closed in June 1849. Little is known about the subsequent career of Thomas Home, pioneer of paid telegrams, except that he was established as a brick and drainpipe manufacturer at Brill, Buckinghamshire in 1865, and died there in 1898.

The provision of a nation-wide telegraph service followed the founding of the Electric Telegraph Co by W.F.

Sending a telegram meant a stiff climb. The world's first paid telegrams were sent from Telegraph Cottage at Slough on 16 May 1843.

Cooke and J.L. Ricardo MP in 1846, Cooke's patents being acquired by the Company for the sum of £168,000. By September 1847, two networks had been established, a northern system, taking in most of the major cities lying between Edinburgh and Birmingham, and a southern system, linking London with Dover, Gosport and Southampton. The two regions were joined at 5pm on 14 November 1847, when the stock-market quotations for the day were transmitted from London to Manchester. Initially, the rates for telegrams were based on distance, the charge for 20 words being calculated at 1d per mile for the first 50 miles, ½d per mile for the next 50 miles and ¼d per mile beyond the first 100 miles. This made long-distance telegrams prohibitively expensive, and in March 1850 the tariff was reduced to a maximum of 10s for any distance. The appearance of rival telegraph companies on the scene in the 1850s forced down the rates so that by the end of the decade most inland telegrams could be sent for either 1s or 2s.

The word 'telegram' was used for the first time in print in the *Albany Evening Journal* (Albany, N.Y.) on 6 April 1852: 'A friend desires us to give notice that he will ask leave . . . to introduce a new word. . . . It is telegram instead of telegraphic dispatch, or telegraphic communication.'

The 'friend' referred to was E.P. Smith of Rochester, N.Y. His suggestion aroused the ire of Classical scholars, who objected that the word was not based on Greek analogies, which would render it as 'telegrapheme'. Smith's term, however, was succinct and easy to remember and by 1860 it had ousted the more cumbersome alternatives.

PRESS TELEGRAM: the first was dispatched from a Congress reporter in Washington, D.C. to the Editor of the *Baltimore Patriot* by Morse Telegraph at 2pm on Saturday, 25 May 1844 and read: '1 o'clock – There has just been a motion in the House to go into Committee of the Whole on the Oregon question. Rejected. Ayes, 79; noes, 86.' The New York *Daily Sun* commented 'This is indeed the annihilation of space.'

GB: The first Press telegram was transmitted from Windsor Castle to *The Times* via the Slough–Paddington telegraph on 6 August 1844 and announced the birth of a son (Prince Alfred) to Queen Victoria. The event took place at 7.50am; the edition of *The Times* containing the news was published 40min later. Next day *The Times* complained rather moodily that despite the fact that they had published the news at 8.30am, the Tower authorities knew nothing about it until 1pm, when they received a command from the Board of Ordnance to fire a salute without further delay.

GPO GREETINGS TELEGRAM: the first was designed by Rex Whistler and launched by Sir Kingsley Wood on 24 July 1935. For an additional charge of 3d the message was delivered on a special festive form enclosed in a golden envelope. The first special-occasion greetings telegram was issued on 14 February 1936 to celebrate St Valentine's Day. Fifty-thousand lovers took advantage of this opportunity to express their sentiments, including one young man who concluded with the words:

And now I've asked you to be mine –
By gosh! it's cost me eight and nine!

The first
TELEPHONE

which may have been capable of transmitting articulate speech by electrical impulses was built by Antonio Meucci of Florence at Havana, Cuba in 1849. With this instrument he claimed to have been able to converse with his invalid wife, whose room was on the third floor, from the basement of his house. Meucci was too poor to patent his invention, but a loan of $20 enabled him to file a caveat in 1871. Though his instrument was never demonstrated publicly, it seems probable from the description in the caveat that it was capable of transmitting articulate but imperfect speech.

TELEPHONE TO BE PUBLICLY DEMONSTRATED: the first was built by Johann Philipp Reis of Friedrichsdorf, near Frankfurt in 1860. The original prototype used a violin-case for a resonator, a hollowed-out beer-barrel bung for a mouth-piece, and a stretched sausage-skin for a diaphragm. An improved model was shown before the Physical Society, Frankfurt on 26 October 1861, when verses of songs were transmitted over a 300ft line between the meeting-room and the Civic Hospital. Listeners claimed to be able to recognize the tunes, though it is doubtful whether they were able to distinguish more than a few of the words. In view of modern tests made with Reis telephones under controlled conditions it seems likely that they were capable of transmitting articulate speech spasmodically.

TELEPHONE CAPABLE OF SUSTAINED ARTICULATE SPEECH: the first was patented by Alexander Graham Bell of Edinburgh on 9 March 1876. The first coherent message was transmitted at 5 Exeter Place, Boston, Mass. on 10 March 1876 by Bell to his assistant Thomas Watson and consisted of the words: 'Come here, Watson, I want you.'

Bell's first speaking telephone was publicly displayed at the Centennial Exhibition, Philadelphia, 25 June 1876. It attracted little attention at first, and would probably have been ignored by the judges then had it not been for the interest of the Emperor of Brazil, who opened the first royal telephone conversation with the words: 'My God – it talks!'

GB: The Bell telephone was first demonstrated by Sir William Thomson (Lord Kelvin) before the British Association for the Advancement of Science, Glasgow, 7 September 1876.

The first telephone line between two separate buildings was laid from the Queen's Theatre, London to Canterbury Hall for a demonstration held on 14 July 1877.

PERMANENT INSTALLATION OF A TELEPHONE: the first for private use was made by Charles Williams Jr at his home in Somerville, Mass. and also at his office, 109 Court Street, Boston, on 4 April 1877. Williams, an electrical engineer, commenced manufacture of Bell's Box Telephone the same month. The first installation of a telephone for business purposes (other than by Bell and his associates) was made by the Cambridge Board of Waterworks in May 1877 and connected their office in Cambridge, Mass. with the works at Fresh Pond. The rental fee for business phones was $40 p.a., twice that of private installations.

GB: The first private connection was made between Osborne House, Isle of Wight, the summer home of Queen Victoria, and Osborne Cottage, the home of Sir Thomas Biddulph, with whom the Queen conversed by telephone on 14 January 1878. Telephones were first offered to the public in a circular issued by Bell's British agent, Col W. H. Reynolds, in October 1877, the advertised cost being £25 for a pair of telephones on a short circuit, or £5 p.a. rent, £35 for a pair on a long circuit, or £10 p.a. rent.

TELEPHONE SWITCHBOARD: the first was installed at the Holmes Burglar Alarm Co, 342 Washington Street, Boston, by the proprietor, Edwin Holmes, and brought into operation on 17 May 1877. Five of Holmes's clients (Brewster, Bassett & Co, bankers, the Shoe & Leather Bank, the National Exchange Bank, the Hide & Leather Bank, and Charles Williams, electrical engineers), were interconnected over the existing burglar-alarm lines. The switchboard was operated during the day only, the lines reverting to their regular function at night. No fee was charged for the service.

GB: As for Telephone Exchange below.

TELEPHONE EXCHANGE: the first was established by Isaac D. Smith, agent for the New England Telephone Co, at the Capitol Avenue Drug Store, Hartford, Conn., following an announcement in the *Hartford Courant* for 17 August 1877:

At the regular meeting of the allopathic physicians on Monday evening experiments were successfully tried with telephones, and it was proposed to have a system of inter-communication between the doctors established by means of the new invention so that by reporting to a central office of the Capitol Avenue Drug Store they can readily exchange views between office and office.

On 8 October 1877 Smith advertised the exchange as a commercial venture, and by the following month there were 17 subscribers.

GB: The Glasgow Medical Telephone Exchange, 140 Douglas Street, Glasgow, established by Messrs D. & G. Graham, electrical engineers, probably in January or February 1879. An unlimited number of calls was allowed for the annual fee of £12. Other specialized exchanges were started for lawyers, stockbrokers and commercial interests.

The first London exchange, and the first exchange in Britain open to general subscribers, was established by the Telephone Co at 36 Coleman Street, in August 1879. By 6 September eight subscribers had rented telephones at £20 p.a., including the Pullman Car Association and the Equitable Insurance Co.

FULL-TIME TELEPHONE-OPERATOR: the first was George Willard Coy, who began operating the District Telephone Co's exchange at New Haven, Conn. on 28 January 1878. At first the usual call signal was 'Ahoy! Ahoy!', but this was abandoned for 'Hallo', probably at the instigation of those who liked to address the operator by name. The first woman telephone-operator was Miss Emma Nutt, who began working for Edwin Holmes's Telephone Despatch Co exchange at Boston, Mass. on 1 September 1878. By the mid 1880s most exchanges employed women; boys were found to be too quarrelsome for the work.

AUTOMATIC TELEPHONE EXCHANGE: the first was patented by Kansas City undertaker Almon B. Strowger on 12 March 1889. Traditionally Strowger was inspired to invent the automatic switchboard because his principal business rival's wife, an operator on the Kansas City exchange, used to put his clients through to her husband. The original prototype of the switching device was worked out with the aid of a collar box and a quantity of spent matches. The first Strowger automatic exchange was opened at La Porte, Ind. on 3 November 1892, and soon came to be known in the American vernacular as 'the girlless, cussless telephone'. Strowger's early system did not incorporate dial telephones, but was operated by a series of three keys, one representing single figures, another units of ten, and the other units of a hundred. To call a number the subscriber depressed each key the number of times required to make up the sequence.

GB: The first experimental automatic switchboard, incorporating 200 lines, was installed at Winchester House, Old Broad Street, London in 1897. The first commercially operated automatic exchange was opened at Epsom on 18 May 1912.

DIAL TELEPHONES: the first were connected to the Private Automatic Exchange (P.A.X.), City Hall, Milwaukee in 1896. The dial was rotated by means of projecting vanes, holes being a later innovation.

The first
TELEPHONE CALL-BOX

for public use was installed by the Connecticut Telephone Co in their office at New Haven, Conn. Service commenced on 1 June 1880.

GB: 'Call Office suites' were installed at the Stock Exchange and Baltic Exchange, London and the Wool Exchange, Bradford, by the National Telephone Co, *c.* 1882. Payment was made to an attendant, who locked the door of the booth when he went off duty. Regular callers were supplied with a 'Subscriber's Trunk Pass' in the form of a key that would permit them access to the telephone at any time. The first Post Office call-boxes, described as 'silence cabinets', were authorized by the GPO in August 1884.

COIN-OPERATED CALL-BOX: the first was installed in the Hartford Bank, Hartford, Conn. by the Southern New England Telephone Co in 1889. In 1891 the inventor of the coin mechanism, William Gray, formed the Gray Telephone Pay Station Co, to rent out coin-operated telephones to store-keepers.

GB: The National Telephone Co and the Post Office both began experimenting with coin-operated telephones in 1904. The first Post Office coin-operated call-box was installed at the Ludgate Circus Post Office by the Western

Electric Co in April 1906. Most early coin-boxes were of the post-payment type, access to the exchange being obtained by lifting the receiver. The caller was asked to deposit the correct number of pennies at the end of the call. The multi-coin, prepayment box was introduced in 1925.
TELEPHONE KIOSKS (outside): the first in Britain were erected by the National Telephone Co in 1908. Although it is not known for certain where the first call-box was sited, there is a strong local tradition in Nottingham claiming the honour for that town. There was no standard pattern, the maker contracting to supply a design suitable to local requirements, so that Folkestone's first kiosk, erected in the public gardens in 1908, was built to look like a rustic arbour. Post Office kiosks, introduced a few months later, were often fitted with a coin-freed lock on the door rather than a coin-box within. Most were made of wood, but galvanized-iron kiosks were supplied for dockland areas, as it was believed that a docker who lost his 2d would try to kick the door down. In 1912 the Postmaster-General authorized the provision of doodling-pads to discourage artistically inclined callers from defacing the walls, but this amenity was abandoned in the sterner atmosphere of World War I. The first standardized design was a prefabricated concrete structure with red wooden door and metal glazing bars introduced by the GPO in 1921.

An early National Telephone Co kiosk, designed to blend with its environment

The first
TELEPHONE: SPEAKING CLOCK
was designed for the French Ministry of Posts and Telecommunications by M. Esclangon, Director of the Paris Observatory, and came into operation in the Paris area on 14 February 1933. The idea of a speaking clock was originally put forward by M. Esclangon because he was tired of telephone subscribers ringing the staff of the Observatory to find out the exact time. By dialling ODEon 84 00 Parisians were able to hear the voice of a well-known broadcasting personality, Marcel Laporte, stating the precise number of minutes and seconds past the hour. Since the Paris *Horloge Parlante* was synchronized with Observatory chronometers, there was no question as to its accuracy. It is apparent that when the system was extended to the provinces a few years later, it was not always so infallible. Shortly before World War II a senior Ministry official visited the postal headquarters in Marseilles and asked the engineer in charge of the speaking clock how he kept it regulated. 'Very easy, Sir,' replied the engineer, 'I keep it adjusted according to the time signals broadcast by Radio Marseille.' The Ministry official then telephoned the radio station and asked them how they knew that their time signals were accurate. 'No difficulty at all,' came the prompt reply, 'We simply ring up the speaking clock.'
GB: Introduced by the GPO at the suggestion of Eugene Wender of Hampstead, TIM, as it was known from the dial letters, was brought into operation on 24 July 1936. The original voice recording, which remained in use for over 20 years, was that of Miss Ethel Cain of the Victoria Telephone Exchange. She was the successful contestant in a nation-wide competition for switchboard-operators judged by John Masefield and Sybil Thorndike and was awarded a prize of 10gns.

Note: In the following Television entries high-definition TV refers to a screen image made up of 100 lines or more; low definition to under 100 lines.

The first
TELEVISION ANNOUNCER
was the German actress Ursula Patzschke, who was engaged by the Reichspost towards the end of 1934 to introduce the experimental programmes transmitted daily from Berlin. At first she only announced the programmes, but later she occasionally recited poetry, or acted monologues which she had written herself. She had a naturally informal manner, and would sometimes be accompanied by her dog or a couple of children.

France followed Germany's lead in choosing a woman announcer, Mlle Suzy Vinker, who introduced her first programme from the Paris PTT Studios in la rue de Grenelle on 1 September 1935. Mlle Vinker was apt to gesticulate in the Gallic manner while making announcements, and had to be restrained owing to the fact that her arms did not show on the vertical screens used on French television sets.
GB: The first television announcer was Leslie Mitchell, who announced the items presented on the first day of BBC high-definition transmissions to Radiolympia, 26 August 1936. Mitchell already had experience as a Movietone News commentator, television actor and radio compère.

The first women announcers were Jasmine Bligh and Elizabeth Cowell, who were selected from 1,222 applicants

Ursula Patzschke (left), the world's first TV announcer (1934), with Annemarie Beck, who joined the German television service as an announcer in 1935

claiming to fulfil the BBC's requirements of charm, tact, personality, a mezzo voice, and attractive features that would appeal equally to both male and female viewers. In addition the candidates had to be exquisitely photogenic, unmarried, and not have red hair. Elizabeth Cowell, the first to make her début as an announcer from Alexandra Palace on 31 August 1936, was a doctor's daughter from Cambridge. Jasmine Bligh was the granddaughter of Lord Darnley. The two female announcers were entitled to £25 p.a. dress allowance; Leslie Mitchell was expected to supply his wardrobe out of his own funds.
NB: Announcers of the Baird and BBC low-definition transmissions from 1928 to 1935 were only heard as voices off. Generally a test- or title-card was seen on the screen while programmes were being announced.

The first
TELEVISION BALLET PERFORMANCE
was rendered by Ailsa Bridgewater in one of the earliest television programmes by the Baird Co involving the services of a professional artiste. Although the date of this transmission from the Baird Studios in Long Acre, London is not recorded, Miss Bridgewater stated in a letter to *Television* written in 1935 that the broadcast 'started at the somewhat untimely hour of midnight'. This would indicate that it took place between 5 December 1928 and 30 September 1929, since the twice-weekly Baird programmes were transmitted at 12pm between these dates. Describing the experience, she wrote:

Owing to the fact that a full-length picture was then impossible, after a short introductory speech I mounted the stage, which was more in the form of a table than anything else, and commenced to show the rudiments of ballet technique within the carefully marked out space. . . . From the moment when the red light showed suddenly and brightly, and the immediate 'all quiet please' came from the announcer, an indescribable feeling of romance inevitably pervaded the next half hour. Despite a certain amount of natural nervousness at facing both the microphone and the televisor, to a far greater extent was the thrill and realization that this was the foundation of a new means of presenting the art of dancing to the public.

Although only one other ballet performance is recorded before 1933, in that year the prima ballerina Adeline Genée made dance history when she chose to make her world farewell by the infant medium of television. The importance of this presentation cannot be over-estimated at a time when the BBC's television service was being denigrated by its opponents as nothing more than a series of laboratory experiments. On 15 March 1933, 11 days after she had given her farewell theatre performance at the Coliseum, Mme Genée danced *The Love Song* opposite Anton Dolin, a short ballet in which two 18th-century lovers dance round a spinet. The transmission, from the BBC television studio in Broadcasting House, was received by Adeline Genée's compatriots in Copenhagen.

The first complete ballet with full cast performed on television was *The Gods Go a-Begging*, with Lydia Sokolova, Stanislas Idzikowski and a Corps de Ballet comprised of pupils from Mme Sokolova's school, presented by the BBC on 26 June 1934.

The first
TELEVISION: CHILDREN'S PROGRAMME
(Series) in Britain was a weekly 20–30min BBC presentation titled *For the Children*, which commenced on Sunday, 7 July 1946. Produced by A. Miller-Jones, the opening programme included Commander A. B. Campbell 'opening a sea chest and showing its treasures to the children' and L. N. and M. Williams of the Junior Philatelic Society 'showing young collectors commemorative stamps'.

The first
TELEVISION: CIRCUS
presentation was transmitted by the BBC for ½hr daily on five consecutive days from Bertram Mills Circus at Olympia commencing 4 January 1938. The commentator was Freddie Grisewood. Since this was the first occasion that television cameras had been turned on to the ordinary paying audience at a public entertainment, some anxiety was felt that it could lead to embarrassment for individual patrons if, for instance, a married man taking his girl friend to the circus should be seen on the television screen by his wife at home. Accordingly Cyril Mills arranged for notices to be displayed warning patrons that there would be television cameras at the performance; and that if they had any reason for not wanting to be seen, they could apply to the House Manager, who would provide seats out of camera range.

The first
TELEVISION COMMERCIAL
The first commercial undertaking to make use of television for advertising purposes was Messrs Eugène Ltd of Dover Street, London. Demonstrations of the 'Eugène Method' of permanent waving were transmitted via closed-circuit Baird television at the Hairdressing Fair of Fashion, Olympia from 5 to 13 November 1930. According to an advertisement in *Television*, viewers would 'learn how the patented Eugène Sachet coaxes the hair into soft, lovely, natural waves'.
COMMERCIAL TELEVISION STATION: the first was the National Broadcasting Company's WNBT New York, whose first commercial was transmitted on 1 July 1941. It showed a Bulova clock on the screen and was accompanied by an audio announcement emanating from Studio 5F in Radio City, New York. The charge for the 20sec spot was $9. The earliest rate-card, issued on 27 June, shows that the cost to an advertiser buying time for NBC's first sponsored programme, a panel game called *Truth or Consequences*, was $120 an hour, plus studio and production costs. Among the advertisers who showed themselves willing to pay this comparatively high rate to reach a maximum of 4,700 television sets were Ivory Soap, Bulova Watches, Adam Hats and Botany Worsted.
GB: The first commercial shown on ITV was an advertisement for Gibbs S.R. Toothpaste produced by AB-Pathé and transmitted at 9.01pm on the opening day of Independent Television, 22 September 1955.
COLOUR COMMERCIAL: the first on British television was an advertisement for Birds Eye Peas made by Lintas, with colour by Technicolor, transmitted by ATV in the Midland Region at 10.05am on 15 November 1969. Cost for the 30sec off-peak spot was £23.

The first
TELEVISION COOK
was Marcel Boulestin, who demonstrated how to cook an omelette in the opening programme of his BBC series *Cook's Night Out* on 21 January 1937.

The first
TELEVISION CURRENT AFFAIRS PROGRAMME
(regular) was *News Map*, a 15–30min feature inaugurated by the BBC in 1938 in which the artist and commentator J. F. Horrabin explained the background to a talking-point in the news with the aid of film-clips, photographs, diagrams, his own animated maps, and guest speakers to give the specialist viewpoint. The first programme, transmitted at 9.45pm on 21 September, was inspired by Neville Chamberlain's return from Berchtesgaden bringing reassuring messages from Hitler, and sought to analyse the Czechoslovakian situation. Horrabin was accompanied

on this occasion by the BBC's Foreign Correspondent, Vernon Bartlett.

The first
TELEVISION DOCUMENTARY FEATURE
was an illustrated lecture on pottery by G. Holme, Editor of the monthly magazine *Studio*, which was transmitted from the Baird Studios at Long Acre, London in November 1928. Holme brought various exhibits to the studio and held them up before the scanner as he described their points of interest. This was the first occasion on which a scheduled programme was transmitted for home viewers.

During the first year of the Baird sound-and-vision experimental public service (1930) programme material was confined almost exclusively to variety acts and instrumentalists, but in the spring of 1931 Mrs Stackpool O'Dell presented an illustrated talk on phrenology, and Mrs Rhoda Flanders a programme about dogs.

The BBC's first excursion into feature programming was a display of art treasures and antiques by Lord Lee of Fareham in November 1932. Despite the limitations of a small vertical screen and 30-line definition, the programme was welcomed as a successful departure from the BBC's more staple television fare of song and dance, and the Producer, Eustace Robb, was encouraged to embark on a number of other documentary presentations. Among the most popular of these programmes were Lord David Cecil's studio tour of the Queen Elizabeth Exhibition held at Grosvenor House in January 1933, the Duke of Marlborough displaying some of his family heirlooms, and a feature by Brig. A.C. Critchley on 11 April 1933, in which he related the story of greyhound-racing and introduced viewers to a number of winners of classic races which he brought with him to the studio, including the celebrated Mick the Miller.

In the USA, the development of television features was pioneered by W2XAB, the CBS station in New York, beginning with a display of oil-paintings in November 1931 and followed the next month by programmes centred round life in Norway and India. An ambitious 25min documentary to celebrate the George Washington Bicentennial was presented on 7 August 1932. On 16 September 1932 W2XAB broke new ground with the start of the first documentary series, which covered the American aviation industry.

The first
TELEVISION, EDUCATIONAL
The first attempt at providing academic instruction via the medium of television was made by the Columbia Broadcasting System's station W2XAB on 5 February 1932. Dr Ernst von Nardoff, Principal of Stuyvesant High School, New York, was invited to the studio to perform a series of experiments with liquid gas for an educational programme on physics presented by Bernard Sachs. The programme formed part of the regular CBS television schedule.

EDUCATIONAL TELEVISION STATION: the first was the University of Iowa's experimental, low-definition station W9XK, which began transmitting ETV programmes on a regular schedule from Iowa City on 25 January 1933. The opening telecast comprised an introductory lecture on the University by Dr E.B. Kurtz, Director of the station and Head of the Department of Electrical Engineering, a violin solo by a student, Irene Ruppert, a lesson in freehand drawing by the Art Department Lecturer, Aden Arnold, and a scene from the play *The First Mrs Fraser*, presented by members of the Speech Department.

During the 1933–4 season instruction was given by University of Iowa lecturers in oral hygiene, botany (identifying trees), engineering (reading architectural drawings), shorthand, French pronunciation, astronomy, drawing, natural history and a number of other subjects. Programmes were aired at 7.30pm on Mondays and Wednesdays, and included a musical item and dramatic sketch or recitation in addition to the lecture. A total of 389 educational television programmes were broadcast during the six years that the station continued in operation. A regular body of viewers quite unconnected with the University was built up over this period, and reception was reported at distances of up to 600 miles from Iowa City. Some of these 'television students' used home-built receiving apparatus, others purchased the $80 commercially produced 45-line Echophone TV set recommended as suitable by Dr Kurtz. The largest catchment area was Chicago, where there were estimated to be 1,000 home-based sets in operation by 1934. A 'large-screen' set was installed in the Iowa Memorial Union for the benefit of students at the University.

STATION TO OFFER HOME-BASED VIEWERS A DEGREE COURSE (by direct television instruction): the first was WTTW Chicago, which inaugurated its 'TV College' in association with Chicago Junior College in the autumn of 1956. During the first three years of the service, 27 different college courses were put on the air, and 'TV College' enrolments averaged 5,000 students per semester. About a quarter of these were enrolled for credit, and were thus eligible to sit the examinations. The television instruction was supplemented by written work submitted for correction by mail, 5–10 meetings with the section teacher each term, and a 'phone-in' service. At the end of the first three years it was found that some 65% of credit students actually completed their courses and sat for the Associate in Arts degree. Of the 200 students securing their degree, 20 had done so solely through the medium of television.

GB: With virtually no previous experience in educational television for adults, Britain went further than anything attempted in America with the creation of the Open University. This was the world's first university to offer home-based viewers the opportunity to take a full honours degree. An autonomous educational institution operated in conjunction with the BBC, the Open University was inaugurated at 11am on Sunday, 3 January 1971 with an address on BBC2 by the University Secretary, Chris Christodoulou, followed by an *Introduction to Mathematics*. The regular courses commenced the following Sunday, 10 January, with *Social Sciences I*, *Science I* and *Mathematics I*.

The first graduates of the Open University were 903 students who received their degrees at a ceremony held at Alexandra Palace on 23 June 1973.

The first
TELEVISION: INTERNATIONAL TRANSMISSION
was made on 9 February 1928 by John Logie Baird, who sent 30-line images of his own face from Motograph House, London by land-line to transmitting station GK2Z at Coulsdon, Surrey, and thence across the Atlantic to a receiving set manned by his assistant, Ben Clapp, at Hartsdale, N.Y. The *New York Herald Tribune* commented the following day: 'It is said that probably one thousand engineers and laboratory-men were involved in the American (Washington–New York) tests. . . . Only a dozen worked with Baird.'

The first entertainment programme designed specifically for an overseas audience was a performance by the Danish film star Carl Brisson, transmitted on 8 November 1932 from Broadcasting House, London to a large-screen receiver at the Arena Theatre, Copenhagen, where Brisson had made his original stage début. The regular transmissions from Baird's Long Acre studio had been received on amateur-built receiving sets as far away as the Mediterranean two years earlier.

HIGH-DEFINITION INTERNATIONAL TRANSMISSION: the first, and also the first programme seen in England from a foreign television station, was received on the Sussex Downs from the Eiffel Tower transmitter, Paris, in an experiment conducted by the *Daily Express* in conjunction with the Marconiphone Co in June 1938. From 1942 to 1944 German television broadcasts from Paris were regularly monitored by British Intelligence on a receiving set located in a shed at Beachy Head on the south coast, and the newsreel films shown provided valuable evidence of British bomb-damage in France. The first public-service television transmission from one country to another was a BBC outside broadcast from Calais of the centenary celebrations of the laying of the first cross-Channel cable held on 27 August 1950.
EUROVISION was inaugurated on 6 June 1954 when television stations in France, Belgium, Holland, Germany, Denmark, Italy, Switzerland and Britain were linked together with a 4,000-mile chain of relays. The first programme showed the Festival of Flowers from Montreux, Switzerland. In the evening the Pope was seen speaking from the Vatican in Italian, French, German, English and Dutch.
TRANSATLANTIC PROGRAMME TRANSMISSION: the first was made by the BBC from London to Montreal, Canada via the Atlantic telephone cable, on 18 June 1959, and showed the departure of HM Queen Elizabeth II and Prince Philip for the opening of the St Lawrence Seaway. It was seen in Canada on the CBC network and in the USA on the NBC network, having been relayed from Montreal to New York by cable. The first transatlantic programme transmission from Canada to Britain was made on 26 June when the Queen performed the opening ceremony.
TRANSATLANTIC SATELLITE TRANSMISSION: the first was made on 11 July 1962 when the American Telephone & Telegraph Co transmitted the image of its Chairman, Frederick Kappel, from Andover, Maine to Goonhilly Downs, Cornwall via *Telstar.*

The first transatlantic programme relay was made on 2 May 1965 via the commercial communications satellite *Early Bird*, linking 300 million viewers in nine countries. The programme, titled *Out of this World*, included scenes of a heart operation from Houston, Texas, Dr Martin Luther King speaking from Philadelphia, the Pope making an address from the Vatican, a bullfight from Barcelona, the Feast of Santa Cruz from Mexico, and scenes from Quebec, Stockholm and Washington. The British contribution included Russian sailors singing and dancing aboard HMS *Victory* at Portsmouth. Pictures of Georges Lemay, wanted by the Canadian police, subsequently led to his arrest in Fort Lauderdale, Florida.
COLOUR TRANSATLANTIC PROGRAMME: the first transmission was made by NBC via *Early Bird* on 17 May 1965 and consisted of a ½hr show for American viewers titled *A New Look at Olde England.*

The first
TELEVISION INTERVIEW
took place at the Ideal Home Exhibition, Southampton on 29 April 1930, when the actress Peggy O'Neil was interviewed by *Southern Daily Echo* columnist 'Patoc'. Miss O'Neil was televised from the temporary studio installed by the Baird Co in the Royal Victoria Rooms and the interviewer spoke to her by cable from the main exhibition hall. The subject's opening words were reported to be:

Television is certainly very fascinating. This is the first time I have been interviewed by television, and it's rather a jolly experience . . . to say the least, it's very wonderful. And what a top-hole present a televisor would make – there's a new idea.

A rather more ambitious experiment took place on 13 May the following year, when Mrs Philip Snowden, wife of the Chancellor of the Exchequer, was interviewed at 11 Downing Street by the journalist Sydney Moseley, who was located at the *Daily Herald* office. The subjects discussed included Mrs Snowden's work on the BBC Board of Control, her husband's health (he had been seriously ill), the pros and cons of Covent Garden opera in English, and State support for the arts.

The first person to be interviewed in a scheduled television programme was Miss Dorothy Stone, who appeared as a guest on photographer Harold Stein's weekly 'chat show' titled *People I have Shot* via W2XCD Passaic, N.J. on 21 June 1931.
GB: The first interviewee to take part in a scheduled programme was the tennis star Fred Perry, who answered questions about Britain's prospects in the Davis Cup competition at the BBC television studio in Portland Place on 1 August 1933.

The first
TELEVISION LICENCES
in Britain were issued on 1 June 1946 at a combined fee of £2 which included radio. The number of television sets in the hands of the public at that time was estimated at 7,500. No licence was required for television during the pre-war years of the service. The number of TV licences current reached the million mark in 1951, while the number of sound-and-vision licences exceeded sound-only licences for the first time in 1957.

Television Detector Vans were first used by the GPO for the detection of licence-evaders in London and the Home Counties in the autumn of 1951. The GPO Investigation Service had first employed this method of detection in 1931 to combat radio licence evasion.

The first
TELEVISION: LOCAL STATION
in Britain was inaugurated by Greenwich Cablevision from a studio behind a corner shop in Plumstead High Street on 3 July 1972. The first programme, titled *Cable Town*, presented a collage of Greenwich life, with guest appearances from non-residents Dame Sybil Thorndike, Glenda Jackson and Barbara Cartland. Designed as a community television service, Cablevision began operations on a budget of £20,000 and with relay subscribers in about 9,000 Greenwich homes.

The first
TELEVISION: MOBILE UNIT
was a 3½-ton Mercedes-Benz Fernseh-Aufnahmewagen equipped with an intermediate-film transmission system by the German Reichs Rundfunk in 1934. It was employed for the first time at the opening of the Berlin television station of the Reichs Rundfunk on 22 March 1935 and from then on it was taken out into the streets daily to gather contributions for a programme called *Spiegel des Tages* (*Mirror of the Day*) that was transmitted in the evenings.
GB: The first mobile unit was designed by T.C. Macnamara, the engineer responsible for planning the BBC television station at Alexandra Palace, and consisted of two Regal vans built by AEC of Southall and equipped by Marconi's Wireless Telegraph Co Ltd. They were delivered on 2 May 1937, just in time to be used for the BBC's first major outside broadcast 10 days later, when the Coronation procession was televised from a vantage point at Apsley Gate, Hyde Park Corner.

The first
TELEVISION NEWS
The first topical event to be televised was the nomination of Alfred E. Smith for the Presidency of the USA at Albany, N.Y., transmitted by WGY Schenectady on 22 August 1928.

The first attempt at presenting news specially filmed for television was made by the BBC on 31 August 1936, when scenes of the *Queen Mary* docking at

Southampton on the return from her maiden voyage to America were transmitted from Alexandra Palace only 4hr later.

The Reich Rundfunkgesellschaft emulated this achievement a fortnight later when a film of the Nuremberg Rally taken on 13 September was flown to Berlin and televised the same evening.

REGULAR TELEVISION NEWS was first transmitted by WCBS and by WNBT New York, both daily for 15min commencing 1 July 1941. The name of the CBS newscaster is not recorded. NBC's newscaster at WNBT was Lowell Thomas and the programme sponsored by Sunoco.

GB: The first regular news programme was BBC Television Newsreel, a 15min news round-up presented twice weekly from 5 January 1948. Although it aimed chiefly at a magazine-type coverage of the events of the previous few days, a number of same-day 'scoops' were achieved within the first few months, including the test flight of the Bristol Brabazon, the Earl of Harewood's wedding, and the St Leger.

The first daily television news was the BBC's Television News and Newsreel, first transmitted from Alexandra Palace at 7.30pm on 5 July 1954. It was introduced by Richard Baker, seen superimposed against a view of Nelson's Column, with the words: 'Here is an illustrated summary of the news. It will be followed by the latest film of happenings at home and abroad.' To begin with television news strove to be entirely illustrative. On the opening night newsreaders John Snagge and Andrew Timothy could be heard but not seen, while the news items they were reading – which included the Petrov spy case in Australia, tests of the de Havilland Comet airliner and the end of meat rationing – were depicted with a sequence of photo stills, maps, diagrams, portraits and film.

The first television newscasters to be seen in vision were Richard Baker and Kenneth Kendall, who presented the late-night summary on alternate nights commencing 4 September 1955.

The first woman television newcaster was Armine Sandford, a 29-year-old doctor's daughter from Exeter, who joined the BBC West Regional news team at Bristol on 30 September 1957. The first woman to read the national news was Nan Winton on 20 June 1960.

The first
TELEVISION: OPERA
was *Carmen* with Heddle Nash and Sarah Fischer accompanied by Cyril Smith at the piano and a three-piece orchestra, presented by the BBC in a 45min production on 6 July 1934.

Televising the 1936 Berlin Olympics (above). Viewing the Olympics on big-screen television (below).

The first
TELEVISION OUTSIDE BROADCAST
(scheduled transmission) was made by the Baird Co during its morning programme on 8 May 1931. Scenes of Long Acre, London were transmitted from a van parked by the kerb outside the television studio. Previously, all programmes had been made under powerful artificial lighting, though a closed-circuit demonstration of open-air scenes had been made as early as 18 June 1928, when Jack Buchanan was televised 'in immaculate white flannels' on the roof of the Baird Studios at 133 Long Acre.

HIGH-DEFINITION TELEVISION OUTSIDE BROADCAST: the first was made at the Berlin Olympiad of 1–14 August 1936. The Reich Rundfunkgesellschaft used two mobile television vans and three cameras to transmit a selection of the most important events live during the mornings and afternoons. These transmissions were witnessed by an estimated 150,000 viewers at the 28 public television-rooms in Berlin.

GB: The first was made by the BBC on 5 September 1936, and showed the comedian Leonard Henry departing from Alexandra Palace in his car. This pioneer effort was quite spontaneous and was carried out at the instigation of the *Daily Telegraph* Correspondent, who happened to be visiting the studios. Its full significance was only realized when Henry's car had disappeared round the corner and the lift-man exclaimed: 'Blimey, we've made an O.B.!'

Other outside broadcasts were made in the grounds of Alexandra Palace during 1936, following the commencement of a regular public television service (*q.v.*) on 2 November. These included Archie Compston demonstrating golf swings, Maj. Faudel-Phillips giving a riding-lesson, Sir Malcolm Campbell showing the latest Motor Show exhibits, model aeroplanes in flight, simulated sheep-dog trials, a parade of vintage motor cars and a display by the Territorial Army. Range was limited by the short lengths of cable available to relay the pictures back to the transmitter, and it was not until the acquisition of two mobile units (*q.v.*), that the cameras were able to move beyond the immediate surroundings of Alexandra Palace. The first first major outside broadcast of a topical event was the Coronation procession on 12 May 1937, with commentary by Freddie Grisewood.

See also Television: Sport.

The first
TELEVISION PANEL GAME
was a six-a-side *Spelling Bee* compèred by question-master Freddie Grisewood and presented by the BBC on 31 May 1938. This was followed by a number of rather more inventive quiz games, including a *General Knowledge Bee* with A. G. Street (15 October 1938), a *Tactile Bee* with Christopher Stone (20 December 1938), a *Tasting Bee* with the television cook, Marcel Boulestin, and a *Musical Bee* with Philip Bate (10 July 1939).

The first
TELEVISION PERFORMER
(professional artiste) was Irish-

American comedian A. Dolan, engaged by the American Telephone & Telegraph Co to provide a 'short act of monologue and song' during an experimental transmission from the A.T.&T. wireless station in Whippany, N.J. to the Bell Telephone Laboratories in New York City on 7 April 1927. This was the first public demonstration of television in the USA, as well as the first occasion on which television had been used as an entertainment medium anywhere in the world. It was viewed by an invited audience in New York, 22 miles from the transmitting station, on a large-screen grid receiver giving an image measuring 2×2½ft. The head and shoulders of the artiste were seen approximately life-size. Interest in the technical achievement eclipsed any attention that Dolan's performance may have deserved, the only facts about it on record being that he wore an Irish costume and side-whiskers, and that the broken clay pipe in his mouth was clearly discernible on the television screen.

GB: The first professional artiste to be seen on television was Miss Peggy O'Neil, the popular actress, who gave a spontaneous entertainment from a temporary studio adjoining Olympia on the first day of the Radio Exhibition, 22 September 1928. The transmission was received at a viewing-room in near-by Maclise Road, where the Baird Co had installed three cubicles, each holding six viewers at a time, to demonstrate the three different television receivers which they proposed putting on the market as soon as service facilities were granted.

Viewers were delighted to find that the image of Miss O'Neil on their screens was 'instantly recognisable without a doubt'. The magazine *Television* reported:

For about half an hour Miss O'Neil gave us a charming entertainment, chatting and smiling at us, telling Irish stories, and, in response to telephone requests, she sang 'I'm a little bit fonder of you' and several other delightful songs.

ARTISTE UNDER EXCLUSIVE CONTRACT FOR TELEVISION APPEARANCES: the first was Miss Natalie Towers, a recent graduate of Wellesley College, Mass., who was introduced to viewers of the Columbia Broadcasting System's Station W2XAB New York by Mayor Jimmy Walker on 21 July 1931.

TELEVISION STAR: the first artiste to be referred to as such was CBS's Grant Kimball by the *New York Sun* in its issue for 12 November 1932. Previous to this date, however, the *New York World Telegram* had said on 2 May 1931: 'A regular Saturday evening feature over W2XCD, Alice Remsen has built a television public for herself distinct from her radio fans.' Alice Remsen was an English actress and singer who also appeared in the weekly WOR radio programme *Footlight Echoes*.

In Britain the term 'television star' was first used in print by *Popular Wireless*, 5 May 1934, in respect of Cochran girl Laurie Devine. Miss Devine was one of the most regular of the early television performers, having made her début on 23 August 1932, the day after the commencement of the BBC experimental service.

Other artistes to make their television début before 1935 included Gracie Fields, Anona Wynn, Sybil Thorndike, George Sanders, Ralph Richardson, Josephine Baker, Arthur Askey and Hermione Gingold.

See also Television Play; Television Service.

The first *TELEVISION PLAY*

was *The Queen's Messenger* by J. Hartley Manners, adapted and produced by Mortimer Stewart and presented by the General Electric Co's Station WGY, Schenectady, N.Y. on 11 September 1928. Izotta Jewell played the lady and Maurice Randall the messenger, while Joyce E. Rector and William J. Toniski doubled for their hands, holding various props in front of the scanner, including cigarettes, glasses, keys and a dispatch-case. Three 'cameras' were used, one for these effects, and one each for the two performers. The play was transmitted on the 24-line low-definition system developed by Dr Ernst Alexanderson, and lasted for 40min. Reception reports came from viewers as far west as the Pacific Coast.

GB: Box and Cox was produced by Gordon Sherry with Lawrence Bascomb as Box, Vivienne Chatterton as Mrs Bouncer and Stanley Vivien as Cox, and presented by the Baird Co from their studios at 133 Long Acre, London on 15 December 1928. The fourth member of the cast, a cat, was the first animal performer to appear on television. Although no commercial receivers were available at the time, a number of amateur constructors had already made their own sets from directions published in *Television*, so it is possible that the production was seen by several dozen viewers in addition to the Baird staff. The dialogue could be picked up on an ordinary radio set, and at least one listener was inspired to make his own television receiver after hearing the broadcast. Vision was transmitted via the Baird Co's own transmitter and would not have extended much beyond a radius of 5 miles from central London.

BBC TELEVISION PLAY: the first was Pirandello's *The Man with a Flower in his Mouth*, produced by Lance Sieveking and transmitted by the Baird Co on 14 July 1930. The 30min production featured Gladys Young, Earle Gray and Lionel Millard, with sets designed by C.R.W. Nevinson. The BBC's pioneer venture in television programme presentation is notable for the first recorded use of special make-up. Owing to the rather fuzzy appearance given to faces by 30-line transmission, it was thought advisable to use heavy blue lines to accentuate the features, while the cheeks and forehead were painted yellow. Only one member of the cast could appear before the scanner at a time, but the action was varied as much as possible by the skilful use of hand-held props in close-up. The narrow vertical screens fitted to early Baird Televisors hampered dramatic effect, but the following year Baird developed a system called 'zone television' which employed three 30-line scanners in conjunction to give a single 90-line picture. On 24 April 1931 he transmitted a play called *Another Pair of Spectacles* by this means, and for the first time the whole cast of three – John Rorke, Dennis Lawes and Dorothy Leave – could be seen on a special 'wide-screen' receiver at the same time.

PLAY WRITTEN SPECIALLY FOR TELEVISION: the first was *The Underground Murder Mystery*, a 30min drama by J. Bissell Thomas, set in Tottenham Court Road Underground Station and starring Lance Lister and Nancy Poulteney, presented by the BBC on 19 January 1937.

The first *TELEVISION PRODUCER*

was Harold Bradly, appointed by the Baird Co as Studio Director in charge of production for the programme service transmitted from the Company's Long Acre Studios commencing 30 September 1929. Sydney Moseley was appointed Director of Television Programmes.

BBC TELEVISION PRODUCER: the first was Eustace Robb, who was full-time Controller of the BBC experimental programme service from its commencement on 22 August 1932 to close-down in September 1935. He was assisted by the Programme Adviser, George Grossmith.

The first *TELEVISION PROGRAMME: NARRATIVE SERIES*

was *The Wide World Review*, presented

by CBS Television from Station W2XAB New York on Monday evenings from 15 August to 12 December 1932. Described by the *New York Sun* as 'a musical drama with a fast moving script', the series starred a well-known English actor and broadcaster, Jack Fleming, who had made his name in the BBC radio feature *London Crime Club*. The first 25min episode was set in Shanghai.

This was the only known dramatic series transmitted in any country during the period of low-definition experimental television broadcasting. *GB:* The first continuous narrative series was *The Grove Family*, written and devised by Michael Pertwee and produced by John Warrington. The first episode, titled 'A House of Your Own' was presented by the BBC on Friday, 9 April 1954, featuring Edward Evans as Mr Grove, Ruth Dunning as Mrs Grove and Nancy Roberts as Grandma. The series ran until 28 June 1957.

See also Television Serial.

The first
TELEVISION RECEIVER
commercially produced, was advertised for sale at $75 by the Daven Corp. of Newark, N.J. in the July 1928 issue of *Television* (New York). These sets were adjustable to receive 24-, 36- or 48-line transmissions. Construction kits were offered for sale at the same time. There was no television service operating in New York City at this time, though a very rudimentary series of experimental transmissions on a scheduled basis had already begun in Schenectady, N.Y. (*see also* Television Service). In August 1931 the New York Correspondent of the *Observer* reported that there were an estimated 9,000 television sets in New York City and approximately 30,000 elsewhere in the USA. Prices of the half-dozen different models available ranged from $80 to $160 for a ready-made set and $36 for a construction kit. The following year W.C. Rawls & Co of Norfolk, Va. put on the market a luxury, large-screen set in fumed oak at $295. 'Large screen' in this case meant one 11·3in square, but this was considerably in advance of previous image sizes.
GB: The first commercially produced television set to be marketed in Britain was the Baird Televisor, price 25gns, announced for sale in a full-page advertisement placed in *Television*, May 1930, by eight radio and television dealers.

Probably the first Televisor to take its place as a piece of living-room furniture was the one installed by John Baird at 10 Downing Street on 31 March 1930. In a letter of thanks the Prime Minister, Ramsay MacDonald, wrote:

When I look at the transmissions I feel that the most wonderful miracle is being done under my eye. . . . You have put something in my room which will never let me forget how strange is this world – and how unknown.

1928 Baird TV set (top left) manufactured but never marketed; the Bush Co's 1933 Baird Television (top right); 1930 Baird Televisor (below) – the first set marketed in Britain. Price 25 gns (then about $130)

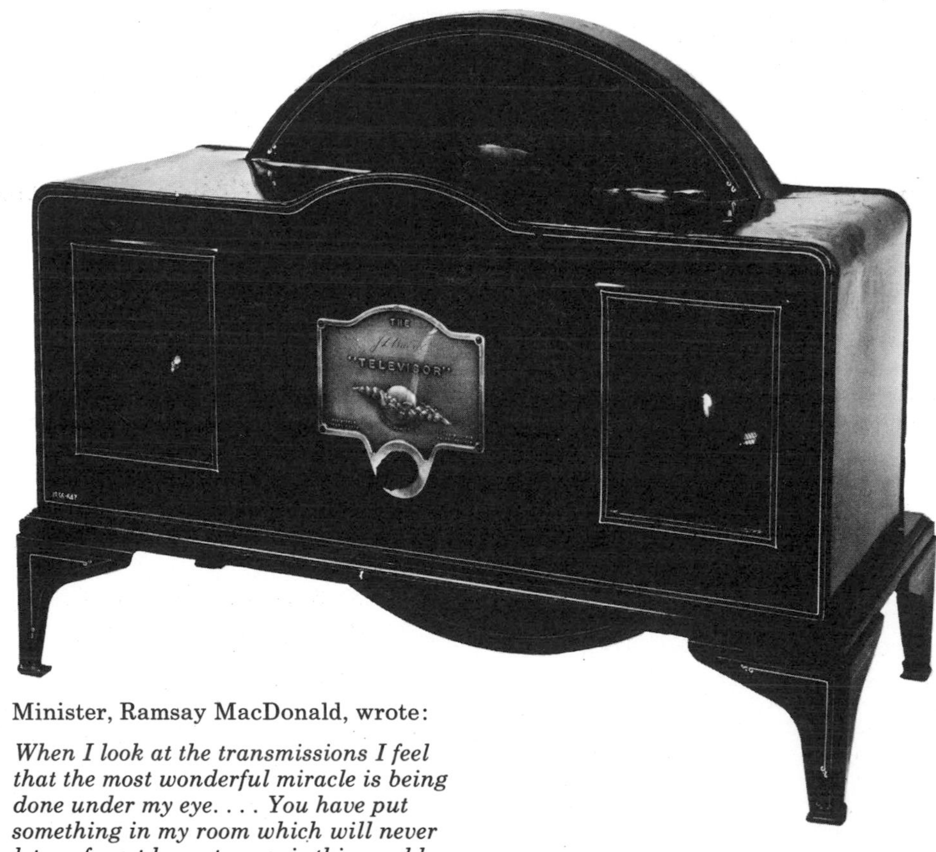

The first television set to be permanently installed in a public place was a Televisor presented by Baird to the Caledonian Club, of which he was a member. Later in 1930 the Prince of Wales (later Edward VIII) was entertained at the Club and watched a programme on the set. By the end of 1931 over 80 radio-dealers were demonstrating Baird televisions.

Baird's Improved Televisor, a mains-operated table model measuring 18×8×13in, with a 9×4in screen, was unveiled to the Press at the Long Acre Studios on 27 June 1932. A free-standing cabinet model with a 16×7in screen was installed in the Press listening-room at Broadcasting House a few weeks later. After modifications, the Baird mirror-drum Televisor was put into commercial production by Bush Radio Ltd and announced for sale at a price of 50gns on 30 June 1933. This was the first commercial receiver with a rectangular screen (9×4in), as opposed to a viewing-lens, and the first to give a clear black and white image without the orange glow that often marred reception on the original Televisor. A rival set, the Ethovisor, was put on the market by Grafton Radio Ltd about the same time. A third contender entered the television market in August 1934, when Plew Television Ltd of Croydon announced three new models at 10gns (vision receiver only), 18gns and 25gns. Probably the cheapest ready-made television set of all time was offered for sale at 65s by the Bennett Television Co of Redhill, Surrey in June 1935 – just two months before the closure of the BBC's low-definition service made the sets obsolete.

The first commercially produced cathode-ray receiver was placed on the market in January 1935 by Gillavision Television of 23 Chilworth Street, London, price 55gns. A 4ft-high free-standing cabinet model with a 5in diameter circular screen, it was designed to receive BBC 30-line transmission on 261 metres, though the manufacturers claimed it could be 'easily converted to any other definition and wavelength'.

Although no reliable figures exist as to the number of receiving sets in use during the years of the low-definition 30-line service of 1928–35, *Television* gave an estimate of 14,000 sets in October 1933 'based on a voluminous correspondence over some years with constructors throughout the country'. In March 1934 the *Daily Express* began sponsoring a construction kit manufactured by Mervyn Sound & Vision Ltd as a 'special offer' to readers, and two months later reported that 5,000 had been sold. Even if these estimates are over-generous, taken with the additional sales up to August 1935 they would suggest a total approaching 20,000 by the end of the service, approximately the same as the number of high-definition sets (*see below*) in use at the outbreak of war.

According to a questionnaire sent out by the Television Society in June 1934, 18% of viewers were interested in television primarily for its entertainment value, 55% regarded it mainly from an experimental standpoint, and 27% answered 'both'.

HIGH-DEFINITION TELEVISION RECEIVERS, commercially produced, were first exhibited at Radiolympia in August 1936, when the public were offered a choice of 17 models by 10 different manufacturers at prices ranging from 85gns to 120gns. According to Sydney Moseley, *Television Today and Tomorrow*, the first of these sets to have been placed on the market was the Baird T5, a mirror-top model with a 12×9in screen. Full public service having begun on 2 November, sales figures totalled a disappointing 280 by the end of the year. It was thought that most potential buyers were waiting to see if the prices would come down, and in February 1937 the manufacturers felt forced to comply, EMI and HMV reducing their 95gn set to 60gns and Baird cutting the 85gn model to 55 gns. Further reductions followed in August and sales began to pick up. One purchaser that year was a Sussex farm-labourer who had never been to London in his life and, having invested his life-savings in a set, said that now he would never need to, as he could sit and watch what was going on 'up there' by his own fireside. By the outbreak of war in September 1939, there were an estimated 20,000 receivers in use, all in the London and Home Counties area, and a probable viewing audience of 100,000.

Luxury TV 1937 style – the Baird Television Radiogram, price 125 gns (about $650)

In Germany and the USA high-definition receivers were not available to the public until 1939. The German radio-manufacturers had been ready to start production of 180-line sets as early as 1935, when 20 different models from 7 firms were exhibited at the Berlin Radio Exhibition. The Nazi authorities, however, were determined that television should not be a preserve of the rich and ordered that production should be halted until the Post Office and the radio-manufacturers had succeeded in designing a 'People's Television Set' which could be sold for about £12. This venture suffered much the same fate as the Volkswagen, which had been inspired by the same motives. The set was put on sale in Berlin on 28 July 1939, but by the outbreak of war a month later only 50 out of a proposed initial production series of 10,000 were in use.

The first TELEVISION RECORDING system was Phonovision, developed by John Logie Baird in London in 1928. It allowed for low-frequency signals to be reproduced on aluminium gramophone records, using either two separate discs for sound and vision, or a single double-tracked disc. The intention was to record programmes which could be purchased by the viewing public and played back by means of a simple attachment to a Baird low-definition Televisor. Baird was anticipating the modern development of video cassettes, but though the principle of his system was perfectly sound, it came too early to be commercially practicable. At least one enthusiastic amateur, however, J. Foster Cooper of Cambridge, was making his own Phonovision recordings of the Baird transmissions from Long Acre, London in 1931. By June 1935, television recordings on disc were being advertised for sale by Major Radiovision Co of Wigmore Street, London. The discs gave 6min of recorded vision on each side and cost 7s each. As Baird had been too precipitant, R.O. Hughes, the initiator of this enterprise, proved to be too late. Four months after he had launched his recordings on the market, Baird low-definition programme transmissions were discontinued and the majority of viewers, many of whom had built their own sets from construction kits, proceeded to dismantle them.

HIGH-DEFINITION TELE-RECORDING: the first was made on 9 November 1947 by Philip Dorté, BBC Television Outside Broadcasts Supervisor. He filmed the Remembrance Day Ceremony at the Cenotaph in Whitehall direct from the TV monitor screen at

Alexandra Palace, using a specially synchronized camera developed after 12 months of experiment. The ceremony having been seen live by viewers in the morning, it was repeated when the recording was transmitted the same evening.

The first
TELEVISION: SCHOOLS SERVICE
was inaugurated by the Philadelphia Board of Education via the Philco Corp's Station WPTZ on 2 March 1949. The project was titled *Operation Blackboard* and consisted of three telecasts a week during the afternoon hours. The programmes, produced under the over-all direction of Martha A. Gable, included 'Young Artists', 'Your Social IQ', 'R for Rhythm', 'Museum Piece' and 'The World at Your Door'. At the start of the first series, 20 Philadelphia public, private and parochial schools were equipped with large-screen television sets donated by the Philco Corp. By 1952 there were 700 classroom sets in the Philadelphia area. Some confusion about the earliest inception of regular schools television has been occasioned by the fact that a number of experiments in televising *from* schools were made in various parts of the USA between 1947 and 1949; these were essentially a public-relations exercise, designed to give parents and citizens an idea of the children's activities in school.
GB: An experimental series of educational programmes was transmitted by the BBC to six north London secondary schools on a daily schedule for four weeks commencing 5 May 1952.

The first regular schools television service in Britain was inaugurated by Associated Rediffusion on 13 May 1957 with daily ½hr transmissions to schools in the London, Midland and central Scotland areas. The first week's schedule included the following programmes, aimed at 14–15-year-olds:

Monday: *Looking and Seeing*
Tuesday: *The Ballad Story*
Wednesday: *On Leaving School*
Thursday: *A Year of Observation* (International Geophysical Year)
Friday: *People among Us* (on immigrants)

The regular BBC Schools Television Service followed on 24 September 1957.

The first
TELEVISION SERIAL
was *Ann and Harold*, a five-part romantic comedy based on the radio play by Louis Goodrich and aired by the BBC in weekly 20min episodes commencing 12 July 1938. Produced by Lanham Titchener, it starred Ann Todd and William Hutchinson in the name-parts, and told the story of a young London couple who meet by chance in Hyde Park through the agency of a Sealyham terrier, their engagement, marriage, life in Bayswater, and their only quarrel.
CONTINUOUS TELEVISION SERIAL: the first was *One Man's Family*, based on the highly successful radio 'soap opera' formula, presented by NBC with Bert Lytell, Marjorie Gateson and Eve Marie Saint from 4 November 1949 until 1 April 1955.
GB: The first continuous television serial was *Emergency Ward 10*, a hospital drama produced by Anthony Kearey and presented by Associated Television twice weekly on Tuesdays and Fridays from 19 February 1957 until 1 October 1966. After that date the show continued in the form of 1hr episodes, each a complete story.

The first
TELEVISION SERVICE
scheduled, was inaugurated by the General Electric Co's Station WGY, Schenectady, N.Y. on 11 May 1928. Transmissions were presented from 1.30 to 2pm on Tuesdays, Thursdays and Fridays using a low-definition system of mechanical scanning developed by Dr Ernst Alexanderson. *Television* reported: 'Only the faces of men talking, laughing or smoking will be broadcast; no elaborate effects are planned at this stage.' Apart from the transmission of a play (*see* Television Play) in September 1928, there is no evidence that WGY ever offered real programmes or attempted to present entertainment by the new medium.
GB: The first regular television service was announced at a meeting of the Television Society on 4 December 1928, members being invited to 'test their apparatus at midnight, when the first of a series of experimental test programmes would be put on the ether for one hour by the Baird Co.'. The midnight programmes were continued every Tuesday and Saturday. They were broadcast via the Baird Co's own 250W transmitting station, 2TV, vision on a wavelength of 200 metres and sound on 250 metres. This meant that the range was extremely limited, and it is improbable that reception could be achieved at a greater distance than 5 miles from central London except in freak atmospheric conditions. Nevertheless it seems likely that there was a small body of regular viewers unconnected with the Company, for Baird had already issued over 2,600 sub-constructor's licences to enthusiastic amateur television hams by the end of 1928.

From the very beginning of the experimental service an attempt was made to show something more than mere moving images on the screen. Although little has been recorded about the early programmes, it appears that they depended largely on the talents of the Baird Concert Party, which included A. Calkin, baritone, and Reginald Shaw, who specialized in minstrel songs. It is possible that Jack Buchanan may have performed, as he was a close friend of Baird's and a frequent visitor to the specially equipped television studio – the first in the world – at 133 Long Acre, London.

A daily service was inaugurated on 30 September 1929, when the Baird programmes were broadcast via a BBC transmitter for the first time. This event was heralded as the beginning of a 'public service'. The transmissions could now be received in any part of Britain, and in some parts of Europe as well, though in every other respect they were still strictly experimental. The opening at 11am was introduced by Sir Ambrose Fleming, inventor of the thermionic valve, and included performances by Lulu Stanley, who sang 'He's Tall, Dark and Handsome' and 'Grandma's Proverbs', and Baird's secretary, Miss King, who gave a spirited rendering of 'Mighty like a Rose'. Sydney Howard contributed a comedy monologue, in which he described the occasion as 'Funny Face Day, or Mug's Monday'. Since there was only one transmitter available, sight and sound had to be broadcast alternately in 2min snatches. For this reason the early transmissions were very restricted in scope, and consisted of little more than holding objects up before the scanner or people pulling faces.

On 31 March 1930, a second transmitter at Brookman's Park was brought into use, and it was possible to broadcast sight and sound simultaneously on 261 metres and 356 metres respectively. The ½hr opening programme included Annie Croft singing 'New Lamps for Old' and Gracie Fields, who sang 'Nowt about Owt'. For the first time, television receivers (*q.v.*) were available to the general public at 25gns each, and a number of home construction kits appeared on the market.

One pioneer viewer, Robert Herring, wrote in the November 1930 issue of the *London Mercury*:

After studying the regular television programmes, I am surprised at the ingenuity shown by the artists. The gestures within the scope of television are few, but they make the most of them. They are as plastic as can be. . . . The other day there was a man playing a musical saw. After he had himself been transmitted, he slipped away from his stool, and we saw the saw, his knee holding it and his hand striking it. He then slid back again; to a film critic, there was quite a hint of 'mounting' here. The same applies to a conjuror, and to Rupert Harvey, a cartoonist, whose drawings appear on the screen while his voice is heard as he goes on. Marionettes have also appeared, and at the end of the programme there is the Television Screen News, which announces what turns will make up the next programme. The news, which is written, not oral, is run on the endless belt system, and the words are drawn by, 'Tomorrow at 11 am. Frank Damer, Baritone, etc.' . . . The programme is for the most part popular, and takes the form of vaudeville.

These variety turns were varied by demonstrations of classical dance and ballet, competitions with prizes for viewers, short plays and sketches, instructional programmes, including lessons in tennis and cricket, illustrated talks on such subjects as 'Dogs', 'Phrenology' and 'English Naval History', dance-bands, keep-fit classes, and a wide range of instrumentalists (*see also* Television Documentary).

The first newspaper to publish daily programme details was the *Daily Express*, commencing on 11 April 1930. Most other national newspapers followed suit, as well as leading dailies in Bristol, Birmingham, Glasgow, Edinburgh and York.

BBC TELEVISION SERVICE (regular) began on 22 August 1932 with four programmes a week from 11 to 11.30pm. The opening programme, transmitted from Studio BB in the basement of Broadcasting House, included Louie Freear singing 'I want to be a Lady' from *The Chinese Honeymoon*, a musical comedy in which she had starred in 1901. The service was inaugurated in co-operation with the Baird Co and superseded their transmissions from the Long Acre Studios. The BBC maintained its 30-line low-definition programme schedule until 10 September 1935, by which time the Selsdon Committee had recommended the setting up of a public high-definition television service.

Prior to 1935 both the BBC and *Television* had been wont to refer to the television audience as 'lookers'. In response to the Selsdon Committee's report in January 1935, the Radio Correspondents of both the *Daily Telegraph* and the *Evening Standard* asked their readers for alternative suggestions. These included such terms as televist, telegazer, radioseer, perceptionist, audoobserver, audovist, beholder, telver, teleite, lustreer, ingazer, telisor, Bairder, telspector, visioner, telscriber, invider, optiphone and opticauris. A *Daily Telegraph* reader sent in 'viewer', but this was only listed under 'other suggestions'. On 25 March 1935 the BBC officially adopted the word 'televiewer' and the *Evening Standard* correctly predicted that it would soon come to be shortened to the more manageable 'viewer'. The *Daily Telegraph* approved the BBC's decision in a leader that said: 'It has . . . a good English appearance, and is not one of those disreputable foreigners like "sabotage" and "Bolshevik" . . . and not the least English thing about it is that foreigners will find it a difficult mouthful.'

HIGH-DEFINITION TELEVISION SERVICE: the first was officially inaugurated by the Director-General of German Broadcasting, Herr Hadamovsky, on 22 March 1935, though in fact 180-line experimental transmissions on a regular schedule had been in progress for about six months. Initially the programmes were broadcast three times a week from 8.30 to 10pm, and the material consisted chiefly of film, including an excerpt from a main feature. There was a change of programme once a week. No television sets were available to the general public, but there were 11 public viewing-rooms in Berlin and 1 in Potsdam, each seating 30 people. There was also a Telecinema with a 4 × 3ft screen in Berlin's Leipzigerstrasse with 100 seats. Free tickets were obtainable in advance from post offices, where most of the viewing-rooms were situated. A contemporary report said that viewing-rooms in the poorer areas were always well attended, particularly in the colder weather; those in residential areas were seldom full.

On 19 August 1935 fire at the Berlin Radio Exhibition destroyed the two ultra-short-wave transmitters then in use, but new ones were quickly completed, and on 15 January 1936 the service reopened with a daily programme from 8 to 9pm, repeated from 9 to 10pm. For the first time, live entertainment transmitted from studios in the Rognitzstrasse supplemented filmed material. The first artiste to make her début on a public high-definition (180-line) service was the soprano, Inge Vesten. At this stage of development only head-and-shoulder images were possible, though on 7 November a play titled *The Rocking Horse* was transmitted, one day after the BBC's first high-definition television play. A typical programme, seen on Saturday, 24 October 1936, consisted of the following:

Newsreel
Therese Crones (extracts from the feature film of that name)
Streets Without Obstacles (educational film)

In the intervals between films Erna Hohberg, violin, played the Czardas by Monti; Carl Sollner sang and accompanied himself on a lute.

After the outbreak of war, the Reich Rundfunkgesellschaft continued transmitting on an increased schedule of up to 6hr a day, principally for the benefit of hospitals and barracks, where receivers were installed for their morale and propaganda value. The service finally closed down on 23 November 1943, when the Berlin transmitter at Witzleben was destroyed by Allied bombing. German-controlled programmes from the Paris Eiffel Tower transmitter continued until 16 August 1944, a week before Liberation.

GB: The first high-definition programmes to be seen by the general public were transmitted from the BBC Television Studios at Alexandra Palace to Radiolympia on 26 August 1936. The BBC had assembled a skeleton staff at the beginning of the month. Gerald Cock was appointed Director of Television, Douglas Birkinshaw became Engineer-in-Charge, and Cecil Madden took on the dual role of Programme Organizer and Variety Producer. The 80min opening programme began at noon with a documentary film titled *Cover to Cover* featuring Somerset Maugham, Julian Huxley, 'Sapper', T. S. Eliot, Rebecca West and A. P. Herbert. This was followed by two songs from Helen McKay, the first live performer, a *Gaumont-British News*, and excerpts from films, including the GPO documentary *Post Haste*.

PUBLIC HIGH-DEFINITION TELEVISION SERVICE: the first was inaugurated by the BBC from Alexandra Palace on 2 November 1936. The claim that this was the first fully public service in the world is based on the fact that high-definition television receivers (*q.v.*) were on general sale, and that the service was recognized by the Government, the Post Office and the BBC as a permanent entertainment medium. Only one aspect of the transmissions can be described as experimental. Initially, the programmes were broadcast by two separate systems on alternate days. The Baird system employed mechanical scanning and transmitted on 240-lines, while the Marconi-EMI system used electronic Emitron cameras and gave a picture with 405-line definition. From 5 February 1937 the latter system alone was used, and remained the standard definition until the introduction of an alternative BBC channel in 1964.

The opening programme of the

service began at 3.30pm and featured introductory speeches by the Chairman of the BBC, the Postmaster-General and others, followed by performances by singer Adele Dixon and two black American dancer-comedians, Buck and Bubbles. The evening programme consisted of a special BBC film, *Television comes to London*, and the second edition of television's first series, *Picture Page*, a topical magazine programme produced by Cecil Madden. Among those appearing were the record-breaking pilot Jim Mollison, the Pearly King and Queen of Blackfriars, writer Algernon Blackwood and the Lord Mayor's coachman. (The first edition had been transmitted to Radiolympia on 8 October 1936.) The first day's transmissions ended with *British Movietone News*.

Originally the BBC television service broadcast on week-days only for 1hr in the afternoon and 1hr in the evening. By the autumn of 1939 there were about 4hr of programmes on a week-day and 90min on Sundays. The service closed down on 1 September 1939 for the duration of the war. There was no closing announcement, and the last words heard by viewers were from Mickey Mouse saying, in imitation of Greta Garbo, 'Ah tink ah go home.'

For the inauguration of the Independent Television service, *see* Television Commercial.

BBC2 began as an alternative programme service transmitting on 625-lines on 30 April 1964. A power service failure having made it impossible to broadcast from Television Centre as planned, Gerald Priestman introduced the first programme with the words: 'Welcome to BBC2 from where it all began – Studio A at Alexandra Palace.'

POSTSCRIPT: OTHER PRE-WAR PROGRAMME SERVICES. Although there were as many as 35 experimental television stations operating in the USA by the end of 1932, only CBS Station W2XAB New York can be said to have provided a regular programme schedule that exceeded the BBC low-definition service in scope. In May 1931 it was reported to be transmitting 3hr of live entertainment every night, including 'singers, instrumentalists, magicians, playlets, boxers, etc.'.

Experimental high-definition television programmes in the USA commenced on 7 July 1936, when the RCA Station W2XBS New York began transmitting on a definition of 343-lines from the Empire State Building. The first full public service was inaugurated by NBC on 30 April 1939 with an outside broadcast of President Roosevelt opening the New York World's Fair.

Apart from Britain, Germany and the USA, the countries with regular high-definition programme services prior to 1940 were France (12 December 1935), Russia (1938), Japan (13 May 1939) and Italy (22 July 1939).

The first
TELEVISION: SPORT
The first telecast of a sporting event took place on 17 February 1931, when a baseball game played by new members of the Waseda University Baseball Club at the Tozuka Baseball Ground, Tokyo, was transmitted by closed circuit to the Electrical Laboratory at Waseda University. The experiment was conducted under the direction of Dr Yamamoto Tadaoki and the 60-line low-definition pictures received on a screen 3ft square. On 27 September 1931 Waseda University presented a public telecast from the Tozuka Baseball Ground in association with the Japan Broadcasting Corporation. This 40min transmission of a match between the Ushigome and Awazi Shichiku Higher Elementary Schools was the world's first telecast of a team game to be watched by viewers in their own homes. The size of the picture on the sets available for domestic use was 8 × 5in. The commentator on this occasion was a Mr Matsuuchi, Japan Broadcasting Corporation announcer.

GB: The first sporting event to be televised was the Derby, transmitted by the Baird Co from Epsom on 3 June 1931. It was also the first transmission of a topical event, and the first outside broadcast (*q.v.*) made in Britain other than street scenes taken in front of the Baird Studios. The race was televised from a caravan stationed by the winning-post and connected by cable direct to the studio in Long Acre, London. From there the signals were broadcast via the BBC's National transmitter at Brookman's Park. The *Daily Telegraph* reported next day: '. . . all the Derby scenes were easily discernible. The parade of the horses, the enormous crowd, and the dramatic flash past at the winning-post.'

Opportunities for showing sport by 30-line low-definition television were naturally limited, though in November 1931 the *Manchester Guardian* reported: 'In order to demonstrate the usefulness of television the programme occasionally includes lessons in tennis and boxing, and an expert has been engaged to give fencing lessons.'

TELEVISION SPORTS COMMENTARY: the first in Britain was given by Amateur Middle-weight Boxing Champion Harry Mallin on the occasion of two England *v.* Ireland amateur contests transmitted by the BBC from the Concert Hall of Alexandra Palace on 4 February 1937. This

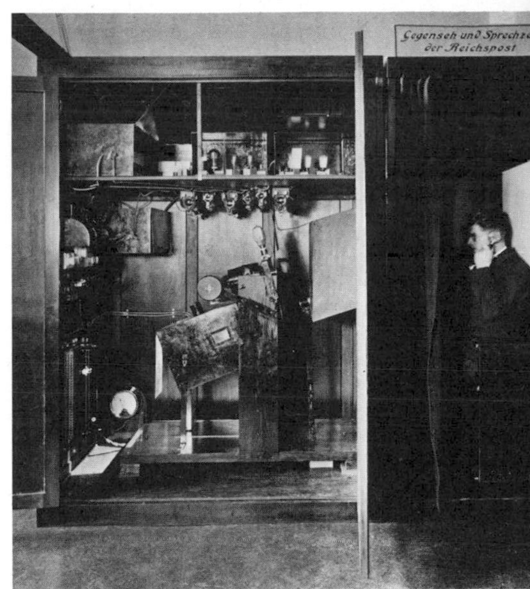

German television-telephone, 1929

was also the first live sports event to be shown on public high-definition television in Britain.

The first
TELEVISION-TELEPHONE
two-way sound-and-vision system, was devised by G. Krawinkel on behalf of the German Post Office and displayed at the Berlin Radio Exhibition in the summer of 1929. The apparatus was subsequently donated to the Deutsche Museum in Munich, where it was employed in demonstrations from 1930 to 1945.

GB: The first British two-way television-telephone system was the Baird Viseotelephone, publicly demonstrated for the first time by H. J. Barton-Chapple in Paris on 19 May 1932. A number of people were able to see and speak to each other in tests conducted between the offices of *Le Matin* and the Galeries Lafayette.

PUBLIC TELEVISION-TELEPHONE SERVICE: the first was opened by the German Minister for Posts and Transport, Freiherr von Eltz-Rübenach, on the opening day of the Leipzig Trade Fair, 1 March 1936. After the coaxial television cable between Berlin and Leipzig had been put through a series of tests, full public service commenced for Aryans only on 25 March. There were three television-telephone booths located in different parts of Berlin and three in Leipzig.

The following year the cable was extended to Nuremberg in time for the NSDAP Rally, and on 12 July 1938 a Berlin–Munich service was started. In Hamburg the Post Office began operating a local service within the city limits on 15 December 1938. The charge for a local call was 1·50 Reichsmarks;

long-distance calls were double the rate of the conventional telephone service.

No public television-telephone system has ever been operated in Britain, but in February 1970 the first permanent inter-office television-telephone system was installed at the headquarters of the Claremont Group in Shrewsbury, Shropshire. The equipment was produced by the Photo-Scan Co, a member of the Group.

The first
TELEVISION TRANSMISSION
of a moving image with gradations of light and shade was made by John Logie Baird in his attic workroom at 23 Frith Street, London, on 30 October 1925. Baird had recently removed from Hastings, where he had built a crude apparatus comprising a tea-chest, an empty biscuit-box for the lamphouse, Nipkow scanning-discs made from cardboard, darning-needles, hat-boxes, cycle-lamp lenses, discarded electric motors, piano-wire, glue, string and sealing-wax to a total value of about 12s 6d. With this primitive machine he had succeeded in transmitting the shadow of a Maltese cross over a distance of about 10ft in February 1924. He was later evicted from this laboratory at 8 Queen's Arcade after an explosion caused by his electrical supply, which consisted of several hundred torch batteries wired together to provide a 2,000V power source.

In a broadcast made in the USA six years later, Baird described the events of the last Friday in October 1925 when the dummy's head he had been using for test purposes suddenly showed up on the screen 'not as a mere smudge of black and white, but as a real image with details . . .'. His first thought was to obtain a living subject and he rushed down to the floor below, occupied by Cross Pictures Ltd. Here the first person he encountered was a 15-year-old office-boy, William Taynton, whom he seized and hustled upstairs.

I placed him before the transmitter and went into the next room to see what the screen would show. The screen was entirely blank, and no effort of tuning would produce any result. Puzzled, and very disappointed, I went back to the transmitter, and there the cause of the failure became at once evident. The boy, scared by the intense white light, had backed away from the transmitter. In the excitement of the moment I gave him half a crown, and this time he kept his head in the right position. Going again into the next room I saw his head on the screen quite clearly. It is curious that the first person in the world to be seen by television should have required a bribe to accept that distinction!

Baird gave his first demonstration of true television to the Press on 7 January 1926, when the *Evening Standard* representative saw the face of Captain O. G. Hutchinson on the screen. On 27 January he gave a public demonstration for some 40 members of the Royal Institution, followed by a series of displays for the technical and scientific Press. Dr Alexander Russell, Principal of Faraday House, wrote a special account of Baird's achievement for *Nature* of 3 July 1926:

We saw the transmission by television of living human faces, the proper gradation of light and shade, and all movements of the head, of the lips and mouth, and of a cigarette, and its smoke were faithfully portrayed on a screen in the theatre, the transmitter being in a room at the top of the building. Naturally, the results are far from perfect. The image cannot be compared with that produced by a good kinematograph film. The likeness, however, was unmistakable, and all the motions are reproduced with absolute fidelity. This is the first time we have seen real television and . . . Mr Baird is the first to have accomplished this marvellous feat.

Baird's system of television employed a mechanical scanner in both the transmitting apparatus and the receiver, and although he was eventually persuaded to develop an electronic receiver, by that time he had already been overtaken by Marconi-EMI in technical quality. Although Baird lost the race to produce a viable system of high-definition television for public service, he had undoubtedly shown others the way and, whether or not he is accepted as the 'inventor' of television, his claim to priority in realizing the dream of 'seeing by wireless' is indisputable.
ELECTRONIC TELEVISION SYSTEM: the first was developed at 202 Green Street, Los Angeles by Philo T. Farnsworth, who succeeded in transmitting a low-definition image of his brother-in-law, Cliff Gardner, in the autumn of 1927. It was not until 1935, however, that he was ready to demonstrate a high-definition receiving and transmission system. Farnsworth's patents were assigned to RCA in 1939.

The first practicable system of electronic high-definition television to be brought into regular use for public-service broadcasting was the work of an EMI research team, which began experiments under the direction of Isaac Schoenberg in 1931. An electronic receiver was soon in operation, while the more difficult problem of electronic scanning had been solved by the spring of 1934 with the development of the Emitron camera. Early the following year Schoenberg decided on 405 lines as the standard of definition, and on 2 November 1936 the EMI-Marconi system came into regular operation with the inauguration of the BBC television service from Alexandra Palace.

The first
TELEVISION TRANSMISSION IN COLOUR
was made by John Logie Baird at the Baird Studios, 133 Long Acre, London on 3 July 1928 and showed red and blue scarves, a policeman's helmet, a man putting his tongue out, the glowing end of a cigarette and a bunch of red roses. *Nature* reported of a Press demonstration: 'Delphiniums and carnations appeared in their natural colours and a basket of strawberries showed the red fruit very clearly.' Baird's low-definition colour-television system employed a Nipkow scanning-disc with red, blue and green filters.
HIGH-DEFINITION COLOUR TELEVISION: the first public demonstration was made by John Logie Baird, whose 120-line system was used to transmit colour films on a 9 × 12ft screen at the Dominion Theatre, Tottenham Court Road, London on 4 February 1938. The first live demonstration was made from the Baird Studios at Crystal Palace on 17 February 1938. Baird employed a mirror-drum scanning system, and though the colour quality was reported to be of a high standard in controlled experiments, his continued refusal to consider electronic rather than mechanical means of transmission limited the possibilities of commercial development.

By January 1941 he had produced a 600-line 2 × 2½ft large-screen colour Tele-Radiogram which could also be used for BBC 405-line black and white transmissions. At the end of the war he formed a company, John Logie Baird Ltd, to produce these giant sets. Within a few months Baird was dead, and with him his dream of large-screen mechanical colour television.
COLOUR-TELEVISION SERVICE: the first scheduled experimental service was commenced by CBS from Station WCBW New York on 1 June 1941. Daily transmissions were made with a 375-line system developed by Dr Peter Goldmark (*see also* Long-Playing Record).

Regular, commercial colour transmissions were inaugurated by CBS from New York on 25 June 1951. The first sponsored colour show was a variety performance featuring Ed Sullivan, Arthur Godfrey and Faye Emerson, which went on the air at 4.35pm. The first colour series, Ivan T. Sanderson's *The World is Yours*, began

the following day. The sale of colour-television sets in the USA advanced very slowly, accounted for partly by high prices and partly by poor-quality colour during the early years of the service. In 1960 there were only 200,000 sets in the whole country; the colour 'explosion' began about 1965, and five years later there were well over 20 million colour sets.
GB: The first public demonstration of colour television by the BBC was made on 2 June 1953, when a special outside broadcast of the Coronation procession was relayed by closed circuit to the wards of the Great Ormond Street Hospital for Sick Children.

The first public reception of the BBC's colour television service occurred unofficially on 19 April 1967, when James Thomas, Television Critic of the *Daily Express*, who had acquired the first Radio Rentals colour set to come on the market, viewed a colour presentation of *Late Night Line Up* on BBC2. The commencement of the service was officially announced for the first time the next day and launched on 1 July 1967 with 7hr of colour transmissions, principally of lawn tennis from Wimbledon.

See also Television, Commercial.

The first
THEATRE
permanent and public, of which record survives was in existence at Ferrara in northern Italy by 1531.
COVERED THEATRE: the first was a converted hall in the Hôtel de Bourgogne in Paris, taken over and adapted for stage plays by the Confrérie de la Passion in 1548. The company had been formed in 1402 for the performance of Mystery Plays, which they continued to do for the next 146 years until their licence was withdrawn. Permission was granted for them to go on presenting plays providing they confined themselves to secular drama, and it was this restriction that encouraged the players to seek a permanent playhouse. After conversion, the theatre in the Hôtel de Bourgogne was furnished with a raised stage faced by a pit for standing patrons, with graduated tiers of benches rising to the back of the hall. The sides of the narrow auditorium were flanked by side galleries containing the most expensive seats. It remained in use as a theatre until the company withdrew to the Comédie-Française in 1673.
PURPOSE-BUILT COVERED THEATRE: the first was the Teatro Olimpico at Vicenza, Italy, designed by Andrea di Pietro (Palladio) shortly before his death in 1580. The building was completed by his pupil Vicenzo Scamozzi and opened on 3 March 1585 with a production of *Oedipus Rex*. The Teatro Olimpico is still in use and is now the world's oldest theatre.
GB: The first building known to have been used regularly for the public performance of plays was the Game Place House in Great Yarmouth, which was leased by the Town Corporation to one Robert Coppyng in 1539 for a period of 30 years at an annual rental of 5s. The terms of Coppyng's lease were that he should

permitt & suffre all suche players as ther audiens to haue the plesure & ese of the seid hows & gameplace at all suche tyme & tymes as eny interludes or playes ther shalbe ministred or played at eny tyme withought eny profight therof by hym or by his assign to be taken.

Prof. Glynne Wickham has written of the Game Place House in his *Early English Stages*: 'Here then, astonishing as it may seem, we have a municipally subsidized theatre legally established in a provincial city nearly forty years before Burbage, with the aid of private enterprise capital, erected his metropolitan house. . . .'

The first purpose-built theatre in Britain was The Theatre, opened at Finsbury Fields, Shoreditch by James Burbage and John Brayne in 1576. Although no details of its construction exist, Burbage's Theatre would probably have been hexagonal, with three tiers of boxes surrounding a pit open to the sky, and an apron stage. Admission to the pit of Elizabethan theatres was 1d, while seats in the gallery cost 2d. The Theatre was demolished in 1598 and its timbers used for the building of the celebrated Globe Theatre.

The first
THEATRICAL KNIGHTHOOD
was conferred on Sir Henry Irving in the Birthday Honours of 24 May 1895. At the time he was playing Don Quixote at the Lyceum and the audience, enraptured when he spoke the line 'Knighthood sits like a halo round my head', broke into spontaneous applause at the Housekeeper's reply 'But Master, you have never been knighted.' Irving received the accolade at Windsor on 18 July and the Queen departed from usual custom by adding after the formal words 'Rise Sir Henry' – 'It gives me very great pleasure, sir.'

The first
TOOTHBRUSH
is claimed by a 17th-century Chinese encyclopedia to have been invented in China in 1498. This prototype toothbrush is described as having bristles set in the handle at right angles and appears to have been of basically the same design as its modern counterpart.
GB: The earliest reference to toothbrushes is contained in a letter addressed to Sir Ralph Verney in 1649, asking him to purchase, during a forthcoming trip to Paris, some of those 'little brushes for making cleane of the teeth, most covered with sylver and some few with gold and sylver twiste, together with some petits bouettes to put them in'.

For how long after this it was necessary to send to Paris for a new toothbrush is not known, though the diary of Anthony à Wood for 1690 records that they could be bought in London from one J. Barret, who also sold shirts and sewing-thread. According to Messrs Floris of Jermyn Street, it was their custom in the 18th century to sell toothbrushes in sets containing five or six different sizes, though the reason for this remains obscure. The bristles were arranged in a circle and were of graduated lengths, coming to an apex in the middle.
NYLON TOOTHBRUSH: the first was Dr West's Miracle Tuft Toothbrush, with bristles made from Du Pont Exton, marketed in the USA in September 1938.
ELECTRIC TOOTHBRUSH: the first was manufactured by the Squibb Co of New York in 1961.

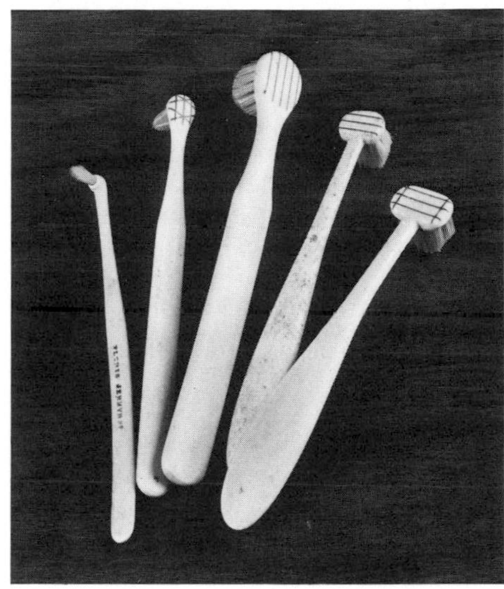

Set of Floris toothbrushes, c. *1800*

The first
TOTALIZATOR, AUTOMATIC
was devised by (Sir) George Alfred Julius of the consulting engineers Julius, Poole & Gibson of Sydney, N.S.W. and first installed at Ellerslie Racecourse, Auckland, New Zealand in March 1913. Julius was the son of the Archbishop of New Zealand. His invention was subsequently taken over by Automatic Totalisators Ltd, which set up machines at Sydney race-track

in 1917–18 and later exported them all over the world.

GB: The first automatic tote was installed at the Stadium Club, Wembley in January 1928 for the use of members betting on the greyhound-races held at Wembley Stadium.

The first tote used for horse-racing in Britain was operated under the control of the newly formed Racecourse Betting Control Board on the occasion of the Old Surrey and Burstow Point-to-Point held at Capt. Woolf Barnato's country estate, Ardenrun, on 25 April 1929.

The first permanent racecourse totalizators in Britain came into use at Carlisle and Newmarket on 2 July 1929. By 1934 the Racecourse Betting Control Board was operating totes on every racecourse in the country.

TOTE DAILY DOUBLE: the first was introduced at Connaught Park Racetrack, Ottawa, Canada at the instigation of Leo Dandurand in 1930.

The first
TRACTOR, AGRICULTURAL

petrol-driven, was the Burger, built in 1889 by the Charter Engine Co of Chicago, Ill., who coupled a single-cylinder Charter gasoline engine to the running-gear of a Rumely steam-traction engine. The fire-box, boiler and smoke-stack, which constituted the frame of the steam-engine, were replaced by a chassis, and a reverse gear was added. This first tractor, which was also the first petrol-engined vehicle in North America, was sold to a wheat-ranch near Madison, S. Dak. the same year. It performed sufficiently well for the Charter Engine Co to build six more, all of which were subsequently employed on wheat-farms in the Dakotas.

The pioneering role of the USA in tractor development is in sharp contrast to her belated acceptance of the petrol engine generally, which was several years behind the leading European nations. Steam-traction, however, had been developed on a fairly extensive scale on the prairies of the West. The flat ground and dry climate, combined with a shortage of manpower, made steam cultivation a practical and relatively economic proposition. Fuel, however, was in short supply and bulky and expensive to transport. With the development of an efficient internal-combustion engine, the substitution of petrol for steam was an obvious step towards effective farm mechanization.

The first production model to be advertised for sale was the Sterling Tractor, produced by the Charter Engine Co in 1893 and marketed by a Mr Hockett with financial backing from the farmers of Sterling, Kans. It is not known how many models were sold, but by this date there were already rivals appearing in the field. William Deering & Co had brought out a prototype in 1891, followed a year later by the Case Co of Wisconsin and by John Froelich of Froelich, Iowa, who formed the Waterloo Gasoline Traction Engine Co in 1893. One of the most successful of these pioneer tractors was the Otto, of which 14 models were sold between 1894 and 1896. Another model of the same period, produced by the Ohio Manufacturing Co, was notable as the first with a chassis specially designed to incorporate a petrol engine. There is no evidence, though, to suggest that any of these tractors was produced in a quantity large enough to be considered other than experimental until the advent of the Huber (prototype 1894), of which 30 were manufactured in 1898.

GB: The first petrol-driven agricultural tractor was the Ivel, a three-wheeler powered by a double-cylindered 8hp engine, which was built by Dan Albone (*see also* Cycle) of Biggleswade at his workshop in Shortmead Street and completed in 1902. 'Smiling Dan', as he was known to patrons of his Ivel Hotel in Biggleswade, was the son of a market-gardener and exemplar of the ingenious, self-taught mechanic. After building up a successful cycle business, producing the first practical ladies' bicycle and the first practical tandem machine, he turned his attention to the development of an agricultural tractor in 1897. Five years later, on 23 July 1902, he gave the first public demonstration of his prototype Ivel at G. Capon's farm at Old Warden, near Biggleswade, the machine being made to cut corn with a reaper. Further trials with a plough were held in August.

Commercial production began with the forming of Ivel Agricultural Motors Ltd in December 1902, a standard $1\frac{1}{2}$-ton 24hp model being offered at £300.

Albone has been described as 'the first to design a tractor rather than convert a traction engine'. Certainly the Ivel was the first light tractor in the world. A particularly advanced feature of the machine was its enclosed engine and transmission, which did not become a standardized part of tractor design until well after World War I. It was also fitted with a power take-off pulley for use with stationary farm machines.

Dan Albone himself died in the autumn of 1906, shortly after he had given a successful demonstration of night harvesting, but the Ivel Co survived until 1921, when it succumbed to the prevailing economic depression. During its 18 years' existence the Company produced about 900 tractors, many of them for the export market.

PNEUMATIC-TYRED TRACTOR: the first was the 17hp French Latil tractor, demonstrated at the World Tractor Trials held at Wallingford, Berkshire in June 1930. Its price in England was £655. Charles Cawood has written: 'With the pneumatic tyre, the tractor became, at last, Albone's universally useful farm machine; it could, for the first time in its life, do everything a horse could do and do it better and faster.'

Firestone in the USA, and Dunlop in Britain both began to manufacture specially designed pneumatic tractor tyres in 1932.

DIESEL-ENGINED TRACTORS were first produced in a number of countries almost simultaneously in 1930. Examples shown at the World Tractor Trials of that year included the Munktell from Sweden, Mercedes-Benz from Germany, and the Hungarian Hofherr-Schrantz. The British examples were the Marshall, the McLaren, the Aveling & Porter, and the Blackstone. The first American diesel-engined tractor was produced the same year by the Cummins Engine Co of Columbus, Ind.

See also Tractor, Crawler.

The first
TRACTOR, CRAWLER

commercially practical, was the Holt Steam Traction Engine No. 77, built by the Holt Manufacturing Co of Stockton, Calif., and tested for the first time on 24 November 1904. This machine was fitted with an endless track made up of wooden slats mounted on a linked steel chain. The first production model was sold to the Golden Meadow Developing Co for $5,500 in 1906 for use in Louisiana delta land. The same year saw the appearance in prototype form of the first petrol-engined crawler tractor, also by the Holt Co, and in 1908 the first production model went to work on the Los Angeles Aqueduct.

The first
TRAFFIC CONTROL: ONE-WAY STREETS

were introduced in London by an Act of Common Council passed in August 1617 to regulate 'the disorder and rude behaviour of Carmen, Draymen and others usinge Cartes'. The traffic order embraced 17 narrow and congested lanes leading into Thames Street, including Pudding Lane, where the Great Fire of London began in 1667. It remained in force for the following two centuries.

No further one-way traffic restrictions were made in Britain until September 1923, when the Birmingham City Corporation introduced what proved to be a very short-lived experiment. The measure aroused such fervent opposition from local traders that it was rescinded after being in operation little more than a fortnight.

The first permanently enforced one-way traffic order of the Motor Age was made in August 1924 by the Metropolitan Commissioner of Police in respect of Mare Street, Hackney, where traffic was only allowed to proceed in a southerly direction between Amhurst Road and Dalston Lane. The first permanent one-way street in the provinces is believed to have been St James Street, Nottingham, towards the end of 1924. As there were no recognized one-way traffic signs at this date, the prohibition was indicated by a large banner suspended across the street bearing the words 'One Way Traffic – No Road This Way'.

One-way gyratory traffic systems were introduced at Hyde Park Corner, Parliament Square, Trafalgar Square and the Buckingham Palace end of the Mall in the summer of 1926.

The first
TRAFFIC CONTROL: PARKING RESTRICTIONS
on motor traffic were imposed under Paragraph 28 of the Paris Police Ordinance of 14 August 1893, which stated:

Vehicles are not allowed to stand on the public way except when absolutely necessary; the standing of the vehicle is prohibited in all cases where it interferes with or impedes general traffic. No vehicle shall stand in a parallel line with another vehicle already standing at the opposite side of the road.

GB: There were no parking restrictions in London other than those relating to obstruction until the spring of 1930, when parking in Jermyn Street, and five other streets in the Piccadilly area, was restricted to one side of the road only on alternate days. This was indicated by signs on both sides of the street, with a single ring showing the days there was no parking on that side, and a double ring when the order applied to the other side.
FIXED-PENALTY PARKING-TICKETS were introduced in Britain under the Road Traffic Act 1960. The first motorist to fall foul of the new regulation was Dr Thomas Creighton, who on 19 September 1960 parked his Ford Popular car outside a West End hotel while he attended a patient suffering from a heart attack. Traffic Warden Frank Shaw issued a parking-ticket in perfect good faith, but there was an immediate outcry in the Press when the circumstances became known, and Dr Creighton did not have to pay the £2 fine.

See also Parking Meters.

The first
TRAFFIC CONTROL: WHITE ROAD MARKINGS
were devised by Edward Norris Hines, Road Commissioner for Wayne County, Mich., whose 'center line safety stripe' was painted on the surface of River Road, near Trenton, Mich. in the autumn of 1911.
GB: The first white lines were laid down on a number of dangerous bends on the London–Folkestone road at Ashford, Kent, in 1914. The idea was originated by County Alderman Amos, a farmer who used the road frequently, though he was not at that time a motorist. The work was undertaken by the County Surveyor for Kent, H. T. Chapman.

White lines became quite common on short stretches of road after World War I, but only in accordance with the Minister of Transport's policy of 'confining white lines to areas where special guidance is called for'. The first continuous centre-line over a distance was laid down on 5¼ miles of the Great West Road in 1931.

The first interrupted centre-line was laid down on 70 miles of the A30 and A38 in Devon in 1935. Double white lines were introduced in accordance with a European Agreement in 1957.
ARROWS AND DIRECTIONAL WHITE LINES were first painted on the road surface at Hyde Park Corner, London, and brought into operation on 22 March 1926. The *Illustrated London News* commented adversely:

The experiment in a gyratory system of traffic at Hyde Park Corner . . . was not altogether a success. There was considerable congestion on the road past St. George's Hospital, and confusion among drivers, resulting in seven minor collisions.

Hyde Park Corner was also designated one-way at this time.

The first
TRAFFIC-ISLANDS
were installed in the streets of Liverpool at the suggestion of John Hastings, a saddler who kept a shop on a busy and potentially dangerous corner. Hastings first put forward his idea of pedestrian refuges in 1860, but it was rejected by both the City Council and the Police Force. The following year, however, a prominent Liverpool stationer, John Walmsley, was knocked down and killed by a bus on the very spot Hastings had warned about, and in 1862 six traffic islands were constructed in various parts of the City, each with twin lamp-posts to light the crossing at night.

The first traffic-island in London was privately installed in St James's Street by Col Pierpoint in 1864, so that he would be able to reach the haven of his club without accident. The Colonel was wont to gaze over his shoulder to admire his island as he crossed the street, which on one notable occasion caused him to be knocked over by a cab.

The first
TRAFFIC-LIGHTS
were erected on a 22ft-high cast-iron pillar at the corner of Bridge Street and New Palace Yard off Parliament Square, London, and came into operation on 10 December 1868. The installation was made at the direction of the Metropolitan Commissioner of Police, Richard Mayne, and was intended principally for the benefit of MPs wishing to gain access to the Houses of Parliament. Manufactured by Saxby & Farmer, the traffic-signal was surmounted by a revolving lantern with red and green signals. Red indicated 'Stop' and green 'Caution'. The lantern, illuminated by gas, was turned by means of a lever at the base of the standard so that the appropriate light faced the oncoming traffic. Manning the lever was not without its hazards. The unfortunate constable assigned to this duty on 2 January 1869 was badly injured when the gas apparatus exploded and blew gravel into his eye. The signal was unpopular with the general public, one hansom-cab driver complaining that it was 'another of them fakements to wex poor cabbies'. It remained the only traffic-light in London, and after it was removed in 1872 there were no similar experiments for over half a century.
ELECTRIC TRAFFIC-LIGHTS DESIGNED TO CONTROL CONFLICTING STREAMS OF TRAFFIC: the first were erected by the American Traffic Signal Co in Cleveland, Ohio on 5 August 1914. The 15ft-high signal stood at the crossroads formed by Euclid Avenue and 105th Street, red and green lights being used in association with a warning buzzer. The French also adopted a sight-sound system, when the first traffic-signal in Paris was erected at the junction of Grands Boulevards and boulevard de Strasbourg in 1923. This consisted of a single manually operated light attached to a lamp-post with the word *HALTE* inscribed on the glass lens and a gong that was beaten to warn motorists when it was about to be switched on or off. The first traffic-signal with red, green and amber lights was brought into use in New York in 1918.
GB: A manually operated set of red, green and amber electric traffic-lights were installed at the junction of St James's Street and Piccadilly, in London's West End, by the Westing-

house Brake and Saxby Signal Co in July 1926.

The first automatic traffic-lights in Britain began functioning on 5 November 1927 at Princes Square crossroads in Wolverhampton. The installation was made by J. Boot, Chief Engineer for the Siemens & General Electric Railway Signal Co, and consisted of an aluminium signal-box, suspended above the centre of the roadway from cables, with red, green and amber lights facing in four directions. It remained in use until 1968.

VEHICLE-ACTUATED TRAFFIC-LIGHTS: the first in Britain, controlled by rubber pads set in the road, were set up at the junction of Gracechurch Street and Cornhill in the City of London by the Automatic Electric Co of Liverpool in 1932.

The first
TRAFFIC-SIGNS
in Britain were erected by local cycling clubs affiliated to the Bicycle Union in December 1879, and consisted of a wooden post with an enamelled iron plate bearing the warning: 'TO CYCLISTS – THIS HILL IS DANGEROUS'. The location of the 25 signs set up during the first year of the scheme is not known, but the minutes of the Bicycle Union for January 1881 record that danger-boards had recently been installed at Garrowby Top on the York–Scarborough road, Stepney Hill, Scarborough, and a hill in Dewsbury on the main road to Leeds.

The first local authority to erect a traffic sign was the Highway Board of Moreton-in-the-Marsh, Gloucestershire, which applied to the Bicycle Union in October 1881 for a warning sign for Bourton Hill.

Early traffic signs sometimes had something in common with modern 'shock' road-safety posters. This one surmounted a dangerously steep hill in Derbyshire at the beginning of the motoring era.

The first warning-sign directed specifically at motorists was erected at the top of Birdlip Hill, Gloucester by the (Royal) Automobile Association with the permission of Gloucestershire County Council in October 1901.

Local authorities were first empowered to erect traffic-signs for the guidance of motorists under the Motor Car Act 1903. A Local Government Board circular issued 10 March 1904 recommended (but did not require) the adoption of an 18in diameter white ring surmounting a plate for speed limits; a solid red disc for signs indicating prohibitions; a hollow red triangle with plate for warning-signs; and a diamond shape to signify crossroads, dangerous corners and 'precipitous places'. Not all local authorities accepted these suggestions, and the motoring organizations designed their own signs. The result was a confused proliferation of notices of varying shape and size and a haphazard choice of wording, often difficult for the passing motorist to assimilate at a glance. Statutory requirements for the employment of a standardized design were enjoined on local authorities under Section 48 of the Road Traffic Act 1930 and implemented in accordance with the *Report of the Departmental Committee on Traffic Signs* (1933).

The first uniform signs with a nationally agreed set of standardized symbols were adopted in France in 1903 at the instigation of the Association General Automobile. The symbols were painted in white on a rectangular black board. Those still in use include: Turn Left, Turn Right, Bridge, Level Crossing and Steep Hill.

The first internationally standardized signs – a red triangle surmounting a plate bearing an agreed symbol – were adopted by most European countries at the Convention on International Circulation of Motor Vehicles held in Paris in 1909. Britain was not a signatory, and it was not until 1929 that five of the international symbols – bend, crossroads, level-crossing with and without gates, and uneven road – were brought into use. The present range of continental signs was adopted by 30 European countries under the Protocol of the UN World Conference on Road and Motor Transport, Geneva, in 1949, and by GB, following the report of the Warboys Committee, in 1964. In Britain the change-over involved the replacement of some 1½ million obsolete signs.

The first
TRAVEL AGENCY TO ENGAGE IN THE TOURIST TRADE
was established by Thomas Cook of Leicester as an outcome of the cheap railway excursions for Temperance galas he had been organizing since 1841. The real beginnings of organized tourism can best be dated from Cook's first holiday excursion to Liverpool and North Wales in 1845, a forerunner of the modern package holiday (*q.v.*). The brochure announced: 'The Train will leave Leicester at Five o'clock in the Morning on Monday, August the 4th. . . . Parties will have to be wide awake at an early hour, or they will be disappointed. Promptitude on the part of the Railway Company calls for the same from passengers.' Later Cook wrote: 'The Advertisement of the trip created such a sensation, that at Leicester the tickets issued at fifteen shillings first class, and ten shillings second, were in many instances resold at double those rates.'

The tourists could choose between spending the four-day holiday in Liverpool, probably at one of the seven Temperance Hotels recommended in the brochure, or they could stay overnight and proceed to Caernarvon at 8am by the specially chartered packet-boat *Eclipse*. The boat returned from Caernarvon on Wednesday morning, the 350 holiday-makers having enjoyed in the meantime the opportunity of visiting Snowdon and 'beholding from its summit the opening dawn and the rising sun'. For this part of the trip Thomas Cook secured the services of the only English-speaking Welshman he could find in Caernarvon to act as guide. Those who were disinclined to spend a night on the bare mountain were assured by their mentor that there were several passable inns at its foot. The indefatigable Mr Cook himself, however, was among those who climbed to the summit, from which point, he wrote afterwards, he 'looked toward Ben Lomond and Ben Nevis, and determined to get to Scotland the next year, or know the reason why'. This decision set the course of his life and established tourism as an industry.

The following year Cook established a booking-office at 26 Granby Street, Leicester, an indication that his activities as an excursionist were becoming more than just a sideline to his main business of printing and publishing Temperance tracts. The first of the Scottish tours began on 25 June 1846, when a party of 350 excursionists departed from Leicester and Derby for five days in Edinburgh, Glasgow and the Burns country. On arrival at Glasgow they were conducted to the Town Hall behind a brass band, and there entertained to a series of morally uplifting speeches, including one on 'The Natural, Moral and Political Effects of Temperance' that lasted a full hour. The inhabitants of

Edinburgh treated them to more speeches, lightened on this occasion by the addition of 'appropriate tunes on the pianoforte' by the Misses Blake. For the rest of the holiday they were free to enjoy themselves. Cook was asked afterwards whether it was safe for women to join his Scottish tours, to which he replied emphatically in the affirmative. 'Despite the trappings of prevailing fashion', which sometimes caused these redoubtable ladies problems when 'climbing over precipices, and among rude blocks of granite and basalt', he considered that 'many of them often put to shame the "masculine" effeminates'.

CONTINENTAL HOLIDAY TOUR: the first was organized by Thomas Cook in 1855, one year after he had discontinued his printing and publishing business to devote himself exclusively to the travel agency. The first of two parties of about 50 tourists left Harwich for Antwerp on 4 July. They were personally conducted by Mr Cook to Brussels, the Field of Waterloo, Aix-la-Chapelle, Cologne, up the Rhine to Mayence, Mannheim, Frankfurt, Heidelberg, Baden-Baden, Strasburg, Paris, and home via Le Havre and Southampton. Cook wrote afterwards a trifle wistfully: 'These were charming Tours, but denuded of much of their enjoyment by pecuniary losses.' He was considerably cheered, however, on receiving a letter of gratitude from

a working man – a model for his order – who having carefully husbanded his surplus earnings, first paid £6 for a Ticket for the long route, and with about £4 additional managed to enjoy a treat. . . . Many a working man who spends £20 a year in 'drink and bacca' would stand appalled at the idea of appropriating half that sum to a trip on the Continent.

By 1865, when he opened his first London office, Cook was offering regular tours to France, Switzerland, Italy, Belgium, the Netherlands, Germany and Austria, and was soon to venture far farther afield, including the USA (1866) and the Middle East (1868). For the next 25 years he enjoyed a virtual monopoly of the holiday-travel business and the phrase 'Cook's tour', used colloquially of any circuitous journey, passed into the everyday currency of the English language.

See also Package Holiday; Air Charter Holiday; Motor-Coach Tour; Ocean Cruise.

The first
TRAVELLERS' CHEQUES
were invented by Robert Herries as a substitute for the Letter of Credit, which could be used only on a pre-planned route. Herries founded the London Exchange Banking Co in St James's Street, London and began issuing his 'Circular Notes' in denominations of £20 and upwards on 1 January 1772. They were negotiable in 90 cities from Moscow to Madrid and guaranteed against theft. No commission was charged, profits coming from the use of customers' capital. The peak year of business was 1839, when notes to the value of £120,000 were on issue.

The present form of travellers' cheque, incorporating the counter-signature system, and negotiable at hotels and ticket agencies as well as banks, was devised by Marcellus Berry of American Express, known as 'The Edison of Finance'. His employer, James C. Fargo, had spent the summer of 1890 on a tour of Europe and complained to Berry that his efforts to secure currency outside the main cities had been continually frustrated. The first American Express travellers' cheque was cashed for $50 at the Hotel Hauffe, Leipzig by Fargo's son William on 5 August 1891.

The first
TYPEWRITER
of practical utility was built in 1808 by Pellegrine Turri of Reggio Emilia, Italy for his blind friend the Countess Carolina Fantoni. The two maintained a regular correspondence and 16 of the Countess's typewritten letters, dating from 1808 to 1810, are preserved at the Reggio State Archives. No details of the construction of the machine are recorded, other than the fact that the type impression was originally made with carbon paper, later with an ink applicator. It may be inferred, though, that the type was arranged on plungers which could be depressed directly down on to the paper. There were 27 characters, the 23 letters of the Italian alphabet in upper case and four punctuation marks.

TYPEWRITER IN REGULAR SERIES PRODUCTION: the first was the Danish *Skrivekugle* (Writing Ball), invented by Pastor Malling Hansen and manufactured by the Jürgens Mekaniske Establissement of Copenhagen in October 1870. Constructed of brass and steel, the flat-bed Hansen machine weighed 165lb and worked on the radial-plunger principle. Its 52 keys were angled in a hemispherical mounting in such a way that each, when depressed, would extend to a common printing point. The paper lay in a flat-bed case which moved laterally along guide rails one character space at a time. The price of the machine was £100 when it was marketed in Britain in 1872, though later versions sold for as little as £17. The Hansen typewriter was sold all over Europe and America and many models were still in use at the time of World War I.

The first commercially produced keyboard machine, forerunner of the modern typewriter, was developed by Christopher Latham Sholes and originally manufactured by his financial backer, James Densmore, in a Milwaukee wheelright's shop in June 1872. To begin with there was no standardized model, each machine incorporating the latest ideas of its promoters.

Although the keys were originally arranged in alphabetical order, Sholes and Densmore decided on a new arrangement based on the order of type in a printer's case. The first machine incorporating the 'universal' keyboard still in use (with only slight amendments) was completed by 8 November 1872, when Densmore wrote a letter to his son on it saying that 'the change was better to be made than not'.

Nearly all Sholes's output during the first year of production was sold to telegraphers, shorthand-reporters, lawyers and other professional men – scarcely any to commercial firms, and only one sale to a Government office is recorded. One of the 1872 models was sold to Allan Pinkerton, founder of the private detective agency that bears his name, and a number of machines were ordered by James O. Clephane, who set up the first commercial typewriting service the same year with offices in Washington and New York. During the course of 1872 James Densmore's brother Emmett sailed for England to take out British patents and arrange a sales agency.

In the winter of 1873 James Densmore opened the first typewriter-shop at 4 Hanover Street, New York, where Sholes's machine, now standardized for series production, was retailed at a price of $125. The basic design features of this model were similar to those of most modern typewriters with three important exceptions – it printed only in capital letters; the text was not visible to the operator while typing; and there was no back space.

Meanwhile the two partners, Sholes and Densmore, had signed a contract (1 March 1873) for the mass production of their machine by the Remington Small Arms Co of Ilion, New York. The Remington model was marketed as the Sholes & Glidden Type-Writer (Carlos Glidden had assisted Sholes at various stages of development) on 1 July 1874. Mechanically, this typewriter (renamed the 'Remington No. 1' in 1876) followed the design of the Milwaukee machines almost exactly, the only significant difference being in the casing, metal having replaced wood. The price remained unchanged at $125.

Of the 400 customers who purchased Remington typewriters during the remaining months of 1874, the most notable was undoubtedly Mark Twain, who saw a model displayed in a store-window in Boston while out for a walk one day with his friend and fellow humorist Petroleum V. Nasby. The two men were unable to agree on what purpose the machine was intended to serve, so they went inside to ask. The salesman explained, adding that it could write at a speed of 57 words a minute. Twain replied that this was quite impossible. A 'lady typewriter' was summoned and began to operate the machine while Twain and Nasby stood by with watches in their hands. At the end of a minute she had written exactly 57 words. Twain said it was a fluke, so she did it again. The rest of the afternoon was happily passed in further demonstrations, the two spectators stuffing the typewritten pages into their pockets as fast as they came off the typewriter, to keep as souvenirs. It was only on returning to their hotel that they looked at the papers closely enough to see that they all contained the same sentence, repeated over and over again, but if Twain felt he had been duped, it was too late to alter the fact that he had already become the first author to possess a typewriter.

During the first 10 years of production, sales of the Remington typewriter were disappointingly small. One of the main reasons for sluggish sales was the use of aniline inks for typewriter ribbons. This retarded the adoption of typewriters by Government departments and other institutions requiring permanent records, as the typescript was liable to fade. The breakthrough came in 1885 with the introduction of permanent inks, which was soon to have the effect (coupled with other improvements) of making the typewriter an essential item of office equipment, rather than a novelty or status symbol. A year later the *Scientific American* estimated that there were approximately 50,000 typewriters of all makes in use in the USA, and by 1890 there were 30 manufacturers competing for custom.

GB: The first typewriter manufactured in Britain was designed by the celebrated magician John Nevil Maskelyne and produced by the Maskelyne British Typewriter & Manufacturing Co Ltd of London in 1889. This model embodied two unusual features – a shift key that could be operated either by hand or foot, according to the customer's preference, and differential spacing, enabling each character to occupy a space appropriate to its width, as in printing. The latter idea was reintroduced by IBM in 1941.

TYPEWRITER INCORPORATING A SHIFT KEY: the first capable of inscribing text in both capital and lower-case letters, was the Remington No. 2 of 1878.

'BAR' TYPEWRITER: the first model designed so that the writing was visible to the typist was the Horton, manufactured in Toronto, Canada in 1883.

PORTABLE TYPEWRITER: the first was designed by George C. Blickensderfer of Erie, Pa. in 1889, and produced by the Blickensderfer Manufacturing Co of Stamford, Conn. in 1893 as the Blick No. 5. Although light-weight typewriters had been produced earlier, some of them, like the 7lb Hall of 1883–4, actually described as portables, the Blick was the first that folded neatly into a carrying-case for easy handling.

ELECTRIC TYPEWRITER: the first in commercial production was a type-bar machine designed by Dr Thaddeus Cahill of Washington D.C. and manufactured by the Cahill Writing Machine Co in 1901. Only 40 units were built at a development cost of $157,000 before the enterprise was abandoned.

The first successful electric typewriter was the Blickensderfer Electric of 1902, a type-wheel machine operating on the same principle as modern 'golf ball' electrics. Very sophisticated technically, it would probably have gained greater recognition if more offices had had mains electricity.

The first
TYPISTS

The earliest record of female office-workers being recruited as typists is contained in an advertisement placed in the New York paper *The Nation* for 15 December 1875 by the Remington agents Locke, Yost & Bates Ltd. 'Mere girls', it ran, 'are now earning from $10 to $20 a week with the "Type-Writer", and we can secure good situations for one hundred expert writers on it in counting-rooms in this City.'

These wages were abnormally high for female workers of the period and probably reflect the scarcity of competent typists only a year after full-scale production of typewriters had been initiated by the Remington Co. By the following decade the beginner's rate had fallen appreciably, but was still favourable compared to that of female shop-assistants. Speaking before a women's club at New Orleans in 1888, a typewriter-salesman called Harry Hodgson said that a typist would start at $6 a week if reasonably proficient, and might eventually earn as much as $20 if she proved her worth. A shop-girl could only expect $6 as a top salary. Moreover the typist only worked from 8.30am to 5.30pm and was given a full ½hr off for lunch; the counter clerk might be on her feet for 12hr or more a day. The effect of the typewriter in liberating young women of the lower middle class from the bondage of the home was immeasurable. Previously the nearest approach they had made to office employment was as telegraphists. With the advent of the typewriter, and soon afterwards the telephone (*q.v.*), women began to take their place in offices, not as a rare, privileged exception, but in order to fulfil tasks that in general they were better fitted to do than their male colleagues.

GB: The first known female office typists to secure employment were two 'Lady Typewriters', who began work at the Inland Revenue Office in London on 12 March 1887. They were segregated from the male workers in a special room of their own, and documents for copying were handed through a hatch. They only became visible once a week, on pay-day, when they were escorted to the cashier's office by two messengers, one going in front and the other behind.

It is possible that some typists may have been employed by commercial firms at an earlier date, though in general, English businessmen were considerably more conservative in their attitude to having women in their offices than their American counterparts.

TRAINING COURSE FOR OFFICE TYPISTS: the first was offered in 1877 by the Central Branch of the YWCA in New York City. The eight pioneer girl students were chosen for physique rather than aptitude, as it was claimed that the arduous six months' course was beyond the capacity of female minds and constitutions. Despite the condemnations from many quarters – one critic described it as 'an obvious error in judgement by well meaning but misguided ladies' – all eight girls survived the course and secured immediate employment on graduation. The YWCA was then inundated with requests for more trained typists and was able to establish the course on a more permanent footing.

The first
TYPIST, TOUCH

was Frank McGurrin, Official Stenographer of the Salt Lake City Federal Court, who demonstrated his prowess in public for the first time in a speed-typing contest held at Cincinnati on 25 July 1888. McGurrin used 10 fingers to operate his Remington and never looked at the keyboard; his opponent, typing-instructor Louis Taub, was a four-finger typist, and kept his eyes on the keyboard of his Caligraph typewriter all the time. Taub lost not only his $500 stake but also his reputation as a speed typist, while the challenger won a victory for his own system of typing that was to have a profound effect on the methods used to train typists all over the world.

The first recorded
UMBRELLAS
(waterproof) are listed in an inventory of the moveable effects of King Louis XIII of France made in 1637. The entry refers to: 'Eleven sunshades in various colours, made of taffeta. Three umbrellas of oiled cloth, trimmed underneath with gold and silver lace.' This is the earliest-known instance of the sunshade, used by ancient civilizations, being distinguished from its counterpart, the waterproof umbrella. Neither the King, nor any of his male courtiers, is likely to have carried one of these decorative trimmed umbrellas, but it is quite probable that Louis's beautiful Queen, Anne of Austria, went abroad under a protective canopy of oiled silk, setting a style that was to be followed assiduously by the women of France.

The prejudice against the use of the umbrella by men was probably dissipated earlier in France than in any other European country. When the Parisian manufacturer Marius produced the first folding pocket-umbrella with a collapsible shaft in 1715, he advertised his wares by means of an illustrated poster which shows a decorative model being carried by a lady of fashion, and a plain, unadorned masculine style of umbrella being held aloft by a man in a tricorn hat.
GB: The earliest reference in English literature that can be taken as an indication that the waterproof umbrella was already in use dates from 1696, and is contained in Jonathan Swift's *A Tale of a Tub*. Swift writes of his character Jack: 'A large skin of parchment . . . served him for a night-cap when he went to bed, and for an umbrella in rainy weather.' From 1708, when Kersey's *Dictionarium Anglo-Britannicum* defined the umbrella as 'a kind of broad fan or skreen, commonly us'd by women to shelter them from the rain', literary references become increasingly frequent, but their emphasis is always on its use as an exclusively female accessory. Umbrellas were commonly kept at coffee-houses to protect the customers as they left to enter their carriages, but for a man to be actually seen carrying one was to invite the kind of ridicule implied in the following advertisement, which appeared in the *Female Tatler* on 12 December 1709:

The young gentleman belonging to the custom house, that for fear of the rain borrowed the umbrella at Will's coffee house, in Cornhill, of the mistress, is hereby advertised that to be dry from the head to foot on the like occasion, he shall be welcome to the maid's pattens.

Umbrellas in the 18th century were comparatively expensive. Ambrose Barnes, writing in 1718, itemized: 'Umbrella for the Church's use 25s', and the Churchwarden's Accounts of Burnley, Surrey record: 'Paid for umbrella £2 10s 6d.' For this reason, umbrellas were often held as common property, to be lent out from coffee-house, club or church porch when the weather demanded. Cambridge University in 1730s maintained one umbrella for the use of all the undergraduates, booking being well in advance.

Not until the closing years of the 18th century did the stronger sex cease to regard the umbrella as an insult to its manhood. The philanthropist Jonas Hanway is often cited as being the first man in London to carry an umbrella with any degree of regularity, adopting the practice after his return from a 7yr journey through Russia and Persia in 1750. According to his biographer John Pugh, 'when it rained, a small parapluie defended his face and wig; thus he was always prepared to enter into any company without impropriety or the appearance of negligence . . . after carrying one near thirty years, he saw them come into general use'. In the meantime he was obliged to suffer the insults of coachmen and the criticism of the Godly, who maintained that he was defying the heavenly purpose of rain, which was to make people wet.

John MacDonald, a footman who wrote his autobiography in 1790, relates that 12 years earlier he used to be greeted with the shout 'Frenchman, Frenchman! Why don't you call a coach!' whenever he went out with his 'fine silk umbrella, newly brought from Spain'. At the date he was writing, said MacDonald, umbrellas had become everywhere accepted and 'a very useful branch of business'.

The 19th century saw an advance from the oily canvas 'gamp' with its bulging whalebone ribs, fit only for the worst of weathers, to a silken, pencil-slim creation suited to the adornment of a gentleman of the highest rank. France again led the way, when in 1829 Messrs Odiot opened a factory in Paris, devoted exclusively to the production of superior-quality umbrella silk. The weight of the average umbrella had been progressively reduced from 3lb 8oz in 1645 to 1lb 13oz in 1740, and 13¼oz by 1840, but only at the cost of less resilient frames. This problem was solved in 1852 by Samuel Fox of Stockbridge in Yorkshire, who was the first to successfully adopt the fluted steel rib for umbrella-manufacture. Since that time there has been no radical change in basic design.

The first
UNDERGROUND RAILWAY
was conceived by Charles Pearson, the City Solicitor and Liberal Member for Lambeth, who submitted plans for the undertaking to the Royal Commission on Metropolitan Railways in 1846. The North Metropolitan Railway Co was founded in 1853, and after a considerable delay because of financial difficulties the first shaft was sunk at Euston Square, London, in January 1860. The 4-mile-long Metropolitan Railway was eventually opened to fare-paying passengers at 6am on 10 January 1863. There were seven stations, with termini at Farringdon Street and Paddington, and the journey took 33min overall. Passenger compartments were lit with gas which, according to the *Daily Telegraph*, 'in some instances was turned on so strong in the first-class carriages . . . that newspapers might be read with ease'. On the opening day, six engines each drawing four carriages left at 15min intervals, and made a total of 120 journeys in both directions, carrying over 30,000 passengers.

The District Line was opened from High Street, Kensington, to Gloucester Road on 1 October 1868. The South Kensington Station also served the Gloucester Road–South Kensington track of the Metropolitan Line, so for the first time it was possible to change from one Underground train to another.
TUBE RAILWAY: the first was the Tower Subway, which ran from the City to South London, passing under the Thames. It was constructed in 1869–70 by James Greathead of Grahamstown, South Africa, using his Greathead Shield which enabled a tunnel to be driven through the earth without the necessity of surface excavation. A cable-drawn railway was operated along the tube, 1,430ft long, from 2 August 1870 to 23 December 1870, with fares of 2d 1st Class and 1d 2nd Class. The service failed to pay its way, and after the removal of the track the tunnel became a pedestrian

subway until the opening of Tower Bridge in 1894.

UNDERGROUND SYSTEM TO BE ELECTRIFIED, and the first successful tube railway, was the City & South London Railway (now the City branch of the Northern Line), officially opened on Tuesday, 4 November 1890, when the Prince of Wales made the first royal progress by Underground from King William Street to the Oval. (The terminus was one stop farther on, at Stockwell.) Passenger service commenced on 18 December 1890 with a flat-rate fare of 2d for any distance. There were no tickets, fares being paid at a turnstile. Fourteen four-wheel 12-ton electric locomotives built by Mather & Platt of Manchester, each drew three carriages at an average speed of $11\frac{1}{2}$mph. The carriages came to be known as 'padded cells' to the travelling public, as they were fitted with 5ft-high upholstered seats for the full length of the car, reaching up to a narrow, horizontal slit of window at eye-level. They were, however, the first carriages on the Underground to be lit by electric light. Sliding doors at the front and rear of the cars let out on to a metal platform, and gatemen were positioned between each carriage to operate the lattice entrance gates.

The first tube trains drawn by motor-cars (locomotive and carriage embodied in one car) were introduced by the Waterloo & City Railway between Waterloo and the Bank on 18 August 1898. The cars were built by Jackson & Sharp of Wilmington, USA.

COIN-OPERATED TICKET-MACHINES were first installed by the Central London Railway (now Central Line) in 1904. These had pull-bar control. The first automatic (electric) ticket-machines were installed on the Hampstead (now Northern), Piccadilly, Bakerloo and District Lines in Jackson & Sharp of Wilmington, USA.

UNDERGROUND MAP: the first to show all lines, with a different colour for each line, was issued in 1908 as a result of the efforts of Albert Stanley (later Lord Ashfield) to co-ordinate the separate lines into a unified Underground system. Six million copies of the map were published during the first year of issue.

CARRIAGES WITH AUTOMATIC DOORS: the first were built by Cammell Laird and introduced on the Piccadilly Line in 1922.

WOMEN EMPLOYED ON THE LONDON UNDERGROUND first began duties as ticket-collectors and porters on 17 September 1940. Their original uniform of white dust-coat and grey kepi was later replaced by blue tunics and berets.

AUTOMATIC TICKET BARRIER: the first on the London Underground was installed at Stamford Brook on 5 January 1964.

AUTOMATIC TUBE TRAINS (driverless): the first on the London Underground began regular trials on the Central Line between Woodford and Hainault on 5 April 1964.

The first *UNIVERSITY MAGAZINE*

was the *Student*, published at Oxford University, with the imprint of the London bookseller and publisher John Newbery (*see also* Children's Magazine) from 31 January 1750 to July 1751. The editor was the poet Christopher Smart, a Fellow of Pembroke Hall, Cambridge, who has been described by one unflattering biographer as a bookseller's hack, who 'made for some years a hard living betwixt improvidence, dissipation, and a wife and children'. The wife was John Newbery's daughter. He was later confined to a madhouse, where he wrote his most famous poem – 'A Song for David' – using a key to scratch its 86 stanzas on the wainscot, writing-paper having been denied him. The *Student* ran for 19 issues and is generally considered to possess little literary distinction other than a contribution from Dr Johnson.

The first distinctively undergraduate magazine was an Oxford publication called *The Undergraduate* which began in 1819.

The first *VACUUM CLEANER*

power operated, was devised by bridge-engineer Hubert Cecil Booth in 1901, after watching an attempt to clean a Midland Railway carriage by compressed air at St Pancras Station in London. The compressed-air method would create clouds of dust, but as there was no way of removing it the dirt simply settled again. Seated in a restaurant with other witnesses afterwards, Booth declared that he believed the answer was to suck the dirt into a receptacle, instead of trying to blow it away. The others were sceptical, so he placed a pocket-handkerchief over the back of the seat, put his lips to it, and sucked. A ring of black spots on the handkerchief showed that his principle was sound. A prototype machine was built and on 25 February 1902 Booth issued a prospectus of his newly formed Vacuum Cleaner Co Ltd.

Since few houses were served with electricity, and the apparatus was expensive and cumbersome, it was decided not to sell cleaners outright but to provide a cleaning-service on demand. A powerful vacuum pump, driven by either a petrol or an electric motor, was mounted on a four-wheel horse-drawn van, and stationed by the kerbside outside a customer's house. The dust was then sucked out of carpets and soft furnishings through 800ft-long hoses which passed through the first-floor windows and thence to any part that needed cleaning. In a BBC radio *Scrapbook* programme Booth recalled that so atrocious was the noise of the machine that he was frequently sued for allegedly frightening passing horses, cab-proprietors being particularly hostile. When finally a test case was taken to appeal, the Lord Chief Justice upheld his right to operate the machines in the street.

One of the earliest successes of the Vacuum Cleaner Co occurred in connection with the Coronation of King Edward VII in 1902. When all the other preparations in the Abbey were complete, it was found that the deep-pile blue carpets under the twin thrones were in a deplorable state, and by this time it was too late to remove them for cleaning by conventional means. Booth heard of the predicament and approached the Board of Works with an offer of assistance. Within hours a machine was standing in the Cloister Quadrangle and the hoses being led into the Abbey. The King was delighted with the story when it came to his ears and commanded a demonstration at Buckingham Palace, which both he and Queen Alexandra watched. Booth was obliged to make an exception to his 'no sales' policy when an order was received for two complete vacuum cleaners, one for the Palace and the other for Windsor Castle.

As a result of this royal patronage vacuum cleaners won rapid favour with society hostesses, not only for their practical utility, but as a tea-party attraction. Soirées were held at which the guests were entertained by a team of Vacuum Cleaner Cooperatives going to work on the carpets and upholstery. As an added novelty Booth provided visible inspection tubes so that the audience could watch the dirt as it was sucked into the machine outside.

The first portable electric vacuum cleaner for domestic use was a 92lb trolley-mounted model marketed by Messrs Chapman & Skinner of San Francisco in 1905. A somewhat similar, though lighter, portable machine was produced in England by the Vacuum Cleaner Co of Victoria Street, London the following year.

The prototype of the modern, upright vacuum cleaner with dust-bag attached to the handle was built in 1907 by J. Murray Spangler, janitor in a department store at New Berlin (now Canton), Ohio. Crudely fashioned out of wood and tin, Spangler's machine was fitted with a broom-handle and an old pillow-case begged from his wife for a dust-bag. Nevertheless, it attracted the favourable attention of W.H. Hoover, a New Berlin harness-maker, who was aiming to diversify, as his business had been hit by the advent of the automobile. Having purchased Spangler's rights he produced the first commercial model in 1908, price $70. So successful was the new venture, that within three years Hoover was able to establish a separate factory in Canada, and it was from here that his Suction Sweeper Co began the export of upright vacuum cleaners to Britain in 1912. While Spangler's name has been largely forgotten, Hoover's has not only become generic but enjoys the rare distinction of having been made into a verb – as in 'hoovering the carpet'.

The first
VENDING-MACHINES
operating on the coin-in-the-slot principle were the so-called 'honesty' tobacco-boxes, which are known to have made their appearance in English taverns by 1615. Insertion of a penny in the slot would release the lock on the lid of the box, enabling the customer to take out a pipeful of tobacco. A strong element of trust entered into this method of vending, relying as it did on the purchaser taking no more than the permissible pipeful, and on his shutting the lid again, though it is unlikely the box was ever allowed out of the publican's range of vision. These primitive vending-machines remained in use until well into the 19th century.
AUTOMATIC VENDING-MACHINE: the earliest capable of working with reasonable proficiency was patented in Germany by Carl Ade in 1867. Though intended for selling handkerchiefs, cigarettes and confectionery, it is not certain whether it was ever actually put into operation.

The first automatic vending-machine to achieve commercial success was a postcard machine designed by Percival Everitt, and set up on the platform of Mansion House Underground Station, London, in 1883. Traditionally this apparatus is supposed to have delivered two postcards for ½d, but in view of the fact that only ½d-stamped postcards were allowed to be sold at this date, it seems more probable that it was a penny-in-the-slot machine. The Victorian public, it would appear, were no better behaved when confronted with slot-machines than the vandals of a later generation. 'It has been found in practice', said Everitt in his American patent application of 1886, 'that although the apparatus is perfectly successful when not designedly misused, articles such as paper, orange-peel, and other rubbish have been maliciously placed in the slit provided for the admission of the coin. . . .' Notwithstanding these discouraging setbacks, he pressed ahead with development and on 25 November 1887, the Sweetmeat Automatic Delivery Co was organized to exploit the machines on a nation-wide basis. The range of goods sold was not as restricted as the title suggests, for within a year or two, commodities available at the drop of a coin in the slot included cigarettes, eggs, quinine, biscuits, scent, handkerchiefs, condensed milk, towels, cough lozenges, sugar and accident insurance.

The spread of automatic vending to other countries followed rapidly, the first American machines, which sold chewing-gum (*q.v.*), starting to do business in 1888, and the first in France, operated by a society for the blind, making their appearance on railway stations the next year. The Americans lost no time in adapting the vending principle for everything from gambling (1889) to the bulk sale of peanuts (1901). By the mid 1890s the citizens of Corinne, Utah, were able to obtain divorce papers automatically from a machine that proffered this service in exchange for two silver dollars in one slot and one half dollar in another. The Germans were equally inventive, pioneering the automat or coin-operated restaurant in 1895, and reaching what may have been ultimate in bizarre slot-salesmanship in 1924, when a Berlin newspaper reported that a machine had just come into operation that would dispense a valid American doctorate for the equivalent of $1.

For other coin-operated machines, *see* Jukebox; Parking Meter; Postage Stamp: Machine; Underground Railway: Ticket-Machine.

The first
VETERAN MOTORING
as an organized activity stemmed from a letter written by H.E. Rendall to an English motor-cycling magazine in 1910. He suggested that motor cycles built *c.* 1900, which were then being sold off for £1 or £2, should be preserved for posterity. The following year some members of the North West London Motor Cycling Club took up the idea by founding an 'Old Tanks Club', limiting themselves to a capital outlay of £7 for the purchase of suitably antique machines. A number of light-hearted racing events were held in the atmosphere of levity that characterized the early veteran motoring movement. The 'Old Tanks' did not remain alone in the field for long, the Streatham Motor Cycling Club organizing a veteran run to Brighton in 1914, for motor cycles over 10 years old.

Eighty-one-year-old Karl Benz participating in the Automobil-Korso at Munich in 1925. The car was only 40!

VETERAN CAR RALLY: the first was held at Munich on 12 July 1925, in celebration of the 25th Anniversary of the Allgemeine Schnauferlklub. The historical Automobil-Korso included the oldest petrol-driven car in the world, a three-wheeled Benz of 1886 (*see also* Motor Car), driven by the 81-year-old Karl Benz himself. Also in attendance, driving or riding in vehicles a little more juvenile, were Karl Opel, Emil Stoewer, Auguste Horch, Heinrich Kleyer and other pioneers of the German motor industry.
GB: In a quite different spirit – the reverence was totally lacking – the *Daily Sketch* organized an Old Cars Competition on 13 October 1927, from the paper's offices in Gray's Inn Road to Olympia. There were 43 starters, and the first prize of £100 went to John Bryce, driver of a Panhard claimed to date from 1893. 'As each old vehicle made its appearance it was a signal for cheers and roars of laughter', the *Daily Sketch* reported the following day. 'Sairey Gamp umbrellas and Victorian fashions were paraded in several of the cars.'

It was on this occasion that the *Daily Sketch* adopted the unfortunate sobriquet 'old crocks', which veteran motorists have been attempting to exorcize ever since. The Olympia rally was followed by the first of the annual

Brighton Runs, also sponsored by the *Daily Sketch*, which was held on 12 November 1927. Out of an entry of 51, only 10 cars failed to arrive at Brighton within the time-limit. Unlike the Brighton Run today, the event was competitive. Once again the winner was John Bryce from Lanark, who announced to reporters afterwards that he had driven his 1893 Panhard over 9,000 miles in the previous two-and-a-half years.

VETERAN CAR CLUB: the first was founded in 1930, at the instigation of Capt. J.H. Wylie, 'to whom', it was said, 'the vulgarity of comic costumes, etc. was little less than nauseating'. His primary intention was to form an association that could take over the management of the Brighton Run from the *Daily Sketch*, and conduct it on more dignified lines. In the event the RAC agreed to take over the sponsorship of the Run, but Capt. Wylie and S.C.H. Davis, the like-minded Sports Editor of the *Autocar*, decided to continue with the idea of forming a club for participants. Accordingly a meeting was held at Brighton on 23 November 1930, following that year's Run, and the Veteran Car Club of Great Britain formally established.

The first
WALLPAPER

known, was uncovered at the Master's Lodgings, Christ's College, Cambridge during the course of restoration in 1911, and is believed to date from 1509. The black and white design was an imitation of Oriental velvet or brocade, with a central motif consisting of a pine-cone surrounded by strap-work and foliage. A Lombardic 'H' appears half way up on the left-hand side, and opposite this the image of a bird. These two variations from the otherwise symmetrical pattern indicate that it was almost certainly the work of the printer Hugo Goes, who employed the mark of an 'H' and a goose as a form of signature. Originally from Beverley, Yorkshire, in 1509 Goes was carrying on his printing business at Steengate, York.

The paper itself consisted of discarded printed documents, the design being printed on the reverse from a woodblock 16 × 11in. These documents include a poem on the death of Henry VII (21 April 1509), a proclamation issued on the accession of Henry VIII, and an indulgence of about the same time embellished with the della Rovere arms. The dating accords with the fact that the building of the Master's Lodgings was completed towards the end of 1509.

In continental Europe there is no authentic evidence of wallpaper earlier than 1568, when one Herman Schinkel of Delft was arraigned for printing an heretical book. According to the records of the trial, Schinkel was in the habit of using up old ballad paper by printing the reverse with a design of stripes or roses and selling it as wallpaper.

The earliest-known Chinese wallpapers date from the mid 16th century, and were usually presented to their foreign customers by Chinese merchants as gifts. There is no evidence that the Chinese used wallpaper in their own homes, which were generally decorated with hand-painted silken wall-hangings. A considerable export trade in wallpaper developed in the 18th century, and the Chinese designs were widely imitated in Europe.

The first
WAR CORRESPONDENT

was John Bell, the Yorkshire-born proprietor of *The Oracle or Bell's New World*. This was a paper which he had founded in June 1789 as vehicle for hurling verbal abuse at his former business partner, the fashionable rake Capt. Edward Topham. In February 1793, the month that France declared war on Great Britain, Bell was called to judgment for libelling the Foot Guards. When he failed to appear in court, his goods were seized and sold by public auction. Describing this turn of events as 'misfortune succeeding injustice', the proprietor of *The Oracle* decided that the only means of restoring his fortunes was to boost the circulation of the newspaper that represented his sole remaining possession. This he proposed to do with on-the-spot accounts of the fighting between the French and British in the Low Countries. His decision to march with the enemy forces rather than with the Duke of York's army may have been made either out of perversity, or from an instinctive flair for the best news angle.

The usual editorial practice at this time was to copy the war news from the foreign Press most closely concerned. A few papers received exclusive reports direct from whichever capital lay nearest the fighting, but at best this was a system founded on rumour. The readers of *The Oracle* knew at first hand the true nature of the war's progress. They were able to follow Bell on what he described as his 'perilous excursion through Flanders', and read his accounts of the British victories at Le Cateau-Cambrésis, Villiers-en-Cauche and Troixelle, followed by the disheartening report of a major defeat at Tournay at the hands of Marshal Pichegru.

The Times, chagrined no doubt that its thunder had been stolen, described the adventurer as 'a bloody satellite of Robespierre and a promoter of Jacobite [*sic*] heresies'. Though there was no foundation for these conflicting accusations, it is an interesting side-light on 18th-century warfare that Bell, as a civilian, was able to mingle freely with the enemy and go unmolested.

When the terrible winter retreat of 1794–5 began, John Bell felt it was time to return to the security of the editorial chair. The precedent he had established was followed in future by other papers, notably his chief critic, *The Times*, which commissioned Henry Crabb Robinson in 1808 to cover the Peninsular War. It was a later representative of *The Times*, William Howard Russell, who was accorded the inscription 'The First and Greatest of War Correspondents' on his memorial in St Paul's Cathedral. Russell, whose reports from the Crimea won him a national celebrity, was indeed the first to telegraph his dispatches from the battle zone, but this was the extent of his role as innovator. That Bell should have been overlooked is not totally inexplicable; he died in such obscurity in 1831 that not one of the five newspapers of which he had been at some time proprietor published an obituary notice.

WAR CORRESPONDENT TO TELEPHONE HIS REPORT: the first was *The Times*' representative at the Battle of Ahmed Khel, fought during the 2nd Afghan War on 19 April 1880. He was able to phone the story of General Sir Donald Stewart's defeat of the Ghilzais to a heliograph station outside the battle area; from here it was flashed to a field telegraph, and then by commercial cable to London, where it was published the next morning.

The first
WATCH

The earliest written record believed to refer to a watch is a letter addressed to the Marchese di Manta in November 1462, by the Italian clockmaker Bartholomew Manfredi, offering to make him a 'pocket clock' better than the Duke of Modena's.

The earliest surviving watch is an iron timepiece made by Peter Henlein of Nuremberg, Bavaria, which dates from the early 16th century, and is now preserved at the Philadelphia Memorial Hall. Although a putative date of c. 1504 has been assigned to the watch, in fact this really only represents the earliest year in which it is reasonably possible it could have been made. Henlein qualified as a master locksmith in 1509, a more likely date for him to have begun his watchmaking activities, and the first certain reference to this branch of his craft dates from 1511. In that year Johannes Cocclaeus, a citizen of Nuremberg, described the innovation in terms that leave little doubt that Henlein was regarded locally as the inventor of the watch:

From day to day more ingenious discoveries are made; for Petrus Hele, [alternative Henlein] a young man, makes things which astonish the most learned mathematicians, for he makes out of a small quantity of iron horologia devised with very many wheels, and these horologia, in any position and without any weight, both indicate and strike for 40 hours, even when they are carried on the breast or in the purse.

This passage has been taken as evidence that the watchmaking industry began in Nuremberg; but even excepting the questionably early allusion to 'pocket clocks' in the Manfredi letter of 1462, there are a number of records of watches in France within a few years of the Cocclaeus account. It is possible that the French introduced watches quite independently and at about the same time.

GB: The introduction of watchmaking in Britain cannot be certainly dated. Francis Noway, originally of Brabant, is known to have been working in London between 1580 and 1583 (possibly later) and at least two watches of his workmanship survive. Queen Elizabeth I's Clockmaker, Bartholomew Newsham, who worked at his trade from 1568 until his death in 1593, is also known to have produced a number of watches. The Queen herself owned a 'watche of gold sett with small rubies, small diamondes and small emerodes' in 1571, but it is probable that this came from the French watchmaking centre of Blois. Nothing more definite can be said about the first native product than that it is likely to have belonged to the period 1575–85. England made up for a late arrival by becoming the leading watchmaking nation of Europe during the first quarter of the 17th century.

WATCH WITH A SECOND HAND: early watches had a single hand only, indicating the hour. With greater precision-work it became possible to add a minute hand, though this is scarcely known before the 1660s. The first watch with a second hand, notable also as one of the earliest examples with a minute hand, was made by John Fitter of Bermondsey c. 1665.

JEWELLED WATCH MOVEMENT was first patented on 1 May 1704 by the Swiss geometrician and optician Facio de Duillier and the French watchmaker Peter Debaufre, both of whom were based in London. Debaufre's first jewelled watch is said to have been worn by Sir Isaac Newton. Jewelling remained rare until after 1825, when the preparing and setting of jewels for watches became a regular industry at La Chaux-de-Fonds in Switzerland.

WRISTWATCH: the first of which there is any record dates from 1790, and is itemized in the accounts of the Swiss watchmakers Jaquet-Droz & Leschot of Geneva as 'a watch to be fixed on a bracelet'. The earliest surviving example is a gold watch set in a jewelled bracelet encrusted with pearls and emeralds, made by the Parisian jeweller Nitot in 1806. It originally belonged to the Empress Josephine. Although a few other examples of early bracelet watches of this type have been noted, mainly from the mid 19th century, they really belong more to the jeweller's than the watchmaker's art. The first wristwatches for men, and the first that were made for convenience rather than display, were ordered from C. Girard-Perregaux of La Chaux-de-Fonds by the German Admiralty in 1880, for the use of naval artillery officers at sea. The watch-cases were made of polished gold and fixed to a black leather strap. Girard-Perregaux subsequently began manufacturing wristwatches for the general market, but it would appear that it was only in Peru that there was any demand for them at this early period. The refusal of US dealers to handle them, and a general lack of enthusiasm elsewhere, brought a premature end to the nascent Swiss wristwatch industry. It was not until Parisian women began to set a fashion for wearing wristwatches c. 1908 that the idea became accepted in Europe.

Wristwatches for men were considered effeminate prior to World War I, but this prejudice was overcome when they were found to be more practical than pocket-watches on active service.

GB: In 1885 the London firm of J. W. Benson Ltd introduced the English Lever Wrist Watch, with a movement by Messrs Rotherham of Coventry. This enjoyed no lasting success and the wristwatch only became firmly established in Britain after its re-introduction by the Swiss watchmaker H. Willsdorf in 1909.

Harington Water Closet, 1596. The unfortunate sitter has invoked the devil by saying his prayers while engaged on less Godly business.

The first
WATER-CLOSET
was designed by the Elizabethan poet Sir John Harington and installed at his country-seat, Kelston, nr Bath, in 1589, by a local craftsman known to the history of sanitation only by his initials, 'T.C.'. In 1596 Harington described his invention in a book called *The Metamorphosis of Ajax* (a pun on 'jakes', the slang word then used for lavatory), which itemized the materials necessary for its construction together with their price – 30s 6d for the complete installation – and included diagrams to show how it worked. Water was drawn from a cistern – depicted with fish swimming in it – into the pan of the bowl, and flushed into a cesspool beneath when a handle in the seat was pulled to release a valve. Harington's water-closet resembled a modern flush lavatory in all important respects, having a reservoir of water constantly in the bowl to prevent foul air rising from the pipe, and a discharge that flushed down all the inside walls.

Despite the practical instructions given in his book, only two Harington water-closets are known to have been built, the Kelston one for his own use, and another at Richmond Palace, installed at the express command of Queen Elizabeth, who was Harington's godmother. Both courtier and Queen were noted in their time for a singular attention to hygiene. The Queen was considered by the rest of the Court to be uncommonly fastidious about her own person, taking a bath once a month 'whether she need it or no'. Harington went further, and had a bath every day, a habit considered by his friends to be a mark of the most eccentric behaviour.

The fact that the royal example was not followed by any other of her subjects is a reflection not on the worth of Harington's innovation, but of the total indifference of the majority of Elizabethans to dirt and its attendant odours. There was, however, a practical consideration that made the installation of flush lavatories difficult. The absence of drains or sewers meant that unless a pipe could be run from the water-closet to a river or stream, the effluent would have to be discharged into a pit – little improvement over the common midden. The water-supply was also extremely limited. The majority of householders relied on a communal pump for their water, drawing it in buckets. Those fortunate enough to have piped water were obliged to refill their tanks by turning on the tap from the main during the 2–3hr that the water was pumped from the water-works on three days of the week. Until the introduction of ball-valves in 1748, this supply depended on the householder or his servants remembering to turn on the tap at the right time, and even more important, to turn it off again. Water being regarded as a precious commodity, the water companies resented any subscriber using more than his fair share. When a Mr Melmouth of Bath installed a flush lavatory in his house in 1770, the company cut off his supply until he consented to remove it again.

Despite these problems, a few rich and enterprising persons did have water-closets built for them during the 17th and early 18th centuries, prior to regular manufacture. One of the most notable of these was an automatically flushing lavatory at the house of Sir Francis Carew at Beddington, Surrey. John Aubrey, who stayed there in 1678, described it as

a pretty machine to cleanse an House of Office, viz by a small stream of water no bigger than one's finger, which ran into an engine made like a bit of a fire-shovel, which hung upon its centre of gravity, so that when it was full a considerable quantity of water fell down with some force.

The first manufacturer to undertake quantity production of water-closets was London cabinet-maker Joseph Bramah, who sold some 6,000 units between 1778 – the year of his patent – and 1797. Bramah closets continued to be manufactured until *c.* 1890.

For a century after the introduction of the Bramah, it was customary for lavatory-bowls to be boxed in with a wooden surround. The first pedestal water-closet was Jennings's Pedestal Vase, which won a Gold Medal when it was unveiled at the Health Exhibition of 1884 and was judged to be 'as perfect a sanitary closet as can be made'.

Jennings was also the first to introduce the oval 'picture-frame' lavatory-seat, which, if credence can be lent to 19th-century legend, was actually used as a handsome surround for family and other portraits by some less sophisticated customers.

RAILWAY CARRIAGE TO CONTAIN WATER-CLOSETS: the first was George Mortimer Pullman's 'Old No. 9', a sleeping-car with a lavatory at either end that was put into service on the Chicago & Alton Railroad on 1 September 1859.

GB: The first sleeping-carriage (*see also* Railway Carriage: Sleeping-Car), introduced by the North British Railway between Glasgow and King's Cross on 2 April 1873, had two lavatories side by side but facing in reverse directions, each letting into a 1st-Class compartment.

The first day carriages with lavatories in Britain were introduced by the East Coast and the Midland Railways in 1881 and 3rd-Class passengers were granted this relief for the first time by the Manchester, Sheffield & Lincolnshire Railway in 1886.

AEROPLANE FITTED WITH A LAVATORY: the first was the giant Russian passenger transport *Russky Vitiaz*, designed by Igor Sikorski and test flown at Petrograd on 13 May 1913. Whether this was a water-closet proper is doubtful, as it seems unlikely that Sikorski would have increased the load by carrying unnecessary supplies of water. It is nevertheless recorded here as a tribute to the first man who concerned himself with the problems of high-altitude sanitation.

The first civil airliner in regular passenger service to contain a lavatory was the Handley Page W.8, introduced on the London–Paris flight route in December 1919.

See also Public Lavatory.

The first
WEATHER FORECASTS

had their earliest forerunner in the reports carried by John Houghton's weekly newspaper *A Collection for the Improvement of Husbandry and Trade.* The issue for 14 May 1692 introduced the subject with the words: 'Twould be of great use to have a true history of the weather, from which it is likeliest to draw prognostications.' Appended was a seven-day table, recording pressure and wind readings for the comparable dates of the previous year. These, Houghton explained, had been obtained from Henry Hunt of Gresham College and were taken from the 'barascope or Quicksilver Weather Glass'. The feature continued weekly, readers being expected to make their own forecast from the data supplied.

Unscientific as it was, Houghton's idea soon found a number of imitators, culminating in 1711 in a journal called the *Monthly Weather Paper* devoted exclusively to meteorological predictions. Long-range forecasting of this kind was generally compounded of a mixture of astrology, guess-work and a very little science, and could seldom produce correct prophecies other than by chance.

Accurate and scientific 'state of the weather' reports were first published by Charles Dickens's newspaper the *Daily News*, commencing 31 August 1848. At 9am every morning, observations were made on a uniform plan at a number of meteorological stations and telegraphed to London, where they were then analysed by James Glaisher of the Royal Greenwich Observatory for inclusion in the following day's issue of the paper. This was a major step forward, but still fell short of true weather forecasting, as the reader was left to draw his own conclusions.

On 6 February 1861 Admiral Robert Fitzroy, Superintendent of the Meteorological Office, began to issue official storm warnings for the benefit of ships putting to sea. At the same time he coined the term 'weather forecast', believing that this smacked less of the soothsayer than 'prophecy' or 'prognostication'. Shortly afterwards the Admiral extended the service offered by the Meteorological Office to include an official daily forecast for public consumption. The first of these was published in *The Times* for 1 August 1861. It optimistically predicted fine weather throughout the country.

BROADCAST WEATHER FORECASTS (vocal): the first were transmitted by the University of Wisconsin's Station 9XM at Madison, Wisc. commencing 3 January 1921. Weather bulletins in Morse code had been broadcast since the Station was established in 1917.

GB: Daily forecasts broadcast by the BBC as from 26 March 1923.

TELEVISED WEATHER FORECASTS were first introduced in Britain by the BBC on 29 July 1949.

TELEPHONE WEATHER-FORECASTING SERVICE: the first in Britain came into operation on 5 March 1956.

The first
WEDDING AT WHICH THE BRIDAL COUPLE LEFT IN A MOTOR CAR
took place in Paris on 27 February 1897. A correspondent wrote in the following week's issue of the *Autocar*:

It was my privilege on Saturday to see the first instance of an autocar ever being used at a wedding. The vehicle was ranged up among the other carriages outside a restaurant in the Boulevard des Patignolles, where the young married couple and their friends were partaking of the wedding breakfast. The autocar was a brougham of the type manufactured by M. L. Fisson. . . . The lamps were adorned with rosettes of white satin. Later on I met the autocar containing the happy couple leading a procession of carriages in the Bois de Boulogne . . . driven by M. Fisson himself.

GB: The first motor-car wedding in Britain took place at St Augustine's Roman Catholic Church, Solihull on 21 April 1897 between Albert Edward Day, son of Edward Day, Assistant Manager of the Anglo-French Motor Carriage Co, and Irma L'Hollier, daughter of Leon L'Hollier, a Director of the Company (*see also* Motor Agent). The three cars present were probably all Roger-Benzs, the make of car in which the Company specialized. 'At the conclusion of the ceremony,' the *Autocar* reported, 'the wedding party adjourned to the house of the bride's father, where autocars were used in the diversion of the company.'

The first
WINDSCREEN-WIPERS
mechanically operated, were introduced in the USA in 1916.
GB: The first manually operated windscreen-wipers were patented by Mills Munitions Ltd of Birmingham on 13 January 1921 and put into production the same month. The first automatic windscreen-wipers were produced by W. M. Folberth in the summer of 1921. The Folberth was powered by a double-acting air engine connected by a tube to the inlet pipe of the car's engine.

The first electric windscreen-wiper unit was the Berkshire, produced in the USA in 1923 and introduced into Britain by the Houdaille Hydraulic Suspension Co of New Bond Street, London, in May of the same year, price £2 15s including motor.

The first
WOMAN AMBASSADOR
was Alexandra Kollantai (*see also* Woman Minister of State), the daughter of a Russian aristocrat who turned her back on her class and joined the Bolshevik Party in 1915. She was appointed to the Legation of the Soviet representation in Norway in the autumn of 1922 and became Head of the Legation the following year. At this time Norway had not recognized the Soviet Union, so that although Alexandra performed ambassadorial duties, she was not officially accredited to the Norwegian Court. On 15 February 1924, Norway recognized the Soviet Union *de jure* and Alexandra Kollantai was appointed chargé d'affaires and officially introduced into the Diplomatic Corps. Her designation as Minister Plenipotentiary followed in August of the same year and she presented her credentials to the King 'with the usual ceremonial' on 8 September 1924. She served in this post until 1926 and as Ambassadress to Mexico and Sweden until her retirement in 1946.
GB: The first woman Ambassador to the Court of St James's was Señora Maria del Carmen Gutierrez Chamberlain de Chittenden, who represented Costa Rica from August 1962 to June 1966. There have been no British women ambassadors.

The first
WOMAN ARCHITECT
professionally qualified in Britain, was Miss Ethel Mary Charles, who was articled for three years to the firm of Sir Ernest George & Peto in 1892 and subsequently employed by Mr Walter Cave. After touring England to study Gothic and domestic architecture, she sat her Finals in June 1898 and was elected an Associate Member of RIBA on 5 December. She was registered as practising in York Street Chambers.

The first
WOMAN BARRISTER or ADVOCATE
was Mrs Carrie Brunham Kilgore, registered as a law student in the State of Pennsylvania at the age of 34 in 1870, but refused admittance to the University of Pennsylvania Law School the following year. She won her battle to gain entry in 1881 and graduated as Bachelor of Laws in 1883. A year later she was admitted to the Delaware County Courts and one Philadelphia Common Pleas Court, and in 1890 to the Supreme Court of the United States.
GB: Miss Fay Kyle and Miss A. K. S. Deverell were called to the Irish Bar on 1 November 1921, Miss Deverell enjoying the added distinction of being called at the same time as her twin brother.

The first woman to be called to the English Bar was Oxford lecturer Dr Ivy Williams on 10 May 1922. She was called by Sir Henry Dickens, who presented her with an inscribed copy of *David Copperfield* to mark the signal event. Although 10 other women law students were called to the Bar in December of the same year, Dr Williams had been enabled to take precedence by securing a Certificate of Honour in the Bar Finals which excused her two terms' dinners. She subsequently returned to teaching at Oxford.
WOMAN BARRISTER TO APPEAR AS COUNSEL IN AN ENGLISH COURT: the first was Miss Helena Normanton, who received her first brief on 18 December 1922, the night she was called to the Bar.
WOMAN KC: the first was Miss Margaret Kidd of the Scottish Bar, appointed on 20 December 1948. The first women members of the English Bar to be appointed KCs were Miss Helena Normanton and Miss Rose Heilbron on 12 April 1949.

The first
WOMEN CHORISTERS
were introduced at St Paul's Pro-Cathedral, Melbourne, Victoria in 1887. They were clad in surplices and rounded trenchers. A contemporary journal reported: 'The effect was admirable on the whole, though Church composure was ruffled in some instances.'

The first
WOMAN DENTAL SURGEON
(professionally qualified) was Miss Lucy B. Hobbs, who graduated from the Ohio College of Dental Surgery, Cincinnati with a DDS degree on 21 February 1866. Miss Hobbs was already a practising dentist at this time, as there was no legal requirement to hold a licence, and due to her previous experience she was only required to attend the Ohio College for one semester.
GB: The first qualified woman dental surgeon to practise in Britain was an American, Dr Olgavon Oertzen, who established a surgery in Kensington in 1886.

The first woman to qualify as a dental surgeon in Britain was Miss Lilian Murray (later Dr Lilian Lindsay), who qualified as LDS Edinburgh on 20 May 1895. Her decision to enter a profession hitherto closed to women was made while still a pupil at the North London Collegiate School. Miss Buss, the Headmistress, had urged her to train as a teacher of the deaf and dumb. Lilian was not enthusiastic, but Miss Buss refused to be put off. Finally the girl cried out in temper 'I would rather be a ——' The expected word was 'hangman', but something prompted her to substitute 'dentist'. On later reflection she decided it was the very thing she would like to be. When Miss Buss heard this, she dismissed the idea with the words: 'How absurd, child! There is no such thing as a woman dentist.'

Lilian Murray entered the Edinburgh Dental Hospital and School in 1892 and, on becoming a Licenciate in Dental Surgery, set up a practice at 69 Hornsea Rise in north London. In 1946 she was elected first woman President of the British Dental Association.

The first
WOMAN DOCTOR
professionally qualified, was Elizabeth Blackwell. She was first encouraged to make medicine her career when a friend, who was dying of cancer, told her that she would have been spared many of her worst sufferings had she been attended by a female medical practitioner. Born at Bristol in 1821, Elizabeth Blackwell emigrated to New York with her family when she was 11 years old. Her initial attempts to enter a recognized medical school proved unsuccessful. She was refused admittance in Philadelphia and New York, and the only encouragement she received was from a professor who said he would allow her to attend his classes if she was prepared to disguise herself as a man. When she applied to the Medical Institute of the small University of Geneva, New York State, the Dean, Dr Lee, turned the decision over to the student body, confident that they would return a negative reply. On 20 October 1847 he replied to her letter, enclosing a copy of the students' Resolution:

Resolved – That one of the radical principles of a Republican Government is the universal education of both sexes; that to every branch of scientific education the door should be opened equally to all; that the application of Elizabeth Blackwell to become a member of our class meets our entire approval; and that in extending our unanimous invitation we pledge ourselves that no conduct of ours shall cause her to regret her attendance at this Institution.

Elizabeth Blackwell entered the Geneva Medical Institute and gained her clinical experience during the summer vacation of 1848 at the Blockley Almshouses in Philadelphia, where she found herself caring for the victims of a typhus epidemic. She graduated MD on 23 January 1849.

After further training at La Maternité in Paris, Dr Blackwell returned to New York, and on failing to obtain a hospital appointment she embarked on private practice in March 1852, most of her early patients being women of the Quaker persuasion. Together with Marie Zakrzewska, a Polish woman doctor, she established the New York Infirmary of Women and Children in May 1857. Settling in England in 1874, she was appointed to the Chair of Gynaecology at the newly founded London School of Medicine for Woman, but retired to Hastings in 1879 after a long period of ill-health.

GB: The first woman doctor to qualify in Britain was Elizabeth Garrett Anderson, daughter of a Whitechapel pawnbroker, who met Dr Elizabeth Blackwell at the house of Mme Barbara Bodichon in London, on 2 March 1859, and was fired with the ambition to follow in her footsteps. After a year as a Surgical Nurse at the Middlesex Hospital, Elizabeth Garrett was admitted to the chemistry lectures of the Middlesex Hospital Medical School on 20 March 1861. Three months later the Medical School Committee refused to afford her full recognition as a medical student following a petition submitted by her fellow students, to the effect that her presence among them exposed the hospital to ridicule. Having been refused by every medical school in London, she approached the Royal College of Surgeons and the examining bodies of Oxford, Cambridge, Glasgow and Edinburgh, all of whom were equally opposed to the admission of women candidates. The only remaining examining body, the Society of Apothecaries, also took an unfavourable attitude, but consulted an eminent QC on the interpretation of its Charter, and was advised that it could not refuse to examine a candidate solely on the grounds of her sex.

In order to qualify for the Society of Apothecaries' examination, Elizabeth Garrett secured a formal apprenticeship to Dr Joshua Plaskitt of the Middlesex Hospital, backdated to 1 October 1860, when she had first begun to receive coaching from him in Latin, Greek and *materia medica*. She also studied with Dr Day of St Andrews, and with Alexander Keiller at the Edinburgh Maternity Hospital, where she was able to obtain clinical experience in midwifery.

Elizabeth Garrett completed her final course of lectures at the beginning of August 1865, and applied to the Court of Examiners of the Society of Apothecaries for admittance to the final examination. The Society, suddenly aware of the odium with which it would be regarded by most of the medical profession if she became a Licenciate, returned her a letter of refusal, but on being threatened with litigation by Elizabeth's father, hastily backed down. On 28 September 1865 she was examined orally by a Mr Wheeler at Apothecaries' Hall, in medicine, midwifery and medical pathology, and was one of three out of seven candidates to receive a Final Certificate, entitling her to practise as a qualified physician and surgeon.

Within a few weeks of qualifying Dr Garrett established a practice at 20 Upper Berkeley Street as a consultant physician to women and children, and in 1866 opened the St Mary's Dispensary for Women and Children in Seymour Place, London.

Elizabeth continued to fulfil a pioneering role. On 15 January 1870 she became the first British woman MD when she passed the final examination of the Medical Faculty of the Sorbonne in Paris, receiving the personal good wishes of the Emperor and Empress. Exactly two months later she was appointed visiting Medical Officer to the East London Hospital for Children, becoming the first woman to serve on the medical staff of any British hospital.

SURGICAL OPERATIONS BY WOMEN SURGEONS in Britain were first performed by Dr Frances Morgan and Dr Elizabeth Garrett Anderson (her married name) at the New Hospital for women, Seymour Place in or before December 1871. The first case to be reported in the medical Press (*British Medical Journal*, 14 December 1871) was of a woman of 50 suffering from ovarian dropsy, successfully operated on by Dr Morgan. This was in fact carried out illegally, as Dr Morgan possessed a foreign qualification that did not entitle her to perform surgery in Britain. Elizabeth Garrett Anderson was the only woman doctor on the British Medical Register, and for the next 20 years was the only woman empowered to undertake major surgery.

The first woman to be admitted to the Royal College of Surgeons was Miss Eleanor Davies-Colley in 1911. In that year there were 477 women doctors in the UK.

The first
WOMAN JOCKEY
The first woman known to have competed in a horse-race was 22-year-old Alicia Meynell, mistress of Col Thornton, who rode the Colonel's horse Vingarillo against Capt. William Flint, mounted on his own horse Thornville, over a 4-mile course at York on 25 August 1804. Riding side-saddle under the name 'Mrs Thornton', she sported leopard and buff colours with blue sleeves and cap and started as 5 to 4 favourite. Although leading for the first 3 miles, her 20-year-old

mount then tired and she was overtaken by Capt. Flint, who won in a time of 9min 59sec. Miss Meynell proved a poor loser, vilifying her opponent in the columns of the *York Herald* for alleged lack of courtesy, and Col Thornton an even poorer one, for he refused to pay up the £1,000 wager on the grounds that the magnitude of the sum had been merely a device to attract a large gathering of spectators.

Miss Meynell competed again at the York August Meeting of 1805, winning two races, the first by default and the second by half a neck. Apart from an Irish lady, Miss Ouzley, who won a race at Loughrea, County Galway in September 1805, no other women are known to have ridden competitively until the following century.

WOMAN JOCKEY TO WIN AN OPEN RACE: the first was Miss Eileen Joel, daughter of the millionaire racehorse-owner Solly Joel, who rode Mrs Earl's Hogier to victory in the 4-mile Newmarket Town Plate on 8 October 1925. Eschewing silks, Miss Joel achieved her historic win attired in a cloche hat. There were eight other competitors in all, five of them women. The Newmarket Town Plate is unusual in being held under its own rules, originally drawn up in 1665 at the personal behest of King Charles II. The articles state that the race is to be open to any amateur rider, and since the word 'rider' is not defined by sex, it was successfully contended in the 1920s that this could be interpreted to include women. The Newmarket Town Plate of 13 October 1927 was the first in which only ladies competed, Miss Iris Rickaby coming first out of a field of three, with Miss Joel second.

WOMAN JOCKEY LICENSED TO RIDE AS A PROFESSIONAL: the first was English-born Miss Judy Johnson, who made her début riding Lone Gallant in a steeplechase at Pimlico Racetrack, Baltimore, Md., on 27 April 1943. She finished 10th out of a field of 11 horses. Her mount was beaten by 30 lengths, though this was an improvement on a previous performance under a male jockey, when it had come in 400 lengths behind the winner. Miss Johnson had first applied to the Maryland Jockey Club for a licence in 1927, but was turned down on the grounds that no woman had been issued with one before. Her renewed application was accepted because of the shortage of jockeys due to enlistment. After riding in a few more races she reverted to her former occupation of trainer.

LADIES' RACE UNDER JOCKEY CLUB RULES: the first in Britain was the Goya Stakes, held over 1 mile 1 furlong, at Kempton Park on 6 May 1972. The winner was 23-year-old Miss Meriel Tufnell of Bishops Waltham, Hampshire on her mother's 50 to 1 outsider Scorched Earth. Prize money for first place was £949. The Goya Stakes was the first of 12 Ladies' Races sanctioned by the Jockey Club for the 1972 flat-racing season.

Cloche-hatted Eileen Joel riding to victory in the 1925 Newmarket Town Plate

The first *WOMEN JURORS*

sat on an all-female jury convened for the trial of Judith Catchpole, accused of murdering her infant child, at the General Provisional Court held at Patuxent, Md., on 22 September 1656. The jury accepted the defendant's plea that far from murdering her child she had never had one, and returned a verdict of Not Guilty.

A mixed jury of six men and six women is recorded at Albany, N.Y. in 1701.

The first legal provision for women to serve on juries was made by an Act of the Legislative Council of the Territory of Wyoming passed on 10 December 1869. Chief Justice J.H. Howe, who empanelled the first women to serve on the juries of the Supreme Court at Cheyenne, wrote in 1872: 'After the grand jury had been in session two days the dance-house keepers, gamblers and demi-monde fled out of the State in dismay to escape the indictment of women jurors.'

GB: The first women jurors were six ladies 'drawn from the middle class' who made up one-half of a jury empanelled at Bristol Quarter Sessions on 28 July 1920. R.E. Dummett, Prosecuting Counsel in the opening case, remarked that he was the first person ever to use the words 'Ladies and Gentlemen of the Jury' in an English court. Six cases were adjudicated, including the trial of a riveter charged with indecently assaulting two girls at Clifton.

The first women to be sworn in as jurors at the Old Bailey were called for service on 11 January 1921. Although about 50 women were summoned, the majority from Hampstead, nearly half of them were excused, many for seemingly trivial reasons. One reluctant nominee pleaded 'I am so awfully nervous I don't think I am suitable', while another was excused after asserting that she thought there were 'others who would enjoy the experience more'. The first to take the oath was Miss Mary Constance Burnett, who sat with one other woman on a jury in the Recorder's Court; the first Forewoman of a jury was Mrs Taylor Bumstead, as the only female member of the jury in the Common Serjeant's Court.

The first *WOMAN MAGISTRATE*

was Mrs Esther Morris, described as 'a large, plain-spoken, warmly witty shopkeeper's wife', who was appointed Justice of the Peace for South Pass, Wyoming on 17 February 1870. She tried 70 cases during her tenure of office.

GB: Miss Emily Duncan was appointed a Justice of the Peace in West Ham on 26 May 1913.

The first *WOMAN MAYOR*

was 27-year-old Susanna Medora Salter, who was elected Mayor of Argonia, Kans. by a two-thirds majority on 4 April 1887. She had been nominated for office by the Women's Christian Temperance Union, who for some reason omitted to tell her that they had done so. It was only on arriving at the polling-station to vote that she discovered she was one of the candidates.

GB: Elizabeth Garrett Anderson (*see also* Woman Doctor), was elected Mayor of Aldeburgh, Suffolk on 9 November 1908, following the death of her husband, the previous holder of the office.

Her first official act as Mayor was to send a telegram of congratulation to King Edward VII for his birthday, the day of her election.

The first *WOMEN MPs*

were elected in Finland on 15–17 March

1907, when 19 constituencies returned woman members to the Diet. Nine were members of the ruling Social Democrat Party, including a journalist, a dress-maker, a school-teacher, a weaver and a women's rights agitator. Of the other nine, six were elected for the Old Finnish Party, the majority being teachers, though there was also a restaurant-proprietor and a clergy-man's wife among their number. The lady members took their seats at Helsingfors on 23 May and appeared, said the *Times* Correspondent, 'quite at their ease'.

GB: The Parliament (Qualification of Women) Act received the Royal Assent on 21 November 1918. Seventeen candidates – 1 Conservative, 4 Labour, 4 Liberal and 8 others – contested seats in the General Election of 14 December 1918. The first and only woman to be elected was Constance, Countess Markievicz, who was returned as Sinn Fein Member for St Patrick's, Dublin, defeating the Nationalist candidate, holder of the seat since 1892, by 7,835 votes to 3,752. The Countess was not present during the election cam-paign, being under detention at Hollo-way Gaol for Irish Republican activities, nor did she take her seat when released in March 1919. She is reputed to have paid only one visit to the Commons during her tenure of the St Patrick's division, going incognito to look at the coat-peg inscribed with her name that was the sole visible evidence of a woman representative in the House.

The first woman MP to take her seat in Parliament was American-born Nancy, Viscountess Astor, who was adopted as Coalition Unionist (Con-servative) candidate for the Sutton division of Plymouth to contest the by-election caused by the succession of her husband, the sitting Member, to the Peerage. Polling took place on 28 November 1919 and she was returned with a 5,203 majority over the Labour candidate. She made her maiden speech on 24 February 1920, speaking in opposition to a motion for the abolition of the Liquor Control Board. Lady Astor retained her seat for just over 25 years, retiring in 1945.

The first Labour woman MP was Miss Susan Lawrence, elected for East Ham North with a majority of 416, 6 December 1923. She was also the first woman returned to the LCC (as a Conservative) in 1910, and the first woman Chairman of the Labour Party in 1930. Among her many idiosyncrasies, which included at various times of her life the wearing of a monocle (as a Conservative) and an Eton crop (as a Socialist), was her steadfast objection to being referred to as a 'woman MP'. She was known to have inquired of those who addressed her thus, whether they called Churchill a 'man MP'. She was also the only woman Member to reveal her age in *Who's Who* (then 52), and listed her recreations as 'parties, Tolstoy, rowdy meetings, mountaineer-ing, and reading Government Blue Books'.

The first Private Member's Bill to be moved by a woman and become law was the Intoxicating Liquor (Sale to Persons under 18) Bill, promoted by Lady Astor and passed on 13 July 1923 by 247 votes to 10.

The first WOMAN MINISTER OF RELIGION

was the Rev. Antoinette Brown, who was born at Henrietta, N.Y. in 1825, entered the Oberlin College Theological Seminary as the first female divinity student, and preached her first sermon in New York in 1848 while still a member of the Seminary. She was ordained minister of the South Butler Congregational Church, N.Y. at a salary of $300 p.a. on 15 September 1853. Although accepted in her parish, reaction outside was not always favourable, and on one occasion when she was sent as a delegate to a Temperance convention she was greeted with hoots and jeers. Later she became a Universalist, married Samuel C. Blackwell, and was still preaching at All Souls' Church, Elizabeth, N.J. in 1912.

The first woman minister of religion in the British Commonwealth was Miss Martha Turner, who was born in England in 1839, educated at Dijon, where she 'early developed high intel-lectual qualities', and emigrated to Australia to join her brother Henry Gyles Turner in October 1870. Turner was a lay preacher at the Unitarian Church in Melbourne, and during a period in 1872 when the minister had to go absent on sick leave, was one of six men who volunteered to conduct the services. In a memoir he wrote:

I preached my first sermon on the 11th February and four more before the end of the year. But the work was a great labour to me owing to my sincere self-criticism, and the limited time I could spare from my anxious business. Happily my sister came to my assistance, and with such general approval, that she was formally called upon to take the position permanently.

The Rev. Higginson being unable to resume his duties, a special meeting of the congregation of the church was held on 26 October 1873, and Martha Turner was elected as their first permanent minister. On Sunday, 23 November Miss Turner gave her inaugural address on accepting the pastorate – for the second lesson she read 1 Cor. 14, in which occurs the verse (34): 'Let your women keep silence in the churches.'

Miss Turner solemnized her first marriage at the Unitarian Church, Grey Street, East Melbourne on 2 November 1876. The couple joined in Holy Matrimony were Joseph Howgate, hotel-keeper, of 38 Swanston Street, Melbourne, and Adeleide Jeanette Wustermann of Shelley Street, Richmond.

Two years later Miss Turner was her-self married to John Webster, and planned to resign her office, but the congregation persuaded her to con-tinue and she did so until 1883, when she resigned in order to make a journey to England with her husband.

GB: The first woman minister of religion was Miss Gertrude von Petzold, who came to Britain from Germany in 1897 and attended St Andrews and Edinburgh Universities, graduating MA in 1901. She proceeded to Man-chester College, Oxford as a theological student and completed the three-year course with 2nd-Class Honours in Philosophy and New Testament Studies. In its issue for 2 July 1904, *The Inquirer*, a Unitarian newspaper, reported:

Miss von Petzold is the first . . . to have been appointed to a charge in this country. She has accepted the pastorate of the Narborough Road Church at Leicester, and we rejoice that the liberal principles of religion, the spread of which in her Fatherland she has warmly at heart, should have given her the opportunity of service among us here.

Miss von Petzold served as pastor of Narborough Free Christian Church from 1904 to 1908, resigning to go on a two-year preaching tour of the USA. On her return she was appointed minister of the Waverley Road Uni-tarian Church, Birmingham, where she remained from 1911 to 1915. In the latter year she was granted a 12-month leave of absence by her congregation, who 'expressed the hope that the separation would be only temporary'. She subsequently left the Unitarian ministry and returned to her native Germany, after which there is little trace of her, though she is believed to have been still alive in the late 1930s.

ANGLICAN WOMAN MINISTER: the first was the Rev. Florence Tim-Oi Lee of Macao, who was ordained priest by Bishop R.O. Hall of the Diocese of Hong Kong and South China as an emergency war measure at Shie Hing in Kwangtung province, China, on 25 January 1944. Owing to the total absence of ordained priests in Macao,

Miss Lee had already been granted the authority to celebrate Holy Communion two years earlier, while still a Deaconess. In 1946 the Diocesan Synod of Hong Kong and South China endorsed Bishop Hall's action and proposed a draft Canon allowing a trial period of 20 years for the ordination of women. The proposal was rejected by Lambeth in 1948, by which time Miss Lee, sensing opposition to her remaining in Orders in peacetime, had returned her licence to the Bishop. She was living in Canton at the time of the Communist take-over, since when nothing more has been heard of her. Hong Kong Diocese reintroduced the practice of female ordination in 1971, when Miss Jane Hwang Hsieu Yeun and Miss Joyce Bennett, the first English-born Anglican woman priest, took Holy Orders. The only other woman to have been ordained a Church of England minister in the meantime was officiating as a parish priest in Kenya.

The first
WOMAN MINISTER OF STATE
was Alexandra Kollantai, appointed People's Commissar (Minister) of Social Welfare with Cabinet rank in the revolutionary Bolshevik Government formed by Lenin on 8 November 1917 (27 October old style).

Born of aristocratic family, Mme Kollantai had rejected her own class to embrace the Socialist cause in 1899 and subsequently spent many years in exile, returning to Russia immediately after the February Revolution. During her six months' tenure of office as People's Commissar she was responsible for disabled ex-servicemen, hospitals, pensions, leper colonies, orphanages, female education and the administration of playing-card factories (already a State monopoly). Her first act as Minister was to compensate an aggrieved peasant for his requisitioned horse. This was not a responsibility of her Ministry, she explains in her autobiography, but the fellow had somehow secured an audience with Lenin, who had sent him round to Madame Kollantai with a scribbled note requesting her to settle the matter somehow, as the Social Welfare Commissariat was the only one with any cash at its disposal.

Other accomplishments included the abolition of religious education, the transfer of priests to the civil service, the introduction of pupil participation in the running of girls' schools, and the setting up of a committee of medical men to plan a national health service. Madame Kollantai considered her most important achievement was the founding of the Central Office for Maternity and Infant Welfare in January 1918.

Madame Kollantai resigned from the Government in March of that year 'on the ground of total disagreement with the current policy'. Always outspoken and independent, from this time forward she became an increasing liability to the Party and in 1922 she was sent out of harm's way as an envoy with the Russian Legation to Norway, later becoming the world's first woman Ambassador (*q.v.*).

GB: The first woman Minister was Miss Margaret Bondfield, appointed Under-Secretary of State to the Minister of Labour in Ramsay MacDonald's first Labour Government on 23 January 1924. On 18 February, she became the first woman to answer a question on the Order Paper, the subject being the cost of Britain's contribution to the International Labour Office in Geneva. She held her post until Parliament was dissolved in October.

On 8 June 1929 Margaret Bondfield became the first woman Cabinet Minister when she was appointed Minister of Labour in Ramsay MacDonald's second Labour Government. She attended her first Cabinet meeting in Downing Street on 10 June.

WOMAN PRIME MINISTER: the first was Mrs Sirimavo Bandaranaike, who took up office as Prime Minister of Ceylon (Sri Lanka) on 21 July 1960.

The first
WOMAN MOTORIST
to drive a motor car was Mme Levassor, wife of one of the partners in the Paris motor-manufacturing concern Panhard et Levassor, but better known by her former name of Mme Sarazin. Prior to her second marriage, and after the death of her first husband, Mme Sarazin had acquired the French and Belgian rights of manufacture for the Daimler petrol engine. The following year, in 1890, she married Emile Levassor, and the patent rights passed to her new husband's firm. They began manufacturing cars under their own name in 1891, and it seems likely that this was the year Mme Levassor learned to drive, though the earliest evidence of her becoming a chauffeuse is a photograph showing her at the tiller of a Panhard car and dated 1892. Although the pioneer woman car-driver, Mme Levassor was not the first member of her sex to take to the highway in a petrol-driven vehicle; this distinction was earned by Mrs Edward Butler, who drove her husband's motor cycle (*q.v.*) at Erith, Kent in 1889.

GB: The first woman car-driver, and also the first woman owner, was the actress Minnie Palmer, who had a French-built Rougement motor carriage delivered to her by the Daimler Co while she was on tour at Aberdeen in September 1897.

WOMAN TO PASS THE DRIVING TEST: the first was the Duchesse d'Uzès, who secured her brevet as a *conducteur d'automobile* in May 1898 after satisfying the examiner of her ability to brave the hazards of the busy Bois de Boulogne. The first Englishwoman to take a test was Miss Vera Hedges Butler in Paris in August 1900.

The first
WOMAN NOVELIST
in Britain was Mrs Aphra Behn (*see also* Woman Playwright), whose first published works of fiction, *The Unfortunate Bride*, *The Dumb Virgin*, *The Wandering Beauty* and *The Unhappy Mistake*, appeared in 1687. Mrs Behn had already established a reputation as a brilliant dramatist, before turning to prose work in about 1683. In that year she is believed to have written her first novel, *The Adventure of the Black Lady*, but it was not published until 1697, eight years after her death. Forced by circumstance to earn her own living, Aphra Behn first took paid employment as a secret agent in Holland, her mission being to spy on certain known regicides and traitors to the Crown. This successfully accomplished, and having brought but small monetary reward, she turned instead to literature and became the first Englishwoman to support herself in this manner.

Her output was prodigious. Between 1670 and 1687 she wrote 19 plays, an average of over one a year, and during the briefer six-year period of her prose work (1683–88), produced 11 novels, 5 volumes of translations and a collection of fictitious *Love Letters between a Nobleman and his Sister*, besides a quantity of poetry. Gildon, in his *Account of the Life of the Incomparable Mrs Behn* (1697), said that 'She always Writ with the greatest ease in the world, and that in the midst of Company, and Discourse of other matters. I saw her my self write *Oroonoko*, and keep her own in Discoursing with several then present in the Room.' *Oroonoko* was Mrs Behn's most successful novel, based on a romantic episode in her own life when, as a young girl living in Surinam, she had encountered the Royal Slave of that name.

The first
WOMAN PHOTOGRAPHER, PROFESSIONAL
was the Parisian daguerreotypist Antoinette de Correvont, who opened a portrait studio at Munich in 1843.

GB: The only woman photographer noted in the 1851 Census was a Miss

Wigley, who maintained a studio at 108 Fleet Street, London. During the ensuing 10 years photography began to attract an increasing number of female practitioners, the Census of 1861 enumerating 204 women photographers, a figure that represented about 8% of the whole profession.

The first
WOMAN PILOT

was Mlle Elise Deroche, better known by her self-assumed title, Baronne de la Roche, who was taught to fly at Châlons in a Voisin biplane by the Chief Instructor of Voisin Frères; she made her first solo flight – a 'straight' of 300yd – on 22 October 1909. The following year she won her brevet, becoming the world's first qualified woman pilot on 8 March.
GB: Miss Edith Maud Cook learned to fly early in 1910 under the name of Miss 'Spencer Kavanagh' on Blériot monoplanes at the Grahame-White School at Pau, France. Well known as a parachute-jumper under another of her pseudonyms, 'Violet Spenser', she was killed making a descent from a captive balloon over Coventry in July 1910.

The pilot's licence issued to Mme de Laroche, 8 March 1910

PROFESSIONAL WOMAN PILOT: the first in Britain was Mrs Buller, who joined the Caudron Co at Hendon early in 1914.

See also Pilot's Licence.

The first
WOMAN PLAYWRIGHT

in Britain was Lady Elizabeth Carew the Younger, whose *Tragedie of Marian the faire Queene of Iewry* was published in London in 1613. Written in rhyming quatrains, the play is described as 'tedious' in the *Dictionary of National Biography*, and there is no evidence that it was ever performed.

The first woman to have a play performed on the stage was Mrs Aphra Behn (*see also* Woman Novelist), whose *The Forc'd Marriage; or, the Jealous Bridegroom* ran for six days at the Duke's Theatre, Lincoln's Inn Fields in December 1670. Described by Montague Summers as 'a good tragi-comedy of the bastard Fletcherian Devenant type', the leading roles were taken by Thomas Betterton and his wife Mary Sanderson, one of the first English actresses. A supporting part was played by the dramatist Thomas Otway, then a boy of 18 just left Winchester, but he was received so poorly that he abandoned all thoughts of becoming an actor. Mrs Behn's many plays – she was the most prolific dramatist of her time next to Dryden – are noted for the robustness of their dialogue and the indelicacy of the situations portrayed. Even in her own day this was an occasion for comment, and Alexander Pope composed the apt couplet:

The stage how loosely does Astrea tread
Who fairly puts all characters to bed.

A later age condemned her out of hand, one mid-Victorian female literary critic recoiling from the mention of Mrs Behn's name with the assertion that 'it is amply evident her mind was tainted to the very core'.

The first
WOMEN STOCKBROKERS

were Victoria Claflin Woodhull and Tennessee Claflin, who opened the brokerage office of Woodhull, Claflin & Co at the Hoffman House, New York on 19 January 1870. The two sisters had been instructed in the art of high finance by Commodore Vanderbilt in return for their services as clairvoyant and mistress respectively. Although neither partner was a member of the New York Stock Exchange, the firm did a brisk business, particularly with lady clients, for whom a special room was reserved at the rear of the office. Not all their attention was reserved for brokerage, as they also edited a magazine called *Woodhull and Claflin's Weekly*, for the propagation of Free Thought and Free Love, and in April 1870 Victoria offered herself as the first woman candidate for the Presidency. They also succeeded in combining stockbroking with an admiration for Marxism, but clients who had been prepared to overlook the sisters' other idiosyncrasies withdrew their support after Victoria had declared herself a free lover from a public platform at the Steinway Hall, and business declined sharply. There was a further scandal when Tennessee assumed the honorary Colonelcy of two Negro regiments and, after three years in operation, the firm of Woodhull, Claflin & Co was obliged to close.
GB: The first woman stockbroker was a Miss Bell, about whom regrettably little is known except that she had an office in Bucklesbury in the City of London in 1890 and was then 'between 30 and 40'.

WOMAN MEMBER OF A STOCK EXCHANGE: the first was Miss Oonagh Keogh of Foxrock, Eire, who was admitted to the Dublin Stock Exchange on 9 July 1925 at the age of 22, and remained an active broker until her resignation in 1939. Miss Keogh was able to make her application under a provision of the Irish Free State Constitution that guaranteed equality of opportunity to every citizen over the age of 21. Since the approval of new members was the responsibility of the Minister of Finance, the Committee of the Exchange was precluded from barring her on grounds of sex, though a number of brokers declared their intention of ignoring her on the floor. To begin with, Miss Keogh confined her activities to recording the deals made by her father, also a member, but when he became ill she took over full responsibility and her aptitude soon won the respect of her male colleagues.
GB: The first woman to be elected to a stock exchange with a trading floor was Miss C. V. Ward, a partner in the firm of Walter Ward, who became a member of the Sheffield Stock Exchange on 10 June 1965.

The first 10 women members of the London Stock Exchange were elected with effect from 25 March 1973. The following day Mrs Susan Shaw became the first woman to set foot on the floor of the Stock Exchange in the 171 years of its history.

The first
WOMAN TO WEAR TROUSERS

as an article of feminine apparel was the French actress Sarah Bernhardt, who was photographed at her Paris studio by Mélandri in 1876 costumed in a jacketed trouser-suit of extraordinarily modern style and appearance. It should be noted that the notorious 'bloomers' introduced by the American feminist Amelia Bloomer in 1848 were baggy pantaloons worn beneath a short skirt, and not trousers in the generally accepted sense.

Women of fashion, ready enough to follow Sarah Bernhardt's lead in other directions, did not emulate her in this. It was women's entry into the world of organized games that eventually allowed for a relaxation of the prevailing code on what was acceptable female wear. The first woman known to have adopted trousers for sporting purposes was 25-year-old Miss Eleonora Sears of Boston, Mass., who in 1909 appeared on the polo ground of the Burlingame Country Club in jacket and trousers and asked to be allowed to participate in a match about to be played against a team from England. It is recorded that the English Captain was rendered speechless and that the Manager of the

American team promptly ordered her from the field. Miss Sears was a superb all-round sportswoman and did much to allow for the active participation of women in games on a par with men. She also believed passionately that they would never attain equality on the playing-field until they discarded the full-length skirts that were still *de rigueur* for most outdoor activities at this date (though knickerbockers were sometimes worn for cycling and athletics).

The reaction to Miss Sears's innovation makes it the more remarkable that when only 10 years later Miss Elaine (later Baroness) Burton became the first sportswoman to wear shorts, at the English Northern Counties Ladies' Athletics Championships, she met with relatively little opposition. What was considered marginally acceptable for athletics in 1919, however, was not allowed as proper for any other sport for at least another decade. Towards the end of the 1920s, a few of the more daring spirits began to adopt shorts for hiking, a craze of the period. Not until July 1933 did Miss Eileen Bennett succeed in breaking down another barrier, when she became the first Englishwoman to appear on the tennis-court in shorts, at a party given by Lady Crosfield in London. As a concession to femininity Miss Bennett's shorts were pleated; the effect on her 'correctly' attired fellow guests was no less electrifying.

The first uniformed women to wear trousers (as opposed to breeches) were conductresses and guards of the Prussian State Railways under a regulation issued in the summer of 1916. It was ruled that female employees on the railways should be issued with the same costume as men, including 'dark grey wide trousers'.

Outside the domains of organized labour and organized sport, trousers for women emerged first as beach pyjamas at fashionable Riviera resorts in the late 1920s, and were followed by the first trousers for street wear in the form of slacks, *c.* 1931. Trouser-suits, not unlike Sarah Bernhardt's, but designed for day wear, burst upon a startled London in 1933.

The first
WOMAN TO VOTE IN A PARLIAMENTARY ELECTION

was Mrs Lily Maxwell, the independent proprietor of a small shop selling kitchenware, who attended the polls on the occasion of the Manchester by-election of 26 November 1867. As a ratepayer – in itself unusual for a woman at this time – Mrs Maxwell had been placed on the electoral register in error. The Secretary of the Manchester Women's Suffrage Society, Miss Lydia Becker, canvassed her vote on behalf of the Liberal candidate, Mr Bright, and received the welcome answer: 'If I'd twenty votes I would give them all to Jacob Bright.' She was escorted to the polling-booth by a bodyguard of Liberal supporters, enlisted to protect her in the event of loutish behaviour by opponents, and made her public declaration in favour of Mr Bright in the manner customary before the advent of the secret ballot. Contrary to expectation, her spoken vote was met by ringing cheers from the whole assembled crowd, irrespective of party persuasion.

Mr Bright, younger brother of John Bright, was returned to Parliament and very appropriately made a name for himself as one of the champions of the women's cause.

Prior to the General Election held in the autumn of 1868, a number of female ratepayers succeeded in having their names placed on the electoral register, the law being as yet untested on the question. Eight women are known to have voted in Manchester and at least three in London. One of the arguments most often advanced in opposition to granting women the right to vote was that they would be subjected to indignities and possibly to actual bodily harm in the rough hurly-burly that characterized the polling-booths of the period. Nothing of this kind happened. Nevertheless the rights assumed by this handful of women voters were immediately called into question, and by a decision of the Court of Common Pleas given on 9 November 1868, female suffrage was declared to be illegal.

WOMEN GRANTED THE RIGHT TO VOTE IN PARLIAMENTARY ELECTIONS: the first were widows and spinsters of the Isle of Man holding real estate to an annual value of £4, who were enfranchised by the House of Keys Election Act passed on 21 December 1880. Women went to the polls for the first time on the occasion of the General Election to the House of Keys held on 5 April 1881. The property qualification was removed in 1892.

NATION TO GRANT ITS FEMALE CITIZENS THE RIGHT TO VOTE: the first was the self-governing colony of New Zealand, the Electoral Reform Act that conferred this privilege receiving the Governor's Assent on 19 September 1893. There was no qualification other than attainment of the age of majority. Although the enfranchisement of women had been proposed as early as 1843 by Alfred Saunders (who happily lived to see its fulfilment 50 years later), there was no organized campaign until the founding of the

Women going to the poll in New Zealand. They were the first representatives of their sex entitled to vote in national elections.

Franchise Department of the Women's Christian Temperance Union under Mrs K.W. Sheppard in 1886. In the comparatively short space of seven years, Mrs Sheppard and her followers succeeded in winning the support of a majority of the Legislative Council, though not of a minority of dissident members who petitioned the Governor against the proposal, on the grounds that votes for women would 'seriously affect the rights and property of Her Majesty's subjects not resident in the colony . . . and may seriously embarrass the finances of the colony'. The Bill, while drawing support from both the ruling Liberal Party and the opposition Conservative Party, passed its Third Reading in the Upper House by the bare margin of two votes.

The first occasion on which the women of New Zealand went to the polls was the General Election of 28 November 1893. William Pember Reeves, the Liberal candidate for Christchurch, wrote:

The women began to vote early – at about nine o'clock – and by amicable arrangement were allowed in the cities to have certain booths pretty much to themselves until noon. . . . Each woman armed herself conscientiously with her number, and on the whole the novices went through the ordeal with much credit. The proportion of spoiled ballot papers was very little larger than at previous elections. When the polls closed at seven o'clock, 90,000 women had peacefully voted.

GB: Women were first permitted to vote in elections to the Parliament at

Westminster under the Representation of the People Act that became law on 6 February 1918. Although technically the Act came into immediate effect, there was a clause precluding electoral registers from being amended until the proper appointed time; newly enfranchised women had no opportunity to exercise their right in any of the by-elections of that year. They voted for the first time in the General Election contested on 14 December 1918, a total of 8,482,528 female electors having registered the previous month. The age qualification was reduced from 30 to 21 in 1928.

The first
WOMEN'S COLLEGE
to admit full-time students was Oberlin Collegiate Institute, Oberlin, Ohio, founded by Theodore Weld and a number of his fellows who withdrew from Lane Theological Seminary, Cincinnati in order to establish a college with neither sex nor colour as an entry qualification. It opened on 3 December 1833 with 44 students, 29 men and 15 women. Although the declared intention of the college was to fit its women students 'for intelligent motherhood and a properly subservient wifehood', Oberlin did in fact become one of the fountainheads of the feminist movement.

The first college exclusively for women was Mount Holyoke Female Seminary, opened under Miss Mary Lyon at South Hadley, Mass. on 8 November 1837. The curriculum included chemistry, astronomy, geology, rhetoric, logic, moral philosophy, natural theology and ecclesiastical history. The 80 students paid annual fees of $64 and the prospectus indicated that they were expected to assist with the housework. The college did not award degrees, but diplomas were awarded to the first four students to graduate on 23 August 1838.
GB: Queen's College, Harley Street, London, opened under the Rev. F. D. Maurice on 1 May 1848. The first two students were Miss Sarah D. Woodman and Miss King, but by the end of the first term 200 students had been enrolled. The College was founded with the intention of raising the educational standard of governesses. Neither Queen's nor Bedford College (founded 1849) were accorded university status. The first women's college in Britain to offer higher education at university level (though not empowered to award degrees) was the College for Women, Benslow House, Hitchin, Hertfordshire. It was founded by Miss Emily Davies, and opened with five students under Mrs Manning in October 1869. It was removed to Girton, near Cambridge in 1873, and has since been known by that name.
COLLEGE TO GRANT DEGREES TO WOMEN: the first was Oberlin Collegiate Institute (*see above*), where Caroline Mary Rudd of Huntingdon, Conn., Elizabeth Smith Prall of New York and Mary Hosford of Oberlin, Ohio graduated as Bachelors of Arts on 25 August 1841.
GB: London University was empowered to grant degrees to women by a Supplementary Charter of 4 May 1878. The first three woman graduates were: Elizabeth M. Creak of Redditch, student at Newnham Hall, Cambridge; Marianne Andrews of 73 Westwick Gardens, London, student at University College, London; Mrs Elizabeth Hills of the East of England Girls' School, Bishop's Stortford, Hertfordshire, private study. They graduated as Bachelors of Arts on 17 November 1880. The first woman MA was Mary Clara Dawes of Newton House, Surbiton, student at Girton College, Cambridge, MA Classics, London University, 1884. At this time London University was solely a degree-awarding body and had no constituent colleges. Consequently its degree examinations were open to anyone in the country who had passed matriculation.

The first
WOMEN'S MAGAZINE
was *The Ladies' Mercury*, a question-and-answer weekly published by the London bookseller John Dunton commencing 27 June 1693. With this periodical Dunton initiated what is known in female journalism today as a 'Problem Page' – indeed it consisted of only this feature and comprised but a single sheet, printed on both sides. 'Ladies are desired to send in their questions to the Latin Coffee House in Ave Mary [*sic*] Lane', wrote Dunton in the first issue. He promised answers 'to all the most nice and curious questions concerning love, marriage behaviour, dress and honour of the female sex, whether virgins, wives or widows . . . with the zeal and softness becoming the sex'. Both questions and answers were generally couched in frank and forceful language, and the Editor evinced no disinclination to admit such subjects as adultery and pre-marital sex into his columns. This full-blooded approach towards matters affecting the feminine psyche remained characteristic of problem pages in women's magazines until their discontinuance in the latter half of the 18th century. The revival of this kind of feature by S. O. Beeton in his *Englishwoman's Domestic Magazine* of 1852 under the title 'Cupid's Letter Bag' was marked by a far more discreet handling of readers' problems.

The first women's magazine edited by a woman and the first to contain articles on miscellaneous topics was *The Female Tatler*, inaugurated in July 1709 by 'Mrs Crackenthorpe'. This pseudonym cloaked the identity of the notorious Mrs Mary de la Rivière Manley, who was arrested for libel in October of the same year for her scandalous work *Secret Memoirs and Manners of Several Persons of Quality*. Similar intimate revelations in *The Female Tatler* caused the magazine to be indicted as a 'nuisance' by a Grand Jury shortly afterwards, and this seems to have effectively altered the character of the paper, which was said to have become 'as insipid as anything in print'.
WOMEN'S FICTION MAGAZINE: the first was *The Records of Love, or Weekly Amusements for the Fair*, which ran for 12 issues in 1710.
FASHION MAGAZINE: the first was the fortnightly *Le Cabinet des Modes*, launched in Paris in 1785. Its novelty may be inferred from the Editor's claim that readers 'will no longer be obliged to maintain commission agents at great expense or to have dolls made, puppets always inadequate and yet extremely dear, which give at best merely a hint of our new modes'.
GB: The Gallery of Fashion, a monthly established by the German artist Nicolaus von Heidoloff in 1794, subscription 3gns a year. It continued until 1803.

The first mass-circulation women's magazine aimed at the middle-class English housewife was launched by 21-year-old Samuel Orchart Beeton as *The Englishwoman's Domestic Magazine* in May 1852. His intention, the young publisher declared, was 'to produce a work which should tend to the improvement of the intellect, the cultivation of the morals, and the cherishing of domestic virtues'. The housewives of England were not in the least put off by this somewhat forbidding recital, and flocked to have their morals cultivated for only 2d a month. Its low price was undoubtedly one of the success factors of Beeton's venture.

By 1856, the year that he married Isabella Mayson (Mrs Beeton of culinary fame), the circulation of *The Englishwoman's Domestic Magazine* had risen to an unprecedented 37,000, and was to reach 50,000 by the end of the decade. Mrs Beeton's contribution's on household management undoubtedly helped to win new readers, but much of its appeal lay in the novel features introduced by Samuel Beeton at the outset, including the first give-away paper dressmaking patterns, the first prize competitions to appear in a women's magazine, and the reintroduction of the 'problem page'. He also credited his female readers with sufficient intelligence to appreciate fiction of a distinctly higher merit than the gothic romances and stories of abducted heiresses that formed the literary staple of other periodicals for women. Considering that this magazine held sway in the front parlours of respectable middle-class villas through what were perhaps the least permissive 25 years of Victoria's reign, it may seem strange to find some of its numbers relegated to the Closed Case at the British Museum as pornography. They contain a continuing correspondence from readers that so caught and enlivened the public imagination as to persuade Samuel Beeton he should issue a special supplement with the letters reprinted under the title 'On the the Whipping of Girls, and the General Corporal Punishment of Children'. The boost in the magazine's circulation might have been less gratifying to its earnest and well-intentioned Editor had he suspected, as the Trustees of the British Museum have since, that the authorship of these letters 'was not confined to those with a genuine interest in juvenile education'.

See also Fashion Photograph.

The first
WORKING-MEN'S CLUB
was the Collonade Working-men's Club, opened in a room in the Collonade, Clare Market, London, under the Presidency of Viscount Ingestre in 1852. Newspapers, books and refreshments were provided, as well as entertainment of a suitably uplifting kind. It differed from previous working-class institutes and fraternities in that its aims were solely recreational, and not educational, political or religious. In spite of this the Club languished after a short time, possibly on account of too much supervision by well-intentioned but overbearing upper-class philanthropists – a constant complaint by members of early working-men's clubs.

The nation-wide club movement dates from the founding of the Working Men's Club and Institute Union by the Rev. Henry Solly on 14 June 1862. Solly rightly believed that working men should be allowed to manage their clubs themselves, but made an initial error by insisting that drink and tobacco should be banned on all club premises. It was only when he was forced to rescind this rule in 1865 that the movement began to make positive headway. His own devotion to the cause, even when he found that it could not be made an instrument of Temperance reform, never wavered. Henry Fawcett, the Postmaster-General, introduced his wife to Solly with the words: 'This is Henry Solly, my dear, who believes that Heaven consists of Working Men's Clubs.'

The first
YACHTS
recorded, were six sailing-vessels that took part in a water festival held at Amsterdam in honour of Prince William I of Orange on 17 March 1580. Originally *jaghts* were small, swift sailing-craft employed as escorts to merchant vessels bound for Portugal or the Baltic. The date at which they were first employed for recreational or sporting purposes is not known, though by the early 17th century they were being used in the annual Admiral Sailing at Amsterdam, a kind of water pageant with a competitive element in which manœuvres were carried out by flag signals, and mock battles fought.
GB: The first yacht to sail in English waters was the 100-ton *Mary*, presented to King Charles II by the Dutch East India Company on 15 August 1660. A 52ft-long single-masted vessel with cutter rig, the *Mary* was described as a 'curious piece' by John Evelyn, who recorded in his *Diary* that the notion of a pleasure-boat was something new to England.

The first yacht to be built in Britain was the *Katherine*, constructed for Charles II at Deptford by Peter Pett, and launched in March 1661. Named after the Queen, she was 49ft long and of 94 tons burthen. Later the same year the King raced the *Katherine* against his brother's yacht *Anne*, from Greenwich to Gravesend, in the first competition of this kind ever held.
STEAM YACHT: the first recorded was the 400-ton *Menai*, built for Thomas Assheton-Smith in 1829. Two years earlier the Royal Yacht Club (forerunner of the Royal Yacht Squadron), of which Assheton-Smith was a leading member, had attempted to forestall any such blemish upon the seas by instituting a rule that 'any member applying steam to his yacht shall be disqualified hereby and shall cease to be a member'. Incensed at what he considered an unwarranted interference with personal choice, Assheton-Smith built the *Menai* apparently as a gesture of defiance and resigned from the Club.

The first
ZIP-FASTENER
was invented by Whitcomb L. Judson of Chicago, and consisted of two metal chains that could be joined together in a single movement by a slide-fastener. Designed for use on boots and shoes, it was exhibited at the Chicago Exposition of 1893 and attracted the attention of Col Lewis Walker, who formed the Automatic Hook & Eye Co at Meadville, Pa. later the same year to undertake manufacture. Judson's device had a number of design defects, the most basic being that it easily came apart. An improved version was manufactured in 1902 by Walker's Universal Fastener Co under the brand-name C-Curity, but the public remained unimpressed. Success was finally achieved by a young Swedish engineer from Hoboken, N.J., Gideon Sundback, who was granted a patent for 'separable fasteners' on 29 April 1913. The first zipper to work on the principle of identical units mounted on parallel tapes, Sundback's invention was marketed by Col Walker as the Talon Slide Fastener. This was the zip as we know it today, simple to operate and completely reliable, though at first it met with the same indifference as Judson's vastly inferior device of 20 years earlier. Then in 1917 America entered the war, and almost overnight a small manufacturing concern became an industry. The US Navy ordered zips for flying-clothes, the Army used them on the pockets of uniforms and the Air Corps adapted them for aeroplane fabric. After the war ex-servicemen spread the zipper habit, and they were incorporated into an assortment of leather goods, footwear and sports clothes.
GB: On its introduction as the Ready Fastener by Kynoch of Birmingham in 1919, the English reacted to the zip much as the Americans had done before the war. Their change of heart was brought about in 1924, when a large zipper on a stand was displayed at the Wembley Empire Exhibition. The sceptical public were invited to try for themselves and by the end of the Exhibition the fastener had been zipped and unzipped 3 million times without catching. The first articles of clothing to be fitted with zips in Britain were sports suits in 1927.

The first couturier to employ zips on women's dresses was Mme Schiaparelli at her Paris fashion house in 1930. When the New York fashion houses followed suit in 1931, the zip at last found its place as a regular fashion accessory and Walker and Sundback rapidly found themselves millionaires.

Zip-fasteners on men's trousers were introduced in 1935.

SOURCES OF ILLUSTRATION

Endpapers (left to right)
Modern reconstruction of Cayley's glider: Anglia Television; the first television commercial, 1930, for Eugène Hair Wave: *Television*, Royal Television Society; one of the original Belgian pillar boxes of 1849: Ministère des Communications et des Postes, Brussels; the first man on the moon, 21 July 1969: NASA, Washington

Title-page
The first petrol-driven car to be manufactured – the 2hp Benz of 1888
Daimler-Benz AG

page 7 *The Parrot*, 11 November 1887
9 Martin-Baker (Aircraft) Ltd
11 John W.R. Taylor
13 United States Information Service
14 United Air Lines
16 Courtesy of The Post Office
17 Courtesy of the Commandant, Royal Army Medical College
23 *Illustrated London News*
24 The Library of Congress, Washington
27 Stanley K. Hunter
29 Oyslager Organization BV
32 (above) from *Cyprus As I Saw It* by Sir Samuel Baker, London 1880; (below) from *The Cruise of the Land Yacht 'Wanderer'* by W. Gordon Stables, London 1886
35 Cadbury Bros
36 *Illustrated London News*
41 *Illustrated London News*
42 New York Public Library
46 *De Natuur* 1881
48 *The London Magazine*
49 Mansell Collection
52 Gestetner Ltd
53 *La Nature* 1890
55 Smithsonian Institution
57 Otis Elevator Co
59 (left) Australian Post Office; (right) *Illustrated London News*
61 Crown Copyright, Science Museum, London
64 Kodak Museum
67 (left) Lent to Science Museum, London by Miss G. M. Le Prince; (right) National Film Collection, National Library of Australia.
69 Kodak Museum
72 from *The Origin of Finger-Printing* by Sir William J. Herschel, London 1916
77 Girl Guides Association
78 from *A Magnificent Man and his Flying Machines*, Anglia Television
81 Royal Aeronautical Society
82 Ladbroke Holidays Ltd
85 Roger-Viollet
87 Museo Nazionale della Scienza e della Tecnica Leonardo da Vinci, Milan
90 By courtesy of Linda Hannas, from her book *The English Jigsaw Puzzle 1760–1890*
93 Ministère des Communications et des Postes, Brussels
94 Mander and Mitchenson Collection
96 Crown Copyright, Science Museum, London
99 Daimler-Benz AG
100 Automobile Club de France
103 Museo del'Automobile, Turin
105 Marconi
106 *Buffalo Evening News*
109 Daimler-Benz AG
111 Daimler-Benz AG
112 Crown Copyright, Science Museum, London
114 City of Liverpool Housing Department
116 Internationales Zeitungsmuseum, Aachen
118 *New York Daily Graphic*
120 *Illustrated London News*
122 *Illustrated London News*
124 *Illustrated London News*
125 Trustees of the Chatsworth Settlement
127 Nottingham Historical Film Unit
129 Willi Bernhard Collection, Hamburg
130 Percival F. Hinton
133 Metropolitan Commissioner of Police
136 *The Strand Magazine* 1896
137 Australian High Commission
139 Trustees of the British Museum
144 The Marconi Co Ltd
146 *Popular Wireless* 1922
148 The Marconi Co Ltd
150 The Marconi Co Ltd
152 *Illustrated London News*
153 Royal Museum, Canterbury
156 Frigidaire, Ohio
160 Dunlop Ltd
162 The Automobile Association
163 Singer
166 (above) Crown Copyright, Science Museum, London; (below) Decca Record Co Ltd
168 NASA, Washington
172 from *A Tour of Teesdale* by Richard Garland, 1848, courtesy of the Durham County Library
175 *Illustrated London News*
177 (above) By courtesy of The Post Office (below) from *Archiv für das Post- und Fernmeldewesen*, courtesy of the Hans Bredow Institute, Hamburg
181 Pressebilderdienst Kindermann & Co, Berlin
183 (above right and left) Royal Television Society; (below) Crown Copyright, Science Museum, London
184 Royal Television Society
187 Deutsches Museum, Munich
189 Author's collection: photo by Derek Witty
192 from *The World on Wheels* by H.O. Duncan
197 from *The World on Wheels* by H.O. Duncan
199 Crown Copyright, Science Museum, London
203 *Illustrated Sporting and Dramatic News*
206 *Illustrated London News*
207 *Auckland Institute and Museum*

CHRONOLOGY

Firsts contained in the text have been printed in *italics* and the page numbers on which they occur are in square brackets.

For reasons of space the following abbreviations have been used:

AA	Automobile Association (GB)
ad	advertisement
adv	advertised
apnt	appointed
archt	architect
Arg	Argentina
arr	arrived
assoc	association
attrib	attributed
Aus	Australia
Aust	Austrian
b	born
battn	battalion
bdcst	broadcast
BEA	British European Airways
Beds	Bedfordshire (GB)
Belg	Belgium
Berks	Berkshire (GB)
Br	British: in brackets after a first signifies the first British (but not world) use of something when this took place outside Britain, as for example the use of particular weapons in warfare
BR	British Rail
Bucks	Buckinghamshire (GB)
Can	Canada, Canadian
C.I.	compression-ignition engine
Co	Company
C of E	Church of England
Con	Conservative Party (GB)
d	dated
Dan	Danish
dem	demonstrated
dept	department
des	designed
desc	described
dev	devised
disc	discovered
ed	editor
edn	edition
EMI	Electrical and Musical Industries (GB)
Eng	England, English
estab	established
exp	experimental
f	founded
FA	Football Association (GB)
Fr	France, French
GB	Great Britain: the British Isles prior to 6 December 1922 and Great Britain and Northern Ireland after that date. GB after a first signifies the first in Britain. Where no place is given under GB entries, it may be assumed to be London
GCE	General Certificate of Education (GB)
Ger	Germany, German
Gk	Greece, Greek
Glos	Gloucestershire (GB)
Govt	Government
GPO	General Post Office (GB)
GWR	Great Western Railway (GB)
Hants	Hampshire (GB)
HE	His Excellency
Herts	Hertfordshire (GB)
HMS	His/Her Majesty's Service
HMV	His Master's Voice (GB)
Hunts	Huntingdonshire (GB)
illus	illustration
inaug	inaugurated
inc	included
inst	instituted
introd	introduced
inv	invented
It	Italy, Italian
IW	Isle of Wight
Lab	Labour Party (GB)
labs	laboratories
Lancs	Lancashire (GB)
Lat	Latin
LCC	London County Council
Lib	Liberal Party (GB)
Lincs	Lincolnshire (GB)
LMS	London Midland & Scottish Railway
MCC	Marylebone Cricket Club
Middx	Middlesex (GB)
mkt	marketed
mnf	manufactured: in brackets after a heading signifies regular commercial production
MoT	Ministry of Transport (GB)
MP	Member of Parliament (GB)
mthly	monthly
NAAFI	Navy, Army and Air Force Institute (GB)
NCO	non-commissioned officer
Neths	Netherlands
NI	Northern Ireland
Nor	Norway
Northumb	Northumberland (GB)
Notts	Nottinghamshire (GB)
NSW	New South Wales (Australia)
NT	New Testament
NZ	New Zealand
orig	originated
org	organized
OT	Old Testament
p.a.	per annum
PABX	private automatic branch exchange
pat	patented
PC	police constable (GB)
Pemb	Pembrokeshire (GB)
PM	Prime Minister (GB)
PO	Post Office
pop	population
pr	printed
prod	produced
PT	physical training
pub	published, publication
p.w.	per week
Qn	Queen
RAC	Royal Automobile Club (GB)
RAF	Royal Air Force (GB)
RAMC	Royal Army Medical Corps (GB)
RASC	Royal Army Service Corps (GB)
RE	Royal Engineers (GB)
rec	recorded
ref	reference
reg	regular
regt	regiment
reprod	reproduced
RFC	Royal Flying Corps (GB)
rly	railway
RMS	Royal Mail Steamer (GB)
RN	Royal Navy (GB)
RNAS	Royal Naval Air Service (GB)
RNVR	Royal Naval Volunteer Reserve (GB)
RSM	Regimental Sergeant Major (GB)
RSPCA	Royal Society for the Prevention of Cruelty to Animals (GB)
Rus	Russian
SA	South Africa
SAS	Special Air Service Regiment (GB)
Scot	Scotland
Sec	Secretary
soc	society
Sp	Spain, Spanish
Staffs	Staffordshire (GB)
STD	subscriber trunk dialling (GB)
Swn	Sweden, Swedish
Swz	Switzerland, Swiss
tr	transmitted
trans	translation
univ	university
USA	United States of America, American
VC	Victoria Cross
vol	volume
VTOL	vertical take-off and landing
V/STOL	vertical/short take-off and landing
wkly	weekly
WRAF	Women's Royal Air Force (GB)
WRNS	Women's Royal Naval Service (GB)
Yorks	Yorkshire (GB)

767
Printed text (known): 1 million dhāranī (thanksgiving prayers) pr on paper by order of Empress Shokutu of Japan

816
Anno Domini system of dating GB: adopted by Council of Chelsea

851
Porcelain (rec): Chinese porcelain drinking vessels desc by traveller Soleiman

868
Printed book: 11 May [139]

969
Playing cards (rec): [131]

983
Canal lock: built by Chiao Wei-Yo on Grand Canal of China, near Huai-yin

1041
Printing from movable type (rec): type cast by Pi Shêng, China

1045
Gunpowder: earliest-known formula pub in the Chinese *Complete Compendium of Military Classics*

1088
Clock (rec): [40]

1103
Fireworks (rec): in use China

1110
Play (rec) GB: *Saint Catherine* by Geoffrey, Abbot of St Albans

1126
Artesian well: bored at Lillers, Artois

1136
Arabic numerals used in Europe: by Gerard of Cremona in his translation of Ptolemy's *Almagest*

1157
Lighthouse: Meloria, Italy

1194
Coroners GB: apnt under Richard I's Article of Eyre

1205
Vicar (non-conventual priest) GB: Standish, Glos, Eng

1217
Treaty (formal and written) GB: England–France, 11 Sept

1226
Glass manufacture GB: by Laurence Vitraerius, Chiddingfold, Surrey. Bottles and window glass

1233
Piped water supply GB: Paddington–Westminster

1258
Document in the English language (known): Henry III's Oxford Provision

1259
Soap manufacture (rec) GB: in Sopar's Lane, London

1266
Blindfold chess match (rec): Bizzecca played two opponents blindfold, Florence, Jan

1269
Gunpowder GB: earliest formula by Oxford monk Roger Bacon in his *De Secretis Operibus Artis*

1279
Glass mirror: desc by John Peckham, Franciscan monk of Oxford, Eng

1283
Clock (rec) GB: [40]

1285
Watermark (known): Fabriano, Italy

1289
Spectacles (rec): [168]

1299
Sugar (rec) GB: Moroccan sugar available in Durham

1301
Prince of Wales: Edward of Caernarvon (later Edward II), 7 Feb

1307
Guillotine (rec): execution of Murcod Ballagh at Merton, Ireland, 1 April

1311
History of the world: *Jami'u't-Tawarikh* (Great Universal History), Rashid-eddin, Persia

1325
Clock dial (rec) GB: [40]

1326
Spectacles (rec) GB: [168]
Guns (rec): [79]

1331
Artillery in warfare (rec): [80]

1337
Duke GB: Edward, Duke of Cornwall, 17 Mar

1338
Hand gun (rec): [80]

1346
Artillery in warfare (Br): 25 Aug [80]

1352
Parliament, upper and lower houses GB: Commons and Lords met separately

1362
Court proceedings in English (rec): Oct

1376
Speaker of the House of Commons: Sir Peter de la Mare, took office 29 April

1384
English Bible: trans by John Wycliffe

1385
Marquis: Robert de Vere, M of Dublin

1388
Bowls (rec): prohibitive statute (12 Richard II)

1389
Comedy play (rec): *Paulus*, by Pier Paolo Vergerio of Bologna, Italy

1392
Type foundry: Korea

1399
English monarch to abdicate: Richard II, 29 Sept

1400
Beer GB: imported to Winchelsea from Flanders

1409
Book printed from movable type (rec): [139]

1411
Hand guns used in warfare: [80]

1413
Club (rec): GB [40]

1414
Passports (rec) GB: issue regulated by Act
Warship to carry heavy armament: 6-gun 760-ton *Holy Ghost*, built Southampton, Eng

1427
Lighthouse (rec) GB: Spurn Point, Yorks

1436
Beer, brewing of (rec) GB: brewers from Holland and Seland accorded royal protection

1451
Book printed from movable type (rec) *Europe:* [139]
Income tax: [86]

1453
Lord Mayor's Show: inst by Sir John Norman, London

1454
Calendar, printed: pr by Johannes Gutenberg, Mainz

1456
Printed Bible: 15 Aug [139]

1457
Golf (rec): prohibitive decree of Scottish Parliament, Mar

1460
Dictionary (printed): *Catholicon* (Lat-Ger), Friar Johannes Balbus Januensis, Mainz

1461
Books printed in vernacular: Ulrich Boner's *Edelstein*; Johann von Tepl's *Ackermann aus Böhmen.* Both pr by Albrecht Pfister, Bamberg

1462
Watch (rec): [198]

1463
Numbering of houses: [119]
Playing cards (rec) GB: [131]

Table fork (rec) GB: 'my silvir forke for grene gyngor' mentioned in will of John Baret of Bury St Edmunds

1465
Roman type: Donatus grammar pr by Conrad Schweynheym (Ger) and Arnold Pannartz (Ger) at Subiaco, Italy
Blotting paper (rec) GB

1466
Advertisement, printed (known): handbill pr by Heinrich Eggerstein, Strasbourg
Bible in the vernacular: pub in Ger by Johann Mentelin, Strasbourg

1470
Page numbers in a printed book: Werner Rolewinck's *Sermo ad Populam*, pr by Arnold ther Hoernen, Cologne

1472
Printed music (known): gradual by unknown Constance printer

1473
Guide book (printed): Benedict's *Mirabilia Romae*, pr by Adam von Rottweil, Rome

1474
Book catalogue: maths books in preparation, issued by Regiomontanus, Nuremberg
Book printed in English: [139]

1475
Illustrated Bible (printed): pr by Jodocus Pflanzmann, Augsburg

1476
Text printed from movable type GB: indulgence pr by William Caxton, Westminster, 13 Dec
Book illustrations printed from plates: copper engravings in Colard Mansion's edn of Boccaccio's *De Casibus Illustrium Virorum*, Bruges

1477
Printed book GB: 18 Nov [139]
Advertisement, printed GB: book ad handbill pr by William Caxton
Dictionary in two living languages: *Vocabolario Italiano-Teutonico* (It-Ger), pub Adam von Rottweil, Venice

1478
Maps, printed: 27 maps of known world by Conrad Sweynheym in Ptolemy's *Cosmographia*, pr by Arnold Buckinck, Rome

1481
Missal (printed): by Jean Dupré, Paris
Printed book, illustrated GB: *The Mirror of the World*, pr by William Caxton, Westminster; 27 diagrams, 11 pictures

1482
Carpets (rec) GB: itemized in accounts of Duke of Bedford – 'xj carpettes bought from Xpofer Colens', 14 Nov

1487
Land mine: used by Genoese against Florentines at Siege of Serezanella

1489
Plus (+) and minus (−) signs: in John Widman's *Mercantile Arithmetic*, Leipzig

1490
Flower painting (known): Vase of lilies, iris and columbines by Hans Memling of Bruges

1491
Copyright: granted to Bernadinus de Choris in respect of *Foenix Magistri Petri memoriae Ravennatis*, Venice, 10 Jan
Illustrated advertisement (known): handbill adv *The Lovely Melusina*; illus showed heroine in bath. Pr in Antwerp

1493
Syphilis (Europe): outbreak in Barcelona, following Columbus's return from New World in Mar

1495
Printed music GB: in Ralph Higden's *Polychronicon*, pr by Wynkyn de Worde
Cookery book: *Honesta Volupate*, Bartholomaeus Platina, Venice
Scotch whisky (rec): mentioned in Exchequer Rolls. The distiller was Friar John Cor
Double-entry book-keeping: expounded by Lucas Paciolus, Venice
Paper mill GB: estab by John Tate, Stevenage, Herts

1496
Dry dock GB: Portsmouth; completed at cost of £193 0s 6¾d April
Compulsory education: for sons of Scottish barons and freeholders; penalty for non-compliance £20

1498
Toothbrush: [189]
Music printed from movable type: part-songs pr by Ottaviano dei Petrucci, Venice

1499
Dictionary (printed) GB: *Promptorium parvulorum sive clericorum* (Lat-Eng), pr by Richard Pynson

1500
Caesarian section: [30]
Italic type: Used in Aldine *Letters of St Catherine of Sienna*, Venice. Type cut by Francesco Griffo

1501
Hymn book: 13 Jan [84]

1504
Coins bearing accurate likeness of reigning English monarch: effigy of Henry Tudor from steel die struck by Alexander de Brugsaal

1505
International postal service: Thurn and Taxis Posts, Belgium–Austria

1508
Theatre scenery (rec): backdrop with houses, churches, etc, painted by Pellegrino da Udine for production of Ariosto's *Cassaria* at Ferrara, Italy

1509
Roman type GB: speech by papal collector Petrus Gryphus pr by Richard Pynson, May
Book printed in roman type GB: *The Ship of Fools*, pub by Richard Pynson 13 Dec
Wallpaper (rec): [198]

1510
Copyright GB: Granted to Thomas Godfry for *The History of King Boccus*

1512
Postal service GB: Royal Mail estab Aug

1514
Author to receive payment for published work GB: Thomas Murner for *Geuchmatt*

1515
Published play GB: Henry Medwall's *Fulgens et Lucres*

1517
Taxidermy: Cassowary birds from E. Indies stuffed at Amsterdam

1518
Professional body to conduct qualifying examination GB: Royal College of Physicians by charter d 23 Sept
Fire engine (rec): [73]

1519
Railway (rec): German mine track illus in *Der Ursprung gemeynner . . .*, Reichnau

1520
Playbill (known): issued Rostock, Ger

1522
Circumnavigation of earth: by Juan de Elcano, Capt. of 85-ton *Vittoria*, and 17 surviving crew; arr San Lucar de Barrameda, Spain after three-year voyage, 7 Sept

1526
New Testament in English (printed): William Tyndale's trans; pub by Peter Schoeffer, Worms, Feb

1527
Knitting (rec): earliest ref in foundation articles of French Stocking Knitters Guild, 16 Aug
Hockey (rec): 'hockie stickes' mentioned in Galway statute, Ireland

1528
Italic type GB: used by Wynkyn de Worde in Robert Wakefield's *Oratio de laudibus Trium linguarum*

1530
Dictionary in two living languages GB: John Palsgrave's *Lesclarcissiment de la langue francoyse* (Eng-Fr), pr by Richard Pynson
Bottle corks (rec): mentioned in Palsgrave's Fr-Eng dictionary

1531
Theatre (rec): [189]

1533
Knitting (rec) GB: ref to '4 peyr of knytt hose' in accounts of Sir Thomas L'Estrange, Hunstanton, Norfolk, 7 Sept

1534
Comma in printed English book: *A Devout Treatyse called the tree and XII frutes of the holy goost*

1535
Complete English Bible, printed: Myles Coverdale's trans; pub Cologne (?) Oct

1537
English Bible printed in Britain: Coverdale's trans; pr by James Nicholson of Southwark

1538
Children's alphabet: *The BAC* [sic] *bothe in Latyn and in Englysshe*, pr by Thomas Petyt

1539
Theatre GB: [189]
English hymn book: [84]
Cabbage GB: introd from Neths by Sir Anthony Ashley of Wimborne St Giles, Dorset

1540
Race meeting (rec) GB: held at Roodeye Fields, Chester, 9 Feb
Plus (+) and minus (−) signs GB: in Robert Recorde's *Grounde of Artes*

1543
Artillery shells: made by Peter Bawd (Ger) and Peter van Collen (Ger) at Royal Foundry, Greenwich, Eng
State schools: Fürsten-Schulen founded at Pforta, Meissen and Grimma in Saxony
Double-entry book-keeping GB: expounded by John Gowghe
University grants: awarded by State of Saxony to graduates of the Fürsten-Schulen
Land yacht: built for Elector Johann Friedrich at Torgau, Saxony

1544
Copyright Act: Venetian Republic

1545
Botanical gardens: at Univ of Padua, It
Conservatory: [45]
Bibliography: Carl Gessner's *Bibliotheca Universalis*, Zurich
Book illustrations printed from plates GB: anatomical engravings by Geminus in Vesalius's *De Humani Corporis Fabrica*

1546
Civil divorce GB: [50]

1547
Marine insurance GB: earliest-known policy issued to John Broke for vessel *Santa Maria*, 22 Sept

1548
Covered theatre: [189]

1549
Book of Common Prayer: adopted throughout Eng, 9 June

1550
Nonconformists GB: group of conventiclers led by Humphrey Middleton; organized Faversham, Kent, 23 June
Refrigeration (rec): [155]

1551
Civil divorce for adultery GB: [50]
Bible with numbered verses: Gk-Lat NT pub by Robert Estienne (Fr), Geneva

1552
Girls' boarding school (secular) GB: Christ's Hospital, London, opened 23 Nov

1553
Exclamation mark: [60]
Joint stock company GB: The Muscovy Co; paid-up capital £6,000 in 240 shares

1554
Sealing-wax (rec): used by Gerard Hermann, London, on letter to Rheingrave Philip von Daun, 3 Aug
Coffee house (rec): [41]
Comedy play (rec) *GB*: *Ralph Roister Doister*, by Southwark schoolmaster Nicholas Udall

1556
Tobacco (Europe): introd from Brazil by André Thevet of Angoulême, Fr

1557
Bibliography of English books: Bishop Bales's *Scriptorum Brytannie Catalogus*, Basle
English Bible with numbered verses: NT pub by William Whittingham, Geneva
English Bible in roman type: NT pub by William Whittingham, Geneva
Poetry anthology: *Songes and Sonnettes*, pub by Richard Tottell, London
Equals sign (=): [59]
Algebra GB: expounded by Robert Recorde, *The Whetstone of Witte*

1558
Doll's House: made for Duke Albrecht V of Bavaria, Munich

1559
Street map of London: engraved by Anthosis van den Wyngaerde

1561
Dredger: built by Pieter Breughel for Brussels municipality; used to excavate Rupel–Scheldt Canal

1562
Conservatory GB: [45]

1563
Children's book (GB): [34]

1564
Road haulage GB: [156]
Sale of copyright (rec) GB: Lucas Haryson to Thomas Marsh, London; rights to Dygges's *Prognostication*

1565
Unitarians: seceded from Polish Reformed Church at Diet of Piotrkow
Pencils (rec): desc by Konrad Gesner

of Zurich in his treatise on fossils
Ambassador (regular appointment): Raymond de Beccaria, Fr A to Spain

1572
Firework display (rec) GB: before Elizabeth I at Temple Fields, Warwick, Aug

1573
Potatoes in Europe (rec): itemized in accounts of Hospital de la Sangre, Seville

1574
Bookplate (known) GB: engraved for Sir Nicholas Bacon, Lord Chancellor

1575
Soft-paste porcelain (Europe): mnf by Bernado Buontalenti, Florence

1576
Observatory (purpose-built): Uraniborg, Denmark, by Tycho Brahe; begun 8 Aug
Theatre (purpose-built) GB: [189]
Autobiography (Eng): [20]

1577
Guide book GB: William Harrison's *Description of England*, with practical hints for travellers

1578
Prefabricated building GB: Nonesuch House, brought from Holland in sections and erected on London Bridge
Glass eyes: made by Ambroise Paré, Venice

1580
Englishmen to circumnavigate the earth: 50 sailors of the *Golden Hind*, arr Plymouth after 33-month voyage under Francis Drake, 26 Sept
Yacht (rec): [209]

1581
Congregationalists: followers of Robert Browne seceded from C of E, Norwich, Mar (?)
Booby trap, explosive: chest with detonator in lid dev by Johann Ostromecki (Pol); sent to Ivan Shujski, defender of Pskov, Russia. Killed Shujski's aides.

1582
Water piped to private houses GB: by London Bridge Waterworks, 24 Dec

1583
Life insurance policy (rec): 18 June [93]

1584
Pencils GB: made from graphite dug at Borrowdale, Cumberland

1585
Covered theatre (purpose-built): 3 Mar [189]
Time bombs: clockwork-actuated floating mines used by Dutch at Siege of Antwerp
Decimal fractions: expounded by Simon Stevin in *Die Thiende*, Leyden

1586
Potatoes GB: brought from Colombia by Sir Thomas Harriot, arr Plymouth 28 July
Learned society GB: Soc of Antiquaries; met wkly at Darby House, London
Tobacco GB: introduction variously attrib to Sir Walter Raleigh, Ralph Lane, Capt. Thomas Price *et al*
Freedom of worship, country to guarantee: Transylvania (Rumania); promulgated by Prince John Sigismund, history's only Unitarian ruler, at Diet of Torda

1587
Marmalade (rec) GB: 5s 3d for 21lb 1oz in accounts of Woolaton Hall, Notts
Asterisk GB: in *Arcadia*, Sir Philip Sidney
Question mark GB: as above

1588
Shorthand: [164]
Artillery shells used in warfare: by Dutch at sieges of Bergen-op-Zoom and Wachtendonck

1589
Knitting machine: inv by William Lee of Woodborough, Notts, Eng
Water closet: [199]

1590
Microscope: made by Hans and Zacharias Janssen, Middelburg, Neths

1591
Fire insurance: 3 Dec [74]
Billiards (rec): in Spenser's *Mother Hubberd's Tale*

1594
Desk diary (rec): *Neu und Alter Schreib Kalender*, pub by Bernhard Cracker, Breslau
Trigonometry GB: expounded by Thomas Blundeville in *Exercises*

1596
Private press: estab by Von Löhneysen at Zellerfeld for printing fine edns on mining and horsemanship

1597
Opera: [121]
Hammocks on RN vessels: authorized by Admiralty

1598
Signpost (rec) GB: in Kent

1599
Auction sale (rec): library of Philip von Marnix sold, Neths

1600
Oratorio: Emilio del Cavalieri's *La Rappresentazione di Anima e di Corpa*, performed Church of Santa Maria della Vallicella, Rome

1602
Abdominal surgery: dagger removed from stomach of sword-swallower Mattheus by Florian Mathis, Prague
Share certificates: issued by Dutch East India Co, 20 Mar

1603
Book translated from English: James I's *Basilicon Dovon*, pub in Fr and Dutch

1604
English dictionary: [49]

1605
Christmas tree (rec): Ger [37]
Railway GB: pit-head rly built by Sir Francis Willoughby at Wollaton, Notts
Passenger vehicles for public hire: Hackney carriages introd in London

1606
Union Jack: adopted 12 April

1607
Guy Fawkes' Day: 5 Nov [80]

1608
Public library GB: [141]
Middle name (rec) GB: [98]
Telescope: dem by Hans Lippershey of Middelburg to Neths States General, 2 Oct
Forks (as companion to table knives) GB: introd from Italy by Thomas Coryate, Oct

1609
Telescope GB: Dutch T used by Thomas Harriott at Syon House, Isleworth for making sketches of the Moon, June
Newspaper: Jan [116]
Tea GB: [173]
English Baptists: baptized by John Smyth, Amsterdam
Cut glass: Caspar Lehmann of Prague granted patent

1611
Baronet: Sir Nicholas Bacon of Redgrove, Suffolk, Eng, 23 May
Service rifles: Danish Army
Bible: King James Version pr by Robert Barker

1612
Flag flown at half-mast: July [75]
Newspaper advertisement: 14 Oct [116]
Baptist congregation GB: formed by Thomas Helwys, Spitalfields, London

1613
Temperature readings (daily): begun by Giovan-francesco Sagredo of Venice with Galileo thermometer, 12 July
Woman playwright GB: [206]

1614
Logarithms: John Napier's log tables pub by Andrew Hart, Edinburgh

1615
Vending machines (rec): [197]
Logarithms, teaching of: by Dr Henry Briggs at Gresham College, London

1617
One-way streets: Aug [190]
Fee-paying boarding-school for girls (known): The Ladies' Hall, Deptford, Eng
Decimal notation GB: by Henry Briggs of Gresham College, London, in his log tables
Microscope GB: Janssen model brought from Neths by Cornelius Drebbel

1618
Dredger GB: pat by Capt. John Gilbert, 16 July

1619
Post Office GB: estab at Royal Exchange for sending and receiving foreign mail; open to public
Compulsory education for all: ages 6–12, introd by State of Weimar

1620
Merry-go-round or carousel (rec): at fair held Philippopolis, Turkey, 17 May
English newspaper: 2 Dec [116]
Curling (rec): mentioned in Henry Adamson's poem *The Muses Threnodie*
Deaf and dumb sign language: desc by Juan Pablo Bonet, Madrid

1621
Newspaper GB: [116]
Fairy tale printed in Eng (known): *The History of Tom Thumbe the Little* . . ., London
Botanical gardens GB: Oxford Physic Garden
Greenhouse GB: [45]
Registration of births, deaths and marriages: [156]
Slide rule: inv by Rev. William Oughtred of Albury, Surrey, Eng
Microscope (mnf) GB: by Cornelius Drebbel (Neths), London

1623
English hymns published: [84]
Adding machine: built by Wilhelm Schickard of Tübingen, Ger

1624
Stamp duty: on all legal and official documents, Neths, 13 Aug
Submarine: [171]

1627
Public postal service (inland): foreign and inland at fixed rates, Fr

1630
Sash windows (rec): installed at Raynham Hall, Norfolk, Eng, by Inigo Jones

1631
Employment Agency: 4 July [58]
Multiplication sign (×): used by William Oughtred of Albury, Surrey, Eng, in his *Clavis Mathematica*

1632
Fire engine (rec) GB: [74]

1633
Bananas GB: exhibited by Thomas Johnson in his shop window, Snow Hill, London, 10 April
Bank GB: Lawrence Hoare, London goldsmith, began accepting cash deposits

1634
Fives (rec): windows of Locking Church, Banwell, Eng, broken by fives players
Cabstand: estab in the Strand, London, by Capt. Bailey

1635
Public postal service (inland) GB: estab by proclamation of 31 July;

rates 2d–8d by distance
Deaf and dumb sign language GB: used by Mistress Babington of Burntwood, Essex to converse with deaf husband

1636
Hospital for incurables: Hospice des Incurables, Paris

1637
Hackney-carriage licences: issued by the King's Master of Horse, July
Opera house: Teatro San Cassiano, Venice; opened with Manelli's *Andromedie*
Umbrellas (rec): [195]

1638
Army List GB: 195 officers named

1639
Milled-edge coins: Fr

1641
Baptist baptized by total immersion: Laurence Blacklock by Richard Blunt, London
Cotton manufacture (rec) GB: 'fustians, vermillions, and dimities' mnf from Cyprus cotton at Manchester

1642
Mezzotint: portrait of Landgravine Amelia Elizabeth reprod by Ludwig von Siegen (Neths), Darmstadt

1643
Medal for gallantry: awarded to Sir Robert Welch and Capt. John Smith for bravery at Edgehill (23 Oct 1642) under Royal Warrant d 1 June
Dictionary in Aboriginal tongue: Roger Williams's *A Key into the Language of America*
Parcel post: Paris

1644
Barometer: inv by Evangelista Torricelli, Florence; desc in letter d 11 June

1646
Newspaper advertisement GB: 23 Nov [116]
Shorthand classes: [164]

1647
Bayonets used in warfare: by Jacques de Chastenet's forces in Bergues and Ypres campaigns
Naval flag code: adopted by English Navy

1648
Quakers: 'Children of Light', an association of ex-Baptists f at Mansfield, Notts, Eng by George Fox
Barometer GB: Torricellian B built by Theodore Haak

1649
Grant aid for education GB: £20,000 p.a. appropriated for teachers' salaries and provision of new schools under Act of 8 June
Employment Agency GB: 12 Aug [58]
Toothbrush (rec) GB: [189]

1650
Daily newspaper: 1 July [116]
Campaign medal: Dunbar Medal (Parliamentary Army), Battle of Dunbar, Scotland, 3 Sept
Marriage bureau: 29 Sept [97]

1651
Tea (mkt) GB: [173]
Conscientious objector GB: George Fox, gaoled at Derby for refusing to join Parliamentary Army

1652
Illustrated newspaper advertisement GB: 2 April [116]
Unitarians GB: congregation formed in London by Gloucester schoolmaster John Biddle

1653
Meritorious service medal: awarded to crew of the *Triumph* for action against Dutch fleet, 31 July
Postage stamp: [137]
Public library open to all GB: [141]
Letter boxes: [92]
Postmen (to deliver inland mail): employed by Petite Poste, Paris

1654
Meteorological office: estab Tuscany under Luigi Antinori with observers in Parma, Milan, Bologna and Florence; daily temperature readings rec from 15 Dec
Air pump: dev by Otto von Guericke, Magdeburg

1656
Women jurors: 22 Sept [203]
English actress: Mrs Edward Coleman, played Ianthe in *The Siege of Rhodes* at Rutland House, Sept
Opera GB: Sept [121]
Pendulum clock: Neths, Dec [40]
Fountain Pen: [75]
Artificial pearls: mnf by M. Jacquin, Paris; pellets of gypsum covered with fish scales.

1657
Classified advertising: 19 May [117]
Reverend: earliest-known use of title by Rector of Tamworth, Staffs, Eng
Chocolate (rec) GB: [35]
Mileometer: Col Blount's 'Waywiser' fitted to coach, Eng
Pineapple GB: presented to Oliver Cromwell
Share dealing GB: East India Co shares became transferable

1658
Pendulum clock GB: [40]
Cheque (rec) GB: 16 Feb [34]
Air pump GB: Guericke pump made by Robert Boyle at Oxford
Debating society: [47]
Slide projector: built by Christiaan Huygens, The Hague
Rates of exchange: reg pub commenced Hamburg

1660
Daily Newspaper GB: 21 Feb [116]
Yacht GB: 15 Aug [209]
Cabinet GB: orig as Foreign Committee of the Privy Council, June
Shakespearian actress: Mrs Norris (?) played Desdemona, 8 Dec
Dentifrice (rec) GB: adv by Robert Turner, London, Dec
Printed wrapper for packaged product (known) GB: Buckworth's Cough Lozenges
Wet dock GB: Blackwall West Dock

1661
Yacht built in GB: Mar [209]
Postmarks: introd by GPO 19 April
Br monarch to attend theatre: 2 July [98]
Banknotes (Europe): issued by the Bank of Stockholm, 16 July
Yacht race: 1 Oct [209]
Dentist (rec): [47]
Coronation mugs: commemorating C of Charles II

1662
Overseas garrison of the Br Army: three regts stationed Tangier, 25 Jan
Lip reading GB: Jan [94]
Bus: 18 Mar [28]
Punch and Judy show GB: rec by Pepys; presented by Pietro Gimonde at Covent Garden, 9 May
Auction sale (rec) GB: *Weymouth, Successe* and *Fellowship* hulks auctioned 3 Sept
Ice skating (rec) GB: skating in St James's Park desc by Pepys, 1 Dec
Catamaran: GB 22 Dec [33]
Life-expectancy table: compiled by London haberdasher John Graunt

1663
Yacht race (open): won by Sir William Petty's catamaran *Experiment*, Dub lin, 12 Jan
Milled-edge coins GB: Feb
Postage due: franks introd by GPO Foreign Branch, 1 June
Fountain pen GB: Aug [75]
Slide projector GB: mnf by John Reeves, London

1664
Barometer with dial face: made by Robert Hooke, London
Theatre curtains: Ichimura-za Theatre, Edo, Japan
Marines: The Duke of York and Albany's Maritime Regt

1665
Periodical: *Journal des Scavans*, ed Denys de Sallo, Paris, 5 Jan (science, literature and law)
Periodical GB: *Acta Philosophica Societas Anglia*, ed Henry Oldenburg, 6 Mar (scientific)

1666
Bookcase (glass-fronted): built for Pepys by joiner Simpson, delivered 17 Aug
Spirit-level: by J. M. Thevenot, Paris
Census (national): New France (Canada); 3,215 European inhabitants

1667
Police force: Mar [134]
Art exhibition: 9 April [19]
Blood transfusion: 12 June [25]
Blood transfusion GB: 23 Nov [25]
Trade union (rec): formed by journeymen hatters, London

1668
Poet Laureate (so titled): John Dryden, apnt 13 April

1669
Lamp-posts (rec): in use Amsterdam by Feb
Businessmen's club: Civil Club, estab at New Corn Exchange Tavern, London, 19 Nov

1670
Medical journal: *Miscellenea curiosa Ephemeridium medico physicorum Germanorum*, Leipzig, May
Play by woman performed: Dec [206]
Megaphone: inv by Sir Samuel Morland; mnf by Simon Beal, Suffolk St, London

1672
Law journal: *Journal du Palais*, Paris, 16 Feb
Magazine: Mar [95]
Bayonet GB: issued to Prince Rupert's Regt under order d 2 April
Public concert GB: 30 Dec [45]
Slide projector used in teaching (rec): by Johann Sturm at Altendorf Univ, Swz
Fire hose: introd by Amsterdam firemaster Jan van der Heiden; 50ft leather length with brass screw joints

1673
Hymns in worship GB: [84]
Wine auction (rec) GB: at Garraway's Coffee House

1674
Fire hose GB: introd by royal enginemaker Isaac Thompson
Service club GB: [40]
Trench mortar: inv by Menno von Cochoorn, Neths

1675
Observatory GB: Greenwich, foundation stone laid 10 Aug

1676
Book auction GB: library of Dr Seaman (5,639 lots) sold by William Cooper, Warwick Court, 31 Aug
Sale catalogue GB: as above
Auctioneer, professional GB: William Cooper as above. Held regular sales for 11 years
Fire insurance Co: 17 Dec [74]

1677
Rainfall records (regular) GB: maintained by Richard Townley of Towneley, nr Burnley till 1703
Trade directory: Samuel Lee's *Collection of Names of Merchants living in and about the City of London* (1,953 entries)

1678
Part-work: *Mechanic Exercises*, pub by Joseph Moxon in 38 mthly parts from 1 Jan
Political parties GB: Whigs and Tories
Jewish newspaper: *Gazeta de Amsterdam* (Ladino)

1679
Hunt (regularly established): Charlton Hunt, Sussex, Eng, f by Duke of Monmouth; first MFH – Squire Roper

1680
Postage stamp GB: 1 April [137]
Postmen (to deliver inland mail) GB: employed by London Penny Post, 1 April
Fire insurance co GB: 13 May [74]
Service rifles GB: eight rifled carbines to each coy of Life Guards
Pressure cooker: inv by Denis Papin (Fr), London

1681
Boxing match (rec): org by Duke of Albemarle between his butler and his butcher, Jan

1683
Museum GB: 6 June [115]

1684
Teacher training college: Institute of the Brothers of the Christian Schools, Rheims, Fr, f by Jean-Baptiste de la Salle, 28 May
Fire Brigade GB: [73]
Cuff links (rec): diamond-studded links mentioned in *London Gazette*
Medical journal GB: *Medicina Curiosa*
Thimble: inv by Nicolas van Benschoten, Amsterdam

1685
Concert hall: opened at York Buildings, London with August Kühnel concert 26 Nov

1686
Convent (post-Dissolution) GB: Bar Convent, York, estab by Institute of the Blessed Virgin
Ice cream (rec) GB: [85]

1687
Woman novelist: [205]

1689
Court martial (peacetime) GB: introd under Mutiny Act, 3 April
Ring bayonets GB: inv by Gen Mackay; first used Battle of Killiecrankie, 27 July

1690
Sale-room GB: The 'Vendu', estab by Edward Millington, Covent Garden
Encyclopedia (alphabetical): [58]

1691
Book reviews GB: by J. de la Crosse in mthly *History of Learning* from July
Nonconformist hymnal GB: [85]

1692
Magazine GB: Jan [95]

1693
Newspaper 'giveaway': *The City Mercury*, London, 7 Mar
Public billiard tables (rec): at Colsoni's Chocolate House, London
Women's magazine: 27 June [208]
Guide to London: *Le Guide de Londres* by F. Colsoni, London; inc five days of planned sightseeing
Gazetteer: *The Gazetteers' or Newsman's Interpreter*, L. Eachard, London ('gazetteer' = journalist)

1694
Lamp-posts GB: erected City of London by Convex Light Co under contract d 25 June

1695
Public drinking fountain: erected Hammersmith, London, by Sir Samuel Morland, 8 July
Matrimonial advertisement: 19 July [98]
Banknotes GB: £10, £20, £30, £40, £50 and £100 by Bank of England
Thimbles GB: mnf by John Lofting, Islington

1696
Strike fund (rec): maintained by Journeymen Hatters' Union (*see* 1667)
Envelope (rec) GB: 15 May [58]
Evening Newspaper: 23 June [118]
Elementary schools (National system) GB: all heritors in Scotland required by Act to estab parish schools
Umbrella (rec) GB: [195]
Metronome: Etienne Loulié, Paris

1697
Sunday schools GB: estab by Congregationalist chapels at Neath and Tirdwyncyn, Wales
Skating boots: made for Peter the Great at Zaandam, Neths

1698
Steam-engine: pat by Thomas Savery, London, 25 July (*see also* 1702)
Police station: [134]

1699
Book of Firsts: *A Pleasant and Compendious History of the First Inventers and Instituters of the most Famous Arts, Mysteries, Laws, Customs and Manners in the whole world*, pr for J. Harris (alphabetical entries), Jan
Dental surgeons (qualified): [47]
Silhouettes: cut by Elizabeth Pyburg (Neths), London

1700
Newspaper theatrical announcement GB: 4 July [117]
Weekly magazine GB: *The Weekly Entertainment*, 24 Oct
Advertisement playing-cards: [131]
School inspector: Rev. Coghan, apnt by SPCK, London
Bathroom with hot and cold running water GB: at Chatsworth, Derbyshire

1701
Naval college: School of Mathematics and Navigation, Moscow, f 14 Jan
Synagogue GB: Bevis Marks, London
Nougat (rec): Montelimar, Fr
Mixed jury: [203]
Seed drill GB: built by Jethro Tull of Basildon, Berks
Provincial newspaper GB: 8 Nov (?) [118]
Illustrated magazine: [95]
Contraceptive sheath (rec): [24]
Woman editor GB: Mrs Ann Baldwin, ed *Memoirs for the Curious*

1702
Daily Newspaper (sustained) GB: 11 Mar [116]
Steam-engine (mnf): by Thomas Savery at 'his Workhouse in Salisbury Ct, London'; des for draining mines, etc
Transatlantic mail service (scheduled): Falmouth–W. Indies, mthly, postage 9d. Inst by Edmond Dummer

1703
Illustrated newspaper advertisement (trade) GB: 17 Mar [116]
School of engineering: Königliche Bergwerkakademie, Freiberg – trained engineers for Saxon mines

1704
Jewelled watch movement: 1 May [199]
English encyclopedia: [58]

1706
Life insurance co: [93]
Reformatory: opened by Jean-Baptiste de la Salle at St Yon, nr Rouen

1707
Pocket diary (rec): pub Stuttgart
Theatre magazine: *The Muses Mercury*, pub by Andrew Bell, London, Jan
Road tunnel: Umer Loch Tunnel (200 ft) St Gotthard road, Swz

1708
Diplomatic immunity: introd GB following arrest of Russian Ambassador for £50 debt, July
Hard-paste porcelain (Europe): made by Walter von Tschirnhaus and Johann Böttger, Dresden, Oct
Numbering of houses (rec) GB: [119]

1709
Piano: built by Bartolommeo Cristofori, Florence
Fire station (purpose-built) GB: Chester
Britain–America mail service (scheduled): Bristol–N.Y., mthly, postage 1s; inst by William Warren

1710
Italian opera GB: Jan [121]
Copyright (statutory) GB: Copyright Act (1709), effective 10 April
House journal: April [84]
Women's fiction magazine: [208]
Bidet (rec): used by Mme de Prie, noted Parisian beauty

1711
Royal Ascot: inst by Queen Anne, 7 Aug
Art School GB: The Academy of Painting, Lincoln's Inn Fields, opened under Godfrey Kneller, 18 Oct
Piano GB: brought from Rome by Samuel Crisp
Tuning-fork: John Shore, London

1712
Literary appreciation society: Spalding Gentlemen's Society, Lincs, Eng, f by Maurice Johnson, 3 Nov
Steam-engine, piston operated: erected Tipton, Staffs, Eng by Thomas Newcomen
Chelsea buns (rec): noted by Swift in *Journal to Stella*

1714
Novel to be serialized: *The Rover*, featured in nos 471–82 of the *British Mercury*, 14 July–29 Sept
Bird's-egg collector (rec): M. Peters of Antwerp
Newspaper, foreign correspondent: London C apnt by *Der Hamburgische*

1715
Diving suit (practical): pat by Andrew Becker 10 Feb; dem in R. Thames. Becker suits still in use in 1754

1716
Competitive rowing event: Doggett's Coat and Badge for apprentice watermen, R. Thames, 1 Aug

1717
Ballet: 2 Mar [21]
Pantomime GB: *Harlequin Executed*, prod by John Rich at Lincoln's Inn Fields Theatre, 26 Dec
Fahrenheit temperature scale: dev by Daniel Fahrenheit, Berlin

1718
Marine insurance co: Mines Royal Society, London
Machine-gun: pat by London lawyer James Puckle, 15 May (*see also* 1721)

1719
School old boys' association: f by alumni of Soho Academy, London
Sequel to a novel: *The Further Adventures of Robinson Crusoe*, Daniel Defoe
Boxing stadium: Figg's Amphitheatre, Tottenham Court Road, London
Cut glass GB: by John Akerman

1720
Yacht club: Cork Harbour Water Club, Ireland, f by Lord Inchiquin *et al*
Mustard paste: [115]

1721
Parliamentary Question: asked by Lord Cowper, answered by Earl of Sunderland, 9 Feb
Prime Minister GB: office generally held to have orig with Robert Walpole's assumption of power, 3 April
Complete English dictionary: [49]
Machine-gun (mnf): by James Puckle at White Cross Alley factory, London

1723
Agricultural society: Honourable Soc of Improvers of the Knowledge of Agriculture in Scotland, f Edinburgh, 8 June
Book illustrated with colour plates: *Coloritto*, London; three-colour engraving process by J.C. Le Blon of Frankfurt
Meerschaum pipe: made by shoemaker Karol Kowates, Pesth, Hungary

1724
Glasshouse GB: [45]
Fahrenheit temperature scale GB: pub by Royal Society

1726
Municipal fire brigade GB: 20 June [73]
Racing calendar: pub by John Cheney of Arundel, Sussex, Eng

1727
Boxing, title fight: James Figg *v* Ned Sutton for Championship of England, Figg's Amphitheatre, London, 6 June. Figg won
Spectacles with side-pieces: [168]
Railway bridge: Tanfield Arch, Eng, built over Cawsey Dell by Ralph Wood; carried double 4ft track colliery rly

1728
Music society: Edinburgh Musical Soc, f 29 Mar
Newspaper interview: conducted by Andrew Brice with condemned man at Exeter Gaol; pub *Brice's Weekly*

Journal, Exeter, Eng, 26 April
Foreign-language newspaper GB: *La Stafetta Italiana*, Dec
Dental Drill (rec): [47]

1729
Sporting journal: *A Historical List of all Horse Matches, Etc*, London
Merry-go-round (rec) GB: St Bartholomew Fair
Methodists: Charles Wesley, William Morgan, Francis Gore (?), founder members of Oxford Univ 'Holy Club'

1730
Newspaper, stock-market quotations: *Daily Advertiser*, London, from 3 Feb
Goldfish bred in GB: from specimens brought from St Helena by Philip Worth

1731
Orchid GB: *Bletia verecunda* cultivated by haberdasher Peter Collinson, Peckham
Piano composition: sonata by Lodorico Guistini, Pistoia, Italy
Lightship: *The Nore*, Thames Estuary
Cigar, Englishman known to have smoked: John Cockburn while marooned on shores of Honduras

1732
Oratorio GB: Handel's *Esther*, performed Crown and Anchor Tavern, Strand, 23 Feb
Angling club: Schuylkill Fishing Company, Philadelphia

1733
Boxing, international contest: Bob Whittaker (Eng) *v* Tito Alberto di Carini (It), Figg's Amphitheatre, London, 6 May; Whittaker won
Perambulator: [125]
Naval college GB: Royal Naval Academy, Portsmouth

1734
Stipendiary magistrate: Thomas de Veil, Westminster, London
Annual trade directory: *Kent's Directory*, London (–1828)
Fire extinguisher: [74]

1735
Parliamentary press report: pub in *Gentleman's Magazine*, 20 Aug
Prime Minister to occupy 10 Downing St: Sir Robert Walpole, 22 Sept
Welsh-language magazine: *Tlysau yr Hen Oesoedd* (one issue)

1736
Field-marshal GB: 12 Jan [60]
Newspaper, gardening feature: commenced in *Northampton Mercury*, Eng

1737
Contour lines: used on chart of English Channel by Fr cartographer Philippe Buache
Medical society GB: Society for the Improvement of Medical Knowledge, Edinburgh

1738
Caesarian GB: Jan [30]

1739
Methodist chapel: The Society-room, Horse-Fair, Bristol, Eng, opened 3 June
Methodist lay preacher: Reading surveyor John Cennick, preached first sermon to 400 miners at Kingswood, nr Bristol, Eng, 12 June
Curling club (rec): Multhill C Soc, Scot, f 17 Nov

1740
Cookery school GB: estab by E. Kidner with branches in Queen St and Holborn

1741
Military college: Royal Military Academy, Woolwich, London, estab 13 April
Centigrade temperature scale: applied to Delisle thermometer by Anders Celsius at Uppsala, Sweden, 25 Dec
Choral society GB: The Madrigal Soc, f by John Immyns at Twelve Bells Tavern, Fleet St, London
Platform scale: weighbridge installed by John Wyatt outside Birmingham Workhouse, Eng
Mineral water (artificial): prepared by Dr William Brownrigg with carbonic acid gas, Whitehaven, Cumberland, Eng

1742
Indoor swimming-pool: 28 May [172]
Suspension Bridge GB: [172]

1743
Rules of boxing: drafted by Jack Broughton; approved 18 Aug
Passenger elevator: [57]
Open-air swimming-pool: [172]
Sheffield plate: dev by Thomas Boulsover, Sheffield, Eng; originally used for buttons

1744
Book of English nursery rhymes: *Tommy Thumb's Song Book*, pub by Mrs Mary Cooper, 22 Mar (inc 'Baa, baa, black sheep')
Golf tournament: won by John Rattray, Leith, Scot 2 April
Cricket match, charge for admission: England *v* Kent at Artillery Ground, Finsbury (2s 6d), 18 June
Cricket club (rec): London Cricket Club
Catherine wheels (rec): at firework display held at Lord Cobham's Head, London
Baseball (rec): picture titled 'Baseball' in J. Newbery's *A Little Pretty Pocket Book*, London

1745
Women's cricket match (rec): Hambledon *v* Bramley, Gosden Common, Eng, 26 July
National anthem: 'God Save the King' performed Drury Lane Theatre 28 Sept (first referred to as Nat Anthem 1822)
Soft-paste porcelain (known) GB: 'goat-and-bee' jugs mnf by the Chelsea Porcelain Manufacture

1747
VD clinic: London Lock Hospital, opened 31 Jan
Boxing gloves: dev by Jack Broughton, London, Feb
Bullfighter killed in ring: Marcos Saenz, picador, Seville, 12 June
Beet sugar: extracted by Andreas Marggraf, Berlin
Raincoat: [154]
Chess club (rec): met at Slaughter's Coffee House, London

1748
Naval uniform (RN): for officers only by Admiralty Order d 13 April
Steel pens: Johann Janssen, Aachen, Germany

1749
Round 'S' (in Eng typography): in Joseph Ames's *Typographical Antiquities*
Bowls club (rec): Croydon Bowling Club, Eng
Census (regular national): Sweden, triennial

1750
University magazine: 31 Jan [196]

1751
Newspaper columnist: 11 Mar [118]
Children's magazine: June [35]

1752
Unsolicited testimonial (rec): 19 Jan [117]
Magazine, colour illustration: *Gentleman's Magazine*, London; hand-painted plate of finches, June
Lightning conductor: Sept [93]
Steeplechase: ridden by Edmund Blake and Mr O'Callaghan 'from the Church of Buttevant to the spire of St Leger Church', Co Cork, Ireland

1753
School cookery class (rec) GB: at Dumfries Burgh School

1754
Rifles used in warfare (Br): 12 rifled carbines issued to French and Indian War expeditionary force

1755
Clubhouse GB: [40]
Iron bridge: [88]
Axminster carpet: Axminster, Eng

1756
Railway turntable: built by John Smeaton on Millbay Works rly, Plymouth, Eng
Keep-left regulation: applied by Act to vehicles crossing London Bridge
Central Statistical Bureau: Stockholm

1757
Private press GB: estab Strawberry Hill, Twickenham by Horace Walpole; first book, Thomas Gray's *Odes*, pub 16 July
Sextant: by Capt. John Campbell RN

1758
Revolving stage: introd at Kado-za doll theatre, Osaka by Namiki Shozo, 22 Dec
Blast furnace: installed by John Wilkinson, Bilston, Staffs
Banknote forgery (rec) GB: draper William Vaughan of Stafford convicted

1759
National museum GB: 15 Jan [115]
Regimental bandmaster GB: (Sir) William Herschel, Durham Militia

1760
Art exhibition GB: 21 April [19]
Hangman's drop: used for execution of Earl Ferrers, Tyburn, London, 5 May
Liquorice (confectionery): mkt by George Dunhill, Pontefract, Eng
Church of England hymnal: [85]
Roller skates: [157]
Art school to teach industrial design: The Trustees' Academy, Edinburgh

1761
Canal (wholly artificial navigation) GB: Bridgewater Canal, Lancs, opened 17 July
Vaulting-horse: Lund Univ, Sweden

1762
Actuary: 7 Sept [93]
Lightning conductor GB: [94]
Veterinary college: École Nationale Vétérinaire, Lyons
Sandwich: dev by John Montagu 4th Earl of Sandwich, during 24hr gaming session, London

1763
Printed cheque (rec) GB: 4 Mar [34]
Classified trade directory: *Mortimer's Universal Director*, London
Jigsaw puzzle: [89]
Written examination GB: introd by Dr Richard Watson for Cambridge Univ Mathematical Tripos

1764
State school for girls: Smolny Institute, St Petersburg
Golf club: Honourable Company of Edinburgh Golfers formally constituted
18-hole golf course: St Andrews, Scot

1765
Fire float GB: Sun Fire Office float operational on R. Thames, Aug
Restaurant: [156]
Church of England Sunday school: held by Rev. Theophilus Lindsey at the Vicarage, Catterick, Eng
Schools for deaf and dumb: Institution des Sourds-Muets, Paris, f by Abbé de l'Epée; Thomas Braidwood's Academy for the Deaf and Dumb, Edinburgh
Casino (legal): opened by M. Chevilly at the Promenade-House, Baden-Baden
Pavements (raised from gutter): laid Westminster, London

1766
Fire escape GB: pat by London watchmaker David Marie, 8 April (wicker basket on pulley and chain)
Paintbox (with watercolour tablets): mkt by William Reeves, London, April
Show jumping: org by Capt. John Knox, Waringsford, Co Down, Ireland, Dec

1767
Concert pianist, English (rec): Mr Dibdin, accompanist at Miss Brinkler's Benefit Concert, London, 15 May
Magazine to feature cartoons: John Almon's *Political Register*, London, from no 2, June
Cast-iron railway track: rails for

Coalbrookdale–Horsehay rly cast at Coalbrookdale Ironworks, Shropshire, Eng, 13 Nov
Long-service medal GB: awarded by CO of Royal Northumberland Fusiliers
Soda water: prepared by Richard Bewley, Gt Massingham, Eng
Woman newspaper editor GB: Mrs Anna Maria Smart, *Reading Mercury*

1768
Hard-paste porcelain (known) GB: blue mug mnf by Plymouth Porcelain Co, d 14 Mar
Encyclopaedia Britannica: Dec [58]
Rubber tubes: súrgical catheters made by P. O. Macquer, Paris
Agricultural show (rec): held by Salford Agricultural Society, Eng

1769
Roman Candles (rec): at benefit held for Mrs Forbes at Marylebone Gardens, London, 27 July
Cremation GB: 25 Sept [46]
Co-operative society: 9 Nov [45]
Infant school: opened by Jean Oberlin at Waldbach, Fr

1770
Welsh-language magazine (sustained): *Trysorfa Gwybodaeth neu Eurgrawn Cymraeg*, Carmarthen, 3 Mar (*see* 1735)
Self-propelled road vehicle: steam-driven gun carriage built by Nicolas Joseph Cugnot, Paris
Lightning conductor on public building GB: [94]
Newspaper, parliamentary reports: *London Evening Post* (*see* 1735)
Breech-loader in service use: Austrian dragoon musket
Eraser: [59]
Club for both sexes GB: [40]

1771
Coloured fashion plate: 'Spring Dress' in *The Ladies' Magazine*, London, April
Matador killed in ring: Jóse Cándido Exposito, by bull, Coriano, at Puerto de Santa Maria, Spain, 23 June
Vaccination: [86]
Trade Union (national): Journeymen Hatters' Trade Union of GB, f by affiliation of provincial trade clubs with those of London and Southwark (*see also* 1667)

1772
Traveller's cheques: 1 Jan [193]
Dial weighing machine: pat by John Clais, London, 30 April
Agricultural journal GB: *The Scots Farmer*, 1 Sept
Keep-left regulation (national): applied to all towns under Traffic (Scotland) Act; 20s penalty
Night school: Dr Henry Clarke's Salford Academy, Eng

1773
Negro author to publish book in English: Phillis Wheatley (a slave) of Boston, Mass., *Poems on Various Subjects, Religious and Moral*, London
Foot and mouth disease: epidemic in France
Medal awarded for overseas service (land): issued by St Vincent Legislative Assembly to participants in Carib War

1774
Hotel: Jan [83]
Unitarian chapel GB: Essex Street Chapel, Strand, registered 17 April
School Magazine: 27 July [161]
State education, national system: implemented Austria under Johann von Felbiger's Educational Statute of 6 Dec
School curriculum, science teaching GB: hydrostatics and chemistry at Laurence Street Academy, Chelsea
Rock garden: laid out by William Forsyth (after whom *Forsythia* was named) with 40 tons of Tower-of-London stone at the Chelsea Physic Garden
Trade Journal: *The Builders Magazine*, London

1775
Regatta (rowing): Westminster Bridge, London, 23 June
Building Society: [28]

1776
Physical training, school to introduce: The Philanthropinum, Dessau, 2 Jan
Steam-engine with separate condenser: built by James Watt at Bloomfield Colliery, Tipton, Eng; operational 8 Mar
Stopwatch: made by Jean-Moyse Pouzait, Geneva; submitted for inspection 9 May
Cricket, three-stump wicket: at Coulsdon *v* Chertsey match, Laleham-Burway, Eng, 6 Sept
Submarine used in warfare: 7 Sept [171]
Stately Home open to the public: [169]
Cricket score-cards: pub by T. Pratt of Sevenoaks, Eng

1777
Army, trained rifle unit: detachment of 100 men from 6th and 14th Regts formed under Capt. Patrick Ferguson, GB, 6 Mar
Iron boat: 20 May [88]
Stars and Stripes: adopted 20 June
Central heating: installed at Château de Pecq, Saint-Germain-en-Laye by architect M. Bonnemain

1778
Skating club: Edinburgh Ice Skating Soc in progress by Jan
State-supported school for the handicapped: Samuel Henicke's school for the deaf, f Leipzig, May
Savings Bank: Hamburgische Allgemeine Versorgungsanstalt Ersparungsklasse, Hamburg, 1 Aug
Water-closet (mnf): [200]
Duplicating machine: [52]
Bucket-chain dredger GB: used by Hull Dock Co to clear Queen's Dock
Brothels, State controlled: registration and inspection of inmates introd Fr

1779
Rotative steam-engine: built by Matthew Wasborough of Bristol, Eng, for Birmingham button-manufacturer James Pickard
Machinery driven by steam power: at Pickard's factory, Birmingham, as above
Newspaper, sports reports (regular): *Whitehall Evening Post*, London
Repeating rifle: 20-shot air rifle mnf for Austrian Army by Bartholomew Girandoni, Nov
Artificial insemination: [19]

1780
Duplicating machine (mnf): 20 Mar [52]
Sunday newspaper GB: *British Gazette and Sunday Monitor*, 26 Mar
Abortion clinic (rec) GB: 28 April [7]
Derby: won by Charles Bunbury's Diomed, Epsom, 4 May
Conductor: baton introd by Anselm Weber at Berlin Opera
Ball bearings (rec): in thrust-race of post-windmill at Sprowston, Norfolk, Eng
Willow-pattern china: Thomas Turner, Caughley, Shropshire, Eng

1781
Iron Bridge GB: 1 Jan [88]
Lighthouse with revolving light: Carlston L, Marstrand, Sweden, 1 Aug
Circular saw: used by Walter Taylor at wood mill nr Southampton, Eng
Artesian well GB: Sheerness, Kent

1782
Slave trade, country to abolish: Aust

1783
Blindfold chess match GB: played by François Philidor (Fr) *v* two opponents at Parsloe's Chess Club, 8 May
Ex-Servicemen's association: Soc of the Cincinnati, f by Gen. Henry Knox, Fishkill, N.Y., 10 May
Steamboat: 15 July [169]
Balloon Ascent (free-flight): François de Rozier and Marquis d'Arlandes in Montgolfier hot-air B, Paris, 21 Nov
High-speed rotative steam-engine: des by James Watt; used to drive tilt-hammer at Bradley Forge, Eng
Piano with foot pedals: by John Broadwood, London

1784
Ploughing match: held Odiham, Hants, Eng, 1 June
Balloon ascent (free-flight) GB: by James Tytler, Edinburgh, 27 Aug
Methodist ministers (ordained as such): Richard Whatcoat and Thomas Wasey ordained for American ministry, London, 1 Sept
Anglican bishop of overseas diocese: Samuel Seabury (US), consecrated Bishop of Connecticut at Aberdeen, Scot, 14 Nov
Shrapnel: inv by Lt Henry Shrapnel RA, tested Carron Ironworks, Stirling, Scot
Company doctor: apnt New Lanark Cotton Spinning Manufactory, Scot

1785
Methodist Church (as independent sect): American Methodists seceded from C of E, 1 Jan
Cross-Channel flight: by Jean-Pierre Blanchard (Fr) and Dr John Jeffries (USA) in hydrogen balloon, 7 Jan
School for the blind: Institution des Jeunes Aveugles, f by Valentin Haüy, Paris, Jan
Beer-pump handles: pat Joseph Bramah, London, 9 May
Bifocals: inv by Benjamin Franklin and first desc in letter d Passy 23 May
Balloon fatality: François de Rozier over Boulogne, 15 June
Anglican priest ordained outside GB: Rev Ashbel Baldwin, ordained by Bishop Seabury (*see also* 1784) at Middleton, Conn., 3 Aug
Fashion Magazine: [208]
Newspaper to employ shorthand reporters: [164]
Textile machinery driven by steam power: Watt rotative engine installed in cotton factory at Papplewick, Eng
Lifeboat: pat by London coachbuilder Lionel Lukin 2 Nov; applied to converted coble, Bamburgh (*see also* 1786)
Soda water (mnf): by H.D. Rawlings, London
Artificial insemination (human): [19]
Bleach (chemical): Count Berthollet's 'Eau de Javelle'; adopted by Lille bleachers

1786
Lifeboat station: estab Bamburgh, Northumb, Eng, by Archdeacon John Sharp (Lukin lifeboat, *see also* 1785)
Threshing machine (practical): built by Andrew Meikle, Haddington, East Lothian, Scot; supplied to Mr Stein of Kilbogie
Book in embossed type for blind: *Essai sur l'Éducation des Aveugles*, Valentin Haüy, Paris

1787
Cricket match played at Lord's: Essex *v* Middlesex at Dorset Sq ground, Eng, 31 May
School magazine GB: 30 July [161]
MCC cricket match: played *v* Islington CC, Eng, 30 July
Registered letters GB: foreign only, 21s fee per piece
Gardening magazine: *The Botanical Magazine*, pub mthly by William Curtis, Lambeth, London
Burglary insurance: introd by General Insurance Office, London
Electric telegraph (working model): inv by M. Lammond, Paris

1788
Daily evening newspaper: *Star and Evening Advertiser*, London, 3 May
Steamboat GB: 14 Oct [170]
Reformatory GB: opened at St George's Fields, London by the Philanthropic Soc
Artillery shells used in naval battle: by Russians against Turks in Sea of Azov

1789
Law Journal GB: *The Templar*, Jan
Public railway: June [154]
Railway company: Loughborough & Nanpantan Railway Co, Eng, June
Rowing club (rec): several 'cutter clubs' in existence on R. Thames (none named)
Official shorthand writer: Thomas Gurney, apnt by House of Commons to report Parliamentary Committees
Bourbon Whisky: distilled from maize by Rev. Elijah Craig, Bourbon County, Ky.

1790
Lifeboat (purpose-built): *The Original*, launched South Shields Eng, 30 Jan

Steeplechase at race meeting: Roscommon, Ireland, 13 April
Sewing machine: 17 July [163]
Steamboat passenger service: 26 July [170]
Semi-detached houses: erected on SE side of Regent's Park, London
VD, free treatment: introd Denmark
Wristwatch (rec): [199]

1791
School for the blind GB: School for the Instruction of the Indigent Blind, Liverpool, f by Edward Rushton, Jan
Semaphore telegraph: dem by Abbé Claude Chappé, Sarthe, Fr, 2 Mar
Veterinary surgeon GB: William Moorcroft, qualified Lyons, Fr, 7 May (practised London)
British Ambassador to USA: George Hammond apnt 5 July
Cricket, school match against outside team: Eton *v* Maidenhead CC, Eng, 19 July
Paper cut-out dolls: on sale London
Contour lines (land map): by Fr surveyor Jean-Louis Dupont-Triel (*see* 1737)

1792
Veterinary college GB: the Veterinary College, Camden Town, opened 4 Jan
Street directory: *Fashionable Court Guide*, pub by P. Boyle, London, 1 Feb
Money Orders: introd GB 1 Oct
Ambulance: [17]

1793
Bank of England £5 note: 15 April
Public zoo: Jardin des Plantes, Paris, estab 10 June
Metric weights: kilo introd Fr, 1 Aug
Conscription (national): all unmarried men aged 18–25, Fr, by decree of 23 Aug
War correspondent: [198]
Revolving stage (full-size): introd at Nakamura-za theatre, Edo, Japan
Referendum (nation-wide): French voters approved Robespierre's new Constitution by 1,801,918 to 11,610

1794
Vet to qualify in GB: Edmund Bond, graduated from the Veterinary College, 2 April (practised Epsom)
Mention in despatches: Capt. Duncan RA for conduct at Siege of Calvi, Corsica, 10 Aug
Military telegraph: Chappe T, Lille–Paris; first message announced capture of Quesnoy, 15 Aug
Science museum: Conservatoire des Arts et Métiers, Paris
Fashion magazine GB: [208]

1795
National anthem (officially adopted): 'La Marseillaise' (composed 1792), Fr, 15 July
Electric telegraph (outdoor lines): Academy of Sciences, Barcelona–Fort Atarazanas (1km); dem by Don Francisco Salvá, 16 Dec

1796
Mental home: The Retreat, York, Eng; opened by William Tuke, 11 May
Cricket, inter-school match: Westminster *v* Eton, Hounslow Heath, Eng, 25 July
Ballet pointes: [21]
Suspension road-bridge: [172]
Ambulance in warfare: [17]
Iron aqueduct: Longden upon Tern, Shropshire, Eng; des by Thomas Telford
Steam dredger: ladle dredger fitted with Boulton & Watt 4hp engine by John Crimshaw; used Sunderland harbour, Eng
Swimming club: Uppsala Simsällskap, Sweden, f by Jöns Svanberg

1797
Top hat: first worn by haberdasher John Hetherington in London, 15 Jan
Volunteer regt to win battle honour (Br): Castlemartin Yeomanry for defence of Fishguard against Fr invasion force, 12–13 Feb
£1 note: issued by Bank of England, 26 Feb
Prisoner-of-war camp GB: 7 April [140]
Parachute (aeronaut): 22 Oct [123]
Iron-framed building: Benyon, Marshall & Bage Flax Mill, Shrewsbury, Eng

1798
American Dictionary: [49]
State subsidy for the arts: Govt grant of £6,500 to San Carlos Opera House, Lisbon
Lithograph: Aloys Senefelder, Munich

1799
Income Tax GB: 9 Jan [86]
Gas fire: 21 Sept [76]
Gymnasium: opened by Franz Nachtegall at 45 Østergade, Copenhagen, 5 Nov
Public weighing machine (rec) GB: operated at Bath by Carl Rosenberg

1800
Police Force (statutory) GB: July [134]
Christmas Tree GB: 25 Dec [37]
Sugar-beet factory: Horowitz, Austria
Bleaching powder: mnf by Charles Smithson Tennant, Glasgow, Scot
Teacher training college for women: f by Ernestine von Krosigk, Berlin
Upright piano: by J.I. Hawkins, Philadelphia
Iron printing press: des by 3rd Earl Stanhope, mnf by Robert Walker of Vine St, London; first model inst at Shakespeare Press, St James's, London

1801
Ordnance Survey map: 1in:1 mile of Kent, pub 1 Jan
Prime Minister of middle-class origin GB: Henry Addington, son of Reading physician, assumed office 18 Mar
Shop with plate-glass windows: 8 April [163]
Self-propelled road vehicle GB: built by Richard Trevithick at Camborne, Cornwall; road-tested 24 Dec
Census GB: returns pub 29 June; pop 8,872,000
Lithograph GB executed from pen drawing by Benjamin West
Electric needle telegraph: dem by Jean Alexandre at Poitiers, Fr, 5 Nov

1802
Threshing machine (wheeled): built by Thomas Wigful, Lynn Regis, Norfolk, Eng
Club badge: adopted by Duddington Curling Club, Midlothian, Scot; worn on jacket
Camping holiday (rec): by Thomas De Quincey (16), toured Wales with tent

1803
Children's library: Jan [34]
Hansard: *Cobbett's Parliamentary Debates*, pr by Thomas Hansard, London (renamed *Hansard's Parliamentary Debates* 1829)

1804
Railway locomotive: 6 Feb [153]
Shrapnel used in warfare: by Br against Dutch in Surinam, 30 April
Steamboat with screw propeller: May [170]
Woman to ride in horse race: 25 Aug [202]
Army physical training: Copenhagen Military Institute estab 25 Aug
Restaurant guide: *Almanach des Gourmands;* listed 500 Paris restaurants
University grants available to all secondary-school pupils (male): under Tsar Alexander I's Education Statute all university education in Russia became free; maintenance grants awarded to children of working-class parents and serfs; special grants to poor undergraduates for textbooks
Water supply (filtered): Paisley, Scot; 6,700 gallons daily
Flea circus: street show in Paris

1805
Trooping of the Colour (Sovereign's Birthday Parade): Horse Guards, London, 4 June
Negro boxer to win prize-fight: Bill Richmond (US) KO'd Jack Holmes (GB) at Cricklewood Green, Eng 8 July
Cricket, Eton *v* Harrow match: Lord's, Eng, 2 Aug. Eton won
Allotments: inaug by Sir George Cayley at Brompton, Yorks, Eng
Gasworks: estab by National Gas Light and Heat Co, London

1806
Aerial propaganda: May [7]
Strawberry, edible scarlet (cultivated): Keens' Seedling, exhib by Michael Keens, Isleworth, Eng, 3 July
Carbon paper: 7 Oct [33]
Rocket missiles (Br): used in naval attack on Boulogne, 8 Oct
Teacher training college GB: Borough Road Training College, Southwark, f by Joseph Lancaster
Cocktail (rec): [40]
Wind-force scale: Force 0–Force 17, dev by Cmdr Francis Beaufort, RN

1807
Passenger railway: 25 Mar [153]
Upright piano GB: pat by William Southwell, London, 8 April
Cricket, round-arm bowling (rec): introd by John Willes of Kent in Kent *v* Eng match, Fenenden Heath, 20 July
Book illustrated with lithographs: John Thomas Smith's *Antiquities of Westminster*, pr by T. Bensley, London
Women's prison GB: London Female Penitentiary, Pentonville
Fruit-flavoured carbonated soft drinks: mnf by Townsend Speakman, Philadelphia

1808
Iron railway points: des by Richard Fothergill, mnf at Tredegar Ironworks for Tredegar–Newport rly, Wales, Aug
Emergency parachute jump: [123]
Typewriter (practical): [193]
Mass production manufacturing process: dev by Marc Isambard Brunel and Henry Maudslay for RN pulley blocks, Portsmouth

1809
Steamboat navigated at sea: 10 June [170]
Railway tunnel: built by Bullo Pill Rly Co on Forest of Dean Rly, Glos, Eng; 1,100yd
PO letter box (rec) GB: [92]
Bank of England notes: printed serial numbers GB

1810
Ombudsman: 1 Mar [121]
Preparatory school GB: [138]

1811
Women's golf tournament: org by Musselburgh GC, Scot, for town fishwives, 9 Jan
Power printing press: steam-driven Koenig press used by Thomas Bensley to print 3,000 sheets of *Annual Register*, London, April
Women's county cricket match: Hampshire *v* Surrey, Newington, Eng, 3–5 Oct
City of 1m population: [39]
Rubber goods (mnf): [159]
Govt grants for school building GB: approx £160,000 p.a. for Irish schools

1812
Prime Minister to be assassinated: Spencer Perceval by John Bellingham, House of Commons, 11 May
Steamboat service GB: Aug [170]
Police Detective: [133]
Canned food: [30]
Cotton sewing thread: mnf by James & Patrick Clark, Paisley, Scot

1813
Chess column: wkly in *Liverpool Mercury*, Eng, from 9 July
Double-headed court cards: [131]
Cartridge (practical): mnf by Samuel Pauly, Paris, for ·59 breech-loading rifle
Ice hockey (rec): orig as 'bandy' at Bury Fen, Hunts, Eng
Soda siphon: Regency Portable Fountain inv by Charles Plinth, London
Craps: adapted from 'hazards' by Bernard de Mandeville, New Orleans

1814
Welsh-language newspaper: *Seren Gomer*, Swansea, 1 Jan
Boxing club: Pugilistic Club, f by 'Gentleman' Jackson, London, 22 May
Cricket match played at Lord's (present site): MCC *v* Herts, 22 June
Historical novel (set in identifiable past): Sir Walter Scott's *Waverley*, pub by Constable, Edinburgh, 7 July
Plastic surgery GB: 23 Oct [131]
Steam-driven warship: US Navy *Demologos*, des by Robert Fulton, launched N.Y. 29 Oct
Newspaper printed on power press:

The Times on Koenig press, London, 28 Nov
Newspaper cartoon: [117]
Art gallery GB: [19]

1815
Steamer to make sea voyage GB: *The Thames*, Glasgow Dublin, May
Written qualifying examination GB: conducted by Society of Apothecaries Court of Examiners, estab 19 July
Pacifist association: the Peace Society, N.Y., f by David Dodge, 14 Aug
Jaunting car: inv by Carlo Bianconi of Milan; introd on Clonmel–Caher route, Tipperary, Ireland
Gas meter: [76]
Cheese factory: estab by R. V. Effinger, Bern, Swz

1816
Infant school GB: The Institution, opened by Robert Owen at New Lanark, Scotland, 1 Jan
Channel steamboat crossing: 17 Mar [170]
Davy Safety Lamp: inv by Sir Humphry Davy; tested Hebburn Colliery, Jan; mnf by John Newman, London
Pacifists Assoc GB: the Peace Society, f by William Allen, 14 June
Fire extinguisher (cylinder model): [74]
Electric telegraph GB: erected by Francis Ronalds in his garden at Upper Mall, Hammersmith
Desk diary GB: pub by John Letts, London
Overseas campaign medal (general issue): Waterloo Medal
Kaleidoscope: inv by Sir David Brewster, Edinburgh
Stethoscope: dev by Rene Laënnec, Hôpital Necker, Paris

1817
Book printed on power press: Johann Blumenbach's *Physiology*, Elliotson, London (Koenig press)
Gasworks, public utility: Manchester Corporation, Manchester, Eng
Flower show: Dannybrook, Co Cork, Ireland

1818
Liner: 5 Jan [120]
Historic buildings scheduled for preservation: Grand Duchy of Hesse-Darmstadt by decree, 22 Jan
National Health Service: free medical treatment for all introd by Duchy of Nassau, 14 Mar
Inter-club golf match: Edinburgh Burgess Golfing Soc *v* Bruntsfield Links GC at Bruntsfield, Scot, 4 June
Steamship service: June [170]
Transfusion of human blood: Sept [25]
Prize-fight fought with gloves: between two unnamed Englishmen, Aix-la-Chapelle, 8 Oct
Anglican parish church choir (surpliced): f by Rev Richard Fawcett, Leeds Parish Church
School examinations (rec): [160]

1819
Atlantic steamship crossing: 20 June [170]
Book for blind in English (raised type): *Extracts from the Best English Authors*, Paris
Canned sardines: by Joseph Colin, Nantes
Iron passenger boat: [88]
Ship canal GB: Exeter Canal
Naval peaked cap: adopted by officers aboard HMS *Phaeton*
Highland Games: held by St Fillans (Perthshire) Highland Society, Scot
Staff canteen: [169]
Chocolate (eating): [35]

1820
Conductor GB: Louis Spohr (Ger) at Philharmonic Soc concert, 10 April
Cricket double century (rec): W. Ward scored 278 for MCC *v* Norfolk at Lord's, London, 25 July
Suspension road-bridge GB: [172]
Cotton reels: introd by J. & J. Clark Co, Paisley, Scot; $\frac{1}{2}$d deposit
Guide-book for English tourists abroad: Marianna Starke's *Travels on the Continent*, pub John Murray, London

1821
Weather chart: drawn by Heinrich Brandes of meterological conditions prevailing in Saxony on 24 Dec
Cigars (rec) GB: Earliest ref to trade in cigars
Book for the blind (raised type) GB: St Matthew's Gospel embossed by Charles Lowther for his own use
Channel steam ferry: [170]
Steam-driven RN vessel: 212-ton 80hp *Monkey*, built Rotherhithe
Raincoat GB: [154]
Rubber-lined fire hose: mnf by James Boyd & Sons, Boston, Mass.
Rubber goods (mnf): [159]
Natural gas (practical use): 30 street lamps at Fredonia, N.Y.
Boxing magazine: *The Fancy*, London
Mouth-organ: inv by Friedrich Buschman, Berlin

1822
Iron steamship: 30 April [171]
Atlantic steamship crossing GB: April [170]
Sheet rubber: [160]
Photographic art reproduction: engraving of Pius VII reprod by Nicéphore Niepce at Chalon-sur-Saône
Aspidistra GB: introd from Canton by John Damper Parkes
Revolver (mnf): by Elisha Haydon Collier (US) of Fountain Ct, London; five-shot flintlock
Physical training, school to introduce GB: Hazlewood, Birmingham; 1 hr daily
Accordion: Friedrich Buschman, Berlin
Cloth-bound books: William Pickering, London, *Diamond Classics* series; red calico

1823
Army uniform, trousers (infantry) GB: replaced breeches by order of 18 June
Locomotive foundry: f by George and Robert Stephenson, Forth St, Newcastle upon Tyne, Eng, 23 June
Birth-control propaganda campaign: launched by Francis Place, London, July
Pier (pleasure): Chain Pier, Brighton, Eng, opened 25 Nov
Jewish magazine GB: *The Hebrew Intelligencer*, 6d mthly
Talking doll (mnf): introd Paris by Johann Maelzel (Ger), price 10 francs; said 'Maman' and 'Papa'
Binoculars: binocular opera-glasses introd Paris; inventor unknown

1824
Rubber galoshes: adv by J. W. Goodrich of Boston, Mass., at $5 pair, 12 Feb
Lifejacket, inflatable rubber: ordered from Charles Macintosh of Glasgow, Scot, by Capt. John Franklin, 30 April
Rubber air-bed: ordered by Capt. John Franklin from Charles Macintosh of Glasgow, Scot, 30 April
Public opinion poll: 24 July [141]
Portland cement: pat by Joseph Aspdin, Wakefield, Eng, 21 Oct
Paintings bought by Nation GB: [19]
Iron railway bridge: Gaunless Viaduct, nr W. Auckland, Co Durham, Eng, built by George Stephenson for Stockton & Darlington Rly
Monorail: built at Royal Victualling Yard, London by Henry Robinson Palmer
Rubber balloons: [160]
Angostura bitters, made by Dr J. G. B. Siegert, Angostura (now Cuidad Bolivar), Venezuela; mkt 1830
Agricultural college: Marymont Institute Veterinary and Agricultural School, Warsaw

1825
Scuba device (for diving): pat GB by William James, 31 May
Public steam railway: 27 Sept [154]
Level crossings: Stockton & Darlington Rly, Eng, 27 Sept
Bottled gas: mkt by Provincial Portable Gas Co, Manchester, Eng
Teaching laboratory: estab by Justus von Liebig, Univ of Giessen, Ger
Gymnasium GB: opened by Carl Voelke in Regent's Park
Army library: estab by 80th Foot at Malta
Canned salmon: prod by John Moir, Aberdeen, Scot
Rubber driving belts (industrial): mnf by Thomas Hancock, Goswell Mews, London

1826
Birth-control manual: *Every Woman's Book*, Richard Carlile, London, Feb
Slate-bedded billiard table: Imperial Petrosian, mnf by John Thurston, London
Tea sold in packets: [173]
Rubber hosepipes: mnf by John Hancock of Fulham, London, for Barclay's Brewery
Telegraph poles: erected at Union Racetrack, Long Is, N.Y., by Harrison Dyar
Co-op dividend: [45]
Chocolate (eating) GB: [35]
Illuminated clock dial: [40]
Photograph from nature: [126]
Gas stove: [76]
Reformatory (state-run): Boston House of Reformation, Boston, Mass.
Capital punishment abolished: [31]
Troopship (steam): Bengal Govt ship *Enterprize*, Calcutta–Rangoon (Burmese War)

1827
Matches: 7 April [97]
Cricket match, Oxford *v* Cambridge: Lord's, London, 4 June
Cricket, wides (first scored as such): Kent *v* Sussex, Brighton, Eng, 17 Sept
Rubber-lined fire hose GB: mnf by John Hancock of Fulham
Photo-engraving: portrait of Cardinal d'Amboise reprod photomechanically by Nicéphore Niepce; prints made by Lemaître of Paris
Army uniform, waterproof cape: made for Duke of York; rubberized blue cloth lined with crimson silk

1828
Railway fatality: driver John Gillespie killed by boiler explosion at Simpasture, Co Durham, Eng; Stockton & Darlington Rly, 19 Mar
Zoo GB: Regent's Park Zoo, opened 27 April
Roman Catholic MP (in Protestant Britain): Daniel O'Connell, elected for Clare, 5 July (took seat 1830)
Christmas annual (children's): *The Christmas Box*, London
School for the mentally handicapped: estab at the Bicêtre, Paris by M. Ferrus
Cocoa: [40]
Complete American dictionary: [49]
Trade exhibition GB: held Royal Mews, Trafalgar Sq
Hypnotist GB: Richard Chenevix introd the art from Paris

1829
Full-page newspaper ad: 1 Jan [117]
Uniformed police force (statutory): 12 Mar [134]
Municipal baths GB: St George's Baths, Liverpool; opened 8 June
Oxford and Cambridge Boat Race: Hambledon Lock–Henley Bridge ($2\frac{1}{4}$ miles); won by Oxford in 14min 30sec, 10 June
Bus GB: 4 July [29]
Inter-school rowing fixture: Eton beat Westminster, Putney–Hammersmith–Putney, London, 27 July
Uniformed police force (statutory) GB: 26 Sept [135]
Hotel bathrooms: 16 Oct [83]
Concertina: Charles Wheatstone, London
Baked Beans (rec): [21]
Passenger lift GB: [57]
Science master GB: Edward Brayley, Hazlewood School, Birmingham
Wrapped soap: James Atkinson's Old Brown London Soap
Book published in braille: *Procédé pour écrire les Paroles . . .*, Louis Braille, Paris
Greetings card: [79]
Steam yacht: [209]

1830
Railway station: Mount Clare, Baltimore, opened 7 Jan
Steam-operated fire-engine: des by John Braithwaite; first used at Argyle Rooms fire, Charles St, London, 5 Feb
Mormons: Church of Jesus Christ of Latter-day Saints estab by Joseph Smith, Fayette, N.Y., 6 April
Steam passenger railway: 6 May [153]
Lawn mower (mnf): 18 May [92]
Policeman murdered on duty GB: 29 June [135]

Long-service medal (official) GB: inst 30 July
Railway passenger fatality: 15 Sept [151]
Mail carried by railway: Liverpool–Manchester, Eng, 11 Nov
Container transport: introd by Pickford's by agreement with Liverpool & Manchester Rly Co, Eng, 22 Nov
Passenger monorail: manumotive system operated at Royal Panarmonium Gardens, London
Sugar-beet factory GB: estab by Marriage, Reid & Marriage at Ulting, Essex
Blind piano-tuner: Claude Montal, Paris
Insurance journal GB: *The Assurance Magazine*
Oyster bed (artificial): Arcachon, Fr
Elastic: [52]
Pictorial matchbox labels: by N. Jones & Co, London and V.R. Powell of Troy, N.Y.
Amateur dramatic society: Shakespeare Club, Cambridge Univ
PO box numbers: introd by Edinburgh PO
Envelopes (mnf) GB: [58]
Paraffin: disc by Baron Karl von Reichenbach (Ger), Blansko, Moravia

1831
Self-propelled road vehicles in regular passenger service: three Gurney steam drags operated by Sir Charles Dance, Cheltenham–Gloucester (9 miles), Eng, 21 Feb–22 June
Troop train: 30 June [154]
Railway Journal: *The Rail-Road Advocate*, Rogersville, Tenn., 4 July
RN long-service medal: inst 24 Aug
Electric transformer: built by Michael Faraday at Royal Institution, London, 29 Aug
Ship to cross Atlantic wholly under steam: 4 Sept [170]
Engineering journal GB: *Civil Engineer's and Architect's Journal*, Oct
Co-operative wholesale society: North of England United Co-operative Co, Liverpool, Dec
Elastic GB: [53]
Steam bus GB: [29]
Sewing machine (mnf): [163]
Electric bell: Joseph Henry, Albany, N.Y.
Plymouth Brethren: assembly formed at Providence Chapel, Plymouth, Eng
Cross-country running (rec): in progress at Shrewsbury School, Eng
Political party HQ: Tory Party, Charles St, London
Dental chair (adjustable): des by James Snell, London; desc in *Practical Guide to Operations on the Teeth*

1832
Newspaper cartoon GB: 8 Jan [117]
Ballet Tutu: 12 Mar [21]
HM inspectors of schools: apnt by Nat Board of Education in Ireland, May
Ballet tutu GB: 26 July [21]
Dynamo: dem by Hypolite Pixii, Paris, 3 Sept
Trams: introd by John Mason, Prince St–14th St, N.Y., 26 Nov
Book dust-jacket: Nov [26]
Constituency Assocs: Rochdale Reform Assoc (Whig); Liverpool Conservative Assoc
Mass circulation magazine (over 100,000): *The Penny Magazine*, London
Newspaper, sports editor: William Trotter Porter, *Baltimore Traveller*, USA
Corrugated iron: mnf by John Walker of Rotherhithe, Eng

1833
Fire brigade (full-time): 1 Jan [73]
Steam bus service: 22 Apr [29]
Flower show GB: held by Royal Horticultural Soc, Chiswick, London, 25 May
Dynamo (rotative) GB: dem at Cambridge by Joseph Saxton, June
Govt grants for school building (Eng and Wales): £20,000 p.a. voted 17 Aug
Co-ed college: 3 Dec [208]
Promenade concerts: held in Champs-Elysées by Philippe Musard
Private detective agency: [140]
Creosote: disc by Baron Karl von Reichenbach (Ger) at Blansko, Moravia (Czechoslovakia)
School science laboratories: Bruce Castle School, Tottenham, Eng
Electric telegraph (permanent): used by C.F. Gauss and W.E. Weber for conveying astronomical information between Physical Cabinet, Göttingen and Weber's observatory (2km)
Performing rights (statutory): under Dramatic Copyright Act
Factory inspectors: first Govt Inspectorate in Eng
Concrete structure: Algiers breakwater, built by M. Poivel

1834
Adhesive postage stamp (essay): Aug [137]
Lacrosse (played on marked-out pitch): between teams of Iroquois and Algonquin Indians at St Pierre Racecourse, Montreal, Sept
Excursion trains: [153]
Wire rope: by Wilhelm Albert, Harz, Ger; also by George Binks, Woolwich, London
Road fatality involving self-propelled vehicle: five killed by John Scott Russell's steam coach, Paisley, Scot 29 July
Books for the blind (published) GB: *St John's Gospel* in raised type pub by James Gall, Edinburgh
Railway signals (fixed): Liverpool & Manchester Rly
Municipal park GB: [115]
Society for the blind: Indigent Blind Visiting Soc, f by Lord Shaftesbury, London
Poker (ref): Mississippi river-boat game desc in *Green's Reformed Gambler*
Preservation society: Société Française d'Archéologie pour la Conservation et la Description des Monuments Historiques, f by Arcisse de Caumont at Caen, Normandy

1835
Chess column in national newspaper: *Bell's Life in London* from 4 Jan
State railway: Brussels–Mechelen, Belgian State Railways, 5 May
Railway journal GB: *The Railway Magazine*, May
Electric lamp: 25 July [54]
Photograph GB: Aug [126]
Bituminous road surface: Vauxhall Rd, London
Gynaecological ward: estab at Rotunda Hospital, Dublin by Evory Kennedy
Railway timetable: *Lacey's Railway Companion* (1s), Liverpool, Eng
Electrical journal: *The Electric Gazette*, London
Children's book, colour illustration GB: [34]
Rifle, bolt-action: Dreyse needle-gun, dev by Johann Dreyse of Sömmerada
Keep-right regulation (national): introd Fr
Keep-left regulation (national): Eng and Wales under Highway Act
Billiard table with rubber cushions: mnf by John Thurston, London

1836
Point-to-point: held at Madresfield Estate by Worcestershire Hunt; won by Capt. Beacher, 2 Mar
Mormon temple: dedicated Kirtland, Ohio, Mar
Steam warship to fire her guns in anger: Spanish Navy's *Isabella Segunda* bombarded Carlists at San Sebastian, 5 May
Electroplating: pat GB by George and Henry Elkington, 24 June
Horsebox: 18 Sept [82]
Provincial newspaper, daily GB: *Cork Daily Advertiser*, 1 Oct
Trained nurses: Kaiserswerth (Ger) Hospital training scheme inaug 20 Oct
Railway derailment (fatal): at Great Corby, Eng, three killed, 3 Dec
Music in raised notation for the blind: *A Selection of Psalm Tunes and Chants*, Rev. W. Taylor, York, Eng
Series of guide-books: *Murray's Handbooks to Travellers*, London
Steamboat with screw propeller: [170]
Author to receive royalties (rec): Charles Knight for *The British Almanac*
Chess magazine: *La Palamède*, Paris
Gas stove (mnf): [77]
Cricket pads: introd by H. Daubeney, Oxford, Eng
Railway sleeping-car: [152]

1837
Magazine for the blind (raised type): *The Student's Magazine*, Philadelphia, Jan
Electric motor: 25 Feb [55]
Police detective GB: Feb [133]
Railway tickets (cardboard, dated and numbered): dev and issued by Thomas Edmondson, booking-clerk at Milton Station, Newcastle & Carlisle Rly, Eng, Apr
Steeplechase racecourse: Hippodrome, Bayswater, opened 3 June
Swimming club GB: National Swimming Soc (London Branch), f 30 June
Registration of births, deaths and marriages GB: 1 July [156]
Recording telegraph: Prof. Steinheil's Munich–Bogenhausen (Ger) T (12 miles) – messages punched on paper tape; operational 19 July
London main-line railway terminus: Euston, opened 20 July
Parachute fatality: Robert Cocking, Greenwich, Eng, 24 July
Mormons GB: nine converts baptized in R. Ribble, Preston, 30 July
Swimming races: org by Nat Swimming Soc in Serpentine, Hyde Park, London 6 Aug
Women's college: 8 Nov [208]
Phonographic shorthand: 15 Nov [164]
School hymnal: *Psalms and Hymns for the Use of Rugby Chapel*, Eng
Shop sale (rec): held by the Bazaar (Kendal Milne), Manchester, Eng
News agency: Agence Havas, Paris
Steam tram: New York & Harlem Rly
Register Office marriages: [156]
Kindergarten: f by Friedrich Froebel at Blankenburg, Swz
Worcester Sauce: made by John Lea and William Perrins, pharmacists of Worcester, Eng, to recipe of Sir Marcus Sandys
Literary work published in braille: *Histoire de France*, Institution Royale, Paris
Deep-sea diving suit (pressurized): inv by Augustus Siebe of London

1838
Railway Travelling Post Office: Birmingham–Liverpool, Eng, 6 Jan
Morse code: dev by Alfred Vail; first message transmitted by Morse telegraph, Morristown, N.J., 8 Jan
Steam liner: 8 April [120]
Ship to cross Atlantic wholly under steam GB: 22 April [170]
Railway race trains: Nine Elms to Kingston-upon-Railway, London & South Western Rly, Eng, Derby Day, 30 May
National sports association: Grand Caledonian (curling), f Edinburgh with 36 clubs, 25 July
Parachute GB: 3 Oct [123]
Prepaid envelope: 1 Nov [58]
Seagoing steamship: Nov 9 [170]
Centre-aisle railway carriage: [154]
Creosote GB: introd by John Bethell
Vaginal cap or pessary: by Dr Friedrich Wilde, Berlin; first use of rubber for 'surgical goods'
Photograph of a living person: [127]
Mechanical excavator: William Otis's American Steam Shovel, mnf by Eastwick & Harrison of Philadelphia; first used for construction of Western Railroad of Massachusetts
Promenade concerts GB: at English Opera House (Lyceum); admission 1s
Blazer (for sportswear): adopted by Mexican Cricket Union

1839
Photograph of the Moon: by Louis Daguerre, Paris, 2 Jan
Indian tea GB: 10 Jan [173]
Grand National: won by Jem Mason on Lottery, Aintree, Eng, 26 Feb
Electric telegraph in regular commercial use: installed Paddington–Hanwell (13 miles) for GWR by Wheatstone and Cooke: operational 6 April
Women PT instructors: trained at the Normalskole for Krindegymnastik, estab Copenhagen 20 Feb
Troop train GB: 24 May [154]
Henley Regatta: 14 June
Photographic exhibition (public): mounted by Hippolyt Bayard at 16 rue de Jeuneurs, Paris, 24 June

Dental journal: *American Journal of Dental Science*, N.Y., July
Negative-positive photographic process: 2 Feb [127]
Rail excursion (special event): 7 Aug [153]
City Police Force GB: Birmingham by Act of 26 Aug
County Constabularies GB: by Act of 27 Aug
Magazine for the blind (raised type) GB: *The Magazine for the Blind*, York, Aug
Photograph reproduced photomechanically: paper proof from etched daguerreotype exhib Paris by Dr Alfred Donne, 23 Sept
Photographic camera (mnf): Sept [128]
Railway hotel: Sept [83]
Studio portrait photograph: 7 Oct [127]
Railway timetable (national): *Bradshaw's Railway Companion*, Manchester, Eng, 25 Oct
Uniform postage rate GB: 4d ½oz; replaced distance rates, 5 Dec
Vulcanized rubber: dev by Charles Goodyear, Philadelphia, Dec (see 1840)
Photograph by artificial light: daguerreotype of coral taken through microscope by L. Ibbetson using oxy-hydrogen limelight, Royal Polytechnic Institution, London, Dec (?)
Cricket practice nets: Eton College, Eng
County cricket club: Royal Sussex CC, Eng
Iron warships: East India Co gunboats *Phlegethon* and *Nemesis*, built Birkenhead, Eng
Electric motor GB: [55]
Electric locomotive: [152]
Bicycle: [23]
Railway signal-box: Corbett's Lane Junction, London & Croydon Rly
Microphotograph: 160× reduction of 20in long document made by Benjamin Dancer, Liverpool, Eng
Foot and mouth disease GB
Artificial fertilizer: superphosphate of lime used by John Bennet Lawes for cultivation of turnips at Rothamsted, Harpenden, Eng

1840
Ocean sounding: depth of 2,425 fathoms sounded by Sir James Ross, HMS *Erebus*, off St Helena, 3 Jan
Correspondence course: 10 Jan [45]
HM inspectors of schools (Eng): Rev. John Allen and Hugh Tremenheere, Jan
Dental college: Baltimore College of Dental Surgery, chartered 1 Feb
Type-composing machine: Pianotyp, pat Eng by James Young and Adrien Delcambre of Lille, 13 Mar (see 1841)
Photographic portrait studio: 4 Mar [128]
Adhesive postage stamp (official): 6 May [137]
Stamp-collector: 7 May [169]
Drama school GB: Miss Kelly's Theatre and Dramatic School, Dean St, opened 25 May
Railway excursion at group rate: 14 June [153]
Dental association: American Soc of Dental Surgeons, f N.Y. 18 Aug
School railway excursion: Gateshead Fell National School to Tynemouth, Eng, 22 Aug
Group photograph: Yale Univ Class of 1810 taken by Samuel Morse, New Haven, Conn., Aug
Bible in raised type for blind: pub by John Alston, Glasgow, Scot; final vol (19th) Dec
Photographs by electric light: arc-lamps used by Benjamin Sillman, N.Y., and Joseph Berres, Vienna
Music-hall (purpose-built): The Star, Churchgate, Bolton, Eng
Photographic society: [128]
Athletics meet: [19]
Ski jump (on to slope): performed by Sondre Nordheim at Mogedal, Norway
Saxophone: inv by Adolphe Sax of Dinant, Belg
Canned lobster: prod by Tristram Halliday, St John, N.B.
Vulcanized rubber (commercial application): Goodyear process used by William Rider of Springfield, Mass. for shirring cloth
Budgerigars GB: pair introd from Australia by John Gould
Photographic developing and printing service: GB inst by John Benjamin Dancer, Liverpool
Convalescent home: Metropolitan Convalescent Institution, Walton-on-Thames, Eng
Nude photographs: by N.P. Lerebours, Paris.

1841
All-metal camera: mkt by Voigtländer, Vienna, 1 Jan
Registered letters (inland) GB: fee 1s; introd 6 Jan
Embossed envelope GB: 29 Jan [59]
Soft-water process: pat GB by Thomas Clark 8 Mar
Photographic portrait studio GB: 23 Mar [128]
Self-propelled fire-engine: completed by Paul Hodge, New York, 25 April
Photographic dealer GB: April [128]
Detective story: April [48]
Women graduates 25 Aug [208]
3-D photograph: taken by Henry Collen for Wheatstone's stereoscope, London, Aug
Collapsible tube: 11 Sept [41]
Express train: London–Brighton commuter service, 105min, 21 Sept
Jewish newspaper GB: *The Jewish Chronicle*, 12 Nov
Football elevens (rec): Wet-Bobs XI *v* Dry-Bobs XI, Eton, Eng, Nov
Cartridges, military issue: by Prussian Army for Dreyse Needle Gun
Electric street lighting: [55]
Paperback book series: [122]
Football club: f at Cambridge Univ, Eng, by Edgar Montagu (Caius) *et al.*
Canned anchovies: prod at Deammen, Norway
Type-composing machine (commercial use): Pianotyp (see 1840) used to set wkly magazine *The Phalanx*, London
Rugby football: handling the ball made lawful at Rugby School, Eng
Photograph of a topical event: presentation of new colours to a regt of the Austro-Hungarian Army at Linz; 14 daguerreotypes by Reisser of Vienna
Chess magazine GB: *British Miscellany & Chess Player's Chronicle*
Christmas cracker (rec): [37]
Street-cleaning machine: inv by Joseph Whitworth; introd by Road & Street Cleaning Co at Manchester, Eng

1842
Anaesthetic: 30 Mar [18]
Public laundry: opened Frederick St, Salford, Eng, 28 May
Br monarch to travel by rail: 13 June [98]
Screw-driven naval vessel: HMS *Dwarf*, adapted June
Full-page illustrated newspaper ad: 10 July [117]
Detective force GB: 15 Aug [134]
Submarine telegraph cable: laid N.Y. Harbour by Samuel Morse 18 Oct
Elementary school to introduce science teaching GB: King's Somborne Village School, Hants, Oct
Screw-driven warship (purpose-built): French Navy's *Napoleon*, launched 6 Dec
Skating-rink: 'miniature Alpine lake' with salts-of-soda surface opened Baker St, London by Henry Kirk, Dec
Photographic society GB: [128]
Electric locomotive GB: [152]
Contributory pension scheme GB: introd for clerical staff of Gas Light & Coke Co, London
Book set by type-composing machine: Edward Binn's *The Anatomy of Sleep*, London
Book illustrated with photographs: two photomechanically reproduced daguerreotypes printed by Hippolyte Fizeau's process in Vol II of N.P. Lerebours's *Excursions Daguerriennes*, Paris

1843
Royal yacht (steam): *Victoria and Albert*, launched Pembroke, 25 April
Vulcanized rubber GB: pat by Thomas Hancock, London, 21 Nov
Theatre matinée: Mitchell's Olympic Theatre, N.Y., 25 Dec
Ski competition: Langlauf (cross-country) held Trömso, Norway
Photographic enlarger: pat by Alexander Wolcott (US) and John Johnson (US) 18 Mar; installed Beard's portrait studio, Royal Polytechnic Institution, London
Dental journal GB: *British Quarterly Journal of Dental Surgery*, 30 Mar
Telegram: 16 May [174]
Telegraph poles GB: West Drayton–Slough, Eng, May
Mechanical excavator GB: Otis Steam Shovel used in building Eastern Counties line at Brentwood, Essex, May
Swimming races held in swimming-bath (rec): four lengths for boys, org by Nat Swimming Soc, National Baths, Holborn, London 18 June
Artificial fertilizer (mnf): by John Bennet Lawes at Deptford Creek, London; superphosphates adv at 4s 6d bushel, 1 July
Trade-union journal: *The Miners' Journal*, pub by the Miners' Assoc, Newcastle, Eng, 2 Oct
Christmas card: Dec [36]
Rugby football club: Guy's Hospital RFC, London
Sidestroke: introd in competitive swimming by George Pewters, London
Soap powder: 'Babbitt's Best Soap', N.Y.
Toy building bricks: Henry Cole's 'Box of Terra Cotta Bricks', mnf by Minton, Eng
Cigarettes (mnf): [37]
Woman photographer: [205]
Season tickets: London & Greenwich Railway

1844
Recording telegraph in commercial use: Morse T from Capitol, Washington–Mount Clare Station, Baltimore, operational 24 May; Morse code on paper tape
Press telegram: 25 May [174]
Book illustrated with photographs GB: William Fox Talbot's *The Pencil of Nature*, first of six parts pub by Longman, London, 29 June
Fog-horn: dem by Capt. J.N. Taylor, London, 12 July. Range 6 miles
Ocean cruise: 26 July [119]
Press telegram GB: 6 Aug [174]
Telegraph arrest: Oliver Martin and 'Fiddler Dick', pickpockets, apprehended at Slough following police wire from Paddington, London, 28 Aug
Detective story GB: 30 Nov [48]
Dental anaesthetic: 11 Dec [18]
Vulcanized rubber (commercial application) GB: Hancock's rubber (*see* 1843) used by GWR for fish-plates
Gummed envelopes GB: [59]
Hotel bridal suite: [83]
Paperback book series GB: [123]
District nurses: Kaiserswerth sisters assigned to Bielefeld and Cleve, Ger
Dynamo (commercial use): built by John Woolrich to supply current to plating vats of Prime & Co, electroplaters, Birmingham, Eng
Day nursery: by Les Soeurs de la Sagesse in Chaillot quarter of Paris
Newspaper directory: *The Advertiser's Guide*, Lewis & Lowe, London
YMCA: f by George Williams, London
Banking journal GB: *The Bankers Magazine*, London
Air conditioning: inst by John Corrie at American Hospital for Tropical Fevers, Apalachicola, Fl.

1845
Anglican sisterhood: Sisters of Mercy, Park Village Community House, Regent's Park, London, Mar
Rubber Band: 17 Mar [53]
Iron Liner: 26 July [120]
Screw-propelled liner: 26 July [120]
Organized holiday tour: 4 Aug [192]
Club colours GB: Aug [40]
Baseball club: Knickerbocker Club, f N.Y. 13 Sept
Pneumatic tyres: 10 Dec [132]
Submarine telegraph cable GB: laid Portsmouth Harbour by Capt. J.N. Taylor
Tarmacadam: laid London Rd, Nottingham, Eng
Glass paperweight: mnf by Pierre Rigaglia, Venice
Aeronautical journal: *The Balloon; or Aerostatic Magazine*, London
Advertising calendar: pub by Auburn, N.Y. insurance co
Book dust-jacket in colour: *Poems by W. W. Lord*, N.Y.
Self-raising flour: mkt by Henry Jones of Bristol, Eng

1846
Field newspaper: 6 June [118]
Baseball match: New York Nine *v* Knickerbocker Club at Elysian Fields Hoboken N.J., 19 June
Magazine photograph: June [95]
Cricket All-England XI (representative): played first match *v* Sheffield, 31 Aug–2 Sept
Civic society GB: estab Sidmouth, 9 Sept
Anaesthetic (major surgery): 16 Oct [18]
Municipal museum GB: 9 Nov [115]
Dental anaesthetic GB: 19 Dec [18]
Anaesthesia (major surgery) GB: 21 Dec [18]
Khaki uniform: Dec [90]
Centrally heated hotel: [83]
Travel agency: [192]
War photographer: studies of Webster's Battn, Gen. Wool, etc taken in Mexico by unknown American daguerreotypist
Rotary-power printing press: Hoe Rotary adopted by *Philadelphia Ledger*
Compulsory education for all (enforced) GB: Scilly Is
Sponge rubber: pat by Charles Hancock, London
Sewing machine (mnf) GB: [163]
Grants for higher education GB: Queen's scholarships to recognized teacher training colleges; av. £25 p.a. maintenance + £25 p.a. tuiton etc
Probation officer (voluntary): John Augustus, Boston Police Court, Mass.
Cricket score-board: Lord's, Eng
Written examination for women GB: conducted by the Governesses' Benevolent Institution
Teletype machine: inv by Royal E. House of Vermont
Rubber tyres: mnf by Thomas Hancock, London

1847
Medical Officer of Health GB: Dr William Duncan, apnt Liverpool 1 Jan
Municipal lending library GB: 14 Jan [141]
Borough Engineer GB: James Newlands apnt Liverpool 26 Jan
Parliamentary Press Gallery: House of Lords, occupied 15 April
Double-decker bus: April [29]
Communist party: 1 June [43]
General Service Medals: Military and Naval GSMs, 1793–1814, sanctioned GB: 1 June
Photographic journal: *Le Daguerreotype*, Paris, June
African colony to secure independence: Liberia, 26 July
Pneumatic tyres (sold): 1 Oct [132]
Birth under anaesthesia: 9 Nov [18]
Communist journal: *Kommunistische Zeitschrift*, London, Sept; first use of slogan 'Workers of the World, Unite!'
Rubber balloons (toy): [160]
School for the mentally handicapped GB: Park House, Highgate, estab by Dr Andrew Reed
Taxi-meter: Patent Mile-Index fitted to London cab
Meat extract: prepared by Justus von Liebig, Royal Pharmacy, Munich
Service revolvers: 1,000 Colt ·45 issued US Army for use in Mexican War
Electric cables (insulated): mnf by the Gutta Percha Co, London
Anaesthetist (full-time practitioner): Dr John Snow, St Thomas's Hospital, London
Municipal water supply GB: Manchester
Steamship to circumnavigate the world: HMS *Driver*, arr Spithead, Eng, 14 May
Building acquired for preservation GB: Shakespeare's birthplace, sold for £3,000 to United Shakespeare Committee, 16 Sept
Ring doughnuts: introd by Capt. Hanson Gregory, Camden, Me.
Woman awarded a medal GB: Jane Townsend, Naval GSM for service at Trafalgar (1805)

1848
Canned sweet corn: first batch sold by Nathan Winslow of Portland, Me., 19 Feb
Mediums: 31 Mar [168]
Women's college GB: 1 May [208]
State-certified teachers GB: 318 names pub 30 June
Coloured MP: 22 Aug [41]
Exclusive Brethren: seceded from Plymouth Brethren (Eng) 26 Aug
Newspaper weather reports: 31 Aug [200]
State school for the mentally handicapped: Massachusetts School for Idiotic and Feeble-minded Youth, estab Boston, 1 Oct
Multiple retailer: 1 Nov [114]
Floodlighting: W.E. Staites floodlit National Gallery with electric arc-lamp, London, Nov 28
Christmas number of a magazine: 23 Dec [37]
Stately home excursion trip: [169]
Chewing gum: [34]
Fire-hydrant (ball-valve): introd at Warrington, Lancs, Eng
Hospital, children's ward GB: Guy's
Oil refinery GB: estab by James Young at Riddings, Derby, Eng
Cricket, wicket-keeper's gloves: mnf by Duke & Son, Penshurst, Eng
Ice skates with steel runners: made by E.V. Bushnell, Philadelphia
Service rifle, bolt-action: Dreyse Needle Gun adopted by Prussian Army
Railcar: [151]
Trained nurses GB: Training Institution for Nurses in Hospitals, estab Fitzroy Sq by Dr Todd
Model aircraft (powered flight): John Stringfellow's twin-screw steam-driven monoplane flew at Chard, Somerset, Eng
Lifebelt (circular cork): inv by Mr Carte, Ordnance storekeeper at Hull, Eng
Department store: [48]
Amateur dramatic society (non-institutional) GB: Manchester Athenaeum Dramatic Soc
Photographically illustrated art book: Sir William Stirling's *Annals of the Artists of Spain*; 66 calotype repros made by Nicolaas Henneman (Neths)
Municipal street-cleaning dept GB: Liverpool; 164 men, 18 sweeping machines

1849
Woman doctor: 23 Jan [202]
Teletype machine commercial operation: by New Jersey Magnetic Telegraph Co, N.Y.–Philadelphia, Mar
Safety-pin: pat by Walter Hunt, N.Y., 10 April (*see also* 12 Oct)
International yacht race: *Pearl of Bermuda* (Bermuda) beat *Brenda* (US), Bermuda, 8 May
Canned tomatoes: prod by Harrison W. Crosby, steward at Lafayette College, Easton, Pa., Sept
Safety-pin GB: pat by Charles Rowley, 12 Oct
Accident insurance: introd by Railway Passengers Assurance Co; first claimant, William Good of Dunstable, awarded £7 6s on 10 Nov
Bowler hat: 17 Dec [26]
Telephone: [175]
Pillar box: [92]
Decimal coins GB: florins, issued in anticipation of proposed decimal changeover
Weather charts GB: prod daily at Greenwich Observatory by James Glaisher
Electric street lighting GB: [55]
Chess tournament: at Simpson's Divan, London; won by Henry Buckle
C.O.D. service: by Swiss Post Office
Coeducational school GB: [41]
Dry cleaner: [52]

1850
Pictorial postage stamp: 1 Jan
Train ferry: 417-ton *Leviathan*, operated Granton–Bruntisland on Firth of Forth, Scot, by Edinburgh, Perth & Dundee Rly, 7 Feb
Day nursery GB: 19 Massay St, Marylebone, cradles 3d per day; 8 Mar
Hippopotamus GB: landed 25 May
Channel telegraph cable: Dover–Cap Gris Nez (Fr), 28 Aug
Photographic slides: pat by Frederick Langenheim, Philadelphia, 19 Nov
External school examination: 23 Dec [161]
Jeans: [89]
Refrigeration plant: [155]
Perambulators (mnf): [125]
Magazine prize competitions: introd by *The Family Friend*, London; 50gns worth of prizes

1851
International Exhibition: Crystal Palace, Hyde Park, London, 1 May
Cocktail bar GB: 1 May [40]
Yale lock: pat by Linus Yale, Newport, N.Y. 6 May
Chess, International Masters Tournament: opened at St George's Club, London 27 May; won by Adolf Anderssen (Ger)
Baseball, inter-club match: Knickerbocker Club *v* Washington BC, Red House Grounds, N.Y., 3 June
Ice-cream factory: 15 June [85]
Weather charts (published) GB: sold daily at Great Exhibition, 8 Aug–11 Oct
International yacht race GB: *America* (USA) won Queen's Cup Race, IW, 22 Aug
Overseas telegrams GB: service introd by Submarine Telegraph Co (20 words Paris 19s; Berlin 32s 6d; Venice 43s) 18 Oct
Urban nation: Britain; 50·6% of population domiciled in towns (USA 15·3%)
Cigarettes (mkt) GB: [37]
Domestic sewing machine: [163]
American tourists, influx of GB: 5,048 Americans visited London for Great Exhibition
Royal cyclist: quadricycle built by J. Ward of Leicester for Prince Consort
Parent-Teacher Association: estab at Ronges Kindergarten, London
Ophthalmoscope: dev by Herman von Helmholtz, Königsberg
International scientific congress: Internat Sanitary Congress, Paris
Kindergarten GB: f Hampstead by Johannes and Bertha Ronges
Self-righting lifeboat: built by James Beeching of Gt Yarmouth, Eng; stationed Ramsgate
Woman photographer GB: [206]
International copyright agreement: Fr-GB
News Agency GB: Reuter's
Tubular steel furniture: rocking chair exhib by R.W. Winfield at Great Exhibition, London

1852
Children's hospital GB: Great Ormond Street. First patient, Eliza Armstrong ($3\frac{1}{2}$), admitted 14 Feb
Public lavatory (Gents): 2 Feb [140]
Public lavatory (Ladies): 11 Feb [140]
Cartridges, military issue GB: for Minié Service Rifle, Feb
Service rifle (standard infantry issue) GB: Belgian Minié issued to 20 regts, Feb
Electric fire-alarm system: 50 signal-boxes operational Boston, Mass., 28 April
Tramp steamer: collier *John Bowes*, launched Jarrow, Eng, 30 June
Free public lending library GB: 6 Sept [141]
Spiritualist medium GB: Oct [168]
House of Commons Press gallery: occupied 4 Nov
Pillar box GB: 23 Nov [92]
Inter-school football match: Westminster *v* Harrow, Eng
Glider flight: [77]
Photographic lantern slides GB: made by John Dancer, Manchester
War photographer (Br): Surgeon John MacCosh, Second Burma War (47 studies survive)
Piano accordion: by M. Bouton, Paris
Business school (collegiate): Higher Institute of Commerce, Antwerp
Working men's club: [209]
Photolitho book illustrations: specimens by N.P. Lerebours and Alfred Lemercier in *Lithophotographie*, Paris
Microfilm: microphotography on collodion film achieved by Benjamin Dancer, Manchester, Eng
Day-release scheme: introd by Cadbury's, Birmingham, Eng, for girl workers
Aeronautical society: Société Aérostatique de France, Paris
Stamp album: pub by A. Oppems, London

1853
Photographic journal GB: *Journal of the Photographic Society of England*, 3 Mar
Aquarium: Aquatic Vivarium, Regent's Park Zoo, London, opened 21 May

Hotel waitresses: May [83]
Printing on tin: litho process pat by Charles Adams, London, 13 Sept
Woman minister of religion: 15 Sept [204]
Provincial daily newspaper (Eng): *Northern Daily Times*, Liverpool, 24 Sept
Branch library GB: Liverpool Northern District Libary, Oct
School football house championship: Harrow, Eng
Nature reserve: Forest of Fountainebleau, Fr
Railway corridor coach: [151]
Hotel private baths: [83]
Book with coloured pictorial cover: *Letters Left at the Pastry Cook's*, shilling novelette pub by Ingram, Cooke & Co, London
Potato crisps: [138]
Wooden pipes (smoking) GB: Norfolk willow, 1s 6d each
Electrical manufacturing company: Société Générale d'Electricité, Paris, mnf of lighthouse generators etc.
Braille GB: specimen inc in Edmund Johnson's *Tangible Typography*

1854
Public school for girls GB: Cheltenham Ladies' College, opened 13 Feb
Perforated postage stamps: Feb [137]
Service revolvers GB: 4,000 American Colts ordered by RN, 8 Mar
Microfilms, commercially produced: scientific subjects mkt by Smith & Beck, London, 29 Mar
VC: Mate Charles Lucas for action aboard HMS *Hecla* at Bomarsund, 21 June (gazetted 1857)
Reformatory (State supported) GB: Saltley, nr Birmingham, Aug
Army VCs: six for gallantry at Alma, 20 Sept
Baby show: 14 Oct [21]
Female military nurses: 24 nurses under Miss Nightingale arr Scutari 4 Nov
Sea cadets: Whitstable Lads Naval Brigade, Eng
Psychiatric nursing: training scheme inaug Crichton Royal Asylum, Dumfries, Scot
Water-softening plant: installed at Plumstead Waterwork, Eng
Hospital for incurables GB: Royal H for Incurables, Putney
Paraffin lamp: Inv by John H. and George W. Austen, N.Y.

1855
Boys' magazine GB: Jan [35]
Field railway: Balaklava–Kadikoi, Crimea, opened 23 Feb
Field-service electric telegraph: inaug by RE at Kadikoi, Russia, 7 Mar
Medical unit of the Br Army: Medical Staff Corps, f 11 June
Continental Holiday Tour: 4 July [193]
Gallantry medal (official issue): Conspicuous Gallantry Medal (RN and Royal Marines), inst 13 Aug
International voluntary organization: YMCA World Alliance, Paris, 19 Aug
Hyde Park orator: a carpenter who spoke on food prices, London, 14 Oct
Anglican bishop consecrated overseas: F.J. MacDougall, B of Labuan, cons at Calcutta, 18 Oct
Symphony orchestra GB: Crystal Palace Orchestra; first concert under August Manns (Ger), 20 Oct
Bunsen burner: by Robert Bunsen, Heidelberg
Water desalination plant: des by S. Sidey, inst at War Office Revictualling Station, Heligoland
Computer: [44]
Safety matches: [97]
Municipal public lavatory: [140]
Aluminium: mnf by Henry Deville at Salindres Foundry, Paris; sold at $60 per lb
Stamp dealer: [169]
War photographer (official): War Office photographers Ensigns Brandon and Dawson, Crimea
Rotary cultivator (self-propelled): built by Robert Romaine, Montreal
Floating mines (contact): laid by Russians in Baltic
Stethoscope, binaural (mnf): by Dr Camman, N.Y.

1856
Victoria Cross (instituted): 5 Feb (retrospective)
Hospital staffed by trained nurses GB: King's College Hospital, London, 31 Mar
Artificial respiration: desc by Dr Marshall Hall of St George's Hospital, London, in the *Lancet*, 12 April
Eight-hour day for adult male industrial workers (permanent): won by stonemasons of Victoria, Australia, 21 May
Detective novel: June [48]
Vote by ballot: 27 Aug [22]
Dental association GB: Odontological Soc of London, f 10 Nov
Book illustrated with photo-engravings: *Photographic Art Treasures*, pub by Photogalvanographic Co, Islington, London, Nov
Industrialist raised to the peerage: cotton-magnate Edward Strutt, 1st Lord Belper
Underwater photograph: study of seaweed by W. Thompson, Weymouth, Eng
Rotary power printing press: Hoe Rotary adopted by *Lloyd's Weekly Newspaper*, London
Lacrosse club: Montreal LC
Gas fire (mnf): [76]
Correspondence school: [45]
Stamp dealer GB: [169]
Clockwork train: mnf by George Browne & Co, Forestville, Conn.
Butter factory: estab by R.S. Woodhull at Campbell Hall, Orange County, N.Y.
Village flower show: org by Henry Cole at Shere, Surrey
Aniline dye: mauve, disc by 17-year-old William Perkin, London
Paraffin (mnf) GB: James Young, Bathgate, Glasgow. Young introd first British paraffin lamp same year

1857
Naval uniform (RN ratings): authorized 30 Jan
Street parade with decorated floats: Mardi Gras, New Orleans, 3 Mar
Department-store elevator: 23 Mar [58]
British army regt to wear khaki: 25 May [90]
Victoria Cross investiture: Hyde Park, London, 26 June
Football club (open membership): Sheffield FC, f 24 Oct
Golf Manual: H.B. Farnie's *The Golfer's Manual*
Lubricating oil: mnf by Price's Patent Candle Co, Battersea, London
Steel railway track: forged by R.F. Mushet; laid Derby Station, Eng
Photolitho book illustrations GB: in J. Pouncy's *Dorsetshire Photographically Illustrated*
Electric street lighting (permanent): [55]
Joker playing-card (rec): [132]
Library for the blind: Lower Sackville St, Dublin
Mechanical vehicles in service use: two Burrell–Boydell traction engines acquired by RE at Woolwich, London
Concrete mixer: used in construction of bridge over R. Tisza at Szeged, Hungary

1858
Divorce court GB: 1 Jan [50]
International swimming championship: Jo Bennett (Aus) beat Chas Stedman (Eng) at St Kilda, Melbourne, 9 Feb
Burglar alarm, electric: installed by Edwin T. Holmes, Boston, Mass. 21 Feb
Steel ship: 6 Mar [163]
Condensed milk: adv by Gail Borden of Burrville, Conn., 22 May
Pencil with attached eraser: pat by Hyman Lipman of Philadelphia, 30 Mar
Magazine regularly illustrated with photographs: 1 July [95]
Baseball match, admission charge: Brooklyn *v* N.Y. All Stars, Fashion Race Course, Long Island, 20 July; 1,500 spectators paid 50c entry
Jewish MP to take seat: Lionel Rothschild, elected MP for City of London, 26 July
Fingerprints: 28 July [72]
Transatlantic telegraph cable: laid by USS *Niagara* and HMS *Agamemnon*; first message sent Newfoundland–Valentia 12 Aug
Transatlantic telegrams: average cost £20; service introd 16 Aug
Aerial photograph: Dec [127]
Lighthouse lit by electricity: South Foreland, Dec
Asphalt street surface: Paris
Woman cigarette smoker GB: [38]
School Certificate exam: [161]
Eight-hour day for adult male industrial workers (permanent) GB: West Yorkshire coal-hewers
Cage bird show: All England Open Canary Show, Sunderland
Black Maria GB: introd by Metropolitan Police
Artiste's agent: [19]
Communication cord (rec): in use on New York Central Railroad
Team photographs (rec): Eton Cricket XI (Eng); Trinity Hall First Boat, Cambridge, Eng

1859
Parish magazine: Jan [124]
Commissionaires (uniformed): Corps of Commissionaires, London, 13 Feb
Labour party: 22 Mar [91]
District nurse GB: Mrs Mary Robinson of Liverpool, apnt May
Dog show: 28 June [50]
Domestic electric lighting: July [54]
London district code: 10 central districts assigned initial letters, 3 Aug (numbers added 1917)
Advertising slogan (regular) GB: Beecham's Pills 'Worth a Guinea a Box', *St Helens Intelligencer*, 6 Aug
Hotel elevator: 23 Aug [58]
Labour MP: 26 Aug [91]
Oil rig: Edwin Drake of Seneca Oil Co struck oil at Titusville, Pa., 28 Aug
Railway carriage lavatory: 1 Sept [200]
Pullman Car: des by George Pullman, introd Bloomington–Chicago line, 1 Sept
Photograph printed in magazine GB: by photoglyphic process in *Photographic News*, 16 Sept
Cricket, overseas tour: Canada and US by Mr G. Parr's XI; first match Montreal, 24 Sept
Maps printed by photolitho: by J.W. Osborne, Govt Survey Office, Melbourne, Aus, Sept
Dental college GB: London School of Dental Surgery, Soho Sq, opened 1 Oct
Flying trapeze: 12 Nov [39]
Mobile library: 'perambulating library for the working classes' inaug by Warrington Mechanics' Institution, Eng
Cottage hospital: estab Cranleigh, Surrey, Eng by Albert Napper; four beds
Postage due stamp (adhesive): France
Children's playground: [115]
Steam-roller: des by M. Lemoime, Paris; used in construction of Bois de Boulogne
School gymnasium GB: Uppingham
Polo club: Cachar PC, Assam
Matchbox-label collectors (rec): noted by Anatole France; known as 'Vulcanites'
Cigarettes (mnf) GB: [38]

1860
RNVR: enrolment 1 Jan
Army cadet corps (permanent) GB: Rossall School Volunteer Corps, 1 Feb
Dental surgeons GB: 13 Mar [47]
Maps printed by photolitho GB: Ordnance Survey, Southampton, Mar
Nurses' home: St Thomas's Hospital, London, 15 June
Baseball tour: by Brooklyn Excelsiors, starting Albany, N.Y. 30 June
Rifle-shooting tournament (long-range): held by National Rifle Assoc at Wimbledon, Eng, 2 July
Breech-loading rifled artillery used in warfare: Armstrong 18-pounders bombarded Sinho, China, 12 Aug
Trams GB: Birkenhead Street Rly, 30 Aug
Professional golf tournament: won by Willie Park of Musselburgh at Prestwick, Scotland 17 Oct
Internal-combustion engine (mnf): 19 Oct [87]
Telephone (dem): 26 Oct [175]
Iron-hulled screw-driven battleship GB: 6,170-ton HMS *Warrior*, launched 29 Dec
Cricket, composition ball: pat by Hamlet Nicholson of Rochdale, Eng
Dry Martini: [41]
Addressograph: inv by Christopher Sholes, Milwaukee; mnf Madison, Wisc.
Pekingeses GB: 4 brought from Peking; 1 to Qn Victoria, 1 to Admiral Lord Hall, 2 to Duchess of Richmond
Pictorial dust-jacket: [26]

Postal Orders: France
Municipal bowling-green: Edinburgh
Press-stud fastener: by John Newnham, Eng

1861
Storm warnings: 6 Feb [200]
Football, inter-club match: Sheffield *v* Hallam, Sheffield, Eng, 12 Feb
Football match, admission charge: as above
Package holiday: 17 May [121]
Colour photograph: 17 May [129]
Weather forecast: 1 Aug [200]
Boys' camp (recreational): org by Frederick Gunn at Milford, Conn., Aug
Post Office Savings Bank: inst GB 16 Sept
Golf, British Open: won by Tom Morris, Prestwick, 26 Sept
Stamp catalogue: *Timbres-Poste*, privately pub by François Berger-Levrault, Strasbourg, Sept
Meat refrigeration plant: estab by Thomas Mort, Darling Harbour, Sydney, NSW
Postcard: [138]
Refrigeration plant GB: [155]
Identity photographs: on Chicago & Milwaukee Railroad season tickets
Warship with turret-mounted guns: Danish Navy's *Rolf Krake*
Ski club: Trysil Skytter og Skilöberforening, Trysil, Norway
Internal-combustion engine (mnf) GB: [87]
Female military nurses (peacetime): Royal Herbert Hospital, Woolwich, Eng
Home for stray animals: Temporary Home for Lost Dogs, Hollingsworth St, London

1862
Stamp catalogue GB: Frederick Booty's *Aids to Stamp Collectors*, pub by H. & C. Teacher, Brighton, April
Baseball stadium: Union Grounds, Brooklyn, opened 15 May
Motor car: May [99]
Stamp magazine: *The Monthly Advertiser*, Liverpool, Eng, 15 Dec
Self-propelled fire-engine GB: $7\frac{1}{2}$-ton steam vehicle (max. 18mph) built by William Roberts of Milwall, sold to C.J. Mare & Co
Health Visitors: employed by the Manchester & Salford Ladies' Sanitary Reform Assoc, Eng
Hockey club: Blackheath HC, London
Women granted municipal vote: ratepayers, Sweden
Thermoplastic: [131]
Christmas card (mnf) GB: [36]
Children's library GB: [35]
Slimming diet: [49]
Doll's pram: [125]
Bicycle manufacturer: [23]
Traffic islands: [191]
Local authority to introduce scholarship system GB: 10 free places annually offered at Doncaster Grammar School by competitive exam; fees paid by Doncaster Corporation
Blazer (for sportswear) GB: adopted by Lady Margaret Boat Club, St John's College, Cambridge

1863
Merry-go-round (power-driven): operated by Thomas Bradshaw at the Pot Market, Bolton, Eng, 1 Jan
Underground railway: 10 Jan [195]
Facsimile transmission by wire, public service: by Pentelegraph system, Paris–Lyons, 16 Feb
International Red Cross: f Geneva, 17 Feb
Rented poster sites GB: inst by Sheldon, Son & Co, Leeds, Feb
Steeplechase under National Hunt Rules: won by Mr Goodman on Socks, Market Harborough, Eng, 26 Mar
Asylum for the criminally insane: Broadmoor, Crowthorne, Berks, Eng; estab 27 May
Athletics club: June [20]
Association Football rules: pub in *Bell's Life*, Eng, 5 Dec
Heavyweight boxing champion of the world: Tom King (Eng) beat John C. Heenan (USA) at Wodhurst, Kent, 8 Dec
Dental drill (power) GB: [47]
Club tie: Eton Ramblers Cricket Club, Eng
Canned peaches: prod by Cutting Co, Calif.
Self-propelled submarine: [171]
Steam-roller GB: des by W.F. Batho of Birmingham for City Engineer's Dept, Calcutta
Steam-roller (mnf): by Gellerat et Cie, Paris
Railway buffet-car: [151]
Oil tanker: *Atlantic*, launched Tyne
Warships with turret-mounted guns GB: HMS *Scorpion* and HMS *Wyvern*
Aerial photograph GB: [128]
Hospital train: 10-ward-car train introd Alexandria, Va.–Washington by Orange & Alexandria Railroad
Roller skates (four-wheel): [157]
Dynamite: made by Alfred Nobel at Ammeberg, Sweden
Harpoon gun (practical): des by Sven Foyn of Tönsberg, Norway; fitted aboard whaler *Spes e Fides* (1864)
Propelling pencil: dev by Johann Faber, Nuremberg

1864
Provincial evening newspaper GB: *Eastern Evening News*, Hull, 26 Jan
Commonwealth VC: Major C. Heaphy of the Auckland Militia for gallantry at Manga Piko River, NZ, 11 Feb (gazetted 1867)
Ship sunk by submarine: 17 Feb [171]
Commonwealth troops to fight in overseas war: 1,130 Australian volunteers arr Auckland, NZ to serve in Maori War, 17 Feb (formed into Auckland Militia)
Inter-varsity athletics meet: 3 Mar [20]
Negro C of E Bishop: Samuel Crowther, consecrated Bishop of the Niger, Canterbury, Eng, 29 June
Cheque, perforated counterfoil: 5 July [34]
Meat extract (mnf): Extractum Carnis Liebig, mnf at Fray Bentos, Uruguay, Sept
Professional baseball player: Al Roach, Philadelphia Athletics, June
Canned asparagus: prod by William Hudson of Hunter's Point, Long Island
Squash courts: built at Harrow School, Eng
Rugby football club (open membership): Liverpool RFC, Eng
Jelly babies: mnf by Herr Steinbeck (Aust), Nelson, Lancs, Eng
Christmas Day dip in Serpentine: [37]
Motor boat: [99]
Policemen's helmets: [135]
Rubber stamp: dev by John Leighton, London
Whaling ship, steam: *Spes e Fides*, built by Sven Foyn, Oslo
Driving chain (practical): introd by James Slater for textile machinery at his Salford factory, Eng
Crammer GB: Dr Frost's (Woolwich and Sandhurst candidates)

1865
Gun-dog field trials: Southill, Beds, Eng, 18 April
Communication cord GB: 'voltaic electric alarm' introd London & South Western Rly, Eng, May
Safe deposit: Safe Deposit Co of New York, 140 Broadway, opened 5 June
Salvation Army: orig with revival meeting held by William Booth at Whitechapel Burial Ground, Eng, 2 July
Speed limit: 2mph country, 2mph towns, under Locomotives and Highways Act, effective GB 5 July
Woman doctor GB: 28 Sept [202]
Oil pipeline: Pithole City-Millers' Farm Depot, Pa. (5 miles); 2in diameter cast-iron pipe, Oct
Pocket lighter: The Erie, mnf by Repeating Light Co of Springfield, Mass. under pat of 7 Nov
Stamp auction: held at Hôtel Drouot, Paris, 29 Dec
Railway tank wagons: (i) des by Hames Densmore, operated Oil Creek, Pa.–New York; (ii) chemical carrier built by Gloucester Wagon Works, Glos, Eng
Croquet club: Worthing, Eng
Gift coupons: [77]
Oyster bed (artificial) GB: South of England Oyster Co, Hayling Island, Eng
Steam-roller used on Br roads: des by Thomas Aveling of Rochester, built by Easton, Amos & Anderson; first used at Erith, Kent
Rubber wellingtons: mnf by North British Rubber Co, Edinburgh

1866
Woman dental surgeon: 21 Feb [201]
Downhill ski races: held on Iverslökken, Norway; won by Elling Beakken of Hönenfoss, 16 Mar
National athletics championship: 23 Mar [20]
Albert Medal: awarded to Samuel Popplestone for rescue at sea, Eng, 14 May
Aeronautical society GB: The Aeronautical Soc, f 27 June
Salvation Army citadel: converted woollen store in Three Colts Lane, Bethnal Green, Eng, June
Indelible pencil: pat by Edson P. Clark of Northampton, Mass., 10 July
Cricket boundaries: Eton *v* Harrow, Lord's, Eng, 13 July
Canoe club: Canoe Club, f by John MacGregor, Richmond, Surrey, Eng, 25 July
Radio telegraphy: Oct [143]
Transatlantic yacht race: won by *Henrietta* (USA), N.Y.–Cowes, 11–25 Dec
Cocoa GB: Dec [40]
Box of chocolates GB: [35]
Steel bridge: built by M. Joret, Paris
British chess championship: opened at St George's Club 19 June; won by Charles de Vere (21)
Newspaper set by type-composing machine: *Eastern Morning News*, Hull, Eng; Hattersley typesetter
Dry cleaner GB: [52]
Plastic goods (mnf): [131]
Roller-skating rink: Atlantic House Rink, Newport, R.I.
Lawn tennis: played by J.B. Perara (Sp) and Maj. T.H. Gem at Fairlight, Ampton Rd, Birmingham, Eng

1867
Condensed milk GB: Milk-Maid brand mkt by Anglo-Swiss Condensed Milk Co, Feb
Canoe race: org by Canoe Club at Thames Ditton (1 mile), Eng, 27 April
Operation performed under antiseptic conditions: Joseph Lister amputated cancerous breast of Isabella Lister (sister) using carbolic acid as an antiseptic, Glasgow Royal Infirmary, Scot, 17 June
Barbed wire: 25 June [22]
Dynamite GB: dem by Alfred Nobel at Merstham Quarry, Redhill, Surrey, Eng, 14 July
Reinforced concrete: pat by Joseph Monier, Paris, 16 July
Croquet tournament: Evesham, Eng, 15–16 Aug
Channel crossing by canoe: *The Octoroon*, Boulogne–Dover, 11hr, 19 Aug
University extension movement: inaug with eight science lectures by James Stuart, Fellow of Trinity, Cambridge, at Manchester, Eng, 10 Oct
Party conference: Conservative, Freemasons' Tavern, Gt Queen St, London, 12 Nov
Woman to vote in Parliamentary Election: 26 Nov [207]
Ticker-tape machine: installed by Gold & Stock Telegraph Co at N.Y. office of David Groesbeck Co, 29 Dec
Decorative biscuit tins GB: by Huntley & Palmer for their Napoleon and Leopold biscuits
Lacrosse GB: introd by W.B. Johnson's touring team of Chaughnawage Indians
Hansard reporters: apnt by NZ Govt, Wellington
Cycling club: Liverpool Velocipede Club, Eng
Railway dining-car (full service): [152]
Steam-roller (mnf) GB: by Aveling & Porter, Rochester; first sale to Liverpool Corp
Vending-machine (automatic): [197]
School meals (in State schools): introd by School Fund Societies, Paris
Daily newspaper to publish regular cartoons: *Evening Telegram*, N.Y.
Commemorative plaque GB: [43]
Lacrosse club GB: Glasgow LC
Department store GB: [48]
Time switch: 8-day clockwork 'Gas Controller' inv by Dr Thurger, Norwich, Eng; inst at Somerset House and the Mint
Dog Licences GB: 5s

1868
Athlete to run 100yd under 10sec: J.P. Tennent at Walham Green, Eng, 3 April

Stapler: pat by C.H. Gould of Birmingham, Eng, 5 Mar
Cricket touring team to visit GB: Australian Aborigines; first match *v* Surrey Gentlemen, 23 May
Cycle race: won by James Moore (Eng), Parc St Cloud, Paris, 31 May
Cycle race GB: won by Arthur Markham, Welsh Harp, Hendon, 1 June
Trades Union Congress: Manchester, Eng, 2–6 June
Cross-country running club (open membership): Thames Hare & Hounds; first run Roehampton, Eng, 17 Oct
Women's cycle race: Parc Bordelais, Bordeaux, Fr, 1 Nov
Indoor athletics meeting: 11 Nov [20]
Traffic lights: 10 Dec [191]
Troop train in warfare (Br): [154]
Athletics track: [20]
Pictorial chocolate box GB: [36]
Torpedo (motor-): Austrian gunboat *Genese* fitted with Whitehead compressed-air torpedoes, Fiume
Direct mail advertising specialists: Smith, Dalby-Welch Ltd, London
Holding company: Pennsylvania Co
Railway air-brakes: inv by George Westinghouse; first used on Pittsburg –Steubenville line
Football tournament: Yorkshire FA Cromwell Cup; won by Sheffield Wednesday

1869
Cyclists to ride from London to Brighton: J. Mayall, R. Turner and C. Spencer in 16hr, 19 Feb
International cycle race: won by Ernest Michaux (Fr), Crystal Palace, 6 Mar
Cremator: 10 Mar [46]
Professional baseball club: Cincinnati Red Stockings, first match as all-pro team *v* Great Western, 15 Mar
Colour photoprint: 7 May [129]
Bicycle manufacturer GB: 10 May [23]
Asphalt street surface GB: Threadneedle St by Val de Travers Asphalte Paving Co, May
Cycling journal: *La Velocipède Illustré*, Paris, 19 June
Probation officers (official): apnt Massachusetts under statute of 23 June
Margarine: 15 July [97]
Operation for removal of kidney: from Margaretha Kleb by Gustav Simon of Heidelberg, 2 Aug
Mountain rack railway: Mt Washington, N.H., opened 29 Aug
Pre-paid postcards: 1 Oct [138]
Cycle road race: won by James Moore (Eng); Paris–Rouen (83 miles), 17 Nov
Cycle show: held at Pré-Catalan, Paris, 1–5 Nov
Women jurors (statutory): 10 Dec [203]
Bicycle with mudguards: mnf by Berruyer of Grenoble
Concrete bridge: built by (Sir) John Fowler, Cromwell Rd, London (temporary)
Novel in raised type for blind: *The Old Curiosity Shop*, Perkins Institution, Boston
Badminton: orig Badminton Hall, Glos, Eng
Novel issued with dust-jacket: *Tom Brown's Schooldays*, Macmillan, London
Rickshaw: [156]
Polo GB: introd Aldershot by 10th Hussars
Bicycle with four-speed gear: mnf by G. Anthoni, Paris
Office elevator: [58]
Municipal housing: [114]

1870
Woman stockbroker: 19 Jan [206]
University grants for women: all Russian secondary schoolgirls with parents in lower-income groups eligible to compete for grants; first State-maintained female undergraduates entered St Petersburg Univ 20 Jan
Post Office telegrams GB: 1s for 20 words, 5 Feb (see 1843)
Women civil servants GB: 201 PO telegraph operators, 5 Feb
Woman magistrate: 17 Feb [203]
Woman on hospital medical staff GB: 15 Mar [202]
Cheese factory GB: by Derbyshire Cheese Factory Assoc, Derby, 8 April
Water polo: rules drafted by London Swimming Assoc 12 May
Tube railway: 2 Aug [195]
Red Cross Society GB: f 4 Aug
America's Cup contest: Mr F. Osgood's *Magic* (USA) beat Mr J. Ashbury's *Cambria* (GB), 8 Aug
State education system GB: inst under W.E. Forster's Education Act, passed 9 Aug
Mechanical vehicles used in warfare: two 20hp Fowler traction-engines delivered to Prussian Army at Pont-à-Mousson, 20 Aug
Red Cross ambulance unit (Br): left Paris 25 Aug
Signals unit of the Br Army: 'C' Telegraph Troop RE, Chatham, Eng, 1 Sept
Postcard GB: 1 Oct [138]
Torpedo (motor-) GB: Whitehead T dem Sheerness 8 Oct
Typewriter (mnf): Oct [193]
Local education authority GB: London School Board, elected 29 Nov
Correspondence school GB: Pitman's Metropolitan School, London
Lorry (self-propelled): [108]
Rubber bicycle tyres: mnf by Thomas Sparrow, London; first tyres with skid-resistant treads
All-metal bicycle: [23]
Books published in braille GB: *Advent Hymns* and *John Gilpin*, British & Foreign Blind Assoc

1871
Dinghy race: org by Thames Sailing Club at Surbiton, Eng, 18 Mar
Rugby International: Scotland beat Eng, Edinburgh, 27 Mar
Women Civil Service clerks GB: recruited by PO Telegraph Clearing House Branch, Mar
Bank Holiday GB: Whit Monday, 29 May
Halftone: May [80]
Cat show: org by Harrison Weir, Crystal Palace, Eng, 13 July
Halftone magazine illustration: July [80]
Mail-order business: 15 Sept [96]
Cycle gear GB: Ariel Cycle (two-speed gear), mnf by Starley, Coventry, Eng, Sept
'Rogues Gallery' GB: all prisoners photographed from 2 Nov
Surgical operation by woman GB: Dec [202]
Machine-gun in service use GB: Gatling
Mechanical vehicle designed for military use: 6hp Aveling & Porter Steam Sapper; in service at RE Depot, Rochester, Eng
Toilet roll: by Seth Wheeler, N.Y.
Women's club: [40]
Model aircraft (rubber-band powered): Alphonse Penaud's *Phlanaphore*, Paris; flew 131ft
Photolitho magazine illustrations: *Canadian Illustrated News*, Montreal
Microfilm used for record-keeping: all policies, etc of a Paris insurance company microfilmed by René Dagron
Circus safety-net: [39]
Book illustrated with half-tone photographs: *Paris Ruiner*, Gustaf Carleman, Stockholm
Margarine (mnf): [97]
School built by local education authority GB: Mount Charles Elementary School, St Austell, Cornwall Capacity 375; cost £940
Wind-tunnel: des by F.H. Wenham, built by Messrs Penn at Greenwich, Eng

1872
National Park: Yellowstone, Wyoming, designated 1 Mar
Cup Final (football): Wanderers beat Royal Engineers 1–0 at Oval, London, 16 Mar
Stamp auction GB: held at Sotheby's, London, 18 Mar
Repeating rifle, bolt-action: Fruwirth Carbine adopted by Austrian Army, May
Keyboard typewriter (mnf): June [193]
Polo match GB: Lancers *v* Life Guards, Woolwich, 16 July
Vote by ballot GB: 15 Aug [22]
Boys' club: Oct [26]
Football International: Eng *v* Scotland at Partick, Glasgow (0–0), 30 Nov
Polo club GB: Monmouthshire PC
RN vessel armed with torpedoes: river launch *Miranda*
National newspaper set by type-composing machine: *The Times*; Kestenbein typesetter
Typewriting service: [193]
State secondary schools GB: Burgh and Parochial Schools passed under control of the School Boards by Scottish Education Act
Mechanical road haulage (long-distance): [156]
Tank-steamer: Red Star Line *Vaterland*, built Jarrow
Picture postcard: [129]
Jehovah's Witnesses: orig as Pittsburg Bible study group under Charles Taze Russell
Lawn tennis club: estab by J.B. Perara (Sp) and T.H. Gem at Manor House Hotel, Leamington Spa, Eng
Passenger monorail, power-driven: cable-drawn system operated at Lyons Exposition
Chewing-gum (chicle): [34]
Reinforced-concrete building: built by William E. Ward, Greenwich, Conn.

1873
Dynamite factory GB: opened by British Dynamite Co, Ardeer, Scotland, 13 Jan
Illustrated daily newspaper: *New York Daily Graphic*, 4 Mar
Railway carriage lavatory GB: 2 April [200]
Railway sleeping-car GB: 2 April [152]
Pocket dictionary (travellers'): John Bellows's *Bona Fide French and English Dictionary* ($4\frac{3}{4} \times 2\frac{3}{4}$in) 340,000 words, Trübner, London
Cable-car: Clay Street Hill Railroad, San Francisco, 1 Aug
Sheepdog trials: Bala, Wales, 9 Oct
American football: rules formulated by Columbia, Princeton, Rutgers and Yale delegates, N.Y., 18 Oct
Typewriter shop: [193]
Badminton club: Folkestone, Eng
Woman appointed to senior Govt post GB: Mrs Nassau Senior (sister of T.E. Hughes), Poor Law Inspector, Local Govt Board
One-man-operated passenger service vehicles: fare boxes introd by Sheffield Tramways, Eng

1874
Pullman cars GB: introd by Midland Rly, London–Bradford, 1 June
Heated railway carriages GB: as above
Dewey Decimal System: dev by Melvil Dewey, student at Amherst College, Mass., June; adopted by Amherst College Library
Osteopath: Dr Andrew Taylor Still, commenced practice Macon, Mo., 22 June
Child kidnapped for ransom: Charley Ross (4), kidnapped at Philadelphia 1 July; $20,000 ransom demand
DDT: disc reported by Othmar Zeidler, Strasbourg, 1 Aug
Summer school: religious knowledge, commenced Fair Point, N.Y. 4 Aug
International rifle competition (long-range): USA beat Ireland 934–931 at Creedmoor, Long Island, 26 Sept
Butter factory GB: Holms Cheese & Butter Factory, Rewlack, Derby, Eng
Working-class MPs GB: [91]
Cloth-covered tennis ball: replaced plain rubber; inv by J.H. Heathcote, first used at Conington Castle, Hunts, Eng
Double glazing (rec) GB: noted at Cranfield Court, Beds
Electric car: 1hp three-wheeler powered from Bunsen cells built by Sir David Salomons at Tunbridge Wells
Women interior decorators: Agnes and Rhoda Garrett (cousins), London
Riveted jeans: [89]
Ladies' bicycle (mnf): [23]
Safety bicycle: [24]

1875
Third-party accident insurance: introd by London & Provincial Carriage Insurance Co, 14 Jan
Disarmament campaign: launched by Peace Soc at Liverpool 23 Jan
Electrical dental drill: 26 Jan [47]
Cabman's shelter (London); Acacia Rd, St John's Wood, 6 Feb
Canadian ice hockey: first organized match played between F.W. Torrance's team and J.G.A. Creighton's team, Victoria Skating Rink, Montreal, 3 Mar
Newspaper to publish daily weather chart: *The Times*, 1 April

Café Chain GB: inst by Peoples Café Co; first branch opened Upper Whitecross St, 16 April
Christian Science: Sunday worship inaug by Mary Glover at Good Templars Hall, Lynn, Mass., 6 June
Railway air-brakes GB: Westinghouse system tested by Midland Railway Co on Nottingham–Newark line, Eng, 9 June
Roller-skating rink GB: Belgravia Skating Rink, 2 Aug
Channel swim: Dover–Calais by Capt. Matthew Webb, 22hr, 24–25 Aug
Factory lit by electricity: Heilman, Ducommun & Steinlein's foundry, Mühlhausen, Ger, Aug; Serrin arc-lamps
Cycling journal GB: *The Bicyclist*, Herne Hill, Nov
Literary agency: [94]
School cookery class (State school) GB: St Luke's Board School, Liverpool
Printing, offset-litho: dev by Robert Barclay, London, for printing on tin; first used Bryant & May tin matchboxes
Factory nurse: Miss Philippa Flowerday, Colman's Mustard Co, Norwich
Milk chocolate: [35]
Female typists: [194]
Snooker: [164]
Canned baked beans: [21]
Station lit by electricity: Gare du Nord, Paris (Lontin arcs)
Chocolate Easter eggs GB: by Fry's, Bristol
Corrugated paper (mnf): Thompson & Norris Co, Brooklyn, N.Y.

1876
Registered trade mark GB: Bass's Pale Ale, 1 Jan
Telephone (practical): 9 Mar [176]
High-jumper to clear 6ft: Hon. Marshall Jones Brooks, Oxford, Eng, 17 Mar
Gorilla GB: landed Liverpool 21 June
Cliff railway: South Cliff Tramway, Scarborough, Eng, 6 July
Steam tram GB: Wantage Tramway, 1 Aug
Mimeograph: 8 Aug [52]
Atlantic crossing, single-handed: by Alfred Johnson (Dan), arr Abercastle, Pemb., Wales, 11 Aug; 57-day voyage
OHMS envelopes: introd by Honourable Artillery Co, Aug
Telephone GB: 7 Sept [176]
Carpet sweeper: 19 Sept [33]
Greyhound race (artificial hare): Hendon Cup, Welsh Harp, Hendon, Eng, 7 Oct
Telephone conversation (sustained): between Bell and Watson, Boston–Cambridge, 9 Oct
Crematoria: [46]
Box-magazine rifle, bolt-action: pat by James Paris Lee of Remington Small Arms Co, USA
Gift coupons GB: [77]
Sex-education manual: *Counsel to Parents on the Moral Education of their Children*, Dr Elizabeth Blackwell, London
Ice rink (artificially made ice): Glaciarium, Chelsea, London
Trouser suit: [206]
Plimsoll Line: Samuel Plimsoll, introd under Merchant Shipping Act, GB

1877
Press report by telephone: filed by *Boston Globe* reporter from Essex Institute, Salem (lecture by Bell), 12 Feb
Cricket, Test Match: Aus *v* Eng, Melbourne, 15–17 Mar
Human cannon-ball: 2 April [39]
Telephone installation (permanent): 4 April [176]
Baseball-catcher's mask: worn by James Tyng (Harvard) at Lynn, Mass., 12 April
Telephone switchboard: 17 May [176]
Torpedoes used in naval action: Whitehead T fired at hijacked Peruvian ironclad *Huascar* by HMS *Shah*, 29 May
Torpedo-boat (purpose-built): HMS *Lightning*, delivered Portsmouth by Thornycroft, May
Office telephone: linked Cambridge Board of Waterworks, Mass., with works at Fresh Pond, May
St John Ambulance Brigade: f as the Ambulance Association by Red Cross, 24 June
Lawn tennis championship: won by Spencer Gore, Wimbledon, Eng, 9–19 July
Telephone-linked buildings GB: 14 July [176]
Boys' camp (recreational) GB: held by St Andrew's Club for Working Boys at Hayling Island, 4–6 Aug
Telephone exchange: 17 Aug [176]
Phonograph: 6 Dec [164]
Liquid oxygen: by Raoul Pictet, Geneva, 22 Dec
Telephones used in warfare: between Pershawar and Sargasha, India during Jowaki campaign, Dec
Railway refrigerator cars: built for Chicago meat-packer Gustavus Smith: employed Grand Trunk Rly, Chicago–Boston
Fingerprinting (official): [73]
Children's art exhibition (reg): [19]
Aluminium GB: mnf by Aluminium Crown Metal Co, Oldbury, nr Birmingham
Shop lit by electricity: Grands Magasins du Louvre, Paris; 80 Jablochkoff Candles
Concrete bridge (permanent): Seaton, Devon, Eng
Steel naval vessel: HMS *Iris*
Department store (purpose-built): [48]
Typists' training course: [194]
Differential gear (practical application): Starley *Wonder* four-wheel sociable, mnf Coventry, Eng
Red Crescent Society: Turkey

1878
Registered-letter envelopes (blue-crossed): introd by GPO, 1 Jan
Woman commoner to receive honour: Cecilia Frances, Lady Northcote; member of the Imperial Order of the Crown of India, 1 Jan
Telephone installation GB: 14 Jan [176]
Press report by telephone GB: filed by *Daily News* reporter from Commons Press Gallery, 22 Jan
Ship sunk by torpedo: Turkish revenue steamer by Russian torpedo boat at Batoum, 25 Jan
Chess match played by telephone: between F. Thompson, ed of *Derbyshire Advertiser*, and friend, Derby, Eng, 25 Jan
Telephone operator (full-time): 28 Jan [176]
Power-driven passenger monorail (permanent): Bradford & Foster Brook Rly, Bradford–Derrick City, Pa. (4miles), Jan
Microphone: dem by Prof. D.E. Hughes at Submarine Telegraph Co offices, London, Jan
Phonograph GB: 1 Feb [165]
Telephone directory: District Telephone Co, New Haven, Conn., 21 Feb
Cycle show GB: Stanley Show, Athenaeum, Camden Rd, London, 12 Mar
Phonograph (mnf): 24 April [165]
Operatic recording: Mme Marie Rose 'warbled a scena' from unidentified opera, N.Y., April
Frozen meat (successful shipment): 5,500 carcasses of mutton aboard SS *Paraguay*, arr Le Havre from Buenos Aires, 7 May
Very pistol: pat Fr by M. Very, June
Theatre lit by electricity (exterior): Gaiety, London, Aug (Lontin arcs)
Salvation Army band: f by Charles Fry at Salisbury, Aug
Women telephone operator: 1 Sept [176]
Floodlit football match: Reds *v* Blues, Bramall Lane Ground, Sheffield, Eng; four Siemens arc-lamps, 14 Oct
Floodlight rugby match: Broughton *v* Swinton at Broughton, Lancs, Eng, 22 Oct
Long-distance telephone call: by Mr Adams from Colman's Mustard Factory, Norwich, to Colman offices, Cannon St, London (115 miles), 11 Nov
Electric street lighting (permanent) GB: 13 Dec [55]
Esperanto: 17 Dec [60]
Incandescent electric light: 18 Dec [54]
Training college for secondary school teachers GB: Bishopsgate Training College for Women
Woman detective writer: [49]
Typewriter shift-key: [194]
First aid: classes held by Surgeon-Maj. Peter Shepherd of the Ambulance Assoc at Woolwich, Eng
Sugar cubes GB: produced by Henry Tate at Silvertown Refinery, London
Musical recording: [165]
Electric fire-alarm system GB: Glasgow
Milking machine (mnf): inv by L.O. Colvin; mnf by Albert Durand, Auburn, N.Y.
Women PT instructors GB: course for elementary school teachers estab by London School Board under Miss Concordia Löfving
Hansard reporters GB
Factory lit by electricity GB: Stanton Ironworks, Derby (arcs)

1879
Phonograph (mnf) GB: 18 Jan [165]
Caravan holiday: 29 Jan [32]
Chain store: 22 Feb [114]
Sacharin: discovery reported by Constantine Fahlberg and Prof. Ira Remsen, Johns Hopkins Univ, Baltimore, 27 Feb
Telephone exchange GB: Feb [176]
Telephone trunk line: Springfield–Holyoke, Mass., District Telephone Co, 2 April
Machine-guns used in warfare (Br): Gatlings by Lord Chelmsford's column at Ginginhlovo, SA, 2 April
Six-day cycle race: Agricultural Hall, London, won by George Waller, 28 April–3 May
Electric passenger railway: Siemens experimental train operated 4mnth at Berlin Trades Exhibition, 31 May
Art gallery lit by electricity: Paris Salon, 7 June
Domestic electric lighting GB: July [55]
Ship lit by electricity: HMS *Dreadnought*, Aug (two arc-lamps)
Ballroom lit by electricity: for Milford Dock Co engineers' dance at Lord Nelson Hotel, Milford Haven, Wales, 1 Sept
Seaside illuminations: Blackpool, 18 Sept
Railway dining-car GB: 26 Sept [152]
Office block with group of elevators: Sept [58]
Station lit by electricity GB: St Enoch's, Glasgow, Sept (Crompton arcs)
Library lit with electricity: British Museum Reading Room, 20 Oct (Siemens)
Liner lit by electricity: Inman Line's *City of Berlin*, Oct (?) (arc-lamps)
Incandescent-filament light bulb: 21 Oct [54]
Photogravure: specimens shown to Vienna Photographic Soc by Karl Klič, Oct
Cash register: 4 Nov [33]
Tube station lit by electricity: Aldersgate, London, Nov
Shop elevator GB: Junior Army & Navy Stores, Waterloo Place, London
Traffic signs GB: Dec [192]
Radio telegraphy GB: Dec [143]
Women's lawn tennis championship: won by Miss M. Langrishe at Fitzwilliam Club, Dublin
Hotel lit by electricity: Langham H, Portland Place, London (arc-lamps)
Technical college GB: City and Guilds Institute, Finsbury
Submarines in regular naval service: [171]
Photographs taken by incandescent electric light: by Herman Krone, Dresden
Theatre lit by electricity (interior): Théâtre Bellacour, Lyons (Jablochkoff Candles)
Cigarette cards: Marquis of Lorne Cigarettes (USA)
Milk bottles: [98]
Steel merchant vessel (ocean-going): *SS Rotomahana*, Union Steam Ship Co of NZ

1880
Telephone directory GB: 6pp (255 names), pub by London Telephone Co, 15 Jan
Theatre lit by electricity (interior) GB: Her Majesty's, Carlisle, Jan (arcs)
Frozen meat GB: 40 tons beef and mutton aboard SS *Strathleven*, arr London from Sydney 2 Feb; sold at $5\frac{1}{2}$d per lb
Radio telephone: 15 Feb [150]
Newspaper photograph: 4 Mar [118]
War correspondent to telephone report from battlefield: 19 April [198]
Salvation Army uniforms: authorized 27 Mar (*see also* 16 June)

Ship lit with incandescent electric lamps: Oregon Rly & Navigation Co *Columbia*, San Francisco, 2 May (Edison)
Telephone call-box: 1 June [176]
Salvation Army bonnet: chosen by Catherine Booth; first worn by 25 'lassies' in Hackney–Whitechapel procession, Eng, 16 June
Military tournament: Grand Military Tournament, Agricultural Hall, Islington, London, 21 June
Ocean liner lit with incandescent electric lamps: Orient Line *Chimborazo*, Gravesend, 24 June (Br Electric Light Co)
College tie: ordered by Exeter C, Oxford, 25 June
Bus tickets GB: 1d, 2d and 3d introd by London & District Omnibus Co, Aug
Cricket, Test Match GB: Eng *v* Aus, Oval, 6–8 Sept
Electric light bulbs (mnf): 1 Oct [54]
Mechanically bored tunnel: 2,024yd of abortive Channel Tunnel bored with Beaumont pneumatic tunneller, Abbotscliffe, Kent, Eng, Oct (–July 1881)
Women graduates GB: 17 Nov [208]
Women's Parliamentary franchise: 21 Dec [207]
Field newspaper (Br): 25 Dec [118]
House lit by incandescent electric lamps GB: Dec [55]
Electric elevator: [58]
Comic postcard: [130]
Miniature electric motors: [55]
Cricket bat with rubber handle-grip: mnf by Page Bros, Kennington, London
Correspondence course for professional qualifying examination: [46]
Pre-stressed concrete: introd by P. H. Jackson, San Francisco
Photogravure (pub): by Klič process in *Photographische Korrespondence*, Vienna
Soft toys: felt elephants mnf by Margarete Steiff, Giengen, Ger
Man's wristwatch: [199]
Safety bicycle (mnf): [24]
Ice-hockey club: McGill Univ Hockey Club
Cyclists to ride from Land's End to John O'Groats: H. Blackwell and C. A. Harman of Canterbury Bicycle Club in 13 days
Universal compulsory school attendance (Eng and Wales): school-leaving age 10
Blowlamp: C. R. Nyberth of the Sievert Co, Stockholm, Sw

1881

Postal Orders GB: introd 1 Jan
Magazine in braille: *Progress*, London, Jan
Electric light bulbs (mnf) GB: Feb [54]
Women to vote by right in Parliamentary election: 5 April [207]
Incandescent electric street lamps: 11 April [55]
Electric tram: Lichterfelde (Berlin)–Anhalt, public service 16 May
Bible, Revised Version: NT pub by Oxford and Cambridge Univ Presses, May (OT May 1885)
Socialist Party GB: 8 June [91]
Electric miners' lamp (practical): Swan bulb lamp des by R. E. Crompton; dem Pleasley Colliery, Mansfield, Notts, Eng 8 June
Hotel lit with incandescent electric lamps: Lamb's Temperance Hotel, Dundee, June (Swan lamps)
Stereophonic sound system: pat Ger by Clement Ader (Fr), 30 Aug; used for telephonic broadcasting service
Colliery lit by electricity (below ground): Earnock Colliery, Glasgow, Scot, Aug
Station lit by incandescent electric lamps: Glasgow Queen Street Station, Scot, Aug (Swan)
Electric power station: 1 Oct [56]
Railway carriage lit by electricity: Pullman parlour-car 'Globe', London–Brighton, 14 Oct
Illustrated daily newspaper GB: *The Evening Illustrated Newspaper*, London, 25 Oct
Clubhouse lit by electricity: Scottish Club, Dover St, London, Nov (?)
Theatre lit with incandescent electric lamps: Savoy, London, 28 Dec (1,158 Swan bulbs)
Art gallery lit with electricity GB: Glasgow Institute of Fine Arts, Dec
Sprinkler system (fire-prevention): installed Edinburgh Rubber Works, Scot
Electric signs: [57]
Round-the-world cruise: SS *Ceylon*
Cyclostyle duplicator: [52]
Steel liner: Allan Line's *Buenos Ayrean* (Canadian)
Naval vessel lit with incandescent electric lamps: HMS *Inflexible* (Swan)
Ski school: estab by Torjus and Mikkel Hemmesvedt, Christiania (Oslo), Norway
Public analyst: Paris
Tobogganing club: Montreal
Blueprints: introd by Marion & Co, London; reprod by ferro-prussiate process
Shops lit by electricity GB: Whiteley's Bayswater; Samuel Bros, Ludgate Hill; Bon Marché, Brixton (all with Jablochkoff Candles)
Photogravure GB: portrait of Mungo Ponson reprod by Klič process in *Yearbook of Photography*, 1882
Hydraulic excavator: mnf by Sir W. & H. Armstrong; first used Alexandra Dock, Hull, Eng

1882

Shop lit by incandescent electric light: Coxon & Co, drapers, Newcastle upon Tyne, Eng, 20 Jan (Swan lamps)
Church lit by electricity: Fifth St Presbyterian Church, Troy, N.Y., 22 Jan
Church lit by electricity GB: City Temple, Holborn, 19 Mar
Pub lit by electricity: 12 April [56]
Trolley bus: Dr Werner von Siemens's Electromote, demonstrated Halensee, Berlin, 27 April
New Zealand mutton GB: arr 25 May
Electric iron: pat by Henry W. Seely N.Y., 6 June
Electrical-engineering school: Hammond Electrical Engineering College, London, opened 1 July
Classified-ad box numbers GB: 6 July [117]
Volunteers on overseas service (Br): 44 men of Post Office Corps served in Egyptian campaign, Aug–Oct
Letter cards: dev by Akin Karoly, Belg; issued Dec 15
Telephone, trunk line (permanent) GB: London–Brighton, 21 Dec
Christmas tree lit by electricity: Dec [37]
Telephone call-box GB: [176]
Boxing manager: Billy Madden, manager to John L. Sullivan
Steel liner GB: Cunard's *Servia*
Electric fan: [53]
Railway corridor-coach GB: [151]
Camera film (mnf): [128]
Ice-hockey club GB: Bluntisham & Erith Skating Hockey Club, Hunts
Naval training ship (ocean-going): *George Stage*, Copenhagen
Local authority evening classes GB: London School Board
Electric mine railway: inst by Siemens & Halske at Zauckeroda coal-mine, Saxony
Judo: dev by Dr Jogoro Kano of the Kadokan Institute, Tokyo
Underground telephone cables: by Northern District Telephone Co, Newcastle upon Tyne, Eng

1883

Children's lending library GB: 10 Jan [35]
Toboggan race: org by John Addington Symonds over 2-mile course on Davos–Klosters road, Swz, 12 Feb
Floodlit baseball match: Fort Wayne, Ind. *v* Quincy, Ill. at Fort Wayne, 2 June
National Insurance: introd under Bismarck's Health Insurance Act, Ger, 15 June
Parcel post GB: introd 1 Aug
Electric passenger railway GB: Volk's Electric Rly, Brighton, 3 Aug
Relay race: 17 Nov [20]
Petrol motor car: [100]
Woman school inspector GB: Miss Emily Jones
League cricket: Heavy Woollen District Cup Competition; won by Heckmondwicke CC, Yorks, Eng
Alpine skiing: introd at Davos, Arosa and St Bernard, Swz
Man-made fibre: [97]
Special Branch: [134]
Vending-machine (automatic) GB: [197]
Visible bar typewriter: [194]
Police college: École pratique de Police municipale, Paris
Game reserve: 880 sq km area of Askonia Nowa in South Russian Steppe
Dustbin (galvanized iron portable container): introd by Eugene Poubelle, Paris Prefect of Police
Spark plug: des for stationary gas-engine by Étienne Lenoir, Paris
Seven-a-side Rugby tournament: org by Melrose RFC, Roxburghshire, Scot

1884

Police whistles GB: replaced rattles, Metropolitan Police, March
Advertising competition: run by Police Plug Tobacco in Pennsylvania press during March
Controlled glider flight: Mar [78]
Oxford English Dictionary: A–Anat pub Jan (completed April 1928)
Switchback: inst Coney Island by L. A. Thompson, June
GPO telephone call-boxes: Aug [176]
Local anaesthetic: 15 Sept [18]
Evaporated milk: pat by John Mayenberg of St Louis, Mo., 25 Nov
Brain surgery: tumour removed by (Sir) Rickman Godlee, London, 25 Nov
Coin-operated weighing machine: pat by Percy Everitt, 13 Dec
Siamese cats GB: Pho and Mia, brought from Bangkok by Owen Gould
Salvation Army social worker (full-time): Maj. James Barker, Melbourne, Aus
Woman MA GB: [208]
Pedestal water-closet: [200]
Summer school GB: held Cambridge Univ for extension-course students from mining areas
Steam turbine (practical): des by Charles Parsons of Gateshead to drive dynamo in local lamp-works
Negroes to play major league baseball: Welday and Moses Walker, Toledo Club
Jehovah's Witnesses GB: group estab Islington
Electric transformer in commercial use: Caulard T used for Metropolitan Rly, Eng, electric lighting system
Library to employ microfilm: Bibliothèque Nationale, Paris
Professional footballer to play for England: J. H. Forrest (Blackburn Rovers)
Youth hostel: estab by Guido Rotter at Hohenelbe, Austria-Hungary (now Cz)
Bananas, regularly imported GB: from Canary I. by Elder Dempster & Co
Woman conductor GB: Viscountess Folkestone
Linotype machine: pat by Ottmar Mergenthaler, Baltimore, 26 Aug (*see* 1886)
Artificial insemination with donor: [19]
School meals (State school) GB: Rousdon Board School, Dorset
Woman barrister: [201]

1885

Electric telegraph used in battle: by Sir John McNeill at Battle of Tofrek, Sudan, to base at Suakin (6 miles), 22 Mar
Crematorium GB: 26 Mar [46]
Commonwealth Expeditionary Force: NSW contingent, arr Suakin for service in Sudan War, 29 Mar
Evaporated milk (prod): mnf by John Mayenberg's Helvetia Milk Condensing Co, Highland, Ill., 25 June
Professional football: legalized by FA, Eng 20 July
World boxing heavyweight championship fought with gloves: John L. Sullivan (USA) beat Dominick McCaffery (USA) at Cincinnati, 29 Aug
Cafeteria (self-service): Exchange Buffet, New St, N.Y., 4 Sept
Petrol pump: 5 Sept [126]
Halftone GB: 5 Sept [80]
Electric street tram GB: Blackpool Electric Tramway Co, 29 Sept
Workmen's compensation: effective Ger, 1 Oct
Motor cycle: 10 Nov [106]
Cream crackers: mnf by William Jacob, Dublin
Private health insurance: introd by Sickness & Accident Assurance Assoc, London
Wheel-shaped ballet tutu: [22]

Ice dancing: ice waltz performed Halifax, N.S.
Motor boat (mnf): [99]
Wristwatch GB: [199]
Snooker GB: [164]
Safe deposit GB: Chancery Lane Safe Deposit
Holidays with pay (manual workers) GB: 1wk+4s 6d gratuity, Gas Light & Coke Co, London
Touring caravan (purpose-built): [32]
Steel-framed building: Home Insurance Co, La Salle St, Chicago; des by William Le Baron Jenney
Sunglasses: mnf from tinted window glass, Philadelphia
Labour Exchange: estab Egham, Eng, by Nathaniel Cohen

1886
The Times *personal column:* 22 Feb [117]
Working-class Minister of State GB: Feb [91]
Member of Royal Family to attend football match: Prince of Wales; Gentlemen *v* Players, Oval, 20 Mar
Coca-Cola: inv by Dr John Pemberton, Atlanta, Ga.; launched as 'Esteemed Brain Tonic and Intellectual Beverage', 29 Mar
Football, international caps: approved by FA Council, 10 May
Linotype machine (used commercially): for setting *New York Tribune* of 3 July
Electric welder: pat by Elihu Thomson of Lynn, Mass., 10 Aug
Dinner-jacket: 10 Oct [50]
Statue to a woman GB: 11 Oct [169]
Bridge (rec): [28]
Holding company GB: Nobel Dynamite Trust Co, London
Petrol motor boat: Aug [99]
School lacrosse GB: introd at Ladybarn House School, Manchester (mixed teams)
Telephone directory, yellow pages: Chicago
Woman dental surgeon GB: [201]
Drinking straws (paper): mkt by Marvin Chester Stone, Washington, D.C.
Photographic package design (rec): Signor Valli Cigarettes, Denmark
Electric light bulb, bayonet cap: introd by Edison & Swan United Electric Light Co, Newcastle upon Tyne, Eng
Torpedo-carrying submarine: [171]
Coin-operated ticket machine: inv by James Longley; installed Leamington Athletic Ground, Leeds, Eng
Book set by Linotype machine: *The Tribune Book of Open Air Sport,* N.Y.
Cycle dynamo: pat by Richard Weber, Leipzig

1887
Telephone-link between capitals: Paris–Brussels, 24 Feb
Female typists GB: 12 Mar [194]
Mimeograph (mkt): 17 Mar [52]
Woman mayor: 4 April [203]
Motor race: 20 April [110]
Appendicectomy: 27 April [18]
Paper napkins GB: at John Dickinson & Co Annual Dinner, Castle Hotel, Hastings, 9 July
Commemorative stamp: July [137]
Newspaper, overseas edition: *New York Herald,* Paris, 4 Oct
Advertisement photography: 11 Nov [7]
Socialist MP GB: [91]
Electrocardiogram: made by London physiologist Augustus Waller
Boxing Manager GB: John Fleming, manager of Jem Smith
Elastic braid GB: [53]
Submarine (powered) GB: [171]
Women choristers: [201]
Skeleton toboggan: introd by L.P. Child (USA) at Clavadel, Swz; first toboggan ridden face-down
Women's cricket club: White Heather Club, Eng
Monotype machine: pat by Tolbert Lanston, Troy, Ohio (*see* 1894)
Electric heater: [53]
Coin-in-slot gas meter: [76]
Correspondence course for degree: University Correspondence College, Cambridge, prepared candidates for London Univ external degrees
Malted milk: Horlick's, Racine, Wisc.
Esperanto text: [60]
Contact lenses: dev by Dr A. Eugen Frick of Zurich; mnf by Zeiss of Jena
Polio epidemic: Stockholm, 44 persons affected

1888
Adding machine (keyboard): mkt by Door Felt, Chicago; first sale to Equitable Gas Light & Fuel Co, Jan
Newspaper to feature political cartoons (reg) GB: 2 Feb [117]
Pneumatic cycle tyre: 28 Feb [132]
Power-driven passenger monorail GB: Listowel & Ballybunion Rly, Co Kerry, 1 Mar
News photograph (pub): Muttra Pigsticking Cup Competition picture in *Illustrated London News* 10 Mar
Motor-car manufacture: 16 Mar [102]
Disc record-player: 16 May [166]
Musical recording GB: 29 June [165]
Appendicectomy GB: 29 June [18]
Petrol-driven tram: Daimler trams operated Stuttgart June
Touch typing (dem): 25 July [194]
Motor tour: Aug [112]
Switchback GB: built for showman George Aspland by Savage & Co, King's Lynn, Aug
Football League matches: played 8 Sept
Beauty contest: 19 Sept [22]
Cinema film: Oct [61]
Celluloid camera film: 7 Nov [128]
Flexible photographic transparencies: 21 Nov [128]
Eight-hour day (national) GB: secured by Gasworkers' Union, Nov
Pneumatic cycle tyres (mkt): 19 Dec [132]
Racing, photo-finish: introd by Ernest Marks at Plainfield Track, N.J.
Service rifle, bolt-action GB: Lee-Remington Magazine Rifle Mk I
Motor bus: electric vehicle built by Ward Electric Car Co, London
Motor agent: [99]
Bob-sled: introd Davos, Swz by S. Whitney (USA)
Working-class dwellings built with bathrooms: Port Sunlight, Cheshire, Eng
Motorcycle GB: [106]
Piano recording: [165]
Christian Scientists GB: Mr and Mrs Graves Colles of Dublin
Electric switch socket: des by Sir David Salomons, Tunbridge Wells, Eng
Chewing-gum vending-machine: [34]
Royal motorist: [197]
Motor boat GB: [99]
Christian Science Reading Room: Boylston St, Boston
Typewriter stencil: [52]
Dinner-jacket GB: [50]
Forensic science laboratory: by Prefecture of Police, Paris
Advertising agency to offer creative services: N.W. Ayer & Son, Philadelphia

1889
Vehicle Excise Tax (motor): 2 gns p.a. for all four-wheeled steam and motor road vehicles; effective GB, 1 Jan
Data processing computer: 8 Jan [44]
Newspaper: overseas edition GB: *New York Herald,* London, 2 Feb
Racing cycle with pneumatic tyres: ridden by W. Hume at Queen's College Sports, Belfast, 18 May
Factory to institute eight-hour day GB: Messrs Beaufroy's, manufacturers of jam and British wine and vinegar, London, June
Photographic picture postcard (rec): 6 July [130]
Hotel private baths GB: 6 Aug [83]
Celluloid rollfilm (mnf): 27 Aug [128]
Esperanto journal: *La Esperantisto,* Nuremberg, 1 Sept
Publicly owned electric power station GB: 20 Sept [57]
Jukebox: 23 Nov [90]
Recording adding machine: Comptograph mnf by Felt & Tarrant Mnf Co, Chicago; first sale to Manufacturers' National Bank, Pittsburgh, Dec
Electric heater (mnf): [53]
Agricultural tractor (petrol): [190]
Rubber heels: introd by Aberdeen Rubber Sole & Heel Co, Scot
Margarine (mnf) GB: by Otto Monsted (Dan) at Godley. Cheshire
Electric elevator (permanent): Demarest Building, Fifth Ave, N.Y.
Electric elevator GB: Otis at Crystal Palace
Mosque GB: Shah Jehan Mosque, Woking, Surrey
Electric oven: [56]
Spark plug GB: des by Thomas Parker of Ewell-Parker Co, Wolverhampton for stationary gas-engine
Hunger strike (rec): [84]
Photomat: dev by T.E. Enjalbert, Paris; independently by J. Raders, Frankfurt
Milking machine (mnf) GB: by William Murchland of Kilmarnock, Ayrshire; first model sold to David Shaw of Haining Mains
Domestic science college: Sheffield Training School of Cookery & Domestic Science
Influenza epidemic GB
Esperanto GB: [60]
Picture postcard art reproductions: [130]
Woven name tapes: J. & J. Cash, Coventry
Dishwashing machine: [50]
Fruit machine: [76]
Coin-operated telephone call-box: [176]
Orchestral recording: [165]
Disc record-player (mnf): [166]
Typewriter (mnf) GB: [194]
Electric sewing machine: [163]

1890
Football goal-nets: dev by Liverpool engineer J.A. Brodie; first used Bolton Wanderers *v* Nottingham Forest match, Bolton, Eng, 1 Jan
Magazine illustrated entirely with photographs: *The Illustrated American,* 22 Feb
Linotype machine GB: used by *Leeds Mercury* Feb
Profit-sharing scheme GB: introd by South Metropolitan Gas Co, Feb
Comic: 17 May [42]
Newspaper headline GB: 16 July [118]
Water-polo International: Scot beat Eng, Kensington Baths, 28 July
Newspaper, women's feature (regular) GB: 2 Aug [119]
Electric chair: 6 Aug [53]
Socialist newspaper GB: *Labour World,* 21 Sept
Submarine telephone cable: laid St Margaret's Bay, Eng–Sangatte, Fr, by Siemens Bros, Sept
Underground railway, electric: 4 Nov [196]
Christian Science worship GB: services held at 48 Stanhope Gdns, London by Anne Dodge (USA), Nov
Power lifeboat: steam-driven *Duke of Northumberland,* stationed Harwich, Eng
Aluminium saucepan: made by Henry W. Avery, Cleveland, Ohio. Prototype used by Mrs Avery till 1933
Epidiascope (electric): built by Dr S. Stricker, Prof. of Pathology, Univ of Vienna, for medical lectures
Rubber gloves (surgical): worn by Nurse Caroline Hampton at John Hopkins Univ Hospital, Baltimore
Photomat GB: introd by Automatic Photograph Co
Petrol motor boat (mnf): [99]
Free State education (primary) GB: fees in Scottish Board Schools abolished below Standard V
Records (mnf): [166]
Woman stockbroker GB: [206]

1891
Old age pensions: 1 Jan [120]
Record magazine: *The Phonogram,* N.J., Jan
Two-way cycle-tyre valve: pat by cotton-spinner Charles Woods, Mar (mkt by Pneumatic Tyre Co, 1892)
Telephone link GB–Continent: 8s 0d for 3min, London–Paris, 1 April
Warship sunk by torpedo: Chilean battleship *Blanco Encalada,* 13 April
Golf, bogey score: inst by Coventry GC, 13 May
Public demonstration of motion picture film: 22 May [62]
World weightlifting championship: held at Café Monico, Piccadilly, 28 May
Stamp-machine: May [138]
Pierrots: Clifford Essex Pierrots, début Henley, 7 July
Traveller's cheque (countersignature type): 5 Aug [193]
Telephoto lens: pat Fr by A. Duboscq, 7 Aug (*see below* 2 Oct)
Police fingerprinting: 1 Sept [73]
Football, penalty kick: taken by Heath of Wolverhampton Wanderers in match *v* Accrington, 14 Sept
Street collection for charity: Lifeboat Day, Manchester and Salford, 8 Oct
Newspaper photograph GB: 4 Nov [118]

Telephoto lens GB: pat by Thomas Dallmayer 2 Oct; dem 10 Dec
Disc record-player (mkt) GB: Dec [166]
Fashion photographs: Dec [60]
Baby incubator: [20]
State Registered Nurses: Cape Colony
Model train set (complete track lay-out): 1¾in gauge clockwork set mkt by Märklin Bros, Göppingen, Ger
Technical correspondence course: [46]
Christian Scientist (England): Miss Catherine Verrall of Falmer, Sussex
Crown Cork bottle cap: inv by William Painter; mnf 1892 by Crown Cork & Seal Co, Baltimore
Trade union closed shop (recognized): operated by Bedstead Workmen's Assoc, Birmingham, Eng
Bird-ringing: inst by Lord William Percy at Alnwick, Northumberland, Eng
Free State education (Eng): introd under Elementary Education Act
Canned baked beans (tomato sauce): [21]
Petrol motor boat GB: [99]
Electric oven (mnf): [56]
Electric torch: [57]
Electrically heated buildings: [54]
Coffee vending-machine: at Palace of Industry, Paris
Record catalogue: [165]
Electric kettle: mkt by Carpenter Electric Mnf Co, St Paul, Minn.

1892

Basketball: dev by Dr James Naismith (Can) at YMCA Training School, Springfield, Mass.; rules pub *Triangle*, 15 Jan
Letter cards GB: introd 11 Feb
Colour halftone: Feb [80]
Corridor train: 7 Mar [151]
Electric oven GB: 11 Mar [56]
Escalator: 15 Mar [59]
Police fingerprint bureau: 31 Mar [73]
Electric iron GB: dem by J.J. Dowsing at Crystal Palace, April
Newspaper in raised type for the blind: *The Weekly Summary* (Braille), Eltham, Kent, Eng, June
Socialist MP elected GB: 4 July [91]
Coloured MP GB: 6 July [41]
Fingerprint detection: 8 July [73]
Monarch to own petrol car: Aug [158]
Floodlit American football: Mansfield Teachers College *v* Wyoming Seminary, Mansfield, Pa., 29 Sept
Musical comedy: Adrian Ross and James Leader's *In Town*, Prince of Wales Theatre, London, 15 Oct
Gymn slip: Oct [80]
Automatic telephone exchange: 3 Nov [176]*
Football, £100 transfer fee: paid by Aston Villa for Willie Groves
Concrete road: Main St, Bellefontaine, Ohio
Toothpaste tube: [41]
Psycho-analysis: 'Elizabeth von R' analysed by Sigmund Freud, Vienna
Mobile bank: operated on Palmerston–Otaki rly, NZ
Advertising copywriter (full-time): John J. Geisinger of N.W. Ayer & Son, Philadelphia
Chocolate wafer biscuits: Cadbury's, 1d each
Thermos flask: (Sir) James Dewar, Cambridge, Eng
International ski meet: held Stockholm; langlauf won by Finland, ski-jump by Norway
Man-made fibre (mnf): [97]
Book matches: [97]
Compression-ignition engine: [43]
Fashion photographs GB: [60]
Motor bicycle GB: [106]
Motor van: [112]
Records (mnf) GB: [165]
Woman car driver: [205]

1893

Electric oven (mnf): Jan [56]
Film studio: 1 Feb [71]
Film close-up: 2 Feb [66]
Box-kite: des and flown by Lawrence Hargrave at Stanwell Park, Sydney, NSW, 15 Feb
Gramophone magazine GB: *The Phonogram*, May
Women's golf championship: won by Lady Margaret Scott, Royal Lytham, Eng, 13 June
Diesel engine: 10 Aug [44]
Parking restrictions: 14 Aug [191]
Motor vehicle registration plates: 14 Aug [112]
Driving licence: 14 Aug [51]
Driving test: 14 Aug [51]
Nation to grant women's franchise: 19 Sept [207]
Destroyer: HMS *Havock*, first trials 28 Oct
Newspaper colour supplement: 19 Nov [117]
Newspaper staff cartoonist GB: [117]
Model soldiers (hollow-cast lead): Life Guards set mnf by Messrs Britain
Petrol GB: Standard Petrol mkt by Carless, Capel & Leonard of Hackney Wick at 11d gallon
Women Factory Inspectors GB: Miss May Abraham and Miss May Paterson
Basketball GB: introd by Mme Bergman-Osterberg at Hampstead Physical Training College
Automatic: Borchardt 'Prometheus' eight-shot magazine pistol (Ger)
Pyschiatric clinic GB: out-patients clinic, Wakefield Asylum
Ferris wheel: erected by George Ferris on Midway at Chicago Exposition
Central heating, electric: introd by American Electric Heating Corp
Electric toaster GB: mkt by Crompton Co, Chelmsford
Railway automatic signalling system (electric): Liverpool Overhead Rly, Eng
Language tuition course on records: [92]
Breakfast cereal: [27]
Electric goods locomotive, GEC No. 1: operated by Manufacturers' Railroad, New Haven, Conn.
Travel association (for promotion of tourism): Kihin-Kai, Tokyo
Criminals fingerprinted GB: [73]
Motor boat (mnf) GB: [99]
Eleven-plus exam: [161]
Public library with open access shelves GB: [141]
Portable typewriter: [194]
Zip fastener: [209]

1894

Striptease: 13 Mar [171]
Racing, starting-gate: inv by J.L. Johnstone of Melbourne; first used Mooney Valley, 22 Mar
Commercial presentation of motion picture film: 14 April [62]
Sports film: 14 June [70]
Motor rally: Paris–Rouen, won by Count de Dion, 22 June
Death duties GB: introd 2 Aug
Main-line rail electrification: 4 Aug [152]
Picture postcard (rec) GB: 14 Sept [129]
British musical presented on Broadway: *A Gaiety Girl*, Daly's Theatre, 17 Sept
Chain store GB: 28 Sept [114]
Commercial presentation of motion picture film GB: Oct [62]
Motor cycle (mnf): Nov [106]
Petrol motor car GB: Nov [101]
Motoring magazine: 1 Dec [108]
Motor show: 11 Dec [111]
Christian Science church (purpose-built): Mother Church, Boston, opened 30 Dec
Petrol motor car (Br): Dec [101]
Football club to make overseas Tour: Sunderland FC to USA
Ferris wheel GB: Earls Court
Passenger elevator with push-button control: built by Otis for Mrs E.I. Shepard's private residence, N.Y.
Photographic press agency: Illustrated Journals Photographic Supply Co, Ludgate Hill, London
University grants GB: eight Senior County Scholarships awarded annually by London County Council; £60 p.a. maintenance + £30 tuition
Coca-Cola, bottled: by Joseph Biedenham, Vicksburg, Miss.
Turbine vessel: *Turbinia*, built by Charles Parsons at Heaton, Co Durham
Municipal sports ground: Franklin Field, Boston (40 acres)
Chewing-gum GB: [34]
Cycle chain-guard: pat GB by Harrison Carter
Minimum wage rates: legally enforced NZ
Electric heater (mnf): GB [54]
Monotype machine (mnf): by Sellers & Co, Philadelphia (*see* 1887)
Series of pictorial stamps: [138]

1895

Hospital almoner: Miss Mary Stewart, apnt to Royal Free Hospital, London at £125 p.a., Jan
Hockey International: Ireland beat Wales 3–0, Rhyl, 25 Jan
Petrol lorry: 10 Feb [108]
Breakfast cereal (flakes): Feb [27]
Petrol bus: 18 Mar [29]
Films screened publicly: 22 Mar [62]
Sports film GB: 30 Mar [71]
Labour Exchange (municipal): estab Frankfurt/Main 1 May
Film screened for paying audience: 20 May [63]
Woman dental surgeon to qualify in GB: 20 May [201]
Theatrical knighthood: 24 May [189]
Horse-race filmed: Derby by Birt Acres, Epsom, Eng, 29 May
Pneumatic motor tyres: 11 June [132]
Motor race (petrol cars): 11 June [110]
News film: 20 June [68]
Chauffeur GB: June [34]
Motor journey GB: 12 July [111]
Rotogravure: dev by Karl Klič; used commercially by Storey Bros, printers of Lancaster, Eng, 1 Aug
Women's chess tournament: won by Lady Thomas, Hastings, Eng, 5 Aug
Sir Henry Wood Promenade Concert: Queen's Hall, London, 10 Aug
Film actor: 28 Aug [64]
Rugby League football: first club matches under Northern Union rules played 7 Sept
Controlled glider flight GB: 12 Sept [78]
Relay race GB: Sept [20]
Golf, American Open (official): won by Horace Rawlins, Newport, R.I., 4 Oct
Motor show GB: 15 Oct [111]
Motoring offence GB: 17 Oct [108]
Rugby League county match: Lancs beat Cheshire, Stockport, Eng, 21 Oct
Motoring association: 1 Nov [107]
Motoring journal GB: 2 Nov [108]
X-ray: disc by Wilhelm Röntgen, Würzburg, 8 Nov
Motoring association GB: 10 Dec [107]
Petrol van (mnf): 25 Dec [112]
Comedy film: 28 Dec [64]
Clinical X-ray: of gunshot wound in forester's hand by Franz Exner, Vienna, 28 Dec
Service station: Dec [162]
Motor agent GB: [99]
C.I.-engined vehicle: [43]
Doctor to use motor car: [102]
Jockey to ride in crouch position GB: Negro rider Sims
Women's football club: The British Ladies' Football Club, f by Lady Florence Dixie
Bible in modern English: Ferrar Fenton's trans of NT (OT 1903)
National Trust property: 4½-acre nature reserve at Barmouth, Eng
Ice dancing GB: ice waltz introd from Paris; performed at the Niagara and Hengler rinks, London
Volley-ball: dev by W. Morgan at YMCA gymn, Holyoke, Mass.
Milking machine (pulsator model): Thistle Mechanical Milking Machine, inv by Dr Alexander Shields, Glasgow, Scot; mkt at £100. Regarded as modern prototype
Rolled asphalt street-surfacing: King's Rd, Chelsea and Pelham St, Kensington
Electric cars (mnf) GB: by Acme & Immisch, Chalk Farm
Golliwog: [79]
Motor ambulance: [17]

1896

X-ray GB: made by Alan Campbell Swinton of contents of locked cash-box, 7 Jan
Public screening of films GB: 14 Jan [63]
Motorist convicted of speeding GB: 28 Jan [108]
Radiation treatment: Mrs Rose Lee treated for carcinoma of the breast by Emile Grubbe, Chicago, 29 Jan
Car hire: Jan [102]
Dental X-ray: by Otto Walkoff, Braunschweig, Ger, Jan
Church of Christ, Scientist GB: branch estab at Portman Rooms, Baker St, London, 7 Feb
Clinical X-ray GB: bullet embedded in wrist, by Sir Oliver Lodge at Royal Southern Hospital, Liverpool; exhib to Liverpool Medical Institution 13 Feb
Member of Br Royal Family to ride in car: 14 Feb [158]
Films screened for paying audience GB: 20 Feb [63]
Women's Hockey International: Ireland beat Eng 2–0, Dublin, 2 Mar
Pneumatic motor tyres GB: Mar [132]
Olympic Games (modern): Athens, 6 April

Olympic Gold Medallist: Harvard student James B. Connolly (USA), hop, step and jump, 6 April
Professional film actor: April [64]
Shipboard film show: presented by Carl Hertz aboard SS *Norman* (Eng–SA), April
Screen kiss: scene from *The Widow Jones*, with May Irwin and John Rice, filmed by Raff and Gammon, N.Y., April
Motor trade show GB: 9 May [111]
Hospital X-ray unit GB: Glasgow Royal Infirmary, May
Cinema: 26 June [38]
Newsfilm GB: 27 June [68]
Motor-car theft: June [105]
Royal Command Film Performance: 21 July [157]
Motoring fatality: 17 Aug [107]
Chop suey: Li Hung-Chang's chef, New York; devised to appeal to both Chinese and American tastes, 29 Aug
Motor cycle (mnf) GB: Aug [106]
Motor-race, track event: 7 Sept [110]
Heart surgery: 9 Sept [33]
Motor-cycle race: 20 Sept [106]
Petrol lorry (mnf): Sept [109]
Br Monarch filmed: 3 Oct [98]
Election motor car: 23 Oct [102]
Election motor car GB: 31 Oct [102]
Motor insurance: 2 Nov [108]
Motor-car manufacture GB: 13 Nov [103]
Film magazine: *The Phonoscope*, N.Y. 15 Nov
Parking summons GB: received by William Marshall, for parking in Tokenhouse Yard, City of London; case dismissed 25 Nov
Motor van GB: Nov [112]
Soccer film: made by R.W. Paul at Newcastle upon Tyne, Eng, Nov
Film studio with artificial lighting: Nov [71]
Electric car-starter: Nov [102]
Radio (public dem): 12 Dec [144]
Car hire GB: Dec [102]
National Trust building: The Priest's House (1350), Alfriston, Sussex, Eng, purchased for £300
Pictorial book-jacket, original design GB: by anon junior member of Fisher Unwin staff – issued with L. Parry Truscott's *The Poet and Penelope*
Invalid carriage, motor: Britannia Bath Chair (electric), mnf by John Ward, London
Factory welfare officer GB: Miss E.M. Wood, Rowntree's of York
Armoured car: four-man 16hp Pennington Military Autocar, built by E.J. Pennington (USA) at Motor Mills, Coventry, Nov; Harveyized steel armour, two machine-guns
Steel-framed building GB: Robinson's Emporium, West Hartlepool; archt Basil Scott
Transatlantic crossing by rowing boat: George Harbo and Frank Samuelson (Nor), N.Y.–Le Havre, 62 days
IQ test: [87]
Chlorinated water supply: Pola, Italy
Taxi: [173]
Woman to smoke in public GB: [38]
Ice-cream cone: [85]
Escalator (installed): [59]
Poodle parlour GB: [136]
Colour photography (commercial): [129]
Operatic record (mkt): [166]
Outboard motor: [121]
Dial telephone: [176]

1897

Motor van built in GB: 2 Jan [112]
Petrol lorry GB: Jan [109]
Petrol van built in GB: 2 Feb [112]
Women's Institute: f Stoney Creek, Ont. by Mrs Hoodless, 19 Feb
Motor wedding: 27 Feb [201]
Wide-screen film: 17 Mar [72]
Motor wedding GB: 21 April [201]
Rugby League club championship: Northern Union Cup Competition; Batley beat Leeds in final at St Helens, Eng, 24 April
Service station GB: April [162]
Taxi fitted with meter: May [173]
Women's international chess championship: opened at Hotel Cecil 23 June, won by Miss Mary Rudge (Eng)
British-built petrol van sold: 6 June [112]
Wireless Co: 20 July [144]
Radio transmission at sea: from St Bartholomew naval arsenal, Italy to tug in Gulf of Spezia by Guglielmo Marconi, 14 July (*see also* 17 Dec)
Advertising film: 5 Aug [64]
Taxi GB: 19 Aug [173]
Motor-coach excursions: Aug [105]
Motor car, hire-purchase terms GB: offered by Yorkshire Motor Car Co, Bradford, Aug
Prime Minister to be filmed GB: Lord Salisbury at Buckingham Palace Garden Party, 28 June
Motorist convicted of drunken driving GB: 10 Sept [108]
Motoring fatality (public highway) GB: 23 Sept [107]
Petrol bus GB: 25 Sept [30]
Woman car driver GB: Sept [205]
Second-hand car dealer GB: Sept [162]
Motor vehicles, military use: eight cars used by Fr Army on 200km exercise, Paris region, 21 Oct
Newspaper comic strip: 24 Oct [42]
Country motor bus GB: Hamilton–Larkhall/Blantyre, Scottish Motor Omnibus Co, Oct
Home movie outfit: Oct [82]
Motor mail van: Oct [109]
Crash between two motor vehicles: two motor vans collided in Charing Cross Rd, London, Oct
Royal Command Film Performance before Sovereign: 23 Nov [157]
Motor-cycle race GB: 29 Nov [106]
Radio station: Nov [144]
Radio transmission at sea GB: Alum Bay, IW to steamer *Solent* in Solent by Guglielmo Marconi, 17 Dec
Christian Science church (dedicated) GB: former synagogue at 57 Bryanston St
Plasticine: mnf by William Harbutt, Bath
C.I.-engined vehicle GB: [44]
Petrol-driven brewer's dray: [109]
Baby incubator GB: [21]
Crown Cork bottle cap GB: introd from USA
Hydrofoil: built by Comte de Lambert, tested on R. Seine
Chlorinated water supply GB: Maidstone, Kent
Land's End–John o'Groats motor journey: by Henry Sturmey in 4½hp Daimler, 929 miles in 93½hr driving-time, 9–19 Oct
Rugby football, numbering of players: for Queensland *v* NZ match, Brisbane
Trailer caravan: [32]
Film studio GB: [71]
Motor mower: [92]
Dress-wear hire: [51]
News film (indoor): [68]
Dust cart (self-propelled): [109]
Recording studio (disc): [166]
Automatic telephone switchboard GB: [176]
Scooter: [162]
Record shop: [166]

1898

Commercial traveller to use motor car: Ralph Foort of Oxford, Eng; began driving Daimler Covert phaeton, 20 Jan
Car driver killed GB: 12 Feb [107]
Badminton tournament: Guildford, Eng, 10 Mar
Whole-day motor-coach excursion: 13 Mar [105]
African game reserve: Sabi Game Reserve, Transvaal; designated 26 Mar
Armoured car (Br design): 3-ton, six-man, 14hp Simms War Car, des by F.R. Simms for Vickers Maxim Ltd, pat 26 Mar; 6ft high steel armour, two Maxim guns
European Monarch to own motor car: Mar [158]
Petrol bus (full-size): Mar [30]
Motor car with mileometer: Benz Ideal fitted by John Hope of Liverpool, Eng, with register of his own invention, Mar
American musical presented in West End: *The Belle of New York*, Shaftesbury Theatre, London 12 April
Coffee vending-machines GB: installed Leicester Sq, London and Queen's Buildings, Southwark by Pluto Hot Water Syndicate, April
Motor-racing fatality: Marquis of Montaignac at Prigueux, Fr, 1 May
Motor-car bumper: 21 May [101]
Articulated lorry: May [109]
Woman to pass driving test: May [205]
Barbed-wire defences: May [22]
Member of Royal Family to travel by car on public highway: 25 June [159]
Motor pantechnikon: Clarke oil-engined removal van acquired by Curtis & Mawes, Lincoln, Eng, June
Motor mail van (regular service): 17 June [109]
Battle scenes filmed: fighting at Siboney, Cuba (Spanish-American War) by J. Stuart Blackton and Albert E. Smith, 17 June
Workmen's Compensation GB: effective 1 July
Motor-bus timetable GB: issued by Mansfield Motor Car Co, 1 July
Car park (non-motoring event) GB: Henley Regatta, 5–7 July
Solo circumnavigation of the earth: by Capt. Joshua Slocum in 36ft oyster boat *Spray*; arr Fairhaven, Mass. after 38mnth voyage, 3 July
Motor-coach tour: 11 July [105]
Press report by radio: Kingstown Regatta report transmitted to *Dublin Daily Express*, 21 July
Whole-day motor-coach excursion GB: 2 Aug [105]
Underground railway motor-cars: 18 Aug [196]
Radio, commercial application: 26 Aug [144]
Motor-coach (inter-urban): Aug [105]
Diesel engine (commercial operation): Sept [44]
Motor fire-engine: Oct [74]
Labour-controlled council: Lab won 29 out of 48 seats in West Ham Borough election, Eng, 1 Nov
Hillclimb: at Chanteloup, nr Paris, 27 Nov; won by Jenatzy electric
Escalator GB: Nov [59]
Woman architect GB: 5 Dec [201]
Ship's radio (permanent): East Goodwin lightship, 24 Dec
Enclosed car GB: Dec [102]
Christmas stamp: Dec [138]
Newspaper van (motor): Daimler used by *Bradford Observer*, Eng, Dec
Epidiascope (mnf): des by Edward Richter; mkt by Zeiss of Jena
Corn flakes: [27]
Car with independent front suspension (mnf): 3½hp Decauville Voiturelle, mnf at Corbeil, Fr
Crawl: introd into competitive swimming by Alick Wickham (7) of British Solomon Islands in 66yd under-10 handicap at Bronte Pool, Sydney
X-ray diagnosis of war wounded: by Br Army surgeons in Tirah campaign
Motor sleigh: built by Dr Casgrain of Quebec; Bollée engine
Rubber-cored golf ball: inv by Coburn Haskell at Cleveland, Ohio
Natural gas (practical use) GB: for lighting of Heathfield Station, Sussex
Professional basketball league: National Basketball League (USA)
Reinforced concrete, multi-storey building GB: Weaver's Mill, Swansea
Trade union closed shop (national): all linotype operators in England and Wales to be members of Typographical Assoc
Home movie outfit GB: [82]
Loudspeaker: [95]
Road bridge in reinforced concrete: built by Francois Hennebique at Chatellerault, Fr
Magnetic recorder: [96]
Man-made textile yarn: [97]
Enclosed car (mnf): [102]
Electric torch (tubular): [57]
Instructional film: [68]
Brewer's dray (self-propelled) GB: 3-ton Thornycroft steam wagon for Messrs Guinness
Picture postcard art reproductions GB: [130]
Table tennis: [172]
Disc record-player (mnf) GB: [166]
Disc recording GB: [166]
Record press: [166]
Slow-motion film: [69]

1899

Radio manufacturer: Wireless Telegraph & Signal Co factory opened Hall St, Chelmsford, Eng, 25 Jan
Motor-cycling fatality: 11 Feb [107]
Car passenger killed GB: 25 Feb [108]
News film (unscheduled event): 17 Mar [68]
Radio distress signal: 17 Mar [149]
International radio transmission: 27 Mar [150]
Motor cycle, military: 30 Mar [106]
Motor milk van: introd by Eccles Co-op, Lancs, Eng, Mar

Motor auction: by Parson & Sons, Brighton, Mar

Anglo-American military alliance: combined land operation by RN and USN forces at Apia during Samoan campaign, 1 April

Mobile post office: Carroll County, Md., 3 April

All-England badminton championship: London Scottish Drill Hall, 4 April

Motor-cycle-racing fatality: M. Chaudron killed at Vincennes, Fr during 20km championship, 14 May

Women's athletic meet (rec): Wellesley College, Mass., 29 May

Aspirin (mnf): May [19]

Motor mower GB: May [92]

Box-kite GB: introd from Aus by Lawrence Hargrave, May

Moving staircase: 9 June [59]

Hillclimb GB: At Petersham Hill 9 June; won by Barrière tricycle (14mph)

Motor-rally GB: org by Automobile Club over 60-mile circuit from Southall; won by M. Heyermanns in 8hp Delahaye, av. 14.77mph, 12 June

Black Maria, motor: Loomis electric acquired by Akron, Ohio, Police Dept, June

Juvenile court: 1 July [90]

Woman motor-racing driver: 1 July [110]

International motor-cycle race: org by London Motor-Car Club and Automobile Club de France at New Brighton, Eng; won by Béconnais (Fr), 8 July

RN ships fitted with radio: HMS *Alexandria*, HMS *Juno*, HMS *Europa*, July

Ship-to-ship radio communication: between the above ships

Long-distance lorry trip GB: 8 Aug [157]

Motor-cycle despatch riders: 6 Sept [106]

Newspaper, motoring feature (regular): 'Motoring Notes' in *Daily Mail*, London, 13 Sept

London motor bus: 9 Oct [30]

School medical inspection (State school) GB: by Dr James Kerr at Usher St Board School, Bradford; report d 10 Oct

Spark plug (mnf): by Frank Wellington, St George's Sq, London, Oct

War scenes filmed (Br): 5th Northumberland Fusiliers at Orange R., SA, by John Bennett Stanford, 12 Nov

Staff suggestions scheme GB: introd by Lever Bros, Port Sunlight, 14 Nov

Ship's newspaper with news bulletins: *The Transatlantic Times*, SS *St Paul*, 15 Nov

Liner, radio messages received aboard: SS *St Paul* from Needles wireless station, Eng, 15 Nov

Labour Prime Minister: 28 Nov [91]

Radio used in warfare: 1 Dec [150]

Motor trade association GB: Motor Trades Assoc, f 13 Dec

Golf tee: pat by George F. Grant, Boston, Dec

Diesel engine (mnf): [44]

Car with sloping windscreen: built by Amedée Bollée of Le Mans, Fr, for Comte de Paiva

Postmark slogan: used by Buffalo, N.Y., PO to adv Pan-American Exposition

Judo GB: introd as music-hall act by Yukio Tani

Motor-car mascot GB: St Christopher des by Chas Sykes for John Scott Montagu's Daimler

Model cars (electric): mnf by Carlisle & Finch, Cincinatti; battery powered, $3.50

Oxo cubes: produced at Fray Bentos, Uruguay

Motor vehicles, army: two 3½hp Woods electric vans acquired by US Army Signal Corps

Rotary duplicator: [52]

Travel association (Europe): Società Italiana degli Albertagori

Naval turbine ships: destroyers HMS *Cobra* and HMS *Viper*

Petrol invalid carriage: [87]

Book matches GB: [97]

Publisher's blurb: [26]

Garage: [76]

Police dogs: [134]

Motor car used by police GB: April [133]

Road-haulage contractor to use motor lorries: [56]

1900

Petrol bus (enclosed single-deck) GB: King's Lynn–Gaywood, Norfolk, Jan

Liner with ship's radio (permanent): *Kaiser Wilhelm der Grosse*, left Bremen in radio contact with shore, 28 Feb

Battle scene filmed (Br): cavalry skirmish nr Kimberley, SA, by Joe Rosenthal of Warwick Film Co, Feb

Radio used in naval warfare: by HMS *Forte*, HMS *Thetis* and HMS *Magicienne* blockading Delagoa Bay, Mar

Sound film: 15 April [69]

Stamp books: 16 April [138]

Motor hearse: May [107]

Member of Br Royal Family to own motor car: 11 June [159]

International motor race: 14 June [110]

Driving tuition GB: June [51]

Tachometer: mnf by Taxameter Syndicate Ltd, London, June

Old school tie: 7 July [121]

Woman motor-racing driver GB: 14 July [110]

Motor ambulance (in service): July [18]

Lawn tennis, Davis Cup: USA beat GB at Brookline, Mass., 8–10 Aug

Long-distance motor coach: 27 Aug [105]

Electric torch (tubular) GB: Aug [57]

Film music: 13 Sept [68]

Labour MP GB: 2 Oct [91]

Radio telephone (conventional system): Dec [150]

Motor lorry used in warfare: SA-built petrol-driven lorry used by Boer commando as ammunition-carrier in Transvaal

Army lorries: two Scotte steam lorries acquired by Fr Army

Petrol-driven vehicles, army: two Panhard troop-carriers, two De Dietrich medical vans, two De Dion-Bouton scout cars acquired by Fr Army

Electrocardiograph (in clinical use): dev by Willem Einthoven for Leiden Hospital, Neths

Flame-thrower: gas-operated instrument inv by Richard Fiedler, Berlin

Judo school GB: opened by Prof S. K. Uyenishi at 31 Golden Sq

Film scriptwriter: [69]

Newsreel: [68]

Motor cycle used in warfare: [106]

Bus with pneumatic tyres: [132]

Record label: [166]

1901

Motor road: 140 mile route, Tamatave–Antananarivo, Madagascar; opened 1 Jan

Front page newspaper headline (national daily) GB: death of Queen Victoria, *Daily Express*, 23 Jan

Electric car starter (mnf) GB: Feb [102]

Radio telegraph service (commercial): between Hawaiian Is, inaug by Inter-Island Telegraph Co, 1 Mar

Truck service GB: 11 Mar [157]

Diesel engine GB: 25 Mar [44]

Motor race, track event GB: 8 April [110]

Liner with ship's radio (Br): SS *Lake Champlain* departed Liverpool 21 May

Motor hearse GB; 15 April [107]

Monarch to drive motor car: April [158]

Multi-storey car park: May [114]

Driving school GB: May [51]

Petrol lorry (mnf) GB: June [109]

Liners to communicate by radio: SS *Lucania* and SS *Lake Champlain*, mid-Atlantic, June

Trolley-bus service: Bielethal, Ger, 10 July

Police fingerprint bureau GB: July [73]

Turbine merchant vessel: passenger steamer *King Edward*, built Denny Bros, Dumbarton, Scot; in service Fairlie–Campbeltown, July

Cinema GB: 6 Aug [38]

Motor fire-engine GB: Aug [74]

Motor vehicle equipped with radio: Fr Army De Dion steam lorry, used on manœuvres Aug (*see also* Sept)

Radio engineering school: Marconi College, Frinton, Eng, Sept

Motor vehicle equipped with radio GB: Guglielmo Marconi's MMC car, Sept

Naval submarine GB: 2 Oct [171]

Traffic sign (warning to motorists) GB: Oct [192]

Getaway car: used by three Paris bandits for shop theft, 27 Oct

Hearing aid (elec): 15 Nov [80]

Motor-cycling club GB: The Motor-Cycling Club, f London 19 Nov

Road tanker (self-propelled): 5-ton steam tanker delivered to Consolidated Petroleum Co by Coulthard & Co, Preston, Eng, Nov

Safety razor: 2 Dec [160]

Nobel Prizes: awarded 10 Dec

Transatlantic radio transmission: Poldhu, Cornwall–St John's, Newfoundland by Guglielmo Marconi, 12 Dec

Table-tennis tournament: 14 Dec [173]

Army lorries, petrol-driven: nine Daimlers delivered Berlin, Dec

Motor-car speedometer (mnf): by Thorpe & Salter, Clerkenwell; 0–35 mph

Table-tennis club: [173]

Building erected from prefabricated concrete sections: cottage built at Cobbs Quarry, Everton, Eng by J. A. Brodie

Peanut vending-machine: inst at Pan-American Exposition, Buffalo N.Y. by Mills Novelty Co

Ambassador to use official car GB: HE Sir Chichen Lofengluh of China

Cardiac massage: woman patient (43) revived by Dr Kristian Igelsrud, Tromsö, Norway

Trade union levy GB: by Miners' Federation; 1d per month towards Parliamentary Fund

Motor-car mileometer (mnf): Bell Odometer by S.H. Davis Mnf Co, Portland, Mass.

Building with basement car park: Christian Science Church, Central Park West, N.Y.

Meccano: dev by Frank Hornby, Liverpool, Eng

Motor oil GB: Mobiloil, mkt by Vacuum Oil Co, Milwall

Fan club: [60]

Motor vehicles used by Br Army: 7hp Panhard, 16hp Napier, 12hp Daimler, 2-ton Milnes-Daimler lorry, used on cavalry manœuvres, Aldershot, 22 July

Municipal bus service: run by Southampton Corporation, Eng with hired vehicles

Motoring map: of Belgium pub by Automobile Club Belgique

Netball: introd by Miss Adair Roberts at Dartford Physical Training College, Eng

Car with front-wheel drive: Korn et Latil 3½hp *voiturette*

Christmas-tree lamps (mnf): [37]

Motor horse-box: [83]

Cigarette coupons: [77]

Signature tune: [164]

Department store moving staircase: [59]

Sound films GB: [69]

Mass-produced motor car: [104]

Electric typewriter (mnf): [194]

Vacuum cleaner: [196]

1902

Army lorries GB: Thornycroft and Foden steam wagons acquired by War Dept, Jan

Motor-cycling magazine: *Motor Cycling*, London 12 Feb

Horse trials: Championnat du Cheval d'Armes, Paris, 29 Mar

Prime Minister to own motor car GB: Lord Salisbury, Locomobile, April

Agricultural tractor GB: 23 July [190]

Crawl GB: dem by Richard Cavill of Sydney at Manchester, July

Breakfast cereal GB: July [27]

Lorry with pneumatic tyres: July [133]

Window envelope: inv by Americus F. Callahan of Chicago; mnf by US Envelope Co, Springfield, Mass., July

Fingerprint conviction GB: 13 Sept [73]

International Court of Justice: Court of International Arbitration, The Hague; in session Sept

Borstal Institution: special wing of Borstal Prison, Rochester, opened 16 Oct

Staff car GB: 10hp Lanchester delivered War Office, Oct

Esperanto club GB: 7 Nov [60]

Cardiac massage GB: male patient (65) revived by Sir William Arbuthnot Lane, London, Nov

Transatlantic radio press report: filed from Glace Bay, Canada by *The Times* correspondent, Parkin, 15 Dec
Automatic tea-maker: mnf by Frank Clarke, Birmingham, Eng; price 30s
Tyre chains: introd by Harry Parsons of City & Suburban Electric Carriage Co, London
Diesel-engined vessel: canal boat *Petit-Pierre*, built by Sautter-Harle et Cie, Paris
Motor caravan: [32]
Motor car with all-metal body: aluminium 9hp Napier, mnf London
Rubber-studded table tennis bat: [173]
Racing-car with fully enclosed body: streamlined Baker Electric Racer, Cleveland, Ohio (max 85mph)
Labour Exchanges (municipal) GB: estab under Labour Bureau (London) Act
Car with silencer (standard): Pan-American, mnf at Mamaroneck, N.Y.
Production car with electric starter: [102]
Motor mower (mnf): [92]
Auction bridge: [28]
Teddy bear: [174]
Khaki uniforms (general service): [91]
Hotel garage: Warne's Hotel, Worthing, Eng
Film Rental: [68]
Motor van with enclosed cab: [112]
Winter sports package holiday: [122]

1903
Saloon car: 16 Jan [102]
Municipal bus company: estab by Eastbourne Corporation, Eng; four Milnes-Daimlers in service 12 April
Postage meter: 15 June [137]
Motor-boat race: 11 July [99]
Trans-USA motor journey: San Francisco–N.Y., Winton car, 23 May–26 July
Western film: 21 Sept [72]
Baseball, world series: won by Boston Red Sox, 13 Oct
Children's theatre: The Children's Educational Theater, N.Y.; first prod *The Tempest*, Oct
Young Liberals: f 19 Nov
Wildlife preservation society GB: Soc for the Preservation of the Wild Fauna of the Empire, f 11 Dec
Usherettes: Majestic Theater, N.Y., 16 Dec
Aircraft flight: 17 Dec [10]
Driving licence GB: 28 Dec [51]
Mechanized army unit: Corps d'Automobilistes Militaire (Fr); Nos 77 and 78 Coys Army Service Corps (Br)
Service automatics: Colt .38 and Luger-Parabellum .30 adopted by US Army
Motor manufacturer's test-track: estab by Wolseley Co on eight-acre site at Adderley Park, Birmingham, Eng
LCC commemorative plaque: Holly Lodge, Kensington (Lord Macaulay)
Motoring maps GB: 100-mile radius of London, pub by Dunlop Co
Mixed bathing GB: permitted at Bexhill, Sussex
Motor caravan GB [32]
Standardized traffic signs: [192]
School bus (motor): 20hp Serpollet acquired by École St Dominique, Paris
Magnetic recorder (mnf): [96]
Public relations consultant: [141]
Police car: [133]
Safety razor (mnf): [160]
Complete opera on disc: [166]

1904
Motor-vehicle registration plates GB: 1 Jan [113]
Newspaper, children's feature GB: initiated by *The Daily Paper*, 4 Jan
Newspaper photographers: Feb [118]
Motor lifeboat: petrol craft built La Rochelle for port of Brest; launched Feb (*see also* May)
Stamp-books GB: 16 Mar [138]
Electric trains (surface) GB: 29 Mar [152]
Rugby League International: Other Nations beat Eng, Wigan, 5 April
Rotogravure magazine illustrations: *Der Tag*, Ger, 26 April
Petrol taxi GB: May [173]
Motor lifeboat GB: *J. McConnell Hussy* (1893) fitted with Fay & Bowen petrol motor, May; stationed Folkestone
Woman minister of religion GB: June [204]
Motor car to travel over 100mph: 13½-litre Gobron-Brillié driven over measured km at 103.56mph by Louis Rignolly, Ostend, 21 July
International radio-telegraph service: Bari, Italy–Antivari, Montenegro, 2 Aug
Photographic picture postcard in natural colour (rec): 16 Oct [130]
Thermionic valve: two-diode, pat by Dr Ambrose Fleming of London, 16 Nov
Crawler tractor: 24 Nov [190]
Film magazine GB: *The Optical Lantern and Cinematograph Journal*, Nov
Electric car lamps GB: Nov [102]
Revolving stage GB: introd by Oswald Stoll at Coliseum Theatre, London 24 Dec
Armoured car (production model): 35hp Austro-Daimler in service with Austrian Army; 30hp Charron Automitrailleuse (Fr) in service with Russian Army
Christian Science church (purpose-built) GB: First Church of Christ, Scientist, Manchester
Diesel-electric vessel: 650-ton tank barge *Vandal*, built for Nobel Oil Co at Sermovo Works, St Petersburg
Floral clock GB: inst at Princes Street Gdns, Edinburgh by James Ritchie & Son
Block of flats built from prefabricated concrete sections: Eldon St, Liverpool, Eng by J.A. Brodie (*see also* 1901)
Processed cheese: mnf by J.L. Kraft, Chicago
Offset-litho printing-press (paper): rotary machine built for Eastern Lithographic Co by Ira Rubel of Nutley, N.J.
Open-air school: at Charlottenburg, Ger
Christmas seals: dev by Danish postmaster Einar Holbøll; in aid of TB campaign
Fire appliance, turntable ladder: built by John Morris & Sons for Manchester Fire Brigade, Eng
Motor-boat passenger service: [99]
Long-playing record: [94]
Film rental GB: [68]
Mass-produced motor car GB: [104]
Colour photographic plates (mkt): [129]
Folding metal push-chair: the Allwin, mnf by Liddle Co, Chicago
Outboard motor: [121]
Double-sided records: [166]
Underground railway ticket-machines: [196]

1905
Children's cinema matinée: *Ubanora* presented by Charles Urban, Alhambra Theatre, London, 9 Jan
Armoured car used in action: Russian Army Charron against St Petersburg rioters, Jan
Mobile library (public library service): inaug by Washington County Free Library, Md., April
Newspaper: overseas edition (Br): *Continental Daily Mail*, Paris, 22 May
Historical pageant GB: org by Louis N. Parker at Sherborne Castle, Dorset, 12 June
Man-made textile yarn (mnf): July [97]
Safety glass: pat by Swindon solicitor John Crewe Wood 2 Oct, and fitted to his own Peugeot *Bébé*
Motor ambulance GB: Nov [18]
Motor ambulance (civilian) GB: 16 Dec [18]
Beauty contest (rec) GB: 23 Dec [22]
Aspirin GB: [19]
Football, £1,000 transfer fee: paid by Middlesborough, for Alfred Common
Judo for women: taught by Mrs Roger Watts at Prince's Club, Eng
Women's lacrosse club GB: Southern Ladies' LC
Turbine liners: Allan Line's *Victorian* and *Virginian* (Canadian)
Milk chocolate GB: [35]
Motor road-roller: mnf by Barford & Perkins, Peterborough, Eng: first sale to Leatherhead Golf Club
Surfing club: Hui Nalu Surf Club, Hawaii
Strip lighting: [57]
Baked beans GB: [21]
Motor-car bumpers GB: [101]
Pre-selective jukebox: [90]
Wafer ice creams: [86]
Helicopter: [80]
Motor hearse (purpose-built): [107]
Petrol pump (motor spirit): [126]
Safety razor GB: [160]
Petrol filling-station: [162]
Police motor-cycle patrol: [135]
Pack parachute: inv by Ralph Carhart, USA
Vacuum cleaner (portable): [196]

1906
Aircraft with pneumatic tyres: 5 Mar [133]
Coin-operated telephone kiosk GB: April [176]
London bus route numbers: introd by London Motor Omnibus Co, 30 April
Grand Prix motor race: 26 June [110]
Socialist daily newspaper GB: *The Majority*, 10 July
Motor-bus fatality GB: 10 killed, 26 injured at Handcross Hill, Sussex, 12 July
Electric motor horn GB: 28 Aug [56]
Permanent wave: 8 Oct [126]
Amplification valve: three-diode Audion pat by Prof. Lee de Forest, N.Y., 25 Oct
Aircraft mnf co: Nov [11]
London Underground, season tickets: Piccadilly Line, 15 Dec
Radio broadcast: 24 Dec [144]
Feature film: 26 Dec [67]
Pentecostal Church: estab by W.J. Seymour at 312 Azusa St, Los Angeles
Crawler tractor (mnf): [190]
Humane killer (practical): des by Maj. Derriman, Secretary of RSPCA, London
Army lorries, petrol-driven GB: RASC 20hp Milnes-Daimlers
Co-operative advertising campaign: Californian Orange Growers
Lifeguards: beach patrols at Sydney, NSW
Psycho-analysis GB: female patient analysed by Dr Ernest Jones, London
Milk cartons: introd by G.W. Maxwell, San Francisco
Record reviews: pub in *Phonographische Zeitschrift*, Ger
Car with front-wheel drive GB: 16hp Pullcar taxi, mnf Preston
Diesel submarines: Fr Navy's *Opale* and *Emeraude*
Safety glass (mnf): by the Safety Motor Screen Co, f by J. Crewe Wood of Swindon, Eng (*see* 1905)
Milk bottles GB: [98]
Loudspeaker (electric): [95]
Disc-playing pre-selective jukebox: [90]
Holiday camp: [81]
GPO stamp-machine: [138]
Vacuum cleaner (portable) GB: [197]
Cartoon film: [65]
Colour photographic portrait studio: [128]

1907
Broadcasting service: Feb [145]
Woman MP: 15 Mar [204]
Motor cab fitted with taxi-meter GB: General Motor Cab Co Renault, London, 22 Mar
Model-aircraft competition: org by *Daily Mail* at Crystal Palace, Eng; won by A.V. Roe's *Avroplane*, Mar
Ship radio telephone: April (?) [151]
Isle of Man TT Races: won by Charles Collier on Matchless (av. 38.22mph), 7 May
Open zoo: Hamburg Tierpark, opened 7 May
Mother's day: initiated by Miss Anna Jarvis; held Philadelphia 10 May
24-hour motor race: 25 May [110]
Detergent (household): Persil, mkt by Henkel & Cie, Düsseldorf, 6 June
Caravan club: f London 14 June
Air Force: 1 July [13]
Motor-racing track (purpose-built): Brooklands, Weybridge, Surrey, opened 6 July
Open-air school GB: Bostall Wood, Plumstead, July
Aerodrome (with hangars): Issy-les-Moulineaux, Fr, Aug
Motor-racing fatality GB: Vincent Hermon, Brooklands, 14 Sept
Repertory theatre company: Manchester Repertoire, Eng, f by Miss A. Horniman; first production – *David Ballard* at Midland Hotel Theatre, 23 Sept
Warships fitted with radio telephones: Sept [151]
Servicewomen (unofficial): FANY

(First Aid Nursing Yeomanry), f by RSM Edward Baker with HQ at Surrey Yeomanry Depot, London, Sept (recognized by War Office 1927)
Pentecostals GB: group f by Rev Alexander Boddy, Sunderland, Sept
Professional artiste to broadcast: Sept [145]
Central cooking depot for school meals GB: estab Green Lane, Bradford by Bradford Education Committee, 28 Oct
Helicopter, free flight: 13 Nov [81]
Boxing referee to officiate inside ring: Eugene Corri at Tommy Burns *v* Gunner Moir fight, National Sporting Club, 7 Dec
Motor gun-carrier used in warfare: Panhard mounted with Hotchkiss machine-gun by Capt. Gentry, Fr 1st Cavalry Division, Casablanca, 18 Dec
Feature film (over 90min): *L'Enfant Prodigue* with Georges and Mendelys Wague, directed by Benoît Lév at Pathé Studios, Paris (*see* 1906)
Newspaper photograph transmitted by wire: portrait of King Edward sent Paris–London in 12min, 8 Nov; pub *Daily Mirror* 9 Nov
Strip lighting GB: Moore Tubing used to illuminate Savoy Hotel Court
Aircraft mnf co GB: [11]
Publisher's blurb GB: on wrapper of George Bourne's *Memoirs of a Surrey Labourer* (Duckworth)
Diesel ship, seagoing: oil tanker *Djelo*, built Kolomna Yard, Russia
Radio Telephone Installation (commercial): GB: [151]
Silk-screen printing process GB: by Samuel Simon, Manchester
Probation officers (official) GB
Canned tuna fish: prod by A.P. Halfhill, San Pedro, Calif.
Electric washing-machine (mnf): The Thor, des by Alva J. Fisher, mnf by Hurley Machine Corp, Chicago
Bakelite (mnf): inv by Dr Leo Baekland (Belg); first used commercially by Loando Co of Boonton, N.J. for moulded electrical insulation components
Free State secondary education (national system) GB: all State-aided secondary schools required to reserve 25% free places
Photocopier: [126]
Radio broadcast GB: [145]
Novel written in Esperanto: Dr Henry Vallienne's *Kastele de Prelongo*, Paris
Cargo vessel with ship's radio: Anglo-American Oil Co tanker *Iroquois*

1908

Scout troop: 26 Jan [27]
Transatlantic radio-telegraph service (public): inaug Glace Bay, Canada–Clifden, Ireland at 15c/7½d word, Feb
Radio magazine: *Modern Electrics*, N.Y., April
Aircraft passenger: 14 May [10]
Court of Criminal Appeal GB: sat 15 May
Diesel submarine GB: D.1, launched Barrow, 16 May
Middle-Eastern oil: first struck in commercial quantities, Masjid-i-Sulaiman, Persia, 26 May
Motor car, supercharged: 30 May [105]
Football International played by England against a foreign country: beat Austria 6–1, Vienna, 6 June
Flying club: Aeronautical Soc of N.Y., f with flying facilities at Morris Park Racetrack, 10 June
Film critic: June [68]
SOS signal adopted: 1 July [150]
Woman aircraft passenger: 8 July [10]
Women Olympic competitors: in figure-skating and lawn-tennis events, IVth Olympiad, London, 13–25 July
International beauty contest GB: 14 Aug [22]
Cartoon story film: 17 Aug [65]
Aeroplane fatality: Lt Thomas Selfridge killed (in crash with Orville Wright), Fort Meyer, Va., 17 Sept
Ship fitted with radio telephone GB: Sept [151]
Aerial film: Sept [65]
Aircraft passenger (Br): 8 Oct [10]
Aircraft flight GB: 16 Oct [10]
Aeroplane flight, cross-country: Mourmelon–Rheims, Fr (20 miles) by Henry Farman in 50hp Voisin, 30 Oct
Woman mayor GB: 9 Nov [203]
Hotel Bibles: Nov [84]
Film music (story film): 17 Nov [68]
American football, numbered players: Univ of Pittsburgh *v* Washington and Jefferson, Pittsburgh, 5 Dec
World heavyweight boxing champion, Negro: Jack Johnson (USA), defeated Tommy Burns (Can), Sydney, 26 Dec
Malted milk GB: mkt by Horlick's Malted Milk Co, Slough, Bucks
Motor vehicles used in warfare (Br): War Department cars used for carrying officers during Mohmand campaign, India
Paper cups: introd by the Public Cup Vendor Co, N.Y.
Aeroplane engine (series prod): 50hp 7-cylinder Gnome rotary (Fr)
C.O.D. service GB: overseas only
Cellophane: pat by Dr Jacques Brandenberger of Zurich
Offset-litho printing press GB: Rubel rotary acquired by Bemrose & Sons, Derby
Oscillating electric fan: [53]
Cinema, sloping floor GB: [38]
Electric car lamps (mnf) GB: [102]
Horror film: [68]
IQ test GB: [87]
Police dogs GB: [134]
Military radio telephone: [151]
Girl Guides: [77]
Outdoor telephone kiosk: [177]
Crawler tractor (petrol): [190]
Underground railway map: [196]

1909

Old Age Pensions GB: 1 Jan [121]
Colour film (commercial): 26 Feb [66]
Aerodrome GB: estab Aero Club at Shellbeach, Kent, Feb
Double-decker bus (enclosed): 9 April [29]
Film censorship: April [66]
Motor lifeboat (purpose-built): SR Lifeboat No. 561, stationed Stromness, Orkney, 2 May
Chemotherapeutic drug: Salvarsan 606 (anti-syphilis), successful trial by Dr Paul Ehrlich, Frankfurt, May
Aerial navigation chart: five-colour map of flight paths out of Paris, pub by Cartes Guides Campbell, May
SOS signal transmitted: 10 June [150]
Diesel passenger vessel: *Romagna*, built by Cantiere Navali Riumiti of Ancona, Italy; delivered to Romagnola SS Co 24 June
Hydrofoil GB: *Miranda III*, des by Sir John Thornycroft, tested June
Hunger strike GB: 5 July [84]
Air display: 'Concours d'Aviation,' Douai, Fr, 28 June–18 July
Weather report by radio: transmitted Sangatte–Dover, 19 July
Cross-Channel aeroplane flight: Baraques–Dover by Louis Blériot in Blériot XI (37min), 25 July
Military aircraft: 2 Aug [14]
Aircraft passenger GB: 14 Aug [10]
Air race: Gordon Bennett Cup Race, Rheims, Fr, 29 Aug; won by Glen Curtiss (USA)
Scout rally: Crystal Palace, Eng, 4 Sept
Pilot killed in air crash: Eugène Lefebvre while testing a Wright A at Juvisy, Fr, 7 Sept
Trolley bus GB: built by Railless Electric Traction Co; dem Colindale, Sept
Rugby match at Twickenham: Harlequins *v* Richmond, Eng; first try by John Birkett (Harlequins), 2 Oct
Air display GB: Doncaster, 15–23 Oct
Woman pilot: 22 Oct [206]
Pilot officer: 26 Oct [14]
Aeronautical engineering school: Sup' Aero, Paris, Oct
Air-speed indicator: pat by Alec Ogilvie, fitted to his Short-Wright biplane at Rye, Sussex, Eng, 3 Nov
Woolworth's GB: Liverpool, 5 Nov
Woman glider pilot: Dec [78]
Professional ice-hockey league: National Hockey Assoc, f Montreal, 2 Dec
Photo taken from Aeroplane: Dec [127]
Coca-Cola GB: imported from USA
Mobile bank GB: Farrow's Motor Bank toured Sussex villages
Diesel warships: Imperial Russian Navy gunboats *Kars* and *Ardagan*
Brassière (rec): 'a brassière for dressy occasions' mentioned in *Vogue* (USA)
Synthetic rubber: Synthesized by F. Hofman of Bayer Co, Elberfeld, Ger
Students' strike GB: at Ruskin College, Oxford following dismissal of left-wing Principal, Douglas Hird
Electrocardiograph (in clinical use) GB: Einthoven electrocardiograph installed University College Hospital, London by Cambridge Instrument Co
Nitrogen fertilizer: disc by Fritz Haber, Karlsruhe, Ger
Buses lit by electricity: 'National' steam bus operated by Thomas Clarkson, London
Swimming-pool, mixed bathing GB: Holborn Baths
Communal Christmas tree: [37]
Super tax GB: [86]
Bus conductress: [30]
Subway escalator: Bowery Station, N.Y.
Gliding club: [78]
Motor hearse (purpose-built) GB: [107]
Broadcast talk: [145]
Motor car with four-wheel brakes (standard) 16hp Arrol-Johnston (Scot)

1910

Pilot's licence: 1 Jan [130]
Juvenile court GB: 4 Jan [90]
Opera broadcast: 13 Jan [148]
Woman granted pilot's licence: 8 Mar [130]
Pilot's licence GB: 8 Mar [130]
Seaplane: des by Henri Fabre; took off from water at Martigues, nr Marseilles, 28 Mar
Frankenstein movie: Edison's *Frankenstein* with Charles Ogle, released Mar
Night flight: Roade, Northants–Lichfield, Staffs, Eng, by Claude Grahame-White, 27–28 April
International driving licences GB: issued by RAC, 1 May
Royal aeroplane passenger: Prince Charles of Roumania, piloted by M. Osmont in Farman at Bucharest, 24 May
Cross-Channel Aeroplane flight (Br): Dover–Sangatte–Dover by Hon. C.S. Rolls in Short-Wright biplane, 2 June
Aircraft reconnaissance: 9 June [12]
Father's Day: inst by Mrs John Bruce Dodd, Spokane, Wash., 19 June
Military aircraft GB: June [14]
Pilot killed in air crash GB: Hon. C.S. Rolls in Wright Flyer, Bournemouth, 12 July
Aircraft radio: 27 Aug [11]
Policewoman: 12 Sept [135]
Aircraft reconnaissance GB: 24 Sept [12]
Aircraft radio GB: 27 Sept [11]
Twin-engined aeroplane: Sommer (Fr), test flown 27 Sept
Photo taken from aeroplane GB: 30 Sept [128]
Aeroplane collision: between M. Thomas's Antoinette and Capt. B. Dickson's Farman, Milan, 2 Oct
Royal pilot: 23 Oct [159]
Sea Scouts: f Oct
Fighter aircraft: Voisin biplane with machine-gun exhibited Paris Aero Show, Oct
Aircraft take-off from ship: 14 Nov [12]
Steel-shafted golf clubs: pat by Arthur F. Knight of Schenectady, N.Y., Nov
Neon lighting: 3 Dec [115]
Aeronautical engineering course GB: at Northampton Institute, Clerkenwell, autumn term
Aeroplane, retractable undercarriage: Short No. 3, built Leysdown, Kent, Eng
Railway milk tanker (glass-lined): Whiting Milk Co wagon, Boston & Maine Railroad
Personnel officer GB: apnt by Hans Renold Ltd, engineers, Manchester
Chemotherapeutic drug, production: Ehrlich's Salvarsan 606 (*see* 1909) by Hoechst Co, Ger
Model aircraft kits: mkt by American Aeroplane Mnf Co, N.Y.
Cycle dynamo (mnf) GB: by Bowden Co
Car with independent front suspension GB: Morgan three-wheeler, mnf Malvern Link
Radio direction-finder: Marconi–Bellini–Tolsi apparatus installed at Boulogne, Fr
Animal cartoon film character: [65]
Sound-on-film: [69]
Car with four-wheel brakes: 12hp Argyll, mnf Glasgow, Scot
Synthetic rubber (mnf): by Bayer Co at Leverkusen, Ger (*See* 1909)
Synthetic-fibre stockings: [97]
Military vehicle with radio: French Signal Corps limousine

Women bank manager: Miss May Bateman, Farrow's Bank Ladies' Branch, New Bridge St, London
Ice-cream cone GB: [86]
Daily broadcasting service: [145]
Broadcasting receiver (kit): [148]
Woman pilot GB: [206]

1911
Bombs dropped from aircraft: by Lt M.S. Sidney at San Francisco, 7 Jan
Aircraft landing on ship: 18 June [12]
Monte Carlo Rally: won by Henri Rougier in 25hp Turcat-Méry, 21 28 Jan
Motor-car mascot (standard): George Synger's *Spirit of Ecstasy*, executed in bronze by Rolls-Royce, 6 Feb
Airmail: 18 Feb [16]
Air force GB: 1 April [14]
Aeroplane flight, London–Paris non-stop: by Pierre Prier in 50hp Blériot, 3hr 56min, 12 April
Military pilot GB: 24 April [14]
Radio journal GB: *The Marconigraph,* April
Aeroplane flight with fare-paying passenger GB: 17 May [10]
Indianapolis 500: won by Ray Harroun in Marmon Wasp (ave 75mph), 30 May
Liner with swimming-pool: SS *Olympic*, delivered to White Star Line, 31 May
Aeroplane flight restrictions: Air Navigation Act, became law 2 June in GB
Trolley-bus service GB: Leeds, 20 June
Charter flight: 28 June [33]
Air freight: box of Osram lamps flown Shoreham–Hove, Eng by Aeronautical Syndicate Ltd; Valkyrie monoplane; freight charge £100, 4 July
Trainer aircraft (dual-control): Short S.32, flown by Frank MacClean at Eastchurch, Eng, 29 July. Used for training Territorial Army pilots
Woman granted pilot's licence GB: 29 Aug [130]
Air-sea rescue; by Hugh Robinson, landed seaplane on Lake Michigan to rescue downed pilot, Aug
Airmail GB: 9 Sept [16]
Service pilot killed in air crash GB: Lt R.A. Cammell of Air Bttn RE, Valkyrie monoplane, Hendon, 17 Sept
Twin-engined aeroplane GB: Short S.39, test flown Eastchurch 18 Sept
Film stunt-man: 30 Sept [71]
Moving staircase GB: 4 Oct [59]
Aeroplane used in warfare: 23 Oct [8]
Air raid: Libya, 1 Nov [8]
Br monarch to visit Commonwealth country: 14 Nov [98]
Seaplane GB: Avro D biplane adapted by Cdr Oliver Schwann RN; flown from Cavendish Dock, Barrow-in-Furness, 18 Nov
Bank hold-up, motorized: Société Génerale Bank, rue Ordener, Paris, by Jules Bonnot gang, 21 Dec
Western film in colour: Kinemacolor's *Fate*, made in Eng
Black Maria, motor GB: Lacre van supplied to Glasgow Police
Flame-throwers in service use: issued to Nos 23, 24 and 25 Pioneer Bttns of the German Army
Aeroplane with enclosed passenger cabin: six-passenger Blériot *Berline* built for M. Henri Deutsch de la Neurthe of Paris
Nursery school GB: Rachel McMillan Open-Air Nursery School, Evelyn House, Deptford
Film-fan magazine: *Photoplay*, Chicago
Portable pack military radio set: [150]
Chewing-gum vending-machine GB: [34]
Veteran motoring: [197]
White lines (road): [191]

1912
Aircraft take-off from ship GB: 10 Jan [13]
Flying boat: des by Glenn Curtiss; maiden flight Hammondsport, N.Y., 10 Jan
Aerial propaganda raid by aircraft: 15 Jan [8]
Diesel ocean liner: Ostasiatiske Komp AB *Selandia*, built Copenhagen; maiden voyage to Bangkok, 22 Feb
Photo reconnaissance in warfare: 24 Feb [12]
Parachute descent from aeroplane: 1 Mar [123]
Casualty in aerial warfare: 31 Mar [8]
Woman pilot to fly Channel: Dover, Eng–Hardelot, Fr by Harriet Quimby (USA) in Blériot monoplane, 16 April
Aeroplane with enclosed cockpit: Avro F, flown Brooklands, Eng, 1 May
Aircraft take-off from ship under way: 8 May [13]
Automatic telephone exchange GB: 18 May [176]
Aeroplane registration numbers: introd under Fédération Aéronautique Internationale's Brussels Agreement, 19 May
Motor museum: 31 May [110]
NCO to qualify as pilot GB: Cpl Frank Ridd RE, Salisbury Plain, 4 June
Motor ambulances in warfare: 8 June [18]
Motor transport used in battle: 44 lorries and 10 ambulances by Italian Lequio Division at Battle of Zanzur, Tripoli, 8 June
Night air raid: on Turkish lines, Tripoli, by 2nd Aerial Coy, Italian Aviation Corps, 11 June
Royal Command Variety Performance: Palace Theatre, London, 1 July
National Insurance GB: payments began 15 July (for benefits *see* 15 Jan 1913)
Pilot captured in warfare: 11 Sept [8]
Feature film GB: Sept [67]
Theatre loudspeaker: Sept [95]
Brassière (rec) GB: '. . . a necessity for those of generous build' – *Queen*, Sept
Three-colour film: 15 Nov [67]
Pilot killed in warfare: Nov [8]
Ice show: *Flirting at St Moritz*, with Charlotte Oelschlagel, Berlin Admiral Palast, Dec
Aircraft carrier: [13]
Armoured cars used in warfare: Isotta–Fraschini *automitraliatrice* and Fiat *autoblindata* by Italians in Tripoli
Film scriptwriter GB: [69]
Test pilot (professional) GB: Gordon Bell for Short Bros, Eastchurch
Service aircraft with radio GB: [12]
Mobile library (motor): Washington County, Md.
Diesel ship GB: 3,150-ton cargo ship *Eavestone*, built by Sir Raylton Dixon Co, Middlesbrough
MPs salaries GB: £400 p.a.
Zips used in clothing: by Firma Vorweck & Sohn, Wuppertal-Barmen, Ger
Horror film GB: [68]
Concrete road GB: Roberts Lane, Saltney, Cheshire
Contract bridge: [28]
Radio direction-finder GB: Marconi–Bellini–Tolsi apparatus inst RMS *Mauretania*
Gliding club GB: [78]
Film awards: [66]
Third-party motor insurance (compulsory): [108]
Slot-car racing: Lionel Racing Automobiles (electric), USA
Neon sign: [115]
Public opinion poll (nationwide): [141]
Diesel locomotive: [152]
Self-service grocery: [171]
Motor car with all-steel bodywork: mnf by BSA, Birmingham, Eng

1913
Film censorship GB: 1 Jan [66]
'U' film: *Mary of Briarwood Dell* (Barker), British censorship, 1 Jan
'A' film: *A Strong Man's Love* (Clarendon), British censorship, 1 Jan
Maternity benefit GB: 30s; introd 15 Jan
Sickness benefit GB: 10s p.w., introd 15 Jan
Unemployment benefit GB: 7s p.w., introd 15 Jan
Road-safety poster GB: issued by Joint Traffic Committees of London, Jan
Repertory theatre (purpose-built): Birmingham Rep, Eng, opened by Barry Jackson with *Twelfth Night*, 15 Feb
Automatic totalizator: Mar [189]
Film archive: 9 April [66]
Night flight by Service aircraft GB: Larkhill–Upavon return by Lt Cholmondeley, RFC in Maurice Farman, 16 April
News film taken from air: 21 April [65]
Aeroplane fitted with lavatory: 13 May [200]
Four-engined aeroplane: Igor Sikorsky's *Grand*, test flown Petrograd 13 May
Airliner: eight-seater Sikorsky *Grand*, Petrograd, 13 May
Chelsea Flower Show: Royal Horticultural Soc, London, 20–22 May
Fly-past (ceremonial): by RFC aircraft before Sir H.L. Smith-Dorrien, Peckham Down, Eng, 22 May
Woman magistrate GB: 26 May [203]
Woman to parachute from aeroplane: 21 June [123]
Colour talkie: June [67]
Pilot to parachute from aeroplane: Adolphe Pégoud from Blériot 700ft over Buc, Fr, 20 Aug
Loop-the-loop by Lt Peter Nesterov (Rus) in a Nieuport, 27 Aug
Stainless steel: first cast by Harry Brearley, Sheffield, Eng, 20 Aug
Automatic pilot: fitted to Curtiss flying boat; dem Hammondsport N.Y. by Lawrence Sperry, Aug
Upside-down aeroplane flight: by Adolphe Pégoud in a Blériot, Juvisy, Fr, 2 Sept
Bomber aircraft: British & Colonial Aeroplane Co's T.B.8, supplied to Rumanian Army, Oct
Feature film on sexual theme: Universal's *Traffic in Souls*, dir by George Tucker, première Joe Weber's Theater N.Y., 24 Nov
Crossword: 21 Dec [46]
Hydroplane passenger service: two craft built by Lambert Co, Paris, operated on Lake Geneva
Glass-bottomed boat: built by author Charles F. Holder, Santa Catalina Is, Calif.
Postage stamps, Charity Issue: Surcharged in aid of children's health organizations, Swz
Cellophane (mnf) by La Cellophane, Paris
Nitrogen fertilizer (mnf): by Badische Anilin & Soda Fabrik, Ger
Flying boat GB: T. Sopwith and Fred Sigrist's *Bat Boat*, built Kingston upon Thames
Boxer to wear gumshield: Br featherweight champion Ted 'Kid' Lewis
Neon sign GB: [115]
Potato crisps GB: [138]
Refrigerator: [155]
Loudspeaker public address system: [95]
Broadcast time signals: [149]
Diesel-electric railcar: [151]
Portable gramophone: [166]
Complete symphony on discs: [166]

1914
Airline: 1 Jan [15]
Aerial torpedo: released from Farman biplane by Gen. A. Guidoni of It Army, Feb
Cub Scouts: Peter's Cub Pack (Peter Baden-Powell), f Robertsbridge, Sussex, Eng, 2 Feb
Citrated blood transfusion: 27 Mar [25]
Gravure colour supplement: 29 Mar [117]
Feature-length colour film: 9 April [66]
Aircraft carriers in warfare: April [13]
Airmail (reg): 18 May [16]
Charter flight GB: 21 May [33]
Military aeroplane with enclosed cockpit: S.E.4 Scout, test flown Farnborough, Eng, June
Full meal served in aeroplane: aboard Sikorsky airliner *Ilya Mourometz I* during Petrograd–Kiev flight, 29 June
Aerial torpedo GB: 810lb Whitehead torpedo released by Sqn-Cdr A.M. Longmore from Short seaplane, Calshot Naval Station, 28 July
Traffic lights (electric): 5 Aug [191]
Submarines in action (Br): E.6 and E.8, N. Sea, 5 Aug
Motor troop transport in warfare (Br): invasion of Togoland by Gold Coast Regt, 7 Aug
Submarine sunk by Royal Navy: U-15 by HMS *Birmingham*, N. Sea, 9 Aug
Shot fired by Br soldier in World War I: by RSM Alhaji Grunshi, Gold Coast Rgt, at Lomé, Togoland, 12 Aug
Air battle: 14 Aug [8]
Aircraft reconnaissance in warfare (Br): 19 Aug [12]
Field postcard GB: issued 21 Aug
Flag day: 21 Aug [74]
Air battle (Br): 22 Aug [9]
Bomb attack by aeroplane (Br): 24 Aug [9]
Aeroplane shot down (Br): 22 Aug [9]
Armoured cars used in warfare (Br): two RNAS Rolls-Royce tourers armoured with boiler plates, delivered Dunkirk, Fr, 19 Sept
Aircraft radio in warfare: 24 Sept [12]

National flag day: 3 Oct [75]
Ship sunk by RN submarine: Ger cruiser *Hela* by E.9, Heligoland Bight, 6 Oct
Armoured car unit: Canadian Motor Machine-gun Corps, arrived Fr with 20 Autocar Co armoured cars, 16 Oct
RN submarine sunk: E.3, torpedoed by U-27 at mouth of R. Ems, Ger, 17 Oct
Aeroplane to shoot down another: 5 Oct [8]
Air raid (Br): 8 Oct [9]
VC and Bar: Lt Arthur Martin-Leake RAMC, South Africa (8 Feb 1902) and Flanders, 29 Oct–8 Nov
Territorial Army regt in action: London Scottish at Wytschaete, Flanders; 321 casualties, 31 Oct
Aerial propaganda raid by aircraft (Br): Oct [8]
Multi-engined heavy bomber: Sikorsky *Ilya Mourometz*, Imperial Russian Air Corps; bombing trials, Oct
Bomber squadron: 1ère Groupe de Bombardement, Aviation Militaire (Fr), formed with 18 Voisins, 13 Nov
Aeroplane to shoot down another (Br): 22 Nov [9]
Policewomen GB: 27 Nov [136]
Fighter aircraft used in warfare (Br): Vickers E.B.5 Gunbus, in service with RNAS, Dec
RFC/RNAS (later RAF) Roundel: adopted for aircraft identification 11 Dec
Air raid on Britain: 24 Dec [9]
Air battle GB: RNAS Vickers F.B.5 engaged enemy over Erith, Kent, 25 Dec
Aircraft carrier in warfare (Br): 25 Dec [13]
Tear gas: xylyl-bromide prepared by Dr von Tappen, Berlin; dem Kumersdorf, Dec
Radio direction-finder, military: installed Blendecques, Fr by Capt. H. J. Round for locating enemy radio and aircraft, 16 Dec
Miniature camera (35mm): Tourist Multiple (USA) and Simplex Multi-Exposure (USA)
Air freight (regular commercial): Aviatik biplane used for transporting diamonds Karibib–Windhoek, SW Africa
Postage-due stamp (adhesive) GB
Foxtrot: devised by Oscar Duryea on roof garden of New Amsterdam Theater, N.Y. and danced to tune by Harry Fox
Die-cast model cars: Tootsietoys by Dowst Mnf Co, Chicago
Synthetic rubber GB: by Synthetic Products Ltd
Mass X-ray: group radiography unit estab Hôtel-Dieu, Lyons, Fr by Auguste Lumière
Electric platform truck GB: introd by Great Central Rly, Immingham Dock
Aspirin (mnf) GB: [19]
Newspaper film critic: [69]
Complete symphony on discs GB: [166]
Aluminium-foil milk-bottle caps: [98]
Record library: [155]
White lines (road) GB: [191]
Professional woman pilot GB: [206]

1915
Gas attack in warfare: tear gas used by Germans against Russians at Bolimow, Poland, 3 Jan
Air-raid casualties GB: 19 Jan [9]
Passport photographs GB: required from 1 Feb
Night air raid (Br): by two RFC B.E.2Cs on Cambrai Aerodrome, 19 Feb
Flame-throwers used in warfare: by German 3rd Guard Pioneer Rgt against French in Malancourt, 26 Feb
Fighter squadron: MS12 Escadrille de Chasse (Fr), in action 1 April
Newspaper comic strip GB: 5 April [43]
Air force VC: 2nd Lt W.B. Rhodes-Moorhouse, RFC, for aerial attack on Courtnai Junction, 26 April
Labour Cabinet Minister: 25 May [92]
Air raid on London: by LZ 38 Zeppelin; first house hit 16 Alkham Rd, Stoke Newington, 31 May
Gas masks: anti-chlorine mask dev by (Sir) Robert Davis; issued to Br troops, May
Civil Defence unit (uniformed) GB: Architectural Assoc Air Raid Section, June
Electric goods train GB: Shildon–Newport ($18\frac{1}{2}$ miles) electrified by North Eastern Rly; open to goods traffic 1 July
Aerial torpedo attack (Br): by Flt-Cdr C. Edmonds, sank Turkish transport, Sea of Marmara, 12 Aug
Tank: des by William Tritton, completed by Foster & Co, Lincoln, Eng, 8 Sept
Women's Institute GB: Llanfairpwll-gwyngyllgogerychwyrndrobwll andysiliogogogoch WI, Anglesey, Wales, f 11 Sept
Fighter squadron GB: No. 24 Sqn RFC, formed Hounslow, 21 Sept
Transatlantic radio telephone transmission (direct): 21 Oct [151]
Catapult launch from ship: 5 Nov [13]
Aeroplane, all-metal: Junkers J.1, test flown Dessau, Ger, 12 Dec
Brownies: constitution pub *Girl Guides' Gazette*, Dec
Multi-engined heavy bomber GB: Handley Page O/100, test flown 18 Dec
Guided missile: 600lb motor-driven gyroscopically controlled 'aerial torpedo' dev by Sperry and Delco companies; dem Long Is
Psychiatric hospital GB: Maudsley H, London
Profits tax GB: levied under Finance (No. 2) Act 1915
Lipstick retailed in metal cartridge container: mnf USA by Maurice Levy
Rent control GB: introd under Rent and Mortgage Restriction Act
Aspirin tablets: [19]
Jazz orchestration (pub): [88]
Motor scooter: [111]

1916
Rationing GB: sugar, London area only, 1 Jan
Fighter squadron, operational (Br): No. 24 Sqn RFC, St Omer, 7 Feb
Conscription GB: Military Service Act effective 9 Feb
National Savings Certificates: on sale 19 Feb in GB
Aircraft radio telephone: Feb [12]
London bus conductresses: Feb [30]
Airlift: 19,000lb supplies carried to besieged garrison at Kut al-Imara, Iraq by 30 Sqn RAF; 140 flights, 15–29 April
Daylight saving: clocks put forward 1hr, Ger, 1 May
Daylight saving GB: introd 21 May
Woman bank cashier GB: Mrs E. Boorer, joined Morgan Guaranty Trust, London at £1 p.w., 29 May
Open-air public address by loudspeaker: 30 June [95]
Tank in series production: Mark I, delivered to Tank Detachment, Bisley, June
Submarine sunk by depth charges: U-boat UC7, 6 July
Feature film presented by Royal Command: 4 Aug [158]
Tank used in warfare: Mark I D1 commanded by Capt. H.W. Mortimore, Machine-Gun Corps, in action nr Delville Wood, Fr, 5.15am 15 Sept
Birth-control clinic: opened 46 Amboy St, Brooklyn by Margaret Sanger, 16 Oct
Election returns broadcast: US Presidential Election by De Forest Radio Laboratories, Highbridge, N.Y., 7 Nov
Road-safety campaign (sustained) GB: launched by London 'Safety First' Council, 1 Dec
Heavy bomber, operational (Br): Handley Page O/100 delivered 5th Wing RNAS Dunkirk, Nov
Nitrogen fertilizer (mnf) GB: at Billingham, Co Durham
Electric mower: mnf by Ransome's, Ipswich, Eng
Nissen hut: [119]
VD, free treatment GB: under Public Health (Venereal Diseases) Regulations
Guide dogs: [79]
Colour cartoon film: [65]
Sub-machine-gun: 9mm Villar Perosa, issued to Italian Alpini troops
Windscreen wipers: [201]
Women's trouser uniform: [207]

1917
Service flier to make parachute jump GB: 13 Jan [123]
Co-operative advertisement GB: by British Ignition Apparatus Assoc, *The Autocar*, 27 Jan
Feature film presented by Command of the Sovereign: 24 Feb [158]
Technicolor film: Feb [67]
Jazz record: 7 Mar [167]
Guided missile GB: radio-controlled 'AT' weapon des by Prof. A. M. Low; flight trials Upavon, 21 Mar
Servicewomen (official) GB: Women's Army Auxiliary Corps (WAAC), f 28 Mar
Air-sea rescue GB: two seaplane crew rescued after five days in N. Sea by Flt-Cdr L. Gordon and Flt Lt G. Hodgson in flying boat, 29 May
Airmail stamp: May [138]
International airmail: May [16]
Dame (of Order): the Hon. Lady Lawley, created GBE 4 June
Air-raid siren GB: Folkestone, June
Women's athletics meeting (open): org by Femina Sport at Stade de la Porte Brançion, Paris, July
Animal clinic GB: estab Liverpool by RSPCA, 20 Sept
Roll-towel cabinet: pat by George Steiner of American Linen Supply Co, Salt Lake City, 10 Oct
Woman Minister of State: 8 Nov [205]
Communist Govt: 8 Nov [43]
Postmark slogan GB: 'Buy British War Bonds Now', 10 Dec
Rationing (national) GB: 8oz sugar p.w., 31 Dec
Ambulance aircraft: biplane adapted by Maj. Chassaing, Fr Army Medical Service; used for evacuating wounded from Loulin Laffaux
Women taxi-drivers GB: employed at Cardiff, Manchester and Edinburgh
Sex-education film: *Birth Control*, made by the Message Photoplay Corp; banned in N.Y.

1918
WRNS: recruiting began 8 Jan
Parliamentary candidature deposit: introd under Representation of the People Act; £150, 6 Feb
Women's franchise (national) GB: 6 Feb [208]
International airmail (reg): 11 Mar [16]
Pilot to bale out in emergency: 1 April [123]
WRAF: f 1 April; first recruit, Miss Sylvia Hodkinson, 2 April
Meat rationing GB: London and Home Counties, 25 Feb; national, 7 April
Tank *v* tank action: 13 Ger A7Vs engaged three Br Mark IVs at Villers-Bretonneaux, Fr, 24 April
National Savings Stamps: on sale 8 July
Women's athletics, national championship: held at Vienna, Austria, 27 July
Feature-length cartoon film: 15 Aug [65]
Airmail stickers: Aug [17]
Woman Parliamentary candidate GB: Miss Mary Macarthur, adopted by Stourbridge Labour Party, Aug
Women's athletics GB: WRAF relay team competed at RAF Sports, Stamford Bridge, 9 Sept
Propaganda broadcast: incitement to insurrection bdcst to Germany from US Naval Transmitter, New Brunswick, N.J., 20 Oct
Woman elected to Parliament GB: 14 Dec [204]
Women to vote by right in British General Election: 14 Dec [204]
Orienteering: dev by Maj Ernst Killander, Sweden
All-metal aeroplane, production model: Junkers J.10 fighter (Ger)
Judo club GB: Westminster Budokwai, f by Gunji Zoizumu
Flying Squad: [134]
Anti-tank weapon: Ger 13mm T-Gewehr 18
Record library GB: [155]

1919
Nazi Party: f Munich by locksmith Anton Drexler, 5 Jan
Coloured Peer: 25 Jan [42]
International air-freight service: Folkestone, Eng–Ghent, Belg by Air Transport & Travel Ltd, Jan (military supplies)
Airline service (sustained): 6 Feb [15]
Transatlantic radio-telephone transmission GB: 19 Mar [151]
International airline service: 22 Mar [15]
Fascist Party: Fasci di Combattimento, by Benito Mussolini, Milan, 23 Mar
Jazz band GB: 7 April [89]

Jazz record GB: 16 April [167]
Air-freight service (regular civil): Paris–Lille by Cie des Messageries Aériennes, 18 April
Civil airport GB: Hounslow; first take-off by Air Transport & Travel de Havilland D.H.9, 1 May
Airline GB: 10 May [15]
Transatlantic aeroplane flight: Newfoundland–Lisbon by Lt-Cdr Albert C. Read, USN, and five crew in Curtiss NC-4 flying boat, 16–27 May (*see also* 14 June)
Royal pilot GB: May [159]
Transatlantic aeroplane flight, non-stop: Newfoundland–Galway by Capt. John Alcock and Lt Arthur Whitten-Brown in Vickers Vimy (16½hr), 14–15 June
Business charter flight: by Maj. Pilkington of Pilkington Glass, St Helens, Lancs, London–Paris, 15 July
International airline service GB: 25 Aug [15]
Church service broadcast: from Trinity Church, Washington D.C. by US Signal Corps, 25 Aug
Intercontinental airline service: 1 Sept [15]
London–Brussels airline service: Handley Page Transport, 23 Sept
London–Amsterdam airline service: British Aerial Transport, 7 Oct
Civil airliner (purpose-designed) to enter service: British Aerial Transport FK 26, Hendon–Amsterdam, 7 Oct
Airline meals: 11 Oct [15]
Jazz musician (Br): 11 Oct [89]
Executive aircraft (for company personnel): de Havilland D.H.4A operated Hounslow–Cardiff and Hounslow–Paris by S. Instone & Co (shipping), 13 Oct
Airmail (reg) GB: 10 Nov [16]
Aeroplane flight, UK–Australia: Hounslow–Darwin by Ross and Keith Smith in Vickers Vimy, 12 Nov–13 Dec
Woman MP (to take seat) GB: 28 Nov [204]
Airliner lavatory: Dec [200]
Trailer caravans (mnf): Dec [33]
Science-fiction magazine: *The Thrill Book*, ed Harold Hersey, N.Y.
Film critic, national newspaper GB: E.A. Baughan, *Daily News*
Housing subsidies GB: paid to builders and Local Authorities
Film society: Stoll Picture Theatre Club, London
All-steel four-door saloon car: Dodge Sedan (USA)
State Registered Nurses GB
Canned grapefruit: introd by Yankee Products Ltd of Puerto Rico
Photomontage: executed by John Heartfield and George Grosz, Berlin
Motor scooter GB: [111]
Police cars GB: [133]
Department store, self-service food dept: [48]
Filmstrip: [71]
Zip-fastener GB: [209]
Sportswoman to wear shorts: [207]

1920
Broadcasting service (exp) GB: Jan [146]
Aeroplane flight, UK–South Africa: Brooklands–Cape Town by Lt-Col Pierre van Ryneveld (SA) and Flt Lt C.J. Quinton Brand (SA), 4 Feb–20 Mar
Air-force college: RAF College, Cranwell, first intake 5 Feb
Greyhound-racing stadium: opened by O.P. Smith at Emeryville, Calif., 22 Feb
Woman to speak in Parliament GB: 24 Feb [204]
Field-Marshal promoted from ranks GB: 29 Mar [61]
Petrol filling-station GB: Mar [162]
Aircraft fitted with radio direction-finder: Handley Page Transport, Cricklewood, Mar
Orchestral concert broadcast: April [148]
Professional artiste to broadcast GB: 15 June [146]
RAF Air Display: Hendon, 3 July
Public radio-telephone service: 16 July [151]
Liner fitted with radio telephone: SS *Victorian* spoke to England and Newfoundland, 21 July
Women jurors GB: 28 July [203]
Airmail stickers GB: 10 Aug [17]
News broadcast: 20 Aug [147]
Newspaper to publish radio programme schedule: 20 Aug [145]
Gliding meet: Aug [78]
Communist MP GB: Aug [43]
Broadcasting receiver (ready-made): 29 Sept [148]
Broadcasting station (commercially operated): 2 Nov [145]
Referendum GB: 500 regional plebicites held in Scotland on prohibition issue; began on 2 Nov
Electrical recording: 11 Nov [167]
Blues recording: 'Crazy Blues', rec by Mamie Smith for Okey Co, N.Y., Nov
Airline disaster: 14 Dec [16]
Car with hydraulic brakes: Duesenberg Model A, mnf Indianapolis, Dec
Surgeon to operate in white cap and gauze mask GB: William Hunter, Charing Cross Hospital
Ambulance aircraft (Br): converted de Havilland D.H.9 bomber used in Somaliland campaign
State scholarships to university GB: 200 grants p.a. awarded by University Grants Committee
Mounted regts of Br Army to be mechanized: eight TA yeomanry regts became armoured car coys
Route numbers GB: A and B roads classified
Nudist camp: Frei-Sonnenland, Motzener See, Ger
Legalized abortion: [7]
Caravan hire: [33]

1921
Car tax discs (windscreen) GB: 1 Jan
Motor-car log-books GB: introd 1 Jan
NAAFI: f 1 Jan
Station broadcast of church service: from Calvary Episcopal Church, Pittsburgh by KDKA, 2 Jan
Broadcast weather forecast: 3 Jan [200]
Prime Minister to occupy Chequers: Lloyd George, 8 Jan
Women Old Bailey jurors: 11 Jan [203]
Windscreen wipers GB: 13 Jan [201]
Charitable appeal broadcast: by Herbert Hoover for war refugees, KDKA Pittsburgh, 15 Jan
Young Farmers' Club: f Hemyock, Devon 31 Jan
Automatic pilot GB: Aveline Stabilizer fitted to Handley Page Transport, Jan
Trans-USA flight: San Diego, Calif.–Jacksonville, Fla. by Lt William Coney, 21–24 Feb
International women's athletics championship: Fr, GB, Swz, It, Nor competed Monte Carlo, 10 Mar
Birth-control clinic GB: The Mothers' Clinic, Holloway Rd, estab by Dr Marie Stopes, 17 Mar
Women's athletic club GB: London Olympiades, f Mar
Tommy-gun: des by Oscar Payne and Theodore Eickoff, mnf Hartford, Conn.; first deliveries made to IRA agent, 2 April
Broadcast sports commentary: 11 April [149]
Feature film with sound sequence: 1 May [70]
Newspaper distribution by air (regular): London–Paris by Cie des Messageries Aériennes daily from 2 May
British Legion: f 14 May
Newspaper comic strip (adult) GB: J. Miller Watt's 'Pop', *Daily Sketch*, 20 May
Air-to-ground traffic control: air patrols reported by radio to police and AA, Derby Day, Eng, 1 June
Insulin: 27 July [87]
Aerial crop-dusting: 3 Aug [7]
Bathing-beauty contest: 7 Sept [23]
Motorway: 10 Sept [113]
Liberal woman MP: Margaret Wintringham, elected Louth, Lincs, Eng, 23 Sept
Woman barrister GB: 1 Nov [201]
Poppy Day: held by British Legion, 11 Nov
Market-research organization: The Psychological Corporation, f USA by Dr J. McKeen Cattell
Mobile library (motor) GB: Ford van in service with Perthshire & Kinross County Library
Point-to-point, ladies' race: South and West Wilts P-to-P, Motcombe, Dorset, Eng; won by Lady Jean Douglas-Hamilton
Choc-bar: [86]
Blood-donor panel: [26]
Concentration camp: [44]
Children's radio programme: [147]
Refrigerator GB: [156]
Diesel train in service: [152]

1922
Airline uniforms: Instone Air Line, Eng, 1 Jan
Slalom race: org by Sir Arnold Lunn at Mürren, Swz; won by J.A. Joannides, 6 Jan
Diabetic treated with insulin: 11 Jan [87]
Prison concert GB: Amy Evans, Fraser Grange and Band of 1st Life Guards, Pentonville, 19 Feb
Broadcast, studio audience: Ed Wynn's *The Perfect Fool*, WJZ New York, 19 Feb
Symphony concert broadcast: Detroit Symphony Orchestra, WWJ, Feb
Dracula movie: *Nosferatu*, with Max Schreck, released Ger, Mar
Airline steward: 2 April [16]
Airliner collision: 7 April [16]
Woman barrister (Eng): 10 May [201]
Broadcast sports commentary GB: 11 May [149]
Car radio: May [104]
Airliner night flight: by Grands Express, Le Bourget, Fr–Croydon, Eng, 9 June
Newspaper photograph transmitted by radio: portrait of Pope Pius XI sent Munich–N.Y. by Dr Arthur Korn in 40min; pub *New York World*, 11 June
Comedy radio programme GB: 29 July [147]
Radio play: 3 Aug [148]
Postage meter GB: 16 Aug [137]
Radio commercial: 28 Aug [147]
Shakespeare broadcast: tent scene from *Julius Caesar* with Robert Atkins (Cassius) and Basil Gill (Brutus), 2LO, Eng, 2 Sept (*see also* 1923)
Sound-on-film (public presentation): 17 Sept [69]
Market research GB: conducted by the Bureau of Advertising Facts, Sept
Royal broadcast: 7 Oct [157]
Gliding meet GB: 16 Oct [78]
Radio play GB: 17 Oct [148]
Original radio script GB: 20 Oct [147]
Woman chartered surveyor: Miss Irene Martin (sister of Kingsley Martin), Chief Assistant House Property Manager, HM Commissioners for Woods and Forests, elected Professional Associate, Surveyors' Institution, London, 1 Nov
Charitable appeal broadcast GB: by (Sir) Frank Gill for London Hospitals, 2WP London, 8 Nov
BBC programme: 14 Nov [146]
News broadcast GB: 14 Nov [148]
Election results broadcast GB: 15 Nov [146]
Communist MP elected GB: 17 Nov [43]
Aircraft carrier (des): 30 Nov [13]
Car radio GB: Nov [104]
Children's radio programme GB: 5 Dec [147]
Woman barrister to accept brief (Eng): 18 Dec [201]
Woman solicitor GB: Miss Carrie Morrison of London, admitted 18 Dec
Orchestral concert broadcast GB: 23 Dec [148]
Daily news broadcasts GB: BBC, 23 Dec
Play written for radio: 24 Dec [148]
Religious programme broadcast GB: talk by Rev. J.A. Mayo, Rector of Whitechapel, BBC, 24 Dec
Cricket, Eng *v* NZ Test: Eng won; Wellington, NZ, 30 Dec–2 Jan
9.5mm projector: Dec [82]
Ice-cream brickettes GB: [85]
Power rammer: inv by Ben Johnson of Bramley, Leeds, Eng
Tank with revolving turret: Vickers Medium Mark I
Water-skis: ridden by Ralph Samuelson (18) at Lake City, Minn.
Canned baby food: mnf by Harold H. Clapp, Rochester, N.Y.
3-D feature film: [72]
Football pool: [75]
Motor car, supercharged (standard): [105]
Tube train with automatic doors: [196]
Riot gas: Delanoy Gas Bombs adopted by N.Y. Police

1923
Opera broadcast GB: 8 Jan [148]
Service parachutes (compulsory): US Army Air Service 15 Jan

Band concert broadcast GB: Irish Guards, 23 Jan
BBC charitable appeal: by Sir Ian Hay for Winter Distress Fund, 13 Feb
MP to broadcast: 22 Feb [147]
Radio discussion programme GB: 22 Feb [147]
Broadcast short story GB: read by Gilbert Frankau, 9 Mar
Broadcast weather forecast GB: 26 Mar [200]
Piped music GB: by Western Electric at Ideal Home Exhibition, Olympia, Mar
Jazz broadcast (live): Original Dixieland Jazz Band from Copley Plaza Hotel, Boston, WNAC, 14 April
Sound-on-film (paying audience): 15 April [69]
Sports programme broadcast GB: football discussion presented by H.S. King, BBC, 20 April
Shakespeare play in modern dress: *Cymbeline*, presented by Birmingham Rep, 21 April
Wembley Cup Final: Bolton Wanderers beat West Ham United, Eng 2–0, 28 April
Broadcast police appeal: by WGY Schenectady, re kidnapping of Verner Alexanderson, 30 April
London–Berlin airline service: Daimler Airway, 30 April
Record reviews GB: by James Caskett in *The Gramophone* from April
Air troop transport: April [17]
Trans-USA flight, non-stop: Long Island–San Diego by Lts O.G. Kelly and J.A. Macready in Fokker T-2, 27hr, 2–3 May
By-pass GB: Eltham By-pass, opened 17 May
Le Mans 24hr Race: won by A. Lagache and R. Leonard in a Chenard-Walcker, 1,373 miles at average speed 57.2 mph, 26–7 May
Shakespeare play broadcast in full: *Twelfth Night* with Herbert Waring and Cathleen Nesbitt, BBC, 28 May (*see* 1921)
Sound-on-film (public presentation) GB: 14 June [70]
Symphony concert broadcast GB: conducted by Percy Pitt, BBC, 21 June
Flight refuelling: by two de Havilland D.H.4Bs over San Diego, Calif., 27 June
16mm ciné-camera: 5 July [82]
BBC film critic: C.A. Atkinson, wkly bdcst from 11 July
Woman Private Member's Bill: 13 July [204]
Portable radio GB: July [149]
Aircraft carrier (des): July [13]
Ship–shore radio-telephone service: Channel ferry SS *Lorina*, Aug
London–Zurich airline service: Handley Page Transport, 16 Aug
Diesel lorry: Aug [109]
Radio book critic GB: John Strachey, *Books of the Week*, BBC, 3 Sept
Supercharged racing-car to win a Grand Prix: 9 Sept [105]
Radio announcer (full-time) GB: J.S. Dodson, joined BBC 12 Oct
Broadcast oratorio: 'The Hymn of Praise', 5NO Newcastle, 14 Oct
Self-winding watch: pat Swz by John Harwood (GB), 16 Oct (*see* 1928)
Planetarium: opened at Deutsche Museum, Munich, 21 Oct
Welsh-language broadcast: 5WA Cardiff, 8 Nov
Prime Minister to broadcast GB: Stanley Baldwin, Armistice Day speech, 11 Nov
Amateur film-making society: Cambridge Kinema Club, f by Peter Le Neve Foster, Nov
Labour woman MP: 6 Dec [204]
Transatlantic radio broadcast: dance music from Savoy Hotel, London, bdcst by WJZ New York, 29 Dec
Transatlantic radio broadcast GB: Dr Henry Davis spoke from Pittsburgh via 2AZ Manchester, 31 Dec
9·5mm ciné-camera: Dec [82]
Crossword-puzzle book: pub Simon & Schuster, N.Y.
Bible in modern American: Dr Edgar J. Goodspeed's trans of NT (OT 1927)
Bulldozer: blade attachment for crawler tractors introd by LaPlant-Choate Co, USA
Armoured security vans: introd by Brink's Inc, Chicago
Chanel Number 5: created by Ernst Beaux, Paris
Nudist camp GB: estab by English Gymnasophist Soc at Wickford, Essex
Speedway racing: org by John Hoskins at West Maitland, Aus
Electronic hearing aid: Marconi Otophone (16lb)
Windscreen wipers (electric): [201]

1924
Church service broadcast GB: from St Martin-in-the-Fields, 6 Jan
Play written for radio (adult) GB: *Danger* by Richard Hughes (one act), BBC, 15 Jan
Labour Govt GB: 22 Jan [92]
Woman Minister of State GB: 23 Jan [205]
Winter Olympics: Chamonix, Fr, 25 Jan–4 Feb
BBC 'pips': 5 Feb [149]
Gas chamber: 8 Feb [76]
Woman to answer Parliamentary Question: 18 Feb [205]
School Broadcasting Service: inaug by BBC, London, with talk on music by Sir Walford Davies, 4 Mar
Broadcast poetry reading GB: by John Drinkwater, 6 Mar
Language tuition by radio: French, WJZ New York, 21 Mar
Army beret GB: adopted by Royal Tank Corps, Mar
Helicopter forward flight: 14 April [81]
Jockey to wear crash helmet: Prince Henry at Bar Point-to-Point, Northaw, Herts, Eng, 17 April
Pictorial postage stamp GB: 23 April [137]
Aeroplane flight, round-the-world: Seattle–Seattle by Lt L.H. Smith in Douglas *Chicago* and Lt Erik Nelson in Douglas *New Orleans*, 24 April–28 Sept; 57 stops
One-way street for motor traffic GB: Aug [191]
Motor-racing magazine GB: *The Brooklands Gazette* (now *Motor Sport*), Aug
Woman ambassador: 8 Sept [201]
Inter-urban motorway: 21 Sept [113]
Racing-driver to wear crash helmet: Sir Henry Segrave at San Sebastian Grand Prix, Spain, 27 Sept
Election address broadcast GB: 13 Oct [147]
Loudspeaker van used for electioneering GB: by J.L. Tattersall, Lib, Stalybridge and Hyde Div (Cheshire), Oct
Newpaper crossword GB: 2 Nov [47]
Broadcast racing-commentary: by Arnold Treloar from Cheltenham Park via 5CL Adelaide, Aus, 29 Nov
Woman Conservative Minister GB: Duchess of Atholl, Parliamentary Under-Secretary, Board of Education, 6 Nov
Teaching-machine: dem by Sidney L. Pressey of Ohio State Univ, Dec
Leica camera: mnf by Leitz Co, Wetzler, Ger
Caravan hire GB: [33]
International airline timetable: *Guides des Voyages Aériens*, Paris
Ambulance aircraft, civilian: Fairey III seaplane adapted by Real Daylight Balata Estates of British Guiana
Municipal parking lot: Flint, Mich.
Language laboratory: estab Ohio State Univ for Spanish teaching with phonographs
Fascist Party GB: British Fascisti, f by dairy farmer Rotha Lintorn-Orman of Langford, Somerset
Six-wheeled motor bus GB: converted single-deck Lancias introd by Barton Transport, Nottingham
Neon advertising sign GB: [116]
Coloured policewomen: Buffalo Police Dept, N.Y.
Car with hydraulic brakes GB: 13/35hp Triumph
Spiral wire binding (for diaries, etc.): Spirex, introd by Staab Co, Ger
Corn flakes GB: Kellogg's
Sound-on-film story film: [70]
Technicolor sound film: [70]
Refrigerator (mkt) GB: [156]
Colour rollfilm: [129]
Freefall parachute descent: [123]
Public-relations consultant GB: [142]
Paper tissues: Kleenex, mkt USA

1925
Choice of BBC programmes: 8 Jan [146]
Electrical recording (mkt): April [167]
In-flight movie: April [68]
Electrical recording (mkt) GB: HMV's 'O, Katerina', June
Woman member of a stock exchange: 9 July [206]
Veteran car rally: 12 July [197]
Alternative BBC channel: 27 July [146]
Language tuition by radio GB: French by Albert Le Grip, 5SC Glasgow, 23 Sept
London double-decker bus (enclosed): 2 Oct [29]
Woman jockey (open race) GB: 8 Oct [203]
Television transmission: 30 Oct [188]
Play written for radio (full-length) GB: *The White Château* by Reginald Berkeley, BBC, 11 Nov
Broadcast cricket commentary: by L.G. Watt, Australia *v* The Rest, 2FC Sydney, 4 Dec
Motel: 12 Dec [99]
Headlight dipper (double-filament bulb) GB: Osram 'Bilux' lamp
Dodgem cars GB: introd Skegness by Billy Butlin
Electric pylons GB: erected by South Wales Power Co
Railway museum: York
Diesel buses: M.A.N. single-deckers operated by Bavarian Post Office
Stereophonic broadcasts: WPAJ New Haven, Conn.
Crop-dusting service (commercial): [7]
24hr clock GB: adopted by armed forces, airlines and for continental rail services
Helicopter free flight GB: [81]
Full-length talking film: [70]
Public Relations Officer GB: [142]
All-electric gramophone: [167]

1926
Arts cinema: 14 Jan [39]
BBC *This Week's Good Cause* broadcast: 24 Jan
BBC shipping forecast: from Daventry 5XX, 26 Jan
Television (public dem): 27 Jan [188]
Liquid-fuel rocket: fired to 41ft altitude by Robert H. Goddard, Auburn, Mass., 16 Mar
Directional road-surface markings GB: 22 Mar [191]
Pilot to bale out in emergency GB: Pilot Officer Eric Pentland, RAF, 17 June
Pop-up electric toaster: mkt at $13.50 by McGraw Electric Co, Minneapolis June
Greyhound-racing stadium GB: Belle Vue, Manchester, opened by Brig. A.C. Critchley, 24 July
Traffic lights (electric) GB: July [191]
Double-decker bus with pneumatic tyres GB: introd by Wolverhampton Corporation, July
Woman to swim English Channel: Cap Gris Nez, Fr–Deal, Eng by Gertrude Ederle (USA), 14hr 34min, 6 Aug
Grand Prix GB: 7 Aug [110]
Promotional tour by London bus: Daimler bus toured Ger, Austria, Hungary to boost exports and tourist trade, Aug
BBC *The Epilogue:* 26 Sept
Sound-on-film talkie, commercially produced GB: comic song by Billy Merson, Sept
Sound-on-film talkie (paying audience) GB: 4 Oct [70]
Betting tax GB: first levied on bets for Estates Selling Plate, Birmingham, 1 Nov
Sound-on-film talking film drama GB: *The Fair Maid of Perth*, starring Louise Maurel, director Miles Mander, Dec
Pedestrian crossing GB: Dec [124]
Containers designed for motor transport: introd by Hays Wharf Cartage, West Smithfield, London
Model agency GB: Cave's Mannequin Bureau, Gt Turnstile, London
Power steering: prototype unit fitted to Pierce Arrow by Francis Davis, Waltham, Mass.
Artificial ski slope: installed by June Boland at London Ski School
C.O.D. service (inland) GB
'Invisible eye' (camera to detect thieves in action): inv by J.E. Seebold, Chicago
Tubular steel chair (cantilevered): des by Mies van der Rohe, mnf by Thonet, Ger
Aqualung: des by Commander Yves Le Prieur, France
Professional lawn tennis players: Suzanne Lenglen, Vincent Richards Mary K. Browne, Howard Kinsey
Car with headlight dippers (standard) GB: Morris Oxford
Microgroove LP: [95]
GB plates: [113]

Motor cars with safety-glass windscreens (standard fitment): Stutz and Rickenbacker cars, USA

1927

Marshal of the Royal Air Force: Lord Trenchard, promoted 1 Jan
Intercontinental airline service GB: London–Cairo, Imperial Airways, 7 Jan
Transatlantic telephone service: London–N.Y., £15 for 3min, 7 Jan
Broadcast rugby commentary GB: 15 Jan [149]
Broadcast football commentary: by Capt. H.B.T. Wakelam, Arsenal *v* Sheffield United, Highbury, London, 22 Jan
Ship's radio, short wave: inst SS *Carpathia* by Siemens, Jan
Space-flight journal: *Die Rakete*, pub by Society for Space Travel, Breslau, Jan
External broadcasting service: 11 Mar [147]
Mille Miglia: won by Ferdinando Minoia and Guiseppe Morandi in an O.M., 26–7 Mar
Fighter aircraft, all-metal GB: Armstrong Whitworth Siskin IIIA; entered service with 41 Sqn RAF, Mar
Oxford *v* Cambridge Boat Race broadcast: by O.G. Nickalls and J.C. Squire, BBC, 2 April
Television performer: 7 April [182]
Airliner, cooked meals aboard GB: 1 May [16]
Speedway racing GB: Camberley Heath, 8 May
Broadcast cricket commentary GB: by Rev. F.H. Gillingham, Essex *v* NZ, Leyton, BBC, 14 May
Solo transatlantic aeroplane flight: Long Is.–Paris by Charles Lindbergh in Ryan monoplane *Spirit of St Louis* (33½hr) 20–21 May (*see below* 4 June)
Broadcast horse-race commentary GB: The Derby, by Meyrick Good, BBC, 1 June
London double-decker bus with pneumatic tyres: introd 4 June
Transatlantic aeroplane passenger: Charles Levine, piloted by Clarence Chamberlain N.Y.–Ger, 4 June
Lawn tennis broadcast commentary GB: by Capt. H.B.T. Wakelam from Wimbledon, BBC 29 June
Disc Jockey GB: 7 July [50]
Promenade Concert broadcast: from Queen's Hall, 13 Aug
Channel swim by Englishwoman: London typist Mercedes Gleitze, Cap Gris Nez–South Foreland, 15hr 15min, 7 Oct
Veteran car rally GB: 13 Oct [197]
Sound newsreel: 27 Oct [68]
First- and second-class airline fares: Oct [16]
Traffic lights (automatic) GB: 5 Nov [192]
Paratroops: Italian Army; first practice drop over Cinisello, 6 Nov
External broadcasting service GB: 11 Nov [147]
Railway milk tanker (glass-lined) GB: United Dairies wagons, Wootton Bassett/Calveley–London, 1 Dec
Wall-mounted can-opener: mkt by Central States Mfg Co, St Louis, Mo.
Athletics, starting-blocks: [20]
Electric blanket GB: mkt by Thermega Ltd, London
Spiral wire binding GB: introd by James Burn & Co, bookbinders, London
All-electric Jukebox: [90]
Double-decker bus with enclosed stairs: London General Omnibus Co LS1 and LS2, Hammersmith–Liverpool St
Diesel road-roller: TH/TW model mnf by Barford & Perkins, Peterborough, Eng
Car radio (mnf): [105]
Electronic TV system: [188]
Diesel lorry GB: [109]
Frogman flippers: des by Louis de Corlieu, Fr
Industrial film (sound): made for Servel Refrigerator Co by De Forest Phonofilm Corp, N.Y.

1928

Adhesive tape, transparent: Scotch Tape mkt by 3M Co, St Paul, Minn., 31 Jan
Totalizator GB: Jan [190]
Transatlantic TV transmission: 9 Feb [179]
Airliner with kitchen: Short *Calcutta* flying boat, launched Rochester, 13 Feb
Graduate in business studies GB: William Wallace of York, granted Master of Commerce degree by London Univ, Feb
Television magazine: *Television*, London, Mar
East–west transatlantic aeroplane flight: Dublin–Labrador by Cmdt James Fitzmaurice, Irish Free State Air Service, and Capt. Herman Köhl in Junkers Bremen, 12–13 April
Budget broadcast: by Rt Hon. Winston Churchill, 25 April
Automatic-change gramophone: April [167]
Television service: 11 May [185]
Flying Doctor: Dr K.H. Vincent Welsh using de Havilland D.H.50 *Victory*; service inaug by Australian Inland Mission, Cloncurry, Queensland, 15 May
Aeroplane flight, trans-Pacific: Oakland, Calif.–Brisbane by Charles Kingsford-Smith in Fokker F.VIIb-3m *Southern Cross*, 31 May–9 June
Woman transatlantic aeroplane passenger: Amelia Earheart, piloted by Wilmar Stulz from Newfoundland to Wales, 17–18 June
Outdoor scene televised GB: 18 June [181]
Cricket Eng *v* W. Indies Test Match: Eng won; Lord's, 23–26 June
Television receiver (mnf): June [183]
Colour TV transmission: 3 July [188]
All-talking feature film: 6 July [70]
16mm colour film: July [82]
Television, daily schedule: inaug by WRNY from Hotel Roosevelt, N.Y., 14 Aug
News event televised: 22 Aug [180]
Television play: 11 Sept [182]
Robot GB: built by Capt. Rickards and A.H. Reffell at Gomshall, Surrey; opened Model Engineering Exhibition, London, 15 Sept
Cartoon talkie: 19 Sept [65]
Television performer GB: 22 Sept [182]
Penicillin: Sept [124]
Hot-air hand-drying apparatus: Elektra Händetrockner, exhib Leipzig, Sept
Iron lung: 12 Oct [88]
16mm colour film GB: 18 Oct [83]
Twins born by Caesarian section GB: delivered to 70lb hunchback by Dr M.R. Soni, Nell Lane Hospital, Manchester, 26 Nov
TV documentary: Nov [179]
Television service GB: 5 Dec [185]
TV play GB: 15 Dec [182]
Western talkie: 25 Dec [72]
Birth control, rhythm method: devised by Dr Harmann Knaus, Berlin; accorded Vatican approval Dec 1930
Self-winding watch (mnf): by Harwood Self-Winding Watch Co, London (*see* 1923)
Cloverleaf intersection: State Highway Routes 4 and 25, Woodbridge, N.J.
Motor-car fog-lamp GB: mnf by Desmo of Birmingham
Cavalry regts mechanized GB: 11th Hussars and 12th Lancers
Sports-coaching film: made by All-England Women's Hockey Assoc
Channel car ferry: The *Artificer*, Townsend Ferries
Lie detector GB: Scotland Yard
Diesel bus GB: Blackstone-engined Lancia run exp by Barton Transport, Nottingham
Football, £10,000 transfer fee; paid by Arsenal, for David Jack (£11,500)
Football, numbering of players: introd by Herbert Chapman, manager of Arsenal
Teletypesetter: installed by *Rochester Times Union*, Rochester, N.Y.
'I speak your weight' machine: inv by Joseph Tripodi; operated Genoa, Italy
PABX telephone exchange GB: Liverpool St Station
Water-ski jump: 25ft by Dick Pope Sr at Miami Beach, Fla.
Diesel locomotive GB: [152]
Motor car with safety-glass windscreen (standard fitment) GB: Hillman
Television recording: [184]

1929

Clinical use of penicillin: 9 Jan [124]
Totalisator (horse-racing) GB: 25 April [190]
Book Society Choice: Helen Beauclerk's *The Love of a Foolish Angel*, April
Football International: English defeat by foreign team: 4–3 to Spain Madrid, 15 May
Academy Awards: 16 May [66]
Full-length colour talkie: 28 May [70]
Labour Govt elected GB: 30 May [92]
Woman Cabinet Minister GB: 7 June [205]
Woman Privy Councillor: Miss Margaret Bondfield, 8 June
Full-length talkie GB: 21 June [70]
Racecourse totalizator: 2 July [190]
Film shown on TV: 19 Aug [71]
Television producer: 30 Sept [182]
Daily TV service GB: 30 Sept [185]
MP to appear on television: Maj. A.G. Church, Wandsworth (Lab), Baird TV, 30 Sept
Wide-screen feature film: Sept [72]
Pony Club: movement f GB 1 Nov
News theatre: 2 Nov [39]
All-talking feature film GB: 16 Dec [70]
Keep-fit classes for housewives GB: inst Sunderland by Miss Norah Reed
Wall of Death GB: Kursaal, Southend
Milk tanker (glass-lined) GB: Express Dairies, AEC Mammoth
Yo-yo: mkt by Louis Marx, N.Y.
TV ballet performance: [178]
Milk cartons GB: introd by Express Dairy, Finchley
Police call-boxes GB: erected Barnes, Kew and Richmond
Station wagon (private car design): Ford Model A
Steel-shafted golf clubs GB: mnf by Spalding's of Putney
'I speak your weight' machine GB: Salter's Auto-Phonograph; Ellaw's Weigh-o-Phone
Car with synchromesh gearbox: GM's Cadillac and La Salle models
Davis Escape Apparatus: des by (Sir) Robert Davis, mnf by Siebe Gorman Ltd (*see* 1931)
Water-ski flight: by Dick Pope Sr on kite des by Harrison Fisher, Winter Haven, Fla.
Travel association GB: Travel Assoc of GB & Ireland
Tape-recorder: [96]
Aluminium-foil milk-bottle caps GB: [98]
Sound newsreel GB: [68]
Military radio telephone (general issue) GB: [150]
Colour rollfilm GB: [129]
Radiogram GB: [167]
Television telephone: [187]
Foam rubber: [160]

1930

Broadcast Stock Exchange prices GB: BBC, 6 Jan
Variable-geometry aircraft: SJ biplane, flown by Hans Körner, Breslau, Ger, Jan
Frozen food: 6 Mar [75]
Glider pilot's licence GB: 30 Mar [131]
Newspaper, television programmes: pub by *Daily Express* from 11 April
Television interview: 29 April [180]
Television receiver (mf) GB: April [183]
Woman glider pilot GB: April [78]
Air hostess: 15 May [14]
Birth-control clinic, State supported: estab at Bangalore and Mysore, India, by order of Mysore Govt d 11 June
BBC television play: 14 July [182]
Green Line bus: Guildford–Charing Cross, 17 July
Football, World Cup: Uruguay beat Argentina 4–2 in final, Montevideo, 30 July
Flash bulb: dev by Johannes Ostermeier (Ger); mkt by GEC, Schenectady, N.Y., 1 Aug
Diesel bus in regular service GB: Benz-engined Karrier introd by Sheffield Corporation 9 Sept
International bridge match: 15 Sept [28]
Television engineering course: 10wk course offered by Coyne Electrical School, Chicago, Sept
BBC Symphony Orchestra broadcast: under Sir Adrian Boult, Queen's Hall, 22 Oct
Advertising by television: 5 Nov [178]
Irish Sweep: held on Manchester November Handicap; first prize (£204,764) to Belfast civil servant Frank Ward, 22 Nov
Veteran car club: 23 Nov [198]
Youth Hostel GB: Pennant Hall,

Conway Valley, Wales, Dec
16mm sound projector: [83]
Channel car-ferry (purpose-built): *The Autocarrier*, Southern Railway, Eng
Riot-control water cannon: introd by Berlin Police
Mobile police patrol GB: 12hp Bean under Sgt White, Hounslow Police
State subsidy for the arts GB: £17,500 p.a. to Covent Garden
News theatre GB: [39]
Film made for TV: [71]
Police motor-cycle patrol GB: [135]
Supermarket: [172]
Tote daily double: [190]
Diesel tractor: [190]
Parking restrictions GB: [191]

1931
Third-party motor insurance (compulsory) GB: 1 Jan [108]
Papal broadcast: by Pius XI, Vatican Radio, 12 Feb
Closed-circuit TV (public dem): Western TV Co system used to transmit share prices, Chicago Stock Exchange, 26 Jan
Sport telecast: 17 Feb [187]
Two-volume London telephone directory: Feb
TV films (regular): 1 Mar [71]
TV film (programme service) GB: 6 Mar [71]
Electric razor (manufactured): Schick Inc, Stamford, Conn., 18 Mar
Amphibious car GB: Riley 13hp Floatercar, tested R. Severn, Mar
Feature film shown on TV: 6 April [71]
Highway Code: issued by Ministry of Transport, 14 April
Unit Trust GB: M & G General Trust Fund; units on sale 1 May
TV outside broadcast (scheduled): 8 May [181]
Open zoo GB: Whipsnade, opened 23 May
Cigarettes, cellophane-wrapped GB: May [38]
Railway train, air-conditioned throughout: *The Columbian*, N.Y.–Washington, 24 May
Sport telecast GB: 3 June [187]
Davis Escape Apparatus used in emergency: six men escaped from HM Submarine *Poseidon*, sunk off Wei-hai-Wei, China, 9 June
Cross-Channel glider flight: 19 June [78]
TV 'chat show': 21 June [180]
TV artiste under exclusive contract: 21 July [182]
Television, wrestling: from Baird Long Acre Studio, London, 29 July
Guide dogs GB: July [79]
Ice vending-machine: Los Angeles, inst by Central Ice Co, July; 25lb for 15c
Boxing-match televised: Mickey Walker *v* Benny Leonard at CBS Studio, N.Y.; W2XAB, 25 Aug
33⅓ rpm LP: 17 Sept [95]
Diesel caterpillar tractor: mnf by Caterpillar Tractor Co, Peoria, Ill., Oct
Mass X-ray of schoolchildren: commenced at Public Day School No 90, Richmond Hill, Long Island, 30 Nov
Diesel-electric railcar GB: Dec [151]
Underground car park GB: opened beneath Carlisle Parade by Hastings Council, Dec
Concrete lamp-standards GB: Liverpool
Exposure meter (photo-electric): Electrophot, des by J. Thomas Rhamstine of Detroit
Farming subsidies (direct) GB: under Wheat Act
Paratroop assault: by Soviet troops against Basmachi insurgents in Central Asia
Diesel bus production model GB: mnf by Crossley Motors, Stockport
Liner with stabilizers: *Conte di Savoia* (It), built GB
Amateur film-making award GB: [83]
16mm sound projector GB: [83]
Blood bank: [26]
Skydiving: [123]
Foam-rubber products: [160]

1932
TV sets in hotel rooms: Feb [84]
Educational TV programme: 5 Feb [179]
Newspaper colour photographs GB: *The Times Weekly Edition,* 17 Mar
Business reply-paid envelopes GB: introd by GPO, 18 April
London–Cape Town airline service: Imperial Airways, 27 April (11 days)
Electric milk-floats GB: built by T.H. Lewis Ltd, Camden Town, for Express Dairy; operational Kenton and Highgate depots, April
Television telephone GB: 19 May [187]
Woman to fly Atlantic solo: Amelia Earheart (USA), Newfoundland–Londonderry, 21 May
Air charter holiday: May [12]
Railway buffet-car GB: 2 June [152]
Cricket, Eng *v* India Test Match: Eng won; Lord's, 25–28 June
Radio Vox Pop interviews: 27 June [149]
Educational cruise: 14 days Baltic and Norway for £5, org by Scottish Secondary Schools Travel Trust; 1,000 boys sailed SS *Neuralia*, 25 July
Film festival: 6 Aug [67]
Olympic village: built for Xth Olympiad, Los Angeles, 30 July–14 Aug
Creaseproof fabric: 9 Aug [46]
BBC Television producer: 22 Aug [182]
BBC Television service: 22 Aug [186]
8mm ciné-camera: Aug [82]
Documentary TV series: 16 Sept [179]
Iron lung GB: 6 Oct [88]
Television, Party Political Broadcast: by Democratic Party, CBS, New York, 11 Oct
Gang Show: *The Gang's All Here*, presented by Ralph Reader, Scala Theatre, London, 30 Oct
Television critic: 'Spectator', *Television*, London, Oct
Petrol pump with automatic price indicator: 1 Nov [126]
Theatre-in-the-Round: four short plays presented by Univ of Washington School of Drama at Edmond Meany Hotel, Seattle, 4 Nov
International TV programme transmission: 8 Nov [179]
Election returns televised: Roosevelt/Hoover Presidential Election, CBS, New York, 8 Nov
Member of Royal Family to attend Rugby League match: Prince of Wales, boys' match in Central Park, Wigan, 23 Nov
TV narrative series: 12 Dec [182]
Floodlit Rugby League match: Leeds *v* Wigan, White City Stadium, 14 Dec
Anti-bacterial chemotherapeutic drug: Prontosil, disc by Prof. Gerhard Domagk of IG Farben, Elberfeld, 20 Dec
Television pantomime: *Dick Whittington*, BBC, 26 Dec
Agricultural marketing board GB: Hops Marketing Board
Mobile: exhib by Alexander Calder (USA) at Galerie Vignon, Paris
Synthetic sponge: mnf by Novacel, France
Diesel lifeboat: Yarmouth, IW
Yo-yo GB: introd from USA
Car with synchromesh gearbox GB: Vauxhall Cadet
Book tokens: [26]
Three-colour technicolor film: [67]
Ski lift: Parsenn ski run, Swz
Car radio (mkt) GB: [105]
Police radio patrol cars GB: [133]
Pneumatic tractor tyres: [190]
School milk (free) GB: introd by Bradford Education Committee
Vehicle-actuated traffic lights GB: [192]

1933
Main-line electrification GB: [152]
Battledress gaiters GB: worn experimentally by 2nd Battn the Queen's Royal Regt, Aldershot, 9 Jan
Educational TV station: 25 Jan [179]
Telephone speaking clock: 14 Feb [177]
Polythene: Mar [136]
Television, high-definition GB: dem by Baird Co at Long Acre Studios; boxing-match transmitted on 120 lines (electronic reception). 4 June
Drive-in cinema: 9 June [39]
Aerogramme: 15 July [9]
Aeroplane flight, round-the-world solo: by Wiley Post in Lockheed Vega *Winnie Mae*, 15–22 July; N.Y.–N.Y., 10 stops
Woman radio announcer GB: Sheila Borrett, BBC, 27 July
Woman to play tennis in shorts GB: July [207]
TV programme interview GB: 1 Aug [180]
Boxing-match televised GB: Freddie Baxter *v* Bill Lewis at Broadcasting House, BBC, 22 Aug
Broadcast police appeal GB: via BBC for Stanley Hobday, wanted for murder, 28 Aug
Police pocket radio sets: 3½lb one-valve Plessey sets issued to 30 Brighton (Eng) PCs, 14 Sept
Television engineering course GB: inaug under J.J. Denton at Borough Polytechnic, 28 Sept
Television, feature film transmission GB: *I Was a Spy*, closed circuit at Baird Studios, Nov
London–Singapore airline service: Imperial Airways and Indian Trans-Continental Airways, 9 Dec
Butterfly stroke: first used in competition by Henry Myers of N.Y. Dragon Club, Brooklyn, Dec
Electron microscope: built by M. Knoll and E. Ruska, Berlin
Airliner with retractable undercarriage: American Airlines Boeing 247
Airliner with retractable undercarriage GB: Portsmouth, Southsea & IoW Aviation Co AS5 Courier monoplane
Remand Homes: Stamford House (boys) and Cumberlow Lodge (girls), estab by LCC
School crossing patrol GB: Oxford
Perspex (mnf): Röhm & Haas GmbH, Ger
Lexicon (card game): inv by David Whitelaw: mkt by Waddington's, Leeds, Eng
Soapless shampoo: Proctor & Gamble's Drene, USA
Comic book: [42]
Military walkie-talkie: [150]
Parachuting club: [123]

1934
Transatlantic airmail (reg): 3 Feb [17]
Radar: 20 Mar [142]
Reflecting road studs: Mar [155]
Launderette: 18 April [92]
Catseyes: April [155]
Police College GB: Hendon, opened 10 May
Quins to survive infancy: Emilie, Yvonne, Cecile, Marie and Annette Dionne, b Callender, Ont., 28 May
TV ballet (complete): 26 June [178]
Television opera: 6 July [181]
Talking book for the blind: anthology of Americana issued on eight 33⅓rpm LPs by American Foundation for the Blind, N.Y., July
Belisha beacon: Sept [124]
Motor cars with automatic overdrive: Chrysler and De Soto (USA)
Die-cast model cars GB: Dinky Toys, mnf by Meccano Ltd
Teletypesetter GB: inst London offices of the *Scotsman*
16mm three-colour film: Dufaycolor mkt by Ilford, GB
Cheap-rate telephone calls GB: Sunday, and after 6pm
Monopoly (game): [98]
Television announcer: [177]
Mobile TV unit: [180]
Adhesive tape (transparent) GB: Durex, mnf by Durex Abrasives Ltd, Birmingham

1935
Perspex GB: vases, candlesticks, etc, exhib Burlington House, 4 Jan
Water-ski club: Juan-les-Pins Water-Skiing Club, f 8 Jan
Legalized abortion on medico-social grounds: 28 Jan [7]
Electronic TV receiver (mnf): Jan [184]
Radar GB: 26 Feb [142]
Driving test GB: 13 Mar [51]
High-definition TV service: 22 Mar [186]
Indoor athletics meeting GB: 6 April [20]
Airline service, UK–Australia: by Imperial Airways and Qantas, 13 April. Fare £195; 12½ days to Brisbane
Theatre-in-the-Round theatre: Penthouse Theatre, Seattle, opened with *The Dover Road*, 18 April
Alcoholics Anonymous: f by 'Bill W' (William Wilson), Akron, Ohio, 12 May
'L' plates GB: compulsory 1 June
Parking meter: 16 July [124]
Greetings telegram GB: 24 July [175]
Penguin book: 30 July [123]
Public opinion poll (sampling method): July [141]
Ship fitted with radar: Sept [143]
Wearable hearing aid (elec): Oct [80]
Quads (to survive infancy) GB: Ann, Ernest, Paul and Michael Miles, b St

Neots, Hunts, 28 Nov
Newspaper to microfilm back issues: *New York Times* 1914–27, Nov
Talking book for the blind GB: *The Story of San Michele* and four other titles issued by RNIB, Nov
Driving simulator: at Central Motor Institute, Hampstead, London
Pedestrian guard-rails GB: Britannia Crossing, Camden Town
Waste-disposal sink unit: mkt by GEC, Bridgeport, Conn.
T-bar ski tows: Davos and Zürs
Tape-recorder (plastic tape): [96]
Stereophonic sound film: [71]
Technicolor feature (three-colour): [67]
Member of royal family to appear on TV: [158]
Public library record section GB: [155]
Foam-rubber mattresses: [160]
Security guards GB: [162]
Trouser zip: [209]
Motor car with windscreen washers (standard): Triumph

1936
Pop-music chart: 4 Jan [137]
British monarch to fly in aeroplane: Edward VIII, Sandringham–London, 20 Jan
Public TV-telephone service: 1 Mar [187]
London–Hong Kong airline service: Imperial Airways, 14 Mar
Cross/Don't Cross pedestrian signals GB: St Helier Ave, Morden, April
Skydiving GB: by Clem Sohn (USA), Hanworth, 2 May
Open prison GB: New Hall, nr Wakefield opened 27 May
Book club: May [26]
GPO speaking clock: 24 July [177]
High-definition TV outside broadcast: 1 Aug [181]
Olympic flame: carried from Greece to Berlin for opening of XIth Olympiad, 1 Aug
BBC high-definition TV programme: 26 Aug [186]
Television announcer GB: 26 Aug [177]
Football match televised: film of Arsenal *v* Everton match at Highbury shown by BBC same evening, 29 Aug
News filmed for TV: 31 Aug [180]
Woman TV announcer GB: 31 Aug [177]
High-definition TV receivers (mnf): Aug [184]
Aerial invasion: Aug [17]
High-definition TV outside broadcast GB: 5 Sept [181]
Coloured newspaper ad GB: 7 Oct [117]
Mobile post office GB: Marden Agricultural Show, Kent, 7 Oct
Radio request programme: 25 Oct [149]
High-definition TV service GB: 2 Nov [186]
High-definition TV play: Jean Clyde and Walter Roy in *Marigold,* BBC, 6 Nov
Football match televised live: Germany *v* Italy, Berlin, 15 Nov
Women's TV programme (regular): *Women's Interests*, BBC, 20 Nov
TV gardening programme: *In Your Garden* with Mr Middleton, BBC, 21 Nov
Fluorescent lighting: 23 Nov [75]
Giant panda in captivity: Sub-Lin, arr N.Y. from Szechuan, China, Dec
Electron microscope GB: Metropolitan-Vickers EMI
Water-skis GB: ridden by Leeds garage-owner Geoffrey Appleyard at Scarborough, Yorks
Trampoline: built by George Nissen, Cedar Rapids, Iowa
8mm colour film: Kodachrome [83]
Ship fitted with radar GB: [143]
Hydraulic lift tractor: des by Harry Ferguson; mnf by David Brown Tractors of Huddersfield, Eng

1937
Gas-masks (civilian) GB: production inaug at Govt Factory, Blackburn, 12 Jan
Public opinion poll GB: 14 Jan [141]
Play written for TV: 19 Jan [182]
Television cook: 21 Jan [178]
TV sports commentary GB: 4 Feb [187]
Nylon: 16 Feb [119]
Hypermarket: H.C. Bohack Co, Brooklyn, N.Y., Mar
Airborne radar: Mar [143]
TV sports series: *Sporting Magazine* (mthly), BBC, 1 May
Mobile TV unit GB: 2 May [180]
Monarch to appear on TV: 12 May [158]
Vox Pop interviews broadcast GB: 12 May [149]
Air-defence radar station: May [142]
Technicolor feature (three-colour): May [67]
Frozen food GB: May [76]
Military walkie-talkie GB: 21 June [150]
Lawn tennis televised: Wimbledon by BBC, 21 June
Telephone, '999' emergency service: 1 July
Prisoners' wages GB: 3d p.w. all gaols from 12 Sept
Sellotape: mkt GB 13 Dec
Feature-length colour cartoon talkie: 21 Dec [66]
Aeroplane with hydraulic retractable undercarriage GB: Armstrong Whitworth Ensign
Five-day working week GB: introd by Marconi Co, Chelmsford, and Alfred Bird Co, Birmingham
Station wagon GB: 10hp Commer
Prime Minister to receive salary GB: Neville Chamberlain; £10,000 p.a.
Roll-towel cabinets GB: Steiner cabinets introd by Advance Laundry and Initial Towel Services
Tape-recorder (plastic tape) GB: [96]
Escort agency: [60]
Police motor cycles with radio telephones: [135]

1938
Foreign-language broadcasting (external) GB: 3 Jan [147]
Television circus: 4 Jan [178]
Radio comedy series GB: 5 Jan [147]
Broadcast serial GB: *The Count of Monte Cristo*, adapted for radio in 12 episodes by Patrick Riddell, 3 Jan–21 Mar
High-definition colour TV: 4 Feb [188]
Nylon product (mnf): 24 Feb [119]
Public air-raid shelter (purpose built) GB: by Westminster City Council, beneath Caxton Hall, Feb
Athletics meeting televised GB: Oxford & Cambridge Inter-Varsity Sports, from White City by BBC, 12 Mar
Rugby match televised: Eng *v* Scot (Calcutta Cup), Twickenham, 19 Mar
Fluorescent lamps (mnf): 1 April [75]
Football match televised live GB: Wembley Cup Final, BBC, 30 April
TV panel game: 31 May [181]
Children's Zoo GB: Regent's Park, opened by Robert and Edward Kennedy, 2 June
Superman comic: June [42]
Television serial: 12 July [185]
Air cadets GB: Leicester Squadron of Air Defence Cadet Corps, 17 July
Marriage guidance counsellors GB: service estab by Br Social Hygiene Council, July
Golf tournament televised: Roehampton, BBC, 15 July
Cricket match televised: Second Test *v* Australians, Lord's, BBC, 24 July (commentator: H.B.T. Wakelam)
Feature film shown on TV GB: 14 Aug [72]
Promenade Concert televised: Queen's Hall, BBC, 22 Aug
Prime Minister to be televised: Neville Chamberlain at Heston Aerodrome, BBC, 16 Sept
TV current affairs series: 21 Sept [178]
Gas-masks issued to civilians GB: distribution began 26 Sept
Nylon toothbrush: Sept [189]
Radio drama, continuous serial GB: *The English Family Robinson*, with Ralph Truman and Megs Jenkins, BBC, wkly from 7 Oct
Motor-racing televised: Imperial Trophy Heats, Crystal Palace, BBC, 8 Oct
Xerox: first successful copy made by Chester F. Carlson of Pittsford, N.Y., 22 Oct (*see* 1950)
Airliner with pressurized passenger Cabin: Boeing 307 Stratoliner (USA), first flight 31 Dec
Breath tests for drunken drivers: Dr R.N. Harger's Drunkometer officially introd by Indianapolis Police Dept, 31 Dec
Coelacanth caught alive: off East London, South Africa, Dec
Plastic toy soldiers: US infantryman mkt by Beton Toys of Carlstadt, N.J.
LSD: synthesized at Sandoz Labs, Swz
Bren gun: originally ZB 26, dev at Brno, Czechoslovakia
Instant coffee: [41]

1939
Nuclear fission: discovery pub by Prof. Otto Hahn of the Chemical Institute, Berlin in *Naturwissenschaften*, 6 Jan
Television, farming programme: *This Month on the Farm*, presented by A.G. Street, BBC, 1 Feb
Anderson shelters: erected by residents of Tober St and Carlsbad St, Islington, London, 25 Feb
Oxford *v* Cambridge Boat Race televised: BBC, 1 April
Battledress blouse and gaiters GB: general service issue from 20 April
President of USA televised: F.D. Roosevelt opening N.Y. World's Fair, WNBT, 30 April
Radio request programme GB: 19 May [149]
N Atlantic airmail (reg): 20 May [17]
Br monarch to visit USA: 7 June [98]
National Serviceman, 10000001: Pte Rupert Alexander, Middlesex Regt, Eng, 26 June
N. Atlantic airline service: 27 June [16]
Air-sea-rescue team: Luftwaffe Seenotstaffel 1, f 1 July
N. Atlantic airmail GB: 4 Aug [17]
Jet aircraft: 24 Aug [10]
Airborne interception radar: Aug [143]
Polythene (mnf): 1 Sept [136]
Citizens' advice bureaux GB: 200 opened 3 Sept
American football televised: Fordham Univ *v* Waynesburg College at Randall's Island, N.Y. W2XBS, 30 Sept
Electric loud hailers GB: used by Metropolitan Police for directing Evacuation, Sept
Nylon yarn: 15 Dec [119]
Pre-cooked frozen food: [76]
DDT used as insecticide: by Dr R. Wiesmann to combat Colorado beetle outbreak in Swz
Batman comic: [42]
Flyover road junctions GB: Winchester By-pass carried over Alton, Alresford and A33 roads

1940
Ice hockey televised: N.Y. Rangers *v* Montreal Canadians, Madison Sq Gdn, W2XBS, 25 Feb
Basketball match televised: Fordham Univ *v* Univ of Pittsburgh, Madison Sq Gdn, W2XBS, 28 Feb
Church service televised: Protestant and RC Easter services from NBC studios, N.Y., via W2XBS, 24 Mar
Paratroop landing in warfare: Ger 1st Parachute Regt, invasion of Denmark and Norway, 9 April
Nylon stockings: 15 May [119]
Paratroopers GB: No. 2 Commando began training at Ringway Airport, Manchester, 8 July
Airliner with pressurized passenger cabin in service: Transcontinental Airways, Boeing 307 Stratoliner, N.Y.–Burbank, Calif., 8 July
Smoke jumpers: Earl Cooley and Rufus Robinson parachuted to fight forest fire in Winthrop, Washington, 12 July
Pure penicillin: 24 Aug [124]
Women employed by London Underground: 17 Sept [196]
George Cross: inst 23 Sept
Jeep: Sept [89]
Power steering GB: Bendix units from USA fitted to British Army Chevrolet armoured cars
Supplementary benefits GB: introd under Old Age and Widows' Pensions Act

1941
Nylon GB: 23 Jan [119]
Paratroop assault (Br): by 11th SAS Battn on Tragino Aqueduct, Italy, 10 Feb
Patient treated with pure penicillin: 12 Feb [124]
Air-sea-rescue team GB: formed by RAF, Feb
Aircraft ejection seat: 2 April [9]
Daily drama serial broadcast (Br): *Front-Line Family*, BBC Overseas Service, 28 April (*see* 1945)
Jet aircraft GB: 15 May [10]
Colour TV service (exp): 1 June [188]
Clothes rationing GB: 1 June
TV commercial: 1 July [178]
Television news: 1 July [181]
Jeep GB: Nov [89]
Aeroplane armed with air-to-ground

rockets: Ilyushin Il-2 Stormovik (Rus)
War Office Selection Board: introd in Scottish Command by Col J.V. Delahaye
Chipboard: mnf by Torfit-Werken G.A. Haseke, Bremen, Ger
Terylene: dev by J.R. Whinfield and J.T. Dickson at Calico Printers Assoc labs, Accrington, Lancs, Eng

1942
Emergency aircraft ejection: 13 Jan [9]
Golden disc: 10 Feb [79]
Self-service grocery GB: 5 June [172]
Nylon parachute: dev by Pioneer Parachute Co, Manchester; first jump by Adeline Gray over Hertford, Eng, 6 June
Bazooka: tested Frankford Arsenal, May; used in action by US troops, N. Africa, Nov
Surface-to-surface guided missile: German V1, ground launched at Peenemünde, 24 Dec
DDT GB: introd from Swz
Helicopter (mnf): [81]

1943
Amphibian (military) GB: Thornycroft Terrapin 1, tested Mar
Professional woman jockey: 27 April [203]
Air hostess GB: 10 May [14]
Ballpoint pen: 10 June [22]
Aerogramme GB: 18 June [9]
Guided missile used to warfare: Luftwaffe's Hs 293 air-to-surface missile; first operational success against HMS *Egret* in Bay of Biscay, 27 Aug
Mass X-ray GB: Lancs, Oct
Adventure playground: inst by Workers' Co-operative Housing Assoc, Copenhagen

1944
Helicopters used in warfare: three Sikorsky R.4s performed patrol duties with Atlantic convoy; departed N.Y., 2 Jan
Woman Anglican Minister: 24 Jan [204]
PAYE GB: 6 April [86]
Jet aircraft (mnf): May [11]
Napalm, use in warfare: by British 79th Armoured Division, Normandy, 6 June
Surface-to-surface guided missile attack: Ger V1s launched from Calais area, towards Eng, 13 June
Jet bomber: June [11]
Jet aircraft (mnf) GB: 18 July [11]
Jet combat: 25 July [11]
Jet aircraft used in warfare (Br): 27 July [11]
Postcodes: introd Germany, 1 Aug
Free secondary education for all GB: implemented under Education Act passed 3 Aug
Jet aircraft shot down in aerial combat: two Messerschmitt Me 262A fighters by 31st Fighter Group, US 8th Air Force, 10 (?) Oct
Hi-fi records (mkt): Dec [167]
Kidney machine: built secretly for Dutch Resistance by Willem Kolff during Ger occupation of Neths
Ballpoint pen (mnf): [22]

1945
Fluoridated water supply: Grand Rapids, Mich., 25 Jan
Aircraft ejection seat (operational): 14 April [10]
Family Allowances GB: 5s per child after first, 15 June
Atomic bomb: detonated Alamogordo Air Base, New Mexico, 16 July
Daily drama serial broadcast GB: *The Robinson Family*, BBC Light Programme, 30 July (*see* 1941)
Atomic bomb used in warfare: dropped on Hiroshima from USAAF Boeing B-29 bomber *Enola Gay*, 6 Aug
Civilian Jeep: 4 Sept [89]
Fluorescent lighting GB: 2 Oct [75]
Air-sea rescue by helicopter: seamen on wrecked oil barge rescued by US Army Sikorsky R-5, Long Island Sound, 29 Nov
Microwave oven: pat USA by Percy LeBaron Spencer
Ballpoint pen (mkt): [22]

1946
TV licences GB: 1 June [180]
Transatlantic airline service GB: 1 July [16]
Bikini: 5 July [24]
Young Conservatives: f 6 July
Children's TV series GB: 7 July [178]
Pope to be televised: Pius XII, by RCA from Vatican, 12 July
Jet take-off from aircraft carrier: 21 July [13]
Ejection seat GB: 24 July [10]
Fluorescent street lighting GB: 1 Aug [75]
Film festival GB: 31 Aug [68]
Church service televised GB: from St George's Chapel, Biggin Hill, BBC, 15 Sept
Vinylite record: Oct [167]
Royal Command Film Performance at public cinema: 1 Nov [158]
New Town: Stevenage, designated 11 Nov
Nylon stockings (mnf) GB: Dec [119]
Outward Bound School: Aberdovey, Wales
Drive-in bank: Exchange National Bank, Chicago
Drive-on, drive-off Channel car ferry: *The Forde*, Dover–Calais
Photosetting machine (practical): Harris-Intertype Fotosetter installed Govt Printing Office, Washington D.C.
Electronic computer: [44]

1947
Covent Garden Opera Company production: 14 Jan [121]
Helicopter (mnf) GB: Jan [81]
3-D colour talkie: Feb [72]
Tubeless tyres: 11 May [133]
Helicopter pilot's licence GB: 14 Mar [131]
Party Political Broadcast GB: by Rt Hon. C.R. Attlee (Lab), 18 Mar
Professional theatre-in-the-round company: Theatre '47, opened with William Inge's *Farther Off From Heaven*, Dallas, Tex., 3 June
Supersonic flight (level): by Capt. Charles Yeager, USAF, in Bell XS-1 rocket plane at 670mph over Edwards Air Force Base, Muroc, Calif., 14 Oct
High-definition TV recording: 9 Nov [184]
Plastic toy soldiers GB: mnf by Malleable Mouldings, Deal, Kent
Microwave oven (mnf): by Raytheon Co, Waltham, Mass.
Fork lift truck GB: Coventry Climax FTD
In-flight magazine: Pan American's *Clipper*
Radio cabs GB: Camtax, Cambridge
All-electric jukebox (mnf) GB: [90]
Tape-recorder (for home use): [96]

1948
TV news programme GB: 5 Jan [181]
Supermarket GB: 12 Jan [172]
Steeplechase televised: Sandown Park, BBC, 24 Jan
Land-Rover: 30 April [89]
Electronically controlled passenger elevators: Otis at Universal Pictures Building, N.Y., April
Carrier-based jet sqn: 5 May [13]
Roll-on, roll-off freight transport ferry service: introd Preston, Eng–Larne, N.I. by Transport Ferry Service, 20 May
Aircraft hijacking: 16 June [10]
Woman vice-chancellor GB: Prof. Lillian Penson, London Univ., 25 June
Transistor: dev by Dr John Bardeen and Dr Walter Brittain, Bell Telephone Labs, Murray Hill, N.J.; dem 30 June
National Health Service GB: operational 5 July
Air car-ferry: Silver City Airways, Le Touquet, Fr–Lympne, Eng, 7 July
Jet aircraft to fly Atlantic: six RAF de Havilland Vampires of No. 54 Sqn, GB–Labrador, 12 July
Alcoholics Anonymous GB: f London 15 July
Turboprop airliner GB: Vickers Viscount V.630, flown 16 July
Documentary feature filmed for TV GB: *Germany Under Control*, written and prod by Robert Barr, tr BBC, 18 Sept
TV western series: *Hopalong Cassidy* with Bill Boyd, NBC, 28 Nov
Polaroid Land Camera: des by Dr Edwin Land, Cambridge, Mass.; mkt Boston, 28 Nov
Woman KC: 20 Dec [201]
Reith Lecture: *Authority and the Individual* by Bertrand Russell, 26 Dec
Photosetting machine GB: Rotofoto, dev by George Westover, London

1949
TV situation comedy: The Goldbergs, CBS, 17 Jan (–25 June 1951)
45rpm long-playing records: by RCA-Victor, Feb
TV thriller series: *Suspense*, CBS, 1 Mar (–17 Aug 1954)
Schools TV service: 2 Mar [185]
Woman KC (Eng): 12 April [201]
Scout Bob-a-job Week: 18–24 April
Badminton Horse Trials: won by Capt. John Shedden on Golden Willow; held 20–22 April
High-altitude liquid-fuel rocket: Viking, fired to 50 miles altitude in 54.5 sec, White Sands, New Mexico, 3 May
Launderette GB: 9 May [92]
Jet bomber GB: 13 May [11]
Heliport: Heliport No. 1, Pier 41, N.Y. 23 May
Emergency aircraft ejection GB: 30 May [10]
Closed-circuit TV (permanent) GB: inst Guy's Hospital by EMI, May
Closed-circuit colour TV: CBS system used to tr appendicectomy performed by Dr David Allman, Atlantic City Hospital, 6 June
Film drama made for TV GB: 11 July [71]
Jet airliner: de Havilland Comet GB flown 27 July
TV weather forecast GB: 29 July [200]
Comprehensive school GB: Holyhead County Secondary, Anglesey, Wales, by amalgamation of St Cybi Secondary Modern and Holyhead Grammar, 21 Sept
Continuous TV serial: 4 Nov [185]
Trampoline GB: at Loxford School, Ilford, Essex
Charity Christmas card: [36]

1950
Election returns televised GB: BBC, 23 Feb
Gas-turbine car: Coventry-built Rover Jet I, dem publicly Silverstone, Eng, 9 Mar
Operational RAF helicopter unit: RAF Casualty Evacuation Flight, Seletar, Singapore, 1 April
Jet airmail: 18 April [17]
Credit cards: issued by Diners Club, N.Y., May
Helicopter passenger service: London–Birmingham during Br Industries Fair, 9 May
Soap coupons GB: Tide, May
Helicopter passenger service (permanent): Cardiff–Wrexham–Liverpool (GB), 1 June
Bikini GB: June [24]
Farnborough Air Display: 7 July
Channel swimming race: won by Lt Abdel Rehim (Egypt), 10hr 50 min, 22 Aug
International TV programme tr (public-service): 27 Aug [180]
33⅓rpm LP GB: Aug [95]
World Championship of Drivers: won by Nino Farina (It) with victory in Italian Grand Prix, Monza, 3 Sept
Legal Aid GB: effective 2 Oct
Railway preservation society: Talyllyn Railway Preservation Soc, f 11 Oct
Jet–jet combat: Korea, 8 Nov [11]
National Park GB: Peak District NP, designated 28 Dec
Automatic service rifle GB: Enfield EM-2
Passenger elevator with self-opening doors: installed by Otis at Atlantic Refining Building, Dallas, Tex.
Xerox (mnf): by Haloid Co, Rochester, N.Y. (*see* 1938)
Air charter holiday company: Horizon, London
GCE 'A' and 'O' level: [161]
Pre-recorded tapes: [96]

1951
'X' film: 9 Jan [66]
Miss World Contest: 19 April [23]
Jet bomber (service) GB: 25 May [11]
Heliport GB: Elmdon H, Birmingham, 1 June
Colour TV service (public): 25 June [188]
Colour TV series: 26 June [188]
Helicopter troop transport combat operation: US Marines, 1st Div, Inje Punch Bowl battle zone, Korea, 13 Sept
Supermarket chain GB: Premier

Supermarkets; first branch Earls Court, London, Sept
Television, Party Political Broadcast GB: by Lord Samuel for Lib Party, 15 Oct
Space flight by living creatures: Dec [167]
Cobalt radiation unit: Victoria Hospital, London, Ont., Canada, 27 Oct
Zebra crossing: 31 Oct [124]
Transistors, commercial application: in Bell Telephone (USA) trunk dialling apparatus, Oct
Rugby League match televised: Eng *v* NZ, Swinton, Yorks, BBC, 10 Nov
Language laboratory (tape-recorders): Louisiana State Univ (*see also* 1924)
Adventure playgrounds GB: inst by Lady Allen of Hurtwood at St Luke's, Peckham and Clydesdale Rd, Notting Hill Gate
Terylene products (mnf) GB: dresses, lingerie, shirts
Electronic computer (mnf): [44]
Ice-cream van chimes GB: introd by Ronald Peters of Tonibell Mnf Co
GPO television detector van: [180]

1952
Transatlantic economy-class air fares: 1 May
Jet airline service: 2 May [16]
Schools TV (exp) GB: 5 May [185]
Drive-on, drive-off Channel car ferry (purpose-built): BR's *Lord Warden*, Dover–Boulogne, 17 June
Cinerama: 30 Sept [72]
Atomic bomb (Br): detonated on Monte Bello Islands off Western Australia, 3 Oct
Documentary TV series GB: NBC's *Victory at Sea*, tr in 26 parts by BBC, starting 27 Oct
Hydrogen bomb: detonated by US at Eniwetok, Marshall Is, 31 Oct
45rpm LP GB: *The Nun's Chorus*, EMI, Oct
Videotape: dem by John Mullin and Wayne Johnson at Bing Crosby Enterprises labs, Beverly Hills, Calif., 11 Nov
Pop-music chart GB: 14 Nov [137]
Air-sea rescue by helicopter GB: four Danish sailors rescued by Flt Lt Daniel Kearns, RAF, off Yarmouth, 3 Dec
Transistor hearing aid: 29 Dec [80]
Son et Lumière: Château de Chambord, Fr
Sex-change operation: George/Christine Jorgènsen, American soldier, operated on at the Serum Institute, Copenhagen by Dr Karl Hamburger
Local Education Authority to go 100% comprehensive: 11+ abolished by Anglesey Education Committee, Eng
Water-ski club GB: Ruislip Lido WC
Tea bags (mkt) GB: [173]

1953
RAF helicopter squadron: No. 194 Sqn, f Seletar, Singapore, 1 Feb
Helicopter troop transport combat operation (Br): by Sikorsky Sqn RN, Malaya, 20 Mar
Turboprop airliner in service: Vickers Viscount on London–Nicosia route, BEA, 18 April
Woman to fly faster than sound: Miss Jacqueline Cochrane (USA) piloting North American F-86 Sabre, 18 May
Hydrofoil passenger service: Swiss 30-seat Surpramar PT 10, Lake Maggiore, Italy, May
BBC colour TV programme: 2 June [189]
Greyhound-racing televised GB: by BBC from Wembley, 14 Sept
Cinemascope: 24 Sept [72]
Televised police appeal GB: photo of William Pettit, wanted for murder, shown by BBC, 1 Oct
Samaritans: f by Rev. Chad Varah, City of London, Nov
Supersonic fighter: North American F-100A Super Sabre
Plastic tube (collapsible): [41]

1954
Electronic business computer: Jan [44]
Nuclear submarine: 21 Jan [171]
Swept-wing fighter GB: Supermarine Swift; entered service with 56 Sqn RAF, Feb
TV narrative series GB: 9 April [183]
Stock-car racing GB: Old Kent Road Stadium, New Cross, 16 April
Four-minute mile: by Roger Bannister in 3min 59.4sec, Oxford, Eng, 6 May
Pre-recorded stereo tapes: May [96]
Passenger conveyor (permanent): Speedwalk at Erie Station, Jersey City, May
Mass polio vaccination programme: 1,829,916 Michigan children immunized with Salk vaccine, 26 April to July
Eurovision: 6 June [180]
Atomic power station: 27 June [20]
Value Added Tax: dev by M. Maurice Laure, introd Fr (wholesale only) 1 July
TV news (daily) GB: 5 July [181]
VTOL aircraft: Rolls-Royce TMR 'Flying Bedstead', flown 3 Aug
Supersonic fighter GB: English Electric P.1 (Lightning), flown Boscombe Down 4 Aug
Comprehensive school (purpose-built) GB: Kidbrooke School, London, opened Sept
Oral contraceptive: [25]
Home stereo tape-recorder: [96]

1955
Luncheon vouchers GB: introd by Luncheon Vouchers Ltd, 1 Jan
Radar speed meters GB: employed in Bucks, Herts and Cambridge, Jan
Pilot to bail out at supersonic speed: George Franklin Smith from F-100 Super Sabre 37,000ft over S. Calif., 22 Feb. Survived but remains unable to drink alcohol
Heliscoop: inv by Lt-Cdr John Sproule RN; first rescue off Ford, Sussex, Eng, 18 Mar
Theatre-in-the round GB: *Circle of Love*, Library Theatre, Scarborough, 14 July
TV newscasters GB: 4 Sept [181]
TV commercial GB: 22 Sept [178]
Fluoridated water supply GB: Anglesey, 17 Nov
Parachute club GB: British PC, Denham, f 19 Nov
Stereophonic tape-recordings: 'Stereosonic' tapes mkt EMI
Armoured security vans GB: introd by Armoured Car Services, London
Non-stick saucepans: mnf by Tefal Co, Paris

1956
Yellow no-parking lines GB: laid Slough, Feb
Weather forecast telephone service GB: 5 Mar [200]
Television, ministerial broadcast: GB: by PM, Rt Hon. Anthony Eden, 27 April
Area of Outstanding Natural Beauty: Gower Peninsula, Wales, designated 9 May
Football, European Cup competition: Real Madrid beat Rheims 4–3 in final, Paris, 13 June
Atomic power station GB: 20 Aug [20]
Go kart: built by Art Ingles, Echo Park Rd, Los Angeles, Aug
Transatlantic telephone cable: Oban–Newfoundland; operational 25 Sept
Premium Bonds: on sale 1 Nov
Supersonic bomber: Convair B-58 Hustler, flown USA 11 Nov
Non-stick saucepans GB: Harbenware
Videotape (mnf): by Ampex Corp, Chicago
Pop group: [136]
Stainless-steel razor blades: [160]
TV degree course: [179]

1957
Portable electric typewriter: mkt by Smith Corona of Syracuse N.Y., 4 Feb
Continuous TV serial GB: 19 Feb [185]
British colony in Africa to become independent: Ghana, 6 Mar
Roll-on, roll-off service to Continent: introd Tilbury–Antwerp by Transport Ferry Service, 12 Mar
Commercially sponsored steeplechase: Whitbread Gold Cup, Sandown Park, 27 April
Schools TV service (regular) GB: 13 May [185]
Hydrogen bomb (Br): dropped over Christmas Is region, 15 May
Premium Bond winner: holder of bond 1KF 341150, 1 June (£1,000)
Xerox GB: first machine sold for £1,250 by Rank Xerox to *The Times* Publishing Co, June
Son et lumière GB: Greenwich Palace, 1 Aug
Intercontinental ballistic missile: successful launching announced by Soviet Govt, 26 Aug
BBC schools TV service (regular): 24 Sept [185]
Woman TV newscaster GB: 30 Sept [181]
Space satellite: Russian *Sputnik I*, launched 4 Oct
Royal Christmas TV broadcast: 25 Dec [158]
Go-kart racing (under rules); held Eastland Shopping Centre, West Covina, Calif., Dec
Microwave oven GB: Artic Cooker, des by R.J. Constable of Lewispoint Holdings, London
Go karts (mnf): by the Go Kart Mnf Co, Azusa, Calif.
Wankel rotary engine: des by Felix Wankel; built by NSU, Neckarsulm, W. Ger
Motor-racing drivers' school: opened Snetterton, Norfolk, by Jim Russell

1958
Planetarium GB: opened at Madame Tussaud's, 19 Mar
Civic theatre GB: Belgrade Theatre Coventry, 27 Mar
Stereo discs (mkt): April [167]
Videotape GB: BBC's VERA, first used for *Panorama*, April
Stereo discs (mkt) GB: May [167]
Woman bank manager (conventional bank) GB: Miss Hilda Harding, Barclay's, Hanover St, London, May (*see* 1910)
Duke of Edinburgh's Award: first Gold Medals presented Buckingham Palace, 4 June
Parking meter GB: 10 July [124]
Go karts GB: five karts imported from USA by Mickey Flynn, Burtonwood Air Force Base, Sept
Transatlantic jet airline service: 4 Oct [16]
Woman high-jumper to clear 6ft: Iolanda Balas of Rumania, 18 Oct
Life Peer to take seat in House of Lords: Lord Parker of Wassington, 21 Oct
Life Peeress to take seat in House of Lords: Baroness Swanborough, 21 Oct
Woman to address House of Lords: Baroness Elliott of Harwood on the developing nations, 4 Nov
Motorway GB: 5 Dec [113]
STD telephone service GB: Bristol, 5 Dec
Patrol car manned by policewomen GB: Miss Mabel Middleton and Miss Mary Walton, Lancs Constabulary, Dec
Go-kart track: opened at Azusa, Calif., Dec
Tea vending-machine (fully automatic) GB: 'Tea Cub' by W.M. Still Ltd, London
Moulton bicycle: [24]

1959
Lunar spaceshot: 2 Jan [168]
Identikit: Feb [86]
Hovercraft: 30 May [84]
Submarine armed with ballistic missiles: *George Washington* (Polaris), launched Groton, Conn., 9 June
Transatlantic TV programme transmission: 18 June [180]
Nuclear warship: 14,000-ton cruiser USS *Long Beach*, launched Quincy, Mass., 14 July
Hovercraft Channel crossing: 25 July [84]
Anti-missile missile: Nike-Zeus, test-fired White Sands, New Mexico, 26 Aug
Spacecraft to land on moon: 12 Sept [168]
Postcode GB: Norwich, 3 Oct
Photograph of far side of moon: transmitted from *Lunik III* (Rus), 7 Oct
Charity walk: 26 Dec [33]
Initial teaching alphabet: pub by Sir James Pitman, London
Hotel or restaurant to install microwave oven GB: Kew Gardens Hotel; Artic Cooker
Drive-in Bank GB: Martin's, Leicester
Motor car with fibreglass body: Lotus Mark 14 Elite, mnf Cheshunt, Eng
Car telephones GB: introd S. Lancs and N. Cheshire via Manchester Peterloo Exchange

1960
Meteorological satellite: American *Tiros I*, launched 1 April
Motor-car seat-belts (across shoulder pattern) GB: des by P.O. Weman (Swn); mkt by Britax of Byfleet, May
Submerged circumnavigation of the earth: by US nuclear sub *Triton*; surfaced at St Paul's Rock after 3-month voyage, 25 April
Language laboratory GB: estab by Shell International Petroleum to teach Indonesian, London, June
Woman Prime Minister: 21 July [204]
Laser: dev by Theodore Maiman at Hughes Research Labs, Malibu, Calif., July
Supersonic fighter in service GB: English Electric Lightnings of 74 Sqn RAF, delivered Coltishall, July
Communications satellite: American *Echo I*, launched 12 Aug
Oral contraceptive (mkt): 18 Aug [25]
Fibre-tip pen: Pentel mkt by Japan Stationery Co, Tokyo, Aug
MoT test: introd 12 Sept
Traffic Wardens GB: London, 15 Sept
Nuclear aircraft carrier: 24 Sept [13]
Passenger coveyor GB: Bank Station 'Travolator', opened 27 Sept
Nuclear submarine GB: *Dreadnought*, Westinghouse reactor, launched Barrow, 21 Oct
Potable water desalination plant GB: opened by States of Guernsey Water Board, 21 Oct
Urban motorway GB: M62 Stretford–Eccles By-pass, 28 Oct
VTOL aircraft (production model): Hawker Siddeley P. 1127 (Kestrel), flown GB 19 Nov
Typesetting by computer: introd at Imprimerie Nationale, Paris

1961
Oral contraceptive (mkt) GB: 1 Jan [25]
GPO Recorded Delivery: 1 Feb
Automatic half-barrier level crossing GB: on B5030 road, Spath, nr Uttoxeter, 5 Feb
Minicabs GB: introd by Carline of Wimbledon, 6 Mar
Women traffic wardens GB: Leicester, 27 Mar
Manned space flight (successful): 12 April [167]
New English Bible: NT pub by Oxford and Cambridge Univ Presses, Mar 14; (OT 16 Mar 1970)
Identikit GB: Mar [86]
School ship: SS *Dunera*, British India Line; maiden educational cruise 12 April
American spaceman: Alan B. Shepard in *Freedom VII*, 5 May
Member of Royal Family interviewed on TV: 29 May [158]
In-flight movies (regular): 19 July [68]
Reading taught by Initial Teaching Alphabet: at 19 Eng infant schools in Oldham, Burton, Stoke, Walsall, Grimsby, Harrow, 4 Sept
Fixed-penalty parking ticket GB: 19 Sept [191]
Channel swim, non-stop double crossing: St Margaret's Bay return by Antonio Albertondo (Arg), 43hr 5min, 20–21 Sept
Self-service petrol filling-station GB: Southwark Bridge, Nov
Electric toothbrush: [189]

1962
Newspaper colour supplement GB: 4 Feb [117]
Nuclear merchant vessel: *Savannah*, launched Camden, N.J.; maiden voyage 23 Mar
Anglo-American space satellite: *Ariel I*, launched from Cape Canaveral 26 April
Orienteering GB: inaug by Scottish Council of Physical Recreation; championship held Dunkeld, Perthshire, May
Casino (legal) GB: Metropole Casino, Brighton, 2 June
Television communications satellite: Bell Telephone *Telstar I*, launched 10 July
Underwater Channel swim: Cap Gris Nez–Sandwich by Fred Baldasare (USA), 18hr 1min, 10–11 July
Transatlantic TV satellite transmission: 11 July [180]
Hovercraft passenger service: 20 July [84]
Briton to swim Channel underwater: Simon Paterson of Egham, 28 July
Interplanetary space shot: 27 Aug [167]
Woman Ambassador to Britain: Aug [201]
Football, £100,000 transfer fee: paid by Manchester United for Denis Law of Turin, July
Parliamentary Commissioner: 1 Oct [121]
School language laboratory GB: Mayfield School, Putney

1963
Woman astronaut: 16 June [167]
Channel crossing by hydrofoil: Ostend–London by two Aquavits, 8 July
Pre-natal blood transfusion: 20 Sept [26]
Football pitch, undersoil heating GB: first used at Leeds Rugby League ground for Leeds *v* Dewsbury match, 21 Dec
Letraset: introd by John Davis and Frederick Mackenzie, London

1964
London Underground automatic ticket-barrier: 5 Jan [196]
Driverless tube trains: 5 April [196]
BBC 2: 30 April [187]
Hydrofoil service GB: Channel Is–France, April
British Week (official): Dusseldorf, Ger, 23–31 May
Topless swimsuit: des by Rudi Gernreich of Calif., June
Postgraduate business school GB: Manchester School of Business, Oct
Commercial radio station GB: Radio Manx, 23 Nov
Orienteering club GB: South Ribble OC

1965
Compensation for victims of violence: NZ; Act effective Jan 1
Member of Br Royal Family to enter commerce: 5 Jan [158]
Space walk: 18 Mar [167]
Capital Gains Tax GB: 6 April
Woman coroner GB: Dr Mary McHugh, apnt C of Bexley, Bromley, Croydon, Sutton, 23 Mar
Transatlantic TV satellite programme transmission: 2 May [180]
Transatlantic colour TV programme transmission: 17 May [180]
Fibre-tip pen (mnf) GB: Penline, mkt by Mentmore of Stevenage, May
Woman member of a Stock Exchange GB: 10 June [206]
Airliner to make automatic landing: Paris–London BEA de Havilland Trident, Heathrow, 10 June
Capital punishment abolished GB: 9 Nov [31]
70mph speed limit GB: introd 22 Dec
Horse-racing, starting stalls GB: Chesterfield Stakes, Newmarket, 8 July
Mini skirt GB: reported 6in above knee in Chelsea, Dec
Panda cars: [133]

1966
Soft landing on moon: 3 Feb [168]
Corporation Tax GB: effective 5 April
Red Arrow buses: Victoria–Marble Arch, London, 18 April
£25,000 Premium Bond winner: Norman Jepson of Sandbach, Cheshire, Eng, 1 Feb
Husband and wife Life Peers: Lord and Lady Brooke of Cumnor (she 1964), 19 May
Telephone directory Yellow Pages GB: Brighton, July
Transatlantic crossing by rowing boat (Br): Capt. John Ridgway and Sgt Chay Blyth of the Parachute Regt; Orleans, Mass–Inishmore, Eire, 4 June –3 Sept
Coloured policeman GB: PC 492 Mohamet Yusuf Daar (Kenya), Coventry Police, 20 June
Racing-car with aerofoils: first to race, Jim Hall's Chaparral 2E at Bridgehampton Can-Am event, 18 Sept
Spacecraft to land on another planet: 16 Nov [168]
International computer chess match: Prof. John McCarthy's computer, Stanford Univ *v* Abram Alikhanov's computer, Russian Institute of Theoretical & Experimental Physics, commencing 23 Nov; USSR won 3–1
Christmas stamp GB: 1 Dec [138]

1967
Hover-freight: load of Atlas bulbs hovered Ramsgate, Eng–Calais, Fr. 23 Jan
North Sea gas: piped ashore by BP at Easington, Co Durham from West Sole, 4 Mar
Parliamentary Commissioner GB: 1 April [121]
Space fatality (confirmed): 24 April [167]
Woman to drive London taxi: Mrs Shirley Preston, April
Space satellite (Br): *Ariel III*, launched from Vandenburg Air Base, Calif., 5 May
Colour TV service GB: 1 July [189]
Value Added Tax (retail): Denmark, 3 July (*see* 1954)
V/STOL combat aircraft: Hawker Harrier (GB), flown July
Government Green Paper: *The Development Areas: a Proposal for a Regional Employment Premium*, 5 Aug
BBC Radio 1: 30 Sept [147]
Conservation Area: Stamford, Lincs designated 3 Oct
Majority verdict GB: wrestler Saleh Kassem, alias 'The Terrible Turk', found guilty of handbag theft by 10–2 majority of jury. Brighton Quarter Sessions, 5 Oct
Breathalyser test (statutory) GB: administered to unnamed motorist at Flax Bourton, Somerset, 8 Oct
Local radio station (BBC): 8 Nov [147]
Heart transplant: 2 Dec [33]
English Mass GB: introd in all RC churches, 3 Dec
Wankel-engined car (production): NSU Spider, mnf Neckarsulm, Ger

1968
Coloured policewoman GB: Mrs Sislin Fay Allen (Jamaica), reported Metropolitan Police Training Centre, Westminster, 1 Jan
Phone-in radio programme GB: *What Are They Up to Now?* Radio Nottingham 4 Feb
Woman airline captain GB: Miss Gillian Cazalet of Skyways Coach Air Ltd, Feb
Decimal cheque GB: 4 Mar [34]
Open lawn tennis championship (amateur/pro): Hard Court Championships of GB, Bournemouth, 22–27 April
5p and 10p decimal coins: issued 23 April
Legalized abortion GB: 27 April [7]
London postcodes: W1 area, 5 June
Woman Governor of a Commonwealth Territory: Dr Hilda Bynoe, Governor of Grenada, 8 June
Motorway warning signals GB: operational Severn Bridge section of M4, 14 June
Two-level motorway viaduct GB: Tinsley Viaduct, Sheffield, June
Channel hoverferry: 1 Aug [84]
Supersonic airliner: Tu-144, (Rus) flown 31 Dec
Wankel-engined car marketed GB: NSU Ro 80 (Ger)

1969
Negro Peer: Baron Constantine, elevated 1 Jan
Passenger hydrofoil built GB: 25-seat *Sea Ranger I* by Southern Hydrofoils; launched Dartmouth, Feb
Supersonic airliner GB: Anglo-French Concorde 002, flown Bristol–Fairford, 9 April
Non-stop solo circumnavigation of earth: by Robin Knox-Johnston (Br) in 32ft ketch *Suhaili*; arr Falmouth after 312-day voyage, 22 April
University broadcasting station GB: University Radio York, 30 April
Transatlantic crossing, solo row: by Dubliner Tom McClean of the Parachute Regt; St John's, Newfoundland–Blacksod Bay, Co Mayo in 20ft dory *Super Silver*, 17 May–27 July
Man on the moon: 21 July [168]
50p decimal coin: issued 14 Oct
Quins (to survive) GB: b to Mrs Irene Hanson of Rayleigh, Essex, 13 Nov
Colour TV commercial GB: 15 Nov [178]

1970
TV-telephone installation (permanent) GB: Feb [188]
Decimal postage stamps GB: 10p, 20p 50p on sale 17 June
Briton to swim Channel both ways non-stop: Kevin Murphy of Kenton,

Middx, 35hr 10min, 4–6 Aug
Aircraft hijacking (Br): 9 Sept [10]
Moon vehicle: Russian *Lunokhod I*, landed Sea of Rains 17 Nov

1971
TV degree course GB: 3 Jan [179]
½p, 1p, 2p decimal coins: issued 15 Jan
Decimal currency system GB: replaced £sd, 15 Feb
Space station: Russian *Salyut*, launched 19 April
Moon vehicle (manned): American Lunar Roving Vehicle, driven by *Apollo 15* commander David R. Scott, 31 July
Tracked hovercraft: 2 Aug [84]
£50,000 Premium Bond winner: Coventry holder of bond 4EW 614665, 2 Aug
Busway: 12-mile bus-only route, Runcorn, Cheshire, Eng, 29 Oct

1972
Plastic warship: 500-ton minehunter HMS *Wilton*, launched Southampton 18 Jan
£500,000 pools winner GB: 4 Mar [75]
Hovercraft fatality: four died aboard Seaspeed SR-N6, Southsea, Eng, 4 Mar
Contraceptives on the rates GB: 1 April [25]
Ladies' race (Jockey Club Rules): 6 May [203]
Local TV station GB: 3 July [180]
Living member of Royal Family portrayed on stage: 19 Oct [158]
Br Monarch to visit Communist country: 17 Oct [98]

1973
Women members of London Stock Exchange: 25 Mar [206]
Value Added Tax GB: 1 April
Open University graduates: 23 June [179]
Radio commercial GB (mainland): 8 Oct [147]
Divorce-by-post GB: decree nisi to Mrs Mary Garrity of London, 19 Dec

1974
Sextuplets (to survive): three boys, three girls born to Mrs Sue Rosenkowitz, Cape Town, SA, 11 Jan
Wankel-engined motor cycle: mkt by Suzuki, Japan, Jan
Backgammon, International Masters' Tournament: org by Br Backgammon Assoc; final at Hilton Hotel, London, 28 June
£75,000 Premium Bond Prize GB: drawn 1 July

INDEX

Italic figures are the page numbers of entries in the text; dates refer the reader to the years in the Chronology. The meanings of any abbreviations used in this index will be found on page 211.

A EUGÈNE WAVE